WORLD TRADE ORGANIZATION

Dispute Settlement Reports

2001
Volume III

Pages 777-1292

CAMBRIDGE
UNIVERSITY PRESS

PUBLISHED BY THE PRESS SYNDICATE OF THE UNIVERSITY OF CAMBRIDGE
The Pitt Building, Trumpington Street, Cambridge, United Kingdom

CAMBRIDGE UNIVERSITY PRESS
The Edinburgh Building, Cambridge CB2 2RU, UK
40 West 20th Street, New York, NY 10011–4211, USA
477 Williamstown Road, Port Melbourne, VIC 3207, Australia
Ruiz de Alarcón 13, 28014 Madrid, Spain
Dock House, The Waterfront, Cape Town 8001, South Africa

http://www.cambridge.org

First published 2003

Printed in the United Kingdom at the University Press, Cambridge

French edition and Spanish edition paperbacks of this title are both available directly from WTO Publications, World Trade Organization, Centre William Rappard, 154 rue de Lausanne, CH-1211 Geneva 21, Switzerland http://www.wto.org

ISBN 0 521 82980 1 hardback

THE WTO DISPUTE SETTLEMENT REPORTS

The *Dispute Settlement Reports* of the World Trade Organization (the "WTO") include panel and Appellate Body reports, as well as arbitration awards, in disputes concerning the rights and obligations of WTO Members under the provisions of the *Marrakesh Agreement Establishing the World Trade Organization*. The *Dispute Settlement Reports* are available in English, French and Spanish. Starting with 1999, the first volume of each year contains a cumulative index of published disputes.

This volume may be cited as DSR 2001:III

TABLE OF CONTENTS

UNITED STATES – DEFINITIVE SAFEGUARD MEASURES ON IMPORTS OF WHEAT GLUTEN FROM THE EUROPEAN COMMUNITIES

Report of the Panel

WT/DS166/R

TABLE OF CONTENTS

I. INTRODUCTION

1.1 On 17 March 1999, the European Community requested consultations with the United States pursuant to Article 4 of the Understanding on Rules and Procedures Governing the Settlement of Disputes (the "DSU"), Article XXII:1 of the General Agreement on Tariffs and Trade ("GATT 1994"), Article 14 of the Agreement on Safeguards ("SA") and Article 19 of the Agreement on Agriculture with regard to the definitive safeguard measures imposed by the United States on imports of wheat gluten (WTO document WT/DS166/1).

1.2 On 1 April 1999, pursuant to paragraph 11 of Article 4 of the DSU, Australia notified its desire to be joined in the consultations under Article XXII:1 of GATT 1994 (WTO document WT/DS166/2).

1.3 The European Community and the United States held consultations on 3 May 1999 in Geneva, but failed to reach a mutually satisfactory solution.

1.4 On 3 June 1999, the European Community requested the establishment of a panel pursuant to Article XXIII of the GATT 1994, Articles 4 and 6 of the DSU, Article 19 of the Agreement on Agriculture and Article 14 SA, with regard to the definitive safeguard measures imposed by the United States on imports of wheat gluten (WTO document WT/DS166/3).

1.5 At its meeting on 26 July 1999, the Dispute Settlement Body (the "DSB") established a Panel in accordance with the request made by the European Community in document WT/DS166/3.

1.6 At that meeting, the parties to the dispute also agreed that the Panel should have standard terms of reference. The terms of reference were, therefore, the following:

> "To examine, in the light of the relevant provisions of the covered agreements cited by the European Community in document WT/DS166/3, the matter referred to the DSB by the European Community in document WT/DS166/3, and to make such findings as will assist the DSB in making the recommendations or in giving the rulings provided for in those agreements". (WTO document WT/DS166/4)

1.7 On 11 October 1999, the parties to the dispute agreed on the following composition of the Panel:

Chairman: Mr. Wieslaw Karsz

Members: Ms. Usha Dwarka-Canabady

Mr. Alvaro Espinoza

1.8 Australia, Canada and New Zealand reserved their rights to participate in the panel proceedings as third parties.

1.9 The Panel met with the parties on 20-21 December 1999 and 1-2 February 2000. It met with the third parties on 21 December 1999.

1.10 Following the resignation on 11 April 2000 of Mr. Wieslaw Karsz as Chairman of the panel originally constituted to consider this matter, the parties agreed, on 20 April 2000, that Mr. Maamoun Abdel-Fattah would serve as Chairman of the Panel (WTO Document WT/DS166/6).

1.11 Accordingly, the composition of the Panel was as follows:

Chairman: Mr. Maamoun Abdel-Fattah

Members: Ms. Usha Dwarka-Canabady

Mr. Alvaro Espinoza

1.12 The Panel in its new composition held one additional meeting with the parties on 18 May 2000. At this meeting, each party was invited to make an oral statement summarizing its case on the basis of evidence already on the Panel record, including correspondence between the Panel and the parties.

1.13 The Panel issued its interim report to the parties on 19 June 2000. On 28 June 2000, the European Community and the United States each submitted written requests for review by the Panel of precise aspects of the interim report. On 5 July 2000, the parties submitted written comments on one another's requests for interim review. Section VII, *infra*, describes the interim review requests and comments received, and the changes made to the report in response to those comments.

II. FACTUAL ASPECTS

2.1 This dispute concerns the imposition by the United States of a definitive safeguard measure, in the form of a quantitative restriction, on certain imports of wheat gluten (HS headings 1109.00.10 and 1109.00.90).

2.2 The United States imposed the measure following an investigation initiated by the United States International Trade Commission (the "USITC") on 1 October 1997 (USITC Investigation No. TA–201–67). The USITC initiated the investigation on the basis of a petition filed by the Wheat Gluten Industry Council of the United States, which consists of two of the four US producers of wheat gluten, Midwest Grain Products, Inc. ("Midwest") and Manildra Milling Corporation ("Manildra").

2.3 In a communication dated 17 October 1997, the United States notified the WTO Committee on Safeguards, pursuant to Article 12.1(a) SA, of the initiation of the safeguards investigation. The notification was circulated as a WTO document on 21 October 1997.[1]

2.4 On 15 January 1998, the USITC determined that wheat gluten was being imported into the United States in such increased quantities as to be a substantial cause of serious injury to the domestic wheat gluten industry. The United States notified the WTO Committee on Safeguards pursuant to Article 12.1(b) SA of these findings in a communication dated 11 February 1998.[2]

2.5 The USITC forwarded its injury findings and remedy recommendations to the President of the United States on 18 March 1998. In a communication dated 24 March 1998, the United States notified to the WTO Committee on Safeguards, pursuant to Article 12.1(b) SA, a finding of serious injury caused by increased imports of wheat gluten.[3] A copy of the USITC Report[4], containing the USITC's analysis and a summary of the information collected during the investigation and excluding information identified as confidential information[5], was provided with the United States notification.

2.6 On 3 April 1998, the United States Trade Representative (the "USTR") requested that the USITC provide additional information on the degree to which the domestic industry's adjustment plan would improve its competitiveness in the mid- and long-term. The additional information was requested to assist the interagency group that was considering what action to recommend that the United States President take. On 8 April 1998, the United States notified the WTO Committee on Safeguards, pursuant to Article 12.1(b) SA, of this request for ad-

[1] G/SG/N/6/USA/4, 21 October 1997.

[2] G/SG/N/8/USA/2, 12 February 1998.

[3] G/SG/N/8/USA/2/Rev.1, 27 March 1998.

[4] USITC Publication 3088, March 1998.

[5] A note on page iv of the USITC Report states: "Information that would reveal confidential operations of individual concerns may not be published and therefore has been deleted from this report. Such deletions are indicated by asterisks."

ditional information and informed the Committee that the United States President would make his determination not later than 31 May 1998.[6]

2.7 Under the "Proclamation 7103 of 30 May 1998 – To Facilitate Positive Adjustment to Competition From Imports of Wheat Gluten"[7] and the "Memorandum of 30 May 1998 - Action Under Section 203 of the Trade Act of 1974 Concerning Wheat Gluten"[8] by the United States President, the United States imposed definitive safeguard measures on imports of wheat gluten effective as of 1 June 1998. In a communication dated 4 June 1998, the United States notified the WTO Committee on Safeguards, pursuant to Article 12.1(c) and Article 9, footnote 2, SA, concerning the taking of a decision to apply a safeguard measure and the non-application of the safeguard measure to developing countries.[9]

2.8 The definitive safeguard measure consists of a quantitative restriction on certain imports of wheat gluten to the United States imposed for a period of three years plus 1 day, with annual increases in such quota limits of six per cent in the second year and the third year. The quantitative restriction is set at 57,521,000 kg for the first year, an amount which represents the total average imports in the crop years ending 30 June 1993 through 30 June 1995. Products from Canada[10] and certain other countries were excluded from the application of the safeguard measure. Within the overall quantitative restriction, the quota is allocated based on average import shares in the period covered by the crop years ending 30 June 1993 through 30 June 1995. The shares of countries excluded from the quota are assigned on a *pro rata* basis to countries subject to the quota.

2.9 Wheat gluten is produced from wheat flour. About 80 per cent of wheat gluten consumed in the US serves as input to the milling and baking industry with year-to-year variations depending upon the quality and protein content of the wheat crop. Wheat gluten must be used in the production of high-fibre and multi-grain breads. Non-bakery uses, including the pet food industry, account for the remaining 15-20 per cent of consumption. The process of manufacturing wheat gluten always results in two products: one part of gluten and approximately five

---

[6] G/SG/N/8/USA/2/Rev.1/Suppl.1, 9 April 1998.

[7] Exhibit US-2. "Proclamation 7103 of May 30 1998 - To Facilitate Positive Adjustment to Competition from Imports of Wheat Gluten", Federal Register, Vol. 63, No. 106, Wednesday 3 June 1998, "Presidential Documents", pp. 30359-30361.

[8] Exhibit US-3. "Memorandum of May 30 1998 - Action under Section 203 of the Trade Act of 1974 Concerning Wheat Gluten", Federal Register, Vol. 63, No. 106, Wednesday 3 June 1998, "Presidential Documents", pp. 30363-30364.

[9] G/SG/N/10/USA/2 and G/SG/N/11/USA/2, 8 June 1998.

[10] In the "Memorandum of 30 May 1998 - Action Under Section 203 of the Trade Act of 1974 Concerning Wheat Gluten", supra note 8, the United States President states: "I agree with the USITC's findings under section 311 (a) of the NAFTA Implementation Act, and therefore determine, pursuant to section 312(a) of the NAFTA Implementation Act, that imports of wheat gluten produced in Canada do not contribute importantly to the serious injury caused by imports and that imports of wheat gluten produced in Mexico do not account for a substantial share of total imports of such wheat gluten. Therefore pursuant to section 312(b) of the NAFTA Implementation Act, the quantitative limitation will not apply to imports of wheat gluten from Canada or Mexico."

parts of starch. Effluents can be sent to a distillery – which may be part of the wheat gluten company itself – for utilization in the production of ethanol or food grade alcohol. It is also possible to use certain parts of the effluents as animal feed stock, and others as wheat feed.

2.10 There are four US producers of wheat gluten: Manildra[11], Midwest, Archer Daniels Midland ("ADM") and Heartland Wheat Growers ("Heartland"). The latter began production in June 1996. Heartland, Manildra and Midwest accounted for the substantial majority of domestic production of wheat gluten during the period of investigation. Each of the companies produces wheat gluten and wheat starch in a joint production process. Heartland, Manildra and Midwest all produce other by-products or derived products. Midwest, in particular, further processes wheat starch into alcohol.

III. PROCEDURES ADOPTED BY THE PANEL CONCERNING PRIVATE CONFIDENTIAL INFORMATION

3.1 In order to facilitate the Panel's obtention of information that had been deleted from the public version of the USITC Report of March 1998, the Panel adopted "Procedures Governing Private Confidential Information" as part of its working procedures on 1 February 2000. Pursuant to these procedures, only "approved persons" – i.e. a Panel member, a representative, or a Secretariat employee - whose selection or authorization has been notified to the Chairman of the Panel were permitted to view or hear information designated by a party as private confidential information in the course of the Panel proceedings. Such approved persons were under an obligation not to disclose that information, or allow it to be disclosed, to any other person other than another approved person, except in accordance with the Procedures. The Panel was under an obligation not to disclose private confidential information in its interim and final reports, but could make statements of conclusion drawn from such information. These Procedures are set forth in Attachment 4.

3.2 The Panel proposed a further procedure to the parties on 24 February 2000.[12] However, in light of communications received from the parties in respect of this proposed procedure, the Panel did not adopt this procedure.

---

[11] Manildra is a wholly owned subsidiary of a United States company which is, in turn, wholly owned by an Australian company.

[12] See infra, para. 8.10, for a description of this proposed procedure.

IV. PARTIES' REQUESTS FOR FINDINGS AND RECOMMENDATIONS

A. *European Community*

4.1 In its submissions made before the Panel, the European Community requests the Panel to find that the United States, by imposing the definitive safeguard measures on wheat gluten, has breached Articles I and XIX of the GATT 1994 and Articles 2.1, 4, 5, 8 and 12 of the Agreement on Safeguards.[13]

B. *United States*

4.2 The United States submits that its definitive safeguard measure on wheat gluten satisfies the United States' obligations under the Agreement on Safeguards and the GATT 1994.

V. ARGUMENTS OF THE PARTIES

5.1 The arguments of the parties are set out in their submissions to the Panel. The parties' submissions as well as their communications and comments in respect of the request by the Panel for certain information that had been identified as confidential information and deleted from the public version of the USITC Report are attached. The communications of the parties concerning newly proposed procedures governing private confidential information are attached as well (see Attachments 1 and 2).

VI. ARGUMENTS OF THE THIRD PARTIES

6.1 The arguments of the third parties, Australia, Canada and New Zealand, are set out in their submissions to the Panel (see Attachment 3).

VII. INTERIM REVIEW

7.1 On 28 June 2000, the European Community and the United States each submitted written requests for review by the Panel of precise aspects of the interim report issued on 19 June 2000. Neither party requested an additional meeting with the Panel. On 5 July 2000, the parties submitted written comments on one another's requests for interim review.

[13] See European Community first written submission, Attachment 1-1, para. 186; European Community second written submission, Attachment 1-4, para. 129. We note that in the request for the establishment of a Panel (WT/DS 166/3) the European Community also alleged a violation of Article 4.2 of the Agreement on Agriculture. The European Community did not submit any arguments in support of this claim. We address this claim infra, para. 8.221 .

7.2 We have reviewed the comments presented by the European Community and the United States and have finalized our report, taking into account those comments by the parties which we considered justified, and also making certain technical and typographical refinements.

A. *Comments by the European Community*

7.3 In general, the European Community disagrees with the thrust of paragraphs 8.1 through 8.127 of the Panel's findings. According to the European Community, the Panel does not draw the necessary negative inferences from the refusal by the United States and its industry to disclose the information requested by the Panel[14] in spite of the fact that procedures for protecting private confidential information had been adopted by the Panel after consulting the parties.[15] The European Community asserts that the Panel report does not correctly appreciate that information was unjustifiably removed from the published version of the USITC Report, whilst it could have been provided in a manner which did not impinge upon business secrets of individual companies, and maintains its request that the Panel find that Article 4.2(c) SA is thereby violated. Moreover, the European Community does not find any basis in the covered agreements for the Panel's view that factors which are not explicitly mentioned in Article 4.2(a) SA only need to be investigated if they have been raised in a certain manner during the national proceedings. We have maintained these paragraphs in our findings, and have added certain clarifying language in paragraph 8.59 pursuant to the EC comment that the Panel does not draw the necessary conclusions in paragraphs 8.57-8.66 from the fact that the allocation *methodology* concerning profits and losses could - and therefore should - have been explained in detail in the USITC Report itself.

7.4 The European Community submits certain detailed comments and suggested textual modifications with respect to paragraphs 8.5, 8.6, 8.91, 8.131, 8.151, 8.175 and 8.176. In addition, according to the European Community, footnote 156 and paragraphs 8.160, 8.177 and 8.182 incorrectly reflected the imports excluded from the application of the measure. We have made certain modifications pursuant to these comments, including in footnote 156.

7.5 With respect to the Panel's exercise of judicial economy in paragraphs 8.184 and 8.220, the European Community requests that the Panel make at least factual findings with respect to the claims of the European Community under Article XIX ("unforeseen developments") and Article I of the GATT 1994 and Article 5 SA. Having determined that the measure at issue is inconsistent with Articles 2.1 and 4.2 SA, and exercising the discretion implicit in the principle of judicial economy, we do not deem it necessary to examine whether the measure is also inconsistent with Article XIX of the GATT 1994 ("unforeseen develop-

[14] See infra, section VIII.B.
[15] See supra, section III.

ments"), nor whether the form, level and allocation of the inconsistent measure are in breach of Article 5 SA or Article I of the GATT 1994. We have clarified our language to this effect in the cited paragraphs and have added footnote 201.

B. Comments by the United States

7.6 The United States suggests certain clarifications to the language in paragraph 8.69 concerning the evaluation of relevant factors in addition to those listed in Article 4.2(a) SA. The United States requests the insertion of certain clarifications of its argument in paragraph 8.134 concerning the USITC's findings relating to other possible causal factors. The United States also comments on the language used by the Panel in paragraph 8.209 concerning the requirement in Article 12.4 to notify the provisional measure before applying it. We have made certain modifications pursuant to these comments, including the insertion of additional language describing the United States argument in paragraph 8.134 and the insertion of footnotes 72 and 129-135.

7.7 The United States further asserts that the Panel should delete certain portions of paragraph 8.151. We have maintained these portions of this paragraph, and have made certain clarifications. With respect to the United States comment concerning the role of footnote 1 SA in the context of the imposition by free-trade area members of a safeguard measure, we have made certain additions to paragraph 8.181.

VIII. FINDINGS

A. Standard of Review

1. Arguments of the Parties

8.1 The parties each made extensive submissions with respect to the standard of review that the Panel should apply. The parties agree that we should not engage in a *de novo* review of the USITC safeguard investigation and determination, and that Article 11 of the DSU articulates the appropriate general standard of review for WTO panels.

(a) European Community

8.2 The European Community, on the basis of Article 11 of the DSU and the panel reports in *Korea-Definitive Safeguard Measure on Imports of Certain Dairy Products*[16] ("*Korea-Dairy Safeguard*") and *Argentina-Safeguard Meas-*

---

[16] Panel Report, *Korea - Definitive Safeguard Measure on Imports of Certain Dairy Products* ("*Korea -Dairy Safeguard*"), WT/DS98/R and Corr. 1, adopted 12 January 2000, DSR 2000:I, 49 as modified by the Appellate Body Report, WT/DS98/AB/R, DSR 2000:I, 3.

ures on Imports of Footwear[17] ("*Argentina-Footwear Safeguard*"), requests that the Panel make an objective assessment of whether: i) the domestic authority has considered all relevant facts as a whole, including specifically each factor listed in Article 4.2(a) SA; ii) the published report of the investigation contains adequate explanation of how the facts support the determination made; and iii) the determination made is consistent with the United States' obligations under the Agreement on Safeguards and the GATT 1994. According to the European Community, the role of the Panel is to determine whether the United States International Trade Commission ("USITC") fully and objectively considered the evidence before it, including any evidence that detracts from an affirmative determination of increased imports, serious injury or causation. The Panel should also verify the adequacy of the USITC's reasoning by reviewing whether the findings and conclusions made by the USITC are consistent with the evidence. The European Community asserts that the Panel cannot be content with a superficial glance at the issues, taking at face value the text of the USITC Report. Rather, the European Community submits that the Panel must concentrate on the substance of the evidence that actually is in the Report or should have been in the Report since it was either considered during the investigation procedure, or should have been considered as pertinent evidence that was publicly available, or had been submitted to the USITC during the investigation procedure. The European Community submits to the Panel Exhibits EC-10, -12, -13 and -14, which are documents not submitted to the USITC during its investigation.

(b) United States

8.3 The United States submits that the Panel should apply the standard of review in Article 11 of the DSU, as articulated by the panel in *Argentina – Footwear Safeguard*.[18] According to the United States, the European Community misrepresents the standard of review that the European Community purports to espouse by advancing arguments that it claims undermine the USITC conclusions. According to the United States, the European Community fails to demonstrate why the USITC's explanation of its decision was inadequate. Instead, the European Community attempts to persuade the Panel to engage in a *de novo* investigation of the underlying facts. The United States asserts that it is inappropriate for a panel to attempt to conduct its own assessment of the raw data reviewed by the competent authority during its investigation. In addition, with reference to Exhibits EC-10, 12, 13 and 14, the United States submits that the European Community should not be permitted to submit data to a WTO panel that it could have submitted to the competent authority during the investigation, but did not. In the

---

[17] Panel Report, *Argentina - Safeguard Measures on Imports of Footwear* ("*Argentina - Footwear Safeguard*"), WT/DS121/R, adopted 12 January 2000, DSR 2000:II, 575, para. 8.124 as modified by the Appellate Body Report, WT/DS121/AB/R, DSR 2000:I, 515

[18] Ibid, para. 8.124.

United States view, this would invite strategic manipulation by parties of the process before the domestic investigating authority.

2. Evaluation by the Panel

8.4 Article 11 of the DSU articulates the appropriate standard of review for panels examining the consistency of a safeguard measure with the provisions of the Agreement on Safeguards.[19] Pursuant to that Article, "a panel should make an objective assessment of the matter before it, including an objective assessment of the facts of the case and the applicability of and conformity with the relevant covered agreements...".

8.5 Thus, we agree with the parties that a *de novo* review would be inappropriate. However, we also consider relevant the view of previous panels that for us to adopt a policy of total deference to the findings of the national authorities could not ensure an "objective assessment" as foreseen by Article 11 of the DSU.[20] In determining whether the United States complied with its obligations under the Agreement on Safeguards and the GATT 1994, our review will consist of an objective assessment, pursuant to Article 11 of the DSU, of: whether the USITC considered all relevant facts, including an evaluation of "all relevant factors of an objective and quantifiable nature having a bearing on the situation of [the] industry" in Article 4.2(a) SA; whether the USITC demonstrated the existence of the causal link between increased imports and serious injury and did not attribute to imports injury caused by other factors; whether the published report on the investigation contains an adequate, reasoned and reasonable explanation of how the facts in the record before the USITC support the determination made with respect to increased imports, serious injury and causation; and, consequently, of whether the determination made is consistent with the obligations of the United States under the Agreement on Safeguards and the GATT 1994. We note that previous WTO panels have adopted a similar approach.[21]

8.6 We do not see our review as a substitute for the investigation conducted by the USITC. Our role is limited to a review of the consistency of the United States measure with the Agreement on Safeguards and Articles I and XIX of the GATT 1994. Within the framework established by the Agreement on Safeguards, it is for the USITC to determine how to collect and evaluate data and how to assess and weigh the relevant factors in making determinations of serious injury and causation. It is not our role to collect new data, nor to consider evidence which could have been presented to the USITC by interested parties in the investigation, but was not. We refer in this regard to Exhibits EC-10, -12, -13 and -14.

---

[19] We find support for our view in Appellate Body Report, *Argentina - Footwear Safeguard, supra*, footnote 17, para. 120.

[20] Panel Report, *Korea – Dairy Safeguard*, supra, footnote 16, paras. 7.26, 7.30-7.31.

[21] Panel Report, *Argentina – Footwear Safeguard*, supra, footnote 17, para. 8.124; Panel Report, *Korea - Dairy Safeguard*, supra, footnote 16, paras. 7.26, 7.30-7.31.

However, we do not consider it necessary here to make a specific finding with respect to the admissibility of the United States government (Department of Agriculture) statistics pertaining to monthly pricing data which the European Community submitted as part of its Exhibits EC-10 and EC-12 in conjunction with its first written submission. These statistics were not part of the record before the USITC, but the European Community argued that, as they were United States government statistics, the USITC could and should have taken them into account. The submission by the United States of Exhibit US-10 provided quarterly pricing data that were in the USITC record but had previously been redacted from the public version of the USITC Report. As both parties subsequently referred to, and relied on, the quarterly pricing data in Exhibit US-10 in the course of these proceedings, we also referred to and relied on these data, which we deemed relevant and sufficient for reaching our determination. It was therefore not necessary for us to consider whether or not to refer to pricing data outside the USITC record in reaching our determination.[22]

B. *Panel Request for Certain Confidential Information Redacted from the Published USITC Report*

8.7 The Panel considered that having access to certain information that had been redacted from the public version of the USITC Report would facilitate its objective assessment of the facts of the case. The Panel also considered that the adoption of certain procedures governing confidential information would facilitate its obtention of such information. Accordingly, on 24 January 2000 the Panel indicated to the parties that it proposed to adopt procedures governing the treatment of confidential information, and sent a draft of the proposed procedures to the parties for their comments. After giving the parties an opportunity to comment on the draft procedures and considering the communications received from the European Community and the United States in this regard, the Panel adopted the "Procedures Governing Private Confidential Information".[23] On 1 February 2000, the Panel transmitted to the parties the following communication, containing a request by the Panel to the United States for certain confidential information that had been redacted from the public version of the USITC Report:

> "The Panel requests the United States to submit the following information furnished by the domestic industry (or derived from information furnished by the domestic industry) that was deleted from the public version of the ITC Report of March 1998:

---

[22] The European Community submitted Exhibits EC-10 and EC-12 in conjunction with its first written submission (Attachment 1-1), and referred to the statistics in EC Exhibit-12 in its first oral statement (Attachment 1-2, paras. 15-16). However, in its second written submission, Attachment 1-4, paras. 34-35, the European Community referred to the USITC quarterly pricing data in Exhibit US-10.

[23] Attachment 4.

-data on p. II-18, including table showing "individual industry costs on a per-pound basis";

-Table 10 on p. II-19;

-data on p. II-20, including table showing "individual industry costs as a percentage of the cost of goods sold" and information on cost allocation methodology (but not including Table 11);

-Table 12 on p. II-21;

-Table 8 on p. II-16;

-Table C-1 (p. C-4); Table C-2 (p. C-6); and Table C-3 (p. C-8).

Having given the parties an opportunity to comment on its "Proposed Procedures Governing Business Confidential Information" and having considered the communications received from the European Communities and the United States in this regard, the Panel has adopted the attached "Procedures Governing Private Confidential Information". These Procedures supplement the working procedures already adopted by the Panel. In accordance with these Procedures, and in anticipation of the submission by the United States of the requested information, the Panel requests that the European Community notify the Chairman of the Panel and the United States of its representatives who are "approved persons".

The Panel is aware of the provisions of Article 3.2 of the Safeguards Agreement. The Panel believes that the procedures in effect in this case are adequate to protect the confidentiality of information submitted to it. The Panel notes the recent statement by the Appellate Body in *Canada – Measures Affecting the Export of Civilian Aircraft* (WT/DS70/AB/R, adopted 20 August 1999, para. 204) that "a refusal to provide information requested by the panel may lead to inferences being drawn about the inculpatory character of the information withheld."

8.8 The United States did not submit the requested information to the Panel. The response by the United States to this request for information, as well as the subsequent related communications of the parties are attached.[24]

8.9 On 24 February 2000, the Panel proposed further procedures to the parties for viewing the requested information. The communications of the parties with respect to these proposed procedures are attached.[25]

---

[24] European Community - Attachments 1-5,1-9 to 1-11; United States -Attachments 2-6, 2-9 to 2-11.

[25] European Community - Attachments 1-12, 1-13; United States -Attachments 2-12, 2-13.

8.10 On 1 March 2000, the Panel communicated the following ruling to the parties with respect to the information requested by the Panel:

> "In its communication to the Panel of 8 February 2000, the United States indicated that the various domestic producers would grant permission for release of all the information the Panel had requested if the Panel amended its Procedures Governing Private Confidential Information as follows:
>
> > "... the procedures should be amended to make clear that: 1) the Panel will review the CBI exclusively *in camera*; and 2) any Panel member, or WTO employee, who views or hears such information shall be under an obligation not to disclose the information, or allow it to be disclosed, to any person. For the reasons set out in the WGIC letter, the companies concerned are not prepared to grant permission for the CBI to be divulged to EC representatives."
>
> In its communication to the Panel of 11 February 2000, the European Community stated, *inter alia*:
>
> > "The course of action suggested by the United States ... would irreparably damage the fairness of this dispute settlement procedure, since the Panellists and the officials of the WTO Secretariat assisting the Panel would have access to *ex parte* communications, in flagrant breach of Article 18.1 of the DSU and of the Rules of Conduct on the appointment of Panellists."
>
> Article 18.1 of the DSU states:
>
> > "There shall be no *ex parte* communications with the panel or Appellate Body concerning matters under consideration by the panel or Appellate Body."
>
> The Panel considered that, in light of Article 18.1 of the DSU and the position expressed by the European Community in this case, it should not view the requested information under the conditions outlined by the United States.
>
> On 24 February 2000, the Panel proposed further procedures to the parties for viewing the requested information, as follows:
>
> > "No more than two representatives of the United States would bring the requested information to a designated location at the premises of the WTO in Geneva on Thursday 2 March 2000. The Panel, two professional staff of the WTO Secretariat, and no more than two representatives of the European Communities would review the information exclusively *in camera*. These individuals would be under an obligation not to disclose the information, or to allow it to be disclosed, to any person. No photocopies of the informa-

> tion would be permitted. The Panel, the two professional staff of the WTO Secretariat, and the representatives of the European Communities may take written summary notes of the information for the sole purpose of the Panel process. Any such notes would be destroyed at the conclusion of the Panel. While the Panel would be under an obligation not to disclose the information in its report, it could make statements of conclusion drawn from such information."

In light of the communications received from the parties concerning these proposed procedures, the Panel has decided not to adopt the proposed procedures.

Accordingly, the Panel has decided to proceed with its examination on the basis of the record as it currently stands."

8.11 In our view, the protracted exchange of communications between the parties about the circumstances under which the Panel should view the requested information demonstrates the existence of a serious systemic issue as to the relationship between, on the one hand, the confidentiality obligations under Article 3.2 SA of a Member's investigating authorities with respect to confidential information obtained in the course of a domestic safeguards investigation and, on the other hand, the duties of Members when faced with a panel request for such confidential information under Article 13 DSU. The Panel's efforts to develop a consensual approach to the conditions under which the Panel might view the requested information were ultimately unsuccessful.

8.12 We remain of the view that having access to the requested information would have facilitated our objective assessment of the facts of this case, and of the matter before us. We recall the view expressed by a previous panel and the Appellate Body that the WTO dispute settlement system cannot function optimally if relevant information is withheld from a panel.[26] While the submission of the requested information would certainly have furnished a more extensive basis for our examination, we consider that the Panel record in this case - including the USITC Report and the oral and written submissions of the parties and third par-

---

[26] In Canada – Measures Affecting the Export of Civilian Aircraft, the Appellate Body observed that the "continued viability of [the dispute settlement] system depends, in substantial measure, on the willingness of panels to take all steps open to them to induce the parties to the dispute to comply with their duty to provide information deemed necessary for dispute settlement" (Appellate Body Report, *Canada – Measures Affecting the Export of Civilian Aircraft* ("*Canada – Aircraft*"), WT/DS70/AB/R, adopted 20 August 1999, DSR 1999:III, 1377, para. 204. See also Panel Report, *Chile – Taxes on Alcoholic Beverages* ("*Chile – Alcoholic Beverages*"), WT/DS87/R, WT/DS110/R, adopted 12 January 2000, as modified by the Appellate Body Report, WT/DS87/AB/R, WT/DS110/AB/R, DSR 2000:I, 303, note 390.

ties - provides sufficient basis for us to conduct the objective assessment of the matter required by Article 11 of the DSU.[27]

C. *Evaluation of Claims*

1. *Claims under Articles 2.1 and 4 SA and Article XIX of the GATT 1994*

(a) Redaction of Certain Confidential Information from the Published USITC Report

(i) Arguments of the Parties

European Community

8.13 The European Community argues that the United States violated Articles 2.1 and 4 SA, as much of the data on which the USITC findings are based have been omitted from the public version of the USITC Report. According to the European Community, the USITC's findings based on secret data are unverifiable and unreviewable. The European Community argues that Article 4.2(c) SA presupposes that the detailed analysis and the demonstration of the relevance of factors are published, unless confidentiality is really an issue. The European Community does not contest that under certain specific circumstances, the protection of certain information regarding individual companies may be justified. However, in the EC view, confidentiality is not an issue in the context of whether or not data in summary form, such as aggregate data, is provided. According to the European Community, the USITC could have disclosed the relevant elements of confidential information while keeping it confidential, by providing aggregate data, or by describing the developments in performance of an individual company by using percentages or by showing trends in indexed form.

United States

8.14 According to the United States, the EC argument that a determination may be found inadequately explained under the Agreement on Safeguards due to failure to disclose confidential information flies in the face of the Agreement's plain terms: Article 3.2 SA prohibits domestic authorities from disclosing confidential information. Article 4.2(c) SA makes clear that the requirement to publish a "detailed analysis of the case under investigation" and "demonstration of the relevance of the factors examined" cannot entail the publication of information

[27] We note that the United States deemed that the published USITC Report "provides sufficient information for the Panel to conduct the analysis required by Article 11 of the DSU." See United States Response to Panel Question 3, Attachment 2-4, para. 7. For its part, the European Community asserted that "...it cannot be admissible for a party to contrive that a Panel is unable to carry out its tasks under Article 11 of the DSU simply by withholding self-proclaimed "confidential information"." See European Community Response to Panel Question 3, Attachment 1-3.

treated as confidential under Article 3.2 SA, as such publication shall be "in accordance with the provisions of Article 3." The United States submits that the use of percentages and indexes, as suggested by the European Community, would not be adequate to alleviate the disclosure problems in this case. According to the United States, when the universe of reporting companies is small, the USITC faces the same problem in reporting data in percentage and index form as it faces in reporting the actual aggregate data – i.e. the disclosure of confidential data.

(ii) Evaluation by the Panel

8.15 The issue before us relates to the nature of the obligations that Articles 2.1 and 4 SA, and specifically Article 4.2(c) SA, imposes upon Members concerning the contents of the published report of the safeguards investigation and their interaction with the obligations imposed upon Members by Article 3.2 SA in respect of the treatment of "confidential" information in a domestic safeguards investigation.

8.16 Several provisions of the Agreement are relevant to our consideration of this issue. Article 4.2(c) SA provides:

> "The competent authorities shall publish promptly, in accordance with the provisions of Article 3, a detailed analysis of the case under investigation as well as a demonstration of the relevance of the factors examined."

8.17 Article 3 SA is entitled "Investigation". Article 3.1 SA provides, in relevant part:

> "The competent authorities shall publish a report setting forth their findings and reasoned conclusions reached on all pertinent issues of fact and law."

8.18 Article 3.2 SA deals specifically with the treatment of "confidential" information by the investigating authorities in the course of the investigation. It reads:

> "Any information which is by nature confidential or which is provided on a confidential basis shall, upon cause being shown, be treated as such by the competent authorities. Such information shall not be disclosed without permission of the party submitting it. Parties providing confidential information may be requested to furnish non-confidential summaries thereof or, if such parties indicate that such information cannot be summarized, the reasons why a summary cannot be provided. However, if the competent authorities find that a request for confidentiality is not warranted and if the party concerned is either unwilling to make the information public or to authorize its disclosure in generalized or summary form, the authorities may disregard such information unless it can be demonstrated to their satisfaction from appropriate sources that the information is correct."

8.19 Thus, Article 4.2(c) SA, including by cross-reference Article 3 SA[28], requires written presentation of a detailed analysis of the case, including the findings and reasoned conclusions reached on all pertinent issues of fact and law and a demonstration of the relevance of the factors examined, while maintaining the confidentiality of certain information. Article 3.2 SA places an obligation upon domestic investigating authorities not to disclose - including in their published report setting forth their findings and reasoned conclusions reached on all pertinent issues of fact and law and demonstrating the relevance of the factors examined - information which is "by nature confidential or which is provided on a confidential basis" without permission of the party submitting it. Article 3.2 SA does not define the term "confidential" nor does it contain any examples of the type of information that might qualify as "by nature confidential" or "information that is submitted on a confidential basis".

8.20 Article 3.2 SA requires that information that is by nature confidential or which is submitted on a confidential basis shall, upon cause being shown, be treated as such by the competent authorities. In the absence of a detailed elaboration or definition of the types of information that must be treated as confidential, we consider that the investigating authorities enjoy a certain amount of discretion in determining whether or not information is to be treated as "confidential". While Article 3.2 does not specifically address the nature of any policies pertaining to the treatment of such "confidential" information which a Member's investigating authority may or must adopt, that provision does specify that such "information shall not be disclosed without permission of the party submitting it". The provision is specific and mandatory in this regard. This furnishes an assurance that the confidentiality of qualifying information will be preserved in the course of a domestic safeguards investigation, and encourages the fullest possible disclosure of relevant information by interested parties.

8.21 Given that the very terms of Article 4.2(c) expressly incorporate the provisions of Article 3, and given the specific and mandatory language of Article 3.2 dealing with the required treatment of information that is by nature confidential or is submitted on a confidential basis, the requirement in Article 4.2(c) to publish a "detailed analysis of the case under investigation" and "demonstration of the relevance of the factors examined" cannot entail the publication of "information which is by nature confidential or which is provided on a confidential basis" within the meaning of Article 3.2 SA.

---

[28] The European Community's request for establishment of the Panel, WT/DS166/3, which establishes the Panel's terms of reference under Article 7 DSU, does not contain a claim under Article 3 SA. Thus, we are not being asked to examine whether or not the United States fulfilled its obligations under Article 3 SA. Nevertheless, as the very terms of Article 4.2(c) expressly incorporate the provisions of Article 3, it is difficult to see how a panel could examine whether a Member had complied with Article 4.2(c) without also referring to Article 3. See, for example, Appellate Body Report, *Argentina – Footwear Safeguard*, supra, footnote 17, para. 74.

8.22 The European Community asserts that aggregate data cannot be considered "confidential" in this sense and that, even if it is "confidential", it could be presented in percentages or indexed form so as to protect its confidentiality.[29] In response, the United States explains its confidentiality policy[30] and appends a copy of a memorandum relating to this policy.[31] The USITC Report contains the following text: "Note – Information that would reveal confidential operations of individual concerns may not be published and therefore has been deleted from this report. Such deletions are indicated by asterisks".[32]

8.23 While the United States has described the USITC's efforts to characterize as much confidential information as possible in its Report without compromising the confidential nature of that information, the USITC might ideally have been more creative in trying to provide the essence of the confidential information in its findings in the published USITC Report. We draw attention to the provision in Article 3.2 SA that parties providing confidential information in a domestic safeguard investigation "may be requested to furnish non-confidential summaries thereof or, if such parties indicate that such information cannot be summarized, the reasons why a summary cannot be provided..." The language of this provision is hortatory.[33] However, this is one vehicle envisaged by the Agreement on Safeguards that may provide a greater degree of transparency while respecting the confidentiality of qualifying information.

8.24 Nevertheless, given the small number of firms comprising the United States domestic industry (and the non-US producers and exporters) in this case; the fundamental importance of maintaining the confidentiality of sensitive business information in order to ensure the effectiveness of domestic safeguards investigations; the discretion implied in Article 3.2 SA for the investigating authorities to determine whether or not "cause" has been shown for information to be treated as "confidential"; and the specific and mandatory prohibition in that

---

29 We observe that the types of information redacted from the published version of the USITC Report are generally the types of information that might be treated as confidential, relating inter alia to profitability data, input costs, value of assets, capital expenditures and R&D expenses, importers inventories and producers' imports. We do not understand the European Community to argue that this type of information would never merit confidential treatment. Rather, we understand the EC to contest the redaction of such information in this case because of the EC's view that it was "aggregate data" which could have been provided in summary form.

30 United States first written submission, Attachment 2-1, para. 156. The United States submits that its applicable domestic rules "assure that the publication of aggregate information does not disclose to competitors the confidential information of any firm. Under that policy, when confidential business data come from one or two firms, the published report does not disclose the data. Moreover, to assure that aggregations do not disclose a particular firm's information, aggregate summaries are not provided when the information comes from three or more firms, but one firm accounts for 75 per cent of the total or two firms account for 90 per cent."

31 Exhibit US-9.

32 USITC Report, p. iv.

33 This contrasts with the mandatory nature of the language in Article 6.5 of the Agreement on Implementation of Article VI of the GATT 1994 (the Anti-dumping Agreement) and Article 12.4 of the Agreement on Subsidies and Countervailing Measures.

provision against disclosure by them of such information without permission of the party submitting it[34], we cannot find that the United States has violated its obligations under Articles 2.1 and 4 SA, nor specifically under Article 4.2(c), by not disclosing, in the published report of the USITC, information qualifying under the USITC policy as information "which is by nature confidential or which is provided on a confidential basis", including aggregate data.[35]

8.25 While we acknowledge the possibility for a Member to misuse the confidentiality provisions in the Safeguards Agreement by withholding non-qualifying information, we presume good faith implementation by Members and we see no basis to conclude that, in this case, the USITC systematically extended confidential treatment to information that did not merit such treatment. We note that the United States supplied in its "corrigendum" (Exhibit US-10) certain information - including quarterly pricing data in Table 18 of the USITC Report – that had originally been identified by the USITC as requiring confidential treatment. The European Community considers that the submission by the United States of its "corrigendum" is an admission of violation of the obligation to publish certain information "promptly" under Article 4.2(c) SA.[36] We view this rather as a correction by the USITC of the application of its own confidentiality policy.[37]

8.26 **For these reasons, we find that the United States has not acted inconsistently with Articles 2.1 and 4 SA, nor specifically with Article 4.2(c) SA, in not disclosing certain confidential information in the published USITC Report.**

(b) "increased quantities" of Imports

(i) Arguments of the Parties

European Community

8.27 The European Community argues that, while Article 2.1 SA refers to imports "in such increased quantities, absolute or relative to domestic production...", the analysis in the USITC Report was limited to a comparison of absolute data, often selectively chosen, and focusing on end-to-end comparison of

---

34 United States Response to Panel Question 3, Attachment 2-4.

35 We are addressing here the EC claim under Articles 2.1 and 4, and specifically Article 4.2(c) SA, concerning the required contents of the published report. We are not ruling here on the impact of Article 3.2 SA on a Member's disclosure of confidential information to a WTO panel.

36 See European Community Response to Panel Question 14, Attachment 1-3.

37 We note in any event the United States permits interested governments access to confidential information under certain circumstances and subject to certain conditions (see United States Response to Panel Question 4, Attachment 2-4) and that although the European Community filed a notice of appearance early in the USITC investigation, the European Community did not avail itself of the opportunity to have access to the confidential information through an administrative protective order.

data.[38] We understand that this particular EC allegation pertains to the USITC finding of "increased imports" at p. I-10 of the USITC Report and is limited to Article XIX GATT 1994 and Article 2.1 SA.

United States

8.28 The United States submits that the USITC concluded that the criterion of "increased imports" was satisfied based on the absolute increase in imports from 128 million pounds in 1993 to 177 million pounds in 1997, as well as the relative increase compared to domestic production. The United States submits that the USITC also analyzed the trends in imports, noting that virtually all of the increase in imports occurred in the last two years of the period, during which imports increased from 128 million pounds in 1995 to 156 million pounds in 1996 to 177 million pounds in 1997. The United States further submits that during the investigation, EU producers conceded that imports had increased.

(ii) Evaluation by the Panel

8.29 Article XIX:1(a) GATT 1994 states, in pertinent part:

> "If ... any product *is being imported* into the territory of that Member *in such increased quantities* and under such conditions as to cause or threaten serious injury to domestic producers in that territory of like or directly competitive products..." (emphasis added)

8.30 Article 2.1 SA states:

> A Member may apply a safeguard measure to a product only if that Member has determined, pursuant to the provisions set out below, that such product *is being imported* into its territory *in such increased quantities, absolute or relative to domestic production*, and under such conditions as to cause or threaten to cause serious injury to the domestic industry that produces like or directly competitive products. (emphasis added, footnote omitted)

8.31 It is clear to us that Article XIX:1(a) of the GATT 1994 and Article 2.1 SA contain the initial threshold requirement that there be an increase in imports. In the absence of an increase in imports, there would certainly be no need to perform any quantitative or qualitative analysis concerning the trends in imports and other factors relating to serious injury or causation under the Agreement on Safeguards. However, we note that Article XIX:1(a) of the GATT 1994 and Article 2.1 SA do not speak only of an "increase" in imports. Rather, they contain specific requirements with respect to the quantitative and qualitative nature of the "increase" in imports of the product concerned. Both Article XIX:1(a) of the

[38] See European Community first written submission, Attachment 1-1, para. 55.

GATT 1994 and Article 2.1 SA require that a product is being imported into the territory of the Member concerned *in such increased quantities* (absolute or relative to domestic production) as to cause or threaten serious injury. Thus, not just *any* increase in imports will suffice. Rather, we agree with the Appellate Body's finding in *Argentina-Footwear Safeguard* that the increase must be sufficiently recent, sudden, sharp and significant, both quantitatively and qualitatively, to cause or threaten to cause serious injury.[39]

8.32 Turning to examine the USITC determination of "increased imports", we note that the USITC determined that there was an absolute increase in imports, as well as an increase in imports relative to domestic production, during the period of investigation ("POI").[40] In support of that determination, the USITC Report referred to data[41], which indicate that imports dropped from 128 million pounds in 1993 to 124 million pounds in 1994 and then rose to 128 million pounds in 1995, 156 million pounds in 1996 and 177 million pounds in 1997. The USITC observed that the volume of imports increased by 38 per cent over the POI[42], and found that "virtually all" of the increase occurred in 1996 and 1997.[43] The USITC also referred to data pertaining to the ratio of imports to production that indicate a drop from 100.6 per cent in 1993 to 88.2 per cent in 1994 and then an increase to 89.7 per cent in 1995, 139 per cent in 1996 and 145.4 per cent in 1997.[44]

8.33 While these data indicate a decrease in imports - both absolute and relative to domestic production - early in the POI, they subsequently indicate a sharp and substantial rise through to the end of the POI. We view this increase in imports reflected in the data before the USITC - both absolute and relative to domestic production - as recent, sudden, sharp and significant.

8.34 **For these reasons, we find that the USITC Report provides an adequate, reasoned and reasonable explanation of how the facts support the determination made with respect to "increased imports" and that the USITC's determination that wheat gluten was being imported in "increased quantities" was not inconsistent with the threshold requirement of Article XIX:1(a) and Article 2.1 SA of imports in "increased quantities".**

---

39 The Appellate Body in Argentina-Footwear Safeguard stated: "And this language in both Article 2.1 of the Agreement on Safeguards and Article XIX:1 (a) of the GATT 1994, we believe, requires that the increase in imports must have been recent enough, sudden enough, sharp enough and significant enough, both quantitatively and qualitatively, to cause or threaten to cause 'serious injury'." Appellate Body Report, *Argentina-Footwear Safeguard*, supra, footnote 17, para. 131.

40 USITC Report, p. I-10. The period of investigation was 1993-1997.

41 USITC Report, pp. II-12.

42 USITC Report, p. II-9.

43 USTIC Report, p. I-10.

44 USITC Report, p. II-15.

8.35 It remains for us to examine whether these imports were in such increased quantities *as to cause serious injury*. This finding must, therefore, be read in light of our findings below with respect to serious injury and causation.[45]

(c) Serious Injury

(i) Arguments of the Parties

European Community

8.36 The European Community argues that, under Article 4.2 SA, a Member must evaluate all factors having a bearing on the situation of the industry and must demonstrate that serious injury has taken place. With respect to the USITC's serious injury finding, the European Community alleges that: (i) the USITC failed to evaluate all relevant factors having a bearing on the situation of the industry under Article 4.2(a) SA; and (ii) the findings and conclusions of the USITC with regard to those factors which it did investigate were not supported by the evidence.

United States

8.37 The United States counters that the USITC's determination was based on the whole record, including an examination of all relevant factors in Article 4.2(a). The United States asserts that the European Community's factor-by-factor review of the evidence largely obscures the USITC's actual reasoning on injury and causation. According to the United States, the European Community takes exception to the weight the USITC gave to each factor and the conclusions the USITC drew from the available evidence. However, the relative weight accorded each factor is within the discretion of the competent authorities, so long as they reach a reasoned conclusion. Moreover, the United States asserts, in its report the USITC noted that "virtually all", but not *all*, factors pertaining to the serious injury analysis were negative.

(ii) Evaluation by the Panel

8.38 Article 4.2(a) SA reads:

> "In the investigation to determine whether increased imports have caused or are threatening to cause serious injury to a domestic industry under the terms of this Agreement, the competent authorities shall evaluate all relevant factors of an objective and quantifiable nature having a bearing on the situation of that industry, in particular, the rate and amount of the increase in imports of the product concerned in absolute and relative terms, the share of the domestic

[45] See, in particular, infra, para. 8.98.

market taken by increased imports, changes in the level of sales, production, productivity, capacity utilization, profits and losses, and employment."

8.39 Article 4.2(a) SA requires that the competent authorities evaluate "all relevant factors of an objective and quantifiable nature having a bearing on the situation of that industry, in particular,..." the factors listed in that provision. We note that the language in this provision is mandatory ("shall..."). Furthermore, this list is preceded by the term "in particular...". On the basis of the text of the provision, we therefore concur with the shared view of the parties[46] that all of the factors listed in Article 4.2(a) must be evaluated.[47] Of course, an examination of any one of those factors in a given case may lead the investigating authority to conclude that a particular factor is not probative in the circumstances of a particular industry or a particular case, and therefore is not relevant to the actual determination. Likewise, factors not enumerated in Article 4.2(a) that are "relevant" must be examined, although examination may lead the investigating authority to conclude that a particular factor is not probative in a particular case.

8.40 In examining the USITC's serious injury determination we examine, first, whether the USITC evaluated "all relevant factors of an objective and quantifiable nature having a bearing on the situation of [the] industry", in particular, the factors listed in Article 4.2(a) SA, as well as other such factors. Second, we examine whether the USITC Report provides an adequate, reasoned and reasonable explanation of how the facts as a whole support the USITC's serious injury determination, and consequently whether the determination made is consistent with the United States' obligations under the Agreement on Safeguards.

Did the USITC Evaluate all Relevant Factors?

8.41 The USITC Report indicates that the USITC considered all the factors expressly enumerated in Article 4.2(a) SA[48], in particular, the rate and amount of the increase in imports of the product concerned in absolute and relative terms and the share of the domestic market taken by increased imports, changes in the level of sales, production, productivity, capacity utilization, profits and losses

---

[46] European Community Response to Panel Questions 6 and 7, Attachment 1-3; United States Response to Panel Question 7, Attachment 2-4, para. 24.

[47] We find support for our view in the Appellate Body Report in Argentina – Footwear Safeguard. There, the Appellate Body stated: "We agree with the Panel's interpretation that Article 4.2(a) of the Agreement on Safeguards requires a demonstration that the competent authorities evaluated, at a minimum, each of the factors listed in Article 4.2(a) ...". Appellate Body Report, *Argentina-Footwear*, supra, footnote 17, para. 136; Panel Report, *Argentina-Footwear*, supra, footnote 17, para. 8.123.

[48] USITC Report, pp. I-10, I-12 to I-14, II-16; pp. II-9-II-21, II-25.

and employment. The parties also do not dispute that the USITC considered wages[49], inventories[50] and price.[51]

Factors Listed in Article 4.2(a)

8.42 The European Community alleges that the USITC has violated Article 4.2(a) SA in its collection and treatment of the data with respect to two of the factors explicitly listed in Article 4.2(a): (i) productivity; and (ii) profits and losses. We turn to examine the EC arguments concerning these factors.

(i) productivity

8.43 With respect to productivity, the European Community argues that the USITC's treatment of this factor is inconsistent with Article 4.2(a), as it embraces only "worker productivity" rather than overall industry productivity. The United States responds that the European Community does not suggest why an analysis of worker productivity does not satisfy the requirement of Article 4.2(a) to consider "productivity" and that, in any event, the USITC did not fail to take into account capital investment, especially capital projects adding production capacity and their effect on capacity utilization rates.

8.44 We note that the Agreement on Safeguards provides no precise definition of the term "productivity" that appears in Article 4.2(a) SA.[52] The context of this term includes the rest of the text of Article 4.2(a) – and in particular, the phrase "all relevant factors of an objective and quantifiable nature having a bearing on the situation of that *industry*"(emphasis added). We consider that this term, read in its context, may refer to the overall productivity of the *industry*.

8.45 It is apparent to us from the USITC Report that the USITC gathered and analyzed data on capital investment in the industry[53] as well as data pertaining to worker productivity. In these Panel proceedings, the United States asserts that "it is simple mathematics that if production declines (as it did in 1996-1997 from 1995 levels), while the amount of capital in the industry increases (as it did from the capital projects adding capacity), the productivity of capital will correspond-

---

[49] USITC Report, p. I-14; pp. II-16, II-17.

[50] USITC Report, p. I-13; pp. II-14, II-16.

[51] USITC Report, pp. I-13, I-14; pp. II-27 to II-37.

[52] In its response to Panel Question 6, Attachment 2-4, para. 23, the United States observed that the EU producers had not raised before the USITC any argument regarding the productivity of capital investment. In response to Panel Question 7, Attachment 2-4, para. 24, the United States states "...there is no doubt that a competent authority should undertake an inquiry as to these specifically enumerated factors [in Article 4.2 SA] regardless of whether they are raised by the parties." We consider "productivity", and the capital component thereof, to constitute a factor that is specifically enumerated in Article 4.2(a) SA.

[53] See p. II-21 and Table 12 of the USITC Report. Data in Table 12 are redacted from the USITC Report as confidential information.

ingly decline."[54] We would have preferred a more integrated examination in the USITC Report of "productivity" that explicitly encompassed *overall* industry productivity - particularly in light of the acknowledgement by the USITC that "production of wheat gluten is extremely capital intensive and requires very few production workers"[55]. Nevertheless, we consider that the data and statements pertaining to worker productivity, in conjunction with those on capital investments, in the overall context of the USITC Report, indicate that the USITC considered industry productivity as required by Article 4.2(a).

8.46 **For these reasons, we find that the United States did not act inconsistently with Article 4.2(a) SA in the treatment of "productivity" in the USITC Report.**

(ii) profits and losses

8.47 With respect to profits and losses, the European Community alleges that the USITC does not provide an adequate explanation for the determination made, in violation of Article 4.2 SA. The European Community's allegations concerning the financial data obtained by the USITC pertain to the coverage of the data and to the unreviewable nature of the data.

8.48 The United States argues that the European Community does not claim that the USITC's findings may not support an injury determination, but faults the USITC's collection of information on this issue without alleging any basis for finding that the USITC's investigation or determination are in violation of the Agreement.

8.49 We turn to an examination of the specific allegations of the European Community concerning the financial data collected and analyzed by the USITC, as reflected in the USITC Report.

data coverage

8.50 Concerning the data coverage of the financial information, the European Community submits that data relating to the whole period of investigation were available for only two of the firms in the industry. The European Community notes that the USITC received usable financial data only from three of the four domestic producers of wheat gluten, and not from ADM.[56] The European Com-

---

[54] United States first written submission, Attachment 2-1, para. 97.

[55] USITC Report, pp. I-13, II-17.

[56] The United States asserts that the EC allegation that the United States violated Article 4.2(a) because of the nature of the financial records of ADM (in response to Panel Question 18 seeking clarification of a statement in the EC first written submission) is outside our terms of reference as it was not included in the EC panel request. See United States second oral statement, Attachment 2-7, para. 20. The EC panel request, WT/DS166/3, alleges that: "...the United States are in breach of the United States obligations under Articles 2.1 and 4 of the Agreement on Safeguards, since the United States disregarded in the investigation fundamental requirements under these provisions". We con-

munity submits that there was no explanation why ADM could not provide separate data on its United States operations, nor does the report detail any USITC efforts to obtain such separate data. The European Community further observes that one of the four firms entered the market in 1996, and new entrants in a market are almost always unprofitable in the first year of their operations.

8.51 The United States asserts that the USITC received usable financial data from three of the four domestic producers of wheat gluten. The fact that it did not obtain information from one producer for a period before it became a producer is not an inadequacy of the USITC investigation. In the view of the United States, the Agreement does not assume that an investigation will obtain perfect data coverage.

8.52 According to the USITC Report, the USITC "received usable financial data on wheat gluten operations from three of the four domestic producers of wheat gluten, Midland [*sic*], Manildra and Heartland. These three firms accounted for the substantial majority of domestic production of wheat gluten."[57] The fourth firm, ADM, provided data on its combined US and Canadian wheat gluten and wheat starch operations.[58]

8.53 Article 4.1(c) SA states that,

> "in determining injury or threat thereof, a "domestic industry" shall be understood to mean the producers as a whole of the like or directly competitive products operating within the territory of a Member, or those whose collective output of the like or directly competitive products constitutes a major proportion of the total domestic production of those products."

8.54 Therefore, the Agreement expressly envisages that, in certain circumstances, the "domestic industry" may consist of those domestic producers "whose collective output of the like or directly competitive products constitutes a major proportion of the total domestic production of those products". This implies that complete data coverage may not always be possible and is not required. While the fullest possible data coverage is required in order to maximize the accuracy of the investigation, there may be circumstances in a particular case which do not allow an investigating authority to obtain such coverage. In this case, the fact that the USITC record included full period data for only two domestic producers was partially a result of the fact that Heartland became part of the domestic industry only in 1996. Furthermore, the profitability data provided by ADM did not pertain specifically to the domestic industry under investigation and was therefore excluded.

---

sider that the EC panel request, which calls into question the USITC investigation and the obligations under Articles 2.1 and 4 SA, is adequately broad to encompass this issue, particularly in light of the fact that "profits and losses" is a factor explicitly listed in Article 4.2(a) SA.

57 USITC Report, p. I-13.

58 USITC Report, p. I-13, note 56, citing USITC Report, p. II-17, note 45.

8.55 Moreover, the USITC found that "[p]rofitability reflected the trends in average unit value prices, which initially rose and then fell."[59] The USITC had before it data pertaining to unit value from all producers, including ADM. The concurrence in trends between these two factors supports the view that the profitability data used by the USITC was representative of the domestic industry's situation.

8.56 **On the basis of the information contained, or referred to, in the sections of the USITC Report relating to profits and losses and the statement by the USITC that the three domestic producers that provided usable financial data on wheat gluten "accounted for the substantial majority of domestic production of wheat gluten"[60], we find that the United States did not act inconsistently with Article 4.2(a) in terms of the coverage of the "profits and losses" data.**

allocation methodologies

8.57 The European Community submits that the USITC finding that profitability had gone down was based on allocation of profits by United States domestic producers between the co-products of wheat gluten and wheat starch, and derived products. According to the European Community, because the wheat gluten/wheat starch industry relies by necessity on a single raw material input (wheat or wheat flour) and utilizes a single production line that results in wheat gluten, wheat starch and effluents suitable for producing e.g. alcohol, any allocation of profitability among the output products is arbitrary. In addition, data provided by United States producers to argue that the profitability of their wheat gluten sales had gone down are unverifiable. For the European Community, the USITC Report does not contain an adequate explanation of how the facts support the determination made with respect to "profits and losses".

8.58 The United States asserts that an authority's determination cannot be found in violation of the Agreement because it does not disclose information that is by nature confidential. The United States submits that the USITC specifically addressed the allocation issue in its report, and took care to ensure the accuracy and probative worth of the information provided to it. According to the United States, the USITC provided specific instructions to domestic producers with respect to the submission of financial data. The firms that did not maintain separate internal profit-and-loss and cost of production data for wheat gluten operations were directed to allocate costs between wheat gluten and wheat starch, to explain their allocation methodology and to provide worksheets with their calculations. Furthermore, the United States submits, the USITC took additional steps to verify the accuracy and reasonableness of the data, including an on-site verification by a USITC auditor at Midwest, the largest producer.

---

59 USITC Report, p. I-13.
60 USITC Report, p. I-13.

8.59 The USITC Report indicates to us that the USITC gathered and analyzed data and information pertaining to the profits and losses of the domestic industry. The lion's share of this information, including not only the profitability data but also the allocation methodologies for the profitability data, is not included in the Report, as the USITC identified the information as confidential and thus redacted it. We recall our finding above that the United States did not act inconsistently with its obligations under the Safeguards Agreement by redacting confidential information from the published USITC Report.[61] However, we do not consider that the non-disclosure of confidential information under Article 3.2 SA excuses a Member from providing an adequate, reasoned and reasonable explanation of how the facts support the determination made. We therefore turn to consider whether the USITC Report provides such an explanation. Concerning the cost allocation methodologies used by the relevant United States domestic producers, the USITC found:

> "[e]ach of the companies [Midwest, Manildra and Heartland] produces wheat gluten and wheat starch in a joint production process. Each of the companies also produces by-products or related products, especially alcohol. We carefully considered the arguments made by the respondents with respect to the allocations made by domestic producers in providing financial data on their wheat gluten operations. Based on a careful review of the allocation methodologies used by domestic wheat gluten producers in responding to the Commission's questionnaire, we find those allocations to be appropriate."[62]

8.60 The above passage demonstrates to us that the USITC considered the arguments made by the EU respondents in the course of the investigation concerning the allocations made by domestic producers in providing financial data on their wheat gluten operations. It also demonstrates that the USITC reviewed the allocation methodologies used and decided that those allocations were "appropriate".

8.61 The Panel asked the United States to clarify the nature of the "careful review" the USITC had performed and to clarify and elaborate upon the "allocation methodologies" referred to.[63] The United States responded that the majority of the responding firms maintained separate internal profit-and-loss and cost of production data for wheat gluten on a regular basis and furnished this data to the USITC. The responding firm that did not maintain separate data made allocations, and provided the USITC with an explanation of the basis for those allocations. The USITC reviewed the accounting methodologies used by all the producers and did an on-site verification of Midwest, the largest producer.[64] Accord-

[61] Supra, para. 8.26.
[62] USITC Report, p. I-13.
[63] Panel Question 26, Attachments 1-3 and 2-4.
[64] US response to Panel Question 26, Attachment 2-4.

ing to the United States, while virtually all of the information in the auditor's report, which formed part of the USITC record, is confidential information, the United States was able to submit before us that:

> "To derive the wheat gluten financial data from the overall corporate financial data, the USITC auditor at the verification conducted a reconciliation which entailed a detailed evaluation of the firm's operations and the accounting system. The USITC auditor reconciled Midwest Grain's questionnaire data on wheat gluten for each period with the product income and loss statements which were derived from the audited financial statements. This was possible as Midwest Grain prepares separate income and loss statements on a monthly basis for each of its divisions, one of which is the wheat gluten division. The USITC auditor reviewed the financial statements for each division and any allocations that might have been used, and tested their reasonableness with alternative allocation methods.
>
> In addition, the USITC auditor confirmed that the allocation methods used by Midwest to measure the financial performance of each division, to the extent allocations were necessary, had been in use for a number of years and were not changed for purposes of the USITC wheat gluten investigation....."[65]

8.62 In response to an additional question put by the Panel[66], the United States explained that "[t]he USITC's staff report reflects its resolution of issues that arose in its careful review of producers' cost allocations, a review that included extensive input from respondents and included scrutiny not discussed in the Report". The United States also indicated that the allocation methodologies had been the subject of questioning by the USITC to the domestic producers, on which the EU producers had an opportunity to comment in the course of the investigation.[67]

8.63 We recognize the fundamental importance of assuring that data gathered in the course of a safeguards investigation is accurate and that any allocation of costs and revenues reflects, to the greatest extent possible, the realities of the domestic industry concerned. However, we note that the Agreement on Safeguards does not set out precise rules on the collection and analysis of data, nor does it require the use of any particular allocation methodology with respect to financial data gathered by the investigating authorities in the course of the investigation.

8.64 We note that the USITC paid attention to the allocation methodologies used by all domestic producers and in the questionnaire requested firms that did

---

65 US response to Panel Question 26, Attachment 2-4, paras. 74-75.

66 Panel Question 2, Attachment 2-15.

67 United States Response to Panel Question 2, Attachment 2-15, para. 5.

not maintain separate records for wheat gluten to make allocations and explain the methodology used.[68] We also note that the USITC conducted certain procedures, including internal analysis by its staff as well as an on-site verification by a USITC auditor, in order to verify the accuracy and the adequacy of the financial information provided. We believe that, in support of the USITC statement concerning the "careful review" and the finding that the methodologies were "appropriate", the USITC Report could have included a description of such procedures and a more detailed explanation as to how and why the USITC considered the allocations to be "appropriate", in addition to a characterization of the redacted confidential information.

8.65 Nevertheless, in light of the indications pertaining to the data actually collected and analyzed by the USITC[69], the findings contained in the USITC Report based upon this data and the clarifications given by the United States in these Panel proceedings pertaining to certain elements appearing on the face of the USITC Report, we consider that there is no reason to doubt the veracity of the USITC findings pertaining to the allocation methodologies, nor to call into question the thoroughness of the scrutiny given by the USITC in reviewing the allocation methodologies and in ensuring that the financial data used in the USITC serious injury analysis pertained to the domestic industry subject to the investigation.

8.66 **For these reasons, we find that the USITC Report provides an adequate, reasoned and reasonable explanation with respect to "profits and losses" and that the United States did not act inconsistently with Article 4.2(a) of the Agreement on Safeguards in this regard.**

Factors not Listed in Article 4.2(a)

Arguments by the Parties

European Community

8.67 The European Community submits that the United States violated its obligations under Article 4.2 SA by not investigating appropriately "all relevant factors" in reaching its determination of serious injury. For the European Community, such "relevant factors" include: (i) new entries/expansion during the investigation period; (ii) developments as to co-products; and (iii) "imports as "positive business strategy" of certain US producers".[70] According to the European Community, all of these factors were raised by the EU producers respondents before the USITC.

---

[68] Exhibit US-1.

[69] USITC Report, pp. II-18 to II-20.

[70] We address EC allegations concerning the USITC's approach to "productivity" in Article 4.2(a) supra., paras. 8.43-8.46.

United States

8.68 According to the United States, the European Community complains that the USITC failed to address factors that are not enumerated in the Agreement on Safeguards. In the view of the United States, while Article 4.2(c) SA requires the competent authorities to publish an analysis of the case that demonstrates the *relevance* of the factors examined, there is no obligation to explain why it found some factors irrelevant and thus did not rely on them.

Evaluation by the Panel

8.69 We have already stated that Article 4.2(a) SA requires a demonstration that the competent authorities evaluated "all relevant factors" enumerated in Article 4.2(a) as well as other relevant factors.[71] We read this requirement in Article 4.2(a) SA as mandating that the investigating authorities evaluate those "factors" enumerated in Article 4.2(a) SA as well as any other relevant "factors" - in the sense of factors that are *clearly* raised before them as relevant by the interested parties in the domestic investigation. Article 3.1 SA provides that a safeguards investigation shall include "public hearings or other appropriate means in which importers, exporters and other interested parties could present evidence and their views, including the opportunity to respond to the presentations of other parties..." This embraces an opportunity for interested parties to bring to the attention of the investigating authorities factors which these interested parties consider to be relevant as having a bearing on the situation of the domestic industry.[72] In addition, the requirement in Article 4.2(b) SA that "the determination in subparagraph (a) [of Article 4.2] *shall not be made*" (emphasis added) unless a causal link is established between increased imports and serious injury constitutes an explicit textual linkage between Articles 4.2(a) and (b) that acknowledges the intertwined nature of the serious injury and causation analysis. An investigating authority must evaluate all relevant factors, but the Agreement leaves a certain amount of discretion as to the manner in which the investigating authority may evaluate a given factor. With this in mind, we turn to an examination of the factors the European Community alleges that the USITC failed to take into account in its serious injury analysis.

(i) New entrants/expansion

8.70 We first address the EC argument concerning the alleged failure of the USITC to evaluate new entrants and expansion of domestic industry.[73]

8.71 In the course of the USITC investigation, the EU producers submitted, in the context of their argument that the United States statutory test for serious in-

---

[71] Supra, para. 8.39.

[72] Also see our related discussion infra, para. 8.121.

[73] European Community first written submission, Attachment 1-1, paras. 74-75.

jury was not met, that decisions to invest and expand capacity were a reflection of industry health that argued against a finding of serious injury.[74] This particular statement is not reflected in the summary of the arguments in the USITC Report relating to "serious injury", nor is it explicitly referred to in the findings in the USITC Report. However, in the context of a consideration of the decrease in the level of capacity utilization over the POI, the USITC Report states:

> "Some of this decrease in capacity utilization is explained by the fact that domestic capacity to produce wheat gluten increased during the period of investigation in anticipation of significant increases in domestic consumption. Most of this increase in capacity was in place by June 1995, that is, before the surge in imports that occurred in crop years 1996 and 1997. Had there been no increase in imports from 1993 levels, the industry likely could have operated at 61 percent of capacity in 1997. Also, one plant in the industry, opened by ADM in 1994, closed in July 1995 as a result of low-priced imports."[75] (footnotes omitted)

8.72 Moreover, the USITC addresses "increased capacity" as a possible other causal factor in its causation analysis.[76]

8.73 We consider that the USITC findings on serious injury could have expressly indicated that the USITC had considered the relevance of the increase in capacity in its finding of serious injury in the precise manner that the issue was raised before it by the EU producers. However, in light of the statement by the USITC that we have cited pertaining to capacity utilization and the fact that attention is paid to this factor in the USITC causation analysis, **we find that the USITC did not fail to consider this factor in its serious injury and causation analysis under Article 4.2 SA**.

(ii) Developments as to co-products

8.74 With respect to the EC allegation that the USITC failed to investigate the effect of co-products on profitability data[77], we observe that, in the course of the USITC investigation, EU producers submitted that the USITC should give no or little weight to the reported profitability data for wheat gluten and wheat starch, that allocation methods based on revenue can affect apparent profitability trends and that the allocation of wheat gluten costs based on sales revenue distorted the profitability data.[78] This argument is reflected in the summary of the parties ar-

---

[74] Exhibit EC-16, p. 5.

[75] USITC Report, p. I-12, including information originally redacted from the published USITC Report as confidential information that was subsequently submitted in Exhibit US-10.

[76] USITC Report, p. I-17.

[77] European Community first written submission, Attachment 1-1, para. 76.

[78] Exhibit EC-18, pp. 34-36.

guments in the USITC Report.[79] We have discussed above[80] the treatment given by the USITC to the "profits and losses" factor in its serious injury analysis, and the reasons for our finding that the USITC's consideration and explanation of this factor was adequate for the purposes of Article 4.2(a) SA. We note, moreover, that the USITC addresses the issue of co-product markets in its causation analysis.[81] In light of the statement by the USITC that we have cited above[82] pertaining to the profitability data before the USITC and the fact that attention is paid to developments in co-product markets in the USITC causation analysis, **we find that the USITC did not fail to investigate developments in co-product markets - including how the fact that co-products are necessarily produced in the course of wheat gluten production influences wheat starch/wheat gluten profitability - in its serious injury and causation analysis under Article 4.2 SA**.

(iii) Importation by domestic producers

8.75 We next consider the EC argument that the USITC failed to address the issue of importation by domestic producers in its serious injury analysis.[83]

8.76 The EU respondents raised this issue in the course of the USITC investigation. However, it appears to have been raised predominantly in the context of "causation"[84], and the USITC addressed it in this context.[85] The fact that the USITC examined this factor in the context of its causation analysis, rather than in its serious injury analysis, does not constitute a violation of Article 4.2 SA. The nature and role of a "relevant factor having a bearing on the situation of the industry" may be either as indicative of serious injury or as a possible causal factor contributing to, or detracting from, serious injury, or both.

8.77 **Therefore, we find that the USITC did not fail to consider this factor in its serious injury and causation analysis under Article 4.2 SA.**

---

79 USITC Report, p. I-12.

80 Supra, paras. 8.59-8.66.

81 USITC Report, pp. I-16-I-17.

82 USITC Report, p. I-13, cited supra, para. 8.59.

83 European Community first written submission, Attachment 1-1, para. 77.

84 In its response to Panel Questions 6 and 7, Attachment 1-3, the European Community indicated that the issue of importation had been raised before the USITC, and referred to Exhibit EC- 16 (pre-hearing brief of the AAC before the USITC), pp. 2 and 24 – 27 and Exhibit EC-18 (post-hearing brief of the AAC before the USITC), pp. 2, 3-5, 32. In the pre-hearing brief, Exhibit EC-16, the subsection in which the EU respondents' argument concerning importation by domestic producers appears ("Domestic producers import [...] because it is more economical than generating co-products where market demand for wheat starch is weak", Section III.D, p. 24) is entitled "Changes in co-product markets have a substantially larger impact on the U.S. industry than do imports of wheat gluten" (Section III, pp. 13 ff).

85 USITC Report, p. I-17.

Is the USITC Overall Serious Injury Determination Consistent with Article 4.2(a)?

Arguments of the Parties

European Community

8.78 The European Community argues that the evidence before the USITC did not support a finding of serious injury. The European Community underlines that in order for the imposition of a safeguard measure to be justified under the Agreement on Safeguards, the domestic industry must be *currently* seriously injured. The European Community asserts that there were upturns in the trends of several factors at the end of the period of investigation which show that the situation in the industry was far from one of serious injury at the end of the period.

United States

8.79 The United States submits that the USITC's determination was based on the whole record, including an examination of all relevant factors in Article 4.2(a). According to the United States, the relative weight accorded each factor is within the discretion of the competent authorities, so long as they reach a reasoned conclusion. The United States argues that a finding of serious injury does not require a decline in every factor evaluated.

Evaluation by the Panel

8.80 Article 4.1(a) SA defines "serious injury" to mean "significant overall impairment in the position of a domestic industry". We are of the view that a determination as to the existence of such "significant overall impairment" can be made only on the basis of an evaluation of the overall position of the domestic industry, in light of all the relevant factors having a bearing on the situation of that industry.[86]

8.81 We also consider that any determination of serious injury must pertain to the *recent* past. This flows from the wording of the text of Article XIX:1(a) of the GATT 1994 and Article 2.1 SA, which requires an examination as to whether a product "is being imported" "in such increased quantities ... and under such conditions as to cause or threaten serious injury...". The use of the present tense of the verb in the phrase "is being imported" in that provision indicates that it is necessary for the competent authorities to examine recent imports.[87] It seems to us logical that if the increase in imports that the investigating authorities must

---

86 We find support for this view in Appellate Body Report, *Argentina – Footwear Safeguard, supra*, footnote 17, paras. 138-139.

87 See Appellate Body Report, *Argentina-Footwear Safeguard*, supra, footnote 17, para. 130.

examine must be recent, so also must be any basis for a determination by the authorities as to the situation of the domestic industry. Given that a safeguard measure will necessarily be based upon a determination of serious injury concerning a previous period, we consider it essential that *current* serious injury be found to exist, up to and including the very end of the period of investigation.[88]

8.82 On this basis, we examine whether the USITC Report provides an adequate, reasoned and reasonable explanation of how the facts as a whole support the USITC's serious injury determination, and consequently whether the determination made is consistent with the United States' obligations under the Agreement on Safeguards.

8.83 The USITC concluded:

> "In summary, by the end of the period examined, virtually all of the factors relevant to industry performance were negative. Industry capacity utilization has declined significantly, production and shipments have declined, end-of-period inventories have more than doubled; the industry has gone from being profitable to operating at a loss, average unit values have declined and were at their lowest level in 1997 at the same time that unit costs were rising, hourly wages have been relatively flat, worker productivity has declined due to the decline in capacity utilization and unit labour costs have almost doubled. While there has been minor improvement in several factors during the most recent year, these improvements are isolated and do not change our conclusion that the domestic industry is presently seriously injured. Thus, we find that the domestic wheat gluten industry is seriously injured."[89]

8.84 In reaching its serious injury determination, it is apparent to us that the USITC took into account trends over the whole 5-year period of investigation, in addition to the specific trends in 1996 and 1997. The USITC found that several indicators rose from 1996 to 1997, including capacity utilization (slightly), production and sales. USITC weighed the factors before it and, in light of the entire record, found that such "minor" improvements were "isolated" and did not change its conclusion that the industry was, and remained, seriously injured in 1997. Before us, the European Community focuses on the 1996-1997 period to argue that the upturns in several injury factors from 1996 to 1997 demonstrates that there was no *current* serious injury to the domestic industry in 1997.

8.85 The information on which the USITC based its serious injury determination indicates that there were identifiable improvements in several factors in 1997: capacity utilization, production and sales were improving, wages were rising and inventories were being depleted, all signs of a positive trend in the indus-

---

[88] Except, of course, in a case involving threat of serious injury, where the issue involves future injury.
[89] USITC Report, p. I-14.

try. We do not consider that a negative trend in every single factor examined is necessary in order for an industry to be in a position of significant overall impairment. Rather, it is the totality of the trends, and their interaction, which must be taken into account in a serious injury determination.[90] Thus, such upturns in a number of factors would not necessarily preclude a determination of serious injury. It is for the investigating authorities to assess and weigh the evidence before them, and to give an adequate, reasoned and reasonable explanation of how the facts support the determination made.

8.86 We consider that the information before the USITC, in its totality, would not preclude a finding by a domestic authority of *current* serious injury, in terms of a continuing "significant overall impairment" of the domestic industry, in 1997. Although certain factors were not declining, the overall picture could nonetheless still demonstrate "significant overall impairment" of the industry. The USITC found that "...by the end of the period examined, virtually all of the factors relevant to industry performance were negative."[91] Capacity utilization remained low in 1997 (44.5%), and its improvement from 1996 to 1997 was slight (2.5 percentage points). While trends in production, sales and inventories fluctuated over the course of the investigation period, the absolute levels were worse in 1997 than in 1993. Data before the USITC indicated that average unit values were declining and reached their lowest level of the POI in 1997 while unit costs were rising, and the industry was still operating at a loss[92] in 1996 and 1997.

8.87 We believe that the USITC Report could perhaps have contained a more thorough explanation of why the decrease in inventories and the upturns in sales, production and capacity utilization towards the end of the period of investigation did not detract from the USITC's determination of serious injury. In particular, the USITC could have provided an explanation as to why it found the upturns in the trends of various factors (sales, production, inventories, capacity utilization) from 1996 to 1997 to be "minor improvements" that were "isolated". Nevertheless, in the light of the indications in the USITC Report pertaining to the information that was before the USITC at the time of the serious injury determination and the findings contained in the USITC Report pertaining to the overall trends in the factors examined over the POI, we consider that, in their totality, the USITC findings on serious injury contain an adequate, reasoned and reasonable explanation of how the facts as a whole support the determination of serious injury made by the USITC, including its determination that the domestic industry remained seriously injured in 1997. It is evident to us from the findings in the

---

90 The Appellate Body has observed that "... a certain factor may not be declining, but the overall picture may nevertheless demonstrate "significant overall impairment" of the industry...". Appellate Body Report, *Argentina-Footwear Safeguard*, *supra*, footnote 17, para. 139.

91 USITC Report, p. I-14.

92 The USITC Report, p. I-13, states: "...gross profit and operating income increased between 1993 and 1994, and then fell sharply in 1995; further declines in 1996 and 1997 resulted in overall industry losses on wheat gluten operations in both of those years".

USITC Report that the USITC has assessed whether the overall picture painted by the totality of the factors examined demonstrated "significant overall impairment" of the industry as required by Articles 4.1(a) and 4.2 SA.

8.88 **For these reasons, we find that the USITC's overall determination of serious injury was not inconsistent with Article 4.2(a) SA.**

8.89 **In sum, we have found that the USITC did not fail to evaluate all relevant factors having a bearing on the state of the industry in determining serious injury and that its overall serious injury determination was not inconsistent with Article 4.2(a) SA.** However, Article 4.2(b) SA requires that a determination under Article 4.2(a) "*shall not be made*" unless the investigation demonstrates a causal link between increased imports and serious injury. We examine this issue below.

(d) Causation

8.90 A demonstration of the existence of a causal link between increased imports and serious injury is a fundamental requirement for the imposition of a safeguard measure. Article XIX:1(a) of the GATT 1994 and Article 2.1 SA require that a product is being imported in such increased quantities and under such conditions as to cause or threaten to cause serious injury to the domestic industry. Article 4.2(a) and (b) SA read:

> "2.(a) In the investigation to determine whether increased imports have caused or are threatening to cause serious injury to a domestic industry under the terms of this Agreement, the competent authorities shall evaluate all relevant factors of an objective and quantifiable nature having a bearing on the situation of that industry, in particular, the rate and amount of the increase in imports of the product concerned in absolute and relative terms, the share of the domestic market taken by increased imports, changes in the level of sales, production, productivity, capacity utilization, profits and losses, and employment.
>
> (b) The determination referred to in subparagraph (a) shall not be made unless this investigation demonstrates, on the basis of objective evidence, the existence of the causal link between increased imports of the product concerned and serious injury or threat thereof. When factors other than increased imports are causing injury to the domestic industry at the same time, such injury shall not be attributed to increased imports." (emphasis added)

8.91 We consider that an appropriate approach for a panel to take in assessing whether a Member has fulfilled the requirements of Article 4.2(a) and (b) SA with respect to causation consists of a consideration of: (i) whether an upward trend in imports coincides with downward trends in the injury factors, and if not, whether an adequate, reasoned and reasonable explanation is provided as to why nevertheless the data show causation; (ii) whether the conditions of competition between the imported and domestic product as analyzed demonstrate the existence of the causal link between the imports and any injury; and (iii) whether other relevant factors have been analyzed and whether it is established that injury caused by factors other than imports has not been attributed to imports. We observe that this three-step approach to causation was also followed by the panel in *Argentina-Footwear Safeguard* and that the Appellate Body saw "no error" in that panel's approach.[93] We note that, before us, the European Community espoused the latter panel's approach and the United States did not specifically object to it.

(i) Whether Upward Trend in Imports Coincides with Negative Trends in Injury Factors

Arguments of the Parties

European Community

8.92 According to the European Community, the USITC failed to satisfy the element of coincidence of trends between serious injury and increased imports. In the view of the European Community, that the injury factors cited to support the finding of serious injury began declining before the increase in imports raises serious questions about the existence of a causal link. The European Community submits that the USITC provides no analysis or reasoning to demonstrate how the negative trends in injury factors could have been caused by the increase in imports which only began later. In the EC view, most factors indicative of injury either moved negatively before the increase in imports in 1996 and 1997, moved positively when imports were rising, or both. In particular, three factors - capacity utilisation, domestic shipments and inventories - worsened before the reference period and actually improved during the period of the alleged "serious injury".[94] The European Community also alleges that the USITC emphasized the absolute increase in imports while downplaying the trends of imports relative to total United States demand and trends in the market share of imports.

United States

8.93 The United States stresses the 38 per cent increase in imports in 1996-1997 from 1995 levels. Moreover, the United States submits, even though consumption in the United States market was rising, imports gained in market share during that two-year period (from 50.1 per cent in 1995 to 58.9 per cent in 1996

---

[93] See Panel Report, *Argentina - Footwear Safeguard, supra*, footnote 17, para. 8.229; Appellate Body Report, *Argentina – Footwear Safeguard, supra*, footnote 17, para. 145.

[94] See European Community first written submission, Attachment 1-1, paras. 79-80; European Community second written submission, Attachment 1-4, paras. 80-83.

to 60.2 per cent in 1997). According to the United States, coming as it did after a period in which import market share fell slightly, such a rise was sudden and significant. The United States submits that the European Community does not explain why the USITC was required to give precedence to the import trends that the USITC allegedly downplayed.

8.94 Moreover, the United States asserts, the European Community ignores the fact that virtually all the factors relating to wheat gluten industry health declined in 1996 and 1997 in the face of the surge in imports. According to the United States, although the domestic industry was profitable from 1993 to 1995, it suffered growing operating losses in 1996 and 1997, when imports, particularly from the European Community, surged and consistently undersold the United States product. The United States argues that, as the USITC found, the industry's gross profit, operating income, and market share all declined in both 1996 and 1997. Likewise, both the domestic industry's production and shipments fell sharply when imports surged, and were at their lowest levels in 1996-1997. The United States submits that while there were slight upturns in sales and production in 1996 and 1997, both indicators remained in 1997 far below their pre-import surge levels.

Evaluation by the Panel

8.95 We consider that a coincidence in the movements in imports and the movements in injury factors would ordinarily tend to support a finding of causation, while the absence of such coincidence would ordinarily tend to detract from such a finding and would require a compelling explanation as to why causation is still present.[95] The issue before us is whether the USITC Report indicates a coincidence between the movements in imports and the movements in injury factors and whether it contains an adequate, reasoned and reasonable explanation of how the facts support the USITC determination of causation of serious injury by increased imports.

8.96 With respect to the relationship between the movement in imports and the indicators of serious injury, the USITC found:

> "This surge in relatively low-priced imports in 1996 and 1997 coincided with the decline in industry performance described above. There is a direct correlation between the dramatic increase in wheat gluten imports and the significant decline in domestic wheat gluten industry performance in 1996 and 1997. In the face of rising domestic demand and consumption, domestic production, shipments, capacity utilization, unit prices, industry financial perform-

---

[95] We found guidance for our view in the Panel Report, *Argentina-Footwear Safeguard, supra*, footnote 17, paras. 8.237- 8.238; The Appellate Body saw "no error" in the Panel's interpretation of the causation requirements, or in the Panel's interpretation of Article 4.2(b) SA in that dispute, Appellate Body Report, *Argentina-Footwear Safeguard, supra*, footnote 17, paras. 144-146.

ance, and worker productivity all declined during the period of greatest import penetration."[96]

8.97 Looking at the *overall* trends in imports and the *overall* trends in serious injury factors pertaining to the *overall* situation of the industry over the period of investigation, we consider that there is a *general* coincidence between the trends in injury factors and the trends in imports which would support a finding by the investigating authority of a causal connection between increased imports and serious injury.

8.98 The USITC found that there was an absolute rise in imports of 38 per cent in 1996/1997 over 1995 levels (from 128 million pounds in 1995 to 156 million pounds in 1996 to 177 million pounds in 1997), and that there was an increase in the market share of imports from 50.1 per cent in 1995 to 58.9 per cent in 1996 to 60.2 per cent in 1997. We note the EC argument that the 1.3 percentage point rise in the market share taken by imports from 1996 to 1997 would not allow a finding of "increased imports" under Articles 2.1 and 4.2 SA. We disagree. In light of the trends over the course of the POI found by the USITC, including the finding that the share of the domestic wheat gluten market held by domestic wheat gluten producers fell to its lowest level of the POI in 1997[97], as well as the finding concerning the rate of the absolute increase in imports between 1996 and 1997[98], we consider that the rate of rise in imports in both absolute and relative terms would not preclude an investigating authority from characterizing this trend, both qualitatively and quantitatively, as sufficiently recent, sudden, sharp and significant to cause serious injury.[99]

8.99 We also note that the information before the USITC indicates that many of the injury factors declined over the period of investigation, as imports were increasing. For example, sales, production, inventories and capacity utilization showed an overall negative trend during the POI. Furthermore, the USITC found that profitability decreased in 1996 and 1997 and the industry was operating at a loss at the end of the POI.[100]

8.100 We observe that the information in the USITC Report indicates that when one looks at the trends of imports *vis-à-vis* the trends in certain *individual* injury factors in *isolation*, several of these injury factors were declining prior to the surge in imports found by the USITC in 1996-1997. In addition, in the face of

[96] USITC Report, p. I-16.
[97] USITC Report, pp. I-16, II-25.
[98] USITC Report, pp. I-10, II-12.
[99] We refer to the language used by the Appellate Body in its Report, *Argentina-Footwear Safeguard, supra*, footnote 17, para. 131: "And this language in both Article 2.1 of the Agreement on Safeguards and Article XIX:1(a) of the GATT 1994, we believe, requires that the increase in imports must have been recent enough, sudden enough, sharp enough, and significant enough, both quantitatively and qualitatively, to cause or threaten to cause "serious injury"". Also see our finding supra, para. 8.34, with respect to "increased quantities" of imports.
[100] USITC Report, p. I-13.

continuing increased imports in 1996 and 1997, the USITC Report indicates that several injury factors actually improved. In particular, information in the USITC Report indicates that profitability rose in 1993 and 1994, fell sharply in 1995 (before the import surge), and continued to decline in 1996 and 1997. Capacity utilization declined from 1993 to 1995 (before the import surge found by the USITC in 1996 and 1997). Sales rose from 1993 to 1994, declined in 1995 (before the import surge) and 1996, but then increased from 1996 to 1997 (during the import surge). Inventories increased between 1993 and 1995, but then decreased in 1996 and 1997 (during the import surge). The ratio of inventories to shipments followed a similar trend. Hourly wages rose from 1993 to 1994, declined from 1994 (before the import surge) to 1996, and increased again in 1997 (during the import surge).

8.101 We consider that in light of the *overall* coincidence of the upward trend in increased imports and the negative trend in injury factors over the period of investigation, the existence of slight absences of coincidence in the movement of *individual* injury factors in relation to imports would not preclude a finding by the USITC of a causal link between increased imports and serious injury.

8.102 **For these reasons, we find that the USITC Report indicates a general coincidence of trends and that it contains an adequate, reasoned and reasonable explanation of how the facts support its findings with respect to this aspect of the causation analysis.**

(ii) "under such conditions" - Conditions of Competition

Arguments by the parties

European Community

8.103 According to the European Community, Article XIX:1 of the GATT 1994 and Article 2 SA require that a product be imported "under such conditions" as to cause serious injury. The European Community also asserts that, pursuant to Article 4.2(b) SA, the USITC should have demonstrated, "on the basis of objective evidence", the existence of this aspect of the causal link between imports and injury. Furthermore, under Article 4.2(c), the USITC was required to publish "a detailed analysis of the case under investigation as well as a demonstration of the relevance of the factors examined". The European Community alleges that the United States has acted inconsistently with these obligations.

8.104 According to the European Community, the USITC appears to believe that the "conditions" under which imports took place which allegedly caused serious injury consisted of the prices of those imports. For the European Community, there was no evidence of consistent underselling of the type necessary to find that imports take place "under such conditions" as to cause injury. The European Community is of the view that there is no evidence of a causal link between imports and price. With respect to the USITC statement that prices were driven down during 1996 and 1997 by relatively low-priced imports, the European Community asserts that increased imports were not the cause of the decline in domestic unit sales values, and that evidence in the USITC Report indicates that prices went down sharply in 1995, before imports increased. Furthermore, the European Community submits, the USITC acknowledges that the price of wheat gluten is directly related to the protein level in wheat.

United States

8.105 The United States submits that the Agreement on Safeguards does not lend itself to giving price analysis the dispositive position that the EC would give it. "Price" is not an enumerated "relevant" factor in Article 4.2(a). The United States asserts that the European Community does not explain why the phrase "under such conditions" in Article 2.1 should be regarded as referring to price at all, much less why it should give to price a relevance greater than the enumerated factors listed in Article 4.2(a). At any rate, the United States asserts, the USITC fully considered the evidence on price in this case and found that it supported an affirmative injury finding. The United States does not deny that factors other than imports, such as the protein content of the domestic wheat crop, can affect domestic demand for, and the domestic price of, wheat gluten. However, according to the United States, the only explanation for the substantial price decline in 1996 and 1997 in the face of rising demand and consumption was the surge in imports.

Evaluation by the Panel

8.106 The issue before us requires a consideration of the nature of the obligation imposed by the phrase "under such conditions" in Article XIX:1(a) of the GATT 1994 and Article 2.1 SA. In particular, we must consider whether the term "under such conditions" requires a price analysis, and whether such price analysis must demonstrate evidence of consistent underselling by the imported product in the domestic market of the importing Member in order to make a finding of serious injury. We must then consider whether the causation analysis performed by the USITC is adequate to comply with the requirement imposed by the phrase "under such conditions" in Articles XIX:1(a) of the GATT 1994 and Article 2.1 SA and with Article 4.2 SA.

8.107 We first examine the nature of the obligation imposed by the phrase "under such conditions" in Article XIX:1(a) of the GATT 1994 and Article 2.1 SA.

8.108 We are of the view that the phrase "under such conditions" does not impose a separate analytical requirement in addition to the analysis of increased imports, serious injury and causation.[101] Rather, this phrase refers to the *sub-*

[101] Two previous panels have come to a similar conclusion about the nature of the obligation imposed by the phrase "under such conditions". Panel Report, *Argentina-Footwear Safeguard*, *supra*, footnote 17, paras. 8.249-8.252. The Appellate Body saw "no error" in the panel's approach to causation in that dispute, see Appellate Body Report, *Argentina-Footwear Safeguard*, *supra*, footnote 17,

stance of the causation analysis that must be performed under Article 4.2(a) and (b) SA. In our view, it must be demonstrated that the conditions under which increased imports are occurring are injurious, that is, that they are *such as to cause* serious injury. Such causation can be ascertained through an examination of the conditions of competition between the imported and domestic product in the importing country's market, and the importing country must therefore perform an adequate assessment of the impact of the increased imports at issue on the domestic industry under investigation. These conditions of competition (i.e. the precise nature of the interaction and relationship between the imported and domestic products) in the importing country's market will determine whether the conditions under which increased imports are occurring are such as to cause or threaten to cause serious injury.

8.109 As for the nature and content of the examination concerning the conditions of competition between the imported and domestic product, we observe that Articles 2 and 4.2 SA make no mention of "price". "Price" is not expressly listed in Article 4.2(a) SA as a "relevant factor" having a bearing on the situation of the domestic industry. However, this is not to say that "price" may not be a relevant factor in a given case. An imported product can compete with a domestic product in various ways in the market of the importing country. Clearly, the relative price of the imported product is one of these ways, but it is certainly not the only way, and it may be irrelevant or only marginally relevant in a given case.

8.110 Therefore, in the context of safeguards measures, the relevance of "price" will vary from case to case, in light of the particular circumstances and the nature of the particular product and domestic industry involved. Given that this is the nature of the "price" factor under the Agreement on Safeguards, we consider that the phrase "under such conditions" does not necessarily, in every case, require a price analysis. Moreover, if a price analysis is performed, we consider that it need not necessarily demonstrate consistent underselling by the imported product in the domestic market of the importing Member in order to make a finding of serious injury.

8.111 In the present case, the European Community focuses upon the "price" aspect of conditions of competition in its arguments concerning the alleged inconsistency of the USITC Report with the requirements imposed by the phrase "under such conditions" in Article XIX:1 of the GATT 1994 and Article 2.1 SA, and by the causation requirements of Article 4.2(a) and (b) SA. The USITC also placed emphasis on "relatively low-priced imports" in its causation analysis.[102] We turn to an examination of the EC allegation that the USITC consideration of price is inadequate for the purposes of establishing a causal link between imports and serious injury under Article 4.2(a) and (b) SA.

---

paras. 140-145. Panel Report, *Korea-Dairy Safeguard*, *supra*, footnote 16, paras. 7.51-7.52. That specific issue was not appealed in that dispute.

[102] USITC Report, pp. I-17, I-18.

8.112 The USITC Report indicates that the USITC examined "price" and found that it supported a finding of serious injury caused by imports. The USITC stated:

> "The ratio of imports to consumption then increased sharply to 58.9 per cent in 1996 and 60.2 per cent in 1997. The record reflects that most of this increase consisted of imports from the EU. The record also shows that imports from the EU consistently undersold domestic wheat gluten. This surge in relatively low-priced imports in 1996 and 1997 coincided with a decline in industry performance."[103]

8.113 The USITC Report contains data that support the USITC statement that EC imports undersold the US product in 1996 and 1997.[104] Such data can be found in Table 18 of the USITC Report, entitled "Vital wheat gluten produced in the United States and the European Union: weighted-average net delivered selling prices and quantities reported by U.S. producers and importers, and margins of under/(over)selling, by quarters, July 1992-June 1997".[105]

8.114 The USITC also found:

> "We note that raw material costs increased over the period examined, particularly in 1996 and 1997. Consumption also increased significantly during this period. Because demand for wheat gluten is relatively insensitive to changes in price, we would expect that wheat gluten producers would be able to pass on these cost increases to their customers. U.S. producers testified that, historically, higher raw material costs had been passed through to their customers. *In 1996 and 1997, however, unit selling values declined* notwithstanding increased demand and higher raw material costs. We find that this unusual development is explained by the dramatic increase in *relatively low-priced imports* during this period, which had the effect of *driving down wheat gluten prices.*"[106] (emphasis added, footnotes omitted)

8.115 The quarterly pricing data in Table 18 of the USITC Report indicate that, during 1994[107], there was a sharp rise in the price of wheat gluten. The USITC

---

[103] USITC Report, p. I- 16.

[104] We note there was an initial difference of views between the parties concerning the period referred to by the USITC when "imports from the EU consistently undersold domestic wheat gluten" (European Community first written submission, Attachment 1-1, paras. 82-83). The United States clarified before us that this reference in the USITC Report to such "consistent underselling" referred to the 1996-1997 period (United States first written submission, Attachment 2-1, paras. 121-123. We consider that this view is supported by the context of the relevant phrase as it appears in the USITC Report.

[105] USITC Report, p. II-33.

[106] USITC Report, pp. I-17 and I-18.

[107] This reference is to USITC reporting years, i.e. 12-month period ending in June of the relevant year.

explicitly acknowledged that this rise in price was caused, at least in part, by the low protein content in the wheat crop.[108] During 1995, prices fell. Prices then increased slightly in 1996 in comparison with the level of the last quarter of 1995.

8.116 While the USITC states that "unit selling values declined" in 1996 and 1997, the data in Table 18 indicate that quarterly wheat gluten prices actually increased in the first three quarters of 1996 from the level of prices in the last quarter of 1995. We recall that the USITC found that the surge in imports occurred in 1996 and 1997. Data in the USITC Report reflect that, on a quarterly basis, prices fell in 1995 (before the surge and at least in part due to the protein content of the wheat crop) and rose in 1996 (during the surge in "relatively low-priced imports").

8.117 Particularly when the USITC itself emphasizes and relies on a decline in unit selling values (in the face of increased demand and higher raw material costs) and on "relatively low-priced imports ... which had the effect of driving down wheat gluten prices" as part of its causation analysis, we believe that the USITC might have provided a more robust explanation in its findings of how pricing data interrelated with the movement of trends in imports. We note that in Part II of the USITC Report, in its description of pricing information obtained in the investigation, the USITC characterizes in considerable detail the quarterly pricing trends during the POI.[109] Such detailed characterization is, however, not reflected in the USITC findings in Part I of the USITC Report, which focus on average annual unit selling values and merely state that "unit selling values declined". However, as the annual average trends in price as found by the USITC support the statement of the USITC[110], we find that the USITC Report contains an adequate, reasoned and reasonable explanation of how the facts support the determination made on this point, and that the USITC Report contains a demonstration of the relevance of this factor.

8.118 **For these reasons, we find that the United States did not act inconsistently in this context with the obligations imposed by the phrase "under such conditions" in Article XIX:1(a) of the GATT 1994 and Article 2.1 SA nor with its obligations under Article 4.2 SA.**

---

108 USITC Report, p. II-9, pp. I-22-I-23: "The increase in demand for wheat gluten in 1994 ... resulted at least in part from a weather-related deficiency in protein content in the wheat crops of the major producing countries, including the United States, during 1993." This is also reflected at note 84 on p. II-32 of the USITC Report.

109 USITC Report, pp. II-32 ff.

110 USITC Report, pp. II-31 and II-32.

(iii) Other Factors and Attribution

Did the USITC Investigate Other Relevant Factors in the Context of Causation?

Arguments of the Parties

8.119 The European Community argues that the USITC failed properly to investigate factors other than the increased imports as possible causes of injury, as required by Article 4.2(b) SA. According to the European Community, these factors include: (i) the effect of wheat protein premiums on the wheat protein price in the US market ; (ii) co-product markets ; (iii) increased capacity ; (iv) input prices ; and (v) imports by US producers. [111] According to the European Community, under Article 4.2(a), the competent authorities must, on their own initiative, identify which factors may be relevant and then, on their own initiative, obtain all information which is necessary to evaluate how that factor developed. In any event, the European Community submits that the EU producer respondents raised all of these factors, including wheat protein premiums, before the USITC as relevant for the whole period of investigation.

8.120 The United States argues that the USITC examined factors other than imports that may be a cause of serious injury to the domestic industry and included such findings in its report. The United States argues that the competent authority should be able to rely on the points raised by the parties, and does not need to investigate other possible causal factors on its own initiative. The United States submits that the EU respondent producers did not raise wheat protein premiums as a possible causal factor for the whole period of the investigation.

Evaluation by the Panel

8.121 As we have indicated[112], we read the requirement in Article 4.2(a) SA as mandating that the investigating authorities evaluate at least all those "factors" enumerated in Article 4.2(a) SA as well as any other relevant "factors" - in the sense of factors that are *clearly* raised before them as relevant by the parties in the domestic investigation. While the investigating authorities certainly enjoy the discretion to investigate other "relevant factors of an objective and quantifiable nature having a bearing on the nature of the industry" beyond those that have been raised by the parties in the course of the investigation, the investigating authorities are not, in our view, obligated *on their own initiative* to seek out and evaluate factors other than those explicitly enumerated in Article 4.2(a) beyond those that are clearly raised before them by the interested parties in the course of the investigation.

---

[111] The European Community also raised the issue of inclusion of imports from Canada in the investigation and the exclusion of these imports from the application of the measure. We discuss this infra., paras. 8.160 ff.

[112] Supra, paras. 8.39, 8.69.

8.122 From the summary of the arguments in the USITC Report, as well as certain EC Exhibits[113] submitted to us that formed part of the record before the USITC, it is apparent that the EU respondents in the USITC proceedings clearly raised factors (ii) through (v) referred to above by the European Community, i.e. developments as to co-products[114], a "new domestic producer, and less than full levels of capacity utilization by domestic producers"[115], rising input costs[116] and "large-scale importing by US producers"[117] before the USITC. It is further apparent to us from a review of the USITC findings that the USITC considered these four possible causes of injury raised by the EU respondents before it and identified by the European Community in these Panel proceedings. The USITC causation findings expressly address co-product markets[118]; capacity utilization[119]; input prices[120] and the importation of wheat gluten by United States producers[121].

8.123 We turn to the remaining factor identified by the European Community in this context before us - the issue of wheat protein premiums.[122] With respect to this factor, the European Community alleges that the USITC failed to collect data and failed to assess correctly any causal link between imports and alleged serious injury, in violation of Article 4.2(a) and (b) SA.

8.124 We therefore consider whether the issue of wheat protein premiums was raised by the EU respondents before the USITC as a relevant factor having a bearing on the situation of the industry that was possibly causing injury to the domestic industry throughout the POI. Before us, there is disagreement between the parties concerning the extent to which the issue of "protein premiums" was raised by the EU producers in the course of the USITC investigation. Both parties agree that the protein content in the wheat crop was a relevant factor in 1993-1994, that this was raised by the EU respondents before the USITC and that the USITC explicitly considered its relevance in the USITC Report. However, with respect to the post-1994 period, the United States submits before us that there was:

> " no evidence before the USITC of a drop in the protein content of the wheat crop in 1996 and 1997, or of any other change relating to the protein content of the wheat crop that would explain the in-

---

113 Exhibits EC 16-18.

114 USITC summary of EU respondents' argument, USITC Report, p. I-15; USITC findings, USITC Report, p. I-16.

115 USITC summary of EU respondents' argument, USITC Report, p. I-16; USITC findings, p. I-17.

116 Exhibit EC-16, "Pre-hearing brief of 11 December 1997 lodged by AAC with ITC", p. 29; USITC findings, p. I-15.

117 USITC summary of EU respondents' argument, USITC Report, p. I-15; USITC findings, USITC Report, p. I-16.

118 USITC Report, pp. I-16 and I-17.

119 USITC Report, p. I-17.

120 USITC Report, pp. I-17 and I-18.

121 USITC Report, p. I-17.

122 The "protein premium" is the price differential between low- and high-protein wheat.

crease in wheat gluten consumption in those two years. Nor did any of the parties in the USITC investigation make the argument the EC has advanced in this proceeding. While EU producers during the USITC proceeding cited the 1993/94 supply shortage, fluctuating prices of wheat, and the price premium of wheat over *corn* as factors affecting the domestic wheat gluten market, they did not allege a "wheat protein premium factor" or protein shortfall in the 1996 and 1997 wheat crops. If the protein factor of wheat during 1996 and 1997 was a serious factor affecting price and demand for wheat gluten, it is surprising that it was only discovered by the EC long after the conclusion of the USITC investigation."[123]

8.125 Before us, in support of its assertion that the issue of the wheat protein premium was raised before the USITC as a relevant causal factor throughout the entire POI, the European Community indicates several places in the USITC record where EU producers mentioned this issue in the oral and written proceedings before the USITC[124], and points to a statement made by the petitioners in the course of the USITC investigation.[125] We have examined this evidence cited by the European Community before us. While this evidence demonstrates to us that the issue of the effect of protein premiums on price during 1993-1994 was certainly raised by the EU producer respondents as relevant before the USITC, we find that the European Community has not demonstrated to us as a matter of fact that the EU producer respondents clearly raised the broader issue of wheat protein premiums as a possible relevant causal factor pertaining to the post-1994 segment of the period of investigation which the European Community raises in these Panel proceedings.

8.126 We note that the USITC expressly acknowledged that the protein content of the wheat crop has an effect on the demand of wheat gluten[126], and we consider that the USITC might have included an explicit and distinct examination of the protein content of wheat as a "relevant factor having a bearing on the situation of the domestic industry" and reflected the results of that examination, including the relevance of that factor, in its Report. However, in light of our finding that the EU producer respondents did not clearly and persistently pursue this issue before the USITC as another possible cause of injury in the post-1994 period, we find that the fact that the USITC did not collect data on this factor and did not include an explicit and distinct examination of this factor in its Report over and above its considerations of price and demand (which would reflect developments

[123] United States second oral statement, Attachment 2-7, para. 25.

[124] See European Community second written submission, Attachment 1-4, para. 54, referring to Exhibit EC-18, pp. 24 and 31; European Community Response to Additional Panel Question 1, Attachment 1-15.

[125] See European Community second written submission, Attachment 1-4, para. 55, referring to Exhibit EC-17, pp. 149-150.

[126] See, for example, USITC Report, p. II-5.

in the protein content of the wheat crop), does not constitute a violation of Article 4.2(a) and (b) SA.

8.127 **For these reasons, we do not find that the failure by the USITC to investigate the relevance of the protein premium issue in the post-1994 segment of the POI constitutes a violation of Article 4.2(a) and (b) SA.**

8.128 It remains for us to examine the consistency with Article 4.2(b) SA of the USITC's examination of the factors that *were* clearly raised before it by the interested parties in the course of the investigation and *were* addressed by it.

Did the USITC's Examination Ensure the Non-Attribution to Imports of Injury Caused by Other Factors?

Arguments of the Parties

European Community

8.129 The European Community alleges that the USITC failed to fulfill the obligation in Article 4.2(b) SA not to attribute to imports injury caused by other factors. According to the European Community, the United States should have provided an objective criterion to demonstrate that the injury attributable to imports, after having deducted the injury caused by other factors, reached the threshold of "serious". On the basis of the objective elements which they examined or should have examined, the USITC should never have reached the conclusion that such injury was "serious".

8.130 The European Community argues that the United States relies on a "preponderance" test when determining the causal link. In the EC view, the United States legislation mandating the United States authorities to examine whether or not increased imports are only a "substantial cause" and whether or not certain factors are "a more important cause of serious injury than increased imports" has no basis in WTO law. In case of concurring causes of injury, the United States law prevents the investigating authorities from verifying the only important issue, i.e. whether increased imports are *per se* the cause of "significant overall impairment of the position of the domestic industry". The European Community argues that Article 4.2(b) requires that a Member demonstrate that "increased imports" caused "serious injury *per se*, i.e. taken alone".[127] In the EC view, the investigating authorities cannot attribute the cause of serious injury to increased imports if the increased imports are a co-cause of such serious injury but do not reach *per se* , in isolation, the threshold of "serious injury". According to the European Community, the United States investigating authorities are limited by the United States law to investigating a different issue, i.e. whether there is a single cause

[127] European Community Response to Panel Questions 8 and 9, Attachment 1-3.

"more important" than increased imports. This is incompatible with Article 4.2 SA.

8.131 The European Community alleges, in particular with respect to increased capacity, that the USITC violated Article 4.2(b) in that it should not have attributed to increased imports "any (easily quantifiable) injury caused by this factor".[128] The European Community urges that the United States should have excluded the injury caused by overcapacity from its determinations of serious injury and causation. In order to do this, it should have determined whether, if capacity had remained the same since 1993, there still would have been "a significant overall impairment of the domestic industry".

United States

8.132 The United States argues that the USITC specifically examined possible alternative causes of serious injury raised by interested parties in the course of the investigation, including: changes in co-product markets; domestic producers' importation of wheat gluten; competition among domestic producers; increased capacity and rising input costs. The USITC included findings on these possible alternative causes of serious injury in its report. According to the United States, in each case, the USITC found that the asserted cause did not have the effect on the industry suggested (*e.g.*, co-production, corn starch competition with wheat starch, importation by domestic producers, rising prices for inputs) or had only a demonstrably minor role in the serious injury suffered by the industry (increased capacity).[129] The United States submits that the European Community seeks to have the Panel re-find the facts as to each of these factors and assess the USITC's weighing of the factors.

8.133 In the United States view, the causation standard relevant to WTO review of an injury determination is set forth in Article 4.2(b). The USITC determination clearly articulates its reasons for finding "the causal link" between the increased imports and serious injury. The United States argues that nothing in the Agreement on Safeguards requires the competent authority to articulate the causation standard at all; Article 4.2(b) requires merely that it be applied.

8.134 According to the United States, the USITC specifically addressed each of the other factors that importers and foreign producers suggested were causing injury, and found that no other factor that might be adversely affecting the wheat gluten industry was more important than the rapid increase in imports.[130] The United States submits that with respect to co-products, the USITC found that: there was no decline in wheat starch prices that either paralleled the sharp decline since 1994 of domestic wheat gluten prices or explained the sharp decline in the

---

[128] European Community second written submission, Attachment 1-4, para. 69.
[129] United States first written submission, Attachment 2-1, para. 125.
[130] *Ibid.*, para. 127.

financial performance of domestic wheat gluten producers; and the relative stability of, and gradual increase in, domestic wheat starch prices suggested that competition between corn starch and wheat starch was not likely to have much, if any, effect on wheat gluten production.[131] The United States further argues that the USITC found that imports by domestic producers were not responsible for the surge in imports that occurred in 1996 and 1997.[132] According to the United States, the USITC also found that unit selling values declined in 1996 and 1997 despite increased demand and higher raw material costs and that this unusual development was explained by the dramatic increase in relatively low-priced imports during this period, which had the effect of driving down wheat gluten prices.[133] To the extent that one other factor - namely, additions to U.S. capacity - contributed to the decline in capacity utilization in that period, the USITC demonstrated why it was a less important factor than imports. Indeed, the United States asserts, the USITC specifically identified the relative contributions to injury of capacity utilization and imports.[134] The United States argues that the USITC specifically found that if the domestic industry filled the growth in demand in 1996 and 1997, instead of the increased imports doing so, the industry would have operated at 61 per cent of capacity instead of 44.5 per cent as it actually did. Under these conditions, domestic production in 1997 would have been well above, rather than below 1996 levels. Capacity utilization in 1997 would have exceeded 1995 levels. In short, according to the United States, "the fall in virtually all indicators of industry performance in 1996 and 1997 compared with prior periods, which the USITC found to constitute serious injury, would not have occurred."[135] For the United States, the history and context of Article 4.2(b) demonstrate why the EC's proposal that the USITC must somehow quantify and deduct from total injury the specific effects caused by other factors is not required.

8.135 The United States submits that the aspect of US law requiring a finding that imports must be a "substantial cause" of injury requires the USITC to make a finding related to causation that, while not required by Article 4.2, helps to ensure that its objectives are realized. The requirement to examine the relative weight of other factors ensures that the USITC both examines the causal link between increased imports and serious injury, as required by Article 4.2(b), and avoids attributing to imports the effects of other causes of injury that are more important. According to the United States, while they result in findings that provide more detail than required under Article 4.2(b), the relevant United States procedures are entirely consistent with its letter and spirit.

---

131 *Ibid.*, paras. 31-32, citing USITC Report, pp. I-16-17.
132 *Ibid.*, para. 33, citing USITC Report, p. I-17.
133 *Ibid.*, para. 35, citing USITC Report, p. I-17.
134 *Ibid.*, para. 127.
135 *Ibid.*, para. 132.

Evaluation by the Panel

8.136 We view the issue before us as whether, in conducting its investigation into whether increased imports were "a cause that is important and not less than any other cause" of any serious injury to its domestic wheat gluten industry, the USITC satisfied the requirements in Article 4.2(b) SA to demonstrate the causal link between the increased imports and the serious injury, and not to attribute to imports injury caused by other factors.[136] We first consider the nature of the obligations imposed by Article 4.2(b) with respect to the causation analysis that the investigating authorities must conduct.

8.137 Article 4.2(b) SA deals specifically with the causal link between imports and serious injury. It requires that the safeguard investigation demonstrate, "on the basis of objective evidence, the existence of the causal link between increased imports of the product concerned and serious injury or threat thereof." It also stipulates that "[w]hen factors other than increased imports are causing injury to the domestic industry at the same time, such injury shall not be attributed to increased imports." Thus, as part of the causation analysis, there must be a sufficient consideration of "other factors" operating in the market at the same time, so that any injury caused by such other factors can be properly identified and attributed.

8.138 As we have previously observed, Article 4.2(b) SA contains an explicit textual link to Article 4.2(a) SA. It stipulates that "[t]he determination made in subparagraph (a) *shall not be made* unless" the investigation demonstrates the existence of the causal link between increased imports and serious injury. Article 4.2(a) and (b) require a Member: (i) to demonstrate the existence of the causal link between increased imports and *serious* injury; and (ii) not to attribute injury being caused by other factors to the domestic industry at the same time to increased imports. We consider that, read together, these two propositions require

[136] The United States asserts that the "EC makes some statements regarding U.S. law, but the EC did not challenge U.S. law thus such claims are not within the Panel's terms of reference" (United States first written submission, Attachment 2-1, footnote 119). In support, the United States cites the Appellate Body Report, *Guatemala – Anti-dumping Investigation Regarding Portland Cement from Mexico* ("*Guatemala – Cement I*"), WT/DS60/AB/R, adopted 25 November 1998, DSR 1998:IX, 3767, para. 73 (the "measure" and the claims concerning that measure constitute the "matter referred to the DSB" which forms the basis for the panel's terms of reference). The United States argues: "The only matter with respect to Articles 2 and 4 of the Safeguard Agreement that has been referred to this Panel is whether the USITC's findings and conclusion comport with the cited articles." We understand that the measure before us is the definitive safeguard measure imposed by the United States, effective 1 June 1998, pursuant to the United States President's "Proclamation 7103 of May 30, 1998 - To Facilitate Positive Adjustment to Competition from Imports of Wheat Gluten", supra, footnote 7 and "Memorandum of May 30 1998 - Action Under Section 203 of the Trade Act of 1974 Concerning Wheat Gluten", supra, footnote 8. The measure before us is not Section 202 of the United States Trade Act. We must examine whether the United States met the requirements in the Agreement on Safeguards for the application of this measure. Accordingly, we must examine the findings and conclusions of the USITC as to the conditions for the imposition of the measure, and the analysis upon which those findings and conclusions are based.

that a Member demonstrate that the increased imports, under the conditions extant in the marketplace, *in and of themselves*, cause *serious* injury. This is not to say that the imports must be the sole causal factor present in a situation of serious injury. There may be multiple factors present in a situation of serious injury to a domestic industry. However, the increased imports must be sufficient, in and of themselves, to cause injury which achieves the threshold of "serious" as defined in the Agreement.

8.139 In our view, where a number of factors, one of which is increased imports, are sufficient *collectively* to cause a "significant overall impairment of the position of the domestic industry", but increased imports alone are not causing injury that achieves the threshold of "serious" within the meaning of Article 4.1(a) of the Agreement[137], the conditions for imposing a safeguard measure are not satisfied. In such a situation, imports may be causing "injury", and there may even be a demonstration of the causal link between increased imports and "injury". However, where this injury does not achieve the threshold of "*serious* injury", as that term is defined in Article 4.1(a) SA, the conditions and circumstances permitting the imposition of a safeguard measure are not present.

8.140 This should not be construed to mean that we view the Agreement on Safeguards as imposing upon the importing Member any particular method for assessing whether any factors other than imports are causing injury to its domestic market at the same time as imports, or how to go about ensuring that injury attributable to other factors is not attributed to imports. The United States remains free to choose a method for making this assessment and ensuring non-attribution.[138] However, while the United States is free to determine an appropriate method of assessing causation, the method it selects must ensure that the injury caused by increased imports, considered alone, is "serious" injury, that is "a significant overall impairment in the situation of the domestic industry". In order to achieve this, the investigating authorities must ensure that injury attributable to other factors is not attributed to imports. While the investigating authorities may not be required in their report explicitly to *articulate* a particular "causation standard" beyond that provided for in Article 4.2(b) SA, the approach that the investigating authorities actually *apply* must nevertheless yield a result that is consistent with the obligations contained in Article 4 SA, including the obligation not to attribute to imports any injury caused by other factors.

8.141 We note that the panel in *United States – Imposition of Countervailing Duties on Imports of Fresh and Chilled Atlantic Salmon from Norway* examined the issue of the treatment to be given to factors other than subsidized imports in

---

[137] Article 4.1(a) SA states: ""serious injury" shall be understood to mean a significant overall impairment in the position of a domestic industry."

[138] A similar view was expressed by the panel in *Korea – Dairy Safeguard*, *supra*, footnote 16, para. 7.96.

the context of Article 6:4 of the Tokyo Round Subsidies Code. That panel considered[139]:

> "... that the primary focus of the requirement in Article 6:4 of a demonstration of a causal relationship between imports under investigation and material injury to a domestic industry was on the analysis of the factors set forth in Articles 6:2 and 6:3, i.e. the volume and price effects of the imports, and their consequent impact on the domestic industry. In this connection, the Panel recalled its conclusions regarding the findings made by the USITC with respect to these factors. Under Article 6:4 the USITC was required not to attribute injuries caused by other factors to the imports from Norway. In the view of the Panel this did not mean that, in addition to examining the effects of the imports under Articles 6:1, 6:2 and 6:3, the USITC should somehow have identified the extent of injury caused by these other factors in order to isolate the injury caused by these factors from the injury caused by the imports from Norway. Rather, it meant that the USITC was required to conduct an examination sufficient to ensure that in its analysis of the factors set forth in Articles 6:2 and 6:3 it did not find that material injury was caused by imports from Norway when material injury to the domestic industry allegedly caused by imports from Norway was in fact caused by factors other than these imports..."

8.142 We consider that significant differences exist between the text of the particular legal provisions that formed the basis for the analysis of the *United States - Salmon* panel and the legal context in which the issues before that panel arose (i.e. subsidization/dumping, as opposed to safeguards). Nevertheless, to the extent it is relevant to our examination in this dispute, we believe that the above passage from the *United States – Salmon* panel report provides guidance. We agree with the view of that panel to the extent that it would require the USITC to conduct a safeguards examination sufficient to ensure that, in its analysis of the injury factors contained or referred to in Article 4.2(a) SA, it did not find that serious injury was caused by increased imports of wheat gluten when injury to the domestic industry allegedly caused by increased imports was in fact caused by factors other than these increased imports. A Member is not necessarily required to quantify, on an individual basis, the precise extent of "injury" caused by each other possible factor. However, a Member must conduct an examination that

[139] SCM/153, adopted by the SCM Committee on 28 April 1994, BISD 41S/576, para. 321. The panel in United States – Antidumping Duties on Imports of Fresh and Chilled Salmon from Norway, ADP/87, adopted by the ADP Committee on 27 April 1994, BISD 41S/229, para. 555 similarly examined the issue of the treatment to be given to factors other than dumped imports in the context of Article 3:4 of the Tokyo Round Anti-Dumping Code.

ensures that any injury caused by such other factors is not attributed to increased imports.[140]

8.143 Thus, Article 4.2(a) and (b) SA require that increased imports *per se* are causing serious injury. Furthermore, the investigating authorities must conduct an examination that ensures that any injury caused by other factors is not attributed to increased imports. Where injury caused by one - or multiple - other factor(s) is attributed to those other factors, any remaining injury caused by increased imports may not reach the threshold of "*serious* injury", within the meaning of Article 4.1(a) SA.

8.144 On this basis, we examine whether the causation analysis applied by the USITC in this safeguard investigation complied with the "non-attribution" requirement of Article 4.2(b) SA.

8.145 In its investigation, the USITC examined whether increased imports were a "substantial cause" of serious injury, i.e. "a cause which is important and not less than any other cause." The USITC found as follows:

> "We reviewed carefully the alternative causes of injury suggested by the parties and other possible causes, and have concluded that increased imports are both an important cause of serious injury and a cause that is greater than any other cause."[141]

8.146 The USITC Report indicates that the USITC weighed individually each of the other causal factors in question against imports in order to find whether any one of these factors, on its own, was "a more important cause of injury" or a "greater cause of serious injury" than increased imports. The USITC determined that none of these factors, on its own, was "a more important cause of serious injury" than increased imports.

8.147 With respect to co-products markets, the USITC found:

> "We carefully reviewed EU respondents' arguments about the co-product markets. While there is evidence that wheat gluten production decisions are affected by market conditions in the wheat starch market, *we conclude that changes in the co-product markets were not a more important cause of serious injury than increased imports.*"[142] (emphasis added, footnotes omitted)

8.148 With respect to rising input costs[143], the USITC stated:

---

[140] We recognize the practical difficulties that may arise in applying this principle. While we make a finding as to the general kind of examination that a Member is required to conduct, we make no pronouncement as to the precise steps that a Member must take in this regard.

[141] USITC Report, p. I-16.

[142] USITC Report, p. I-16.

[143] In light of our finding below, we do not believe it is necessary to examine that EC assertion that the USITC failed to fulfill the requirements of Article 4.2(b) SA by basing itself on oral assertions by "persons interested in the outcome of an investigation" (i.e. the presidents of two of the US producers, Midwest and Manildra) for the proposition that "[b]ecause demand for wheat gluten is relatively

"Nor do we consider rising prices of wheat and wheat flour, which are the major inputs into wheat gluten/wheat starch production, to be a more important cause of injury than increased imports."[144]

8.149 With respect to the importation of wheat gluten by United States domestic producers, the USITC found:

"*We do not regard the ongoing importation of wheat gluten by domestic producers as being a more important cause of the serious injury*, as argued by respondents."[145] (emphasis added, footnotes omitted).

8.150 With respect to capacity utilization and increased capacity, the USITC found:

"We considered other possible causes of injury, including competition among domestic producers, increased capacity and rising raw materials (wheat and wheat flour) costs. The domestic wheat gluten market is very competitive. Producers have ample excess capacity to meet higher demand. Also, wheat gluten is a commodity product that sells primarily on the basis of price, and wheat gluten from different sources is highly interchangeable. One new domestic producer, Heartland, entered the market in 1996. In addition, the domestic industry added substantial new capacity early in the period of investigation. This increased capacity was added in anticipation of continued strong growth of domestic demand and consumption. Industry projections of continued growth in demand and consumption were largely correct, as apparent consumption increased nearly 18 percent between 1993 and 1997. As indicated above, but for the increase in imports, the industry would have operated at 61 percent capacity in 1997, which is much closer to the level at which the industry operated early in the investigative period when it operated reasonably profitably. We therefore conclude that *neither* domestic competition *nor increased domestic capacity was a more important cause of serious injury than increased imports.*"[146] (emphasis added)

8.151 As we have already observed, Article 4.2(b) SA prohibits the attribution to increased imports of injury caused by other factors. We take this to imply that

insensitive to changes in price, we would expect that wheat gluten producers would be able to pass on these cost increases to their customers. U.S. producers testified that, historically, higher raw material costs had been passed through to their consumers." According to the EC, the USITC could not rely on these oral assertions without verifying the correctness of such "interested" allegations through other sources. See first written submission of the EC, paras. 97-100; Oral Statement of the EC at the first meeting with the Panel, paras. 84-86; second written submission of the EC paras. 29-30, 45.

144 USITC Report, P. I-17.

145 USITC Report, p. I-17.

146 USITC Report, p. I-17.

a given factor is either a cause of injury, or it is not. If a given factor *is* a cause of injury (even a minor cause), then, under Article 4.2(b) SA, such injury "shall not be attributed to increased imports". We note the United States assertions that increased capacity had a role (characterized by the United States in these proceedings as a "demonstrably minor role")[147] in the serious injury suffered by the industry; that "to the extent that one other factor, namely additions to US capacity - contributed to the decline in capacity utilization [in 1996 and 1997], the USITC demonstrated why it was a less important factor than imports"[148]; and that the USITC specifically identified the relative contributions to injury of capacity utilization and imports.[149] To us, these assertions constitute an admission by the United States that at least one factor other than increased imports also contributed to the serious injury experienced by the domestic industry. However, we see no indication in the USITC Report that imports were not also held responsible for the injury caused by this factor. As a result of the USITC causation analysis that weighed each other factor individually against imports to determine whether such factor was "a more important cause of injury" and then excluded such other factor as a "cause of injury" when it did not, on its own, satisfy this standard, the USITC held that imports were effectively the sole remaining cause of injury, which the USITC presumed remained "serious". However, we see this approach as the converse of ensuring that it was the increased imports alone which were causing *serious* injury. A demonstration that a given causal factor did not make an equal or greater contribution to serious injury than imports does not demonstrate that such factor made no contribution *at all* to serious injury.

8.152 The USITC examination as to whether each other factor individually constituted "a greater cause of injury than imports" is not such as to ensure that "serious injury", within the meaning of Article 4.1(a) SA, would necessarily still exist after injury attributable to such other causes was not attributed to imports. In our view, under the USITC causation analysis applied in this case, it is not clear that the increased imports of the product concerned cause "*serious* injury" to the domestic industry. We consider that the USITC's causation analysis does not ensure that imports, in and of themselves, are sufficient to cause *serious* injury to the domestic industry once injury caused by other factors is not attributed to imports.

8.153 **For these reasons, we find that the examination of the USITC into whether increased imports were "a cause that is important and not less than any other cause" of serious injury and the resulting conclusion of the USITC in the investigation that led to the imposition of the safeguard measure at issue that increased imports are "an important cause of serious injury and a cause that is greater than any other cause" are not consistent with**

[147] United States first written submission, Attachment 2-1, para. 125.

[148] United States first written submission, Attachment 2-1, para. 127.

[149] *Ibid.*

Article 4.2(b) SA as they do not ensure the non-attribution to imports of injury caused by other factors.[150]

(iv) Summary with Respect to Causation

8.154 In sum, we have found that the USITC Report indicates a general coincidence of the upward trend in imports with the negative trends in the injury factors and that it contains an adequate, reasoned and reasonable explanation of how the facts support the USITC findings with respect to the first aspect of the causation analysis.[151] With regard to the second aspect of the causation analysis relating to the conditions of competition between the imported product and the domestic product, we have found that the United States did not act inconsistently with the obligations imposed by the phrase "under such conditions" in Article XIX:1(a) of the GATT 1994 and Article 2.1 SA nor with its obligations under Article 4.2 SA. However, we have found that the USITC examination into whether increased imports were "a cause that is important and not less than any other cause" of serious injury and the resulting conclusion of the USITC that increased imports are "an important cause of serious injury and a cause that is greater than any other cause" are not consistent with Article 4.2(b) SA as they do not ensure the non-attribution to imports of injury caused by other factors.

(e) Exclusion of Certain Imports from the Application of the Measure on the Basis of Origin

(i) Arguments of the Parties

European Community

8.155 In challenging the safeguard investigation and the measure imposed by the United States in this case, the European Community raises the issue of the inclusion of imports of wheat gluten from all sources in the investigation, but the exclusion of certain imports from the application of the measure on the basis of origin (in particular, those of Canada, a NAFTA partner) in several contexts under Articles XIX:1 of the GATT 1994 and Articles 2.1 and 4 SA[152] - in particular, "increased imports", "serious injury" and "causation". The European Com-

[150] We do not by our finding intend to express any view as to whether or not, had the United States conducted an examination that ensured that any injury caused by such other factors is not attributed to increased imports, it could have properly found that there was serious injury caused by increased imports. As the United States has itself argued, our task is to review the determination of an investigating authority, rather than to engage in a de novo review or to conduct our own assessment on the basis of the raw data that was before the investigating authority. See supra, para. 8.3.

[151] See supra, para. 8.91 for the three parts of the Panel's approach to causation.

[152] See infra, paras. 8.184 and 8.220 with respect to the EC claims in this context under Article 5 SA and Article I of the GATT 1994.

munity also argued that the procedure followed by the USITC "does not correctly apply the fundamental MFN provision under Article 2.2 of the SA".[153]

8.156 The European Community asserts that the United States found serious injury or threat thereof caused by imports from all sources, including imports from NAFTA countries including Canada, but then imposed its safeguard measure on wheat gluten only on non-NAFTA countries, thus excluding Canada. In the view of the European Community, this constitutes a breach of the principle of "parallelism" that was recognized in the *Argentina - Footwear Safeguard* case.[154] According to the European Community, nothing in Article 4.2 SA allows a Member to conduct a separate examination of serious injury based on the origin of the imported products concerned. The European Community asserts that Article 2.1 SA, and in particular its footnote 1, does not support the arguments made by the United States (and Canada) in this case. In the view of the European Community, the "generic reservation" contained in footnote 1 to Article 2.1 concerning the interpretation of the relationship between Articles XXIV and XIX of the GATT 1994 has no bearing on the interpretation of Article 4.2 SA.

United States

8.157 The United States contends that, in its investigation, the USITC found that the serious injury sustained by the domestic wheat gluten industry was attributable to a surge in imports from the EU in 1996 and 1997, accompanied by sustained underselling from EU producers.[155] In a second step, the USITC examined Canadian imports alone and determined that they were not a significant cause of serious injury. This separate causation analysis of NAFTA imports was conducted pursuant to US law, as required by Article 802 of the NAFTA. According to the United States, the USITC's finding make clear that, unlike in *Argentina – Footwear Safeguard*, the injury determination was not based on effects ascribable to Canadian imports.

8.158 The United States does not understand the Appellate Body to have established a broad requirement of "parallelism". Nevertheless, the United States asserts that the procedures contemplated by Article 802 of the NAFTA, and employed by the United States in this case, satisfies the purpose of the "parallelism" notion articulated in *Argentina-Footwear Safeguard.*

8.159 The United States argues that nothing in the Agreement on Safeguards proscribes an independent causation analysis for imports originating in the territory of another free trade area participant, or suggests that only a single causation analysis is appropriate. According to the United States, specific provisions on the

---

[153] EC second written submission, Attachment 1-4, para. 123.

[154] EC second written submission, Attachment 1-4, para. 118 – 128. The European Community refers to Panel Report and Appellate Body Report, *Argentina - Footwear Safeguard, supra*, footnote 17.

[155] United States Response to Panel Question 29, 17 January 2000.

application of safeguard measures by members of a customs union or free trade area are in footnote 1 of the Agreement on Safeguards. The United States asserts that the applicable provisions of the GATT 1994, namely Articles XIX and XXIV:8, determine Members' rights and obligations regarding the application of a safeguard measure in the context of an FTA. In particular, the footnote makes clear that the non-discrimination requirement of Article 2.2 SA is not pertinent in assessing the safeguards treatment accorded by a customs union or FTA member to goods originating in other participant countries. According to the United States, Article XXIV does not address the sequencing, or number, of causation analyses that may be undertaken as part of an Article XIX safeguards investigation.

(ii) Evaluation by the Panel

8.160 We see the issue before us as whether, in this case, the United States, after including imports from all sources in its investigation of "increased imports" of wheat gluten into its territory and the consequent effects of such imports on its domestic wheat gluten industry, was justified in excluding imports from Canada from the application of the safeguard measure following a separate and subsequent inquiry concerning whether imports from Canada accounted for a "substantial share" of total imports and whether they "contributed importantly" to the serious injury caused by imports.[156]

8.161 In the course of the present Panel proceedings, the United States confirmed that the USITC first conducted a "global" investigation concerning injury and causation that included imports of wheat gluten *from all sources*, regardless of their origin. Following an affirmative determination that wheat gluten was being imported *from all sources* into the United States in such quantities as to cause

[156] In its first written submission, the European Community challenged the exclusion from the application of the measure by the United States of imports from Canada "and certain other countries" (EC first written submission, Attachment 1-1, para. 103); the subsequent EC arguments focused on imports from Canada in this context (see e.g. EC first oral statement, Attachment 1-2, paras. 87 ff.; EC second written submission, Attachment 1-4, paras. 118 ff.). We note that imports from Mexico were also excluded from application of the measure pursuant to NAFTA and the US implementing legislation. According to the USITC Report, "there were no reported imports from Mexico during the period examined" (USITC Report, p. I-19). Imports from Israel and CBERA and ATPA countries were also excluded from the application of the measure. According to the USITC Report, there were also "no reported importations of wheat gluten from any of these countries during the period of investigation" (with the exception of one importation from Ecuador which may have been the result of a data entry error) (USITC Report, p. I-29). Thus, in addition to imports from those countries excluded from the application of the measure pursuant to Article 9.1 SA, imports from Canada, Mexico, Israel, CBERA and ATPA countries were also excluded from the measure. Of these latter countries, only Canada in fact had imports into the United States during the period examined by the USITC. Therefore, imports from Canada were in fact the only imports that were actually included in the USITC investigation but subsequently excluded from the application of the measure (again, apart from imports from those countries excluded from the application of the measure pursuant to Article 9.1 SA). For this reason, we focus our examination here on imports from Canada.

serious injury to the United States domestic wheat gluten industry[157], the USITC conducted a separate and subsequent examination of whether imports from Canada accounted for a substantial share of total imports, and whether imports from Canada contributed importantly to the serious injury caused by imports.[158]

8.162 The USITC Report contains the following account of the USITC finding made with respect to imports from Canada (and Mexico) in the separate causation analysis conducted with respect to these imports:

> "We make a negative finding with respect to both Mexico and Canada. There were no reported imports of wheat gluten from Mexico during the period examined. Thus, Mexico does not account for a substantial share of total imports. Having found that the first prong of the test is not met, we have made a negative finding with respect to Mexico. Canada, on the other hand, was the third largest supplier (after the EU and Australia) of wheat gluten imports during the most recent 3-year period, accounting for an average of 10.2 percent of imports. Therefore, we find that imports from Canada account for a substantial share of total imports. However, imports from Canada declined significantly during the period examined, while imports overall increased, and by 1997 Canada accounted for 8.9 percent of total imports. In addition, petitioner stated in its petition that imports from Canada are not contributing importantly to the serious injury caused by imports. We therefore find that imports from Canada are not contributing importantly to the serious injury caused by imports."[159] (footnotes omitted)
>
> and,
>
> "Having made negative findings with respect to imports of wheat gluten from Canada and Mexico under section 311 of the NAFTA

[157] In response to a question from the Panel, the United States confirmed that an affirmative determination under Section 202(b)(1)(A) of the United States Trade Act of 1974 is a determination "that a product is being imported into the United States in such quantities as to cause or threaten to cause serious injury to a US industry producing a like or directly competitive product". See United States Response to Panel Question 15, Attachment 2-8. The USITC Report states, at p. I-10: "Because section 202 is a global safeguard law, the Commission considers imports from all sources in determining whether imports have increased."

[158] The United States excluded imports from Canada from the application of the safeguard measure on the basis of Section 311(a) of the NAFTA Implementation Act, which, according to the USITC Report, p. I-18, provides that if the Commission makes an "affirmative injury determination" in an investigation under section 202 of the United States Trade Act, the Commission must also find whether: (i) imports of the article from a NAFTA country, considered individually, account for a substantial share of total imports; and (ii) imports of the article from a NAFTA country, considered individually or, in exceptional circumstances, imports from NAFTA countries considered collectively, contribute importantly to the serious injury, or threat thereof, caused by imports.

[159] USITC Report, p. I-19.

Implementation Act, we recommend that such imports be excluded from the quantitative restriction."[160]

8.163 The President's "Memorandum of 30 May 1998 -Action Under Section 203 of the Trade Act of 1974 Concerning Wheat Gluten" states:

> "I agree with the USITC's findings under section 311(a) of the NAFTA Implementation Act, and therefore determine, pursuant to section 312(a) of the NAFTA Implementation Act, that imports of wheat gluten produced in Canada do not contribute importantly to the serious injury caused by imports and that imports of wheat gluten produced in Mexico do not account for a substantial share of total imports of such wheat gluten. Therefore, pursuant to section 312(b) of the NAFTA Implementation Act, the quantitative limitation will not apply to imports of wheat gluten from Canada or Mexico."[161]

8.164 We understand, therefore, that the United States applied the safeguard measures at issue after conducting an *initial* global investigation of the product (wheat gluten) being imported into the territory of the United States *from all sources* and the effects of those imports on the United States' domestic industry. Thus, the overall affirmative determination of serious injury to the domestic industry caused by increased imports was made on the basis of imports *from all sources.*

8.165 We turn to examine the nature of the legal obligations imposed by the Agreement on Safeguards with respect to the scope of the imports subject to the investigation and the scope of the imports subject to the application of the measure.

8.166 Several provisions are relevant to our examination, in particular, Articles 2.1 and 4.2 SA. Article 2.1 SA provides as follows:

> *Conditions*
>
> 1. A Member[1] may apply a safeguard measure to a product only if that Member has determined, pursuant to the provisions set out below, that such product is being imported into its territory in such increased quantities, absolute or relative to domestic production, and under such conditions as to cause or threaten to cause serious injury to the domestic industry that produces like or directly competitive products.
>
> ---
>
> [1]A customs union may apply a safeguard measure as a single unit or on behalf of a member State. When a customs union applies a safeguard measure as a single unit, all the requirements for the determination of serious injury or threat thereof under

---

[160] USITC Report, p. I-21.

[161] Supra, notes 8 and 10.

this Agreement shall be based on the conditions existing in the customs union as a whole. When a safeguard measure is applied on behalf of a member State, all the requirements for the determination of serious injury or threat thereof shall be based on the conditions existing in that member State and the measure shall be limited to that member State. Nothing in this Agreement prejudges the interpretation of the relationship between Article XIX and paragraph 8 of Article XXIV of GATT 1994.

Article 4.2 SA states, in part:

> "(a) *In the investigation to determine whether increased imports have caused or are threatening to cause serious injury to a domestic industry* under the terms of this Agreement, the competent authorities shall evaluate all relevant factors of an objective and quantifiable nature having a bearing on the situation of that industry, in particular, the rate and amount of the increase in imports of the product concerned in absolute and relative terms, the share of the domestic market taken by increased imports, changes in the level of sales, production, productivity, capacity utilization, profits and losses, and employment.
>
> (b) The determination referred to in subparagraph (a) shall not be made unless this investigation demonstrates, on the basis of objective evidence, the existence of the causal link between increased imports *of the product concerned* and serious injury or threat thereof. When factors other than increased imports are causing injury to the domestic industry at the same time, such injury shall not be attributed to increased imports." (emphasis added)

8.167 In our view, the text of Articles 2.1 and 4.2 contains a requirement of symmetry between the scope of the imported products subject to the investigation and the scope of the imported products subject to the application of the measure. Article 2.1 SA refers to "a product". In order for a Member to apply a safeguard measure, this provision requires that "*such product*" (emphasis added) "is being imported into its territory in such increased quantities ... and under such conditions as to cause or threaten to cause serious injury to the domestic industry that produces like or directly competitive products." There exists a basic symmetry between the terms "a product" and "such product" in Article 2.1 SA. Both terms must refer to the *same* thing. That is, a safeguard measure must be applied to a *product*, and it is increased imports of *such product* into the territory of the importing Member that must have been determined to cause or threaten to cause serious injury. In our view, there is no basis in Article 2.1 SA for a distinction to be drawn on the basis of origin between the "product" subject to the investigation and the "product" subject to the application of the measure, and thus there is an implied symmetry with respect to the product that falls within the scope of a safeguard *investigation* and the product that falls within the scope of the *application* of the safeguard measure.

8.168 Similarly, Article 4.2(a) refers to "the investigation to determine whether increased imports have caused or are threatening to cause serious injury to a domestic industry....". Article 4.2(b) stipulates that this determination "shall not be made unless this investigation demonstrates ... the existence of the causal link between increased imports *of the product concerned* and serious injury or threat thereof ....". (emphasis added) These provisions indicate that it is increased imports of "the product concerned" that must form the basis for the determination of serious injury and causal link. In our view, there is no basis in Article 4.2 SA for a distinction to be drawn on the basis of the origin of a product when examining the element of causation in a safeguards investigation.

8.169 We find contextual support for our view in Article 2.2 SA, which mandates that:

> "Safeguard measures shall be applied to a product being imported irrespective of its source."

8.170 We find further confirmation of our view that there is a requirement of symmetry between the imports subject to the scope of the investigation and the imports subject to the scope of the measure in the Appellate Body Report in *Argentina-Footwear Safeguard.* There, the Appellate Body stated the following:

> "We now turn to examine whether the Panel was correct in its interpretation that there is an implied "*parallelism* between the scope of a safeguard *investigation* and the scope of the *application* of safeguard measures."[162] Article 2.1 provides that:
>
> > A *Member may* apply a safeguard measures ... *only* if *that Member* has determined ... that such product is being imported into *its territory* in such increased quantities ... and under such conditions as to cause or threaten to cause serious injury to the domestic industry ... (emphasis added)
>
> Article 4.1(c) defines "domestic industry" as meaning "the producers as a whole of the like or directly competitive products operating *within the territory of a Member ...*". (emphasis added) Taken together, the provisions of Articles 2.1 and 4.1(c) of the *Agreement on Safeguards* demonstrate that a Member of the WTO may only apply a safeguard measure after that Member has determined that a product is being imported *into its territory* in such increased quantities and under such conditions as to cause or threaten to cause serious injury to *its* domestic industry *within its territory.* According to Articles 2.1 and 4.1(c), therefore, all of the relevant aspects of a safeguard investigation must be conducted by the Member that ultimately applies the safeguard measure, on the basis of increased imports entering its territory and causing or threatening to cause serious injury to the domestic industry within its territory.

[162] Panel Report, *Argentina – Footwear Safeguard, supra,* footnote 17, para. 8.87.

> While Articles 2.1 and 4.1(c) set out the conditions for imposing a safeguard measure and the requirements for the scope of a safeguard *investigation*, these provisions do not resolve the matter of the scope of *application* of a safeguard measure. In that context, Article 2.2 of the *Agreement on Safeguards* provides:
>
> > Safeguard measures shall be applied to a product being imported irrespective of its source.
>
> As we have noted, in this case, Argentina applied the safeguard measures at issue after conducting an investigation of products being imported into Argentine territory and the effects of those imports on Argentina's domestic industry. In applying safeguard measures on the basis of this investigation in this case, Argentina was also required under Article 2.2 to apply those measures to imports from all sources, including from other MERCOSUR member States.
>
> On the basis of this reasoning, and on the facts of this case, we find that Argentina's investigation, which evaluated whether serious injury or the threat thereof was caused by imports from *all* sources, could only lead to the imposition of safeguard measures on imports from *all* sources. Therefore, we conclude that Argentina's investigation, in this case, cannot serve as a basis for excluding imports from other MERCOSUR member States from the application of the safeguard measures."[163]

8.171 Having established that there is a requirement of symmetry under Articles 2.1 and 4.2 SA between the scope of the imports subject to a safeguards investigation and the scope of the imports subject to the application of the measure[164], we examine whether the approach of the USITC in its investigation achieved this symmetry.

8.172 The United States argues that "the procedures contemplated by NAFTA Article 802, and employed by the United States in the case of its wheat gluten safeguard, satisfies the purpose of the "parallelism" notion the *Footwear* panel articulated".[165] According to the United States, this purpose "is to ensure that when a Member attributes serious injury to imports originating in the territory of a country that is a party to a customs union (or FTA, in this case), those imports

---

[163] Appellate Body Report, *Argentina-Footwear Safeguard*, *supra*, footnote 17, paras. 111-113.

[164] The only explicit departure from this principle in the Agreement on Safeguards is in Article 9.1 SA, which provides that a safeguard measure "shall not be applied against a product originating in a developing country Member as long as its share of imports of the product concerned in the importing Member does not exceed 3 per cent, provided that developing country Members with less than 3 per cent import share collectively account for not more than 9 per cent of total imports of the product concerned."

[165] United States Response to Panel Question 30, Attachment 2-4, para. 108.

should be included in the safeguard measure the Member determines to apply."[166] The United States argues that "Article 802 and US implementing provisions provide for the exclusion of Mexican and Canadian imports from an eventual safeguard measure where they did not play a significant role in causing serious injury or threat of injury."[167]

8.173 We do not agree with the United States that, in this case, the treatment of imports from Canada in the investigation and in the subsequent exclusion of those imports from the application of the measure comports with the symmetry that we have found to be required by Articles 2.1 and 4.2 SA.

8.174 We recall that the term "serious injury" is defined in Article 4.1(a) SA as "a significant overall impairment in the position of a domestic industry". In this case, the USITC made a global determination of "serious injury". This determination was one of serious injury caused by total imports of the product into its territory *from all sources*. After the USITC had determined serious injury to have been caused by increased imports of the product concerned *from all sources*, it *subsequently excluded* from the application of the measure imports from certain sources (in this case, particularly, Canada). It is our understanding that the USITC initially attributed injury to imports from all sources, including imports from Canada, in order to reach its overall finding of "serious injury" caused by imports, and then, on the basis of a *separate and subsequent* analysis concerning imports from Canada, excluded imports from Canada from the application of the measure.

8.175 The United States contends that, because of the USITC's separate and subsequent analysis of imports from Canada, "the USITC's overall causation finding did not depend on the inclusion of Canadian imports."[168] However, the fact that the USITC found that imports from Canada - which it deemed to constitute a "substantial share" of total imports - nevertheless did not "contribute importantly" to the serious injury caused by imports does not, in our view, demonstrate that imports were causing "*serious* injury", within the meaning of Article 4.1(a) SA, after the exclusion of imports from Canada (at the time, the third largest supplier of wheat gluten to the United States) and the consequent effects of these imports. Under these circumstances, there is no demonstration that the remaining imports of the product concerned would still be sufficient to cause "*serious* injury" to the domestic industry. Our view is not changed by the fact that imports from Canada declined in the years in question as they still accounted for 11.0 per cent and 8.9 per cent of total imports into the United States domestic market in 1996 and 1997, respectively.[169]

---

166 *Ibid.*

167 *Ibid.*, para. 109.

168 United States Response to Panel Question 29, Attachment 2-4, para. 93.

169 As the USITC found, such imports accounted for an average of 10.2 per cent of the subject imports over the "most recent 3-year period". USITC Report, p. I-19.

8.176 The unsupportability of the United States' approach can be demonstrated by taking it to its logical extreme. An approach that excludes from the application of the measure imports of certain countries if they do not account for a "substantial share" of total imports and do not "contribute importantly" to the serious injury caused by imports might also result in a situation where, after multiple minor quantities of imports are excluded from the application of the measure, which *collectively* accounted for a major proportion of imports, it would no longer be clear that any injury remaining that was due to the remaining imports would still achieve the threshold of "serious" as that term is defined in Article 4.1(a) of the Agreement on Safeguards. For example, assume that the imports of 5 countries, each accounting for approximately 10% of total imports, were all deemed individually not to account for a "substantial share" of total imports" and not to "contribute importantly" to serious injury and on this basis were thus excluded. Collectively, such imports account for 50% of total imports. There is no demonstration that any injury caused by imports remaining after the exclusion of 50% of total imports would still reach the threshold of "*serious* injury".

8.177 We consider that in the circumstances of the present case, in applying safeguard measures on the basis of this investigation in this case, the United States was also required under Articles 2.1 and 4.2 SA to apply those measures to imports from all sources, including from Canada, another NAFTA member State. On this basis, we conclude that the United States, on the facts of this case, cannot justify the non-application of its safeguard measures to imports from Canada, another NAFTA member state, on the basis of an *initial* global safeguard investigation that found serious injury, within the meaning of Article 4.1 SA, *caused by* increased imports *from all sources*, including imports from Canada.

8.178 We turn now to the argument of the United States that "Article XXIV provides an exception to Article XIX of the GATT 1994"[170] and that "[a]n examination of Article XXIV demonstrates that the United States' treatment of Canada both with respect to the injury investigation and the remedy applied are consistent with Article XXIV".[171] According to the United States, the last sentence of footnote 1 SA contains specific provisions on the application of safeguard measures by members of a customs union or free trade area. The United States asserts that the question of how a free trade area member may/must treat imports from its free trade area partners cannot be answered by reference to the Agreement on Safeguards, but rather by reference to GATT Articles XXIV and XIX. In particular, the United States continues, footnote 1 SA makes it clear that the non-discrimination requirement of Article 2.2 SA is not pertinent in assessing the safeguards treatment accorded by a customs union or FTA member to goods originating in other participant countries.[172]

---

[170] United States Response to Panel Question 8, Attachment 2-8, para. 13.

[171] *Ibid.*, para. 15.

[172] US Response to Panel Question 30, Attachment 2-4, paras. 99-100.

8.179 In addressing this argument, we note first that the obligations in Article XIX of the GATT 1994 and Agreement on Safeguards are *cumulative.*[173] Thus, "any safeguard measure imposed after the entry into force of the *WTO Agreement* must comply with the provisions of *both* the *Agreement on Safeguards and* Article XIX of the GATT 1994."[174] (footnote omitted, emphasis added)

8.180 Furthermore, we understand that Article XXIV of the GATT 1994 may provide a defence to a claim of violation of a provision of the GATT 1994[175], and may also provide a defence to a claim of inconsistency with a provision of another covered agreement if it is somehow incorporated into that provision or agreement.[176]

8.181 In the present case, while the United States has argued that Article XXIV of the GATT 1994 would provide it with a defence to a violation of Article XIX of the GATT 1994, it has confirmed in these proceedings its understanding that "Article XXIV provides neither an exception nor a derogation to the provisions of the Safeguards Agreement".[177] Therefore, the United States is not arguing that Article XXIV of the GATT 1994 would provide it with a defence to a violation of a provision of the Agreement on Safeguards. We therefore do not examine whether Article XXIV of the GATT 1994 may provide a defence to a violation of a provision of the Agreement on Safeguards. In any event, contrary to the argument of the United States[178], we do not read the last sentence in footnote 1 SA[179] as establishing that the question of how a free trade area member may/must treat imports from its free trade area partners cannot be answered by reference to the Agreement on Safeguards, but rather only by reference to GATT Articles XXIV and XIX. As we have already indicated, we believe that the symmetry that we have found to be required by Articles 2.1 and 4.2 of the Agreement on Safe-

---

173 We find support for this view in Appellate Body Report, *Korea – Dairy Safeguard*, *supra*, footnote 16, para. 77; Appellate Body Report, *Argentina-Footwear Safeguard*, *supra*, footnote 17, para. 84.

174 *Ibid.*

175 We find confirmation for this view in Appellate Body Report, *Turkey – Restrictions on Imports of Textiles and Clothing Products* ("*Turkey - Textiles*"), WT/DS34/AB/R, adopted 19 November 1999, DSR 1999:VI, 2345, para. 58. There, the Appellate Body expresses the view that "Article XXIV may justify a measure which is inconsistent with certain other GATT provisions".

176 In its Report in Turkey –Textiles, the Appellate Body noted that "legal scholars have long considered Article XXIV to be an "exception" or a possible "defence" to claims of violation of GATT provisions" (*supra*, footnote 175, para. 45, note 13). However, the Appellate Body also observed that the chapeau of para. 5 of Article XXIV refers only to the provisions of the GATT 1994 (and not to the provisions of other WTO Agreements). Because the Appellate Body viewed Article 2.4 of the Agreement on Textiles and Clothing as incorporating Article XXIV of the GATT 1994 into that Agreement, it noted that Article XXIV "may be invoked as a defence to a claim of inconsistency with Article 2.4 of the ATC, provided that the conditions set forth in Article XXIV for the availability of this defence are met".

177 United States Response to Panel Question 8, Attachment 2-8, para. 13.

178 Supra, para. 8.178; US Response to Panel Question 30, Attachment 2-4, paras. 99-100.

179 The last sentence of footnote 1 SA reads: "Nothing in this Agreement prejudges the interpretation of the relationship between Article XIX and para. 8 of Article XXIV of GATT 1994."

guards between the scope of the imported products subject to the investigation and the scope of the imported products subject to the application of the measure is also relevant in this context. Our view is not changed by footnote 1 SA.

8.182 **For these reasons, we find that, in this case, the United States has acted inconsistently with Articles 2.1 and 4.2 SA by excluding imports from Canada from the application of the safeguard measure (following a separate and subsequent inquiry concerning whether imports from Canada accounted for a "substantial share" of total imports and whether they "contributed importantly" to the "serious injury" caused by total imports) after including imports *from all sources* in its investigation of "increased imports" of wheat gluten into its territory and the consequent effects of such imports on its domestic wheat gluten industry. We are of the view that, in this case, the United States was not justified in departing from the explicit provisions of Articles 2.1 and 4.2 SA by excluding from the application of its safeguard measure imports from Canada after having included such imports for the purposes of reaching its overall finding of serious injury caused by increased imports of the product concerned**.

8.183 We do not believe that we have been asked to rule, and consequently make no ruling, on whether or not, as a general principle, a member of a free trade area can exclude imports from other members of that free trade area from the application of a safeguard measure.

8.184 In light of our findings on Articles 2.1 and 4.2 SA, and in light of our overall conclusion, we do not find it necessary to address, in this context, the EC's claims under Article 5 SA or Article I of the GATT 1994. That is, having determined that the measure at issue is inconsistent with Articles 2.1 and 4.2 SA, and exercising the discretion implicit in the principle of judicial economy, we do not deem it necessary to examine whether the inconsistent measure is further in breach of Article 5 SA or Article I of the GATT 1994. We therefore make no pronouncement on the admissibility of the EC claim concerning Article I with respect to the United States treatment of imports from Canada, in light of the terms of the panel request[180] which alleges that "the measure was designed and applied in order to breach the most-favoured-nation principle under Article I of GATT 1994, particularly since Australia is favoured in terms of impact on trade", but makes no mention of Canada in this context.[181]

---

[180] WT/DS166/3.

[181] See European Community second oral statement, Attachment 1-6, para. 127.

2. *Claims under Articles 8 and 12 SA*

(a) Type and Timing of Notifications

(i) Arguments of the Parties

European Community

8.185 The European Community alleges that the United States did not make timely notifications of the steps associated with the imposition of its safeguard measure in accordance with Article 12 SA. In particular, the European Community asserts that the United States did not make timely notifications of:

- the initiation of the investigation under Article 12.1(a) (1 October 1997[182]; notification 17 October 1997; WTO document dated 21 October 1997)[183];
- the determination of serious injury caused by increased imports under Article 12.1(b) (15 January 1998; notification 11 February 1998; WTO document dated 12 February 1998); and
- the decision to apply the measure under Article 12.1(c) (the United States President took the decision to apply the measure on 30 May 1998; the United States imposed its final measure effective 1 June 1998; the United States notified this under Article 12.1(c) in a document dated 4 June 1998; and the WTO document was dated 8 June 1998).

8.186 The European Community asserts that according to the plain text and meaning of Article 12 SA, these procedural steps, findings and decisions had to have been made at a date that would have allowed the Committee on Safeguards and, possibly, the Council for Trade in Goods, to request additional information and hold a meaningful discussion. The European Community argues that the United States notifications under Article 12.1(a) and (b) SA fail to comply with the requirement of immediate notification under Article 12.1 SA.

8.187 The European Community further argues that the United States failed to provide meaningful and timely notification of the proposed measure as required by Article 12 of the Agreement on Safeguards. According to the European Community, Article 12 SA establishes a sequence of events starting with the notification under Article 12.1(c) SA providing information to the Committee on Safeguards and the Council for Trade in Goods under Article 12.2 SA and consulta-

[182] We note that the notice of institution and scheduling of the USITC investigation which was attached to the notification under Article 12.1 (a) SA mentions 19 September 1997 as the effective date of institution. The date of 1 October 1997 is the date of publication of the initiation of the investigation in the Federal Register.

[183] The European Community cites the date of WTO circulation of the documents, rather than the date that appeared on the communication from the US to the WTO. We have conducted our examination on the basis of the date of notification to the WTO, rather than on date of circulation of WTO document.

tions under Article 12.3 SA on the proposed measure. The European Community asserts that the United States did not comply with its obligation under Articles 12.1(c) and 12.2 SA to notify the *proposed* final measure to the Committee on Safeguards *before* implementing that final measure.

United States

8.188 The United States argues that, consistent with the requirements of Article 12 SA, it made timely notifications. The United States argues that the text of Article 12.1 SA makes it clear that notification can only be made *after* the finding or the decision concerned has been made. The United States submits that it notified the Committee on Safeguards of the initiation of the investigation under Article 12.1(a) only days after its publication in the Federal Register. With respect to its Article 12.1(b) notification of finding of serious injury, the United States argues that Article 12.1(b) SA clearly provides that a Member's obligation to notify only arises *after* it has made a serious injury determination. Similarly, the United States asserts that Article 12.1(c) SA requires notification once the decision to apply the measure is taken: in this case, the United States President took the decision to apply the measure on 30 May 1998 and the United States notified this decision on 4 June 1998. While the United States disputes the existence of an obligation to notify a proposed measure *before* any measure is taken, in the alternative, it asserts that the notification of 24 March 1998, made under Article 12.1(b) SA, nevertheless complies with this alleged requirement. The United States submits that the Agreement on Safeguards does not preclude the alteration of a proposed measure following an Article 12.1(b) notification.

(ii) Evaluation by the Panel

8.189 We will examine the provisions of Article 12 of the Agreement on Safeguards detailing the requirements concerning notifications to the Committee on Safeguards. In relevant part, Article 12 SA provides as follows:

> "Article 12
>
> *Notification and Consultation*
>
> 1. A Member shall immediately notify the Committee on Safeguards upon:
>
> (a) initiating an investigatory process relating to serious injury or threat thereof and the reasons for it;
>
> (b) making a finding of serious injury or threat thereof caused by increased imports; and
>
> (c) taking a decision to apply or extend a safeguard measure.
>
> 2. In making the notifications referred to in paragraphs 1(b) and 1(c), the Member proposing to apply or extend a safeguard measure shall provide the Committee on Safeguards with all pertinent information, which shall include evidence of serious injury or threat

thereof caused by increased imports, precise description of the product involved and the proposed measure, proposed date of introduction, expected duration and timetable for progressive liberalization. In the case of an extension of a measure, evidence that the industry concerned is adjusting shall also be provided. The Council for Trade in Goods or the Committee on Safeguards may request such additional information as they may consider necessary from the Member proposing to apply or extend the measure.

3. A Member proposing to apply or extend a safeguard measure shall provide adequate opportunity for prior consultations with those Members having a substantial interest as exporters of the product concerned, with a view to, inter alia, reviewing the information provided under paragraph 2, exchanging views on the measure and reaching an understanding on ways to achieve the objective set out in paragraph 1 of Article 8.

4, A Member shall make a notification to the Committee on Safeguards before taking a provisional safeguard measure referred to in Article 6. Consultations shall be initiated immediately after the measure is taken.

5. The results of the consultations referred to in this Article, as well as the results of mid-term reviews referred to in paragraph 4 of Article 7, any form of compensation referred to in paragraph 1 of Article 8 and proposed suspensions of concessions and other obligations referred to in paragraph 2 of Article 8, shall be notified immediately to the Council for Trade in Goods by the Members concerned...."

8.190 We consider that Article 12 SA refers to two different points in time which determine the timeliness of the notification of any decision or finding by a Member. First, Article 12.1 SA refers to the actual decision or finding. The notification is to be made *immediately following* this decision or finding. Second, we consider that Articles 12.2 and 12.3 SA provide that the notifications of Article 12.1 are to be made *in any case before* the implementation of the measure in order to allow for prior consultations on the proposed measure. In sum, we find that the notifications of Article 12.1 are situated in time between the moment of making the decision or finding to be notified and the final application of the measure concerned.

Compliance with Article 12.1 SA: the Requirement of Immediacy

8.191 For the sake of clarity, we recall that the United States made the following notifications to the Committee on Safeguards regarding its wheat gluten investigation:

notification under Article 12.1(a) SA

- On *1 October 1997*, the United States decided to initiate a safeguards investigation regarding imports of wheat gluten. In a communication dated *17 October 1997* (i.e. 16 days later), the United States notified the Committee on Safeguards, under Article 12.1(a), of its decision to initiate an investigation.[184]

notifications under Article 12.1(b) SA

- On *15 January 1998*, the USITC found that there was evidence of serious injury caused by increased imports and the United States notified the Committee on Safeguards pursuant to Article 12.1(b) SA of these findings in a communication dated *11 February 1998* (i.e. 26 days later).[185]
- On *18 March 1998*, the USITC forwarded its Report containing its injury findings and remedy recommendations to the President of the United States. In a communication dated *24 March 1998* (i.e.6 days later), the United States notified to the Committee on Safeguards, pursuant to Article 12.1 (b) SA, a finding of serious injury caused by increased imports of wheat gluten.[186] A copy of this USITC Report, also containing the USITC's analysis and a summary of the information collected during the investigation and excluding information identified as confidential information, was provided with the United States notification.
- On *3 April 1998* the USTR requested that the USITC provide additional information on the degree to which the domestic industry's adjustment plan would improve its competitiveness in the mid and long-term. The additional information was requested to assist the inter-agency group that was considering what action to recommend that the President take. On *8 April 1998*, the United States notified the Committee on Safeguards pursuant to Article 12.1 (b) SA of this request for additional information and informed the Committee that 31 May 1998 was the ultimate date for the President to determine what safeguard action would be taken.[187]

notification under Article 12.1(c) SA

- On *30 May 1998*, the United States President decided to apply a safeguard measure and on *1 June 1998*, the United States imposed quantitative restrictions in the form of a quota on imports of wheat gluten for a period of just over three years. On *4 June 1998* (i.e. 5 days after the decision was taken),

---

184 G/SG/N/6/USA/4.

185 G/SG/N/8/USA/2.

186 G/SG/N/8/USA/2/Rev.1.

187 G/SG/N/8/USA/2/Rev.1/Suppl.1.

the United States notified the Committee on Safeguards pursuant to Article 12.1(c) SA of the decision to apply a safeguard measure.[188]

8.192 We recall that Article 12.1 SA contains an explicit temporal guideline that applies to the three types of notifications explicitly enumerated in that Article. It states that "a Member shall *immediately* notify the Committee ... *upon*": (a) "initiating" a safeguard investigation; (b) "making a finding of serious injury or threat thereof caused by increased imports"; and (c) "taking a decision to apply or extend a safeguard measure."

8.193 The panel in *Korea – Dairy Safeguard* found that the term "immediately" implies a certain urgency and is a function of the content of the notification itself:

> "Article 12.1 provides that "A Member shall *immediately* notify the Committee on Safeguard upon ..." (emphasis added). The ordinary meaning of the term "immediately"[189] introduces a certain notion of urgency.... We note finally that no specific number of days is mentioned in Article 12. For us this implies that there is a need under the agreement to balance the requirement for some minimum level of information in a notification against the requirement for "immediate" notification. The more detail that is required, the less "instantly" Members will be able to notify. In this context we are also aware that Members whose official language is not a WTO working language, may encounter further delay in preparing their notifications."[190]

8.194 We consider that the text of Article 12.1 SA is clear and requires no further interpretation. The ordinary meaning of the requirement for a Member to notify immediately its decisions or findings prohibits a Member from unduly delaying the notification of the decisions or findings mentioned in Article 12.1 (a) through (c) SA. Observance of this requirement is all the more important considering the nature of a safeguards investigation. A safeguard measure is imposed on imports of a product irrespective of its source and potentially affects all Members. All Members are therefore entitled to be kept informed, without delay, of the various steps of the investigation.

8.195 We will now consider the United States notifications under Article 12.1 SA which the European Community alleges were not made immediately after the decision or the finding was made. These are the notification under Article 12.1(a) SA of the initiation of the investigation and the notification under Article 12.1(b) SA of the finding of serious injury caused by increased imports.

---

[188] G/SG/N/10/USA/2 and G/SG/N/11/USA/2.

[189] Original footnote: "The New Webster Encyclopaedic Dictionary defines immediately as "without delay, straightaway"; the New Shorter Oxford Dictionary defines it as "without delay, at once, instantly".

[190] Panel Report, *Korea –Dairy Safeguard*, supra, footnote 16, para. 7.128

8.196 According to the date mentioned on the United States notification under Article 12.1(a) SA of the initiation of the investigation, the United States initiated a safeguards investigation on imports of wheat gluten into the United States on 1 October 1997. The United States notified the initiation of this safeguards investigation on 17 October 1997, i.e. 16 days later. The information contained in the notification is minimal. A copy of the notice of institution and scheduling of the investigation by the USITC is annexed.

8.197 **We therefore find that the delay of 16 days between the initiation of the investigation and the notification thereof does not satisfy the requirement of immediate notification of Article 12.1 (a) SA.** [191]

8.198 On 15 January 1998, the USITC found that wheat gluten was being imported in such increased quantities as to be a substantial cause of serious injury to the domestic wheat gluten industry. The United States notified this finding of serious injury caused by increased imports under Article 12.1 (b) SA to the Committee on Safeguards only 11 February 1998, i.e. 26 days later. This one-page notification refers to the USITC Report, which was to be published on 18 March 1998.

8.199 **We therefore find that the delay of 26 days between the finding of serious injury and the notification thereof does not satisfy the requirement of immediate notification of Article 12.1 (b) SA.**

Requirement to Make Notification under Article 12.1(c) SA Before Implementation of the Measure.

8.200 As we established above, a Member is required to notify the decision to apply a measure immediately after the decision is made. However, we consider that Article 12.1(c) SA as informed by Articles 12.2 and 12.3 SA requires that the notification of the decision to apply a measure is to be made in any case before the measure is implemented.

8.201 Article 12.2 SA provides that a Member proposing to apply or extend a safeguard measure shall provide the Committee on Safeguards with all pertinent information. The information required shall include a precise description of the product involved and of the proposed measure, the proposed date of introduction, its expected duration and the timetable for a progressive liberalization of the measure. Article 12.3 SA requires a Member proposing to apply or extend a safeguard measure to provide adequate opportunity for prior consultations.

---

[191] As noted above, note 182, the notice of institution and scheduling of the investigation which was attached to the notification under Article 12.1 (a) SA mentions 19 September 1997 as the effective date of institution. If one were to take this date as the date of initiation, the delay between the initiation of the investigation and the notification thereof of 27 days would be even less "immediate".

8.202 Articles 12.2 SA and 12.3 SA thus stipulate that the notifications under Article 12.1(b) and (c) which are to be made immediately following the decision or the finding shall contain information concerning the *proposed measure* and shall be made at such time as to provide adequate opportunity for *prior* consultations. The language of Article 12.2 SA and Article 12.3 SA therefore confirms the importance of notifying a *proposed* measure before it is applied in order to allow adequate opportunity for prior consultations, that is, consultations before the measure is effectively applied. With reference to the notifications under Articles 12.1(b) and Article 12.1(c) SA concerning respectively the finding of serious injury caused by increased imports and the decision to apply a measure, Article 12.2 SA refers, *inter alia*, to "the Member *proposing* to apply or extend a safeguard measure", "a precise description of ... the *proposed* measure", and the "*proposed* date of introduction" of the measure (emphasis added). Article 12.3 refers to "the Member *proposing* to apply or extend the measure" and requires that the Member "shall provide adequate opportunity for *prior* consultations..." (emphasis added).

8.203 The reports of the panel and the Appellate Body in *Korea – Dairy Safeguard* provide relevant guidance. The panel in *Korea-Dairy* concluded that Articles 12.2 and 12.3 SA implicitly require that any *proposed* measure be notified *before* the consultations referred to in Article 12.3 SA in order to allow for meaningful and informed consultations. In this respect, the panel stated[192]:

> "Thus, Article 12.1, 12.2 and 12.3 taken together makes it clear that before a definitive safeguard measure may be applied, the Member proposing to apply it must notify all the pertinent information regarding the proposed measure and the factual basis (the injury finding) for applying it, and must provide an opportunity for consultations with Members whose trade will be affected by the proposed measure. In other words, details of the measure proposed must be notified before it is applied, so that affected Members may consult about it before it takes effect."

8.204 We recall that the Appellate Body agreed with the panel in *Korea – Dairy Safeguard* that[193]:

> "... the notification serves essentially a transparency and information purpose. In ensuring transparency, Article 12 allows Members through the Committee on Safeguards to review the measures. Another purpose of the notification of the finding of serious injury and of the proposed measure is to inform Members of the circumstances of the case and the conclusions of the investigation together with the importing country's particular intentions. This allows any interested Member to decide whether to request consultations with

---

192 Panel Report, Korea –Dairy Safeguard, supra, footnote 16, para. 7.120.

193 Appellate Body Report, *Korea –Dairy Safeguard*, supra, footnote 16, para. 111.

the importing country which may lead to modification of the proposed measure(s) and/or compensation".

8.205 The text of Article 12.2 SA speaks of *proposed* measures in the context of both Article 12.1(b) *and* (c) notifications. That is, a measure that is notified under Article 12.1(c) SA would still be a "proposed" measure. Article 12.2 SA requires that information be given in an Article 12.1(c) notification on the "proposed" date of introduction and the "expected" duration and timetable for progressive liberalization. The purpose of notifying a proposed measure *after* taking a decision to apply it and *before* it is applied is in order to "provide all pertinent information" in order to furnish a basis for the consultations referred to in Article 12.3 SA.[194]

8.206 Article 12.1(c) SA, read in conjunction with Article 12.2 and 12.3, refers to a final proposed measure, i.e. the measure that the WTO Member concerned intends to adopt and not one that the Member has already implemented. Otherwise, the requirements of transparency and information would not be fully served. It should be recalled that the objective of the prior consultations as set out in Article 12.3 SA is to review the information provided in the notifications, exchange views on the measure and reach an understanding on ways to achieve the objectives of Article 8.1 SA. The latter provision requires a Member *proposing to apply* a safeguard measure to endeavour to maintain a substantially equivalent level of concessions and other obligations to that existing under the GATT 1994. The Agreement on Safeguards thus requires a Member when proposing to apply a safeguard measure to provide an adequate opportunity to consult with affected Members prior to the application of the measure *inter alia* to discuss ways to maintain an equivalent level of concessions and perhaps agree on adequate means of trade compensation. The requirement to endeavour to maintain a substantially equivalent level of concessions between the Member proposing to apply a measure and exporting Members affected by such a measure is intrinsically linked with the fact that "taking a safeguard action results in restrictions on imports arising from 'fair' trade". [195] The obligation to provide adequate opportunity for *prior* consultations is therefore essential to the proper application of the safeguard mechanism.

8.207 We recall that the United States applied the safeguard measure at issue on 1 June 1998. However, it notified its decision of 30 May 1998 to apply a measure under Article 12.1(c) SA only on 4 June 1998, i.e. three days after the measure was effectively imposed. We note in passing that the delay of 5 days between the

---

[194] It is thus irrelevant to our examination of the timeliness of the United States notification under Article 12.1 (c) SA that the United States notified the USITC's remedy recommendation to the Committee on Safeguards on 24 March 1998. The language of Article 12.2 and 12.3 SA makes it clear that the measure notified under Article 12.1 (c) SA is still a proposed measure and that its notification has to be made before the implementation of the measure in order to allow for an adequate opportunity for consultations.

[195] Appellate Body Report, *Korea –Dairy Safeguard*, supra, footnote 16, para. 87.

decision to apply a safeguard measure and the notification thereof might well satisfy the requirement of immediate notification of Article 12.1 SA. **However, we find that the United States notification of this decision after the measure had been implemented, violated the United States obligation under Article 12 SA to make timely notification under Article 12.1 (c) SA of its decision to apply a measure.**

8.208 We will briefly address two other arguments of the United States in support of its position that the Agreement on Safeguards does not require a Member to notify its proposed measure before it is applied. First, the United States points to the notification provision concerning provisional safeguard measures. The United States argues that if such an obligation of prior notification were to exist with regard to final measures, the Agreement would have explicitly stated so as is the case in Article 12.4 SA concerning provisional safeguard measures. Second, the United States asserts that the obligation to notify the proposed measure would run counter to the purpose of encouraging positive consultations with interested Members since no Member would be inclined to change the measure as a result of consultations with other Member since any change would lead to a new round of notifications of the new proposed measure. This, the United States asserts, cannot have been the intention of the drafters.

8.209 Article 12.4 SA requires Members to notify any provisional safeguard measure before it is taken and provides that consultations be initiated immediately after the measure is taken. According to Article 6 SA, a Member may only take provisional safeguard measures pursuant to a preliminary determination that there is clear evidence that increased imports have caused or are threatening to cause serious injury. Article 12.4 SA thus requires a Member to notify the decision to apply a provisional safeguard measure after a preliminary determination of increased imports causing or threatening to cause serious injury is made but before taking the measure. We consider therefore that Article 12.4 SA in fact strengthens the general rule that a Member is to notify its decision to apply a safeguard measure before it is applied, even if it is only a provisional safeguard measure. What is different from the notification requirements concerning final measures is the obligation to initiate consultations only *after* the (provisional) measure is taken. It seems logical to us that it may well have been the absence of a requirement for prior consultations regarding provisional safeguard measures that led to the explicit requirement of Article 12.4 SA to notify the provisional measure before applying it.

8.210 Finally, we do not believe that, as the United States is arguing, the obligation to notify the proposed measure would give rise to a long chain of new notifications in case the measure is amended as a consequence of the consultations. We refer to Article 12.5 SA which provides *inter alia* that the results of any consultations shall be notified immediately to the Council for Trade in Goods through the Committee on Safeguards. This would imply that in case consultations lead to a modification of the measure, the modification is to be notified under Article 12.5 SA. Members are entitled to assume that in the absence of any notification under Article 12.5 SA, the safeguard measure applied is the measure proposed and notified under Article 12.1 (c) SA.

Summary

8.211 In sum, we have found that the United States violated the requirement concerning timely notification of Article 12 SA. Both its notifications of the initiation of the investigation and of the finding of serious injury caused by increased imports of 17 October 1997 and 11 February 1998 respectively were not made immediately after the decision or the finding as required by Article 12.1 SA. Moreover, and more importantly, we have found that the United States did not provide a timely notification under Article 12.1(c) SA of its proposed final measure since the United States notified its decision to apply a measure three days after the measure had been implemented.

(b) Adequacy of Consultations

(i) Arguments of the Parties

European Community

8.212 The European Community acknowledges that consultations took place between the parties on 24 April 1998 and 22 May 1998. The European Community emphasizes that such consultations only dealt with information provided by the United States in its Article 12.1(b) notifications and therefore cannot be considered prior consultations on the final proposed measure, i.e. the measure in its final form, in terms of form, level and duration.

8.213 The European Community further submits that the United States did not make a genuine endeavour to maintain a substantially equivalent level of concessions and never offered a meaningful opportunity for consultation and negotiation, thereby violating Articles 8.1 and 12.3 SA. The European Community argues that the obligation to engage in meaningful consultations prior to altering the balance of negotiated concessions, even temporarily, is fundamental to the functioning of the WTO system. According to the European Community, the United States failed to demonstrate that it has actively and concretely offered adequate compensation and that compensation was rejected (or at least not accepted) by the Member concerned.

United States

8.214 The United States asserts that it held consultations with the European Community on 24 April 1998 and 22 May 1998 in accordance with Article 12.3 SA. The United States argues that the European Community acknowledged that consultations concerning the wheat gluten investigation took place under Article

12.3 SA in two letters dated 8 May 1998[196] and 21 May 1998[197] respectively. Finally, the United States considers that the Panel should reject the European Community's claim that a Member is required to provide concessions before it can take a safeguard action.

(ii) Evaluation by the Panel

8.215 Article 8.1 provides as follows:

> **Article 8**
>
> *Level of Concessions and Other Obligations*
>
> 1. "A Member proposing to apply a safeguard measure or seeking an extension of a safeguard measure shall endeavour to maintain a substantially equivalent level of concessions and other obligations to that existing under GATT 1994 between it and the exporting Members which would be affected by such a measure, in accordance with the provisions of paragraph 3 of Article 12. To achieve this objective, the Members concerned may agree on any adequate means of trade compensation for the adverse effects of the measure on their trade."

8.216 The principal issue confronting the Panel is whether Articles 12.3 SA and 8.1 SA require that the consultations referred to in these provisions must include consultations on the *final* proposed measure. Clearly, consideration of this issue is intimately intertwined with the Panel's view of the requirements of Article 12 SA concerning the type and timing of notifications.[198] As we established above, consultations on the proposed measure under Article 12.3 SA would necessarily take place *after* a Member has notified the "proposed" measure but *before* that measure is actually applied.

8.217 In this case, the United States applied its safeguard measure effective 1 June 1998, 2 days after the United States President had decided upon the safeguard measure to be applied and had "taken the decision" to apply that measure on 30 May 1998. While the parties have confirmed that consultations did take place on the basis of the United States notifications under Article 12.1(b) concerning the USITC's finding of serious injury and the USITC's recommendations on remedy, no consultations were held on the final proposed measure as approved by the United States President on 30 May 1998. Therefore, the Panel considers that, while consultations may have been held on the basis of the notifications made by the United States under Article 12.1(b) SA, the United States did

---

196 Exhibit US-11.

197 Exhibit US-12.

198 See discussion supra, paras. 8.189-8.211.

not provide "an adequate opportunity for prior consultations" on this final proposed measure, within the meaning of Article 12.3 SA. This necessarily implies that the United States did not fulfil its obligations under Article 8.1 SA to endeavour to maintain a substantially equivalent level of concessions and other obligations, in accordance with the provisions of paragraph 3 of Article 12.

8.218 The fact that consultations took place between the United States and the European Community on 24 April 1998 and 22 May 1998 does not affect this finding. It should be recalled that Article 12.1(b) SA, read together with Articles 12.2 and 12.3 SA, envisages that consultations may also be held on the basis of Article 12.1(b) notifications concerning a finding of serious injury. Members are encouraged to consult with each other before a final decision on whether to apply a measure is taken. Such consultations could fulfil part of the aims of Article 12.3, i.e. to review the information contained in the notifications and possibly exchange views on the measure. However, one of the important objectives of the consultations under Article 12.3 SA is to reach an understanding on ways to achieve the objective of Article 8.1 concerning compensation. We consider that it is only after a decision to apply a measure is taken and information is given on the final proposed measure, that informed and meaningful consultations can be held under Article 12.3 and 8.1 SA. Another interpretation would mean that WTO Members would be consulting on a hypothetical measure that might not come into effect.

8.219 We found above[199] that the United States did not provide a timely notification under Article 12.1 (c) SA of its proposed final measure since the United States notified its decision to apply a measure three days after the measure had been implemented. **For the same reason, we find that the United States violated the obligation of Article 12.3 SA to provide adequate opportunity for prior consultations on the measure. Hence, we find that the United States also violated its obligation under Article 8.1 SA to endeavour to maintain a substantially equivalent level of concessions and other obligations to that existing under GATT 1994 between it and the exporting Members which would be affected by such a measure, in accordance with Article 12.3 SA.**

3. Claims under Article XIX of the GATT 1994 ("unforeseen developments"); Article 5 SA and Article I of the GATT 1994

8.220 The European Community also makes claims under Article XIX:1(a) ("unforeseen developments"), Article 5 SA and Article I of the GATT 1994. We note that a "panel need only address those claims which must be addressed in

[199] See supra, para. 8.207.

order to resolve the matter in issue in the dispute".[200] As we have found that the United States definitive wheat gluten safeguard measure based on the United States investigation and determination to be inconsistent with Articles 2.1 and 4.2 of the Agreement on Safeguards, we do not consider it necessary to examine these claims of the European Community under Article 5 SA and Articles I and XIX of the GATT 1994. That is, having determined that the measure at issue is inconsistent with Articles 2.1 and 4.2 SA, and exercising the discretion implicit in the principle of judicial economy, we do not deem it necessary to examine whether the measure at issue is also inconsistent with Article XIX of the GATT 1994 ("unforeseen developments") nor whether the form, level and allocation of the inconsistent measure are in breach of Article 5 SA or Article I of the GATT 1994.[201]

4. *Claim under Article 4.2 of the Agreement on Agriculture*

8.221 The European Community included a claim under Article 4.2 of the Agreement on Agriculture in its panel request. However, the European Community did not develop this claim in any of its written or oral submissions to the Panel. We thus consider that this claim has been abandoned.

IX. CONCLUSIONS AND RECOMMENDATION

9.1 In light of the findings made in section VIII above, we conclude that the United States has not acted inconsistently with Articles 2.1 and 4 of the Agreement on Safeguards or with Article XIX:1(a) of the GATT 1994 in:

(i) redacting certain confidential information from the published USITC Report; or

(ii) determining the existence of imports in "increased quantities" and serious injury.

9.2 In light of the findings made in section VIII above, we conclude that the definitive safeguard measure imposed by the United States on certain imports of wheat gluten based on the United States investigation and determination is inconsistent with Articles 2.1 and 4 of the Agreement on Safeguards in that:

---

[200] Appellate Body Report, *United States – Measure Affecting Imports of Woven Wool Shirts and Blouses from India* ("*US – Woven Wool Shirts*"), WT/DS33/AB/R and Corr. 1, adopted 23 May 1997, DSR 1997:I, 323, at 340.

[201] We find support for our approach in Appellate Body Report, *Canada - Certain Measures Affecting the Automotive Industry* (" *Canada – Autos*"), WT/DS139/AB/R, WT/DS142/AB/R, adopted 19 June 2000, DSR 2000:VI, 2995, paras. 112-117. In this Report, the Appellate Body cites its previous Reports in *US - Woven Wool Shirts*, *supra*, footnote 200, at 339 and Appellate Body report, *Australia - Measures Affecting the Importation of Salmon* ("*Australia – Salmon*"), WT/DS18/AB/R, adopted 6 November 1998, DSR 1998:VIII, 3327, para. 223, and confirms that, "[i]n discharging its functions under Articles 7 and 11 of the DSU, a panel is not … required to examine all legal claims made before it. A panel may exercise judicial economy."

(i) the causation analysis applied by the USITC did not ensure that injury caused by other factors was not attributed to imports; and

(ii) imports from Canada (a NAFTA partner) were excluded from the application of the measure after imports from all sources were included in the investigation for the purposes of determining serious injury caused by increased imports (following a separate inquiry concerning whether imports from Canada accounted for a "substantial share" of total imports and whether they "contributed importantly" to the "serious injury" caused by total imports).

9.3 In light of the findings made in section VIII above, we also conclude that the United States failed to notify immediately the initiation of the investigation under Article 12.1(a) and the finding of serious injury under Article 12.1(b) SA. We further conclude that, in notifying its decision to take the measure after the measure was implemented, the United States did not make timely notification under Article 12.1(c). For the same reason, the United States violated the obligation of Article 12.3 SA to provide adequate opportunity for prior consultations on the measure. Hence, the United States also violated its obligation under Article 8.1 SA to endeavour to maintain a substantially equivalent level of concessions and other obligations to that existing under GATT 1994 between it and the exporting Members which would be affected by such a measure, in accordance with Article 12.3 SA.

9.4 Under Article 3.8 of the DSU, in cases where there is an infringement of the obligations assumed under a covered agreement, the action is considered *prima facie* to constitute a case of nullification or impairment of benefits under that agreement. Accordingly, we conclude that the United States has nullified or impaired benefits accruing to the European Community under the Agreement on Safeguards within the meaning of Article 3.8 of the DSU.

9.5 The Panel *recommends* that the Dispute Settlement Body request the United States to bring its measure into conformity with the Agreement on Safeguards.

ATTACHMENT 1-1

FIRST WRITTEN SUBMISSION OF THE EUROPEAN COMMUNITY
(15 November 1999)

TABLE OF CONTENTS

1. OBJECTIVES OF THE EC AND METHODOLOGY

1. The European Communities submit at the outset of this procedure that, in their view, this case goes far beyond the economic issue as such and is exemplary of a distorted use of legitimate procedures under the WTO Agreements. In fact, it appears from objective facts as they will be shown during this procedure that the United States, by taking the safeguard measure on wheat gluten (hereinafter: the US WGS) was driven by political and protectionist aims, rather than WTO-compatible preoccupations concerning its domestic industry.

2. *Firstly*, the EC will demonstrate that behind the choices made in this matter by the US authorities most likely lies the WTO-incompatible attempt to protect some egregious errors in the economic strategy of the US wheat starch/wheat gluten producers and to influence the competitive relations between the wheat

starch/wheat gluten producers and the corn starch/corn gluten producers in the US, at the expense of the EC originated wheat gluten, its producers and its exporters.

3. As a *second* main issue, the conduct of the investigation by the US authorities was turned in such a way as to make the facts say what they cannot objectively say. Internal contradictions, voluntary silence on decisive relevant issues of fact and law, and even unsupported "*petitiones principii*" (i.e. non-demonstrated sweeping assertions) punctuate the ITC report[1], which the US President took as a basis for his decision to apply the US WGS.

The EC will demonstrate that a good faith consideration of the facts as exposed in the ITC report itself together with the facts that the private participants have publicly submitted to the US authorities should have led the US government to the opposite conclusion, i.e. the rejection of the petition requesting the application of the US WGS.

In this respect, the EC would like to clarify immediately an issue of procedural nature, whose importance has however a bearing on the conduct of this Panel and ultimately on its final findings.

The EC does not request the panel to engage in a *de novo* exercise. It would not only be inappropriate in terms of WTO procedure; it would also confuse the repartition of responsibilities between the WTO Member that applies the safeguard measure, *in casu* the US, and the Panel, whose task is, according to Article 11 of the DSU, "to assist the DSB in discharging its responsibilities under this Understanding".

The EC expects therefore that this Panel will make an objective assessment of whether

- the domestic authority has considered all relevant facts as a whole, including specifically each factor listed in Article 4.2(a) of the WTO Agreement on Safeguards ("SA"),
- the published report of the investigation contains adequate explanation of how the facts support the determination made, and finally,
- the determination made is consistent with US obligations under the Safeguards Agreement, the GATT 1994 and the Agreement on Agriculture.[2]

---

[1] Exhibit EC-1.

[2] See Panel Report, *Korea - Definitive Safeguard Measure on Imports of Certain Dairy Products* ("*Korea –Dairy Safeguard*"), WT/DS98/R and Corr. 1, adopted 12 January 2000, as modified by the Appellate Body Report, WT/DS98/AB/R, DSR 2000:I, 49, para. 7.29 and Report by the Panel on *Argentina - Safeguard Measures on Imports of Footwear* ("*Argentina – Footwear Safeguard*"), WT/DS121/R, adopted 12 January 2000, DSR 2000:II, 575, para. 8.124.

In this respect, the role of the Panel is to determine whether the ITC fully and objectively considered the evidence before it, including any evidence that detracts from an affirmative determination of increased imports, serious injury or causation.[3]

The Panel should also verify the adequacy of the ITC's reasoning by reviewing whether the findings and conclusions made by the ITC are consistent with the evidence.[4]

4. As a *third* main issue, the US WGS is a clearly disproportionate and unbalanced measure. The EC will demonstrate that, on the one hand, the US measure is built upon the WTO-incompatible design to re-determine the competitive relations between third country products and producers in the US, thus blatantly violating the MFN provisions of the GATT/WTO. On the other hand and in any case, the extent of the US WGS goes far beyond what even the erroneous conclusions in the ITC report could justify.

5. As a *fourth* and final main issue, the US failed to notify the Committee on Safeguards in a timely manner of each and every step of the procedure as required by the SA and never engaged in good faith consultations with a view to re-establish the balance of concessions undermined by the US WGS. The imperative procedural guarantees contained in Articles 8 and 12 SA were in fact repeatedly disregarded. Moreover, and if possible even more seriously, the US WGS is a *unilateral* attempt to bring a negotiating position of the US back to before the conclusion of the Uruguay Round tariff negotiations. Any WTO Member can always achieve such a result by engaging in *bona fide* negotiations and by offering adequate compensation with the aim to preserving the balance of concessions achieved in the multilateral rounds of tariff negotiations. However, the US has clearly failed to do that.

2. FACTS CONCERNING THE PROCEDURE

2.1 The US WGS procedure

6. This dispute concerns a definitive safeguard measure imposed by the United States on imports of wheat gluten classified under tariff headings HS 1109.00.10 and 1109.00.90.

7. The Wheat Gluten Industry Council of the United States, which consists of only two of the four US producers[5], filed a petition with the US International Trade Commission (ITC) on 19 September 1997 requesting a safeguard action against imports of wheat gluten.

---

3 *Korea - Dairy*, *supra*, footnote 2, para. 7.30.

4 *Argentina - Footwear*, *supra*, footnote 2, para. 8.124.

5 ITC report at I-5 and II-6.

8. The ITC initiated an investigation on 1 October 1997 to determine whether wheat gluten was being imported into the United States in such increased quantities as to be a substantial cause of serious injury, or the threat thereof, to the domestic industry producing an "article" (i.e. a product) like or directly competitive with the imported article (USITC Investigation No. TA-201-67). The period of investigation used by the US authorities was July 1992 to June 1997.[6]

9. On 21 October 1997, the United States notified the WTO Committee on Safeguards pursuant to Article 12.1 (a) of the Agreement on Safeguards of the initiation of the safeguard investigation.[7]

A public hearing in connection with the injury phase was held on 16 December 1997.

10. On 15 January 1998, the ITC voted that wheat gluten was being imported into the United States in such increased quantities as to be a substantial cause of serious injury to the domestic wheat gluten industry. A hearing on the question of remedy was held on 10 February 1998.

11. On 12 February 1998, the United States notified the Committee on Safeguards pursuant to Article 12.1(b) of the finding of serious injury.[8]

12. The report of the investigation, including the remedy recommendations of the ITC, was published on 18 March 1998 and forwarded to the president of the United States. The report was notified to the Committee on Safeguards on 27 March 1998.[9] The report (hereinafter referred to as "the ITC-report" or "ITC-report") is annexed as Exhibit EC-1.

13. On 9 April 1998, the United States notified the Committee on Safeguards pursuant to Article 12.1 (b) that the US Trade Representative had requested additional information from the ITC on the degree to which the domestic industry's adjustment plan would improve its competitiveness in the mid- and long-term.[10]

14. On 1 June 1998, the United States imposed quantitative restrictions in the form of a quota on imports of wheat gluten from the European Communities, Australia and other countries for a period of just over three years. The US president's decision is annexed as Exhibit EC-2.

15. On 4 June 1998, the United States notified the Committee on Safeguards pursuant to Article 12.1(c) and Article 9, footnote 2, of the decision to apply a safeguard measure and to exempt imports from developing countries from the application of the measure.[11]

---

[6] ITC report at II-3. The ITC used the "marketing years" in that industry, i.e. 12-month periods running from July to June. The "marketing year 1997" is therefore the period from 1 July 1996 to 30 June 1997.

[7] See WTO doc. G/SG/N/6/USA/4.

[8] See WTO doc. G/SG/N/8/USA/2.

[9] See WTO doc. G/SG/N/8/USA/2/Rev.1.

[10] See WTO doc. G/SG/N/8/USA/2/Rev.1/Suppl.1.

[11] See WTO docs. G/SG/N/10/USA/2 and G/SG/N/11/USA/2.

2.2 A description of the US wheat gluten safeguard measure

16. The total quota is 57.521 metric tonnes (126.812 million pounds)[12] in the first year of its application.[13] The quota became effective 1 June 1998.

17. The country quotas for the first year of application were allocated as follows:

Australia	28,315 t (62.425 million pounds) (49 per cent)
EC	24,513 t (54.041 million pounds) (43 per cent)
Others	4.695 t (10.346 million pounds) (5 per cent)

Certain countries are exempt from the quota, notably Canada, the third largest supplier of wheat gluten to the US during the period of investigation (10 per cent of imports).

18. The relief period is currently aimed to expire on 1 June 2001.

2.3 The reactions by the EC

19. On 3 August 1998, the European Communities notified the Committee on Safeguards pursuant to Article 12.5 of its proposed suspension of concessions and other obligations referred to in Article 8.2 of the Agreement on Safeguards to be applied from 1 June 2001 or five days after the date of a decision from the WTO Dispute Settlement Body that the safeguard measure imposed by the United States is incompatible with the WTO Agreements.[14]

20. On 17 March 1999, the European Communities requested consultations with the United States regarding the definitive safeguard measure on wheat gluten.[15] The request for consultations was made under Article 4 of the Understanding on Rules and Procedures Governing the Settlement of Disputes (DSU), and pursuant to Article XXII:1 of the General Agreement on Tariffs and Trade (GATT 1994), Article 14 of the Agreement on Safeguards, and Article 19 of the Agreement on Agriculture.

21. Consultations were held in Geneva on 3 May 1999 but no mutually satisfactory solution was reached. On 3 June 1999, the European Communities requested the establishment of a panel and this Panel was established on 26 July 1999.[16] Australia, Canada and New Zealand reserved their third-party rights.

---

[12] The ratio of a US pound to a kilogram is 2.2046.

[13] The quota will increase six per cent annually for the duration of the relief period.

[14] See WTO doc. G/L/251 and G/SG/N/12/EEC/1.

[15] See WTO doc. WT/DS166/1.

[16] See WTO doc. WT/DS166/3.

22. On 9 June 1999 the US notified to the WTO its decision to reduce the quota allocated to imports originating in the EC for the 2nd quota year due to an alleged "overfill" of the quota during the first quota year.[17]

23. On 11 October 1999, the parties agreed on the composition of the Panel.[18]

3. FACTS CONCERNING THE WHEAT STARCH/WHEAT GLUTEN INDUSTRY

3.1 Description of the product, its production process, its applications, the co-product nature of the industry, and a number of other factors

3.1.1 The product

24. Wheat gluten is a high protein product produced from wheat flour. It is described by the ITC as "the natural protein portion of wheat that is extracted after wheat is milled into flour".[19]

25. "Vital" wheat gluten means wheat gluten which still has all its original characteristics (they can be lost for instance due to overheating). These include what the ITC calls "visco-elastic properties"[20]. Simply put, when wheat gluten is mixed with water, it forms a dough (see Exhibit EC-3, picture on right-hand side). It is then a tough, elastic greyish substance resembling chewing gum. In the bakery process, its main application in the US, it is the gluten in flour that, when dough is kneaded, helps hold in the gas bubbles formed by the leavening agent. Gas contained within the dough helps the bread or other baked good to rise, creating a light structure.

3.1.2 The production process

26. Exhibit EC-4 provides a flowchart of the production processes by which wheat starch and wheat gluten are produced.

An unprocessed wheat kernel, commonly known as a wheat berry, is made up of three major portions: bran (the rough outer covering), germ, and endosperm (see Exhibit EC-5). The wheat endosperm, which makes up the majority of the kernel, is full of starch, protein, niacin, and iron. It is the protein in the wheat endosperm, which constitutes the wheat gluten. During the so-called "dry milling" process the wheat is separated into three fractions: bran, germ, and flour.

---

[17] See WTO doc. G/SG/N/10/USA/2/Suppl.1 and G/SG/N/11/USA/2/Suppl.1. Subsequently, the US provide a corrigendum to these notifications (G/SG/N/10/USA/2/Suppl.1/Corr.1 and G/SG/N/11/USA/2/ Suppl.1/Corr.2).

[18] See WTO doc. WT/DS166/4.

[19] ITC report at I-3, footnote 1.

[20] ITC report at II-5.

27. The flour is then made into dough by mixing it with water. As a result, the links between the gluten polymers become stronger resulting in the formation of gluten lumps in the dough slurry. The formation of gluten lumps makes it possible to separate the gluten from the other flour components.

28. Then, the dough is separated into gluten, starch, and effluents. The process is described by the ITC as "somewhat akin to taking a ball of dough (flour and water), and rinsing it until all the starch is washed away, leaving only the gluten".[21]

29. During refining, starch and effluents still present in the gluten are washed out, and after dewatering the gluten is dried.

3.1.3 Applications (uses) of wheat gluten

30. According to the ITC about 80 per cent of the wheat gluten consumed in the United States serves as an input to the milling and baking industry to supplement the gluten in the flours used to make baked goods.[22] The function is mainly to increase the protein content (for instance in years where the protein content of wheat is low), or to influence the volume/structure/softness of the baked goods. (See Exhibit EC-6). Non-bakery uses, including in the pet food industry, account for the remaining 15-20 per cent of consumption[23]. (See for a description of the various uses Exhibit EC-7).

3.1.4 The co-products nature of the wheat starch/wheat gluten industry

31. A very important point, which should be made clear from the outset, is the *co-product nature* of the wheat starch/gluten industry. As the ITC itself observes:

> "The process of manufacturing wheat gluten *always* results in two products: one part of gluten and approximately five parts of starch".[24] (emphasis added)

Moreover, there are always effluents, which can be sent to a distillery for utilisation in the production of ethanol or food-grade alcohol.[25] This is confirmed by figure 1 in the ITC report, a wheat gluten production schematic drawn up by one of the US producers, in which it is indicated that part of the starch slurry waste stream goes to distillers.[26] It is also possible to use certain parts of the effluents as animal feed stock, and others as wheat feed. (See Exhibit EC-8)

---

21 ITC report at II-5.
22 ITC report at I-6.
23 ITC report at II-5.
24 ITC report at II-5.
25 ITC report at II-5.
26 ITC report at II-7 right hand side.

32. Furthermore, the fact that much more wheat starch than wheat gluten is produced should be underlined. One hundred kilograms of flour will yield approximately 11 to 13 kilograms of wheat gluten and 63 to 65 kilograms of starch.[27]

33. Because of the integrated nature of the production process, the financial performance of the industry is determined by

(1) sales of *all* products – wheat gluten, wheat starch, alcohol products derived from wheat starch (including ethanol), and other derivatives (e.g. feedstuffs); and

(2) total operating costs, mainly raw materials and energy.

Revenues from wheat gluten generally account for 20-35 per cent of total revenues, with wheat starch and alcohol products accounting for 65-80 per cent of revenues.[28]

3.1.5 Factors influencing demand for and price of wheat gluten; competing products

34. The price of wheat gluten is directly related to the protein level in wheat.[29] As we have seen, wheat gluten is the only product that can be used as a supplement to wheat flour used in bread making in order to attain the desired level of protein for the baking purpose. In general, bread making requires a high level of wheat protein.

Therefore, in years when the general protein level in harvested wheat is low, demand for wheat gluten goes up - since more wheat gluten is needed to supplement the protein level of wheat used in bread making and therefore upward pressure is exerted on price. In contrast, when the general protein level in harvested wheat is high, demand for wheat gluten goes down, and therefore downward pressure is exerted on price .

35. As the ITC itself put it, in particular with respect to the milling and baking industry:

> "Demand for wheat gluten increases during periods when the protein level in wheat is low, since more wheat gluten is needed to supplement the protein level in wheat flour used for baking bread. In contrast, when the protein level in wheat is high, less wheat gluten is demanded to add to the baking flour".[30]

---

27 ITC report at II-6.

28 This can be deducted from Table 9 to the ITC report (at II-19).

29 See for instance ITC report at I-23.

30 ITC report at I-23.

36. Thus, in those cases where wheat gluten is used as a protein supplement in the baking sector, high-protein wheat flour can be substituted.[31] The competition between these two products thus plays a pivotal role on the US market.

37. Furthermore, since – as was explained above – the industry is necessarily a co-product wheat starch/wheat gluten industry, the competition between *wheat* starch and *corn* starch in the US market should be emphasised from the outset. Corn is the most economical and consequently the most commonly used raw material for starch production in the United States. Much more starch can be produced from corn than from wheat; the raw material cost in the US of corn starch had a 45 per cent competitive advantage during the period of investigation. The EC will return to this below when it will discuss factors which the US authorities did not (or at least not adequately) investigate.

3.2 Description of the wheat gluten market, in particular in the US

3.2.1 The US industry

38. There are four US producers of wheat starch/wheat gluten:

- Archer Daniel Midland (" ADM ");
- Heartland Wheat Growers (" Heartland ");
- Manildra Milling Corporation (" Manildra "); and
- Midwest Grain Products, Inc. (" Midwest ").[32]

39. With respect to Heartland, Manildra and Midwest the ITC stated:

> "These three firms accounted for the substantial majority of domestic production of wheat gluten. Each of the companies produces wheat gluten and wheat starch in a joint production process. Each of the companies also produces other by-products or related products, especially alcohol".[33]

Of course, also ADM necessarily produces both wheat starch and wheat gluten.[34]

40. It is important to note at this stage that US domestic production capacity was substantially increased during the investigation period. For instance, Heartland began producing wheat starch and wheat gluten in June 1996. Manildra has two plants, one of which is a new facility which began production in May 1994.[35] Midwest's plants also underwent several expansions and upgrades during the investigation period.[36]

---

[31] ITC report at II-27.
[32] ITC report at I-5-6.
[33] ITC report at I-13.
[34] This is confirmed by the description of ADM in the ITC report at II-8.
[35] ITC report at II-17.
[36] ITC report at II-6.

41. Finally, it is necessary to draw attention to the fact that Manildra is the daughter company of an Australian group, which owns two Australian producers of wheat gluten[37], which may explain the discriminatory structure given to the safeguard measure by the US (see below Chapters 5 and 7).

3.2.2 The US market

42. As a result of the Uruguay Round negotiations, the US granted tariff concessions on wheat gluten. These are described in Exhibit EC-9. The duty applied in 1993 and 1994 for wheat gluten was 8 per cent, unless the wheat gluten was destined to be used as animal feed, in which case it was 4 per cent. These duties are gradually reduced as from 1995 until the year 2000, when the duty will be 6.8 per cent, and 1.8 per cent if destined for animal feed.[38]

43. Apparent consumption of wheat gluten in the US increased nearly 18 per cent between 1993 and 1997.[39] According to the ITC,

> "US demand for wheat gluten, as measured by total US apparent consumption, increased significantly during 1993-1997, from 249.7 million pounds in 1993 to 294.2 million pounds in 1997, or by about 18 per cent".[40]

44. Wheat gluten is imported into the US from many countries[41], including Australia, Canada, the EC, and other countries. During the period of investigation, imports of wheat gluten into the US increased from 128 million pounds in 1993 to 177 million pounds in 1997. Thus, the market share of imported wheat gluten increased from 51.26 per cent in 1993 to 60.16 per cent in 1997 of the total US apparent consumption (i.e. increasing by 8,9 percentage points in volume). In particular in 1996 imports from significant suppliers (i.e. Australia, Canada and the EC) increased.[42]

4. THE COMPELLING CONDITIONS UNDER ARTICLE XIX GATT 1994 AND ARTICLES 2 AND 4 OF THE AGREEMENT ON SAFEGUARDS. THE US WGS CASE

45. According to Article XIX.1 (a) of the GATT,

> "If, as a result of unforeseen developments and of the effect of the obligations incurred by a contracting party under this Agreement, including tariff concessions, any product is being imported (...) in

[37] ITC report at II-8. Two of the companies in the Manildra group (Manildra US and Shoalhaven Starches Pty.) account for the dominant share of exports of wheat gluten from Australia to the US
[38] ITC report at II-6.
[39] ITC report at I-17.
[40] ITC report at I-22.
[41] ITC report at top of page I-6.
[42] ITC report at II-25.

> such increased quantities and under such conditions as to cause or threaten serious injury to domestic producers in that territory of like or directly competitive products, the contracting party shall be free (...) to suspend the obligation in whole or in part or to withdraw or modify the concession".

A WTO Member, *in casu* the US, planning to introduce a safeguard measure must therefore show that the increased imports are the result of "unforeseen developments".

46. Article 2:1 Agreement on Safeguards (footnote omitted) reads as follows:

> "A Member may apply a safeguard measure to a product only if that Member has determined, pursuant to the provisions set out below, that such product is being imported into its territory in such *increased quantities*, absolute or relative to domestic production, and *under such conditions* as to *cause or threaten to cause serious injury* to the domestic industry that produces like or directly competitive products." (emphasis added).

Therefore, the safeguard investigation had to establish in this case that wheat gluten was being imported into its territory in such *increased quantities*, absolute or relative to US production, and *under such conditions* as to *cause serious injury* to the US industry.

47. According to Article 4 SA, second paragraph,

> "(a) In the investigation to determine whether increased imports have caused or are threatening to cause serious injury to a domestic industry under the terms of this Agreement, the competent authorities shall evaluate all relevant factors of an objective and quantifiable nature having a bearing on the situation of that industry, in particular, the rate and amount of the increase in imports of the product concerned in absolute and relative terms, the share of the domestic market taken by increased imports, changes in the level of sales, production, productivity, capacity utilisation, profits and losses, and employment.
>
> (b) The determination referred to in subparagraph (a) shall not be made unless this investigation demonstrates, on the basis of objective evidence, the existence of the causal link between increased imports of the product concerned and serious injury or threat thereof. When factors other than increased imports are causing injury to the domestic industry at the same time, such injury shall not be attributed to increased imports.
>
> (c) The competent authorities shall publish promptly, in accordance with the provisions of Article 3, a detailed analysis of the case under investigation as well as a demonstration of the relevance of the factors examined."

Thus the US authorities should have complied with a number of detailed obligations as set out in this provision, some of which complement the abovementioned conditions under Article 2 SA.

48. The US has repeatedly and seriously violated its obligations resulting from the above-mentioned provisions, as the EC will demonstrate in the following sub-chapters:

4.1 ITC uses, without justification, unverifiable data

49. Practically all the data in the ITC report on which its findings are based, have been omitted from the version of the report available for scrutiny. The reader will find very often "***" where facts are discussed which are relevant for determining whether a safeguard measure may be taken.

The EC does not contest that under certain very specific circumstances the protection of certain information regarding *individual* companies may be justified. However, not even *aggregate* data for the whole US wheat gluten/wheat starch industry are provided, even though the ITC sees no problem whatsoever in providing aggregate data with respect to the *EC* industry. A particularly flagrant example is the historical dataset for the price of wheat gluten on the US market, which is held to be confidential in respect of US product while the parallel price data for the EC product on the same US market are published.[43]

The ITC's findings based on secret data are entirely unverifiable, without sufficient justification. They are also unreviewable.

The US authorities are required to provide "a detailed analysis of the case under investigation as well as a demonstration of the relevance of the factors examined". This requirement presupposes that the detailed analysis and the demonstration of the relevance of factors are published and not held secret, unless confidentiality is *really* an issue. If analyses based so completely on undisclosed data as in the present case were accepted, the stringent requirements to motivate and justify such findings would become void of effect.

The US has violated therefore Articles 2 and 4 of the SA.

4.2 "Unforeseen developments"

50. It clearly results from the wording of Article XIX.1 (a) GATT 1994 that in order to allow the imposition of a safeguard measure, not any increase in imports is relevant, but only those which result from both "unforeseen developments" and "compliance with GATT obligations", including tariff liberalisation according to a Member's Schedule of Concessions.

51. Increased imports as a consequence of the obligations incurred under GATT 1994, including the tariff concessions agreed for wheat gluten during the Uruguay Round cannot be considered "unforeseen" within the meaning of Article

[43] ITC report at II-33.

XIX:1(a) GATT 1994.[44] If it were otherwise, a WTO Member would be allowed to withdraw the very benefits which it had agreed to when entering into tariff commitments. This would neither be consistent with a good faith interpretation of that provision nor with the liberalisation aims pursued by the GATT 1994 and the WTO Agreement overall.[45]

52. In essence, Article XIX requires a logical chain which starts with incurring obligations under GATT 1994, followed by an intervening unforeseen development, which results eventually in increased imports, causing serious injury. It should be noted that not the increase in imports must be unforeseen but rather the "development" which has led, together with GATT obligations, to increased imports.

53. In addition, as stated above, safeguard measures are by definition "emergency" measures. The very nature of a safeguard measure is to tackle an urgent situation which was not expected. Thus, a WTO Member wishing to impose a safeguard measure must prove that an "unforeseen development" was the cause, or at least the determining cause, of the increased imports.

However, in the present case, the events leading eventually to the application by the US President of the US WGS were entirely foreseeable. They were the combined effect of free economic choices of the US domestic industry to increase production (which turned out to be nothing less than an unconsidered gamble) and of the competition on the US internal market between the US produced wheat starch and US produced corn starch.

As the EC will explain later in this document, safeguard measures cannot be used to protect domestic suppliers who increased their capacity in an irrational manner. They neither took into account that the favourable market conditions stemming from the low protein content of the wheat harvest for two years would be unlikely to continue, nor that in view of the tariff bindings which the US had accepted, increased domestic demand could very well turn to foreign suppliers. Also, a safeguard measure cannot be used in order to establish artificial conditions of competition between domestically produced competing products (in casu, wheat starch vs. corn starch) at the expense of the entirely legitimate importation from other WTO Members, in casu the EC, of a co-product, the wheat gluten.

54. The EC submits therefore that, by imposing safeguard measures in the absence of an increase in imports of wheat gluten resulting from "unforeseen

---

[44] This also reflects a generally accepted tenet of economic theory, i.e. that tariff protection can be measured in advance according to specific formulas: see B. Hoekman, M. Kostecki, The Political Economy of the World Trading System, Oxford, 1995, pp. 88, 93.

[45] See the Preambles of the Agreement establishing the World Trade Organisation and of GATT 1994, both referring to "reciprocal and mutually advantageous agreements directed to the substantial reduction of tariffs and other barriers to trade."

developments", the US violated the obligations which it assumed under Article XIX:1(a) GATT 1994.

4.3 *"Increased quantities"*

55. According to Article 2 of the SA, one of the conditions for applying a safeguard measure is that a product is being imported

> "in such increased quantities, absolute or relative to domestic production" as to cause or threaten to cause serious injury to the domestic industry.

However, the ITC's analysis was limited to a comparison of absolute data, often selectively chosen[46], and focusing on end-to-end data.[47] Moreover, by so doing the US authorities included imports from Canada and certain other countries which were eventually excluded from the application of the safeguard measure.

This is in breach of the principle of parallelism that was recognised by the *Argentina- Footwear* panel report.[48]

> "This result supports the interpretation that the two options offered by the footnote to Article 2.1 read in conjunction with Article 2.2 imply a *parallelism* between the scope of a safeguard *investigation* and the scope of the *application* of safeguard measures. Thus, in the light of the context of the footnote to Article 2.1, a member-state-specific investigation in which serious injury or threat thereof is found based on imports from all sources could only lead to the imposition of safeguard measures on a MFN-basis against all sources of intra-regional as well as extra-regional supply of a customs union."

Even if NAFTA is not a customs union, the EC does not see any reason why this specific principle should not apply equally to free-trade areas. Thus, the US breached Articles XIX GATT and 2 SA.

4.4 *"Under such conditions"*

56. Another condition for being allowed to take a safeguard measure, found both in Article XIX GATT 1994 and in Article 2 SA, is that the product is being imported "under such conditions" as to cause or threaten to cause serious injury. However, this should be read in the light of two important facts:

---

[46] The ITC report sometimes refers to the whole of the 1993-1997 period, i.e. the investigation period, some other times it takes other references arbitrarily chosen within that period which probably was considered as suiting better a pre-constituted line of reasoning.

[47] This approach must be wrong: imagine for example that a Member had imported only one ton of wheat gluten. Would an increase of 200 per cent of imports, i.e. by two tonnes, justify a safeguard measure?

[48] At para. 8.87; see also 8.102.

- The ITC appears to believe that the "conditions" under which imports took place which allegedly caused serious injury consisted of the prices of those imports.[49] It is however clear from the ITC report that prices of EC imports went up and then decreased during much of the period of investigation, and were virtually the same at the end of the period for which the ITC assembled data as at the beginning.[50]
- Moreover, in 35 per cent of the cases, the EC imports quarterly selling price was as high or higher than the US price.[51] Furthermore, in probably[52] the majority of cases the price difference was only a few per cent, which would not be statistically significant. There was, therefore, no evidence of consistent underselling of the type necessary to find that imports take place under such conditions as to cause injury. The ITC therefore violated Art. XIX GATT and 2 SA by nevertheless finding that that was the case. The EC will come back to this issue in the "as to cause" chapter below.

4.5 "Serious injury"

57. In this respect, Article 4 paragraph 2(a) of the Safeguard Agreements is important. It provides that

> "In the investigation to determine whether increased imports have caused or are threatening to cause serious injury to a domestic industry (...), the competent authorities shall evaluate *all* relevant factors of an objective and quantifiable nature having a bearing on the situation of the industry (...)".

Accordingly, procedural and substantive obligations are imposed upon a Member wishing to introduce a safeguard measure: that Member *must*, on the one hand, evaluate *all* factors having a bearing on the situation and consequently, on the other hand, it *must* demonstrate that *serious* injury has taken place.

58. The EC's complaints with respect to the ITC's serious injury finding can be structured under the following two headings:

(i) the findings and conclusions of the ITC with regard to those factors which it did investigate were not supported by the evidence;

(ii) moreover, the US authorities failed, contrary to their obligations under Article 4.2 SA, to evaluate *all* factors having a bearing on the situation of the industry.

---

[49] ITC report at I-16.

[50] ITC report at II-33 and Figure at top of page II-35.

[51] ITC report II-36.

[52] As noted above, historical price data of US product is, unjustifiably, held secret; ITC report at II-33.

The EC considers it appropriate to apply, on this point, the clarifications of the standards with respect to a serious injury finding/investigation, which were provided by the Panels in *Argentina-Footwear*[53] and *Korea-Dairy.*[54]

4.5.1 The evidence gathered by the ITC did not warrant a "serious injury" finding

4.5.1.1 The rate and amount of the increase in imports of the product concerned and the share of the domestic market taken by increased imports

59. These conditions are developed in Art. 4.2 (a) of the SA, which provides that the competent authority must evaluate

> "the rate and amount of the increase in imports of the product concerned in absolute and relative terms" as well as "the share of the domestic market taken by increased imports".

60. The ITC places great emphasis on the fact that imports into the US had increased by almost 38 per cent during 1993 to 1997.[55] However, in considering this figure the ITC unjustifiably downplayed a number of key elements. In particular, US demand went up by 18 per cent in the same period.[56] As a result, the *market share* of imports from all sources into the US only went up by approximately 9 percentage points, both in terms of quantity and value, during the entire period.[57] In other words: on average, imports increased by less than 2 percentage points per year, relative to total US demand.[58] Furthermore, the market share of imports was level from 1993 to 1995, before increasing by 6.8 percentage points from 1995 to 1996 and 2.4 percentage points from 1996 to 1997. Since increased imports are a necessary condition for taking a safeguard action, any evidence of injury prior to 1996 is not relevant to a determination that increased imports caused serious injury and should not have been relied on by the ITC in its findings.

However, the US authorities clearly failed to take that into account.

Moreover, as was discussed under "increased imports" above, the ITC failed to apply the parallelism principle since, on the one hand, it included Canada and certain other countries when it considered the rate and amount of increase of imports as well as their market share during the "serious injury" exami-

---

53 Para. 8.123.

54 Para. 7.29.

55 ITC report at I-23.

56 ITC report at I-22.

57 From 51.4 to 60.2 per cent in terms of quantity, and from 49.1 to 58.3 per cent in terms of value. See ITC report at II-25.

58 The EC notes at this stage that the US has decided that an annual increase of 6 per cent in imports was acceptable when it adopted the US WGS.

nation. On the other hand, the US authorities excluded Canada and certain other countries from the application of the US WGS. This is not only in contradiction with Articles XIX GATT and 2 SA, as discussed above, but also with Article 4 SA.

4.5.1.2 Sales

61. Changes in the level of sales are explicitly mentioned in Art. 4.2 (a) SA as a factor to be investigated.

The ITC addresses this issue in a contradictory way. On the one hand, the ITC states that "Domestic shipments..." (by which is apparently meant sales on the US home market) "...followed a similar trend [as production], initially rising and then falling, and they were at their lowest level of the investigative period in 1996 and 1997".[59] On the other hand, sales are mentioned in Part II of the report (information obtained in the investigation), in which the ITC states: "The ending period sales quantity is about 24 per cent higher than the sales quantity at the beginning of the 5-year period".[60]

This last piece of objective evidence shows unequivocally that the US industry was not suffering any injury. It is also in conformity with evidence provided elsewhere in the ITC report[61] from which it appears that in 1997 domestic shipments had increased by 7.7 per cent compared to 1996.

4.5.1.3 Production

62. Between the first and the last year of the investigation period, US production decreased only very slightly, namely by 4.5 per cent, from 128 million pounds in 1993 to 122 million pounds in 1997.[62] This is already in itself an entirely normal fluctuation and certainly does not warrant a finding that an industry is suffering serious injury, i.e. a significant overall impairment.

Moreover, production declined in only one year (1996) of the investigation period. It was going up again at the end of the investigation period, from 112 million pounds in 1996 to 122 million pounds in 1997.[63] The reason for the one-time decline was - as becomes clear upon close reading of the ITC report - that in the two years before, demand had been *exceptionally* high mainly due to "a weather-related deficiency in protein content in the wheat crops of the major producing countries, including the United States, during 1993".[64]

Data on production thus do not warrant any finding of "serious injury".

---

59 ITC report at page I-13.

60 ITC report at II-32.

61 ITC report at page II-16.

62 ITC report at I-12/13. See also table 5 to the ITC report at II-15.

63 ITC report at Appendix C, page C-4.

64 ITC report at I-22/23.

4.5.1.4 Capacity utilisation

63. Capacity utilisation is defined as production (which was just discussed) divided by production capacity.

An important factor in the ITC injury-finding was that capacity utilisation fell substantially in the period of investigation.[65] However, in the previous paragraph it was noted that US wheat gluten production hardly fell in the period of investigation. This means that the fall in capacity utilisation was almost entirely due to increase in US production capacity over the period of investigation. Indeed, as the ITC itself states, "a large increase in capacity by US producers" was one of the major reasons why available supply in the US market increased.[66] US capacity increased by no less than 68.2 per cent, or 111 million pounds, during the 1993-1997 period of investigation.[67] The ITC refers to this as "ample excess capacity of domestic producers".[68] This increase in US capacity took place – again in the words of the ITC – "in anticipation of significant increases in domestic consumption".[69] Most of this increase in capacity was in place by June 1995".[70]

Thus, the US wheat gluten industry constructed additional capacity (apparently) assuming that it, and it alone, would be the one to satisfy the increase in domestic consumption. When however it turned out that many US wheat gluten buyers chose foreign suppliers, including EC suppliers, to satisfy their increase in demand, two of the four US producers turned to the ITC. The US authorities then engaged in a process to protect the US industry from the consequences of the poor investment decisions of two producers.

There exist perfectly legitimate means by which the US could have ensured that their domestic suppliers could compete with foreign suppliers on terms which allowed them to expand their capacities and resist competition from US produced corn products. In particular, during the Uruguay Round[71], it could have renegotiated its tariff binding for imported wheat gluten upwards. But, as is apparent, the US failed to do so probably because it would have been at a cost.

The EC cannot accept that afterwards, safeguard measures without compensation are used to protect domestic suppliers who increased their capacity in

---

65 From 78.3 per cent in 1993 to 42.0 per cent in 1997. However, as the ITC itself acknowledges, capacity utilisation was going up again by 1997 (the last year of the period investigated by the ITC).

66 ITC report at I-22.

67 ITC report at I-24.

68 ITC report at I-27.

69 ITC report at I-12.

70 ITC report at I-12. It may be that the reason for this decision by US wheat gluten producers to increase capacity was the fact that in 1994 demand for and the price of wheat gluten went up. See ITC report at I-23. If this is the case, and given that the 1994 phenomena was due to a weather-related deficiency in protein content in the wheat crops, the US producers were in effect staking their prospects on either continued poor quality harvests or securing unjustified governmental protection.

71 Which ended on 15 April 1994.

an irrational manner[72], i.e. not taking into account that, in view of the tariff bindings which the US had accepted, additional domestic demand could very well turn to foreign suppliers.

64. The ITC also states that

> "... but for the increase in imports, the industry would have operated at 61 per cent of capacity in 1997, which is much closer to the level at which the industry operated early in the investigative period when it operated reasonably profitably".[73]

In other words: the US industry had apparently so much over-invested in new capacity in the beginning of the period of investigation, that – even if imports had not increased at all during that period – nevertheless a significant reduction in capacity utilisation would have been found in 1997. This means that the increase in imports was not the cause of the reduction in capacity utilisation.

Expressed in figures: if US capacity had not increased since 1993, at the end of the period of investigation capacity utilisation would have been 74.8 per cent, a decline of less than 4 percentage points. In fact, over the period under examination, capacity utilisation decreased from 78.3 per cent to 44.5 per cent, a fall of 34 percentage points. Thus, almost 89 per cent per cent of the decline in capacity utilisation is the result of the US industry's own decision to expand capacity without having a reasonable prospect that US buyers of wheat gluten would turn to them for the increased needs. This is shown in the following table and figure.

[72] For instance, Heartland began construction of its Russell plant in July 1993, well in the middle of the negotiations on agricultural products in the Uruguay Round. See ITC report at II-8.

[73] ITC report at I-17.

	1993	1994	1995	1996	1997
Capacity (1,000 pounds)	162.856	208.832	253.712	267.168	273.895
Production (1,000 pounds)	127.525	140.745	142.650	112.167	121.762
Capacity utilization %	78,3%	67,4%	56,2%	42,0%	44,5%
Capacity utilisation, if capacity had been held at 1993 level %	78,3%	86,4%	87,6%	68,9%	74,8%
Table: US wheat gluten capacity, production and capacity utilization					

source: ITC II-15

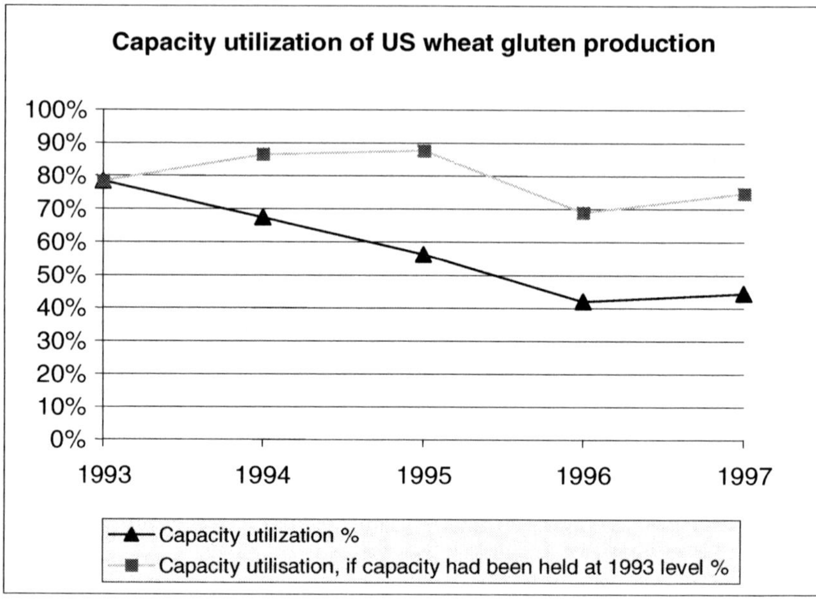

The US authorities fail to explain why an industry allegedly suffering "serious injury" would be increasing its production capacities when it is already operating at substantially less than full capacity.

This badly planned investment has resulted in an increase of production costs and has had a negative impact on profits.

By failing to take all factors mentioned above correctly into account, the US authorities have violated Articles 2 and 4 SA.

4.5.1.5 Profits/losses

65. It should be noted that the ITC states that it received usable financial data only from three of the four domestic producers of wheat gluten, and not from ADM.[74] Furthermore, one of the firms which did provide usable financial data

[74] ITC report at I-13.

only started producing wheat gluten in June 1996, the last month of the fourth year of the period of investigation. In other words, only for two of the firms in the industry were data available relating to the whole period of investigation.

66. Moreover, the finding of the ITC that profitability had gone down was based on allocation of profits by the US producers between the co-products of wheat gluten and wheat starch and derived products. Obviously, the manner in which financial factors such as costs and revenues are allocated can have a tremendous impact on the perceived profitability of the individual segments within an industry. However, because the wheat gluten/wheat starch industry relies by necessity on a single raw material input (wheat or wheat flour[75]) and utilises a single production line that results in wheat gluten, wheat starch, and effluents suitable for producing e.g. alcohol, any allocation of profitability among the output products is arbitrary.

Moreover, the fact that the US industry has heavily invested to increase its production capacity has had a negative impact on production costs and profits. The ITC fails to take that element into account in its analysis.

67. In addition, the data provided by US producers to argue that the profitability of their wheat gluten sales had gone down, are entirely unverifiable for anybody outside the ITC. The ITC limits itself to observing that "based on a careful review of the allocation methodologies used by domestic wheat gluten producers (...), we find those allocations to be appropriate".

Which methodologies were used remains entirely unclear.

In a safeguard investigation, the competent authorities are required to provide an adequate explanation of how the facts support the determination made.[76] With regard to profitability the ITC has not done so, which constitutes another violation of Article 4.2 SA provisions.

68. The EC will return to the issue of profitability when discussing the factors which the ITC *failed* to investigate.

4.5.1.6 Employment

69. During the period examined the average number of production and related workers as well as the number of hours worked increased.

Such data are clearly not an indication of "serious injury". Whilst there are some allegations in the report of losses of managerial and administrative jobs, the ITC-report does not contain any verifiable data whatsoever on that issue.

It is also telling in this respect that the ITC expects that imposition of the safeguard measure will increase, in the short term, the number of US workers

---

75 At least one of the major US producers concerned purchases wheat flour as the raw material rather than wheat grain. This means it loses the margin reserved to the miller, thus squeezing profits further. This fact was not taken into account by the ITC.

76 *Argentina-Footwear, supra*, footnote 2, para. 8.124.

producing wheat gluten in the range of merely ten to fourteen.[77] It is therefore clear that employment was hardly affected, let alone *seriously* affected, by the increased imports.

4.5.1.7 Other Factors – Wages

70. During the period examined, hourly wages rose in three of the five years, in particular *also* in 1997, which shows that there is no connection between imports and wages. Moreover, overall wages paid increased and certain salary cuts were restored by the end of the investigation period.[78]

Thus, the situation was far from one of "serious injury".

1,000 pounds	1993	1994	1995	1996	1997
Imports into US	128.337	124.188	127.912	156.024	177.073
Inventories (end-of-period)	4.539	7.085	13.883	11.491	9.137

Table: US wheat gluten imports and inventories, 1993-1997

source: ITC II-12,16

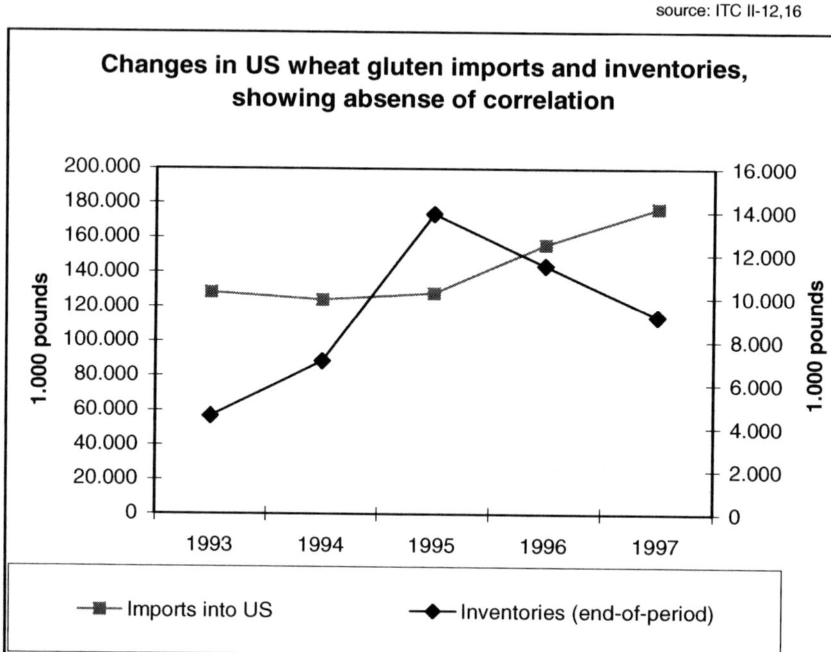

[77] ITC report at I-30.

[78] ITC report at II-17, see also page I-13.

4.5.1.8 Other factors – Inventories

71. A rise in inventories is another factor cited in the ITC report as evidence of serious injury.[79] Inventories rose by 101.3 per cent from 1993 to 1997. However, all of the increase occurred from 1993 to 1995, when inventories increased by over 200 per cent. In the only two years in which imports increased, 1996 and 1997, inventories declined by 34.2 per cent, as shown in the table below. Clearly, the fact that inventories went down during the last two years in which imports increased not only fails to support a finding of serious injury, but instead provides cogent evidence to the contrary. In this respect, it is clear from the rationale of the safeguard instrument as an emergency measure that particular consideration must be given to the most recent time periods. In fact, a safeguard measure can only be imposed if there is *present* serious injury or threat thereof.

4.5.2 Not all relevant factors were appropriately investigated by the ITC

72. As the EC has already observed, the role of the Panel is to determine whether the ITC fully and objectively considered all the evidence before it, *including any evidence that detracts from an affirmative determination of serious injury or causation.*[80] The EC will show that the ITC has failed to do so.

4.5.2.1 Productivity

73. Under Art. 4.2 (a) SA, the ITC was required to evaluate all relevant factors having a bearing on the situation of the US wheat gluten/wheat starch industry, and in particular those explicitly mentioned in that provision.[81] Developments in *productivity* in the US wheat starch/gluten industry should therefore no doubt have been considered in the investigation and in the report.

Productivity refers to the ratio of output to *all* inputs. The ITC's analysis is, however, limited to analysing *worker* productivity[82], even though it acknowledges that "production of wheat gluten is extremely capital intensive and requires very few production workers".[83] Thus analysing worker productivity cannot possibly be sufficient to evaluate overall industry productivity, it must take into account in particular capital investment.

The US therefore failed to meet its obligation to investigate overall industry productivity and it consequently violated Article 4 SA.

---

79 ITC Report at I-13.
80 *Korea - Dairy, supra*, footnote 2, para. 7.30.
81 This was confirmed by Korea-Dairy, paras 7.55 and 7.68.
82 See ITC report at I-14 top of page, which only contains references to "worker productivity".
83 ITC report at I-13.

4.5.2.2 New entries/expansion while injury is supposedly taking place

74. The ITC notes: "[O]ne new domestic producer, Heartland, entered the market in 1996. ".[84] It is incomprehensible that a domestic producer would enter a market which was at that point in time allegedly being *seriously* injured by imports. However, the ITC doesn't provide any explanation how, in spite of this fact, it could find that the domestic industry was, at that time, being seriously injured by imports.

75. Midwest's Atchison plant underwent several expansions and upgrades throughout the period examined.[85] What happened exactly is (once again) removed from the ITC report. However, the text ("In 1996, ***. In 1997, ***") implies that this took place in the years subsequent to the period when the alleged serious injury had taken place. Again, the facts argue against a serious injury finding.

4.5.2.3 Developments as to co-products were completely ignored.

76. As set out above, the production of wheat gluten always involves, at the same time, the production of other products, and even – as far as starch is concerned – in much greater quantities than wheat gluten. In its injury-analysis[86], the ITC acknowledges this fundamental fact:

> "Each of the companies produces wheat gluten and wheat starch in a joint production process. Each of the companies also produces other by-products or related products, especially alcohol".[87]

Nevertheless, the ITC completely failed to investigate how this fact that necessarily co-products are produced influence US wheat starch/gluten producers profitability, even though this fact incontestably – using the terms of Art. 4 para. 2 of the SA - has "a bearing on the situation of [the US wheat starch/gluten] industry".

This omission provides another reason to reject the ITC's final report as flawed, since in their pre-hearing report the ITC's staff had stated : "Because of the joint cost allocation used to determine profitability of the wheat gluten industry, the revenue flow from wheat starch that the US producers can obtain affects wheat gluten profitability".[88]

---

84 ITC report at I-17.

85 ITC report at II-6.

86 ITC report at I-12 through 14.

87 ITC report at I-13.

88 Pre-hearing staff report II-30.

4.5.2.4 Imports as positive business strategy of certain US producers

77. One important US producer of wheat starch/wheat gluten is Manildra, which is part of the US branch of an Australian group owning two Australian companies manufacturing wheat gluten.[89] It is a fair assumption that large parts of imports of wheat gluten from Australia were attributable to this particular company. In fact, because of the company structure, the Manildra group can decide entirely freely whether to produce wheat gluten in Australia and bring it over to the US, or to produce it in the US, depending on the market situation. Moreover, by importing wheat gluten from its Australian sister-companies, rather than producing it domestically, a company like Manildra avoids having to dispose of the co-products and by-products, starch and alcohol in the US, when the US market conditions for those products are not profitable over time. This situation was objectively present during (at least part of) the period of investigation.

A considered deliberate policy of importation by a domestic company, which corresponds to its business strategy optimising profits cannot, by definition, be considered an injury, let alone a serious injury in order to justify a safeguard measure.

The ITC report completely fails to address this issue. The US thus violated Articles 2 and 4 SA.

4.6 "As to cause"

78. The ITC failed to establish a causal link between increased imports and serious injury to the domestic industry as required by Articles 2 and 4.2 of the Safeguards Agreement. Article 4.2(b) is very specific in its requirement for the competent authority to demonstrate, "on the basis of objective evidence", the existence of a causal link. For a causation analysis to meet the requirements of Articles 2 and 4.2 SA, it must consist of at least three elements:

(i) an analysis of whether the upward trend in imports coincides with negative trends in injury factors;

(ii) an analysis of whether the conditions of competition between the imported product and the domestic product demonstrate, on the basis of objective evidence, a causal link between increased imports and serious injury; and

(iii) an analysis of other relevant factors and their proper attribution.[90]

---

[89] ITC report at II-9.

[90] *Argentina - Footwear*, *supra*, footnote 2, para. 8.229.

4.6.1 Does upward trend in imports coincide with negative trends in injury factors?

79. The ITC states: "This surge in relatively low-priced imports in 1996 and 1997 *coincided with* the decline in industry performance described above. There is a direct correlation between the dramatic increase in wheat gluten imports and the significant decline in domestic wheat gluten industry performance in 1996 and 1997"[91] (emphasis added).

80. The EC considers that the facts relating to most of the factors invoked by the ITC to find injury show otherwise. Most factors indicative of injury either moved negatively before the increase in imports in 1996 and 1997, moved positively when imports were rising, or both. In particular, three factors (capacity utilisation, domestic shipments and inventories) worsened *before* the reference period and actually improved during the period of the alleged "serious injury".

Capacity utilisation consistently declined from 1993 to 1995, so before what the ITC describes as a "dramatic" increase in imports, and then improved from 1996 to 1997.[92]

Domestic shipments first declined in 1995, again before what the ITC describes as a "dramatic" increase in imports, but increased from 1996-1997.[93]

Equally, the negative trend for *end of period inventories* lasted until 1995 but was reversed in 1996 and 1997 when the situation clearly improved.[94] The ratio of inventories to US shipments and production followed a similar trend..[95]

Profitability began to decline in 1995, before the increase in imports, and hourly wages declined in 1995 but were increasing in 1997.

With respect to *employment*, the only two declining factors identified are hourly wages and worker productivity. Hourly wages began declining in 1995 and were rising by 1997. Data relating to worker productivity is held secret and therefore unverifiable.[96] Finally, *annual average unit shipment values* for US wheat gluten already declined in 1995.[97]

The ITC failed to satisfy the first element of the causation analysis, a coincidence of trends between serious injury and increased imports. The evidence that the injury factors cited to support the finding of serious injury began declining before the increase in imports raises serious questions about the existence of a causal link. The ITC provides no analysis or reasoning to demonstrate how the negative trends in injury factors could have been caused by the increase in imports which began later.

---

91 ITC report at I-16.
92 ITC report at II-15.
93 ITC report at II-16.
94 ITC report at page II-16.
95 ITC report at page II-14.
96 ITC report at page II-16, table 8.
97 ITC report at II-16.

4.6.2 Conditions of competition

81. Under Article XIX GATT as well as Article 2 SA, in order for safeguard measures to be allowed, products must be not only be imported in strongly increased quantities, but also

> "*under such conditions* as to cause or threaten to cause serious injury".

Pursuant to Art. 4.2 (b) of the SA, the ITC investigation should have demonstrated, "on the basis of objective evidence", the existence of this aspect of the alleged causal link between imports and injury.

Under Art. 4.2 (c) of the SA, the US was under the obligation to publish

> "a detailed analysis of the case under investigation as well as a *demonstration* of the relevance of the factors examined". (emphasis added)

82. The US has not fulfilled this obligation. In the part of the ITC report on causation[98], the ITC states:

> "The record also shows that imports from the EU *consistently* undersold domestic wheat gluten". (emphasis added)

The statement as such is unverifiable, since the relevant data on US domestic producers' sales prices have been removed from the public version of the ITC report, even in the aggregate format.

However, the few data which the ITC does mention show that this statement represents a distortion of the facts. Elsewhere in the report[99] it is clearly stated that out of twenty quarterly price comparisons between domestic and imported EU vital wheat gluten, in six cases the imported EU product was priced *higher* than the US produced product, and in one case at the same price.

In this respect, it is also noteworthy that at the end of the period for which the ITC gives EC prices (first half 1997), those were practically the same as at the beginning of that period (second half 1992).[100]

Finally, one should take into account that price competition between imported and US wheat gluten was also entirely legitimate.

83. As it appears, the assumption in the ITC's reasoning is that it was the price of EU imports which forced US producers to sell at prices which resulted in losses, thus causing serious injury.[101] The EC has already shown, in the previous paragraph, that there was no question of consistent underselling by EC imports, as the ITC alleges in its findings. Indeed, decline in domestic shipment values

---

98 ITC report at I-16 to I-18.

99 ITC report at II-36.

100 ITC report at II-35.

101 ITC report at I-16, in conjunction with I-13 2nd full para.

began in 1995, the year before the increase in imports.[102] One cannot conclude that increased imports were the cause of the decline in domestic unit sales values.

Moreover, the ITC acknowledges that the price of wheat gluten is directly related to the protein level in wheat.[103] When the protein level in wheat is low, demand for wheat gluten goes up – since more wheat gluten is needed to supplement the protein level of wheat used in bread baking - and therefore the price goes up. In contrast, when the protein level in wheat is high, demand for wheat gluten goes down, and its price goes down. Bread baking accounts for 80 per cent of US wheat gluten use. In other words, the ITC was well aware that the price prevailing on the US market was due to be influenced by developments in the protein level of US wheat crops.

4.6.3 Insufficient weight given to analysis of other factors which caused US wheat starch/wheat gluten industry difficulties

84. In order to warrant a safeguard measure, an investigation must, on the basis of objective evidence, demonstrate "the" causal link between increased imports and (threat of) serious injury. If other factors are causing injury at the same time, such injury shall not be attributed to increased imports. (Art. 4.2 (b) SA). The ITC has not properly fulfilled its obligations in this respect.

In the present case, the consideration of other factors takes on a heightened importance for three reasons. First, the very nature of a the wheat gluten/wheat starch industry is such that other factors, i.e., the conditions in the wheat starch and alcohol markets, are critical to the overall situation of the industry. Second, the overwhelming evidence that the injury experienced by the industry began before the increase in imports is strongly suggestive that factors other than increased imports caused the injury. Third, analysis of the relevant data demonstrate that domestic prices were not affected by imports. In light of this, the causation analysis required careful scrutiny and evaluation of other relevant factors to meet the requirements of Article 4.2(b). The evaluation of other factors in the ITC Report did not meet the standard required.

4.6.3.1 Wheat protein premiums determine the wheat gluten price on the US market

85. In the previous sub-chapter, the EC already explained that – as the ITC itself acknowledges - the price of wheat gluten is directly related to the protein level in wheat. However, contrary to its obligation under Art. 4.2 (a) of the SA to evaluate *all* relevant factors, the ITC has completely omitted to examine this issue. The EC attaches a detailed analysis of this question. (Exhibit EC-10)

[102] ITC report, Appendix C, at page C-4, under US shipments unit value.

[103] For instance ITC report at I-23.

This analysis shows that the primary factor affecting unit sales values was the protein level of US wheat/wheat flour as measured by protein premiums for US wheat.[104] It appears from this analysis that wheat gluten imports had virtually *no* effect on US wheat gluten prices. Movements in wheat gluten prices during the 1993 to 1997 period were explained primarily by wheat protein premiums.

In other words, the ITC has not only failed to evaluate this factor, which is in itself already a violation of Art. 4.2 (a) of the SA, but such evaluation should also have led it to a different conclusion.

4.6.3.2 The situation in the co-products markets

(A) Wheat starch

86. With respect to wheat starch, the analysis of the ITC – consisting of only a few sentences - is in fact limited to two points:

(i) wheat starch prices were at their highest level at the end of the investigative period in 1997;

(ii) that fact suggests that competition between corn starch and wheat starch is not likely to have had much effect on wheat gluten production.[105]

87. This is, of course, an evident over-simplification of a very important issue. All US producers concerned produce, from the same wheat, both wheat gluten and wheat starch, in the same production facilities.[106] As was explained before, for every kilogram of wheat gluten produced, about 5 kilograms of wheat starch are produced. Anything which influences the profitability of the starch part of their business therefore necessarily influences the profitability of their entire operations.

88. The wheat starch price at the end of the investigative period is, of course, a factor in the analysis of the profitability of wheat starch production, but clearly only one of many. Other relevant factors were however completely ignored by the ITC in its analysis. For instance, US wheat starch prices fell after 1992/1993 until 1994/1995 and still remained below 1992/1993 levels in 1995/1996. (See Exhibit EC-11). Also, US wheat starch consumption was much less – compared to 1995 - in 1996 and 1997, the exact same years in which allegedly increased wheat gluten imports caused serious injury. Apparent consumption of wheat starch was about 12 per cent and 7 per cent below the 1995 level in 1996 and

[104] The protein premium is a measure of the level of protein in wheat. One common measure is the difference between Kansas City prices for hard red winter wheat, ordinary protein, and 13 per cent protein wheat. When the protein content of ordinary wheat is low, buyers will pay more for higher protein wheat and the premium increases.

[105] ITC report at I-16-17.

[106] Description in ITC report at II-7-8.

1997, respectively.[107] Furthermore, wheat starch production capacity had increased by 93 per cent from 1993 to 1997.[108]

89. At the same time, as was already stated in Part 3 of this submission, wheat starch had to face fierce competition from corn starch during the whole of the period of investigation. Wheat starch has similar physical characteristics as starches derived from other raw materials and is used for most of the same purposes. (Except that in the US, wheat starch is not used to make sweeteners, a point to which the EC will return in a moment).

However, average annual monthly cash wheat prices during the 1993 to 1997 period ranged from 26 per cent to 58 per cent above cash corn prices. (Exhibit EC-12 for wheat prices and Exhibit EC-13 for corn prices). Moreover, nearly 25 per cent more starch is produced from a ton of corn than a ton of wheat – about 690 kilograms of corn starch vs. 575 kilograms of wheat starch. Thus, in the US the raw material cost of wheat starch is 45 per cent higher than for corn starch. This appears from the following table:

US produced Wheat and Corn Starch
Competitive advantage of corn over wheat
(average cash prices over the 1993 to 1997 period)

	Wheat	**Corn**	**Competitive advantage of corn over wheat** (%)
Starch yield %	57.5	69	20%
Weight of wheat/corn to yield 1 Kg of starch (Kg)	1.74	1.45	
Cash price ($/Kg)[109]	0.159	0.105	34%
Cost of wheat/corn input to produce 1 Kg of starch ($/Kg)	0.277	0.152	45%

90. On top of this, two US policies encourage and favour corn starch producers and the expansion of corn wet milling capacity. The first is a tax benefit for ethanol, which works out in practice to be more beneficial to corn wet millers than for wheat starch/wheat gluten producers.[110]

The second is US sugar policy, which has provided incentives for substantial growth in production and consumption of high fructose corn sweetener (HFCS) – a product made from corn starch - over the past 20 years. The US

[107] See on this point also table C-2, at page C-6 of part II of the ITC report, from which it appears that US wheat starch production was about 447.000 pounds in 1995, then fell to about 421.000 in 1996, and in 1997 slightly climbed again to about 430.000.
[108] ITC report at Appendix C, page C-6.
[109] Cash prices for #2 yellow corn in central Illinois and cash prices for wheat, Kansas City, ordinary protein hard red winter.
[110] Gasoline marketers that blend their fuels with ethanol are eligible for a $0.054 per gallon reduction from the federal excise tax on gasoline (about $0.183 per gallon).

sugar policy keeps US sugar prices well above world prices, allowing HFCS to be produced profitably and to substitute for sugar as an ingredient in products such as soft drinks. Over the period 1985/86–1996/97, wholesale refined sugar prices ranged from $0.25-0.29 per pound, compared with wholesale HFCS prices of $0.16-$0.21 per pound.[111] With the high price umbrella provided by the US sugar policy, HFCS producers have been assured of profitable prices for HFCS and a growing demand for HFCS.

The expansion of corn wet milling capacity encouraged by these two policies favourable to corn starch has resulted in the availability of abundant supplies of corn starch on the US market.

91. It should be noted that two thirds of the wheat gluten importers/purchasers responding to the questionnaires in the ITC investigation reported that the most significant factor affecting the competitiveness of wheat gluten in the US market was the difficulty of selling wheat starch in the US market, where cheaper corn starch is the predominant starch sold.[112]

92. In the light of all these factors, which had been brought to the attention of the ITC before it made its findings[113], it is clear that the ITC has not fulfilled its obligation under Article 4 of the SA to seriously and thoroughly evaluate the situation with regard to wheat starch, even though it clearly is one having a bearing on the US wheat starch/wheat gluten industry.

(B) Ethanol/alcohol

93. Ethanol and food-grade alcohol are products of the wheat gluten/wheat starch production process. The wheat starch slurry that results from the first step of the production process is further processed into either wheat starch or alcohol products.[114] From the description of the US producers, it also clearly appears that many of them even have their own facilities to produce (food-grade and fuel-grade) alcohol and ethanol.[115] Therefore, as the ITC itself acknowledges,

> "the volume and valuation of " B " starch (slurry) internally transferred to make alcohol products have varying effects on the profitability of each of the producers".[116]

94. The net sales data reported in the ITC report[117] for one of the US producers, Midwest, show the importance of alcohol products to a wheat gluten/wheat starch operation (59 per cent of total net sales over the period of investigation,

[111] USDA/ERS Sugar and Sweetener Situation and Outlook Year Book 1998 and supplemental data from ERS.

[112] ITC report at II-37.

[113] ITC report at I-15 2nd full para.

[114] ITC Report at II-5 and II-6 for a description of the production process.

[115] ITC report at II-6- and II-7.

[116] ITC report at II-20.

[117] ITC report at II-19.

more than twice as much as for wheat gluten). Furthermore, the ITC notes that "there is evidence that Midwest reduced its wheat gluten production in 1995, for reasons related at least in part to conditions in the alcohol market (...)".[118]Indeed, US ethanol production had gone down severely in 1995 and remained below the 1994 level at least until 1997 (see Exhibit EC-14). Nevertheless, even though the EC industry had explicitly pointed out to the ITC that there was a weakness in the ethanol market[119], the ITC found it unnecessary to investigate this issue further. Instead, it downplayed the issue as a problem only facing Midwest, without giving any serious explanation.[120]

95. Clearly, this constitutes, again, a failure by the ITC to comply with its obligation to evaluate *all* relevant factors.

4.6.3.3 Capacity utilisation

96. As has already been explained above, the reason why capacity utilisation has gone down was not increased imports, but ill-timed and ill-considered industry decisions to expand capacity. In fact, capacity was expanded by 68 per cent[121], while apparent consumption of wheat gluten grew only by 18 per cent over the period of investigation.[122] It is clear therefore, that under Article 4.2 (b), last sentence, of the SA, the reduction in capacity utilisation cannot be attributed to imports.

4.6.3.4 Input prices

97. As the ITC acknowledges, wheat and wheat flour represent the predominant raw material cost to produce wheat gluten.[123] The ITC also notes that these raw material costs generally rose in the US during the entire period examined[124], and "particularly in 1996 and 1997".[125] In fact, wheat prices jumped from $132/ton in June 1994 to $258/ton in May 1996, an increase of 95 per cent.[126] The timing of this huge price increase coincides with the sharp decline in profitability reported in 1995.[127]

98. The ITC wipes this issue off the table by stating that demand for wheat gluten is relatively insensitive to price, and that it would expect that wheat gluten producers would be able to pass on these cost increases to their customers.[128] The

---

[118] ITC report at I-17.
[119] ITC report at I-15.
[120] ITC report at I-17.
[121] ITC report at II-14.
[122] ITC report at I-17.
[123] ITC report at II-27.
[124] ITC report at II 37.
[125] ITC report at I-17.
[126] These data derive from Exhibit EC-12. In practice, Exhibit EC-12 provides for monthly prices in US$ per bushel. The conversion rate from bushel to ton is MAIZE: 1 metric ton = 39.37 bushels; WHEAT: 1 metric ton = 36.75 bushels.
[127] ITC report at II-18.
[128] ITC report at I-17 bottom of page.

only basis for this expectation appears to be oral statements during the investigation by the two companies seeking import relief. There is no objective or quantifiable evidence to support these assertions.

99. In fact, it is completely at odds with the acknowledgement by the ITC, elsewhere in the report, that "[W]hen wheat gluten is used primarily as a protein supplement in the baking sector, high-protein wheat flour can be substituted".[129]

As stated in the factual part of this submission (Part 3.1.3), about 80 per cent of wheat gluten is bought by the baking sector for this purpose.[130] Reported contract periods for wheat gluten sales were generally 3-12 months contracts for the US producers, with prices and quantities fixed for the period of the contract.[131] Nothing prevented US bakers, therefore, from keeping their wheat gluten supplier to the price fixed in the contract for the duration thereof, and then turn to a high protein wheat or wheat flour supplier if the wheat gluten supplier wished to raise his price. Following the 1993/1994 crop, the protein content of US wheat generally improved. Significantly, US imports of high protein wheat from Canada over the 1993 to 1997 period averaged about 1.44 million tons annually, compared to about 0.412 million tons annually in 1991-1992 (Exhibit EC-15).

100. The ITC has therefore also clearly failed in examining seriously and thoroughly whether high[132] wheat and wheat flour prices in the US were not the real cause of the (alleged) injury.

4.6.3.5 Imports by US producers themselves

101. The EC has already noted that part of the imports was imported by US wheat starch/wheat gluten producers themselves.[133] Unfortunately, again, all relevant data are removed from the public version of the ITC report. The ITC does state, however, on the one hand that the part of imports by US producers themselves rose in 1994 relative to 1993, and on the other hand that that part remained relatively stable during the period examined. It furthermore explicitly acknowledges that the US market depends in part on imports to meet domestic demand.

102. The EC has already discussed the question of imports by US wheat starch/wheat gluten producers themselves under "serious injury" above. These facts of course also have a bearing with respect to the causation analysis. Again, by importing wheat gluten from its Australian sister-companies, rather than producing it domestically, a company like Manildra avoids having to dispose of the co-product, starch, and alcohol on the US market when the conditions in that market for those products are not good. Furthermore, Australian production conditions favour wheat starch, owing to a lack of competition from corn, and demand for

[129] ITC report at II-27.
[130] ITC report at II-27.
[131] ITC report at II-30.
[132] In absolute terms as well as relative to corn.
[133] ITC report at I-17 and II-14.

wheat gluten is relatively weak, again favouring export of the latter product to the US

Therefore the data for the imports from Australia to the US by US producers should have been excluded entirely from the causation analysis and findings. The failure to do so constitutes a violation of the entire Article 4.2 SA.

4.6.3.6 Imports by countries excluded from the application of the US WGS were not excluded from the investigation

103. Canada and certain other countries have been excluded from the application of the US WGS. The Panel in *Argentina- Footwear* has already ruled that, in the light of Article 2 of the SA, a safeguard measure only on *certain* sources of supply cannot be justified on the basis of an investigation which finds serious injury caused by imports from *all* sources of supply.[134]

Thus, what a WTO Member clearly cannot do, is find that *total* imports cause or threaten to cause serious injury, and then exclude one of the biggest suppliers from the safeguard measure. However, that is exactly what the US has done.

All the ITC's determinations on increased imports, serious injury, and causation are based on total imports into the US. Moreover, Canada was the third largest supplier of wheat gluten imports during 1995-1997, accounting for an average of 10.2 per cent of imports. For instance, imports from Canada amounted to 7,788.31 tons in 1996.

4.6.4 No standard of causality was used by the US

104. The US seems to rely on a vague notion of preponderance when determining the causal link between increased imports and "serious injury". However, nowhere does the US spell out any objective criteria justifying the implementation of such notion.

More importantly, after having recognised that other factors[135] contributed to injury, nowhere does the US indicate how it came to the conclusion that the injury attributable, in its - erroneous - view, to increased imports could be defined as "serious injury". To put it another way, the US should have provided an objective criterion on the basis of which it could be demonstrated that the injury attributable to imports, after having "deducted" the injury caused by other fac-

---

[134] See the Panel's reasoning starting at para. 8.75. Of course, the Panel was dealing with a situation involving a customs union, but there is no reason whatsoever not to require the same parallelism in the case of a WTO Member which is a member of a free trade area. It is noteworthy that the Panel rejected the Argentinean argument based on US practice, and particularly the wheat gluten safeguard measure, para. 8.100.

[135] In the sense of Article 4.2 (b), last sentence, SA.

tors, reached the threshold necessary for being qualified as "serious", i.e. a "significant overall impairment in the position" of its domestic industry.

The US clearly failed to do that. This is in itself a violation of Article 4.2 (b) and (c) SA. In addition, it is the EC's view that the US, on the basis of the objective elements which they examined or should have examined, should never have reached that conclusion.

4.7 Conclusion as regards this chapter

105. The US authorities have not fulfilled their obligations in determining whether serious injury occurred, and whether increased imports caused this injury. In fact, few factors suggest any form of injury, and as far as they do, it is clear that they have not been caused by increased imports, nor by the conditions under which those have taken place. The US WGS is therefore in breach of Articles XIX of GATT 1994, as well as Articles 2 and 4 of the SA.

5. THE US WGS IS IN BREACH OF ARTICLE 5 OF THE SA

106. Article 5 of the SA contains a number of obligations, which are binding upon each and every WTO Member upon applying a safeguard measure.

5.1 Article 5, paragraph 1, 1st sentence

107. The Panel report on *Korea- Dairy* has partially addressed the interpretation of this provision. It is worth reminding here certain of its conclusions.[136]

> "The first sentence of Article 5.1 does contain a very specific obligation. This obligation is to apply a measure that is commensurate with the goals of preventing or remedying the serious injury suffered by the domestic industry and of facilitating the adjustment of the domestic industry. Our interpretation of this obligation is bolstered by the last sentence of Article 5.1, which provides that Members "should choose measures most suitable for the achievement" of the objectives of preventing or remedying the serious injury and facilitating adjustment."
>
> "In our view a measure is defined by the following elements: product coverage, form, duration and level. Thus, in order to comply with Article 5.1 a Member must apply a measure which in its totality is no more restrictive than is necessary to prevent or remedy the serious injury and facilitate adjustment. In addition, it must be possible for a Panel to evaluate, in accordance with the applicable standard of review, whether a Member has acted in compliance

[136] Paras. 7.100 and 7.101.

with Article 5.1. Therefore, the Member applying the measure must provide a reasoned explanation as to how the authorities reached the conclusion that the particular measure in question satisfies all the requirements of Article 5.1. We consider that the obligations of the first sentence of Article 5.1 apply to all safeguard measures in their entirety."

5.1.1 General overview of the issue in the context of the present dispute

108. According to Article 5, paragraph 1, 1st sentence

> "A Member shall apply safeguard measures only to the extent necessary to prevent or remedy serious injury and to facilitate adjustment".

109. This provision introduces in the SA the so-called "proportionality rule" that compels the WTO Member wishing to apply a safeguard measure to limit the application of such a measure (that must in any case comply with the other obligations under the SA) to the following:

(a) the application must ("shall")

(b) be limited to measures "only"

(c) "to the extent" "necessary to prevent or remedy"

(d) "serious injury"

(e) and "to facilitate adjustment".

The EC would recall at this juncture that the Appellate Body in its "*US-Underwear*" report has defined the possibility for a WTO Member to adopt a safeguard measure as

> "(...) an (...) ability to restrict the entry into its territory of goods in the exportation of which no unfair trade practice such as dumping or fraud or deception as to origin, is alleged or proven".[137]

110. As far as points (a) and (b) above are concerned, the expressions are self-explanatory: they clearly set an unsurpassable limit for the Member applying the safeguard measure.

111. Within the imperative limits under (a) and (b), point (c) introduces the proportionality test: only insofar as the safeguard measure - which the Member

[137] Appellate Body Report, *United States – Restrictions on Imports of Cotton and Man-made Fibre Underwear* ("*US – Underwear*"), WT/DS24/AB/R, adopted 25 February 1997, DSR 1997:I, 11, at page 23. The AB ruling holds entirely its validity for this case even if in the US–Underware case it was taken in the context of a specific transitional safeguard measure under the Agreement on Textiles and Clothing.

plans to apply - is "necessary" to prevent or remedy a serious injury, it can be admitted.

The ordinary meaning of the word "necessary" is "requiring to be done, achieved, requisite, essential".[138] Thus, the Member wishing to apply the safeguard measure is obliged to provide justification on whether the proposed measure is "necessary", i.e. is "required to be done", in order to prevent or remedy serious injury. The *Korea-Dairy* panel indicated that the investigating authority must demonstrate that it has

> "considered all relevant information and explained [its] decision that the measure chosen was no more restrictive than necessary to prevent or remedy serious injury ... and to facilitate the industry's adjustment".[139]

112. On point (d), the term "serious injury" should be understood not only in accordance with the definition in Article 4.1 (a) of the SA[140] but also in their immediate context and in light of the object-and-purpose pursued by the WTO Contracting Parties. As the Panel final report on *US - Sections 301-310* rightly indicated at paragraph 7.19:[141]

> "(...) the elements referred to in Article 31 [of the Vienna Convention] – text, context and object-and-purpose as well as good faith – are to be viewed as one holistic rule of interpretation rather than a sequence of separate tests to be applied in a hierarchical order.[142] Context and object-and-purpose may often appear simply to confirm an interpretation seemingly derived from the "raw" text. In re-

---

[138] Oxford English Reference Dictionary, Oxford University Press, 1995, page 968.

[139] *Korea - Dairy*, *supra*, footnote 2, para. 7.101.

[140] "Serious injury" shall be understood to mean a significant overall impairment in the position of a domestic industry".

[141] Not yet adopted

[142] [original footnote] As noted by the International Law Commission (ILC) – the original drafter of Article 31 of the Vienna Convention – in its commentary to that provision:
"The Commission, by heading the article 'General Rule of Interpretation' in the singular and by underlining the connection between paras. 1 and 2 and again between para. 3 and the two previous paras., intended to indicate that the application of the means of interpretation in the article would be a single combined operation. All the various elements, as they were present in any given case, would be thrown into the crucible and their interaction would give the legally relevant interpretation. Thus [Article 31] is entitled 'General rule of interpretation' in the singular, not 'General rules' in the plural, because the Commission desired to emphasise that the process of interpretation is a unity and that the provisions of the article form a single, closely integrated rule" (Yearbook of the ILC, 1966, Vol. II, pp. 219-220).
See also, Sinclair, I., The Vienna Convention on the Law of Treaties, 2nd Edition, Manchester University Press, 1984, p. 116:
"Every text, however clear on its face, requires to be scrutinised in its context and in the light of the object and purpose which it is designed to serve. The conclusion which may be reached after such a scrutiny is, in most instances, that the clear meaning which originally presented itself is the correct one, but this should not be used to disguise the fact that what is involved is a process of interpretation".

> ality it is always some context, even if unstated, that determines which meaning is to be taken as "ordinary" and frequently it is impossible to give meaning, even "ordinary meaning", without looking also at object-and-purpose".

In this perspective, Article 4.2 (b) of the SA, in regulating causation, defines which serious injury is relevant in order to allow a WTO Member to take safeguard action. It clearly indicates that, *on the one hand*, the determination of serious injury can only be made when the existence of the casual link between increased imports of the product concerned and serious injury is demonstrated on the basis of objective evidence. *On the other hand*,

> "[W]hen factors other than increased imports are causing injury to the domestic industry at the same time, such injury shall not be attributed to increased imports".

In other words, "necessary to prevent or remedy serious injury" in Article 5.1 SA means "serious injury" attributable to "increased imports" *only*.

113. Thus, according to Article 5.1 SA, the extent of the measure *must* be limited to the remedy or prevention of the serious injury, which is demonstrated to be its cause. The imported products cannot bear the consequences of injuries, which cannot be attributed to them: this is not permitted unless a *bona fide prior* negotiation under Article XXVIII of the GATT 1994 is followed (which in turn implies that an adequate compensation is offered).[143]

114. Finally, in accordance with point (e), the future adjustment of the domestic industry shall also be considered.

115. Consequently, as the above mentioned panel in *Korea - Dairy* indicated, the investigating authority must demonstrate that it has "considered all relevant information and explained [its] decision that the measure chosen was no more restrictive than necessary to prevent or remedy serious injury ... and to facilitate the industry's adjustment."

The requirement to justify that the measure chosen is applied only to the extent necessary applies to all elements of the measure: product coverage, form, duration, and level.[144]

116. Moreover and in any case, the safeguard measure can only be justified if it remedies or prevents the serious injury which was objectively demonstrated as having been the effect of the increased imports and that could not be attributed to other factors other than increased imports.

---

143 Panel report on Newsprint

144 See *Korea - Dairy*, *supra*, footnote 2, para. 7.100.

5.1.2 Application to the present dispute: the form and the extent of the US WGS.

117. The European Communities submits that the United States has failed to provide sufficient justification for the *form* of the measure.

118. The ITC Report acknowledges that of the three possible import relief measures – tariffs, tariff-rate quotas, and quotas – a tariff is the least trade distortive.[145]

Since the first sentence of paragraph 1 of Article 5, as interpreted by the *Korea-Dairy* panel report, requires the use of the least trade restrictive import measure, a tariff should be used unless, as provided by the third sentence of paragraph 1, a tariff would not be suitable to remedy the serious injury and facilitate adjustment.

119. The explanation provided by ITC Report for choosing quantitative restrictions is less than adequate.[146]

120. The first factor considered in rejecting a tariff, as an appropriate relief measure, was the co-product nature of the industry. The ITC concluded that since demand for wheat starch has an effect on the production and price of wheat gluten, it would be impossible to calculate an appropriate tariff level that would limit imports of wheat gluten if global wheat starch demand were to rise, leading to increased supplies of wheat gluten available for export.

However, this relationship between wheat starch and wheat gluten, when raised by the EC industry during the investigation as a causal factor for injury, was rejected by the ITC.[147] The ITC Report is thus based on an inconsistent analysis of the underlying facts.

121. The US cannot have it both ways: *either* it considers (as it should) the co-product nature of the industry when determining the "serious injury" and the causal link with the imported products. However, in this case, as the EC has explained above, the US WGS would no longer be justified.

122. *Or*, the US (erroneously) does not take into account the co-product nature of the industry. In this case, however, that element cannot justify later the choice of the form of the safeguard measure in order to remedy a serious injury allegedly concerned only with the imported products. In other words, the imported products cannot be made to bear the consequences of injuries that the applying Member does not consider the cause of the serious injury.

123. Moreover, the US offers no evidence to indicate that wheat starch demand outside the US is expected to rise. This is again a *petitio principii*. The conclusion that a tariff would be ineffective as a relief measure because of the co-

145 ITC report at I-26.
146 ITC report at I-26-27.
147 ITC Report at I-16 - 17.

product nature of the industry is thus based on unsupported speculation about what *could* happen rather than a reasoned analysis supported by evidence.

124. The second factor considered in rejecting a tariff is the alleged price underselling of EC wheat gluten in the US market, the evidence for which has already been shown inadequate.[148] Again, the ITC report offers no evidence to support its allegation that prices for wheat starch in the EC market allow for cross-subsidisation of wheat gluten in the US market.

This unsupported allegation is cited as evidence, along with capacity expansion in the EC, that "even a 50 *per cent ad valorem* increase in tariffs (...) would be inadequate".[149]

Moreover, the report fails to indicate, in the context of a *necessarily co-product* industry such as the wheat gluten/wheat starch industry, what would be wrong if companies exploited their wheat gluten/wheat starch combined production in order to maximise their profits. In fact, given the identical nature of the co-product wheat gluten/wheat starch industry in the US and in the rest of the world, including the EC, the ITC report fails to indicate why the US industry *itself* does not exploit that combined production.

The ITC asserts its belief that "it is possible that EC exporters would choose to absorb any tariff increase permitted under current law" .[150] Beliefs and unsupported allegations can not satisfy the requirement to provide a reasoned explanation of how the ITC reached its conclusion that a tariff would not offer adequate protection. The Panel is invited to consider the fact that, if the US position as expressed by the ITC were retained, tariff measures could always be avoided (and thus quotas always be imposed) by simply "guessing" that the exporters could "absorb" the additional costs deriving from the increased tariff. This outcome would however be contrary to text and the spirit of Article 5.1 as interpreted by the "*Korea-Dairy*" panel.

125. The third factor cited is that "a high tariff would be inequitable in that it is likely to further drive [other foreign] suppliers from the US market". This explanation for rejecting a tariff is very troubling.

The ITC clearly sees its role as protecting the market share of other importers against the EC. This is blatantly inconsistent with Article I of the GATT 1994 and Article 2.2 of the SA. The purpose of a safeguard action is solely to protect a *domestic* industry from injury. A safeguard measure has to be applied to all imports irrespective of source. Article 5.2(b) establishes the strict conditions under which a country may be discriminated against in the application of a quantitative restriction.

---

148 Section 4.4 above.

149 ITC-Report at I-26.

150 ITC report at I-26.

However, that provision only comes into play once a decision to impose a quantitative restriction has been made in full compliance with Article 5.1. Nothing in Article 5.1 permits a Member to consider, in selecting the appropriate remedy, the extent to which the remedy permits discrimination among Members or, worse, permits that Member to establish its own agenda with respect to its "preferred" importers as compared to "less preferred" importers. The ITC Report provides no reasoned explanation to demonstrate that it is necessary to discriminate against imports from the European Communities in order to prevent or remedy serious injury to the US industry.

The EC will examine this issue further in the context of the examination of the violation by the US WGS of Article I of the GATT 1994

126. Finally, assuming *arguendo* that the US WGS is at all justified, *quod non*, the United States has in any case failed to examine a fundamental element under Article 5.1, i.e. the fact that the safeguard measure must be applied "only **to the extent** necessary to remedy the serious injury" for which a causal link could be established with the increased imports of wheat gluten.

127. While reading the ITC report, the Panel will immediately notice that the ITC[151] refers itself to the fact that it "reviewed carefully the alternative causes of injury suggested by the parties and other possible causes". This review prompted the ITC into affirming that "[W]hile there is evidence that wheat gluten production decisions are affected by market conditions in the wheat starch market, we conclude that changes in the co-product markets were not *a more* important cause of serious injury *than* increased imports" (emphasis added). The ITC added further on that "[W]hile there is evidence that Midwest reduced its wheat gluten production in 1995 for reasons related at least in part to conditions in the alcohol market, Midwest's action explains, at most, *only part of the problem* faced by one producer" (emphasis added). The ITC insisted then on the fact that "(...) neither domestic competition nor increased domestic capacity was *a more important* cause of serious injury than increased imports" (emphasis added).

128. It appears evident from the above that the US authorities are instructed by their internal legislation to follow a notion of preponderance when determining the causal link for the application of a safeguard measure: the "more important" cause of injury thus determines their decision. The EC has already indicated above the ITC report's deficiencies in this respect. In any case, whatever the WTO-compatibility *as such* might be of sections 201 and following of the US Trade Act of 1974 (which is not under the scrutiny of this Panel), the application of the notion of preponderance in the determination of the causal link (under Article 4.2 SA) cannot be used *at all* to assess necessity under Article 5.1: preponderance is in fact *not* equal to (rather, it contradicts) the rule of proportionality required under Article 5.1 of the SA.

[151] ITC report at I-16 to I-18.

129. The form and the extent of the US WGS are thus clearly in breach of Article 5.1, 1st sentence, of the SA.

5.2 Article 5, paragraph 1, 2nd sentence of the SA

130. According to Article 5, paragraph 1, 2nd sentence of the SA

> "If a quantitative restriction is used, such a measure shall not reduce the quantity of imports below the level of a recent period which shall be the average of imports in the last three representative years for which statistics are available, unless clear justification is given that a different level is necessary to prevent or remedy serious injury".

131. This provision is the application of the proportionality principle examined above to the specific case of a quantitative restriction. As the ITC itself acknowledged in its report, a quantitative restriction is the most extreme and restrictive measure that a Member could take.[152] It is the most trade-disruptive measure of all possible measures. It is the least likely to develop trade relations between Members, as the reading of Article XI of GATT 1994 confirms. Thus, the proportionality rule in article 5.1, 1st sentence, needs to be read in an even more rigorous way when referred to the hypothesis covered by the 2nd sentence, i.e. the quantitative restrictions.

132. The US authorities have disregarded all obligations flowing from this provision.

133. The second sentence of Article 5.1 states that a "clear justification" is necessary to use a period other than the previous three years as the basis for establishing a quota. The provision requires *much more* than a simple allegation: the ordinary meaning of the term "clear" justification is providing a reason that is more evident, straightforward, indisputable than a simple *obiter dictum* or a vague reference to economic events.

134. In the case of the US WGS, the ITC has referred to an increase in imports[153] as sole justification for using a representative period different from the one based on the last three years for which statistics were available. This justification is not only "unclear", it is absurd since a safeguard measure can *only* be applied if imports have increased.

As a matter of logic, if an increase in imports were a "clear" justification for using a representative period other than the "last three representative years for which statistics are available", this situation would *always* apply, rendering incomprehensible the provision as it stands. If the US were correct, the WTO Contracting Parties would have drafted the text as follows: "the three most recent years *prior to the increase in imports*". However, the term "last three representa-

---

152 ITC report at I-26.
153 ITC report at I-28.

tive years for which statistics are available" is not qualified by the words "prior to the increase in imports" in Article 5.1.

Moreover, the EC recalls that the Panel report on *"EC - Bananas - Recourse to Article 21.5 by Ecuador"*[154] stated that

> "If data from a period are out of date or imports distorted because the relevant market is restricted, then using that period as a representative period cannot achieve the aim of the chapeau. Thus, under GATT practice it is necessary that the "previous representative period" for purposes of Article XIII:2(d) be the most recent period not distorted by restrictions."

Of course, there was no restriction or distortion in imports of wheat gluten from the EC, which entered entirely legitimately into the US customs territory in application of entirely valid tariff concessions made by the US as a result of the Uruguay Round.

135. It is as much a matter of ordinary meaning as a matter of logic to conclude that a Member applying a safeguard measure is required by Article 5.1, 2nd sentence, to demonstrate *something more* than an increase in imports in order to establish a "clear justification" for using a different representative period.

136. This "something more" is clearly lacking in the case of the ITC report. The ITC report states that "in the absence of anomalous circumstances that render any of [the most recent three] years unrepresentative of imports, any quantitative restriction should take into account average import levels during the most recent three years".[155] The report then concludes that a quantitative restriction based on the average of the most recent three years would not remedy the serious injury and therefore a different quantity is clearly justified. In recommending a quota based on 1993-95 import levels, the entirety of the reasoning provided is the following: "[O]ur economic analysis indicates that a quota that restores imports approximately to the relative market shares prevailing in 1993-95 would allow the domestic industry to return to reasonable operating profits".[156]

137. This statement does not demonstrate *how* the ITC arrived at its conclusion that this level of imports would allow the industry to return to profitability, it merely restates its conclusion that this is the appropriate level. It is a self-contained circular reasoning that does not provide any meaningful criterion that could assure the reader that the US indeed had a "clear" justification allowing it to depart from the rule.

---

[154] Panel Report, *European Communities – Regime for the Importation, Sale and Distribution of Bananas – Recourse to Article 21.5 of the DSU by Ecuador* ("*EC – Bananas III (Article 21.5 – Ecuador)*"), WT/DS27/RW/ECU, 12 April 1999, DSR 1999:II, 803, para. 6.39. That Panel referred expressly to the previous panel reports on "EEC - Apples from Chile" and *Japan – Measures Affecting Agricultural Products ("Japan – Agricultural Products II"*), WT/DS76/R, adopted 19 March 1999, DSR 1999:I, 315 that decided along the same lines.

[155] IbIdem.

[156] ITC report at I-28.

138. Consequently, the United States has failed to satisfy its obligation to provide a reasoned explanation of its conclusion that a "clear justification" exists for using a representative period other than the three most recent years.[157]

5.3 Article 5, paragraph 1, 3rd sentence

139. In the light of the above, it becomes inevitable also to conclude that the US has not chosen "the most suitable" measure "for the achievement of [the objectives in Article 5.1]". Thus, the US has violated also Article 5.1, 3rd sentence SA.

5.4 Article 5, paragraph 2(a)

140. According to Article 5.2 (a) of the SA

> "In cases in which a quota is allocated among supplying countries, the Member applying the restrictions may seek agreement with respect to the allocation of shares in the quota with all other members having a substantial interest in supplying the product concerned. In cases in which this method is not reasonably practicable, the member concerned shall allot to Members having a substantial interest in supplying the product shares based upon the proportions, supplied by such members during a previous representative period, of the total quantity or value of imports of the products, due account being taken of any special factors which may have affected or may be affecting the trade in the product".

5.4.1 No prior consultation and no justification

141. The provision above is taken word for word from the text of Article XIII.2 (d) of GATT 1994 which deals with the "Non discriminatory Administration of Quantitative Restrictions". The Panel report on *EC- Bananas* stated[158] the following:

> The text of Article XIII:2(d) provides that where the first "method", i.e., agreement, is not reasonably practicable, then an allocation must be made. Thus, in the absence of agreements with all Members having a substantial interest in supplying the product, the Member applying the restriction must allocate shares in accordance with the rules of Article XIII:2(d), second sentence.

---

[157] The Presidential Proclamation implementing the safeguard measure (Fed. Reg. Vol. 63, No. 106, pp. 30363-30364, 3 June 1998) and the Memorandum in support of the Proclamation (Fed. Reg. Vol. 63, No. 106, pp. 30357-30360, 3 June 1998) provide no further explanation of the US reasoning for establishing a quota based on 1993-95 imports.

[158] Para. 7.72.

142. The US opened consultations with none of the Members having a substantial interest in supplying the product concerned with a view to achieving an agreed allocation.[159]

143. Moreover, no explanation is given as to why that method was not "reasonably practicable".[160]

5.4.2 The US WGS unfairly reallocates market share between WTO Members

144. The remedy applied by the United States unfairly reallocates market share from one WTO Member to another. Paragraph 2(a) of Article 5 requires a quantitative restriction to be allocated among substantial suppliers on the basis of proportional shares in a previous representative period for which reliable statistics are available. In this case, the previous representative period was 1995-97.

145. During this period, the average import shares were as follows:

Australia	38%
Canada	10%
EC	47%
Others	5%

146. Despite having a 47 per cent share of the market in the previous representative period, the EC was allocated only a 43 per cent share of the quota. Australia, on the other hand, was allocated a share of 49 per cent, compared to its share in the previous representative period of 38 per cent.

147. The US has thus clearly and repeatedly breached Article 5.2 (a) of the SA.

5.5 Article 5, paragraph 2(b)

148. According to article 5, paragraph 2 (b)

> "A Member may depart from the provisions in subparagraph (a) provided that consultations under paragraph 3 of Article 12 are conducted under the auspices of the Committee on Safeguards provided for in paragraph 1 of Article 13 and that clear demonstration is provided to the Committee that (*i*) imports from certain Members have increased in disproportionate percentage in relation to the total increase of imports of the product concerned in the representative period, (*ii*) the reasons for the departure from the provision in subparagraph (a) are justified and (*iii*) the conditions of such departure are equitable to all suppliers of the product con-

159 ITC report at I-29.
160 Ibidem.

cerned. The duration of such measure shall not be extended beyond the initial period under paragraph 1 of Article 7 (...)".

149. The United States have failed to meet the requirements of paragraph 2(b).

150. *Firstly*, the obligatory pre-condition set out in the *incipit* to Article 5.2 (b) ("*provided that* consultations under paragraph 3 of article 12 are conducted under the auspices of the Committee on Safeguards") was not fulfilled.

151. To satisfy the requirements of paragraph 2(b), consultations should have been held with the EC, *at the initiative of the applying Member*, i.e. the US, during which the specific details of the allocation of the tariff-rate quota were made known to the EC.

The United States should have also presented its justifications for departing from the provisions of paragraph 2(a) and provided a satisfactory explanation of how the allocation of the tariff-rate quota is equitable to all suppliers. A mere notification of the safeguard action to be taken does not satisfy the consultation requirement. Article 12.3, which is referenced in paragraph 2 (b) of Article 5, specifically states that the consultations should provide for an exchange of views.

A mere notification is not the same as an exchange of views at the initiative of the applying Member.

152. *Secondly*, paragraph 2(b) of Article 5 permits a Member to deviate from the formula in paragraph 2 (a) only if three conditions, *taken together*, are met among which (*iii*) if the conditions of the departure are equitable to all suppliers of the product concerned.

153. Because of the exceptional nature of this provision, Members should be held to the strictest standard when applying this provision.

A safeguard action requires no finding of wrongdoing on the part of the exporting countries. In fact, exporting Members are penalised for engaging in precisely the activity that the rules of the WTO are designed to facilitate. The equity argument for allowing a Member taking a safeguard action to discriminate against efficient suppliers of the product concerned is not sustainable. In fact, Article 5.2 (b) (iii) refers to conditions, which are "equitable to **all** suppliers of the product concerned" (thus including the most efficient) and not just to "more equitable conditions".

154. A superficial approach to this issue might suggest that a Member whose exports of the product have increased relative to other suppliers could be said to have contributed more to the injury.

155. However, a more careful regard of the issue excludes such an apparently "obvious" (in fact, erroneous) reading. The exporting Member has exercised its *right* to increase imports in *full* legality, i.e. under non-discriminatory, valid and applicable multilateral tariff concessions. If this perspective is considered, it becomes apparent that upon the application of the special provision under Article 5.2(b), the more efficient Member does not suffer less or like any other exporter, it suffers doubly. Not only is the efficient exporting Member punished by the establishment of the safeguard measure for being more competitive than the

domestic industry, it is also punished for being more efficient than other suppliers.

156. In order to avoid unjustifiable violation of the MFN clause and in line with the second and third conditions in paragraph 2 (b), this reallocation should only be allowed where the applying Member has "clearly" demonstrated in the investigation report that it has a direct bearing with the benefits for the domestic industry.

157. Otherwise, using a safeguard action to reallocate import market shares is both unjustifiable and inequitable and thus in violation of, inter alia, Article 5 SA. In fact, it would be extraordinary to provide the importing Member, in the context of an emergency action to protect its own domestic industry, with the unrelated power to organise the trade relations between other Members.

158. In the current case, the United States has provided no justification for reallocating market shares from the EC suppliers to the Australian suppliers, nor has there been any attempt to demonstrate how such a reallocation of market share is equitable to all suppliers of the product concerned. The reallocation is patently inequitable because it discriminates against the EC in favour of Australia.

The method for allocation of the tariff-rate quota is all the more suspect because one of the four companies comprising the US industry is owned by the same Australian company that owns two of the Australian wheat gluten producers who export to the United States.[161] While an important US producer has a clear interest in this reallocation, this interest is not protected, and cannot be protected, by making use (in fact, abuse) of Article XIX GATT or the SA.

159. It is thus more than justified to assert that the US authorities discriminated in favour of an Australian wheat gluten producer (in its capacity of owner of a US producer) when favouring the wheat gluten sources where that company has significant economic interests. This, of course, has nothing to do with the protection of the domestic industry from serious injury caused by increased imports.

160. The United States has failed to provide a justification for reallocating market share other than the increase in imports. Nor is any evidence provided that the allocation is equitable to all suppliers.[162] Absent a clear demonstration of benefit to the domestic wheat gluten industry from the reallocation of market share from the EC to Australia, the panel should find that the United States has failed to meet the burden imposed by Article 5.2 (b) for deviating from the normal process of allocating tariff-rate quotas.

[161] ITC report at II-8.
[162] ITC report at I-29.

6. THE US WGS IS IN BREACH OF ARTICLES 8 AND 12 OF THE SA

161. Article 12 of the SA provides mainly for procedural rules to be followed during the process of investigation and application of a safeguard measure. Moreover, it obliges the Member concerned to a transparent conduct vis-à-vis not only the Members whose exports are targeted by the on-going procedure but also the entire Membership of the WTO. Finally, by imposing a procedure in order to consult the targeted Members, the combination of Articles 12 and 8 provide for the legal framework for re-establishing the balance of concessions that is breached by the emergency action put in place through the safeguard measure.

162. As is apparent, these rules are central in the pursuance of the objectives set out in the Preambles to the SA, in particular "to re-establish multilateral control over safeguards", "eliminate measures that escape such control" and "enhance rather than limit competition in international markets".

6.1 Immediate notification and prior consultation

163. According to Article 12.1

> "A Member shall *immediately* notify the Committee on safeguards upon (...)
>
> (a) initiating an investigatory process relating to serious injury (...)
>
> (b) making a finding of serious injury (...) and
>
> (c) taking a decision to apply or extend a safeguard measure". (emphasis added)

164. According to Article 12.2,

> "(...) the Member *proposing* to apply a safeguard measure shall provide (...) all pertinent information, which shall include evidence of serious injury or threat thereof caused by increased imports, precise description of the product involved and the *proposed* measure, proposed date of introduction, expected duration and timetable for progressive liberalisation. (...) The Council for Trade in Goods or the Committee on Safeguards may request such additional information as they may consider necessary from the Member *proposing* to apply (...) the measure" (emphasis added).

165. Paragraph 3 of Article 12, which incorporates Article 8.1 by reference, provides further clarification that the measure should be notified immediately when it is proposed, not after it has been put into place.

166. The United States failed to notify each and every step in Article 12.1 SA in a timely manner. It initiated the investigatory process on 1 October 1997, but notified such action to the Committee on Safeguards only on 21 October 1997.[163] It then made findings of serious injury on 15 January 1998, but notified the WTO only on 11 February 1998.[164] Finally, it implemented the measure on 1 June 1998, but did not notify the Committee on Safeguards until 4 June 1998.[165]

167. However, according to the plain text and meaning of Article 12 of the SA, all these procedural steps, findings and decision had to have been made at a date that would have allowed the Committee on Safeguards and, possibly, the Council for Trade in Goods to request additional information and hold a meaningful discussion in a multilateral forum.

168. In particular, the US notifications of the findings of serious injury and of the decision were effected after the findings had been made and the measure was enacted. The plain language of paragraph 2 makes clear that the *proposed* measure has to be notified. Paragraph 2 refers to "the Member *proposing* to apply or extend a safeguard measure," the "*proposed* measure," and the "*proposed* date of introduction." Once a measure has been implemented, it is no longer a proposed measure, but an actual measure and the objective of allowing for an opportunity to request additional information as contemplated in the last sentence of paragraph 2 has been thwarted.

169. Moreover, the panel in *Korea - Dairy* supported these views:

> "Article 12.3 requires that the notifying Member provide an adequate opportunity for 'prior consultations' with interested Members, that is, consultations prior to the actual application of the measure".[166]

It then recognised with respect to a measure notified after its entry into force:

> " [T]his notification can only be viewed as a notification of the final decision taken since it was notified and circulated only after the final decision was put into force; this notification cannot be taken into account for the purpose of assessing whether Korea complied with its obligation to notify its *proposed* measure since this notification took place after the consultations, and therefore cannot remedy the flaws in the previous notification"[167].(emphasis added)

170. The US thus clearly violated Article 12 SA by systematically not notifying timely the Committee on Safeguards under that provision.

---

[163] G/SG/N/8/USA/2.

[164] G/SG/N/8/USA/2.

[165] G/SG/N/10/USA/2 and G/SG/N/11/USA/2.

[166] *Korea - Dairy, supra*, footnote 2, para. 7.119.

[167] *Korea - Dairy, supra*, footnote 2, footnote 481.

6.2 Inadequate consultations

171. A Member proposing to a apply a safeguard measure is required by Article 8.1 to

> "endeavour to maintain a substantially equivalent level of concessions".

172. This provision is reinforced by Article 12, and in particular paragraph 3 that provides that a Member proposing a safeguard measure

> "*shall* provide" adequate opportunity for "reaching an understanding on ways to achieve the objective set out in paragraph 1 of Article 8."

173. The obligation on Members to engage in meaningful consultations and negotiations prior to altering the balance of negotiated concessions, even temporarily, is fundamental to the GATT.[168] For example, Article XXVIII.3 explicitly provides for such a *prior* procedure. This fundamental rule is, if possible, even more central to the system of the WTO: the rejection by the WTO Members of any sort of unilateralism in favour of multilateral, organised, non-discriminatory and transparent rules rests at the source of this consistent approach.

174. Consequently, when, as in the case of safeguard measures taken consistently with the provisions of the SA, a Member is given the right to unilaterally alter the balance of concessions, the burden on the Member to engage in transparent, timely and meaningful consultations and negotiations is not reduced, it is indeed heightened. Meaningful consultations and negotiations are a necessary counterbalance to unilateral action for affected Members.

175. The question may arise as to how a substantially equivalent level of concessions and other obligations can be maintained given conditions on the right to immediately withdraw concessions in the SA. This is not a question the panel needs to answer. It is precisely the question to be addressed in consultations and negotiations between the Members. However, it is the duty of this Panel to clarify and apply the existing provisions under the covered agreements[169], including Articles 12 and 8 of the SA. A rigorous interpretation of these rules must be made if a meaningful balance of rights and obligations under the WTO, in particular the GATT Articles I, II, XI, XIII and XXVIII and the SA, is maintained.

176. The process of altering the balance of negotiated concessions is well defined in Article XXVIII of the GATT. The provisions of Article 8 of the Agreement mirror those of Article XXVIII. This process envisions the withdrawal of substantially equivalent concessions as the last step in the process.

177. By imposing certain specific conditions on the right of an affected Member to withdraw substantially equivalent concessions, paragraph 3 of Article 8 is addressing only the last step of the process. It does not relieve Members from the

---

[168] Panel on Newsprint.

[169] Article 3.2 of the DSU.

obligation to make every effort to maintain a substantially equivalent level of concessions when imposing a measure under the Safeguards Agreement. An affected Member would be fully within its rights to request temporary concessions on other products to offset the concessions impaired by the safeguard measure.

178. The United States, by failing to offer a meaningful opportunity, indeed any opportunity at all, for consultations and negotiations, has denied the EC its rights under the SA and therefore violated Articles 8 and 12.3 SA.

7. THE US WGS IS IN BREACH OF ARTICLE I OF GATT 1994

179. Article I of the GATT provides that

> "with respect to all rules and formalities in connection with importation and exportation any advantage, favour, privilege or immunity granted by any WTO Member to any other country shall be accorded immediately to the like product originating in all other WTO Members".

180. By applying the US WGS, the US is treating the EC in a flagrantly discriminatory manner. In the way it divides up the quota, it consciously grants an advantage to Australia, consisting of the right to maintain exports to the US at virtually the same level as immediately previously. The EC refers to the facts already discussed in the context of chapter 5 above. Australia's exports increased continuously in the last three years of the investigative period, by almost 21 per cent.[170] In other words, if there really was an import surge causing serious injury, *quod non*, Australia contributed to that substantially. In fact, the ITC did include Australian imports in all its findings on increased imports, serious injury and causation. It appears from the ITC report that for instance in 1996, in which according to the ITC there was such a sharp increase in the ratio of imports to consumption[171], Australian imports constituted practically the same share of US consumption as imports from the EC.[172]

181. However, by taking average import shares in the period June 1993-June 1995 as a basis for dividing up the quota, the US managed to allow Australia to maintain its exports at 1997 levels, their highest level during the whole period of investigation[173] Moreover, since the country quotas are increased by 6 per cent each year, Australia could even start increasing its exports even further as from the second year of the quota.

---

170 ITC report at II-12.

171 ITC report at I-16.

172 ITC report at II-25, in the year ending June 1996, imports from Australia constituted 23.4 per cent of US apparent consumption in terms of quantity and 21.7 per cent in terms of value, against respectively 26.5 per cent and 24.9 per cent for imports from the EC.

173 Australia exported 62.496 million pounds in the year ending June 1997 (ITC report at II-12). Its quota in the first crop year thereafter was 62.425 million pounds, so practically the same.

182. In contrast, the way the US calculated the country quotas ensured that the EC's exports were reduced by 16,816 t, a 41 per cent reduction. The EC reminds the Panel that US producer Manildra is the subsidiary company of an Australian producer of wheat gluten, which exports to the US. Both the discriminatory effect and intent of the US WGS are therefore clear. The US WGS constitutes a flagrant violation of Article I of the GATT.

8. CONCLUSIONS

183. In light of the above, the EC respectfully requests the Panel to find that the US by imposing the US WGS has breached Articles I and XIX of the GATT 1994 and Articles 2, 4, 5, 8 and 12 of the Agreement on Safeguards.

LIST OF EC EXHIBITS

Exhibit EC 1:	**ITC Report March 1998**
Exhibit EC 2:	**Presidential Proclamation 30 May 1998**
Exhibit EC 3:	**Image of wheat gluten**
Exhibit EC 4:	**Wheat gluten/starch production process**
Exhibit EC 5:	**Wheat kernel**
Exhibit EC 6:	**Wheat gluten in bakery**
Exhibit EC 7:	**Other wheat gluten applications**
Exhibit EC 8:	**Wheat process – effluent treatment**
Exhibit EC 9:	**US schedule of concessions**
Exhibit EC 10:	**Analysis of factors affecting US price of wheat gluten**
Exhibit EC 11:	**US wheat starch prices**
Exhibit EC 12:	**Statistics on wheat prices**
Exhibit EC 13:	**Statistics on corn prices**
Exhibit EC 14:	**US ethanol production**
Exhibit EC 15:	**Statistics on US wheat imports from Canada**

ATTACHMENT 1-2

ORAL STATEMENT OF THE EUROPEAN COMMUNITY
(20 December 1999)

Mr. Chairman, distinguished Members of the Panel,

1. This dispute settlement procedure is about drawing a safe and sound line between:

- what is a genuine emergency action by a Member in case of demonstrated serious injury attributable to increased imports and
- what are nothing else than disguised attempts to unilaterally withdraw concessions granted during the multilateral tariff negotiations without undertaking an Article XXVIII GATT procedure and without providing adequate compensation.

The US safeguard measure under scrutiny in this dispute settlement procedure belongs, in our view, to this second category.

Exceptional nature of the safeguard instrument

2. Before entering into the detail of this case, it is important to recall the exceptional nature of the safeguard instrument.

The fact that imports may increase is the *expected* effect of the entirely legitimate use of a *right* provided for under the covered agreements, and in particular Articles I and II of the GATT. The market access rights are negotiated during the multilateral tariff negotiations and constitute the core of the multilateral trading system.

As the Appellate Body has indicated in its very recent report on *Korea - Dairy* (paragraph 87),

> "We should not lose sight of the fact that taking safeguard action results in restrictions on imports arising from "fair" trade. The application of a safeguard measure does not depend upon "unfair" trade actions, as is the case with anti-dumping or countervailing measures".

3. Thus, the possibility that is provided to Members to provide relief to their domestic industry in case of unforeseen developments provoking a proven urgency and economic distress to domestic industry *must* be maintained in balance with the need to preserve and protect the equivalent level of negotiated concessions that lies at the heart of the multilateral trading system (see in the same line of reasoning the AB report on *Argentina - Footwear* at paragraph 93).

4. It is in this specific framework that the Panel on *Argentina-Footwear*[1] has correctly stated that " in order to give this object and purpose [of the Safeguards Agreement] meaning, a strict interpretation and implementation of the disciplines provided for in the Safeguard Agreement is needed. Otherwise, the reinforcement of disciplines, re-establishment of multilateral control and elimination of so-called "grey-area" measures could not be achieved (...)".

Standard of review and the role of this Panel

5. The role of the Panel when examining the compatibility of safeguard measures with the covered agreements is to determine whether the Member's authorities fully and objectively considered the evidence before it, including any evidence that detracts from an affirmative determination of increased imports, serious injury or causation[2]. The Panel should also verify the adequacy of the Member's reasoning by reviewing whether the findings made and conclusions reached are consistent with the evidence.[3]

6. As the Appellate Body confirmed in its very recent report on *Argentina - Footwear* (at paragraph 118), Article 11 of the DSU contains the guiding principles for Panels when pursuing such an examination in substance. This provision clarifies that

> "(...) a panel should make an objective assessment of the matter before it, including an objective assessment of the facts of the case and the applicability of and conformity with the relevant covered agreements (...)".

7. This is the main feature that distinguishes the exercise of a discretionary power subject to multilateral review from arbitrariness. It sets the dividing line between a thorough examination by a panel in accordance with Article 11 of the DSU and a travesty of justice.

8. In this context, it is worth noting that the same Appellate Body report (see paragraph 117) has clearly rejected any parallelism in the standard of review between this case and some obsolete previous cases under the Tokyo Round Agreements, like the *US - Salmon* case. However, it is exactly on this latter case that the US arguments on the standard of review are based (see paragraph 61 of the US first written submission).

9. The EC submits that the primary burden of proof that the conditions set out in Article XIX GATT and the SA have been fulfilled rests of course on the Member adopting the safeguard measure, since it is *that* Member that is bound to

1 Para. 8.88.

2 Panel Report, *Korea - Definitive Safeguard Measure on Imports of Certain Dairy Products* ("*Korea –Dairy Safeguard*"), WT/DS98/R and Corr. 1, adopted 12 January 2000, DSR 2000:I, 49, para. 7.30.

3 Panel Report, *Argentina - Safeguard Measures on Imports of Footwear* ("*Argentina - Footwear Safeguard*"), WT/DS121/R, adopted 12 January 2000, DSR 2000:II, 575, para 8.124.

show in detail in its report that it has followed the conditions required for applying the *exceptional* trade defence instrument under Article XIX GATT and the SA.

10. The EC on its side has demonstrated *prima facie* that an objective assessment of the facts shows

- that the US administration failed to consider all the evidence, as it should, and
- that the conclusions drawn from the partial evidence that was considered were either inadequate or incorrect because they were based on a deficient, or biased or subjective presentation of the facts.

Moreover, the EC has also demonstrated *prima facie* that the measure taken was disproportionate and was adopted in breach of substantive and procedural rules under the SA.

11. The United States attempts to confuse the important issue of the standard of review of this Panel by advancing an over-restrictive interpretation of your powers and of your terms of reference. For example, in paragraph 59 of its first written submission, the US would make you believe that verifying the adequacy of the USITC reasoning by assessing whether its findings are consistent with the evidence provided to the authority during the investigation or publicly available and entirely accessible to it, as the EC suggests, would engage you in a *de novo* review of the evidence.

12. The EC firmly disagrees with this approach.

> In our view, a *de novo* review can be defined as re-assessing the facts and drawing conclusions therefrom as if the Panel would substitute itself to the competent authorities. This would happen if this Panel engaged itself in re-doing the Member's procedure, thus getting to "its" decision on the appropriateness to adopt "that" or "another" safeguard measure. This is certainly not what the EC asks you to do.

13. What the EC requests this Panel to do is to examine whether the US authorities, in their investigation report and in the legal act applying the safeguard measure, *have complied with the rules* under Article XIX GATT and the SA. As the Appellate Body has indicated in its *Argentina - Footwear* report (paragraph 95)

> "[A]s such, safeguard measures may be applied only when [compliance with] *all* the provisions of the *Agreement on Safeguards* and Article XIX of the GATT 1994 are clearly demonstrated."

14. In order to achieve that result, the Panel is thus required to examine the following issues

- Have the US authorities demonstrated, as they should, that the conditions under Article 2 SA and Article XIX GATT 1994 have been fulfilled? The EC submits that they have not.

- Have the US authorities considered, as they should, "*all* pertinent issues of fact and law" (Article 3.1 SA) including "*all* relevant factors of an *objective* and *quantifiable* nature *having a bearing* on the situation of that industry" (Article 4.2 (a) SA)? The EC submits that they have not.
- Have the US authorities presented, as they should, their findings, conclusions and determinations in a "reasoned" (i.e. rational, non contradictory and clear) way (Article 3.1 DSU), based on "objective evidence" (i.e. based on criteria that are not biased by subjective, political or unrelated aims) (Article 4.2 (b) SA)? The EC submits that they have not.
- Have the US authorities established, as they should, the "*existence* (i.e. a positive and irrefutable evidence of its reality) of the causal link between increased imports of the product concerned and serious injury" (Article 4.2 (b) SA)? The EC submits that they have not.
- Have the US authorities applied the safeguard measure, as they should, "*only to the extent necessary*" (i.e. proportionate or commensurate to) to prevent or remedy serious injury and to facilitate adjustment (Article 5.1 SA)? Have the US authorities provided "a clear justification" (i.e. a detailed objective and unbiased explanation) when deciding to apply quantitative restrictions and when choosing a period different from the last three representative years for which statistics are available? Moreover, Have the US authorities fulfilled the other substantive and procedural obligations under Article 5.2 of the SA and under Article I of GATT 1994? The EC submits that they have not.
- Have the US authorities complied with the procedural obligations under Articles 8 and 12 of the SA? The EC submits that they have not.

15. For a full examination of the matter, the EC submits also that the Panel should not stop on the surface of these issues by taking for granted the text of the investigation report, as the US would have it. Rather, it must concentrate on the *substance* of the evidence that actually *is* in the report or *should have been* in the report since it was either considered during the investigation procedure or should have been considered as pertinent evidence that was *publicly* available.

16. Let me provide you with a telling example. The US claims in paragraph 150 of its first submission, "although wheat price data were submitted to the ITC, they were not presented on a monthly basis". Implying that this Panel should not consider the effect of the wheat price on the US market for this reason, is plainly absurd.

The US attempts to dismiss the increase in wheat prices as an unsubstantial allegation by the EC when in fact the increase is indisputably documented by official US statistics (Exhibit EC-12, concerning statistics on wheat price which are regularly published since the 1950s, is an *official document of the US government* (USDA)). Therefore, as a matter of fact, these publicly available statistics are *very pertinent* evidence that the ITC should have considered in its investigation but did not.

17. To continue with another telling example, the Panel should not be satisfied by "a reasonable explanation of the conclusions reached" (as the US insists in paragraph 117 of its first submission). The "reasonable explanation" comes from the Member adopting the safeguard measure, i.e. the interested Member. Therefore, the "reasonability" test can only be passed if the Panel, as neutral judge of the case in a multilateral dispute settlement procedure, can form its *own* judgement on whether the elements provided in the report or in the decision of the Member applying the safeguard measure can convince it that what was decided is *indeed* reasonable.

18. The EC submits that without a full picture, only deference or superficiality is possible.

In order to illustrate this point, Mr. Chairman, allow me to make a final example, based on common sense.

19. Let's imagine that today is a bright mid-summer day after a night of heavy thunderstorms. Let's also imagine that looking from your window you could see children playing wearing rubber boots (to protect themselves from the humidity of the wet grass), that in the shadow the ground is drenched and that some people walk around protecting themselves from the strong mid-summer sun with an umbrella.

If a report was based on the evidence that the grass is wet and the ground is drenched, children wear rubber boots and some people stroll around with their umbrellas, that report stating that it is a rainy day could seem at first sight reasonable. But it would not be correct, since the objective, unbiased, clear reality is that it is a sunny summer day. However, if you were to follow the over-restrictive standard of review suggested by the US you should accept by deference to the report that it is a rainy day and the EC would thus be prevented from showing that the report failed to consider the reality, i.e. that it is a sunny day, and failed also to draw the necessary conclusions from that reality.

Well, Mr. Chairman, this outcome would be the opposite of what the WTO Members negotiated and decided upon when they adopted the DSU *and* the SA.

20. As we have seen, the function of this Panel (under Article 11 of the DSU) is to make an objective assessment of the matter before it. The US itself has supported recently the EC's present views in another panel procedure:

> "(...) nothing in the text of GATT or any other part of the WTO Agreement supported the notion that measures could be excluded from dispute settlement merely because a Member *made an argument* about the justification of a measure. Quite the reverse: (...) If a Member could prevent a panel from issuing rulings merely by

making arguments about its measures, then dispute settlement would grind to a halt".[4]

We could not agree more.

Mr. Chairman, distinguished Members of the Panel,

21. We will now present in some detail the major violations committed by the US when adopting its safeguard measure on wheat gluten. It is *not* our intention to repeat each and every argument that was already analysed in the EC's first written submission but it is appropriate to already respond to some incorrect statements made by the US in its first written submission. The EC is of course ready to answer any question or clarify further any issue you may deem appropriate.

22. With your agreement, it is our intention to proceed now as follows: I will start with the examination of the violation by the US of Article XIX of GATT 1994. Then, my colleague Mr. Van Vliet will address the issues related to the findings and determinations of the US authorities concerning increased imports, serious injury, the causal link and the violation of the MFN principle. I will conclude the EC's statement by addressing the EC's claims concerning the violation by the US of Articles 5, 12 and 8 of the SA.

Violation of Article XIX of GATT 1994: "Unforeseen developments"

23. According to the Appellate Body report on Korea - Dairy at paragraph 77,

> " (...) any safeguard measure imposed after the entry into force of the *WTO Agreement* must comply with the provisions of *both* the *Agreement on Safeguards* and Article XIX of the GATT 1994."

The Appellate Body has therefore definitively rejected the interpretation suggested by the US in its defence. It has also stated that

> "(...) we believe that the clause in Article XIX:1(a) – "as a result of unforeseen developments and of the effect of the obligations incurred by a Member under this Agreement, including tariff concessions ..." – must have meaning. (paragraph 82)".
>
> (...) [I]t seems to us that the ordinary meaning of the phrase "as a result of unforeseen developments" *requires that the developments which led to a product being imported in such increased quantities and under such conditions as to cause or threaten to cause serious injury to domestic producers must have been "unexpected"* (paragraph 84). (...) "
>
> "Although we do not view the first clause in Article XIX:1(a) as establishing independent *conditions* for the application of a safe-

[4]Panel Report, *Turkey – Restrictions on Imports of Textiles and Clothing Products* ("*Turkey - Textiles*"), WT/DS34/R, adopted 19 November 1999, DSR 1999:VI, 2363, para. 7.117.

guard measure, additional to the *conditions* set forth in the second clause of that paragraph, we do believe that the first clause describes certain *circumstances which must be demonstrated as a matter of fact in order for a safeguard measure to be applied consistently with the provisions of Article XIX of the GATT 1994*" (paragraph 85).

24. As the Appellate Body has recognised, the very nature of a safeguard measure is to tackle an urgent situation, which was not expected. Thus, a WTO Member wishing to impose a safeguard measure must prove that an "unforeseen development" was the cause, or at least the determining cause, of the increased imports.

As was indicated in the EC's first written submission, the United States has breached Article XIX.1 (a). The US authorities have not "demonstrated" as a matter of fact that any unexpected development had occurred which led to increased quantities and under such conditions as to cause serious injury to domestic producers.

25. In addition, in the present case there are no unforeseen, i.e. unexpected, developments described in the record of the investigation, which could have led to any increased imports causing serious injury. Furthermore, there is no indication that such unforeseen circumstances were in fact present at all. The EC reserves the right to come back in more detail, if need be, on this issue in its second written submission.

I will now pass the floor to Mr. Van Vliet.

26. Mr. Chairman, as a point of methodology for this presentation, you should be aware that when reference is made to marketing years it means a twelve months period ending 30 June of the year concerned.

Violation of Article 2 and 4 of the SA. unverifiable data

27. The EC believes it appropriate to continue its presentation with the examination of a US violation of a more general nature having a great impact on the entire procedure.

In the ITC report, in almost all cases where data, which are essential for determining whether a safeguard measure can be taken, are discussed, the reader is confronted to typing symbols " *** " that mean that those data are omitted from the text.

28. Under Article 4.2 (c) of the SA, the US is obliged to "publish" "a detailed analysis of the case under investigation as well as a demonstration of the relevance of the factors concerned".

Article 3.1 of the SA imposes moreover that "the competent authorities shall publish a report setting forth their findings and reasoned conclusions reached on all pertinent issues of fact and law".

As the Appellate Body in its *Argentina - Footwear* report has indicated, Article 4 of the SA is violated when a report does not show that the competent authorities "had considered all the relevant facts and adequately explained how the facts supported the determinations that were made."[5]

Article 3.2 of the SA certainly allows that information, which *truly* must be kept confidential, is not included in the public version of the report of a safeguard investigation without permission by the company concerned. However, the ITC report oversteps this provision by not even providing *aggregate* data.

29. The EC submits that the US refusal to disclose pertinent information even in an aggregate form constitutes a very serious violation of the US WTO obligations for the following reasons:

- Transparency vis-à-vis the Member whose exports suffer from the implementation of the safeguard measure is not ensured.
- Transparency vis-à-vis the Membership of the WTO in general is also not ensured.
- The Panel is prevented from performing its task under Article 11 of the DSU, namely to make an objective assessment of all facts relevant in this dispute.
- Finally, the procedural obligations under Article 3 and 4 of the SA are not respected.

30. The US has explicitly recognised in its first written submission that it has "misapplied" the provisions of Articles 3 and 4 of the SA (see paragraph 158). As the Appellate Body has clarified in its report on *Korea- Dairy* (paragraph 98) when addressing a similar issue

> "We agree with the Panel that this "clear justification" has to be given by a Member applying a safeguard measure *at the time of the decision, in its recommendations or determinations on the application of the safeguard measure*" (original emphasis).

31. Contrary to this indication from the AB, the US aims at retro-actively "healing " its violation of the relevant provisions of the SA by submitting, in Exhibit 10 to its submission, a revised version of parts of the ITC report containing data which it had earlier on withheld from the public version of the ITC report.

32. In the light of this established interpretation, the Panel should reject this belated attempt. Otherwise Articles 3 and 4 of the SA would become entirely useless. Their violation cannot be retrospectively "healed".

33. The Panel should therefore find that the US itself admits that by removing certain information from the public version of the ITC-report, it has failed to live up to its obligations under Articles 3 and 4 of the SA.

---

[5] Para. 121.

Violation of Article XIX GATT 1994 and 2 of the SA: alleged underselling

34. According to Art. XIX GATT 1994 and 2 SA increased imports can justify the adoption of a safeguard measure only if they take place "*under such conditions* as to cause or threaten to cause serious injury" (emphasis supplied).

35. The only factor which the ITC mentions in this respect is that prices were allegedly driven down during 1996 and 1997 by "relatively low-priced imports".

36. The AB has confirmed the EC's position that the fact that a product is imported "under such conditions" as to cause serious injury or threat thereof, is one of the *conditions* whose presence *must* objectively be demonstrated in order to be able to apply a safeguard measure[6]. An investigating authority *must* look at the "conditions of competition" between imports and domestic products, one of them being price[7]. The US authorities did not fulfil such obligation. The US admits that fact, by trying to convince you that it is not necessary for you to examine this point.

37. Thus, the US cannot contest now that it failed to fulfil such condition and thus violated Article 2 and 4 of the SA.

38. Turning to the substance with regard to prices, the EC has explained in detail in its 1st written submission why the prices do not show that imports took place "under such conditions as to cause" serious injury to the US industry.[8]

The ITC report indicates[9] that "the US producers selling prices (...) of vital wheat gluten generally *rose from July – September 1992 through January-March 1994*, and reached their peak (...) during this latter quarter, *prices then fell through April – June 1995*". The Exhibit EC-10, figure 4, shows that this drop in prices was by far the most significant during the POI. However, during the period 1993 to 1995 imports remained stable. Thus, the findings of the ITC confirm that there cannot be any significant correlation between price levels of vital wheat gluten on the US market and the level of imports.

Slide No. 1

is taken from the ITC report itself. It shows that the prices of EC imports at the end of the POI were practically the same at they were at the beginning of the POI.

---

6 Appellate Body Report, *Korea - Definitive Safeguard Measure on Imports of Certain Dairy Products* ("*Korea -Dairy Safeguard*"), WT/DS98/AB/R, adopted 12 January 2000, DSR 2000:I, 3, para. 100.

7 Appellate Body Report, *Argentina - Safeguard Measures on Imports of Footwear* ("*Argentina - Footwear Safeguard*"), WT/DS121/AB/R, adopted 12 January 2000, DSR 2000:I, 515, para. 145.

8 See in particular point 4.6.2 and 4.6.3.1 of EC's 1st written submission.

9 II-32.

39. The US evidently cannot contest these plain facts now. In the light of this indisputable evidence the ITC could not reasonably have reached the conclusion that the price level of imports had a significant impact on US domestic prices.

40. The US indirectly recognises this by belatedly turning to an unpublished *revised* version of the ITC report to which we referred before.

41. The EC has just recalled that the AB has taken position on this issue in its recent *Korea – Dairy* report (paragraph 98), flatly rejecting any such attempt. The ITC report itself, at the time, should have provided the relevant information. This failure cannot be "healed" retrospectively. This is established WTO case law.[10]

42. In any event, these inadmissible data do not contradict the established fact that there is no significant correlation between the prices of wheat gluten on the US market and the level of imports.

Violation of articles 2 and 4 of the SA: Serious injury

43. The US determination that serious injury occurred does not meet the standards of Articles XIX of GATT 1994 and the SA. The EC has shown that the US did not adequately investigate all relevant factors and/or did not adequately explain how the facts supported the determinations that were made.

Thus, it is sufficient to recall here only certain points that were developed in our first written submission.

Market shares

44. Under Article 4.2 (a) of the SA, a WTO Member, before taking a safeguard measure, must investigate the share of the domestic market taken by increased imports. The US consumption during the period 1995 to 1997 went up strongly. In fact, consumption rose by 18 per cent during the Period Of Investigation (POI). To no surprise, imports followed this trend. Therefore, the increase of imports in terms of domestic market share cannot support a finding of injury, let alone serious injury.

Slide No. 2

illustrates that the market share taken by imports during the period concerned does not reveal injury nor shows any emergency situation.

45. A number of other factors make clear that the US domestic industry was not suffering any serious injury.

---

[10] See also Panel report, *Korea Dairy*, *supra*, footnote 2, para. 7.24, and Panel Report *United States – Measure Affecting Imports of Woven Wool Shirts and Blouses from India* ("*US – Woven Wool Shirts*"), WT/DS33/R, adopted 23 May 1997, DSR 1997:I, 343, para. 6.8.

Sales (Domestic sales by the US industry)

46. Sales by US industry (what the US calls "domestic shipments ") were up in 1997 compared to 1996. If a larger picture is taken, even though there were variations in the domestic sales by the US industry, the trend has remained relatively steady.[11]

Production (production by the US industry)

47. Exactly the same goes for US *production*. US production was up in 1997 compared to 1996[12]. If a larger picture is taken, even though there were variations in the production of the US industry, the trend has remained relatively steady.[13]

Inventories

48. Also developments with respect to US producers' inventories were satisfactory. These were strongly going down in 1996 and 1997.

Slide No. 3

illustrates this.

It also shows, by the way, that inventories went up before imports went up, so that the increase in inventories cannot possibly have been caused by imports. In fact, this factor is consistent with the data concerning sales and production.

49. On the basis of these consistent data the investigating authorities could not reasonably conclude that the US industry was suffering serious injury.

Mr. Chairman, the data above illustrate in a very clear way a major point of principle. As the Appellate Body has recalled, safeguards are *emergency* measures. The condition of the US industry improved in the recent period preceding the adoption of the safeguard measure. Therefore, there was no "emergency" warranting safeguards.

Profit and losses

50. This brings us to another factor mentioned in Article 4.2 of the SA, which the US authorities did not properly explain in their report.

51. The finding of the ITC that profitability had gone down was based on allocation of profits by the US producers between the co-products wheat gluten and wheat starch and derived by-products.

---

[11] ITC Report at II-16.

[12] ITC Report at II-15.

[13] ITC Report at II-15.

Obviously, the manner in which financial factors such as costs and revenues are allocated has a tremendous impact on the profitability of the individual segments within that industry. This is certainly the case here, given that the wheat gluten/wheat starch industry relies by necessity on a single raw material input (wheat or wheat flour[14]) and utilises a single production line that results in wheat gluten, wheat starch, and effluents suitable for producing e.g. alcohol.

In such a situation, any allocation of profitability among the output products is arbitrary if no objective and verifiable criteria are used.

52. Contrary to the US obligations under the SA, the ITC report provides no explanation whatsoever regarding what methodology was used by the ITC in this respect. The impression is given that the cost allocation between co- and by-products of the wheat gluten production suggested by the plaintiffs was accepted by the ITC with no further examination. In fact, the ITC simply states that it has reviewed that methodology, and finds it "appropriate". What the methodology was, or why it was deemed appropriate by the ITC remains utterly unclear.

53. Any profitability assessment in the report that does not demonstrate *objectively* (i.e. on the basis of a reasoned explanation) how the cost allocation is made is economically arbitrary. It can therefore never be used to support allegations of injury to the industry concerned.

54. The ITC report failed exactly in this way to provide any *objective* evidence of injury. Therefore, the ITC's findings on serious injury based on this factor are completely unjustified.

Import by US producers

55. The US has not contested that large parts of imports of wheat gluten from Australia were attributable to a particular company, Manildra, which, because of the company structure, could decide entirely freely whether to produce wheat gluten in Australia and bring it over to the US, or to produce it in the US, depending on the market situation.

A considered deliberate policy of importation by a domestic company, which corresponds to its business strategy optimising profits cannot, by definition, be considered an injury, let alone a serious injury in order to justify a safeguard measure.

56. Concluding on injury, Mr. Chairman, despite the number of pages devoted to the subject by the ITC, its report contains no genuine in-depth investigation on whether the US domestic industry was *really* suffering serious injury, as defined by the SA ("significant overall impairment in the position of the domestic industry"). Rather, well known facts and publicly available official data that the ITC

[14] At least one of the major US producers concerned purchases wheat flour as the raw material rather than wheat grain. This means it loses the margin reserved to the miller, thus squeezing profits further. This fact was not taken into account by the ITC.

has either superficially reviewed or failed to review point exactly to the opposite direction. The ITC did not adequately investigate and consequently show that US industry was suffering a serious injury as defined under the SA.

Violation of Articles 2 and 4: Causation

57. The EC has demonstrated that there was no sharp increase in the market share taken by imports and no serious injury that could justify the application of a safeguard measure in this case. As the Appellate Body recalled in its report on *Argentina – Footwear* (paragraph 145)

> "it would be difficult indeed to demonstrate a 'causal link' between 'increased imports' that did not occur and 'serious injury' that did not exist".

Thus, the EC will examine the following deficiencies in the US findings and determinations in case the Panel were to reject the EC's claims on those above-mentioned points.

58. The EC submits that the US findings and determinations on causality have no rational justification. Indeed, as our presentation will show now, the main factors having a determinant effect on the position of the wheat gluten domestic industry on the US market were either not examined at all or not objectively assessed.

Inherent competitive disadvantage of US wheat processors in their competition with US corn processors

59. The EC would like to recall a particular feature of the production process of wheat gluten. It is not physically possible to produce wheat gluten without at the same time producing, in much bigger quantities (approximately 5 times), its necessary co-product, wheat starch.

60. On its side, starch and its derived products are interchangeable, whether made from wheat or corn and are used for most of the same purposes. Wheat starch, the necessary co-product of wheat gluten, has therefore to face fierce competition on the US market from corn starch. In such an economic situation, it is stating the obvious to say that the economic effects of that competition have necessarily a direct and very significant impact on the profitability of wheat gluten operations on the US market.

61. It is also a fact that on the US domestic market, the US wheat starch/gluten industry is in an inherent competitive *disadvantage* in comparison with corn millers and this for the following main reasons:

- on the US market, the price of wheat is up to 34 per cent higher than the price of corn. The differential was particularly significant in 1997.

Slide No. 4

- Moreover, the yield of starch per tonne of wheat is much lower than that of corn.

Slide No. 5

This slide also shows that the combined effect of these factors is that the US wheat starch/wheat gluten producers face a massive 45 per cent competitive disadvantage as compared with corn starch producers. The first column on the left-hand side shows how much more starch can be produced from a tonne of corn than from a tonne of wheat. The middle column shows how much cheaper corn is than wheat on the US market. The third column shows the combined effect of these two factors.

62. A factor having such a bearing on the economic viability of the US wheat gluten/wheat starch industry should have been investigated in a thorough and objective way by the US authorities. But it was not. This point shows again that the US wheat gluten/wheat starch industry suffered from an inherent weakness that was totally independent from any increase in imports.

Protein premium

63. The EC has already provided detailed evidence and explanations in its 1st written submission on the fact that variations in the US producers' wheat gluten prices are directly affected by protein levels of the US wheat crop, and *not* by imports.

Slide No. 6 *(taken from Exhibit EC-10)*

64. It shows an economic analysis of the very significant degree of correlation between developments in the protein – i.e. gluten – content of US wheat and US wheat gluten prices. The difference between US prices for high protein and standard protein wheat is what the EC calls "wheat protein premium" or "premium".

65. When the "premium" goes up, the underlying economic situation is that protein levels in normal wheat are low, so that bakers' demand for higher protein wheat – and therefore its price – goes up. As soon as the "premium" increases, the competitiveness of the natural substitute of high protein wheat, wheat gluten, also increases. Thus, demand for wheat gluten also goes up.

66. Consequently, an increase in the "premium" entails that the price of wheat gluten also increases. This alone accounts for instance for high prices in 1994.

67. This graph shows that the US producers' wheat gluten price is basically dependent on the protein level of US wheat crops, and *not* on quantities or price

levels of imports. If one reads the ITC report[15] carefully one finds that the ITC confirms this view. The ITC in particular confirms that the peak in wheat gluten price around 1994 was a direct result of deficiency in protein content in wheat crops during 1993. As the graph illustrates, there is an undeniable long term correlation between the wheat gluten prices and the protein content of wheat.

68. This long-standing correlation shown by statistics available to the ITC should have been examined by the US authorities when they examined the causality condition. The ITC has however decided unreasonably to jump to the conclusion that the imports were the cause of falling prices without considering the high level of protein content in the US wheat crops at the end of the POI.

The increase of capacity of the US industry

69. In the years 1993 to 1995 the US industry increased its capacity by almost 70 per cent. As the US itself admits, most of this capacity was in place *before* the increase in imports occurred.

70. As a result of the US wheat starch/wheat gluten industry construction of additional capacity, by 1995 that industry's capacity utilisation had collapsed from 78,3 per cent (in 1993) to 56,2 per cent.

71. That is more than 20 per cent *less* than the level at which the ITC considered that the US wheat gluten industry could operate "reasonably profitably".[16]

72. By 1995 the US wheat gluten/wheat starch industry had already constructed so much additional capacity that it was at a utilisation level which is far from what the ITC itself considered profitable. It is clear therefore, that contrary to what the US authorities have found, imports cannot be the cause of capacity under-utilisation.

73. The *ex post facto* justification provided by the US in its first written submission (paragraph 34) can be summarised as follows: this capacity was built in anticipation of significant increases in domestic consumption. If there had been no increase in imports, the US industry would have operated at 61 per cent of its capacity, which is much closer to the level at which industry operated profitably.

74. The EC responds that, as we have demonstrated in the previous chapter, demand of wheat gluten is primarily dependent on the protein level of wheat crops. This level is by definition unpredictable. No sensible operator on the wheat gluten market would program large investments 3 years ahead on such an unpredictable event. The US *ex post facto* explanation amounts in fact to accepting that the US industry took a gamble without knowing the odds.

[15] ITC Report at I-22 bottom of page, I-23 top of page.

[16] ITC Report at I-17.

75. Moreover, the US defence assumes illogically and unrealistically that the *entire* domestic consumption or, at the very minimum, the entire increase in US domestic demand should have turned to US domestic suppliers.

76. This argument is a clear expression of the protectionist aims that are behind the US safeguard measure. The argument in fact assumes that foreign producers could not have benefited at all from the increased domestic demand. The US tells us that as soon as they do, a safeguard measure will be imposed. This assumption thus necessarily implies that the US tariff concessions under the WTO could never result in an increased market access and would become worthless.

77. This assumption is fundamentally at odds with the basic objective of the WTO agreements to ensure the expansion of trade in goods and services as expressed in the Recital n. 1 to the Marrakech Agreement. It confirms the real objective pursued by the US authorities when they adopted their safeguard measure, namely to go back from their tariff concession without opening an Article XXVIII of the GATT negotiation and without offering adequate compensation.

78. In addition, the objective facts plead against the US assumption. Imports already provided half of US domestic consumption before 1996-1997. Therefore, the US could not reasonably have expected that all increased consumption would be supplied by US producers[17]. The assumption also unreasonably requires that US purchasers of imported wheat gluten should have altered their long-time commercial relationships with foreign suppliers, and shift their purchases to domestic producers in order to cover increased sales. However, the ITC report provides no explanation of why this obviously curious economic behaviour should have occurred.

79. The conclusion is thus clear: the ITC had no sound economic basis to attribute the under-use of capacity of the US domestic industry to increased imports and its reasoning also on this point is entirely unjustified.

Input costs

80. The major raw material cost in order to produce wheat starch/wheat gluten is the cost of wheat or wheat flour (75 per cent)[18].

81. The ITC failed to objectively examine the fact that the input cost went up significantly in the exact same period during which – according to the ITC itself – serious injury allegedly occurred. The EC has already provided statistical evidence of this with its 1st written submission[19].

---

17 ITC Report at II-25.
18 ITC report at page II-27.
19 See Exhibit EC-12.

Slide No. 7

shows that US wheat prices peaked in the period between July 1995 and June 1997.

82. You will recall that the ITC report claimed that until that period the US wheat gluten production was profitable, and that in the period July 1995- June 1997, it turned unprofitable.

83. A reasonable and objective examination of these two facts taken together should have prompted the ITC to justify the absence of a causal link between the increase of input costs having such a large impact on the overall costs, and the alleged loss of profitability during that period.

84. However, the ITC put to a side this obvious conclusion on the only basis that allegations were made orally by the plaintiffs. Oral assertions by persons interested in the outcome of an investigation clearly do not fulfil the US obligations under Article 4.2 (b) of the SA. In any case, this cannot correspond to an objective assessment of the factual situation given also that the ITC failed to verify through other sources the correctness of such interested allegations.

85. If the ITC had done so, it would have found that the allegations by the plaintiffs are factually incorrect and are inconsistent with the reality of the market.

86. The plaintiffs alleged that wheat gluten producers would have been able to pass on these cost increases to their consumers, since demand for wheat gluten is relatively insensitive to price [20]. However, the ITC explicitly states that high protein wheat or wheat flour is "commercially substitutable" for wheat gluten in baking uses[21]. As the EC has already explained in its 1st written submission[22] there is no reason why US bakers (by far the greatest users of wheat gluten on the US market, purchasing over 80 per cent of the product each year) would not turn to high protein wheat or wheat flour in case US producers' wheat gluten prices went up. Therefore, the ITC could not have logically accepted the plaintiffs' assumption.

Violation of Article 2 and 4 of the SA. The exclusion of Canada: failure to observe the principle of parallelism

87. The US has excluded Canada from the application of its safeguard measure. It should be recalled that the ITC acknowledges[23] that during the POI Canada contributed to imports in a substantial way.

---

20 ITC Report at I-19.

21 ITC Report at I-22.

22 Para. 97-100.

23 ITC Report at I-19: "(... we find that imports from Canada account for a substantial share of total imports").

88. It is a fact, that Canada was the third largest supplier of wheat gluten to the US. Moreover, Canadian imports were higher both in 1996 and 1997 when compared to 1995. The US authorities had therefore no objective reason to exclude Canada from the US safeguard measure.

89. The AB in its Argentina-Footwear report has unequivocally confirmed the existence of a principle of parallelism between the determination of serious injury and causation and the imposition of a safeguard measure:

> "As we have noted, in this case, Argentina applied the safeguard measures at issue after conducting an investigation of products being imported into Argentine territory and the effects of those imports on Argentina's domestic industry. In applying safeguard measures on the basis of this investigation in this case, Argentina was also required under Article 2.2 to apply those measures to imports from all sources, including from other MERCOSUR member States.
>
> On the basis of this reasoning, and on the facts of this case, we find that Argentina's investigation, which evaluated whether serious injury or the threat thereof was caused by imports from *all* sources, could only lead to the imposition of safeguard measures on imports from *all* sources. Therefore, we conclude that Argentina's investigation, in this case, cannot serve as a basis for excluding imports from other MERCOSUR member States from the application of the safeguard measures. "

(paragraphs 112 and 113).

90. The ITC report and the US safeguard measure have breached the principle of parallelism.

91. The US attempts a defence by arguing that "its determination did not attribute injury from NAFTA imports to third countries".

This is factually incorrect. In determining whether its industry was suffering serious injury, the US clearly took into account also the substantial imports from Canada as the ITC's findings regarding serious injury show[24].

Violation of the MOST-FAVOURED-NATION provisions under Articles 5.2 of the SA and I of the GATT 1994

92. The EC claims that the US safeguard measure on wheat gluten was consciously construed in such a way as to grant an advantage to Australia that is not extended, as it should, to all the other WTO Members. The underlying substantive reason for such behaviour of the US is that one of the main US producers

[24] ITC Report at II-12-14.

and also a plaintiff in the US domestic procedure leading to the adoption of the safeguard measure, Manildra, is owned by an Australian holding company. The EC understands that this company holds a controlling share of Australia/US trade in wheat gluten.

93. The breach of the MFN provisions under the SA and the GATT 1994 consisted of the following US actions.

94. On the one hand, the US failed to implement correctly Article 5.2 (a) of the SA when it distributed the QR among the suppliers having a substantial interest in supplying the product concerned. As the EC has indicated in its first written submission, Article 5.2 (a) of the SA is taken word for word from the text of Article XIII.2 (d) of GATT 1994 which deals with the "Non discriminatory Administration of Quantitative Restrictions". It is the lex specialis that is applicable in the case of QRs or TRQs in the context of the adoption of a safeguard measure.

95. The EC draws the attention of the Panel on the fact that the US does not contest the claims made by the EC in its first submission, namely that the US opened consultations with none of the Members having a substantial interest in supplying the product concerned with a view to achieving an agreed allocation. Moreover, the US accepts that no explanation is given as to why that method (reaching agreement) was not "reasonably practicable". As a matter of fact, my colleague Mr. Gussetti will describe to you in a moment how the US refused to negotiate on anything.

Insofar as the US has not fulfilled its obligations under Article 5.2 (a), the equivalent of Article III.2 (d) of the GATT 1994, it has therefore allocated the QR in clear breach of the US MFN obligations.

96. On the other hand, the US has breached also the provisions under Article 5.2 (b) of the SA. Despite having a 47 per cent share of the market in the previous representative period, the EC was allocated only a 43 per cent share of the quota. Australia, on the other hand, was allocated a share of 49 per cent, compared to its share in the previous representative period of 38 per cent. This allocation has preserved entirely the 1997 high levels of imports from Australia despite the fact that Australia's exports increased continuously in the last three years of the investigative period, by almost 21 per cent.[25]

97. In the light of these arguments, the US defence according to which only Article XIII of the GATT should be applicable to this case is clearly incorrect. Article 5.2 of the SA is the lex specialis applicable to the allocation of QRs and TRQs in the context of a safeguard measure and the US has breached it.

98. With respect to the fundamental MFN provision under Article I of the GATT 1994, the EC submits once more that the US has re-introduced selective

[25] ITC report at II-12.

withdrawal of tariff concessions and other obligations which clearly discriminates between WTO Members without any justification under the WTO.

This certainly constitutes a violation of Article I of the GATT 1994. The defence by the US in its submission (paragraphs 210 to 213) thus misses the point. The misrepresentation of our arguments does not provide any further support for the US defence. The EC will come back on this incorrect presentation in its second written submission.

With your permission, I will now pass the floor again to Mr. Gussetti.

Mr. Chairman, distinguished Members of the Panel,

Violation of Article 5.1 of the SA: the proportionality rule

99. The *Korea - Dairy* panel stated[26] in its report

> "The first sentence of Article 5.1 does contain a *very specific obligation*. This obligation is to apply a measure that is *commensurate* with the goals of preventing or remedying the serious injury suffered by the domestic industry and of facilitating the adjustment of the domestic industry. Our interpretation of this obligation is bolstered by the last sentence of Article 5.1, which provides that Members "should choose measures *most suitable for the achievement" of the objectives of preventing or remedying the serious injury and facilitating adjustment*".

100. The Appellate Body's recent decision in that case has unambiguously confirmed this approach (paragraph 96). The EC's presentation in paragraphs 107 to 126 of our first written submission follows exactly this pattern of interpretation.

101. However, the US contests in its first submission (at paragraph 165 and following) the very existence of a proportionality rule in Article 5.1, which it claims it is of "EC's invention".

102. With due respect, Mr. Chairman, the US statement is incomprehensible.

In its submission, the US relies explicitly on an (incorrect) interpretation of the *Korea-Dairy* panel report. By reading that report, the US representatives must have noticed, therefore, what that Panel indicates explicitly in the finding that we have just quoted, namely that

> "This obligation is to apply a measure that is *commensurate* with the goals of preventing or remedying the serious injury suffered by the domestic industry and of facilitating the adjustment of the domestic industry".

103. The term "commensurate" is synonymous with the term "proportionate". They both correspond to the ordinary meaning of the terms "only to the extent to"

[26] para. 7.100.

as the AB report on Korea-Dairy has confirmed at paragraph 96. The proportionality rule is thus well present in Article 5.1 and cannot be contested.

104. Notwithstanding, the US unreasonably states in paragraph 167 of its submission that Article 5.1 provides no support for the notion that remedy selected must be "proportional" to the serious injury that the authorities have found.

the proportionality rule: the extent of the measure

105. Without any need to recall entirely the arguments advanced in our first written submission, the EC would like to draw the attention of the Panel on two major points:

(a) the scope of a safeguard measure cannot go beyond what is needed in order to prevent or remedy the serious injury *that is attributable to the increased imports*. Not only the combined reading of Articles 4.2 (b) and 5.1 SA does not allow any doubt about this interpretation. It is also a matter of common sense: the *legitimate* imports from WTO Members can *not* be restricted in order to remedy an injury that is *not* attributable to them.

In other words, if a causal link were established between the serious injury and the imported products (which in our view is *not* the case in this procedure), the safeguard measure should be commensurate or proportionate to that injury, i.e. to the exclusion of factors other than increased imports. If a combination of causes creates the serious injury but only part is attributable to increased imports, only that part could justify a safeguard measure, whose scope should be also limited to the remedy *of that part* of the injury. The Member proposing the safeguard measure must provide for a meaningful and reviewable criterion that permits the correct application of this fundamental principle.

Reasoning otherwise, as the US suggests in its submission and implemented in the case of the wheat gluten, would amount to over-restrict and over-protect the domestic industry; it would amount in fact to an unjustified withdrawal of tariff concessions and other obligations without pursuing an Article XXVIII of the GATT negotiation and without offering adequate compensation.

Evidence of this unjustified objective exists in the US legislation itself that is quoted by the US in footnote 119 of its first submission. According to that footnote, in order to be indicated as the cause of serious injury Section 2252 (b) (1) (A) of chapter 19 of the US Code requires that increased imports must be a 'substantial cause'. The definition of "substantial cause" (in Section 2252 (b) (1) (B)) is "a cause which is important and not less than any other cause".

An example is again more telling than a long story and is useful to underscore the consequences of the US suggested approach.

Let's imagine that three main causes are creating serious injury to a domestic industry, but that approximately half of that is due to a significant increase in imports. The other two causes (for example a natural disaster and labour unrest) make up approximately the other half. In such an example, under the US law the increased imports would be the substantial cause pursuant to the US Code's definition and a safeguard measure can be taken. However, if we applied to this example the interpretation presented by the US before this panel, with only *half* of the serious injury attributable to imports the US could adopt a safeguard measure restricting imports (i.e. market access for *foreign* products) in order to remedy *100* per cent of the injury.

In the EC's view, this is not compatible with Article 5.1 SA. However, this is exactly what the US has done in the case of the wheat gluten safeguard measure.

(b) The US complains that the EC has not addressed in its claim under Article 5.1 the fact that the safeguard measure shall not only be commensurate to the purpose of preventing or remedying serious injury but also facilitate industry adjustment.

The answer to this argument from the US can be very brief. The text of Article 5.1 clearly indicates that the two conditions must be complied with *simultaneously* ("prevent or remedy serious injury *and* to facilitate adjustment"). The US has clearly breached the proportionality rule with respect to the first leg. Thus, the EC considered it unnecessary to elaborate on whether it complied with the second leg.

However, if the US argument were to be understood as implying that the purpose of "facilitating adjustment" under Article 5.1 could take precedence over the proportion to be kept between imported products and the serious injury attributable to them, that interpretation should be rejected. The consequence of such interpretation would in fact be that a Member would be allowed to impose a safeguard measure that will restrict *foreign* products more than the increased imports justify in terms of serious injury. *Again, the US suggests that a protectionist measure could be applied at no cost, with no compensation.* The EC firmly disagrees.

the proportionality rule: the form of the measure

106. With respect to the form of the measure chosen by the US, a QR, the only argument advanced by the US is that "no textual support for its assertion that the

Safeguards Agreement indicates a preference for, or requires an explanation of, a choice of a form of measure over another" (paragraph 172).

107. It is apparent that the provisions of the SA are "based on the basic principles of GATT 1994"[27] and that the WTO Members recognise "the need to enhance rather than limit competition in international market"[28].

As the recent panel report on *Turkey - Textiles* has found[29]:

> "The prohibition on the use of quantitative restrictions forms one of the cornerstones of the GATT system. A basic principle of the GATT system is that tariffs are the preferred and acceptable form of protection. (...) Two fundamental obligations contained in Part II are the national treatment clause and the prohibition against quantitative restrictions. The prohibition against quantitative restrictions is a reflection that tariffs are GATT's border protection "of choice". Quantitative restrictions impose absolute limits on imports, while tariffs do not. In contrast to MFN tariffs which permit the most efficient competitor to supply imports, quantitative restrictions usually have a trade distorting effect, their allocation can be problematic and their administration may not be transparent."

108. Thus, it is simply untrue to assert, as the US does, that the SA does not provide for a preference for tariff measures on quantitative restrictions. In fact, in opposition to the US suggested interpretation, both the object and purpose of the Agreement as spelled out in its recitals and the proportionality rule in Article 5.1 do provide for such a preference.

109. The US would like you to believe that quantitative restrictions could become the rule rather than the exception. This is incorrect, and the ITC short arguments aimed at supporting that choice are completely inadequate to comply with the US's obligations under the SA, as the EC's submission at paragraphs 119 to 129 demonstrates.

the proportionality rule: the inherent inconsistency in the US approach as regards the remedy

110. The EC does not wish to revert once more on the issue of the relations between the necessary co-products wheat starch and wheat gluten. Mr Van Vliet has already examined this point. I will therefore only draw your attention to the fact that, no matter how many dialectical contortions the US attempts at paragraphs 183 to 186 of its first submission, a patent contradiction persists in its position as expressed in the ITC report.

---

[27] recital 4 to the SA.

[28] recital 3 to the SA.

[29] at para. 9.63.

111. On the one hand, the US authorities have excluded from their reasoning concerning causality the effects of the inherently weak position of the US wheat gluten/wheat starch industry on the US domestic starch market, when determining whether a serious injury could have been caused by imported wheat gluten.

112. On the other hand, the US authorities have included as one of their key considerations the wheat starch market conditions in the US when considering the form, the scope and the extent of the safeguard measure against foreign wheat gluten[30].

113. This inconsistent way of proceeding of the US authorities has doubly prejudiced the market access conditions for EC produced wheat gluten. The EC maintains that the US cannot have the cake and eat it.

Violation of Article 5.1 of the SA: the representative period

114. Another issue of importance is the choice of the period that the US selected as a basis for the import quota. The Unites States insists that the EC has "ignore[d] the language and purpose of Article 5.1, as well as the USITC's explicit findings" (US first submission at paragraph 191).

115. The EC would like to draw the attention of the Panel to the ordinary meaning of Article 5.1, second sentence of the SA. The "last three representative years for which statistics are available" means what it says, namely that the US should have based itself on the last three-year period for which statistics were available at the time of the adoption of the measure (30 May 1998).

116. The US does not contest that 1997, 1996 and 1995 statistics were available.

117. Are these statistics "representative"? Of course they are, since they represent exactly the pattern of trade on-going before the entry into force of the measure, as Article 5.1 requires. As the EC indicated in its first written submission, the US could point to no exceptional circumstances and no violation of WTO obligations as evidence that the pattern of trade that is represented by the 1997-1995 statistics was distorted.

118. The US submits that "representative" "would normally be a period in which imports did not cause serious injury" otherwise "the import level would not remedy the serious injury and facilitate adjustment".

119. The EC responds that there is no textual or logical basis in the SA for such self-serving interpretation. As a matter of logic, if an increase in imports were a "clear" justification for using a representative period other than the "last three

[30] ITC report at page I-26 on "selection of import quota" as recommended relief: "Because of the co-product nature of wheat gluten production, the supply and price of wheat gluten is dictated in part by demand for wheat starch".

representative years for which statistics are available", this situation would always apply, rendering the provision meaningless.

120. In fact, what Article 5.1 requires is that the "representative" period be selected in an objective way. That being done, the Member applying the safeguard measure can then consider which measure is best suited to remedy the serious injury generated by the imported products and to facilitate adjustment of its domestic industry. There is a logical chain of actions that must be respected in its order.

121. The US interpretation distorts the plain text of Article 5.1 SA, second sentence. It confuses the definition of the representative period (an objective, factual issue) with the scope and the extent of the measure.

This is erroneous in law and leads to the implementation of over-restrictive safeguard measures.

The real aim of the US "interpretation" in this case is to turn the clock back to a market situation which was in place before the Uruguay Round, as if the multilateral tariff negotiations did not take place, and that at no cost.

Violation of Article 5.1 of the SA: the absence of a "clear justification"

122. Contrary to the impression given by the US submission at paragraphs 196 and 197, the burden of proof still rests on the US. It is the US that must demonstrate that 1997-1995 period was not representative. This is not the usual burden of proof, since the text of Article 5.1 requires a "clear justification" before departing from that rule. As the Appellate Body has stated in its report on Korea-Dairy (paragraph 98),

> "We agree with the Panel that this "clear justification" has to be given by a Member applying a safeguard measure *at the time of the decision, in its recommendations or determinations on the application of the safeguard measure*."

123. A self-serving and incorrect interpretation of the text of the SA is clearly not appropriate and not enough to fulfil such an obligation.

124. By contrast, the EC has satisfied its procedural obligations by making the US acknowledge that 1997-1995 statistics were available, that no exceptional events occurred and no violation by the EC of its WTO obligation distorted the trade patterns during that period.

Our *prima facie* case on this issue is thus firmly established.

Before concluding this presentation, the EC would like to briefly draw the Panel's attention on the EC's claims under Articles 12 and 8 of the SA.

Violation of Article 12 of the SA: the US has illegally delayed notification

125. The EC's claims under Article 12 SA are confirmed by the first written submission of the US.

126. The United States dedicates long pages to try to defend the indefensible. For instance, its interpretation of the ordinary meaning of the term "immediately" is much closer to "may be one day" than to the text of Article 12 SA.

127. The EC refers the Panel to the findings in the Korea Dairy panel report that condemned Korea on this very issue: for the notifications on initiation, a delay of 14 days was found not to qualify as "immediate". In the present case, the US delayed its notification by 16 days. It also delayed the notification of finding of serious injury by as much as 26 days. In light of the Korea – Dairy standard there can be no doubt that the US notifications breached Article 12 of the SA.

Violation of Article 12 of the SA: the US has not notified the proposed measures and actions

128. Another issue concerns the fact of whether the US has timely and properly notified the WTO relevant Committees and the EC on the proposed measures, as is required under Article 12, paragraphs 1 and 2. As the Korea-Dairy panel report stated

> " [T]his notification can only be viewed as a notification of the final decision taken since it was notified and circulated only after the final decision was put into force; this notification cannot be taken into account for the purpose of assessing whether Korea complied with its obligation to notify its *proposed* measure since this notification took place after the consultations, and therefore cannot remedy the flaws in the previous notification"[31].

129. The US acted in this case exactly as Korea did in that case. As was recalled in the EC's first written submission, the United States made findings of serious injury on 15 January 1998, but notified the WTO only on 11 February 1998. It then implemented the measure on 1 June 1998, but did not notify the Committee on Safeguards until 4 June 1998. All these notifications were thus effected ex post facto, i.e. after the action or the measure had been adopted and not at the stage of proposed action or measure, in clear breach of the letter and the spirit of Article 12 SA.

Violation of article 8 of the SA

130. As far the EC's claim on Article 8 SA is concerned, in a letter of 12 March 1998 by Ambassador R. Hayes, the US informed that "the United States is prepared to consult fully with all Members having a substantial interest as exporters of wheat gluten, including the European Community (…). However, we believe these consultations should be held only after the Article 12.1 (b) notification is

[31] *Korea - Dairy*, *supra*, footnote 2, footnote 481.

supplemented with the USITC report". The report was notified to the WTO on 27 March 1998.

131. An informal meeting was held on 19 - 20 May 1998, i.e. just prior to the adoption of the measure. On 20 May, the representative of the US Trade department, Mr. Jim Murphy, is quoted in a report prepared by the Deputy Director-General of the Directorate General of Agriculture of the Commission of the European Communities to have stated that "he was not in a position to 'negotiate' ". This confirmed the position expressed, albeit in less blunt terms, by the Deputy USTR, Mr. Peter Scher, the day before. The EC can provide the relevant excerpt of that otherwise confidential report, if necessary.

132. Despite formal claims of deference to its WTO obligations under the SA, the US representative is thus on the record expressing the US administration's unwillingness to negotiate, either the scope of the measure or any possible compensation. It is interesting to compare this information with the statement in the US first submission, paragraph 206, that "Article 8, when read in conjunction with Article 12.3, imposes on a Member the obligation to hold consultations".

133. The facts thus confirm that the US did not comply with its obligation under Article 8.1 of the SA since it never "endeavoured to maintain a substantially equivalent level of concessions". Its representatives entered into consultations under instruction not to negotiate on anything. They thus transformed a substantial obligation into, to put it diplomatically, a dubious PR action. The Panel should conclude therefore that the US has also breached Article 8 of the SA.

This point concludes our presentation.

Mr. Chairman, distinguished Members of the Panel, thank you for your attention.

ATTACHMENT 1-3

EUROPEAN COMMUNITY'S REPLIES TO QUESTIONS FROM THE PANEL
(17 January 2000)

Question N. 1

We note that the ITC Report (p. I-9) states: "[w]e find that domestically produced wheat gluten is "like" imported wheat gluten and that the domestic industry consists of the domestic producers of all forms of vital wheat gluten, including modified wheat gluten that is used in the baking and pet food industries." Do the parties agree that, for the purposes of this proceeding, the domestic industry consists of the domestic producers of all forms of vital wheat gluten?

Reply

Yes, the EC agrees that for the purposes of this proceeding, the domestic industry consists of the domestic producers of all forms of vital wheat gluten.

However, since *necessarily* in the production of wheat gluten always co-products are produced, the ITC also should have adequately investigated to what extent developments related to those co-products caused injury, which the ITC did not do. The EC refers to its joint reply to questions 8 and 9 below.

Question N. 2, 4, 14, 15, and 16

In para. 9 of its third party submission, New Zealand asserts: "New Zealand does not contest that the protection of such confidential information, including from the respondents in the safeguards investigation, may be appropriate at the time of the investigation. However, New Zealand considers that a Member cannot justify a measure as being consistent with its obligations under the WTO without disclosing to the panel and the parties the information on which it relies." How do the parties react to this statement?

Could the parties clarify whether the EU had access to the "confidential information" in question in the domestic proceedings before the ITC? If the EC did have access, under what conditions?

In its first written submission, the United States indicates that the ITC has now prepared a corrigendum to the public report that provides the portion of the pricing data and certain other information that can be disclosed, and attached it as Exhibit 10. The United States also expresses that it is "confident that this greater degree of disclosure will allay the EC's concerns." How does the EC react to this statement? What, in your view, is the status of this corrigendum in these proceedings?

What is the motivation underlying the assertion in paragraph 49 of the EC first written submission that "[t]his requirement presupposes that the detailed analysis and the demonstration of the relevance of factors are published and not held secret, unless confidentiality is really an issue"? Is the EC asserting that confidentiality is not really an issue here?

Is the EC arguing that it was/is prejudiced in any way in these WTO dispute settlement proceedings from the ITC's treatment of confidential information in the public version of its report? If so, in what way?

Joint Reply

Since in the EC's view these questions are related, it will provide a joint answer.

As an answer first to question N. 14, the EC has argued in its first written submission and oral statement at the first substantive meeting that the failure to provide relevant data, not even in aggregate form, in the original ITC March 1998 Report constitutes a violation of Article 4.2 (c) SA. Under that provision, the US is obliged to publish a detailed analysis of the case, as well as a demonstration of the relevance of the factors examined. Such a report is to be published "promptly", and must set forth findings and reasoned conclusions on all pertinent issues of fact and law.

The fact that the US now, in the context of these panel proceedings, with regard to a very limited number of points, provides some data which were kept out of the public version of the March 1998 ITC report, does not at all "allay the EC's concerns". Rather, this fact proves that in particular with regard to those data now newly disclosed in Exhibit US-10, there never was any objection to publishing them on grounds of business "confidentiality" in the first place.

The fact that the US feels free to provide these data shows that they could and therefore should have been given at the time of the original ITC-report, since the exception of Article 3.2 of the SA never was an issue. The fact that the US provides these findings stating explicitly that soon they will be made public, proves that the US has violated Article 4 of the SA by not publishing these data "promptly" at the time.

On the issue of *the status of the corrigendum*, in the EC's view, the Panel must draw the conclusion *that the fact that the US has provided the corrigendum*, proves that Article 4 SA has been violated by the US by not providing the information contained in the corrigendum "promptly" at the time of the investigation. The purpose for which the US are providing that corrigendum is evidently inadmissible, in the sense that it could never "undo" the violation of Article 4.2 SA consisting of not providing the relevant information in the *report made public at the time*[1].

The EC would underline that the corrigendum only provides a very limited amount of data; much data which should have been disclosed in the ITC's report is still not made available. In particular, citing "confidentiality", the ITC

---

1 The information contained in the "corrigendum", however, can be used by the Panel as evidence.

omitted any qualitative discussion of the method by which the industry allocated profits and losses between the various operations. This was a crucial piece of evidence relied on by the ITC in determining both injury and causation.

Concerning the *presentation of aggregate data*, the following were deleted from the public version of the ITC Report:

- Cost allocations[2];
- Producers' imports and exports[3];
- Profitability data[4];
- Input costs, including raw material and fuel costs[5];
- Employment data[6];
- Value of assets, capital expenditures, and R&D expenses[7];
- US importers' inventories[8].

Most of these data sets would have had a strong bearing on any objective assessment of the state of the industry.

In addition to consolidated data on the US industry, the ITC, through its questionnaires, gathered a considerable amount of data about the EC and other WTO Members' industries. By also withholding much of this data with no justification possible based on confidentiality, the ITC has concealed a formidable amount of information about the wheat processing industries, which would undoubtedly have had a bearing on the analysis of the case.

In withholding relevant data, the US has relied on the basis that there are few wheat gluten producers in the US (or Australia, etc.). Were this basis to be allowed to pass unchallenged, a Member proposing a safeguards action, whose industry comprised only a few operators, could be allowed to contrive an investigative report, secure in the knowledge that the data on which the action was based could never be scrutinised. This outcome would however evidently *not* comply with the *explicit* requirements of the SA.

As an answer to question N. 15, the EC's position is that confidentiality is not an issue in the context of whether or not data in summary form, such as is the form of aggregate data, is provided in the investigation report. Article 4 requires that any information relevant for the investigation must be found in the published report. The issue of whether or not such pertinent information is "confidential" is only relevant for the question whether it is provided as such *or* only in summary form.

---

2 ITC report at II 20.
3 ITC report at II 14.
4 ITC report at Annex C-4.
5 ITC report at II 18-20.
6 ITC report at II 16-17.
7 ITC report at II 21.
8 ITC report at II 23-24.

Hence, the US is not allowed to withhold aggregate data, i.e. in summary form, from the public version of the ITC report on confidentiality grounds. In part, by providing the corrigendum, the US accepts that it could have given those data at the time, which means the US violated Article 4 of the SA by not doing so.

As an answer to question N. 16, the EC submits that not only it, but that potentially all WTO Members are prejudiced by the fact that the US withholds, on almost all relevant issues indicated above, contrary to Article 4 of the SA, substantial data from the public version of the ITC report, without there being a justification for doing so.

All WTO Members are potentially prejudiced because the absence of this information makes the reasoning of the ITC in coming to its conclusions completely unverifiable. The EC would stress that potentially all WTO Members can be negatively affected by safeguard measures taken by another WTO Member.

This can be either directly because their industry is limited in its possibility to export to the WTO Member applying the safeguard measure, or indirectly because of diversion of trade (when goods which were before exported by other WTO Members to the Member taking the safeguard measure are now exported to third WTO Members).

Thus all WTO Members have a strong interest in being provided, at the time that the measure is taken, with all information relevant for judging its legitimacy (the only exception being information which cannot possibly be provided without infringing on *individual* companies' business secrets). Applying Article 4.2 SA by its terms will moreover, on the one hand, enhance WTO Members' abilities to assert their rights – since they will be provided with all relevant information -, and on the other hand avoid useless litigation – since that information will also allow them to judge whether the safeguard measure is legitimate.

The EC takes this opportunity to stress the obvious fact that, consistent with the well-established principles associated with Article XXIII of GATT 1994 and Article 3.8 of the DSU, any *prima facie* violation of the obligations in the GATT 1994 and/or in the SA is considered a case of nullification or impairment of benefits accruing *directly or indirectly* to WTO Members under these Agreements.

The Appellate Body stressed in its decision on "*Argentina-Footwear*"[9] that the competent authority has, under Article 4, not only an *obligation* "to consider all the relevant facts" but also an *obligation* to "*adequately explains* how the facts support the determination". Since in the present case most of the facts are unjustifiably labelled as "confidential" even in their summary form, it is impossible to verify whether the conclusions of the ITC are supported by its reason-

[9] Appellate Body report, *Argentina - Safeguard Measures on Imports of Footwear* ("*Argentina - Footwear Safeguard*"), WT/DS121/AB/R, adopted 12 January 2000, DSR 2000:I, 515, paras 121 and 145.

ing. It is therefore clear that the US authorities have failed to "adequately explain" how the facts support the determination.

As an answer to question N. 4, at no time did the European Commission, nor any other institution of the European Community, have access to the confidential data. Neither was the EC given any confidential information in the course of meetings held with USTR officials on the subject.

On a point of principle, while it is clearly a positive development that, pursuant to Article 3 of the SA, Members must be allowed to intervene in the domestic safeguard proceedings of other Members (provided the responsible authorities proceed in a fair and reasonable manner), this cannot excuse the Member considering a safeguards action from discharging its full responsibilities under the SA, and in particular Article 4 thereof, in particular by arguing that it is not obliged to investigate relevant issues since that it has not been asked to do so during the national proceedings.

Finally, *as an answer to question N. 2*, the EC submits that the US has violated its obligations under Article 4 of SA, by not publishing data which are relevant to certain essential elements of the ITC's reasoning, without there being any justification for not providing these data. This lack of essential information meant that the ITC report failed to give "detailed analysis ... as well as a demonstration of relevance" required by Article 4.2 (c) SA. This cannot be "rectified" by giving data now which should have been provided in the public version of the ITC-report at the time, i.e. by attempting to undo the wrong.

New Zealand's point concerns a different situation, which is not the case here. That is the case that data regarding *individual* companies are, with proper justification, kept confidential and not included in the published report of a safeguard investigation. New Zealand may be correct in arguing that, in certain circumstances, such information should be provided at the Panel stage, in order to allow a Panel to review whether a safeguard investigation was correctly performed and whether the safeguard measure was justified.

However, the issue in the case of the US wheat gluten safeguard measure concerns *the absence of data in summary form,* whether in aggregate form or otherwise summarised: the withholding of information *in summary form* from the public version of the ITC report *was never justified in the first place.*

Providing that information now, *ex post facto* and one and half year later within the closed doors of a confidential panel procedure, does not change the fact that Article 4 SA was violated by the US that did not "*promptly*" provide it in a *published* report.

Question N. 3

In the view of the parties, is the Panel able to perform an "objective assessment of the matter before it" within the meaning of Article 11 of the DSU on the basis of the ITC Report issued in March 1998 (with the "corrigendum" submitted by the United States in these proceedings)?

Reply

According to the Appellate Body report on "*Guatemala - Cement*"[10], the "matter" before a panel

> "(...) consists of two elements: the specific "measure" and the "claims" relating to it, both of which must be properly identified in a panel request as required by Article 6.2 of the DSU."

Thus, in order to perform an "objective assessment of the *matter* before it", as required by Article 11 of the DSU, this Panel must examine

- the measure **and**
- the claims relating to it as they were brought forward by the EC in its request of establishment of the Panel[11].

The measure is constituted by the US Proclamation 7103 of 30 May 1998 and the US Memorandum of 30 May 1998.

The claims are listed in the request of establishment of the Panel and thoroughly analysed in the written and oral submissions[12] of the EC. They are entirely confirmed here.

As the EC has already indicated in its first oral statement on 20 December 1999, the role of the Panel when examining the compatibility of safeguard measures with the covered agreements is to determine whether the Member's authorities fully and objectively considered the evidence before it, including any evidence that detracts from an affirmative determination of increased imports, serious injury or causation[13] (Articles 2 and 4 of the SA). The Panel should also verify the adequacy of the Member's reasoning by reviewing whether the findings made and conclusions reached are consistent with the evidence[14].

Moreover, compliance with all the other provisions under the GATT Articles I and XIX and the Safeguard Agreement should also be checked, including

---

[10] Appellate Body Report, *Guatemala – Anti-dumping Investigation Regarding Portland Cement from Mexico* ("*Guatemala – Cement I*"), WT/DS60/AB/R, adopted 25 November 1998, DSR 1998:IX, 3767, para. 76.

[11] WT/DS166/3.

[12] See for example para. 14 of the EC first oral statement.

[13] Panel Report, *Korea - Definitive Safeguard Measure on Imports of Certain Dairy Products* ("*Korea – Dairy Safeguard*"), WT/DS98/R and Corr. 1, adopted 12 January 2000, DSR 2000:I, 49, para. 7.30.

[14] Panel Report, *Argentina - Safeguard Measures on Imports of Footwear* ("*Argentina - Footwear Safeguard*"), WT/DS121/R, adopted 12 January 2000, DSR 2000:II, 575, para. 8.124.

Articles 3, 5, 8 and 12. The EC reiterates that the US measure is incompatible with all the above-mentioned provisions. As the Appellate Body has found in its "*Argentina-Footwear*" report,

> "(...) safeguard measures may be applied only when [compliance with] *all* the provisions of the *Agreement on Safeguards* and Article XIX of the GATT 1994 are clearly demonstrated".

Finally, as far as the so-called "corrigendum" of the ITC-Report is concerned, as the Appellate Body has clarified in its report on *Korea- Dairy* (paragraph 98) when addressing a similar issue

> "We agree with the Panel that this "clear justification" has to be given by a Member applying a safeguard measure *at the time of the decision, in its recommendations or determinations on the application of the safeguard measure*" (original emphasis).

Contrary to this indication from the AB, the US aims at retro-actively "healing" its violation of the relevant provisions of the SA by submitting, in Exhibit 10 to its submission, a revised version of parts of the ITC report containing data which it had earlier on withheld from the public version of the ITC report.

In the light of this established interpretation, the Panel should reject this belated attempt. Otherwise Articles 3 and 4 of the SA would become entirely useless. Their violation cannot be retrospectively "healed".

As a matter of principle, the EC would like to stress that it cannot be admissible for a party to contrive that a Panel is unable to carry out its tasks under Article 11 of the DSU simply by withholding self-proclaimed "confidential information".

Question N.5

We note the recent statement of the Appellate Body that the phrase "as a result of unforeseen developments and of the effect of the obligations incurred by a Member under this Agreement, including tariff concessions" in Article XIX:1(a) of the GATT 1994 does not establish independent conditions for the application of a safeguard measure additional to the conditions set out in the second clause of Article XIX:1(a), but it "describes certain circumstances which must be demonstrated as a matter of fact in order for a safeguard measure to be applied consistently with the provisions of Article XIX of the GATT 1994."[15] $

What could constitute such "unforeseen developments"? By whom must such developments be "unforeseen"? In this case, what precisely were the cir-

[15] Appellate Body Report, *Argentina - Footwear Safeguard, supra*, footnote 9, paras. 92 ff.; Appellate Body Report , *Korea - Definitive Safeguard Measure on Imports of Certain Dairy Products* ("*Korea – Dairy Safeguard*"), WT/DS98/AB/R, adopted 12 January 2000, DSR 2000:I, 3, paras. 85 ff.

cumstances constituting "unforeseen developments" and where are these addressed in the ITC Report?

Reply to sub-question 1

The circumstances shall be unforeseen, i.e. unexpected[16]. Examples of "*unforeseen developments*" range from past historical events such as the sudden collapse of the Soviet Union, to less dramatic ones like a massive shift in taste for a particular consumer good (as in the "*Hatters' Fur*" case[17]), an unpredictable collapse of the currency of an exporting nation, or the discovery of a new and revolutionary product which reduces in a very short period of time the use of the traditional product (for example, long-playing records and CDs) and that is mainly imported. However, none of such unexpected circumstances ever happened.

When addressing the issue of the interpretation of Article XIX.1 of the GATT, the attention of the Panel is also drawn to the useful paragraph 94 of the AB report on "*Argentina-Footwear*"

> " (...) In perceiving and applying this object and purpose to the interpretation of this provision of the *WTO Agreement*, it is essential to keep in mind that a safeguard action is a "fair" trade remedy. The application of a safeguard measure does not depend upon "unfair" trade actions, as is the case with anti-dumping or countervailing measures. Thus, the import restrictions that are imposed on products of exporting Members when a safeguard action is taken must be seen, as we have said, as extraordinary. And, when construing the prerequisites for taking such actions, their extraordinary nature must be taken into account."

Reply to sub-question 2

In its report on "*Argentina-Footwear*" the AB states that

> " certain circumstances which *must be demonstrated as a matter of fact* in order for a safeguard measure to be applied consistently with the provisions of Article XIX of the GATT 1994."

Demonstrate means "show evidence of" or "describe and explain". "As a matter of fact", means by providing factual evidence.

The AB has also indicated that

> "The first clause in Article XIX:1(a) – "as a result of unforeseen developments and of the obligations incurred by a Member under the Agreement, including tariff concessions ... " – is a dependent clause which, in

[16] Appellate Body Report, *Argentina - Footwear, supra*, footnote 9, para. 91.

[17] Working Party Report on Withdrawal by the United States of a Tariff Concession under Article XIX of the GATT, GATT/CP/106, adopted on 22 October 1951. See AB report on "Argentina-Footwear" at para. 96.

our view, is linked grammatically to the verb phrase "is being imported" in the second clause of that paragraph.(...) In this sense, we believe that there is a logical connection between the circumstances described in the first clause – "as a result of unforeseen developments and of the effect of the obligations incurred by a Member under this Agreement, including tariff concessions ... " – and the conditions set forth in the second clause of Article XIX:1(a) for the imposition of a safeguard measure."[18]

It has moreover clarified[19] that

""(...) safeguard measures may be applied only when [compliance with] *all* the provisions of the *Agreement on Safeguards* and Article XIX of the GATT 1994 are clearly demonstrated".

It has then concluded that

" we do not believe that it is necessary to complete the analysis of the Panel relating to the claim made by the European Communities under Article XIX of the GATT 1994 by ruling ***on whether the Argentine authorities have, in their investigation,*** *demonstrated that the increased imports in this case occurred "as a result of unforeseen developments and of the effect of the obligations incurred by a Member under this Agreement, including tariff concessions ...* ". (emphasis added).

Therefore, in this case the burden rests *on the US* to show where it has demonstrated *in the ITC report* or in the legal act adopting the safeguard measure that unexpected circumstances had "led to a product [wheat gluten] being imported in such increased quantities and under such conditions as to cause or threaten to cause serious injury to domestic producers"[20]. This is reinforced by the language of Article 3.1 last sentence which requires the published report to contain findings on all pertinent issues of law and fact, irrespective of whether those issues have been raised by any party. The US has not lived up to this obligation. Its violation cannot be retrospectively healed.

Reply to sub-question 3

There is no demonstration of the existence of unforeseen, i.e. unexpected, developments described in the record of the investigation, which could have led to any increased imports causing serious injury. Furthermore, there is no indication that such unforeseen circumstances were in fact present at all.

Questions N. 6 and 7

In paras. 73-77 of its first written submission, the EC argues that the ITC failed to take several "relevant" factors into account in its "serious injury"

18 at para. 92.
19 at para. 95.
20 Appellate Body Report, *Argentina - Footwear, supra*, footnote 9, para. 91.

analysis (i.e. capital investment; new entries/expansion; developments as to co-products, "imports as positive business strategy"). We note that, in the summary of parties' arguments in the relevant section of the ITC Report (pp. I-11, I-12), while it appears that the EC raised arguments concerning "profitability" with respect to wheat starch/wheat gluten, it is not clear that the EC raised the other factors just mentioned as "relevant" in this context in the ITC proceedings. Can the parties clarify whether or not the EC did raise these issues in this context before the ITC? If the EC did not raise them before the ITC in this context, what considerations should guide the Panel in any examination of these factors or of their "relevance" in this context?

Does the language of Article 4.2(a) of the Safeguards Agreement ("...the competent authorities shall evaluate all relevant factors of an objective and quantifiable nature having a bearing on the situation of that industry") impose an obligation on the competent authorities to themselves undertake an inquiry into "all relevant factors ..." even if these are not raised in the proceedings before it? If so, what is the nature and scope of this obligation?

Joint Reply

The language of Article 4.2 (a) SA clearly states that

> "(...) the competent authorities *shall* evaluate *all* relevant factors of an objective and quantifiable nature having a bearing on the situation of that industry, in particular (...)" (emphasis supplied).

Additionally, Article 3.1 SA states that

> "The competent authorities shall publish a report setting forth their findings and reasoned conclusions reached on *all pertinent issues* of fact and law." (emphasis added).

This obligation to evaluate *each* factor of *objective* and *quantifiable* nature *having a bearing* on the situation of the industry concerned applies to the competent authorities, regardless of whether or not a particular factor has been raised by any party during the proceedings referred to in Article 3.1 of the SA. If the drafters of the Safeguards Agreement had wanted to make it conditional on whether the necessity to evaluate the factor concerned had been claimed during those proceedings, nothing would have been easier for them than to include language to that effect in Article 4.2 (a).

The Appellate Body shares this view:

> "We agree with the Panel's interpretation that Article 4.2 (a) of the Agreement on Safeguards requires a *demonstration* that the competent authorities evaluated, at a minimum, each of the factors listed

in Article 4.2(a) *as well as all other factors that are relevant to the situation of the industry concerned.*"[21] (Emphasis supplied).

Therefore, under Article 4.2 (a) SA, the competent authorities must *of their own initiative first* carefully identify which factors may be relevant to the situation of the industry concerned, and *then, again of their own initiative*, obtain all information which is necessary to evaluate how that factor developed. This is reinforced by the language of Article 3.1, last sentence, which requires the published report to contain findings on all pertinent issues of law and fact, irrespective of whether those issues have been raised by any party.

Quite apart from the fact that Article 4.2 (a) SA simply does not make this obligation dependent on whether an issue was raised by any party during the proceedings foreseen in Article 3 of the SA, the aim of the SA could also be undermined if the obligation to investigate a factor having a bearing on the situation of the industry was to be made conditional on the issue having been raised.

Article 4.2 SA requires a good faith evaluation of all relevant factors before a safeguard measure can be taken. The aim of the SA in general is to ensure that safeguard measures can only be taken if certain strict conditions, which are the same for every WTO member, are met. If an interpretation were adopted which made the obligation to investigate a relevant factor dependent on whether it was mentioned during the national proceedings, this could create disparity between WTO Member as to the conditions under which they can take safeguard measures. A WTO Member could choose to provide only very short and limited means for interested parties to provide their views, and then choose not to investigate relevant factors, arguing that they have not been mentioned before it.

This would clearly be an unacceptable result.

In this context the EC would take the opportunity to comment on certain points made by the US in its oral presentation on 21 December 1999 [22] with respect to the issue raised by the Panel's questions.

The EC is *not* arguing, as the US has made it, that new evidence, in the sense of information on factual developments that occurred after the investigation was closed, should play a role in determining whether a safeguard measure was justified. (Provided that the safeguard measure was taken shortly after the period investigated, which was *not* the case here: the EC refers to Item 3 "Injury", point 4.2 of its second written submission).

The EC is arguing that the evidence on the facts occurring during the period investigated, which was obtained by the ITC at the time, or at least should have been obtained by it, does not support the conclusions that the ITC has reached. Contrary to what the US apparently wishes to imply, the slides shown at the first substantive meeting are based either on information contained in the ITC

---

21 Appellate Body Report, *Argentina - Footwear, supra*, footnote 9, para.136.
22 Pages 2 to 5.

report itself, or on information which must have been available to the ITC (such as US Department of Agriculture - USDA - information on corn and wheat prices), since it was *all* of US Government's source.

At this juncture, it is useful to analyse in more detail the particular claim of the US that the EC should not be allowed to bring in *monthly* wheat prices during the period of investigation in relation with its argument that – assuming that injury occurred – higher input (wheat) prices was the main cause of it.

The ITC explicitly *accepts* that "particularly in 1996 and 1997" wheat prices rose. In fact, it possessed (some) relevant data, albeit on a quarterly basis[23], which must have made the price jump in 1996 and 1997 very clear to it.

Contrary to Article 4 of the SA, none of these data, not even on an aggregate basis, were provided in the ITC-report. (The Panel will notice the great number of "***" under Table 22 and Figure 12 on that page. Now, as its "corrigendum"[24], the US tries to bring in that part of information which it thinks is helpful to its case).

Especially in these circumstances there could be no objection whatsoever to the EC's reference to *official USDA* statistics merely to confirm a point – the wheat price jump in 1996 and 1997 – that, as is clear from the ITC report, was known to the US at the time of the investigation on the basis of the information provided by US producers. The reasoning of the United States would in effect deprive other WTO Members from the right to demonstrate that it had *not* analysed all relevant factors.

WTO Members must therefore, under Article 4.2 SA, of their own initiative determine and evaluate all relevant factors, demonstrate the causal link between increased imports and serious injury, and demonstrate the relevance of the factors examined.

According to public international law, WTO Members must perform their WTO obligations in good faith[25].

In the case at hand, this means that the fact that during the proceedings referred to in Article 3 of the SA the interested parties made comments which put elements of the investigation into question, and in particular gave rise to doubt as to whether (the threat of) serious injury existed and whether increased imports were the cause thereof, is relevant in determining whether the US competent authorities have complied with Article 4 SA.

Factors can only be deemed to have been properly "evaluated", and their relevance can only be deemed to have been "demonstrated" by the competent authorities in their report, if in that report those authorities explain in a properly reasoned fashion why the arguments detracting from a serious injury and/or cau-

---

[23] see ITC report II-37 top of page.

[24] pages II-37 and II-37a.

[25] Article 26 of the Vienna Convention on the Law of Treaties.

sation finding which have been raised during the proceedings before them, are not valid.

The ITC has not only completely failed to investigate certain factors, but it failed also to properly explain its conclusions as to other factors, especially since EC producers had during the ITC proceedings explained in detail why those factors detracted from a finding of serious injury and/or causation.

In fact, by its question N. 6, the Panel very rightly points the finger to another unacceptable aspect of the ITC report: it does not correctly and fully address the major points which have been made by the EC's exporters during the hearings. For the benefit of the Panel, the EC submits, as Exhibits EC-16, EC-17 and EC-18, the pre-hearing brief submitted on behalf of EC producers, the report of the December 1997 hearing before the ITC and the post-hearing brief submitted on behalf of EC producers.

For instance, the point that imports by US producers themselves were a positive business strategy since it avoids having to dispose of necessary co-products in an adverse market situation in the US was made very explicitly in those briefs.

The EC refers to the pre-hearing brief, Exhibit EC-16, on pages 2 and explained in detail in pages 24-27.

The point was repeated in the post-hearing brief, Exhibit EC-18, at page 2 (first bullet point), page 3-5, and repeated on page 32 footnote 84. In the post-hearing brief, the statement made by Mr. Stout, president of the Manildra Milling Corporation, that Manildra had been an importer of wheat gluten (from Australia) for many, many years and that it therefore would go on importing in the future as well is cited literally.

However, as the Panel has rightly observed, the ITC conveniently failed to mention that this issue had been brought up by EC exporters, and of course did not provide any explanation whatsoever as to why, in its view, this factor does not detract from a finding of serious injury.

Also, the argument on capacity expansion was explicitly brought forward on behalf of EC exporters. The EC refers to page 5 of the pre-hearing report (Exhibit EC16), where it was explicitly argued that "decisions to invest and to expand capacity are a reflection of industry health".

Questions N. 8 and 9

Article 4.2(b) of the Safeguards Agreement states : "When factors other than increased imports are causing injury to the domestic industry at the same time, such injury shall not be attributed to increased imports." We note that the term used in this sentence is "injury" rather than "serious injury". What is the meaning and relevance, if any, of this distinction?

What is the legal basis in the Safeguards Agreement for a causation analysis that examines whether or not certain factors are "a more important cause of serious injury than increased imports"? What guidance, if any, can be found on this issue in past GATT/WTO practice?

Joint Reply

The Panel's question N. 8 correctly draws the attention to the fact that while the explicit condition under Article XIX of the GATT and Article 2.1 of the SA is that a "*serious* injury" must be caused by increased imports if a Member wishes to apply a safeguard measure, Article 4.2 (b), last sentence, refers only to "injury". "Serious injury" is defined in Article 4.1 of the SA as "a significant overall impairment in the position of a domestic industry".

In the EC's view, the reason for such a different wording resides in the fact that a Member is only allowed to impose a safeguard measure if its investigation demonstrates, by the evaluation of *all* the relevant factors of an objective and quantifiable nature having a bearing on the situation of the industry concerned, that "increased imports" caused "serious injury" (i.e. an "overall impairment in the position of a domestic industry") *per se*, i.e. taken alone. This can only be achieved by demonstrating, again in the investigation report,

- that other factors which contributed to the injury did not cause by themselves the "*serious* injury", and
- that after the factors other than increased imports which (also) cause injury have been removed from the analysis, still increased imports, *alone*, cause *serious* injury.

In such a case, however, the specific provisions contained in the SA impose that the safeguard measure can only remedy the serious injury caused *by imports*, to the exclusion of other factors co-causing injury (Article 5.1 SA).

If a number of events, one of which is the increased imports, amount *together* to a "significant overall impairment of the position of the domestic industry" but none of them can cause *per se* a "significant overall impairment" but only "injury", the Member concerned *is not allowed to* implement a safeguard measure.

As an answer to question N.9, in the only previous report concerning a safeguard measure under the GATT 1947, the "*Hatter's Fur*" case between Czechoslovakia and the US, a Working party confirmed such a reading. It stated[26] the following

> "The United States contention that the domestic production of plain felt hat bodies was "to some extent" affected by the increased imports of velours does not bear examination. (...) The actual development of the domestic United States production of women's fur felt hat bodies from 1947 to the end of 1950 was such that *there was no **serious** injury caused to it by the increasing imports of ve-*

[26] October 1951, at para. 22 (b), page 12.

> *lours*. The Czechoslovak representative referred to a graph drawn by him from the United States data showing the actual development of the United States production. What in fact happened was that the change in fashion created a new market and the demand was such that in 1949 and in the first half of 1950 the exporters and also the domestic producers were unable to fulfil all the orders they received for the special finishes. The market for plain felt hat bodies remained stationary; the domestic production of these types was estimated in thousand dozens by the Czechoslovak representative at 487 in 1947, 614 in 1948, 541 in 1949 and 550 in 1950. The action taken by the United States Government operated not to protect the domestic industry from a threat of injury but to protect an attempt by the domestic producers to capture and monopolize the new market by killing the import trade and to accumulate profits which previously never came their way. The application of Article XIX in this respect was improper." (emphasis added)

In this very relevant precedent (quoted also by the AB in its report on "*Argentina - Footwear*"), the working party follows the correct logic of evaluating whether increased imports have caused "*serious* injury" *per se*. The fact that they contributed to injury caused by other factors is not enough to render the safeguard measure compatible with the GATT (now GATT/WTO provisions).

The EC is in fact convinced that the present wording of Article 4.2 (b) was inspired by such previous report.

With the above-mentioned elements in mind, there can be no doubt that the US legislation (US Trade Act of 1974, Sections 201 and following, as amended) mandating the US authorities to examine whether or not increased imports are only a "substantial" cause" and whether or not certain factors are "a more important cause of serious injury than increased imports" has no basis whatsoever in WTO law.

Indeed, such US internal statutory provision establishes a rule of preponderance which is clearly in conflict with the SA, both Article 4.2 (b) and 5.1. In case of concurring causes of injury, the US law prevents the investigating authorities from verifying the only important issue, i.e. whether increased imports are *per se* the cause of "significant overall impairment of the position of the domestic industry". The US investigating authorities are limited by the US law to investigating a different issue, i.e. whether there is a single cause "more important" than increased imports.

This is incompatible with Article 4.2 SA, because it confuses "injury" with "serious injury", and produces in any case as a consequence a disproportionate extent of the safeguard measure, also in breach of Article 5.1 of the SA. This WTO-incompatible way of evaluating the causes of injury was followed by the US investigating authorities in the case of wheat gluten. The safeguard measure taken as a result of such investigation is clearly disproportionate.

Question N.10

What is the legal relationship between Article 5.2 of the Safeguards Agreement and Article I of the GATT 1994? What legal principles and/or past GATT/WTO practice give guidance in this context?

Reply

According to the Appellate Body report on "*Bananas*" at footnote 138

> "In addition to Article I (the fundamental MFN provision of the GATT), Articles III:7, IV(b), V:2 and V:5, IX:1 and XIII:1 are also MFN-type obligations in the GATT 1994."
>
> According to the Panel report on "*Bananas - Complaint by the United States*"[27]
>
> "Article XIII's general requirement of non-discrimination is modified in one respect by Article XIII:2(d), which provides for the possibility to allocate tariff quota shares to supplying countries. Any such country specific allocation must, however, "aim at a distribution of trade ... approaching as closely as possible the shares which Members might be expected to obtain in the absence of such restrictions" (chapeau of Article XIII:2(d)).
>
> Article XIII:2(d) further specifies the treatment that, in case of country-specific allocation of tariff quota shares, must be given to Members with "a substantial interest in supplying the product concerned". For those Members, the Member proposing to impose restrictions may seek agreement with them as provided in Article XIII:2(d), first sentence. If that is not reasonably practicable, then it must allot shares in the quota (or tariff quota) to them on the basis of the criteria specified in Article XIII:2(d), second sentence.
>
> (...) [i]n the absence of agreements with all Members having a substantial interest in supplying the product, the Member applying the restriction must allocate shares in accordance with the rules of Article XIII:2(d), second sentence".

Finally, according to the Panel report on "*EC - Bananas - Recourse to Article 21.5 by Ecuador*"[28]

> "We have taken appropriate account of the EC's admonition that we should not interpret Article XIII so as to reduce [the Lomé waiver or] Article I to inutility."

Article 5.2 (a) of the SA is the reproduction *word by word* of Article XIII.2 (d) of the GATT 1994. Article 5.2 (b) is a provision specific to the SA that

---

[27] DS27, at paras. 7.70 to 7.72.

[28] at 6.32.

allows a Member applying a safeguard measure to derogate from the general rules under Article XIII and 5.2 (a). This exceptional possibility is however subject to imperative procedural requirements that must be accurately followed.

Thus, in the EC's view, Article 5.2 of the SA is the *lex specialis* applicable when the allocation of a quota is considered. The interpretation of 5.2 (a) should logically follow the interpretation given to Article XIII.2 (d) by previous panel and Appellate Body reports.

In the case of the US safeguard measure on wheat gluten, the US has indicated in its oral statement on 21 December 1999 that

> "Article 5.2(a) does not establish a duty to consult"[29]

As the plain text of Article 5.2 (a) and the interpretations of Article XIII.2 (d) demonstrate, this assumption is doubly incorrect. On the one hand, these provisions impose an obligation to "seek to reach agreement". This is much more than a mere obligation to consult. In any case, without a consultation in good faith on a proposed agreement, the EC fails to see how the US could claim it has fulfilled this obligation. On the other hand, an obligation of providing reasons as to why this method was not "reasonably practicable" is also imposed. In this respect again, the US did not live up to its WTO obligations.

> " [t]he reality is that GATT Article I is not implicated because the US measure is a quota and not a tariff."[30]

This statement is incorrect. As the above mentioned panel and AB reports[31] show, Article I, as the "fundamental" MFN obligation, is not set aside by the existence of Article XIII (or in the case of a safeguard measure, by the corresponding provisions in Article 5.2 of the SA). Article XIII (and Article 5.2 SA) is limited to the specific issue of how the allocation of a quota or a tariff quota is implemented by the Member adopting such a measure. Article I is in general applicable "to *any* advantage, favour, privilege or immunity granted". In the case of the safeguard measure on wheat gluten, the EC has demonstrated that the US has protected Australian exports to the US and so not accorded the same treatment to like products imported from the EC.

This protection goes beyond the WTO-inconsistent distribution of the WTO-inconsistent quota on wheat gluten. For example, a considered policy of importation of wheat gluten from Australia by Manildra, the Australian owned *US-based* company and petitioner, which corresponds to its business strategy of optimising profits cannot, by definition, be considered an injury, let alone a serious injury, for the purposes of justifying a safeguard measure. However, the US

29 at page 8.

30 IbIdem.

31 The Appellate Body Report, *European Communities – Measures Affecting the Importation of Certain* Poultry *Products* ("*EC - Poultry*"), WT/DS69/AB/R, adopted 23 July 1998, DSR 1998:V, 2031 further demonstrates the inconsistency of the US assertions.

authorities did not consider this element when assessing the injury allegedly resulting from increased imports.

While Manildra was complaining of capacity under-utilisation to the US investigating authorities it was at the same time increasing its imports into the US from Australia. In spite of this contradictory behaviour, the US authorities examined and accepted the complaint while ignoring the imports.

These and other facts already submitted to the Panel have the effect to constitute *de facto substantial* "advantages", "favours" and "privileges" granted to Australian exports of wheat gluten not immediately and unconditionally accorded to EC's imports of wheat gluten into the US.

> "The EC cites Article 5.2(b), but that Article is irrelevant because the United States did not take action under Article 5.2(b)."[32]

Article 5.2 (b) is certainly not irrelevant in this context, since it is the only provision that could justify, under strict procedural conditions, a deviation from the requirements of Article 5.2 (a). As a result of the above quotation, the US confirms that it has not followed such a procedure, as the EC has claimed before the Panel.

Since it did not follow the procedures under Article 5.2 (b), the US has no explanation left as to how it can justify that despite having a 47 per cent share of the market in the previous representative period, the EC was allocated only a 43 per cent share of the quota. Australia, on the other hand, was allocated a share of 49 per cent, compared to its share in the previous representative period of 38 per cent. More importantly, *this allocation has preserved entirely the 1997 record levels of imports from Australia despite the fact that Australia's exports increased continuously in the last three years of the investigative period, by almost 21 per cent*[33]. In fact, the ITC report[34] clearly indicates the ITC's intent to target "the disproportional growth and impact of imports of wheat gluten from the European Union".

Regardless of whether the US has proved that the EC wheat gluten exports' increase was disproportionate, *quod non*, without recourse to Article 5.2 (b) procedures, which are specifically designed to address well-documented cases of "disproportionate increase", the result obtained by the US authorities could be achieved in a WTO-consistent manner.

Outside the scope of this exceptional provision, the SA does not provide for the protection of the market share of third countries. Article 2 expressly requires equal treatment for imports from *all* sources. The SA is intended to allow for relief and facilitate adjustment to be provided to the *domestic* industry, and *only* the domestic industry. Relief can be provided only to the extent necessary to

---

32 US oral statement on 20 December 1999, at page 12.

33 ITC report at II-12.

34 at I-21.

alleviate injury and facilitate adjustment to the *domestic* industry. The US argued in its first oral statement[35] that the years 1996 and 1997 were not "representative" because imports from the EC "distorted the relative distribution of market shares among foreign suppliers."

The redistribution of market shares through the quota allocation, therefore, is not justified on the basis of alleviating any injury to the domestic injury, but on the intent to restore Australia's market share relative to the United States.

> "the disproportional growth and impact of imports of wheat gluten from the European Union."

As explained above, without recourse to Article 5.2 (b) procedures, which are specifically designed to deal with such alleged "disproportionate increase", this result cannot be achieved in a WTO-consistent manner.

Questions N. 11 and 24

Can the parties indicate whether consultations took place on 24 April 1998 as the United States is suggesting, and, if so, whether the parties discussed the measure proposed in the United States notification of 24 March 1998?

Does the EC agree with the United States that consultations within the meaning of Article 12.3 of the Safeguards Agreement were held on 24 April 1998 regarding the proposed wheat gluten safeguard measure?

Joint Reply

Consultations under Article 12.3 SA took place between the parties on 24 April 1998 and 22 May 1998 in Geneva. During the consultations the US explained the recommendations of the ITC and referred to the power of the US president to adopt any of the recommended measures or none of them. These consultations only therefore dealt with information provided by the US in the notifications under Article 12.1(b) SA.

The EC does not agree that these consultations were consultations on the "proposed measure" since at the time of the consultations the US had not yet notified any proposal either to the EC as a Member having a substantial interest as exporter of the product concerned or to the WTO.

Internal recommendations, in particular if they are subject to full discretion by the deciding authority, cannot constitute such "proposed measures". In this respect, Article 12 SA establishes a sequence of events starting with the notification of Article 12.1 (c), providing information to the Committee on Safeguards and the Council of Trade in Goods under Article 12.2 and consultations under Article 12.3 SA on the proposed measure.

Only after "taking a decision to apply a safeguard measure" and its notification under Article 12.1(c), a Member is considered "proposing to apply" a

[35] Pages 11and 12.

safeguard measures since Article 12.2 first sentence explicitly refers to this notification.

Clearly, a Member which only notifies a finding of serious injury under Article 12.1(b) does not yet "propose to apply a safeguard measure". Furthermore, consultations under Art. 12.3 on the proposed measure can only be held once a decision to take a safeguard measure has been made and notified (Article 12.3 SA refers again to a Member "proposing a safeguard measure").

In this case, the Article 12.1(c) notification of the US President's decision to apply safeguard measures was made after the two rounds of consultations were held.

Question N. 12

On page 34 of its oral statement, the EC refers to an "informal meeting" held on 19-20 May 1999. Do the parties consider that this meeting constituted "consultations" within the meaning of Article 12.3 of the Safeguards Agreement?

Reply

The EC confirms that these consultations were *not* consultation held within the meaning of Article 12.3 of the SA.

Question N. 13

With respect to production, capacity and capacity utilization, what is the meaning and relevance of the following statement at p. II-14 of the ITC Report: "ADM, Manildra and Midwest reported that dryer capacity defines the limit on production capacity for wheat gluten."

Reply

Since this is an ITC-statement, the EC considers it appropriate that in the first instance the US itself explains its meaning and relevance; however, the EC reserves the right to revert to this point at the second substantive meeting.

Question N. 17

We note that the EC did not refer to Article 3 of the Safeguards Agreement in its panel request. In what way and on what legal basis is the EC referring to Article 3 of the Safeguards Agreement in these proceedings?

Reply

As the Appellate Body stated in paragraph 74 of its report on "Argentina-Footwear"

> "We note that the very terms of Article 4.2(c) of the *Agreement on Safeguards* expressly incorporate the provisions of Article 3. Thus, we find it difficult to see how a panel could examine whether a Member had complied with Article 4.2(c) without also referring to the provisions of Article 3 of the *Agreement on Safeguards*. More

particularly, given the express language of Article 4.2(c), we do not see how a panel could ignore the publication requirement set out in Article 3.1 when examining the publication requirement in Article 4.2(c) of the *Agreement on Safeguards*. And, generally, we fail to see how the Panel could have interpreted the requirements of Article 4.2(c) *without* taking into account in some way the provisions of Article 3. What is more, we fail to see how any panel could be expected to make an "objective assessment of the matter", as required by Article 11 of the DSU, if it could only refer in its reasoning to the specific provisions cited by the parties in their claims."

The EC refers to Article 3 exactly in this manner and to the effect indicated by the AB.

Question N. 18

At p. I-13 of its Report, the ITC states that it "received usable financial data on wheat gluten operations from three of the four domestic producers of wheat gluten....The three firms accounted for the substantial majority of domestic production of wheat gluten." Why precisely does the EC object to this degree of data coverage and on what legal basis?

Reply

Indeed, the EC objects to the fact that the ITC collected only insufficient financial data on US producers' wheat gluten operations[36]. There are at least two cumulative issues here.

First of all, one of the only four firms constituting the US wheat starch/wheat gluten industry only entered the market in June 1996. Obviously it therefore only reported financial data for the last year of the PoI.

New entrants in a market due to start-up difficulties practically always are unprofitable in the first year of their operations. This new entry in the last year of the PoI therefore must have had a negative impact on the overall US wheat starch/wheat gluten producers' situation as reported by the ITC. It gives the impression of a negative trend in 1996 and 1997 compared with 1995, although the new entrant simply was not there in 1995.

The second issue is that ADM, according to the ITC itself, "did not provide usable financial data on its US wheat gluten operations, but rather provided combined data on its US and Canadian wheat gluten and wheat starch operations[37]. There is no explanation in the ITC report as to why ADM could not provide separate data on its US operations, nor does the report detail any efforts made by the ITC to obtain US specific data from ADM. Therefore, with regard to

[36] See in particular para. 65 of its first written submission.

[37] ITC report at I-17 and at II-17, footnote 45.

ADM, one of the three main operators, the US authorities failed to comply with their obligation under Article 4.2 (a) of the SA to obtain relevant data.

Questions N. 19, 20, 21 and 22

In paragraph 165 of its first written submission, the EC argues that paragraph 3 of Article 12 "provides further clarification that the measure should be notified immediately when it is proposed, not after it has been put into place". Does the EC consider that both the proposed measure and the final measure have to be notified?

If a proposed measure is altered before it is imposed, must the modification be notified prior to imposition of the measure?

In paragraph 166 of its first written submission, the EC submits that the United States failed to notify each and every step in Article 12.1 Safeguards Agreement in a timely manner. In paragraph 200 of its first written submission, the United States is arguing that the EC's interpretation of Article 12 Safeguards Agreement suggests that a Member is obliged first to issue "preliminary" findings of serious injury that the Committee would then examine and ratify. Does the EC agree with this interpretation of its argument?

The United States argues that it notified the proposed measure and that consultations were held. The United States refers to its notification pursuant to Article 12.1 (b) of the Safeguards Agreement of 24 March 1998 (United States Exhibit 6). Could the EC explain why it does not consider this notification to be a notification of the proposed measure?

Joint Reply

The provisions under Article 12 of the SA aim at ensuring the achievement of two fundamental objectives:

(a) that meaningful and timely consultations are opened with the exporting Members in order "to endeavour to maintain a substantially equivalent level of concessions and other obligations to that existing under GATT 1994";

(b) that transparency is ensured vis-à-vis the Membership of the WTO in general. This is not a mere formality. It is a response to the very concrete preoccupation that other (non-exporting) Members could indirectly suffer from the imposition of a safeguard measure because of diversion of trade into their territories that could be caused by the restricted access to the market of the Member adopting the safeguard measure.

In order to achieve these fundamental objectives, *good faith*, *timeliness* and *transparency* are the three musts of the required notifications and consultations under Article 12 of the SA. This explains in particular the repeated reference in paragraphs 2 and 3 to "proposed" measures or Member "proposing" the measure.

Any meaningful and good faith consultation must take place in time and before the measure is adopted, on the basis of timely notified texts, at each and every step of the procedure. If such consultations and notifications are reduced to pure formalities, the objective pursued by WTO Members through the agreement in Marrakech on the text of Article 12 of the SA are irreparably lost. The same consideration can be made with respect to the term "immediately" in Article 12.1. This is also the core of the findings of the "*Korea-Dairy*" panel that were not overturned by the AB recent report[38]. In this case, Korea notified a proposed measure under Article 12.1(c) on 21 January 1997, held consultations under Article 12.3 thereafter, and finally notified the final measures under Article 12.1 (c) on 24 March 1997.

In the light of the above, the EC can answer the panel's questions as follows:

(19) Article 12 imposes explicitly (and thus undisputedly) an obligation to notify "proposed" measures, i.e. after a decision to apply them is taken and *before* they are applied. For transparency reasons, the final adopted measure should also be notified to the WTO "immediately" upon "taking a decision to apply (...) a safeguard measure". In the present case, the US made its first notification under Art. 12.1 (c) on 8 June 1998, i.e. after the measure was applied on 1 June 1998.

(20) Yes. This is confirmed by the precedent in *Korea-Dairy*. Korea notified a proposed measure under Art. 12.1 (c) on 1 January 1997, which was different from the final measure notified on 24 March 1997.

(21) The US position in paragraph 200 of its first written submission appears much more an attempt to re-negotiate Article 12's wording than a reading of its plain text or of the corresponding EC's claims. The US comment in paragraph 200 refers to paragraph 168 of the EC's first written submission which is made up, in its two thirds, by a paraphrase of Article 12.2 of the SA. The plain text of Article 12 imposes the notification of the "proposed" measures. The final measure must also be notified.

(22) *First*, the format of the US notification on 24 March 1998 does not allow the information contained therein to be regarded as "proposed measures."

As it appears from the text of the notification[39], the US notified the ITC report (also containing certain recommendations on the remedy) under Article 12.1 (b), i.e. "upon making a finding of serious

[38] See para. 169 of the EC first written submission.

[39] Cf. title and the third para. of page 1 of the WTO doc. G/SG/N/8/USA/2/rev. 1.

injury caused by increased imports". It is clear from the legal basis referred to by the US for this notification that it cannot contain "proposed measures". Such a proposal must be based on Article 12.1 (c) (taking a decision to apply a measure). By not doing so, the US implied that the statements contained in this notification on the ITC recommendations could not be considered "proposed measures" in the meaning of Articles 12.2 and 12.3 SA.

Second, the information referred to in the Article 12.1 (b) notifications only contained recommendations by the ITC to the US President.

However, to qualify as "proposed measures" in the meaning of Article 12.2 and 12.3 SA, measures must be proposed by a WTO Member to the WTO Committee on Safeguards and the Council of Trade in Goods, not by one governmental authority to another within the institutional framework of the same WTO Member. The fact that in the Article 12.1 (b) notifications the heading for the ITC's statements on the possible remedies states "proposed measures" does not affect their nature as purely internal, non-binding recommendations which did not constitute a proposal of the WTO Member "United States of America" to the WTO.

Third, under US implementing legislation the US President has full discretion whether or not to follow the ITC recommendation.

This was even stressed by the US during the consultations under Article 12.3 SA on the content of the Article 12.1(b) notifications on 24 April 1998. Therefore, it was entirely uncertain before measures were actually applied, whether or not, and in which form, measures would be imposed. Consequently, it was not possible to achieve the purposes of Article 12.3, in particular the objective set out in Article 8.1 SA on trade compensation. Assuming *arguendo* that an understanding on ways to achieve the objective set out in Article 8.1 is proposed (and the US did *not* propose anything in the case of wheat gluten) WTO Members cannot agree on re-balancing their concessions unless they are certain which concessions and to what extent they will be withdrawn.

As a conclusion, it is clear that the procedures laid down in US legislation as applied in this case, cannot permit meaningful consultations on the remedy as provided for in Article 12.3 SA. To this extent, the US practice is in violation of the SA.

Questions N. 23 and 25

The United States is suggesting in paragraphs 205 and 208 of its first written submission that the EC is claiming that Article 8 of the Safeguards Agreement requires that substantially equivalent concessions be provided before a Member, in casu the United States, can take a safeguard action. Is this a cor-

rect reflection of the EC's argument under Article 8 of the Safeguards Agreement?

Could the EC expand on the relationship between Article XXVIII of the GATT 1994 and Article 8 of the Safeguards Agreement?

Joint Reply

The Appellate Body has reminded in its recent "*Korea-Dairy*"[40] report that

> "We should not lose sight of the fact that taking safeguard action results in restrictions on imports arising from "fair" trade. The application of a safeguard measure does not depend upon "unfair" trade actions, as is the case with anti-dumping or countervailing measures".
>
> In its "*Argentina - Footwear*" report at paragraph 93 the AB has significantly added that
>
> "The remedy that Article XIX:1(a) allows in this situation is temporarily to "suspend the obligation in whole or in part or to withdraw or modify the concession". Thus, Article XIX is clearly, and in every way, an extraordinary remedy."

Such an extraordinary remedy "in every way" to the detriment of "fair" trade cannot be interpreted, as the US does, as a three years window of opportunity to go back from its GATT concessions at no cost, without genuinely and effectively offer adequate compensation capable of maintaining "a substantially equivalent level of concessions and other obligations to that existing under GATT 1994 between it and the exporting Members which would be affected by such a measure" (Article 8.1 of the SA). This is the textual and substantial meaning both of Article 8.1 and of Article 12.3 of the SA ("with a view (...) to reaching an understanding on ways to achieve the objective set out in paragraph 1 of Article 8").

Such a *genuine* endeavour to reach an understanding on the ways to maintain a substantially equivalent level of concessions or other obligations is not fulfilled by a mere convening of an informal meeting were the Member wishing to adopt the measure politely listens to the exporting Member's complaints.

The adopting Member, *in casu* the US, must *demonstrate* to the Panel that it has *actively* and *concretely offered* an *adequate* compensation and that that compensation was positively rejected or at least was not accepted by the exporting Member concerned. The US cannot prove this in this case for the simple reason that it never endeavoured in good faith to "maintain a substantially equivalent level of concessions or other obligations". In fact, the US officials were not in a position to negotiate at all. Articles 8.1 and 12.3 of the SA have been drafted

[40] Para. 87.

with Article XXVIII of the GATT 1994, and in particular Article XXVIII.2, and with the findings of the Panel on "*Newsprint*" in mind. Any compensation should of course, as is the case when Article XXVIII is applicable, be offered on a MFN basis.

ATTACHMENT 1-4

SECOND WRITTEN SUBMISSION OF THE EUROPEAN COMMUNITY
(17 January 2000)

1. Introduction

1. This second submission serves mainly two functions:

- to rebut certain statements and affirmations by the US which were expressed during the first substantive meeting with the Panel and
- to recall the main claims and arguments of the EC in this case.

Of course, the other points of law and procedure which were advanced by the EC during the first stages of this dispute settlement procedure (including the answers to the questions from the panel) should also be considered entirely confirmed here. This is true in particular for the EC's claims and arguments concerning the violation by the US safeguard measure on wheat gluten of Article I of the GATT 1994 and Articles 12 and 8 of the SA.

2. The EC will thus proceed as follows: a number of items will be listed, under which some of its major claims and arguments will be recalled and summarised, and through which rebuttals of US arguments will be made.

2. Item N. 1: Standard of review of this Panel

3. As the Appellate Body confirmed in its very recent report on *Argentina - Footwear* (at paragraph 118), Article 11 of the DSU contains the guiding principles for Panels when pursuing an examination of a case in its substance:

> "(...) a panel should make an objective assessment of the matter before it, including an objective assessment of the facts of the case and the applicability of and conformity with the relevant covered agreements (...)".

4. In the case of this dispute settlement procedure, the Appellate Body has also set out the Panel's task in clear words[1]

> "So far as fact-finding by panels is concerned, their activities are always constrained by the mandate of Article 11 of the DSU: the applicable standard is neither *de novo* review as such, nor "total deference", but rather the "objective assessment of the facts". Many panels have in the past refused to undertake *de novo* review, wisely, since under current practice and systems, they are in any

[1] Appellate Body Report, *EC Measures Concerning Meat and Meat Products (Hormones)* ("*EC – Hormones*"), WT/DS26/AB/R, WT/DS/48/R, adopted 13 February 1998, DSR 1998:I, 135, para. 117.

case poorly suited to engage in such a review. On the other hand, "total deference to the findings of the national authorities", it has been well said, "could not ensure an 'objective assessment' as foreseen by Article 11 of the DSU".

5. This is exactly what the EC requests this Panel to do. In particular, the Panel will need to verify whether the US has fulfilled its obligations under the SA and the GATT 1994 before resorting to its safeguard measure on wheat gluten. As the EC has already indicated in its first oral statement, in order to achieve that result, the Panel is thus required to examine the following issues:

- Have the US authorities demonstrated, as they should, that the conditions under Article 2 SA and Article XIX GATT 1994 have been fulfilled? The EC submits that they have not.
- Have the US authorities considered, as they should, "*all* pertinent issues of fact and law" (Article 3.1 SA) including "*all* relevant factors of an *objective* and *quantifiable* nature *having a bearing* on the situation of that industry" (Article 4.2 (a) SA)? The EC submits that they have not.
- Have the US authorities presented, as they should, their findings, conclusions and determinations in a "reasoned" (i.e. rational, non-contradictory and clear) way (Article 3.1 DSU), based on "objective evidence" (i.e. based on criteria that are not biased by subjective, political or unrelated aims) (Article 4.2 (b) SA)? The EC submits that they have not.
- Have the US authorities established, as they should, the "*existence* (i.e. a positive and irrefutable evidence of its reality) of the causal link between increased imports of the product concerned and serious injury" (Article 4.2 (b) SA)? Have the US authorities ensured that injury caused by other factors was not attributed to increased imports? The EC submits that they have not.
- Have the US authorities applied the safeguard measure, as they should, "*only to the extent necessary*" (i.e. proportionate or commensurate to) to prevent or remedy serious injury and to facilitate adjustment (Article 5.1 SA)? Have the US authorities provided "a clear justification" (i.e. a detailed objective and unbiased explanation) when deciding to apply quantitative restrictions and when choosing a period different from the last three representative years for which statistics are available? Moreover, have the US authorities fulfilled the other substantive and procedural obligations under Article 5.2 of the SA and under Article I of GATT 1994? The EC submits that they have not.
- Have the US authorities complied with the procedural obligations under Articles 8 and 12 of the SA? The EC submits that they have not.

6. In order to examine the matter according to the standard required by WTO law, the EC submits again that the Panel cannot be content with a superficial glance at the issues, taking at face value the text of the investigation report, as the US would have it. Rather, it must concentrate on the *substance* of the evidence that actually *is* in the report or *should have been* in the report since it was either considered during the investigation procedure, or should have been considered as pertinent evidence that was *publicly* available, or had been submitted to the ITC during the investigation procedure.

7. The US has tried to push the Panel off-track on this crucial issue by making the following incorrect assertions:

(a) *US assertion*: some previous panel reports on anti-dumping should serve as a basis for setting the standard of review of this Panel.[2]

As the AB report on "*Argentina-Footwear*"[3] has indicated, this approach is incorrect. The particular legal nature of anti-dumping measures as compared with safeguard measure[4] , the existence of provisions specific to the SA which are not reproduced in the WTO Agreement on Implementation of Article VI of the GATT 1994 and the self-standing obligations flowing from Article 11 of the DSU exclude such a cross-reference.

(b) *US assertion*: the Safeguards Agreement does not impose an obligation on competent authorities to explain why they found some factors irrelevant and thus did not rely on them.[5]

This is also incorrect. As the Appellate Body stressed in "*Argentina-Footwear*"[6], the Safeguard Agreement imposes on the competent authority not only an obligation to evaluate all the relevant facts but requires the authority to "**adequately explain** how the facts support the determination". Therefore the SA does impose an explicit obligation to justify *how* a certain result is achieved in the investigation. The US authorities are obliged to "publish a report setting forth their findings and reasoned conclusions reached on all pertinent issues of fact and law" (Article 3.1 SA).

In order to determine what is pertinent and what is not, the US should have indicated in a "reasoned" (i.e. expressed as a coherently argued case) the standard for determining which facts should be considered pertinent. In light of such standard, the US should have logically indicated why it believed that certain other facts were not pertinent. Without such an ex-

---

[2] Para. 61 of the US first written submission, pages 7 and 8 of the US first oral statement on 20 December 1999.

[3] Appellate Body Report, *Argentina - Safeguard Measures on Imports of Footwear* ("*Argentina - Footwear Safeguard*"), WT/DS121/AB/R, adopted 12 January 2000, DSR 2000:I, 515, para 117.

[4] Appellate Body Report , *Korea - Definitive Safeguard Measure on Imports of Certain Dairy Products* ("*Korea – Dairy Safeguard*"), WT/DS98/AB/R, adopted 12 January 2000, DSR 2000:I, 3, para. 87.

[5] Para. 58 of the US first written submission.

[6] *Argentina-Footwear, supra*, footnote 3, paras 121 and 145.

planation, the Panel would have no room for independent judgement and only *deference* to national authorities would in fact be possible. Thus, the US suggested interpretation of this Panel's standard of review would have the result that there could be no real "objective assessment of the facts" as Article 11 of the DSU requires.

Article 4.2 SA goes further. It imposes upon the US the obligation to "evaluate all relevant factors of an objective and quantifiable nature having a bearing on the situation of that industry, in particular (...)".

The US authorities should have provided "a detailed analysis of this broad and thorough examination that includes *all* the elements, including those that are susceptible to lead to a decision *not* to adopt a safeguard measure[7], as well as a demonstration of the factors examined" (Article 4.2 (c) SA). , In fact, the US authorities have breached these rules by systematically suppressing, downplaying or otherwise misrepresenting in their report relevant objective facts which indicated that there was no ground to proceed to the adoption of any safeguard measure on wheat gluten.

(c) *US assertion*: the national investigative authorities are limited by the evidence and the views presented before them and have no duty themselves to search "somewhere" for any other information.[8]

This assertion should be rejected as erroneous and in order to avoid setting a troubling precedent. Firstly, it is clear from the text of both Articles 3 and 4 of the SA that there is a positive obligation for national investigative authorities to look into "*all* pertinent issues of fact and law" and "*all* relevant factors of an objective and quantifiable nature having a bearing on the situation" of the industry concerned. Any suggestion that the national authorities are limited by the scope of the complaint which initiated the domestic procedure or by specific rebuttal arguments made during the domestic procedure is without foundation in WTO law.

Secondly, the EC has shown that what the US competent authorities have ignored or suppressed or downplayed or otherwise misrepresented in this case, are pertinent and publicly available data whose source is the US government itself. In other words, the US authorities had themselves gathered those facts and put them in the public domain. They cannot pretend now that they were not aware of them or that they could not examine and consider them.

Thirdly, the US investigative authorities have in any event failed even by the standard of evidence postulated by the US above. The ITC disregarded pertinent information and data provided by the industry during the

---

7 See Panel Report, *Korea - Definitive Safeguard Measure on Imports of Certain Dairy Products* ("*Korea – Dairy Safeguard*"), WT/DS98/R and Corr. 1, adopted 12 January 2000, DSR 2000:I, 49, para. 7.55 ("or detracts from").

8 Pages 4 and 5 of the US oral statement on 21 December 1999.

procedure before it, as will be shown in examining Items N. 3 and 4 below.

The troubling aspect of the US interpretation is that the US is in effect suggesting to the Panel that in the international trade relations between the US and the other WTO Members there could be a reversed hierarchy of norms, according to which the US internal domestic practices (based on its domestic law) would prevail over US WTO obligations under the SA. The EC disagrees with this approach, which would undermine a fundamental principle of the WTO legal system as expressed in Article XVI.4 of the Marrakech Agreement.[9] The WTO obligations on a Member to discharge its duties under the SA cannot be diminished by the implementation procedures instituted by that Member.

(d) *US assertion*: the US claims in paragraph 158 of its first written submission that it has only misapplied its own policy concerning reporting of aggregate data.[10] It denies that it has misapplied the provisions of Articles 3 and 4 of the SA.

In paragraph 1 58 of its first written submission, the US has declared that "(...) the policy guidelines were not met as to some of the pricing data that were withheld from disclosure. Consequently, the USITC has now prepared a corrigendum to the public report that provides the portion of the pricing data and certain other information that can be disclosed (attached as Exhibit 10 to this submission)."

The obligation flowing from Articles 3 and 4 to publish *all* relevant factors of an objective and quantifiable nature having a bearing on the industry concerned is binding on the US regardless of its internal domestic legislation. By the statement above, the US has accepted that it has violated its WTO obligations. Its attempt to heal the breach retrospectively is legally impossible, since the obligation refers to timely publication ("promptly"). Its attempt to make the Panel abstain from looking into this issue on the pretext that it concerns only "USITC own policy" has no merit under the WTO and cannot limit in any way the scope of the Panel's review pursuant to Article 11 of the DSU.

3. Item N. 2: the US has breached Article XIX of the GATT 1994 ("Unforeseen developments")

8. As the EC recalled in its oral statement on 20 December 1999, the burden rests *on the US* to show where it has demonstrated *in the ITC report* or in the legal act adopting the safeguard measure that unexpected circumstances had "led

[9] "Each Member shall ensure the conformity of its laws, regulations and administrative procedures with its obligations as provided in the annexed Agreements".

[10] Pages 5 and 6 of the US oral statement on 21 December 1999.

to a product [wheat gluten] being imported in such increased quantities and under such conditions as to cause or threaten to cause serious injury to domestic producers."[11]

9. The AB has further indicated that

> "The first clause in Article XIX:1(a) – "as a result of unforeseen developments and of the obligations incurred by a Member under the Agreement, including tariff concessions ... " – is a dependent clause which, in our view, is linked grammatically to the verb phrase "is being imported" in the second clause of that paragraph.(...) In this sense, we believe that there is a logical connection between the circumstances described in the first clause – "as a result of unforeseen developments and of the effect of the obligations incurred by a Member under this Agreement, including tariff concessions ..." – and the conditions set forth in the second clause of Article XIX:1(a) for the imposition of a safeguard measure.".[12]

10. It has moreover clarified[13] that

> "(...) safeguard measures may be applied only when [compliance with] *all* the provisions of the *Agreement on Safeguards* and Article XIX of the GATT 1994 are clearly demonstrated."

11. The EC maintains that there are no unforeseen, i.e. unexpected, developments described in the record of the investigation on wheat gluten, which could have led to any increased imports causing serious injury. Furthermore, there is no indication that such unforeseen circumstances were in fact present at all.

12. The US claims in its oral statement on 20 December 1999[14] that the EC allegedly agrees with the US "that the US wheat gluten producers did not foresee the import surge when they added production capacity during 1993 to 1995 in anticipation of a large increase of domestic demand."

13. The EC responds that such a claim is entirely incorrect.

The US approach to the issue is not in line with the interpretation by the AB of the "unforeseen developments" requirement. As indicated above, the AB stated that the Member applying the safeguard measure, *in casu* the US, should have demonstrated in its investigation report that unexpected circumstances "led to a product [wheat gluten] being imported in such increased quantities and under such conditions as to cause or threaten to cause serious injury to domestic producers."

Thus, the ITC report should have shown the existence of an (unexpected) circumstance that *caused* ("led to", in the AB's words) increased imports "under

---

[11] Appellate Body Report, *Argentina-Footwear, supra*, footnote 3, para. 91.

[12] *Ibid.*, para. 92.

[13] *Ibid.*, para. 95.

[14] At page 2.

such conditions as to cause (...) serious injury". The US authorities cannot fulfil their obligations under Article XIX by referring to an alleged "sudden" nature or size of the increased imports themselves. It is the sudden nature of what might have prompted the "increased imports" that is the relevant issue under Article XIX of the GATT.

14. In the present case nothing "unexpected" of that sort has happened: indeed, the uncompetitiveness of the US wheat gluten/wheat starch industry was evident well before 1993, during the whole investigative period and in any case before 1996 and 1997, given its intrinsic weakness vis-à-vis its US competitors on the US starch market. It was aggravated by the higher input costs of wheat. Furthermore, the corn sector, given its competitive advantage, accrued the benefits from US government support policy in relation to ethanol and sugar to the exclusion of the wheat sector. The ill-considered gamble taken by some US domestic companies, a wilful business strategy, of substantially increasing their production capacity during the investigative period led to a (predictable) deterioration in their position.

4. Item no. 3: the ITC did not show that "serious injury" occurred

15. The EC will not, here, repeat the arguments it has made earlier on in this procedure. It will limit itself to the following points.

4.1 Profitability

16. The EC reiterates that it is impossible for any WTO Member to verify, on the basis of the ITC report, whether, as the ITC asserts, the wheat gluten aspect of US wheat gluten/wheat starch producers' operations became unprofitable in 1996 and 1997. The EC reserves the right to come back to this issue in the light of the US answer to Panel question no. 26.

4.2 The reversing "upwards" of the industry's situation during last year of the POI

17. Both in its first written submission[15] and in its oral statement at the first substantive meeting[16], the EC stressed that many factors improved at the end of the period of investigation. The Panel has rightly, in its question no. 27 to the US, noted that the ITC does not explain at all in its report why – in spite of those recent improvements - serious injury in the sense of Article 4.1 (a) of the SA was still found to have occurred at the end of that period.

---

[15] See in particular paras. 57-71.

[16] Paras. 45-48.

The EC reserves the right to come back to this question in the light of the US reply to question no. 27. Nevertheless, the EC would already at this stage draw the Panel's attention to the following points regarding this issue.

18. The Appellate Body has recently stressed that Articles XIX.1 (a) and 2 of the SA are in the present tense: "such product *is being imported* in such increased quantities" as to cause or threaten to cause serious injury. It has explicitly stated that therefore competent authorities need to examine the most recent situation: "We believe that the relevant investigation period should not only *end* in the very recent past, it should *be* the recent past".[17] Especially in view of the fact that by the time the safeguard measure entered into force—1 June 1998—some of the factors indicating the financial condition of the industry had already started moving in a positive direction two years before, the fact that the ITC report contains no data whatsoever on the year preceding the measure's entry into force does not comply with that standard.

19. In this respect, it is also noteworthy that the US invoked in its first oral statement the AB statement that Article 2.1 of the SA "requires that the increase in imports must have been recent enough, sudden enough, sharp enough, and significant enough, both quantitatively and qualitatively, to cause or threaten to cause serious injury.[18] In the last year of the PoI, 1997, the market share of imports increased by a mere 1.3 per cent compared with 1996.[19] The US industry's sales, production, and inventory situation were improving. There simply was not a situation of recent sharp significant increase in imports causing injury warranting a safeguard measure.

20. EC producers moreover explicitly pointed out to the ITC the fact that positive developments occurred in 1997.[20]

21. All this taken together means that the ITC report does not adequately demonstrate that imports were occurring ("is being imported" - Article XIX of the GATT 1994 and 2.1 SA) in such increased quantities and under such conditions as to cause serious injury at the time the safeguard measure was taken.

5. Item N. 4: the ITC's failure to correctly address the causation issue

5.1 Introductory remarks

22. Regarding the issue of causation it is important to refer back to two general issues, on which the Panel asked very pertinent questions.

---

17 Appellate Body Report, *Argentina –Footwear, supra*, footnote 3, para. 130 and footnote 130.

18 Ibidem at para. 131.

19 ITC II-25, 58.9 per cent compared to 60.2 per cent.

20 Exhibit EC-16 at p. 37.

5.1.1 The ITC's investigative obligations

23. The first one, even though it is general, is especially important with regard to the way in which the ITC disposed of the causation issue in its investigation and report. At issue is the duty of the ITC under Article 4.2 of the SA to investigate correctly, in good faith, all pertinent matters.[21] Nevertheless, because the adequacy of the ITC investigation is central to the case before this Panel, the EC considers that the essence of its points about the failure of the ITC investigation to meet the standard in Article 4.2 of the SA bear repeating.

24. This duty to investigate includes obtaining and reviewing evidence on all relevant factors, including those which might detract from a serious injury and causation finding, and providing a solidly reasoned explanation of the findings in a publicly available report which includes all relevant information (with the sole exception of legitimate business secrets of individual companies for which a summary of the confidential information must be provided).

As required under Art. 4 2 of the SA, this must be done on the ITC's own initiative. However, the record shows that several pertinent (and as a matter of fact *crucial*) issues, which had moreover been raised before the ITC, were not dealt with in the report. This is evidence of the failure of the ITC to live up to the obligations imposed by the SA. In the following sections, the EC refers in particular to information which was provided to the ITC during its proceedings, and which was made available to the Panel pursuant to its questions on that point (Exhibits EC-16 to EC-18).

5.1.2 Article 4.2 (b) of the SA.

25. In its reply to the Panel's questions N. 8 and 9, the EC has already explained what the standard for causation analysis under the SA is. The section below will show that the US has not met this standard.

5.2 Input cost increases/alleged possibility to pass those on

26. As the EC has explained, wheat prices jumped in 1996 and 1997. The ITC states that, moreover, fuel costs (partially weather related in 1997) increased and depreciation rose because of increased capital expenditures.[22]

The US alleges that these increased costs in 1996 and 1997 were not the cause of any injury to the industry, since – absent imports – no matter how high the increase in input costs, they could have been passed on to buyers since "demand [for wheat gluten] *is not sensitive* to price changes in wheat gluten because wheat gluten represents only a small cost of producing downstream products and

[21] See also the EC's answer to Panel questions Nos. 6 and 7.

[22] ITC report at II-18.

generally lacks substitutes.[23] This sweeping statement implying zero elasticity of wheat gluten demand to wheat gluten price is inconsistent with the evidence on record before the ITC. The ITC offers no reasonable explanation for this inconsistency.

27. Leaving aside the point that general economic logic dictates that almost no commodity exists for which demand is completely insensitive to price, the US omits to mention that the ITC *itself* acknowledged in its report that wheat gluten competes with high-protein wheat and wheat flour.[24]

In fact, the ITC had stated: "*Demand for wheat gluten is closely tied to the protein content of each year's wheat crop.* Should the quantity and quality of wheat protein naturally occurring in the wheat supply be low, then bakers consume more wheat gluten to supplement the lack of protein in wheat.".[25]

This raises the question: how, if the ITC acknowledges that high-protein wheat can substitute for wheat gluten in bread baking (which constitutes 80 per cent of US wheat gluten consumption), can it assert that demand for wheat gluten is insensitive to price changes?

28. As with other issues, the reasons why the allegation by US producers that – absent imports - they would have been able to pass on to consumers increased input costs of any magnitude is incorrect, were also pointed out explicitly and extensively to the ITC[26] during the investigation, and nevertheless completely ignored by it.

29. Without any explanation or discussion, the ITC ignored the evidence detracting from its findings and accepted the US industry's statements without any supporting evidence (In fact, it relied on two oral statements by the petitioners requesting safeguard measures). For the benefit of the Panel, the EC mentions some of the points which were made to the ITC:

- one cannot expect to pass on all increased cost in a competitive market like the US wheat gluten market, in particular since structural changes in the US wheat gluten industry (e.g. significantly increased wheat gluten capacity and new entrants[27] have intensified intra-industry competition since 1994"[28]
- competition with high-protein content wheat flour[29];
- difficulty in passing on increased input costs immediately due to long-term sales contracts.[30]

---

23 Para. 149 of the US first written submission, emphasis supplied.

24 ITC report at I-22.

25 ITC report at II-9, emphasis supplied. See also at II-27.

26 Pre-hearing brief, Exhibit EC-16, pages 27-35.

27 On the point of the influence of new entrants on profitability of the industry as a whole, the EC refers the Panel to its answer to question 18.

28 Pre-hearing brief, Exhibit EC-16, page 27.

29 IbIdem, page 28.

30. In the light of the US insistence in paragraph 148 of its first written submission that it could rely on oral statements by the two petitioners at the hearing that historically they had been able to pass on higher input cost, the following is particularly relevant.

Midwest, one of those two petitioners claiming, before the ITC, that it could pass on increased input cost without any limits, had stated exactly the opposite in a submission[31] filed in 1993 with the US Securities and Exchange Commission: "Vital wheat gluten's contribution to the Company's profitability during fiscal 1993 (July '92- June '93) *was negatively impacted due primarily to the increased cost of wheat* (...).[32]

Why would Midwest state this to the SEC if it was able to pass on increased input cost without problems? The EC points the Panel's attention to the fact that this statement was clearly pointed out to the ITC during its proceedings, but was ignored by the ITC.

5.3 Protein premium

5.3.1 Introduction

31. This brings the EC to the protein premium issue. The EC has shown that it is the protein level in wheat which is the most important factor determining how wheat gluten prices develop.[33]

32. Indeed, one of the most serious failures of analysis by the ITC concerns its misrepresentation of the reasons for wheat gluten price movements over the period of investigation, and its failure to investigate this issue adequately. According to all price data, from whatever source, there was an extremely sharp increase, and then decrease, in price in the period surrounding the first half of 1994.[34] The ITC itself explicitly attributes the increase to the shortage of high-protein (i.e. high gluten content) wheat on the market in that period.[35]

5.3.2 The ITC's statements

33. For the period of the alleged injury to the US industry, 1996-97, the price of wheat gluten was lower than in 1994. The ITC states on this issue, literally: "In 1996 and 1997, however, unit selling values declined, notwithstanding increased demand and higher raw material costs. We find that this unusual devel-

---

[30] IbIdem, page 31.

[31] Known as a "10-K form".

[32] Pre-hearing brief, Exhibit EC-16 at p. 29, repeated in the post-hearing brief, Exhibit EC-18 at p. 11.

[33] See EC's 1st written submission, Exhibit EC-10.

[34] As always except where specifically otherwise indicated, the EC is using "ITC-years". For example, the period running from e.g. 1 July 1993-30 June 1994 is called "1994".

[35] E.g. ITC II-32, footnote 84.

opment is explained by the dramatic increase in relatively low-priced imports during this period, which had the effect of *driving down* wheat gluten prices.[36] This statement creates the impression of prices being forced to come down during a certain period due to increased imports. Thus, the ITC attributes an alleged US producers' selling price decrease to increased levels of imports, disregarding the developments in protein level in wheat during the PoI.

5.3.3 The information from the ITC

34. The Figure below shows actual US producers' wheat gluten selling price movements. They are derived from the data unjustifiably omitted from the ITC's 1998 March report (wherein table 18 on page II-33 was left blank). The US has now belatedly provided these data in the so-called "corrigendum".[37]

Whilst the EC has already pointed out that the withholding of this information from the public version of the ITC's report constitutes a violation of Article 4 of the SA which cannot be undone since that report had to be published "promptly"[38] and *was not*, the EC has also accepted that it is evidence before the Panel and therefore can be used.

35. The EC notes that, although deleted from the public version of the March 1998 report, the data here presented are the same data which the ITC possessed when it considered the changes in price of the US product. The quarterly wheat gluten price data made available only now by the US reveal a telling pattern of wheat gluten price movements which is contrary to the US statement that wheat gluten prices fell in 1996 and 1997 because of wheat gluten imports.

36. As a last point before discussing the evidence which have only now been produced by the US, the EC underlines that those data entirely confirm the data which the EC has already submitted to the Panel.[39]

[36] ITC I-18, emphasis supplied.
[37] US Exhibit 10, page II-37a.
[38] In the EC's joint reply to questions 2, 4, 14, 15 and 16.
[39] Exhibit EC-10, in particular Figure 2.

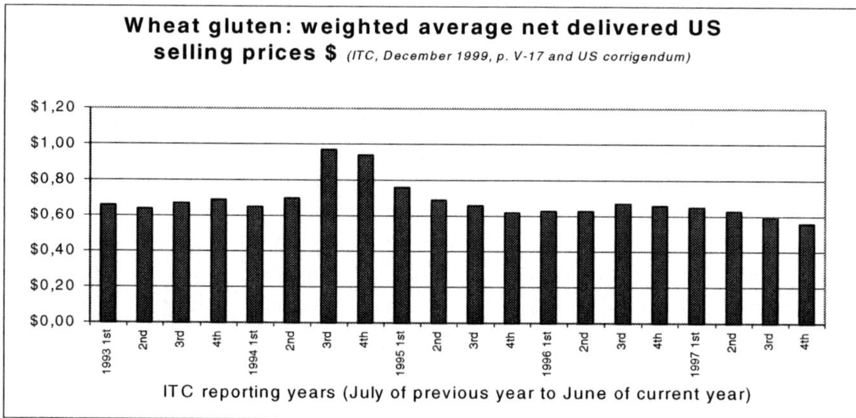

ITC reporting year	1993				1994				1995			
Quarter	1st	2nd	3rd	4th	1st	2nd	3rd	4th	1st	2nd	3rd	4th
Price $	$0,66	$0,64	$0,67	$0,69	$0,65	$0,70	$0,97	$0,94	$0,76	$0,69	$0,66	$0,62
ITC reporting year	1996				1997							
Quarter	1st	2nd	3rd	4th	1st	2nd	3rd	4th				
Price $	$0,63	$0,63	$0,67	$0,66	$0,65	$0,63	$0,59	$0,56				

37. The above graph shows, in the first place, that during the "reporting year" 1994 (the 12-month period ending June 1994), the price of wheat gluten *jumped sharply*. This was the year for which the ITC explicitly acknowledges that low protein content in the wheat crop drove up prices. During the 1995 reporting year however, US producers' selling prices *fell sharply*. The EC underlines that during that same year imports increased only very slightly compared to 1994.[40] Quarterly wheat gluten prices *increased* in 1996 from the level of prices in the last quarter of 1995. (Once again, for clarity, all these years refer to ITC reporting years.) In fact, also in the first and second quarters of 1997 quarterly wheat gluten prices were higher than at the end of 1995. Therefore, wheat gluten prices were above last quarter 1995 prices for six consecutive quarters.

5.3.4 The conclusions which necessarily flow from that information

38. There are three important conclusions to be drawn from these data, which all come from the ITC itself.

39. The *first* is that, looking at the 1994 part of the Figure, protein premium is the most important factor in deciding wheat gluten prices. In its report, the ITC acknowledged that the sharp price increase in 1994 (36 per cent *higher* in the last quarter of 1994 than in the last quarter of 1993) was caused by a shortage of high-protein wheat.[41]

---

40 See ITC II-12 and 13.

41 ITC II-9 and II-32 footnote 84.

40. The *second* is that, looking at the 1995 part of the Figure, it is not increased imports that drive down prices. After all, during the price fall in 1995 (34 per cent *lower* in the last quarter of 1995 as compared with the last quarter of 1994), imports hardly increased (2.9 per cent)[42] compared with the previous year.[43]

41. And the third is that, looking at in particular the 1996 but also the 1997 part of the graph, it was certainly not increased imports which "drove down" prices during those years. Prices were lower at the end of 1995 than for the whole of the 1996 period. In fact, compared to the last quarter of 1995, US producers' selling prices improved throughout the first three quarters of 1996—the year in which the strongest increase in imports occurred—and were still higher during the 2nd quarter of 1997 than during the last quarter of 1995.

5.3.5 The US defence in its 21 December 1999 Oral Statement is unconvincing

42. In its oral statement on 21 December 1999, pages 4 to 5, the US argues that it was increased imports which caused low prices at the end of the PoI because "something must have been happening on the supply side."

43. The EC responds that something was indeed happening on the supply side during the last three years of the PoI. However, in contrast to what the US asserts, what was happening on the supply side in 1996 and 1997 (and for that matter in 1995), as compared with 1994, was the following:

- supplies of high-protein wheat were good;
- the offer of high protein wheat was therefore high, and
- consequently, the protein premium (difference between price of high-protein wheat and low-protein wheat) was low, in particular when compared with record high levels at the end of 1994.

The EC refers in this context to the evidence contained in Exhibit EC-10, in particular Figure 3 thereof.

44. In the latter period of the PoI, bakers in the US[44] were thus able to force wheat gluten suppliers to keep their prices down, by confronting them—in price negotiations—with the concrete alternative that they (the bakers) could also turn to relatively cheap high-protein wheat as a substitute for wheat gluten in baking.

45. The US wheat gluten producers had no choice but to price wheat gluten at the low level determined by the protein premium. This depressing effect on prices affected equally domestic *and* imported wheat gluten.

---

42 ITC report p. II-12 and 13, 127.912 thousand pounds compared with 124.188 pounds.

43 See in particular ITC p. II-13.

44 Bakery makes 80 per cent of consumption of wheat gluten in the US.

Given this market reality, the declarations made by the two petitioner wheat gluten producers before the ITC that they could pass on costs to their main purchasers (the bakers) are evidently incorrect (and inconsistent with earlier declarations before the US Securities and Exchange Commission).[45]

More seriously, the US authorities should never have relied on oral statements which were inconsistent with earlier written statements without duly and thoroughly investigating developments in prices of high and low protein wheat in the US market.

46. Thus, the US statement made before the Panel on 21 December 1999 does not refute the EC's basic claim based on statistical evidence that there is an obvious correlation between protein premium levels and the price of wheat gluten. What it does is distort the EC's argument by quoting the EC as having stated that "demand" rose[46] , implying a shift in the demand curve to the right. In fact, the EC's statement[47] (based on the terminology used in the ITC's report) was that *consumption*—or more precisely, apparent consumption—rose, at a time when wheat gluten prices were lower than in 1994.

After all, since the wheat gluten price was kept relatively low by the pressure resulting from the low protein premium, bakers could—and did—turn to wheat gluten when that was more profitable than buying high protein wheat. Other users, including pet food producers, also could purchase more wheat gluten at the relatively lower prices.

47. The conclusion to be drawn from the above with regard to *causality* are the following.

Wheat gluten prices were low during the last three years of the PoI compared with 1994 as a result of the protein premium factor.

At the same time, input costs (wheat price, fuel and depreciation)[48] were rising.

Thus, US wheat gluten producers were caught in a cost-price squeeze caused by domestic factors. That was the main reason for any difficulties which US wheat gluten producers might have had.

5.3.6 The complete failure of the ITC to investigate the protein premium issue

48. In its findings on the description of the wheat gluten market, the ITC recognises the primary importance of the baking industry as the main outlet for wheat gluten.[49] According to the information considered by the ITC, baking ac-

---

45 See para. 30 of this submission.

46 Page 6 of the US oral statement of 21 December 1999.

47 Para. 44 of the EC's first oral statement.

48 ITC report at II-18.

49 ITC I-9-10.

counts for four-fifths of the wheat gluten market.[50] The ITC was also aware of the basic fact, understood by all wheat gluten processors, including the petitioner companies in the present case, that the protein (i.e. gluten) quality of wheat harvested in a year has a direct effect on conditions for sale of wheat gluten.[51]

49. However, the ITC did not attribute any price movement subsequent to 1994 to the availability of high-protein wheat. Despite its evident relevance, the ITC did not give any data on the price of wheat in its report, nor especially data on the relative prices of high-protein and low-protein wheat.

50. The ITC did not provide any evidence that it performed any statistical analysis whatsoever showing a causal link between imports and price. Indeed, there is no correlation between the two.

The ITC has only shown a marginal *coincidence in time* of an increase in imports and developments in price levels in one sole year, the last, of the PoI. However, during the third and fourth year of the POI price levels moved opposite to import levels. In effect, in the third year, prices declined sharply but imports remained practically stable. In the fourth year, imports increased but prices went up.

This clearly shows that the level of imports did not determine the level of prices. Thus, the US has *not* shown any *causal link* between the level of imports and the level of prices. It has also not provided an explanation anywhere in its report on why the fact that prices fell strongly in 1995 even though imports remained stable was not a reason to detract it from its—incorrect—conclusion that it was imports which "drove down" prices in 1996/7. It finally did not explain how it came to the conclusion that increased imports "drove down" prices in 1996 while they were actually rising.

51. The ITC's analysis has been inadequate in not considering the influence of high-protein wheat on the wheat gluten market. Given the importance of high-protein wheat availability on wheat gluten market, and that evidence of this importance was made available to the ITC—the EC will return to this below—this failure to conduct an analysis by the ITC is unacceptable. By omitting consideration of the effect of the availability of high protein wheat on the wheat gluten market, the ITC's findings on the cause of the price movements, attributed to increased imports, are unsound.

5.3.7 As to the ITC's allegation that it did not need to investigate the protein premium issue since nobody had claimed it was a more important cause of injury

52. At the end of point 135 of its first written submission, the US in fact admits that the ITC did not investigate whether developments in wheat protein con-

---

[50] E.g. ITC II-5 and II-9.

[51] Idem.

tent were not the *real* cause of lower wheat gluten prices during the end of the PoI. By asserting that nobody had claimed during the investigation procedure that the protein premium factor was a "more important cause of the serious injury" the US implies that under US domestic law it was not necessary for the ITC to investigate it. This is evidently not in line with Article 4.2 of the SA.

53. As a general matter, the EC refers in this context to its answers to questions 7 and 6 of the Panel. It is clear from the ITC report itself that the ITC was aware that wheat protein content influenced wheat gluten prices. The ITC should therefore have investigated properly whether developments in wheat protein content were not the real reason that price levels were what they were during 1996 and 1997. Nevertheless, by its own admission, it failed to do so.

54. Moreover, the issue *was* explicitly raised many times on behalf of EC industry during the hearings.

- "Petitioners' regression model ignores other significant supply and demand actors that also affect vital wheat gluten prices, including the protein content of wheat. (emphasis supplied)[52];
- In the discussion on the influence of protein levels in wheat on prices of wheat gluten, the concept of "protein premium" was also specifically explained.[53]

55. If the evidence from the respondents was not sufficient for the ITC, it should have heeded the views of one of the petitioner companies: in a letter from Manildra which was read out by the EC industry before the ITC Commissioners, this petitioner recognised the following:

> "While I understand the situation is drastically different within the community, *the market in the US appears to be headed for further decreases for July forward due to softening demand resulting from weakening high protein premiums* and capacity increases in the US and production increases in Australia" (emphasis supplied).[54]

5.3.8 Conclusion on protein premium

56. The ITC has, as it admits, completely failed to investigate a major factor having an objective and quantifiable bearing on the situation of the US wheat starch/wheat gluten industry, i.e. how protein premiums developed during the POI. This failure prevented the US authorities from *correctly* assessing whether any causal link existed between increased imports and the alleged serious injury (i.e. "a significant overall impairment in the position of the domestic industry"). If the US had considered the protein premium factor, it could not have reached the conclusion that increased imports were the cause of serious injury. This is

[52] Page 24 of the post-hearing brief, Exhibit EC-18.
[53] Page 31 of the post-hearing brief, Exhibit EC-18 under "A" and in footnote 81.
[54] Exhibit EC-17 p. 149-150.

contrary to the US obligations under Article 4.2, and in particular Article 4.2 (a) of the SA.

57. In the light of the above and in any case, the ITC has also illogically failed to exclude the influence of the protein premium factor on wheat gluten prices, and thus on the US industry's situation, since it did not collect any information on that issue. This constitutes a second violation of Article 4.2, and in particular Article 4.2 (b), second sentence, of the SA.

5.4 Creation of overcapacity

5.4.1 Introduction

58. It is clear from the facts on the record that one of the most important reasons why the US industry had problems at the end of the PoI – assuming *arguendo* that they indeed did have problems – was that they had manoeuvred themselves into an impossible position by creating enormous overcapacity in the beginning of the POI. The EC has already dealt with this issue in its first written submission[55] and oral statement at the first substantive meeting.[56] It will only add a few remarks.

59. The US position on this point seems to boils down to stating that, first of all, the US industry had correctly predicted an increase in demand and consumption, and secondly, that it is somehow "unfair" that - the EC quotes from the statement made by the US on 20 December 1999 - "imports increased at a rate greater than the growth in demand.[57] . This is an indefensible position.

5.4.2 The inherent unpredictability of wheat gluten demand

60. Contrary to what the US implies, it is impossible to predict in the long-term with precision what the demand for wheat gluten will be on the US market, since demand for wheat gluten is primarily dependent in the US on the protein level of wheat crops.[58]

Interestingly enough, the ITC itself explicitly says so in its report: "Demand for wheat gluten is closely tied to the protein content of each year's wheat crop. Should the quantity and quality of protein naturally occurring in the wheat supply be low, then bakers consume more wheat gluten to supplement the lack of protein in the wheat"..[59]

---

[55] Paras. 63 and further and 96.

[56] Paras.. 69-79.

[57] Page 2, in fine.

[58] See also para. 74 of EC first oral statement on 20 December 1999.

[59] ITC report at II-9.

61. The assertion by the ITC that "industry *projections* of continued growth in demand and consumption were largely correct"[60] (emphasis supplied) is thus contradicted by its own explicit finding in the factual, second, part of the report, that demand for wheat gluten will be strongly dependent on the protein content of each year's wheat crop. There cannot be any precise "projections" of how wheat gluten demand will develop.

62. That the assertion by the ITC that US industry "predicted" future demand and consumption correctly is unjustified, becomes all the more clear if one reads, again in the factual part of the ITC report, that among the factors contributing to increase in US wheat gluten consumption from 1996 to 1997 was "anticipatory behaviour of purchasers and importers in response to the section 301 action taken by the domestic industry in *January 1997*".[61] Is the ITC telling us that US producers could predict this as well when they increased capacity massively from *1993-1995*?

5.4.3 US producers themselves thought the capacity increase was irrational

63. Moreover, contrary to what the US would want the Panel to believe, even US producers themselves thought this capacity increase early on in the POI was irrational and unwarranted. In the pre-hearing brief[62], counsel for the EC industry explicitly quoted newspaper information, stating that "Midwest expressed concern in 1992 when the Heartland capacity expansion was announced, indicating that the expansion was not warranted based on *existing* US capacity being sufficient to meet market needs."

5.4.4 Capacity increase drives up intra-industry competition and thus drives down prices

64. Also in this context, the earlier quote from a Manildra letter which was read out to the ITC Commissioners during its hearing, and handed over to them is relevant. Not only does Manildra state that protein premium influences price. It also explicitly states that capacity increases drive down prices: "While I understand the situation is drastically different within the community, *the market in the US appears to be headed for further decreases for July forward due to* softening demand resulting from weakening high protein premiums and *capacity increases in the US* and production increases in Australia." (emphasis supplied).[63]

---

[60] ITC report at I-17.
[61] ITC report at II-9.
[62] Exhibit EC-16 at page 31.
[63] Exhibit EC-17, at pages 149-150.

5.4.5 The problems inflicted by US industry upon themselves by the capacity increase were extensively pointed out to ITC.

65. The EC stresses that the fact that it was irrational construction of enormous overcapacity which caused additional problems for the industry, was a point which was explicitly pointed out by EC industry to the ITC during the hearings, and nevertheless disregarded by the ITC without adequate justification.

In the pre-hearing brief, one of the arguments made by counsel for the EC industry on this point was the following: "Capacity increases that result in excess capacity will result in more intense competition, particularly if the capacity expansion is capital intensive, since there is pressure to price at a level to cover variable costs, and a portion of fixed costs".[64]

5.4.6 No basis for assumption that the US industry alone would supply increased consumption

66. Regarding the other aspect of the US position on overcapacity – i.e. the completely unreasonable assumption that in spite of the fact that in the GATT/WTO negotiations a tariff concession on wheat gluten has been exchanged with other WTO Member, all increased domestic consumption should be supplied by domestic producers – the EC refers to its earlier statements.[65]

In summary:

(i) it is economically completely illogical to assume that all increased consumption will be supplied by US industry alone where imports historically provided about 50 per cent of consumption;

(ii) under WTO rules, it is impossible to base oneself on the assumption that all increased consumption will be supplied by domestic industry alone in the situation that a tariff binding has been granted – due to the MFN clause - to all other WTO Members.

5.4.7 Overcapacity was not properly excluded from the causation analysis

67. As a final point on overcapacity the EC would like to comment on point 127 of the US first written submission. The US explicitly admits that an "other factor"- overcapacity - in the sense of Article 4.2 (b) SA, caused (self-inflicted) injury when it uses the words: "[T]o the extent that one other factor – namely, additions to US capacity – contributed to the decline in capacity utilisation (…)".

---

[64] Exhibit EC-16, at pages 30-31.

[65] EC's first written submission, at page 21 and further; EC's oral statement at para. 69 and further.

The US continues by stating that the ITC demonstrated that additions to US capacity "was a less important factor" in causing injury "than imports".

68. As the EC has explained in its answer to question 9, this is not enough. In order to comply with its obligations under Article 4.2 (b), second sentence, of the SA, the US should have *excluded* the injury caused by overcapacity from its determinations on injury and causation. In order to do that, it should have determined whether, if capacity had remained the same since 1993, there still would have been a "significant overall impairment in the position of the industry".

Performing this analysis is simple: one merely has to divide production in 1997 by capacity in 1993. Doing so results in a capacity utilisation level of 75 per cent.[66] In other words: if capacity had not increased during the PoI, the US industry would have been at almost exactly the same level of capacity utilisation in 1997 as it was in 1993 (78.3 per cent)[67] when, according to the ITC, everything was fine.

5.4.8 Conclusion on overcapacity

69. Assuming US industry was in difficulty in 1996 and 1997, overcapacity was certainly one of the main reasons. As explained in particular under the previous paragraph, the ITC should not have attributed to increased imports any (easily quantifiable) injury caused by this factor. By not conforming to this rule in their determination of serious injury and causation, the US authorities breached Article 4.2 (b), in particular the second sentence thereof, of the SA.

5.5 Situation in co-products markets

70. The EC has explained why the situation in the co-products (especially wheat starch and alcohol/ethanol) markets was an additional cause of any impairment in its position that the US industry might have suffered in the relevant period.

5.5.1 The information provided by the EC was or should have been available to the ITC at the time

71. The US defence on this issue starts with implying that Exhibits EC-10 through 14 should be disregarded by the Panel since this information was not submitted to the ITC by EC industry during the ITC's hearings.[68]

The EC would stress once more that all these exhibits are based *on official US government data*, in some cases even the ITC report. For the rest, the ITC

---

66 ITC Report at I-17, 121.792 pounds divided by 162.856 pounds.

67 ITC report at p. II-15.

68 Para. 138 of the US first written submission.

could have easily obtained the information (and should have obtained it; the EC will come back to this in a moment).

It would also like to stress that under WTO rules, the US government is *one* entity. It would be absurd if the US were allowed to defend itself by saying that the *US* ITC did not possess the relevant data, although the *US* Department of Agriculture did.

72. Moreover, much, if not all, of this information should have been available to the ITC already from the replies to its questionnaires (e.g. regarding wheat and wheat flour purchase prices and wheat starch selling prices see ITC II-37).

5.5.2 The US misinterprets and misapplies Article. 4 2 of the SA

73. The US also claims, as a more general point, that the adequacy of the analysis performed by an investigative authority is to be judged "on the basis of the evidence *collected and considered* by that authority" (emphasis supplied), i.e. only on the basis of what the ITC actually obtained and not on what it should have obtained.

It cites the "*Korea-Dairy*" Panel report claiming that that report would support its position. However, in the paragraph quoted by the US[69], that Panel clearly – and rightly stated:

> "For us, an objective assessment entails an examination of whether the KTC had examined all facts in its possession or which it should have obtained in accordance with Article 4. 2 of the SA (including facts which might detract from an affirmative determination (…).[70] (emphasis supplied).[71]

74. Moreover, extensive arguments were made on this point before the ITC. For example, "changes in co-product markets have a substantially larger impact on the US industry than do imports of wheat gluten" was the title of a part of the EC industry's pre-hearing brief comprising 15 pages[72], and a similar part in the post-hearing brief comprised 9 pages.[73] The EC refers the Panel to these pages, but will cite a few of the arguments that were made, often based on information provided by US producers themselves:

- the integrated nature of the production process means that production decisions must also be made on an integrated basis;

[69] 7.30.

[70] Not overturned by the AB and rather supported by AB in *Argentina - Footwear, supra*, footnote 3, para. 136 where AB states that authority must "at a minimum (…)" investigate also "all other factors (…) relevant" than those explicitly listed in Article 4.2 (b).

[71] See also the EC's reply to questions N. 6 and 7 from this Panel.

[72] Exhibit EC-16, at pages 13-27.

[73] Exhibit EC-18, at pages 14-22.

- "from a common sense perspective, how can co-products that absorb 90 per cent of the raw material used to produce wheat gluten *not* have an effect on wheat gluten output and profitability?";
- "the weakness in the wheat starch market is further reflected by the fact that end of period inventories for wheat starch have doubled from 1995 to 1997, while end of period inventories for wheat gluten have declined";
- "with the exception of 1994, over the entire 1993-1997 period, Midwest's alcohol sales exceeded its wheat gluten and wheat starch sales combined.

75. Furthermore, the ITC itself acknowledged that "there is evidence that Midwest reduced wheat gluten production in 1995, *for reasons related in part to conditions in the alcohol market"*.[74] (emphasis supplied).

76. In the light of these points, how can the US assert that the ITC was not under the obligation, pursuant to Article 4.2 (a) and 4.2 (b) SA, to investigate the situation in the co-product market further and acquire the necessary information?

5.5.3 The data on profitability are not verifiable

77. This failure to comply with its Article 4.2 SA obligations is worsened by the fact that the method by which US producers constructed their profitability data regarding wheat gluten remains totally unclear. It is unacceptable, and contrary to Article 4.2 of the SA, that a Member can take a safeguard measure even though it does not investigate the situation on the co-product market, and the method by which the petitioning industry allocates costs among its co-products in its profitability calculation is not explained.

5.5.4 Alcohol prices do not only affect Midwest but all US wheat starch/ wheat gluten in what they obtain for their wheat starch slurry waste

78. Finally, the US also either misses the point or misrepresents some of the arguments which have been made on this issue by the EC. For instance, in paragraph 144 of its first written submission, the US puts forward the incorrect reasoning that since only Midwest *internally* processes a significant amount of wheat starch slurry into alcohol-related products, conditions in the alcohol market would not affect other US wheat starch/wheat gluten producers.[75]

---

[74] ITC report at I-17.

[75] The US appears to mis-construe the ITC report at page I-17 in asserting that Midwest alone processes starch into alcohol. The US (and indeed the ITC) may be confusing starch produced as the main product of wheat processing where it is extracted from starch slurry, and the starch slurry waste resulting from this starch extraction. Both the starch slurry (main product) and the waste slurry (waste or by-product) can be used as raw material for distilling.

However, in describing the production processes in general (i.e. not only those of one company) the ITC itself explicitly states that "[A]ny remaining starch slurry is sent to either a waste processing plant or to a distillery for utilisation in the production of ethanol or food-grade alcohol".[76]

79. This makes clear that it does not make much difference whether a wheat starch/gluten producer itself processes the wheat starch slurry waste into alcohol-related products; even if it sells starch slurry to a processor, its income will nevertheless be negatively affected by lower prices in the alcohol market. The waste slurry has a value on the US market which is dependent from alcohol price levels. If those are high, wheat starch/wheat gluten producers may obtain much income from wheat starch slurry waste; if they are low, they might be forced to pay waste processors to dispose of it.

5.6 No coincidence in time

80. Finally, the EC would reiterate three points regarding the argument already made[77] by the EC that the ITC could not reasonably have concluded that increased imports caused injury, since the movements in injury factors did *not* coincide with the increase in imports.

81. *Firstly*, as was stated above, on the basis of ITC-evidence exclusively, prices went down sharply in 1995 *before* imports increased.

82. *Secondly*, as was also stated above, again on the basis of ITC-evidence exclusively, the 1995 fall in prices was reversed in 1996, when prices even went up slightly, although imports increased.

83. *Thirdly and finally*, the EC calls to the Panel's attention to the fact that evidence was provided on this point to the ITC but was completely ignored.

For instance, the EC industry's pre-hearing brief explicitly noted, with data, that Midwest's wheat gluten sales revenue had already dropped sharply in 1995 compared with 1994. This happened *before* imports increased. Moreover, the decline in 1995 was much greater than in 1996, the year in which the largest increase in imports during the PoI took place.[78] Again, although these facts were available to the ITC, it did not analyse them in any way in its report, thus failing to comply with its obligations under Article 4.2 of the SA.

6. Item N. 5: the US did not respect the proportionality rule

84. A fundamental principle of the SA is that a safeguard measure must be *proportionate* to the serious injury caused by increased imports.

---

76 ITC report at II-5.
77 See in particular paras.. 79 et seq. of the EC's first written submission.
78 Exhibit EC-16, at page 20.

This principle derives from the exceptional nature[79] of safeguard measures which are designed to restrict "fair" trade.[80] A safeguard measure permits exceptionally a "lawful" breach of Article II of the GATT 1994 without the need to pursue the otherwise necessary procedures under Article XXVIII. Its "lawfulness" is however directly dependent not only to the full respect of *all* the requirements under the GATT and the SA but is warranted *only* if the measure is strictly limited to what is necessary to remedy the serious injury *caused by the increased imports* and to the possibility of adjustment of the domestic industry.

85. In other words, when adopting a safeguard measure a Member cannot abuse this temporary withdrawal of tariff concessions bound in its GATT Schedule as a pretext for surreptitiously implementing protectionist policies. Making imports from other Members bear the burden of adjustment of the domestic industry to factors *other* than "increased imports" would surely be an act of protectionism, in violation of Articles I, II and XI of GATT 1994.

86. This principle finds its concrete application in two provisions of the SA, Articles 4.2 and 5.1.

87. According to Article 4.2 (b) last sentence, when considering whether "serious injury" was caused by "increased imports" (the only possibility that allows a Member to impose a safeguard measure), the investigating authorities shall not attribute to increased imports injury caused by other factors, which are causing injury at the same time.

88. This provision has two important consequences: on the one hand, the investigating authorities cannot attribute the cause of serious injury to increased imports if the increased imports are a co-cause of such serious injury but do not reach *per se*, i.e. in isolation, the threshold of "overall impairment in the position of the domestic industry". In order to reach such a conclusion the competent authorities are obliged to scrutinise *each and every* ("all") objective and quantifiable factor having a bearing on the situation of the industry concerned. They must provide a *reasoned* demonstration that they verified and weighted each factor in order to reach their findings.

On the other hand, a combination of causal factors (one of which being increased imports), none of which could be indicated with certainty to create alone, or in isolation, overall impairment in the position of the domestic industry concerned, does not allow that Member to take any safeguard measure.

89. Article 5.1 of the SA is the second textual application of the principle of proportionality and provides that a Member shall apply safeguard measures "only to the extent necessary to prevent or remedy serious injury and to facilitate adjustment".

---

[79] Appellate Body Report, *Argentina - Footwear, supra*, footnote 3, para. 93.

[80] Appellate Body Report, *Korea – Dairy, supra*, footnote 4, para. 87.

90. This provision has numerous consequences on the action of the Member wishing to apply a safeguard measure.

- The measure must be limited to the serious injury caused by imports. Assuming *arguendo* that a Member has correctly attributed the cause of the serious injury to increased imports (and this hypothesis is certainly *not* correct in the case of the US's safeguard measure on wheat gluten), the corresponding safeguard measure must be commensurate or proportionate to that injury, to the exclusion of any injury caused by other factors.

  It is thus out of the question that a Member, *in casu* the US, could be allowed to remedy the intrinsic uncompetitiveness of its domestic wheat gluten/wheat starch industry relative to the corn milling industry, or to remedy the increase in input costs, or to overcome fluctuations in price due to fluctuations in the protein premiums, or to compensate for failed business strategies such as over-expansion of production capacity by the adoption of a safeguard measure.

  Lawful trade from other Members cannot be made to bear the burden in patent breach of Articles II and XI of the GATT 1994 and the provisions of the SA.

- The safeguard measure must be limited "only to the extent necessary" to remedy the serious injury *and* to facilitate adjustment (*only* to the competitive pressure coming from increased import).

  The objective of adjustment has to be taken *together* and *at the same level* as that to remedy the injury. It cannot justify any measure that would go beyond the remedying of the serious injury caused by increased imports on the pretext of adjustment. This approach would breach the principle of proportionality and violate Article 5.1.

- the form of the safeguard measure must be the least restrictive possible ("only to the extent necessary"). The Member is in fact bound to choose measures most suitable for the achievement of these objectives (Article 5.1, third sentence).

  The "suitability" should not be judged, as the US authorities seemed to believe when they adopted their safeguard measure on wheat gluten, upon the *subjective* appreciation by the Member applying the measure on what best suits that Member's interests or its domestic industry. The "suitability" must be judged upon the *objective* standard of "only to the extent necessary" to "remedy of serious injury" together with "facilitat[ion] to adjustment" to the injury caused by increased imports *only*.

In the WTO system, there can be no doubt that quantitative restrictions are the most restrictive measures possible.[81] They thus constitute an *extrema ratio*, applicable only when positive demonstration by the applying Member is given as to the unsuitability of the other tariff-based measures (tariff increases or tariff-rate quotas). That demonstration must of course be complete and non-contradictory.

91. The application of the above-mentioned principles and criteria, which are set out *explicitly* in the SA, to the case of the US safeguard measure on wheat gluten shows without any possible doubt that the US has not implemented the proportionality principle, thus breaching Articles 4.2 and 5.1 of the SA.

92. The EC's first written submission[82] and the EC's first oral statement on 20 December 1999[83] have shown that the US has omitted, under-estimated or misrepresented a number of relevant factors of an objective and quantifiable nature having a bearing on the situation of the domestic industry.

These factors clearly pointed in the direction *opposite* to the existence of a causal link between increased imports and "serious injury". In particular, those factors excluded that increased imports alone could be the determining cause of the "overall impairment in the position of the domestic industry".

93. In any case, the US authorities' report does not provide a single explanation of where and how it weighed these factors (and according to what criteria) in order to come to the conclusion that increased imports were the cause of the alleged serious injury after having deducted the injury caused by (the well documented) other factors.

94. This way of proceeding constitutes a breach of Article 4.2 (a) SA. It is also a clear violation of the principle of proportionality in-built in Article 4.2 (b) and (c).

95. The EC's first written submission[84] and the EC's first oral statement on 20 December 1999.[85] have also clearly shown that the US has repeatedly breached Article 5.1's principle of proportionality on *all* accounts. This was done in spite of this explicit and specific provision of the SA[86]:

- The US did not justify the suitability of the form of the measure taken, which is the most restrictive possible. Rather, the short generic explanation indicated that the investigating authorities relied on that form to remedy injury and facilitate adjustment with respect to factors *other* than increased imports. The EC recalls here that

81 See Panel Report, *Turkey – Restrictions on Imports of Textile and Clothing Products* ("*Turkey - Textiles*"), WT/DS34/R, adopted 19 November 1999, DSR 1999:VI, 2363, para. 9.6.

82 Sub-chapter 4.5.2.

83 paras. 57 to 86.

84 Section 5.

85 Para. 60 et seq.

86 Which has no corresponding equivalent in similar context in other covered agreements.

the US authorities have *included* as one of their key considerations the *wheat starch market* conditions in the US when considering the form, the scope and the extent of the safeguard measure against *foreign* wheat gluten.[87] . This was done in contradictory fashion at the very moment when the same authorities considered (unreasonably) the starch market irrelevant for their determinations on causation.

- The US justified the recourse to a quantitative restriction by stating that "a high tariff would be inequitable in that it is likely to further drive [other foreign] suppliers from the U.S. market". This explanation for rejecting a tariff is not only inconsistent with Article I of the GATT 1994 and Article 2.2 of the Safeguards Agreement. It also shows that the choice of a QR was based on factors other than the need to remedy serious injury and to facilitate adjustment of the *US* industry. That is in contravention of Article 5.1, first sentence, of the SA. It also constitutes unauthorised circumvention of the provisions of Article 5.2 (b).
- The US determined the serious injury and consequently determined the extent of its safeguard measure without deducting the injury caused by other relevant and well-documented factors as the inherent competitive weakness of the US wheat gluten industry vis-à-vis its corn starch competitors, the increase in input costs, the voluntary unconsidered increase in production capacity of the US industry with no relation to the share of the increase in domestic consumption that the US industry could reasonably obtain and, finally, the level of wheat premiums. In short, the US has taken the opportunity of the complaint of its wheat gluten industry to go back from its tariff commitments bound in its GATT Schedule without any coverage in the SA.

96. In its oral statement on 21 December 1999, the US has attempted a defence as follows

> "[T]he EC's position is directly contrary to the Appellate Body's findings in *Korea – Dairy*. The Appellate Body specifically found, and I quote "a Member is *not* obliged to justify in its recommendation or determination a measure in the form of a quantitative restriction which is consistent with the average of imports in the last three representative years for which statistics are available." (AB Report at para. 99). The United States imposed a safeguard measure in the form of a QR set *above* the level of imports in the last

[87] ITC report at page I-26 on "selection of import quota" as recommended relief: "Because of the co-product nature of wheat gluten production, the supply and price of wheat gluten is dictated in part by demand for wheat starch".

three representative years. Thus, the Appellate Body has held that the United States was *not* required to justify the measure. The EC's arguments that the United States has the burden of proof to justify the level of the measure it imposed is incorrect."

97. The Appellate Body's report on "*Korea-Dairy*" does not support the US argument. Paragraph 99 of that report deals with the obligation under Article 5.1, *second sentence*, of providing a "clear justification" when a Member departs from the allocation of a quantitative restriction based on the last three representative years for which statistics are available.

In this case, however, the quota was not based on the last three representative years but on a 1993-1995 period. Hence, a "clear justification" for such a different level was required and the US failed to comply with this obligation.

98. Additionally, the above quoted US statement is unrelated to the issue of whether Article 5.1, *first* and *third* sentence, requires the Member upon adoption of its safeguard measure

- to have recourse to quantitative restrictions only as an *extrema ratio* and
- to justify the "suitability" of such measure on the *objective* factors involved through consideration of the three elements in Article 5.1, first sentence, i.e. "only to the extent necessary" "to remedy serious injury" from increased imports *only* "*and* facilitate adjustment".

99. The US has clearly violated such obligation.

7. Item N. 6: when allocating the quantitative restriction on wheat gluten, the US has manipulated the reference period in such a way as to reduce unjustifiably the level of imports from the EC and to affect trade shares among importing Members (in particular between the EC and Australia)

100. Article 5.1, second sentence, of the SA provides that if quantitative restrictions are used, "such a measure shall not reduce the quantity of imports below the level of a recent period which shall be the average of imports in the last three representative years for which statistics are available unless a clear justification is given (...)".

101. The US confirmed again in its oral statement on 21 December 1999[88] that it was *not* obliged to provide any such "clear justification" in the ITC report or in the act adopting the safeguard measure.

102. As was explained in the EC's first oral statement on 20 December 1999[89], the ordinary meaning of the terms in Article 5.1, second sentence of the SA "last

[88] Page 9.

three representative years for which statistics are available" means what it says, namely that the US should have based itself on the *last* three-year period for which statistics were available at the time of the adoption of the measure (30 May 1998).

103. The US does not contest that 1997, 1996 and 1995 statistics on imports of wheat gluten were available.

104. These statistics are "representative" of the trade concerned. As was already abundantly recalled, the trade involved in a safeguard measure is a fair and legitimate trade and its possible increase is the consequence of entirely legitimate use of market access rights deriving from trade concessions under the GATT Schedules. For a period to be considered *not* "representative", the Member wishing to implement a quantitative restriction must show the existence of exceptional circumstances. The US authorities themselves agree with this interpretation and excluded the existence of any "anomalous circumstances that render any of those years [1995 to 1997] unrepresentative of imports"[90] of wheat gluten in the US.[91]

105. Moreover, violations of WTO obligations can be advanced as evidence that the pattern of trade that is represented by the last three representative years for which statistics are available was distorted. The EC has recalled in its first written submission the Panel report on *"EC - Bananas - Recourse to Article 21.5 by Ecuador"*[92] which stated that

> "If data from a period are out of date or imports distorted because the relevant market is restricted, then using that period as a representative period cannot achieve the aim of the chapeau. Thus, under GATT practice it is necessary that the "previous representative period" for purposes of Article XIII:2(d) be the most recent period not distorted by restrictions."

106. This is clearly *not* the situation in the case of the US safeguard measure on wheat gluten.

107. The logic of this provision and of the entire procedure established by the WTO Contracting Parties under Article 5 of the SA is very transparent.

If a Member chooses lawfully to implement a quantitative restriction (which is *not* the case of the US measure), it has to determine the quantity of im-

---

89 At paras. 114 and following.

90 ITC report at page I-28.

91 The ITC report thus contradicts the latest defence of the US at page 11, in fine, of its oral statement .on 20 December 1999. What counts in this proceedings is, of course, what can be found in the investigation report and not the ex post justification trying to rewrite the facts a posteriori.

92 Report by the Panel on *European Communities – Regime for the Importation, Sale and Distribution of Bananas – Recourse to Article 21.5 of the DSU by Ecuador* ("*EC – Bananas III (Article 21.5 – Ecuador)*"), WT/DS27/RW/ECU, 12 April 1999, DSR 1999:II, 803, para 6.39. That Panel referred expressly to the previous panel reports on "EEC - Apples from Chile" and and *Japan – Measures Affecting Agricultural Products ("Japan – Agricultural products II*"), WT/DS76/R, adopted 19 March 1999, DSR 1999:I, 315, that decided along the same lines.

ports *in an objective way*, i.e. with reference to very recent ("last") statistics available. Such statistics are in principle representative of the legitimate trade in the product concerned unless an exceptional event or a violation of WTO rules has distorted the trade. The Member departing from the available statistics for the *last* three years must prove the existence of such exceptional event or violation.

108. The level of the restriction established in this objective way may *then* be adjusted downwards *in an MFN fashion* provided that "a clear justification is given that a different level is necessary to prevent or remedy injury".

109. If the Member adopting the safeguard measure wishes in addition to distinguish among supplying countries, and thus depart from the specific MFN rule applicable to the allocation of quotas, it must also follow the specific procedures under Article 5.2 (b).

110. In the case of the safeguard measure on wheat gluten, the US has manipulated the representative period in order to achieve both a reduction of the quantities that could be imported (thus over-protecting its industry) *and* a selective allocation among major suppliers (in particular to the detriment of the EC and to the benefit of Australia)[93] without following the procedural and substantive rules under Article 5.1, second sentence, and 5.2 (b).

111. In this context, it is a gratuitous remark for Australia to state that it "recognises[d] that the [US] measure had to be imposed on imports from all sources and not just from the EC"[94] when the US measure had the remarkable effect of reducing Australia's 1997 record level of exports to the US of 62.496 million pounds by no less than 0,0011 per cent.[95]

112. According to an established principle of WTO law, an interpreter cannot attribute to a provision in a covered agreement a meaning that will transform such a provision, in whole or in part, in a redundancy or inutility. The principle *ut magis valeat quam pereat* has been again recalled and applied by the AB in its "*Argentina-Footwear*"[96] report.

113. If an increase in imports were *ipso facto* a "clear" justification for using a representative period other than the "last three representative years for which statistics are available", this situation would *always* apply, rendering useless and redundant the provision as it stands.

---

[93] The findings of the ITC at page I-28 should also be considered in the light of the findings at I-26, last para., were a tariff safeguard measure was excluded on the grounds of protection of other Members trade. The ITC clearly sees its role as protecting the market share of other importers against the EC. However, the purpose of a safeguard action is solely to protect a domestic industry from injury. A safeguard measure has to be applied to all imports irrespective of source. Article 5.2(b) establishes the strict conditions under which a country may be discriminated against in the application of a quantitative restriction. The manipulation of the "representative period" is not a lawful substitute for that exceptional procedure.

[94] Australia oral statement as third party on 21 December 1999, at para. 2.

[95] ITC report at II-12.

[96] Para. 88.

114. The US claims now in its oral statement on 20 December 1999[97] that it "clearly justified this choice of a period in its findings that setting a quota level at the average of 1995 to 1997 would not remedy the serious injury". However, the text of the ITC report[98] states only that "the continued imports at or above this level would not remedy the serious injury to the domestic industry. Accordingly, we believe that a different quantity is "clearly justified" in this case". Such a justification not only is not "clear", it constitutes no justification at all. It is a *petitio principii.* It amounts to saying that, "I like blue eyes because I like them". The US has thus breached Article 5.1, second sentence, of the SA.

115. The US comes also with an additional defence according to which "the last three representative for which statistics are available" should mean a "period 'representative' of conditions in which the industry can survive".[99]

116. Nothing of the sort can be read in Article 5.1, second sentence, of the SA: the term "representative" is grammatically linked to "average of imports". There is no reference whatsoever in that provision to the conditions under which the industry can survive. Even more interestingly, the US defence is contradicted by the ITC report[100] that clearly refers to years "[un]representative *of imports*" and not to the conditions of survival of the industry.

117. The EC thus fully maintains that the US has breached Article 5.1, second sentence, of the SA.

8. Item N. 7: the US has breached the principle of parallelism with respect to imports from Canada.

118. According to the Appellate Body report on "*Argentina-Footwear*"[101],

> "We conclude that Argentina, on the facts of this case, cannot justify the imposition of its safeguard measures only on non-MERCOSUR third country sources of supply on the basis of an investigation that found serious injury or threat thereof caused by imports from all sources, including imports from other MERCOSUR member States."

119. During its oral statement on 21 December 1999, Canada stated as third party the following:[102]

> "The U.S. wheat gluten case is radically different from the *Argentina – Footwear* case (...). The USITC report clearly shows that while the United States conducted a global investigation and exam-

97 At page 11.
98 At I-28.
99 First oral statement on 20 December 1999, at page 11.
100 At I-28.
101 Para. 114.
102 Pages 4 and 5.

ined imports from all sources, its determination did not attribute injury from NAFTA imports to third countries. After the USITC made an affirmative injury determination, it conducted a separate analysis of imports from Canada and Mexico. Its separate examination demonstrated clearly that Canadian imports declined significantly during the period of investigation, while overall imports increased.[103] The USITC rightly concluded that imports from Canada did not contribute importantly to the serious injury. Based on this conclusion, the United States exempted imports from Canada from the safeguard measure".

120. The US defence before the Panel on 20 December 1999 followed substantially the same line of argument.[104]

121. It is the EC's position that, contrary to the incorrect assertions of both the US and Canada, the facts of the *Footwear* case are, with respect to the application of the principle of parallelism, identical to those of the US safeguard measure on wheat gluten.

As in the *Footwear* case, the US's investigation "found serious injury or threat thereof caused by imports from all sources, including imports from" NAFTA countries *including* Canada but then imposed its safeguard measure on wheat gluten only on non-NAFTA countries, thus *excluding* Canada.

122. As is apparent from the Canadian statement, the ITC made "an affirmative determination of injury". In WTO terms, this means that the ITC considered the imports from *all* sources, including Canada and arrived at the (erroneous) conclusion that the increased imports were the cause of "serious injury" affecting the US wheat gluten industry. As Canada states explicitly, it is "*after*" such "affirmative determination" that the ITC "conducted a separate analysis of imports from Canada and Mexico" (i.e. the US NAFTA partners) from which the ITC "concluded that imports from Canada did not contribute importantly to the serious injury".

123. The procedure followed by the ITC, as described by Canada, is clearly not in line with Article 4.2 of the SA, breaches Article 2.1 and 5.2 of the SA and does not correctly apply the fundamental MFN provision under Article 2.2 of the SA.

124. Nothing in Article 4.2 allows a Member to conduct a separate examination of serious injury based on the origin of the imported products concerned. Quite the opposite, the Appellate Body has interpreted the SA[105] as implying that, in the case of measures imposed by a WTO Member which is also a member of a customs union, Article 4.2 requires the Member concerned to verify whether "in-

[103] [original footnote] USITC Report, submitted as U.S. Exhibit 4, p. I-19.

[104] At pages 12, in fine, and 13.

[105] Appellate Body Report, *Argentina-Footwear, supra*, footnote 3 paras. 106 to108.

creased imports" caused serious injury, by pursuing one of the following options (which implement the principle of parallelism)

- *either all* imports taken together, are considered the cause of an "overall impairment in the position of the domestic industry" *or,*
- in the alternative, imports from the countries constituting the customs union are excluded from the scope of the investigation.

125. If such a causal link is established, then the issue of the *application* of the safeguard measure consistent with the principle of parallelism is relevant.[106]

Under the first option, the safeguard measure will have to be applied also vis-à-vis the products originating from the other members of the customs union.

Under the second option, the products originating from the other members of the customs union will not be subject to the measure.

126. In this clear legal framework, a determination of serious injury caused by imports from all sources followed by a second investigation on injury caused by increased imports from NAFTA members only finds no basis whatsoever in the SA and is clearly WTO-incompatible.

127. It is worth noting that the application of safeguard measures[107] is covered by Article 5 of the SA. Article 5.2 (b) of the SA allows for a differentiated allocation of the QR (or a TRQ), in partial breach of the MFN requirements, *provided that* the Member applying the measure follows the very detailed and specific procedure thereof. A differentiated treatment in allocation is however not equal to exclusion from the application of the safeguard measure.

128. However, the US has stated[108] that

> " The EC cites Article 5.2(b), but that Article is irrelevant because the United States did not take action under Article 5.2(b)."

Thus, the US had no legal basis or any justification whatsoever that would allow its authorities to breach the principle of parallelism.

9. Conclusions

129. In the light of the above and of all the claims and arguments made before the Panel in its first written submission, during the first substantive meeting on 20 and 21 December 1999 and when answering to the questions from the Panel, the EC requests the Panel to find that, the US has breached Articles I and XIX of the GATT 1994 and Articles 2.1, 4, 5, 8 and 12 of the Agreement on Safeguards by adopting its safeguard measures on wheat gluten.

---

[106] See, confirming this approach, the AB report on Argentina-Footwear, paras. 111 and following.
[107] This is the title of that provision.
[108] US first oral statement on 20 December 1999, at page 12.

It further requests the Panel that it recommends the DSB that the US WTO-incompatible safeguard measure be withdrawn without delay.

ATTACHMENT 1-5

COMMUNICATION OF THE EUROPEAN COMMUNITY CONCERNING PROPOSED PROCEDURES REGARDING PRIVATE CONFIDENTIAL INFORMATION

(26 January 2000)

As requested, the EC has examined the proposed procedures for the treatment of business confidential information in these proceedings.

As a general comment, it is for the Panel to determine whether such procedure is at all required in the present case. The EC reserves the right to come back on this issue, if necessary.

As far as the proposed text is concerned, the EC has the following comments.

With regard to point V.3, the EC notes that the proposed procedures do not contain, neither in point I nor in point II, any explicit criteria which the Panel could apply if there were a disagreement between the parties to the dispute whether information designated as business confidential information by one of the parties is "reasonably entitled to such treatment". The EC therefore suggests to amend the definition and the term "Business confidential information in point II as follows (changes indicated in "strikeout" and "underline"):

> "Private confidential information" means any information that has been designated as private information by the party submitting it ~~and~~ that is not otherwise available in the public domain *and whose release to interested private parties would seriously prejudice the interests of the private party or parties who originally supplied the information to the party submitting it to the Panel.*

In points V.6 and IX.1, the EC would request the Panel to specify that these rules do not amount to an amendment or a waiver to the existing working procedures with regard to the schedule and the requirement for early submission of factual evidence. Moreover, these rules should not be implemented in such a way as to affect the fairness of the procedure or due process.

With regard to point II, "capital city office", the EC indicates "buildings and grounds of the European Commission in Brussels, Belgium".

Finally, the EC would like to indicate that a determination of a document as "private confidential" cannot in any way prejudice a substantial obligation under the WTO Agreement, where applicable, to make the information publicly available at the time provided for under that Agreement.

ATTACHMENT 1-6

EUROPEAN COMMUNITY'S ORAL STATEMENT, SECOND MEETING

(1 February 2000)

Mr. Chairman, Distinguished Members of the Panel,

1. As we approach the end of this procedure, the European Communities would like to take this opportunity to address once more the most important points of law and fact that are concerned with the violation of several provisions of the GATT 1994 and the Agreement on Safeguards (SA) by the US safeguard measure on wheat gluten.

2. It is stating the obvious to affirm that the role of the complainant, in this case the EC, is to clarify the issue before the Panel while the defendant, *in casu* the US, sometimes attempts to raise a smoke screen or a cloud of dust in order to hide, for as long as it is possible, its misdoing. This tactical scenario was certainly repeated during this procedure.

3. We feel confident however, that the Panel will make sure that the US will not achieve its objective of confusing the issues on which your examination is required. As our presentation will confirm, the US has not succeeded in hiding the *prima facie* violation of Articles I and XIX of the GATT 1994 and Articles 2.1, 4, 5, 8 and 12 of the SA that the EC has demonstrated.

4. In the EC's view, the US safeguard measure on wheat gluten is exemplary of omission and misrepresentation of facts and arguments by a WTO Member during its investigation procedure. It is also paradigmatic of protectionist and discriminatory measures, taken in breach of fundamental principles of the GATT/WTO such as the maintenance of the balance of concessions agreed during multilateral tariff negotiations and the Most-Favoured-Nation treatment. These WTO-inconsistent actions have the effect of seriously distorting the multilateral trading system.

5. The fact that New Zealand, as a third party *not* involved in the trade of wheat gluten, considers it necessary to come forward and to draw your attention to the same matters is further evidence of this very serious, and indeed justified, concern.

6. The EC will proceed in its statement as follows: after re-examining briefly the standard of review of this Panel and the requirements under Article XIX of the GATT 1994, my colleague Mr. Van Vliet will guide you once more through the facts of this case concerning confidentiality, injury and causation and the omissions in the US authorities' investigation. I will then conclude this presentation by recalling other outstanding issues of this case.

7. The EC confirms entirely what it said during the previous stages of this procedure, and will only focus on some issues today, with a view also to rebut points made by the US.

Of course, we are happy to answer any additional question that you may have.

1. STANDARD OF REVIEW

8. On the standard of review of this Panel, the EC would like to add the following.

9. According to Article XVI.4 of the Marrakech Agreement establishing the World Trade Organisation,

> "[E]ach member shall ensure the conformity of its laws, regulations and administrative procedures with its obligations as provided in the annexed Agreements".

10. The US, regardless of how it tries to present its defence, cannot justify a limitation of the terms of reference of this Panel as set out in WTO document WT/DS166/3 of 4 June 1999 and Articles 6.2, 7 and 11 of the DSU by referring to the way in which its internal administrative procedures are organised, or how its domestic authorities view their role in the US domestic legal system.

11. Since the entry into force of the WTO Agreement, when a Panel examines whether a WTO Member is in compliance with any WTO rule, there cannot be any doubt that the WTO obligations of that Member must take precedence over its domestic procedures.

12. It is stating the obvious to affirm that the US domestic procedural rules, or their interpretation, cannot limit the tasks of this Panel whose function is to assist the DSB by performing "an objective assessment of the matter before it". The mission of the Panel cannot consist of a mere "rubber-stamping" of an investigation report.

13. It is also plain from our position that the EC is not asking the Panel to conduct an investigation of any kind. Like any WTO Member in a similar situation, the EC has to indicate to the Panel the information that the ITC should have properly considered but did not, and the importance of that information to the findings and conclusions made by the US authorities.

14. This is entirely consistent with what the Appellate Body considered the correct way of proceeding in its "*Argentina - Footwear*" report, at paragraph 121, third sentence:

> "Rather, the panel examined whether, as required by Article 4 of the Agreement on Safeguards, the Argentine authorities had considered *all* relevant facts and had *adequately explained* how the facts supported the determinations that were made".(emphasis added)

15. As a matter of fact, the objective evidence, which the US authorities have omitted or misinterpreted or downplayed in their investigation and that the EC has submitted to your attention, was prepared by the US authorities themselves before or during the investigation procedure and was in the public domain.

2. THE US SAFEGUARD MEASURE ON WHEAT GLUTEN IS INCONSISTENT WITH ARTICLE XIX.1 OF THE GATT 1994

16. With regard to the violation of Article XIX.1 of the GATT 1994, the latest exchange of written submissions has, in the EC's view, contributed to definitively clarifying that issue.

> That provision requires that a safeguard measure be implemented only if the Member concerned demonstrates *in the report* of its investigation, among other things, that the increase in imports was the result of "unforeseen developments and of the effect of the obligations by a contracting party under this [i.e. the GATT 1994] Agreement".

17. The US claims now that, after all, it had demonstrated in the ITC report that "unforeseen developments", i.e. unexpected circumstances, led to the increase in imports. To that effect, the US points in particular to page I-24 of the ITC report.

18. What the US is doing now is nothing less than an *ex post facto* reconstruction of an examination of unforeseen developments that the US in fact never performed before adopting the safeguard measure.

19. This is, again, a violation of the obligation under Article 4.2 (c) SA, which refers to Article 3, to provide the relevant explanations and proper analysis in the report published before the measure is taken. In the "*Argentina - Footwear*" report, the AB stated[1] that

> "(...) we do believe that the first clause [of Article XIX.1 of the GATT 1994] describes certain *circumstances* which *must be demonstrated* as a matter of fact *in order* for a safeguard measure *to be applied* (...)" (italics in original, emphasis added).

By its findings, the AB has indicated that the "demonstration" must logically *precede* the "*application*" of the safeguard measure. To achieve that result, it could therefore take place only in the investigation report.

1 Appellate Body Report, *Argentina - Safeguard Measures on Imports of Footwear* ("*Argentina - Footwear Safeguard*"), WT/DS121/AB/R, adopted 12 January 2000, DSR 2000:I, 515, para 92. See also para. 95 where the AB states that "(...) safeguard measures may be applied only when all the provisions of the Agreement on Safeguards, and Article XIX of the GATT 1994 are clearly demonstrated" (italics in original, emphasis added).

20. The EC also notes that the US argument[2], that US producers when they increased production capacity did not "foresee" an increase in imports, is simply irrelevant for the issue of whether "unforeseen developments" are present. It is not the increase in imports which needs to be unforeseen, but the *developments leading to it.*[3]

21. The EC will now demonstrate that also the substance of the US argument is without merit.

I would like to suggest that you, Mr Chairman and Members of the Panel, take Exhibit EC-1, the March 1998 ITC report, and reach page I-24.

22. The US would like you to believe that a speculative estimate, made in early *1998*, by the ITC on what could be the possible effects of additional capacity being "brought on line" in the EC in *1999* constitutes the unexpected (i.e. sudden) circumstances that led to the increase in EC imports in *1996*.

23. Moreover, the EC does not deny that there was an increase of capacity of the EC industry in order "to meet demand for wheat starch in the EC market"[4], as the US itself recognises. However, the US has also stressed earlier that a long time is required from the start of construction until the entry into operation of a wheat gluten facility:

> "Although it emphasizes that Heartland entered the market in 1996, (...) the EC omits that construction of the plant began in 1993, long before the import surge and serious injury. Similarly, the EC stresses upgrades of Midwest's Atchison plant in 1996 and 1997, but omits to mention that this was part of a staged series of upgrades that began in 1992, and continued in 1994 and 1995, before the import surge. Thus, the EC's position relies on selective use of evidence while ignoring evidence to the contrary".[5]

24. Therefore, for the same reasons invoked by the US in its defence, the US must recognise now that any increase in capacity of the EC industry during the later part of the PoI could not constitute an "unforeseen development", i.e. an *unexpected* circumstance that led to increased imports.

25. Mr. Chairman, nothing unexpected, no unforeseen developments occurred that led to the 1996 increase in imports. In fact, already on 6 July 1992, in a testimony before the Section 301 Committee of the USTR, Mr. Ladd Seaberg, President of the Wheat Gluten Industry Council and President and CEO of Midwest Grain Products, Inc., stated the following

> "In Italy a new 22 million pound plant is on stream already and another 35 million pound plant is under construction. In France, a

---

2 US answer to question 5 para. 19.

3 See also EC second written submission, para. 13.

4 US second written submission, para. 16.

5 US first written submission, para. 115.

> new plant with 33 M pound capacity is under construction and in Holland an expansion for 33 million pounds is also under way. Then a new plant in East Germany with a capacity of 77 million pounds will be ready by 1994".[6]

This shows that both the US industry and the US Government were fully aware *during the Uruguay Round negotiations and as early as the 6th day of the PoI* of the future developments in the EC industry. The testimony also stresses[7] that

> "The USDA conservatively estimates that EC gluten production could reach 300,000 tons by 1995, roughly double its present capacity(...)".

Therefore, the events which are now invoked by the US cannot be characterised as "unforeseen developments".[8] They do not pass the AB test according to which compliance with Article XIX of the GATT 1994 "*requires* that developments which led to a product being imported in such increased quantities (...) *must* have been *unexpected*"[9] (emphasis added).

26. Furthermore, Mr Chairman, the US surreptitiously suggests that something "unexpected" could also stem from the EC's support to its domestic wheat starch production.

27. *First of all*, the EC draws the attention of the Panel to the fact that the ITC report at page I-24, footnote 119, states that

> "the effect of these programmes *has not been examined by the Commission*" (Emphasis supplied).

28. We fail thus to see how this issue can now be invoked in a credible way by the US authorities.

29. *Secondly*, the reality is that there was no change in the EC policies on this matter since the conclusion of the Uruguay Round negotiations.

30. Given this objective situation, does the US imply by its argument that it recognises that it abused the safeguard mechanism because earlier on it realised that it could not successfully challenge these WTO-consistent EC policies under the WTO SCM agreement? The EC recalls that before filing the petition which led to the safeguard measure, the US industry had first filed a petition under Sec-

---

6 Pages 3 and 4. The EC is of course ready to provide the Panel with a copy of the entire document if it so wishes.

7 Page 17.

8 The US specialised press covered extensively these issues. See, for example, World paper magazine, July 1994, at page 42.

9 Appellate Body Report, *Korea - Definitive Safeguard Measure on Imports of Certain Dairy Products* ("*Korea – Dairy Safeguard*"), WT/DS98/AB/R, adopted 12 January 2000, DSR 2000:I, 3, para. 84.

tion 301 of the US Trade Act which led to an investigation which later had to be dropped by USTR.[10]

31. *Finally*, does the US imply that the implementation of a WTO-consistent policy whose terms are published in English in the Official Journal of the EC, which were very well known during the Uruguay Round multilateral negotiation by all WTO Members including the US, and are also well known by all operators around the world could constitute an "unforeseen development" leading to an increase in imports *four* years after that publication?

32. In summary, Mr. Chairman, Members of the Panel, the last attempt by the US to convince you that it complied with Article XIX of the GATT 1994 is no better than the previous ones. It is now firmly established that the US has not lived up to its obligations under that provision.

I will, with your permission, now pass the floor to Mr. Van Vliet.

Thank you. Mr. Chairman, Distinguished Members of the Panel, I will focus on the issues of confidentiality, injury and causation.

3. CONFIDENTIALITY

33. The EC will come back to the issue of confidentiality when dealing with "profitability" under "injury", but would like to make the following general points. The plain wording of Article 4 of the SA, which refers to Article 3 of the SA, requires the "prompt" publication of a report analysing the case, demonstrating the relevance of the factors examined, and containing reasoned conclusions on "*all pertinent issues*" of fact and law.

34. The ITC report with all its 3-asterisk "***" and with the refusal to provide data in non-confidential form, i.e. by aggregate data or other methods, does not pass that test. This, evidently, is not affected by the US attempt[11] to misrepresent the EC's claim on this matter as meaning that an investigative authority is obliged to publish every piece of non-confidential data which it receives. The EC never made such an absurd statement.

35. Also contrary to what the US asserts[12], the EC does suggest (well-known) ways in which the ITC could have disclosed the relevant elements of confidential information whilst keeping it confidential. Aggregate data is the first obvious way. Alternatively, the developments in performance of an individual company can be described by giving percentages (for example, company Y's sales were x per cent higher in 1997 than in 1996) or by showing trends in indexed form (e.g. 1996: 100, 1997: 110 etc.).

---

[10] See p. II-9 footnote 34 of the ITC report. See also p. 7-8 of EC industry's post-hearing brief, Exhibit EC-18.

[11] Para.21 2nd US written submission.

[12] US answer to question 15, para. 49.

36. Finally, on this point, the EC has to correct a misrepresentation by the US in its second submission.[13] As the EC's joint reply to questions No. 2,4,14,15 and 16 of the Panel shows[14], the EC has provided a long list of omissions of data in the ITC report, which all constitute a breach of Article 4 of the SA, and has thus not limited its claim to the omission of data concerning sales prices, as the US would have it now.

4. INJURY

37. It is worth repeating, very briefly, that many factors indicated that the state of the US industry was in fact improving at the end of the PoI.

For instance, in its answer to question 27, the US states that production was only 4.5 per cent less at end than at the beginning and was rising in comparison with 1996.

Capacity utilisation was (therefore) also going up.

Also, existing inventories were being sold. Contrary to what the US implies[15], the selling out of inventories is a positive and not a negative sign. For instance, for 1997 compared to 1996, it means that US producers were not only producing and selling more, but also receiving income out of selling out their inventories.

38. At the same time, compared with 1996, the market share of imports was hardly increasing in 1997. At the *end* of the PoI, there was therefore, as the EC explained especially in its second written submission, no major import surge, nor any evident sign of serious injury deriving from imports that could justify adopting a safeguard measure.

In this context, your attention is drawn to the fact that the AB emphasised[16] that

"the title of Article XIX is "Emergency Action on Imports of Particular Products".

39. This brings us to another main issue concerning injury. The EC has explained to you earlier, at length, why the absence of data in the ITC report makes the actual situation of the US wheat starch/wheat gluten industry, especially with regard to profitability, unverifiable which is in breach of Article 4 of SA. The way costs were allocated is not explained at all in spite of protests by the EC industry's counsel during the investigation.[17]

---

[13] US second submission at para. 22.

[14] See in particular the answer to question No. 14.

[15] In para. 33 of the US second written submission.

[16] Appellate Body Report, *Argentina – Footwear, supra*, footnote 1, para 93.

[17] Referred to in the ITC report at I-12.

40. At your request, the US has now provided some further explanations.[18]

All these explanations should, and as a matter of fact could, have been given in the ITC report *at the time of its release*, especially since "profits and losses" are explicitly mentioned in 4.2 (a) SA.

41. Therefore, it is now too late for the US to attempt to answer the still unresolved following fundamental questions:

> How was the cost allocated exactly, on the basis of production, sales or any other basis?
>
> Which are the "commercial realities" that were allegedly "reflected" in the differences in the way the various US companies allocated cost?

42. In any case, notwithstanding the explicit request by the Panel, an explanation of exact method by which the companies arrived at their figures is still missing and the "explanations" given now do not provide any concrete clarification.

5. FAILURE OF THE US TO CORRECTLY ADDRESS THE CAUSATION ISSUE

43. The ITC did not fulfil its duty under Article 4.2 of the SA to correctly investigate all pertinent matters. As required under this provision, this should have been done on the ITC's own initiative, and the fact, if proved, that the parties did not bring them to its attention, as suggested by the US, can be no excuse.[19]

44. In this respect the "*United States - Salmon*" case on Anti-dumping cited by the US is not relevant in this case. It is not all other "possible" factors which need to be addressed (as stated in that report),but "*all* relevant factors of an objective and quantifiable nature having a bearing on the situation of the [domestic] industry", which is evidently a different standard. The US authorities did not live up to this obligation.

45. The violation of Article 4.2 (a) is all the more serious since many points were specifically raised before the ITC.[20]

5.1 Input costs went up strongly during the later part of the PoI

46. There is no discussion that wheat is the largest part of industry raw material costs and its price will therefore be determinative of the wheat starch/wheat gluten industry performance.

---

[18] US answer to question No. 26.

[19] US answer to question 7, para. 25.

[20] See Exhibits EC-16 to EC-18.

US wheat prices rose very strongly at the end of the PoI, thus impacting negatively on the US industry's situation.

47. In the EC's view, the US arguments on this point, especially in its second written submission[21], are without merit.

For example, regardless of the fact that the EC is entitled to provide *monthly* wheat prices taken from official USDA statistics to confirm this point, the US' procedural objections against these data cannot detract from the fact that the ITC itself, already in original report[22] acknowledges that these input prices rose. This is corroborated by the US "corrigendum" at II-37a.[23]

48. The US also invokes that some US producers buy wheat *flour* as raw material in order to claim that EC data on raw material costs "are not probative".

This is a remarkable argument: are we to assume that even though wheat prices jumped, by a stroke of magic US wheat starch/wheat gluten producers were still able to buy the flour made from that wheat at low prices?

Even the ITC[24] disagrees with the US present position:

> "purchase prices of wheat *and wheat flour* generally rose during the entire period."(emphasis added)

5.2 Increased costs could not be passed on in prices at the end of the PoI

49. The ITC "reasoned away", in its report, the very real negative effects of higher wheat costs, energy prices and depreciation costs on industry financial performance by assuming that all these costs would have been passed on to buyers, had it not been for increased imports.

50. The fallacy of the ITC's assumptions about passing on input costs was however pointed out explicitly and extensively to the ITC during its investigation and explained in EC's submission. It is worth noting that the US contradicts now those assumptions by stating in its second written submission[25] that if domestic producers raise their prices

> "(...) they would be foregoing some increase in sales, and consequently in production and capacity utilization".

51. The EC recalls that wheat gluten demand is sensitive to the price of wheat gluten because, as acknowledged also by the ITC, high protein wheat/wheat flour and wheat gluten are substitutes in bread baking (which accounts for 80 per cent of apparent US wheat gluten consumption).

---

21 In particular paras. 11-12.
22 II-37.
23 Exhibit US-10.
24 Ibidem.
25 Para. 64.

Bakers have a clear choice: either to use wheat gluten to increase the protein content of low protein wheat/wheat flour or to purchase high protein wheat/wheat flour and thereby substantially reduce the amount of wheat gluten they need. The use of high protein wheat/wheat flour therefore significantly reduces demand for wheat gluten. This is the point the EC always made before the Panel, which is different from the incorrect representation of our position.[26]

The bakers' choice is of course based on profitability: they will choose one or the other – high protein wheat/wheat flour or wheat gluten – depending on their relative price. The mere possibility of using high protein wheat when the protein levels of wheat/wheat flour rise has thus inevitably a depressing effect on the price of wheat gluten. The EC has already explained in its second written submission, at paragraphs 44 to 46, how this particular market works.

52. The EC has also shown[27] that over 86 per cent of the variation in quarterly US wheat gluten prices over the PoI was explained by the protein content of wheat as measured by wheat protein premiums. No other single factor, including imports of wheat gluten, had any statistically significant effect on wheat gluten prices.

53. The reason that protein premiums determine wheat gluten prices has just been explained: *high protein wheat is the only substitute for wheat gluten in bread baking.* All producers/sellers and buyers of wheat gluten face this fundamental reality of the US wheat gluten market.

54. Also the ITC was aware of this: it explicitly acknowledges[28] that crops particularly low in protein content (which generated high protein premiums) drove up wheat gluten prices around 1994.

55. However, the US authorities did not investigate the protein premium developments, especially for the period 1996-1997. This would have required examination of price differences between high protein and low protein wheat on the basis of publicly available data. But the ITC unreasonably did not even request such data.

56. Therefore, in the causation section of the ITC-report[29], the US authorities did not consider, as they should have, whether it was not in fact high protein content of wheat crops (so low protein premium) which was keeping prices relatively low.

---

[26] See para. 48 of the US second written submission: "The EC implies that high gluten wheat flour has a sufficiently high gluten content so as not to require the addition of wheat gluten to enhance the gluten level".

[27] Exhibit EC-10.

[28] I-22 to 23.

[29] I-16 to 18.

5.3 The movements of prices compared with level of imports show that prices moved independently from imports

57. It was in particular the failure to investigate the wheat protein premium issue which resulted in the incorrect and unjustified assertion by the ITC that increased imports "drove down" prices.

58. As its only defence, the US asserts now that "trends speak for themselves"[30], thus implying that it did not need to inquire that issue, and that it draw firm conclusions from the mere coincidence in time during some quarters of the POI of slightly lowering prices and slightly increasing imports Although the EC has already explained in some detail in its written submissions and earlier oral statement that coincidence in time is not automatically proof of a causal link, some brief additional considerations are appropriate.

59. In its "*Argentina-Footwear*" report[31], the AB agreed with the Panel that in an analysis of causation

> "it is *the relationship* between the *movements* in imports (volume and market share) and the *movements* in injury factors that must be central to a causation analysis and determination."

The term "relationship" is of course not equal to "coincidence", as the US would have it. In support of its finding, the AB approvingly cited the "*Argentina-Footwear*" panel statement according to which a coincidence in time of such movements cannot by itself *prove* causation.

60. The ITC's determination is contrary to these principles.

In 1994, wheat gluten prices jumped because of the low protein content of wheat crops, while imports remained practically stable.

In 1995, wheat gluten prices fell from 1994 levels as the protein levels of the wheat crop rose[32], although imports remained practically stable.

In 1996, the wheat gluten price went *up* from the last quarter 1995 level (and remained higher than that level up until the first two quarters of 1997) even though imports were also increasing.

61. All these movements show that there was no relationship between the level of imports and the wheat gluten price. Imports did not "drive down" wheat gluten prices. At the very least, the ITC should have investigated and explained why the protein premium which, as it acknowledges, controlled prices early on in the POI was not relevant later on. It completely failed to do so.

---

30 US second written submission, at para. 27.

31 Para. 144.

32 See Exhibit EC-10 Figure 3.

5.4 *Industry Cost-Price Squeeze*

62. Three defining events impacted the US wheat gluten/wheat starch industry over the PoI:

- wheat gluten prices jumped on the US market to very high levels in 1994 because of the low protein content of wheat;
- wheat gluten prices declined on the US market in 1995, and – although they increased somewhat in the first three quarters of 1996 – remained low in 1996 and 1997, because of the improving protein content of wheat as reflected by declining protein premiums;
- the costs of producing wheat gluten in the US rose in particular since wheat prices increased significantly.

63. Declining wheat gluten prices and rising input costs caught US wheat gluten/wheat starch producers in a cost-price squeeze. Higher costs and lower wheat gluten prices, not imports, were the causes of any deterioration of the US industry financial performance after 1994.

Prices were low due to low protein premium. Furthermore they were influenced by increased intra-industry competition, which brings the EC to the over-capacity issue.

64. The ITC claimed that the US industry would have been able to capture all of the growth in the US wheat gluten apparent consumption in 1996 and 1997, if imports had remained stable at 1995 levels.

This claim is based on the assertion that the industry had expanded production capacity in expectation of increased consumption over the PoI. However, the decision by the US industry to over-expand capacity cannot be explained in any way except that it was a bad business decision.

65. There is no *a priori* reason why US producers would have captured all of the increase in apparent consumption of wheat gluten in 1996 and 1997. US purchasers of imported wheat gluten would have to alter their commercial relations with suppliers and shift to domestic producers to cover increased sales. The ITC provides no explanation of why this curious economic behaviour should have occurred. In fact, the US now contradictorily asserts in its second written submission[33] that

> "[T]his analysis did not assume that the domestic industry would capture all of the increase in domestic demand in 1997 from earlier levels".

66. The US wheat gluten/wheat starch industry found itself with substantial and costly newly installed production capacity at the time when on the one hand wheat gluten prices were declining from the peak levels in 1994, caused by the improving protein content of wheat, and on the other hand production (in particu-

---

33 Para. 63.

lar input) costs were rising. Because of the cost-price squeeze, US wheat gluten/wheat starch producers were unable to take advantage of their expanded production capacity.

67. It is therefore the combination of excessively increased capacity and particularly high input costs which led to any difficulties that the US industry might have had during the latter part of the PoI.

68. Being aware of the existence of all these "relevant factors", it is not understandable how the US authorities could reach the unreasonable conclusion that increased imports were the sole cause, in isolation, of the alleged "serious injury" to the US wheat gluten/wheat starch industry.

69. Now, in its answer to question No. 2, the US admits that the ITC never analysed whether the US industry, could have been profitable at 61 per cent of capacity utilisation when considered *in combination with the high wheat prices during last two years of the PoI*. In other words: the US authorities never analysed whether the cause of the (alleged) unprofitability was imports, or the combination of over-capacity, high input cost, and difficulties in co-product markets, to which we will turn in a second.

70. Thus, the US authorities did not fulfil the requirements under Article 4.2 of the SA, in particular under (b), which prohibits the attribution of injury caused by other factors to increased imports.

5.5 Co-products

71. The EC will not explain again in detail why developments in the necessary co-products of wheat gluten influence the profitability and business decisions of wheat starch/wheat gluten producers. Its analysis will be limited today to the following points concerning mainly starch (for alcohol, we refer you to our earlier statements).

72. The EC has proved by reference to the *ITC's own data* that in comparison with corn starch producers, the competitive position of the wheat starch operations of US wheat starch/wheat gluten producers deteriorated during the PoI. This is the opposite of what the US incorrectly asserts.[34]

73. Since wheat starch and wheat gluten are necessarily produced due to one and the same production process, not only was wheat gluten production capacity irrationally increased by US wheat starch/wheat gluten producers, but so was by necessity wheat *starch* production capacity (by 93 per cent).[35]

74. This worsened the competitive conditions between wheat starch and corn starch for US wheat starch/wheat gluten producers, because it increased the

[34] In particular para. 44 of second US written submission.

[35] See Table C-2 at C-5 of ITC-report.

amount of wheat starch that they had to sell in competition with – cheaper – corn starch.

75. The situation deteriorated even more because input costs – wheat (flour) – also increased. Like with wheat gluten, these increased costs could not be passed on into wheat starch prices because of the weak competitive position in comparison with corn starch.

76. The above combination of factors led to decreasing sales and doubling inventories of wheat starch during the later part of the PoI.[36]

77. Both the ITC's analysis[37] and US defence[38] on this point are totally inadequate. It is in fact limited to noting that wheat starch selling prices showed a gradual increase over the PoI.

78. However, the mere fact that there was some increase in wheat starch prices does not mean at all that this increase was sufficient to offset the negative impact of the strongly increased input prices.

79. The additional argument developed by the US[39], that the fact that wheat prices are higher than corn prices will result in prices of the so-called "A" wheat *starch* being higher than corn starch prices, is devoid of economic logic.

The fact that the price of wheat is higher than that of corn *does not mean* that prices of products *derived* from wheat are higher than prices of products *derived* from corn. Economic logic dictates that it is demand for the derived products that determines their price. This is of course true also for the so-called "A" wheat starch.

6. THE US SAFEGUARD MEASURE ON WHEAT GLUTEN IS A PROTECTIONIST MEASURE IN DISGUISE

80. The EC has explained that the US safeguard measure on wheat gluten is in fact *a protectionist measure* in disguise, that is a measure that goes far beyond the exceptional remedies which a WTO member is allowed to adopt in case of proved serious injury caused by increased imports.

The US has gone back from the concessions bound in its GATT Schedule beyond what it could possibly be allowed to under the SA and without any justification for doing so. The EC has brought to the Panel's attention in the earlier stages of this dispute settlement procedure numerous elements supporting its claim. They can be summarised as follows:

[36] See Table C-6 at C-5 of ITC-report. Note in particular how sales ("US shipments") strongly dropped in 1996 compared to 1995 and inventories more than doubled in 1997 compared with 1995.

[37] I-16-17.

[38] Para. 43-44 of the second US written submission.

[39] US second written submission, at para. 44.

6.1 The US has breached the proportionality principle under Articles 4.2 of the SA

81. Making imports from other Members bear the burden of adjustment of the domestic industry to factors *other* than "increased imports" would surely be an act of protectionism, in violation of Articles I and XIX of GATT 1994 and of all the procedural and substantive requirements under the SA.

82. According to Article 4.2 (b) last sentence, when considering whether "serious injury" was caused by "increased imports" (the only possibility that allows a Member to impose a safeguard measure), the investigating authorities shall not attribute to increased imports injury caused by other factors, which are causing injury at the same time.

83. As was indicated in the EC's second written submission, this provision has the important consequence that an investigative authority can only find that "serious injury" is caused by increased imports if it is found that the increased imports alone cause "significant overall impairment", even after taking all injury caused by other factors out of the analysis.

84. The analysis that my colleague Mr. Van Vliet has just made before you this morning provides the clearest possible confirmation that the US authorities did not comply with the proportionality principle. The effect of this WTO-inconsistent action is that the US authorities have attributed with no justification to increased imports the cause of an alleged serious injury of US domestic wheat gluten/wheat starch industry.

85. In fact, the US authorities, when examining the alleged "significant overall impairment in the position of the domestic industry", have completely disregarded the effects that the other co-causes were producing. An objective examination of "all factors having an objective and quantifiable bearing on the situation of" the wheat gluten/wheat starch industry would inevitably have led to the conclusion that none of the causes was sufficient, *taken in isolation*, to create such serious injury.

86. The "preponderance test" applied by the US pursuant to its internal legislation is inconsistent with the principle of proportionality set out in article 4.2 of the SA.

Its application to the wheat gluten safeguard procedure has produced the effect of prompting the implementation of a safeguard measure in a situation where the US was not in a position to demonstrate objectively that the alleged "significant overall impairment in the position of the domestic" wheat gluten/wheat starch industry could have been caused by "increased imports" taken in isolation, i.e. after having deducted the effects of the other co-causes.

6.2 The US has breached the proportionality principle under Article 5.1, first and third sentence, of the SA

87. Article 5.1 of the SA is the second textual application of the principle of proportionality and provides that a Member shall apply safeguard measures "only to the extent necessary to prevent or remedy serious injury and to facilitate adjustment".

88. Even if one were to assume *arguendo* that a Member has correctly attributed the cause of the serious injury to increased imports (and this hypothesis is certainly *not* correct in the case of the US's safeguard measure on wheat gluten), the corresponding safeguard measure must be commensurate or proportionate to that injury, to the exclusion of any injury caused by other factors.

89. The EC repeats once more that using the pretext of a safeguard measure in order to remedy the intrinsic uncompetitiveness of the US domestic industry (*in casu* the wheat gluten/wheat starch industry) relative to other domestic competing industry, like the corn milling industry, constitutes a violation of the SA.

90. Neither can a WTO Member abuse a safeguard measure, in order to remedy situations unrelated to increased imports such as increase in input costs, or fluctuations in price due to variations of protein premiums, or failed business strategies such as over-expansion of production capacity. However, this is exactly what the US did.

91. The issue of principle that commands this case is that lawful trade from other WTO Members cannot be made to bear the burden of factors allegedly causing injury, which are unrelated to imports. This would be in patent breach of Articles I and XIX of the GATT 1994 and the provisions of the SA.

92. In its second written submission, (paragraphs 64 and 65) the US has attempted a defence by stating that

> "(...)The remedy analysis assumed that domestic producers, relieved from pressure from low-priced imports, *would prefer to raise their prices above their operating costs*, even though this meant that they would be foregoing some increase in sales, and consequently in production and capacity utilization. (...) Because this estimate assumes that the U.S. industry will sell at a price *that covers its operating costs*, it seeks to ensure that the U.S. industry will operate at a level at which it will achieve a reasonable profit".

93. The EC responds that by this statement the US is effectively admitting that its safeguard measure on wheat gluten serves exclusively to keep imports out of the US market in order to allow US producers to surmount purely *internal* problems.

94. In fact, to adopt a safeguard measure whose main effect consists in keeping prices "above operating costs" in a situation where those costs are directly dependent on

- insufficient capacity utilisation due to its irrational increase,

- developments in wheat prices and input costs in general, and
- the burden of disposing of wheat starch in a high competitive market determined by corn starch low prices

effectively amounts to shifting the burden of the inherent uncompetitiveness of the US industry onto imported wheat gluten.

95. There is a WTO-consistent and transparent way open to the US if it wants to reduce imports in order to help its industry deal with internal competitive difficulties. It could start GATT Article XXVIII negotiations in order to raise the tariff protection for its domestic wheat gluten. However, this implies that it must offer first an adequate compensation. The US cannot expect to achieve that result "for free" by abusing the safeguard mechanism.

96. If the factors leading to the situation in which the US industry found itself in the later period of the PoI were still to prevail at the end of the three years of the current safeguard measure, the US industry's situation will be unchanged. Therefore, the current reduction in import levels is not at all justified by an emergency situation and reasonable doubts could be raised as to whether it could effectively be removed in 2001.

97. The *ex post facto* explanation provided now by the US is thus a confirmation that the US safeguard measure goes beyond what is necessary in order to remedy injury allegedly caused by increased imports and to facilitate adjustment of the industry to that injury *only*.

6.3 Article 5.1 did not allow the US to choose a quantitative restriction without having demonstrated that that was the least trade restrictive measure possible

98. The principle of proportionality under Article 5.1 did not allow the US to choose a quantitative restriction without having demonstrated that the applied measure was the least trade restrictive measure possible.

99. The EC would like to recall once more that the explanation provided by the ITC (I-26) for choosing a quantitative restriction refers *only* to the wheat starch market and to the alleged need to avoid "inequitable" distribution of burden between suppliers from third countries.

There is no explanation on the only relevant issue, i.e. the "suitable" remedy for the alleged serious injury to the US wheat gluten industry caused by increased imports only and the need to facilitate adjustment of that industry to increased imports only.

The ITC's unrelated statements or "*petitiones principii*" do not reach the minimum standard of "reasoned conclusions" required under the SA.

100. As a concrete consequence of these violations of the SA, imports of wheat gluten from the EC suffer in a disproportionate manner from the restriction of trade with the US. Or, in other words, the protection provided to the US domestic industry is exaggerated and exceeds what is permissible under the SA.

101. Please allow me to react briefly to a misinterpretation of the SA by the US.

In the EC's view, the comparison between Article 6 SA and Article 5.1 which is made in its second written submission is incorrect[40] and thus provides no support for the US defence. The first provision imposes tariffs as provisional safeguard measures because that allows refund in case no definitive measure is taken. By contrast, Article 5.1 imposes a proportionality obligation. It provides for the possibility of adopting definitive safeguards also in the form of a quantitative restriction, but only if the investigation report demonstrates that this is indispensable in order "to remedy serious injury and to facilitate adjustment" to increased imports.

6.4 The US has applied the safeguard measure on wheat gluten inconsistently with the findings of the US authorities about injury and causation.

102. The US authorities have *excluded* from their reasoning concerning causality the effects of the inherently weak position of the US wheat gluten/wheat starch industry on the US *domestic* starch market, thus incorrectly determining that a serious injury was caused solely by the imported wheat gluten.

103. However, the US authorities have *included* as one of their key considerations the wheat starch market conditions in the US when considering the form, the scope and the extent of the safeguard measure against *foreign* wheat gluten.

104. This inconsistent way of proceeding of the US authorities has *doubly* prejudiced the market access conditions for EC produced wheat gluten by first indicating imports as the sole cause of serious injury and then increasing the restrictions flowing from the safeguard measure in order to remedy other causes.

105. This constitutes further evidence that the US abused the safeguard instrument when it adopted the safeguard measure on wheat gluten.

6.5 The US has manipulated the "representative period"

106. The EC reiterates here briefly its position of principle on the interpretation of Article 5.1, second sentence, of the SA.

107. If a Member chooses to implement a quantitative restriction, it has to determine the quantity of imports *in an objective way*, i.e. with reference to the most recent ("last") statistics available.

108. Such statistics are representative of the legitimate trade in the product concerned *unless* an exceptional event or a violation of WTO rules has distorted

---

40 US second submission, para. 69.

the trade. The Member departing from the available statistics for the *last* three years must prove the existence of such exceptional event or violation.

109. As was mentioned in our second written submission[41], the "*Bananas - Recourse to Article 21.5 by Ecuador*" panel report and the ITC itself have confirmed the correctness of the EC's position.

110. When the objective level of imports is set, it may be adjusted *in a MFN fashion* provided that "a clear justification is given that a different level is necessary to prevent or remedy injury".

111. A "*clear*" justification corresponds to a *reinforced* burden of proof upon the Member using that possibility. It is not the "*US - Shirts and Blouses*"[42] standard according to which

> "the party who asserts a fact, whether the claimant or the respondent, is responsible for providing proof thereof".

It is a much higher, more demanding standard. Generic explanations or statements do not fulfil that standard.

112. Therefore, a correct implementation of Article 5 of the SA imposes that the two *successive* and *separate* steps that we have just examined are not confused.

113. The US has not followed this correct line of action. Rather, it has argued even in its second written submission that it was entitled to invent a new rule and read in Article 5.1, second sentence, the possibility of choosing another representative period of its choice.

114. The practical consequence of such action is that the quantities of imports allowed into the US are unjustifiably lower than the level at which they should have been set. In other words, the US domestic industry on wheat gluten is overprotected by the US measure, which is a protectionist measure in disguise. This corresponds to a violation of Article 5.1 of the SA.

7. THE US SAFEGUARD MEASURE ON WHEAT GLUTEN IS A DISCRIMINATORY MEASURE

115. The EC has also indicated that the US safeguard measure on wheat gluten is in fact *a discriminatory measure*, i.e. a measure that was designed with the aim of treating in a differentiated fashion imports from different origins. This discrimination is however inconsistent with Articles I of the GATT 1994 and 2.1, 4.2 and 5.2 of the SA.

116. The EC has brought to the Panel's attention in the earlier stages of this dispute settlement procedure numerous elements supporting its claim. The an-

41 Paras. 104 and 105.
42 At page 15.

swers by the US and Canada to the questions from the Panel have shed new interesting light on this issue.

117. Discrimination between products based on their origin constitutes a breach of the fundamental principle of MFN treatment.

118. According to Article 4.2 (a) SA

> "In the investigation to determine whether *increased imports* have caused (...) serious injury to a domestic industry under the terms of this Agreement, the competent authorities shall evaluate all relevant factors (...), in particular the rate and amount of the *increase in imports* of the product concerned in absolute and relative terms, the share of the domestic market taken by *increased imports* (...).

119. According to Article 4.2 (b) SA

> "The determination referred to in subparagraph (a) shall not be made unless this investigation demonstrates (...) the existence of a causal link between *increased imports* of the product concerned and the serious injury (...). When factors other than increased imports are causing injury (...), such injury shall not be attributed to *increased imports*".

120. The US[43] and Canada[44] have confirmed in their latest submissions that the US authorities have performed the injury and causation investigation in two steps.

121. They have first (unjustifiably) attributed alleged "serious injury" to increased imports regardless of their origin.

122. However, the US authorities have then performed a *second causation* investigation and have excluded Canada because its imports allegedly did not contribute "substantially" to the injury.

123. Finally, they have implemented the allocation of the quantitative restriction in order to reallocate shares among foreign suppliers (ITC I-21 and I-26, *in fine*).

124. The text of Article 4.2 (a) and (b) on its face obliges *all* the Members, including the US, to consider "imports" or "increased imports" as a whole, *without* discrimination among such imports based on the origin of the product.

125. Indeed, *in view of the clear text of the SA*, a departure from such a fundamental principle of the GATT/WTO cannot be based on unjustified statements such as that "nothing (...) proscribes" deviating from that rule, as the US asserts in its answer to question No. 29 .

---

43 US answer to question No. 29, at para. 93.

44 Canada's answer to questions from the Panel and the EC, at para. 2.

126. Notwithstanding, this is exactly how the US authorities operated. The US latest defence is moreover in conflict with the ITC's statement at I-18 of its report:

> "Nothing in Article 4 of the Agreement, which defines key terms and sets out the factors to be considered in determining whether imports are a substantial cause of serious injury (...) suggests that a country should look at anything else than *all* imports when determining whether imports have increased, and whether increased imports cause or threaten serious injury to a domestic industry."(emphasis added).

127. The EC therefore concludes that the unequivocal text of Article 4.2 of the SA and of Article I of the GATT clearly prohibit that the US perform a two step injury and causation analysis, and include Canadian imports when determining whether "serious injury" has occurred but exclude Canada from the scope of the safeguard measure.

128. The facts also contradict that possibility since imports from the EC, Australia as well as Canada increased in 1996, and the level of imports from all these sources into the US in 1997 were in any case higher than in 1995 (ITC II-10, Table 1).

129. The US has admitted that it ignored these facts and isolated imports originating in the EC in its investigation.[45] The US has no justification under the SA or under any other WTO agreement for having breached the principle of parallelism and the fundamental principle of the MFN treatment.

130. As is apparent, Article 2.1 SA, and in particular its footnote, does not support at all the US' (and Canada's) case.

131. Free trade areas such as the NAFTA are not even mentioned in that text.

132. The generic reservation contained in footnote 1 to Article 2.1, concerning the interpretation of the relationship between article XXIV of the GATT 1994 and Article XIX of the same agreement, has evidently no bearing on the interpretation of *Article 4.2 of the Safeguards Agreement*. This is all the more so in light of the General Interpretative note to Annex 1A to the WTO Agreement.

133. The uneven allocation of shares of the quantitative restriction in favour of Australia and to the detriment of the EC is another plain example of discriminatory treatment without justification.

134. The US has explicitly stated before you that "The EC cites Article 5.2(b), but that Article is irrelevant because the United States did not take action under Article 5.2(b)".[46]

---

[45] See US answer to question 29 at para. 92: " In its analysis the Commission found that the serious injury sustained by the domestic wheat gluten industry was attributable to a surge in imports from the EU in 1996 and 1997, accompanied by sustained underselling by EU producers."

[46] US oral statement on 20 December 1999, at page 12.

135. Since, by its own spontaneous admission, it did not follow the procedures under Article 5.2(b), the US has no explanation left as to how it can justify that despite having a 47 per cent share of the market in the previous representative period, the EC was allocated only a 43 per cent share of the quota. Australia, on the other hand, was allocated a share of 49 per cent, compared to its share in the previous representative period of 38 per cent. More importantly, this allocation has preserved entirely the 1997 record levels of imports from Australia despite the fact that Australia's exports increased continuously in the last three years of the investigative period, by almost 21 per cent.[47] In fact, the ITC report[48] clearly indicates the ITC's intent to target the allegedly "disproportional growth and impact of imports of wheat gluten from the European Union".

136. Finally, the manipulation of the "representative period" by the US authorities, that was examined above, has provided *de facto* a better treatment of wheat gluten of Australian origin when compared to wheat gluten of EC origin. That manipulation is therefore not only a breach of Article 5.1 of the SA but also of Article I of the GATT 1994.

137. In summary, the EC reiterates that the US safeguard measure on wheat gluten is inconsistent with Article I of the GATT 1994 and Articles 2.1, 4.2 and 5 of the SA.

138. Before concluding this oral statement, the EC would draw the attention of the panel to the fact that the US has not contested that during the meetings held between the US and the EC prior to the entry into force of the safeguard measure, the US officials were instructed "not to negotiate on anything". For the rest, the documents cited by the US[49] only confirm the fact that the EC never considered these consultations as covering either proposed measures or trade compensation. The breach of Articles 12 and 8 of the SA has thus been definitively established.

Mr. Chairman and distinguished Members of the Panel, thank you for your attention.

---

[47] ITC report at II-12.
[48] At I-21.
[49] US Exhibits 11 and 12.

ATTACHMENT 1-7

EUROPEAN COMMUNITY'S COMMENTS ON US EXHIBIT 13

(2 February 2000)

The table submitted by the US as US Exhibit 13 at the last minute on 1 February 2000, at the end of the session with the panel, is misleading. The US intention was to show that the allocation of the quota adopted as a safeguard measure on wheat gluten is not discriminating against the EC or in favour of Australia and Canada.

The EC has the following comments concerning that table:

- The table is based on "crop years" which means *1 July* of one year to *30 June* of the following year.
- The "quota year" is based on the Proclamation by the US President, i.e. *1 June* of one year to *31 May* of the following year.
- Therefore, there is a one month overlap between the two referenced years.
- The management of the quota (which was decided by the US) is based on a "first come – first served" system, which means that the quota will remain open until the quantities are filled. As soon as the quantities are completely used, no more imports are allowed for the remaining part of the quota year.
- Given that, unlike for Australia and Canada, the over-restrictive size of the quota allocated to the EC has substantially reduced the room of manoeuvre of the importers from the EC, experience of the first two "quota years" shows that a substantial part or even the totality of the share of the quota allocated to the EC is filled in a very short period of time, at the beginning of the quota year, *i.e. during the month of June*. This is possible because wheat gluten can be easily stored in warehouses in the US territory and shipped to US customers according to sales contracts over the remaining part of the "quota year".
- The market share of the EC imports in "crop year" *1999* (i.e. July 1998-June 1999) which is shown in the US Exhibit 13 includes not only part of the quantities for the quota year 1998/1999 but also practically *all* the quantities which may be imported from the EC until 31 May 2000, which pertain to "quota year" 1999/2000 (i.e. June 1999-May 2000). Evidence of this is provided by statistics concerning *June 1999*: 97 per cent of the total quantities granted to the EC for the "quota year" 1999/2000 were imported within that first month.
- Therefore, **the statistics based on "crop years" provided by the US in its Exhibit 13 create a major statistical distortion that renders them totally unusable for the purpose pursued by the US. In fact, at least the 1999**

"crop year" includes a volume of imports which is equivalent to almost two "quota years".

- The real import shares of the EC, Australia and Canada can only be appreciated if import shares are calculated on the basis of "quota years". The table annexed to this document provides such correct statistics.
- If we now take the US Exhibit 13 for the "crop year" 1995, the Panel can easily appreciate that Australia had a share of 40.5 per cent of the imports into the US. However, it was provided 49 per cent of the quota.
- In the meantime, the exclusion of Canada from the scope of the quota has resulted in a spectacular gain in market share, as the EC has relentlessly repeated as from the start of this procedure. The US Exhibit 13 and the EC statistics show that Canada more than doubled its exports when compared with the last year preceding the entry into force of the safeguard measure on wheat gluten.

COMPARISON IMPORTS "CROP YEAR" VS. "QUOTA YEAR" IN METRIC TONS

	Crop year 01 July 98-30 June 99		**Quota year 01 June 98-31 May 99**	
	Volume	%	Volume	%
Total imports	96,636.5	100.00	77,576.9	100.00
EC*	46,587.8	48.21	30,867.4	39.79
Australia	31,345.8	32.44	28,341.4	36.53
Canada	13,179.9	13.64	12,753.1	16.44

IMPORTS ACCORDING TO US CUSTOMS IN METRIC TONS

Imports by:	**EC**	**Australia**	**Canada**
June 98	5,397.9	2,194.6	621.1
Crop year 1998/99			
July 98	5,461.7	3,169.7	669.4
August 98	6,729.4	2,131.2	638.8
September 98	7,166.0	2,828.4	928.3
October 98	5,517.2	2,508.1	1,475.6
November 98	595.1	2,239.0	900.0
December 98	0.0	3,354.3	1,195.3
January 99	0.0	2,107.1	1,240.5
February 99	0.0	2,866.9	1,212.7
March 99	0.0	3,104.6	1,195.9
April 99	0.0	1,680.6	1,320.0
May 99	0.0	156.9	1,355.4
June 99	21,118.2	5,199.0	1,047.9
TOTAL	46,587.75	31,345.8	13,179.9

* The quantity for the quota year 1998/99 i.e. 30,867.4 tons is exceptionally higher than the EC quota by 5,402 tons due to mismanagement of the quota by the US customs.

ATTACHMENT 1-8

RESPONSES OF THE EUROPEAN COMMUNITY TO THE ADDITIONAL QUESTIONS FROM THE PANEL (4 February 2000)

Questions No. 2 (EC) and 3 (EC and US)

Q2. "Please comment on the US statement on page 9 of its oral statement at the second substantive Panel meeting that "the relevant question is whether the USITC demonstrated in its investigation that unforeseen developments occurred, not whether the USITC made a specific determination regarding unforeseen developments....""

Q3. "In connection with question 2 above, could the parties please indicate to the Panel what, if any, they consider the difference between "demonstrating" such unforeseen developments in an "investigation" – the terms used by the Appellate Body at para. 98 of the Argentina – Footwear report – and "making a specific determination" regarding such unforeseen developments."

Joint Reply

In the "*Argentina - Footwear*" report, the AB stated that

> "(...) we do believe that the first clause [of Article XIX.1 of the GATT 1994] describes certain *circumstances* which *must be demonstrated* as a matter of fact *in order* for a safeguard measure *to be applied* (...)" (italics in original, emphasis added).

By its findings, the AB has indicated that the "demonstration as a matter of fact" must logically and chronologically *precede* the "*application*" of the safeguard measure. To achieve that result, it can therefore take place only in the investigation report. Moreover, it necessitates an examination in fact that can take no other form than a reasoned development in writing. This is entirely missing in the ITC report.

Moreover, in the same report, the AB has reminded that:

> "This suggests that Article XIX continues in full force and effect, and, in fact, establishes certain *prerequisites* for the imposition of safeguard measures."

Finally, in the "Korea-Dairy" report, at paragraph 84, the AB has also indicated that

> "(...) it seems to us that the ordinary meaning of the phrase 'as a result of unforeseen developments' *requires* that the developments *which led to* a product being imported in such increased quantities and under such conditions as to cause (...) serious injury to domestic producers *must* have been 'unexpected'".

In the light of these interpretations, the US should have demonstrated in the ITC report the existence of 'unforeseen developments'. In order to be demonstrated, that "prerequisite" should have been examined by the investigative authorities which should have analysed whether the circumstances "that led to a product to be imported in such increased quantities (...)" were "unexpected".

This inevitably implies that it is not possible to try to reconstruct *ex post facto* a justification on the existence of a "prerequisite" that was patently neglected during the investigation.

Paragraph 98 of the "*Argentina – Footwear*" report contains the conclusions of the AB on this issue. To no surprise, its careful wording, including the terms "in their investigation" constitutes the consistent and logical confirmation of the interpretation of Article XIX that the same AB had adopted in the above-mentioned paragraphs of the same decision and of the contextual "*Korea – Dairy*" decision.

The EC would like to repeat once more that, in substance, the *ex post facto* explanations by the US do not stand up to serious scrutiny, as the EC's second oral submission has demonstrated.

Question No. 4 (US)

"How does the United States respond to the statements of the European Community at para. 25 of its oral statement to the second substantive Panel meeting concerning "unforeseen developments"?"

Comments by the EC

The EC recalls the co-product nature of wheat gluten and wheat starch: when 5 kg of wheat starch a re produced, necessarily 1 kg of wheat gluten is produced. Therefore, it is not unexpected that any increase in wheat starch capacity of production automatically leads to an increase in wheat gluten production capacity. Moreover, the statement referred to by the EC was made by the President of the Wheat *Gluten* Association and specifically referred to increases in wheat *gluten*capacity.

Questions No 5 (EC) and 6 (EC and US)

Q5. "How does the EC respond to the US statement in its first written submission (para. 79) that "...the EC advances no reason why a rise in imports relative to consumption should be given greater weight than the absolute rise in imports and their rise relative to production"?"

Q6. "In connection with question 5 above, please comment on the relevance of the fact that Article 2.1 SA refers to the increase in imports relative to domestic production only. (We note that the Anti-Dumping Agreement (article 3.2) and the SCM Agreement (article 15.2) refer to the amount of imports relative both to production and consumption)."

Joint Reply

Under the Safeguards Agreement, in order to be able to take a safeguard measure, it is required that the domestic authorities demonstrate that imports increased in absolute or relative terms (Art. XIX and Art. 2.1of the SA). However, this is *not* sufficient to justify the imposition of a safeguard measure.

Safeguard measures can only be taken if increased imports cause serious injury to a domestic industry, i.e. a "significant overall impairment" in its position. The relevant requirements for such a "serious injury" determination are contained in Article 4.2 (a) of the SA.

Article 4.2 SA explicitly requires an evaluation of the increase in imports "in absolute *and relative terms*" as well as "the share of the domestic market taken by increased imports" (in terms of consumption).

The same injury factors are referred to in Article 3.2 of the Anti-Dumping Agreement and Article 15.2 of the SCM Agreement ("a significant increase in dumped [subsidised] imports, either in absolute terms or relative to production or consumption (...)"). This shows that these three injury factors are identical in the three provisions of the various agreements.

Therefore, in order to establish whether a "significant overall impairment" has occurred, it is not sufficient to demonstrate that imports have increased only in absolute terms or relative to domestic production. The investigative authority has also to examine the share of the domestic market taken by increased imports.

In this case, the EC in paragraph 60 of its 1st written submission has demonstrated that the ITC's examination was deficient because it did not consider that domestic consumption increased strongly during the PoI. Had the ITC done so, it would have found that the share of the domestic market taken by increased imports was not indicative of serious injury.

Consequently, what the EC argued was not that increase in terms of consumption must be given greater weight than other injury factors but that it has to be appropriately considered in the injury determination, which the ITC did not.

Question No. 8 (EC and US)

"Could Article XXIV of the GATT 1994 provide an "exception" or "derogation" to provisions of the Safeguards Agreement? Please give the legal basis for your response."

Reply

The EC would like to recall that it is in the context of the issue of whether Article XXIV of the GATT 1994 could justify that Argentina exclude the Members of the MERCOSUR customs union from its safeguard measure on footwear, that the issue of the correct implementation of the principle of parallelism was examined by the AB.

In that framework, the AB stated the following (paragraph 109)

> "we also are not persuaded that an analysis of Article XXIV of the GATT 1994 was relevant to the specific issue that was before the Panel. This issue, as the Panel itself observed, is whether Argentina, after including imports from all sources in its investigation of "increased imports" of footwear products into its territory and the consequent effects of such imports on its domestic footwear industry, was justified in excluding other MERCOSUR member States from the application of the safeguard measures."

The situation in the present panel procedure is identical to that examined by the AB, with the sole exception that NAFTA is not a customs union but a free-trade area, which is not covered in Article 2.1 and footnote 1 of the SA.

In fact, the US has conducted an examination of injury and causation under Article 4.2 "including imports from all sources in its investigation of "increased imports" of [wheat gluten] into its territory and the consequent effects of such imports on its domestic [wheat gluten] industry" but then, using as a pretext a second injury examination discriminating the imported products by their origin, it has excluded Canada "from the application of the safeguard measures".

The AB had also indicated that

> "According to Articles 2.1 and 4.1(c), therefore, all of the relevant aspects of a safeguard investigation must be conducted by the Member that ultimately applies the safeguard measure, on the basis of increased imports entering its territory and causing or threatening to cause serious injury to the domestic industry within its territory."

The statement of the AB can not be reconciled with any discrimination between increased imports covered by the investigation made on the basis of the origin of the products. However, the US has recognised that it did just that in its investigation procedure.

The AB concluded in its report that

> "On the basis of this reasoning, and on the facts of this case, we find that Argentina's investigation, which evaluated whether serious injury or the threat thereof was caused by imports from *all* sources, could only lead to the imposition of safeguard measures on imports from *all* sources."

The EC submits that this Panel has no reason to take a different decision in the present case that is identical, in its substance, to the case that was examined by the AB. Like in the "*Argentina – Footwear*" case, Article XXIV of the GATT provides no coverage for the WTO-inconsistent action of a WTO Member, like the US, aimed at breaching the principle of parallelism.

Questions No. 9 (US) and 15 (US)

Q9. "How do you react to the argument made by the European Communities concerning "discrimination" at paras. 115-137 of its oral statement at the second substantive Panel meeting, particularly with respect to GATT Article I?"

Q15. "We note that Section 311(a) of the NAFTA Implementation Act provides for certain actions to be taken after the Commission makes an affirmative determination in an investigation under Section 202 of the Trade Act. Please clarify what elements comprise an "affirmative determination" under section 202 of the US Trade Act. Is it a determination that the domestic industry is "seriously injured"? Or is it a determination that the domestic industry is "seriously injured" and that this "serious injury" is caused by imports? Please cite the relevant portions of your legislation."

Joint comments by the EC

The principle of parallelism is clear and simple:

- either imports from a certain origin are integrated from the start in the safeguard investigation on whether increased imports have caused serious injury, in which case the measure taken must apply to all imports, or
- imports from a certain origin are excluded *from the start* from such investigation, in which case the principle of parallelism would allow exclusion of those imports from the measure.

The US is however prevented by its own legislation of following the principle set by the Appellate Body, and has therefore failed to do so in this case.

Indeed, section 202(b)(1)(A) of the US Trade Act of 1974 requires that the ITC shall determine "(...) whether an article is being imported into the United States in such increased quantities as to be a substantial cause of serious injury, or the threat thereof (...)," without making any reference to the origin of the product. (See also the similar language in Section 201 (a) of that Act). It is clear from the ITC report that the affirmative determination made by the ITC under Sec. 202 consisted of finding that serious injury occurred due to the effect of all imports of wheat gluten taken together (i.e. not excluding imports from Canada). The ITC explicitly states this on several occasions[1] Since Canadian exports are excluded from the safeguard measure pursuant to section 311(a) of the NAFTA Implementation Act, this is a clear breach of the principle of parallelism, and violates in particular Art. 4.2 SA and Art. I of GATT 1994.

---

[1] See e.g. p. I-18: "We find no basis in the statute for the disaggregated analysis that Shoalhaven avocates." "That Article [5.2 of the Safeguards Agreement] does not provide authority for examining only certain imports in determining whether increased imports are a substantial cause of serious injury or the threat of serious injury to the domestic industry." See also page I-10: "Because Section 202 is a global safeguard law, the Commission considers imports from all sources in determining whether imports have increased." (Emphasis supplied).

Question No. 10 (EC and US)

Q10. "Is the causation analysis under Article 4.2 SA to be conducted in terms of imports as a "necessary" or "sufficient" condition (or both) for serious injury?"

Reply

An increase in imports is a "necessary" condition for taking safeguard measures. However, the mere coincidence in time between increased imports and "serious injury" is not "sufficient" for to prove causation because, *inter alia*, Art. 3 SA requires an explanation i.e. "findings and conclusions" on the existence of a causal link[2] Pursuant to Article 4.2 of the SA, the investigation must "demonstrate, on the basis of objective evidence, the existence of "the causal link" (not: "a" causal link) between increased imports and serious injury. Injury caused by other factors must not be attributed to increased imports.[3]

This means that increased imports *in isolation*, i.e. taken alone, must be demonstrated to cause "serious injury". They must be "sufficient" by themselves to cause "serious injury". It is not enough under the Safeguards Agreement that increased imports are a "necessary" element among a number of factors which together cause "serious injury". Another interpretation would deprive the words "*the* causal link" (emphasis supplied) in Art. 4.2(b) SA, as well as the entire second sentence of that provision, of any meaning.

The application in this case by the US of the test contained in section 202(b)(1)(B) of the US Trade Act of 1974 violates Art. 4.2(b) of the SA. The ITC has failed to investigate whether the increased imports *alone* caused injury which can be qualified as "serious".

Question No. 13 (EC)

"How do you react to the statement by the United States at para. 53 of its oral statement at the second substantive Panel meeting that "there is no provi-

---

[2] See Panel Report, *Argentina – Safeguard Measures on Imports of Footwear* ("*Argentina – Footwear*"), WT/DS121/R, DSR 2000:II, 575, para. 8.238.

[3] The EC refers in this respect to the report of the Panel on Canada-Countervailing Duties on Grain Corn from the US. Adopted by the Committee on Subsidies and Countervailing Measures on March 26, 1992, BISD 39S/411. (The EC is aware that the AB has stressed that the reasoning of Panels under pre-WTO Agreements cannot always be applied to WTO rules (Argentina-Footwear at para. 117). However, since the test under Art. 6 para. 4 second sentence of the Tokyo Round Subsidies Agreement is very similar to the one under Art. 4.2(b) of the Safeguards Agreement, the citation is relevant). "(…)[T]he Panel noted that the CIT acknowledged the existence of factors other than subsidized imports having an effect on the price of Canadian grain corn, but made no effort to ensure that the injuries caused by other factors were not attributed to the subsidized imports." Similarly, in the US-wheat gluten case, the US failed to ensure that the effect on prices of in particular intra-industry competition due to overcapacity and of the availability of low-priced high-protein wheat was not attributed to increased imports.

sion in Article 12 that requires or suggests that a Member is obliged to notify its proposed measure under Article 12.1(c)"?"

Reply

The EC recalls that it has argued in its joint answer to the Panel's questions No. 11, 12 and 22 raised during the first substantive meeting, that one of the reasons why the US notification under Art. 12.1 (b) cannot be considered a notification of "proposed measures", was that its heading (and therefore its legal basis) was "Article 12.1 (b) notification upon making a finding of serious injury or threat thereof caused by increased imports".

First of all, the EC's claim that a notification of "proposed measures" must not be made under Article 12.1 (c) is based on the relation between the wording of Articles 12.1 (b) and 12.1 (c). While the former provision is concerned with "finding of serious injury (...)", only the latter Article 12.1 (c) requires a notification "upon a decision to apply or extend a measure".

Second, since both Articles 12.2 and 12.3 refer to notifications under Articles 12.1 (b) and 12.1 (c) as being made by a "Member proposing to apply or extend a safeguard measure", the notification under 12.1 (c) can only be a notification of a "proposed measure", not the notification of a measure which is already being applied, as the US argues.

Third, reference is made to the format for notifications adopted by the Committee on Safeguards (G/SG/W/1, 23 February 1995). The headings contained in the format for "Notifications under Article 12.1 (b) and (c)" pertain only to three distinct categories of information:

1. Evidence of serious injury and increase in imports, and description of the product concerned.
2. Information concerning the *proposed* measures only: description, date of introduction and expected duration and timetable of liberalisation and date of mid-term review.
3. Information on measures to be extended.

This list of categories of information to be notified clearly shows that information pertaining to the "proposed measure" must be made available in a notification under Article 12.1 (c).

If information on the "proposed measures" were notified under Article 12.1 (b), there would be no information left to be notified under Article 12.1 (c) (with the exception of extension of measures) rendering this provision meaningless.

In conclusion, the EC maintains its argument that the US notification under Article 12.1 (b) was not a prior notification of the "proposed measures" both with regard to the format as well as to the substance of the notification.

For the rest, the EC refers the Panel to the EC's answer to the Panel's question No. 22.

Question No. 14 (EC)

"Please comment on the statement by the United States at para. 57 of its oral statement at the second substantive Panel meeting that "...the EC's view makes it very unlikely that a government would ever modify its measure because under the EC's reading a Member would have to re-notify the new proposal and start the consultation process again. That is because if the Member decided to change its proposed measure, the new measure would then be its proposed measure. This could lead to an endless round of consultations and notifications...". "

Reply

According to the second preambular sentence of the SA, the WTO Members recognise the need to

> "re-establish multilateral control over safeguards and eliminate measures that escape such control"

One of the key provisions, which are designed to achieve such an objective, is Article 12 of the SA. By imposing an obligation of notification of each successive step of the procedure leading to the adoption of a safeguard measure, it provides the opportunity to all Members in the relevant WTO Committees to scrutinise the action of the Member wishing to adopt the safeguard measure. It also provides the opportunity to hold "prior" consultations. Last but not least, it provides in Article 12.3 the possibility of

> "(...) reviewing the information provided under paragraph 2, exchanging views on the measure and reaching an understanding on ways to achieve the objective set out in paragraph 1 of Article 8".

In summary, the overall objective of Article 12 is to ensure transparency through formal and timely notification before any definitive decision is taken and to constitute the legal and factual framework within which the maintenance of "a substantially equivalent level of concessions or other obligations to that existing under GATT 1994 between ["the member proposing to apply a safeguard measure"] and the exporting Members" will be achieved.

In this legal framework, the EC is of the view that the US arguments quoted by the Panel are at best irrelevant.

A measure which is modified in its substance *after* the notifications, consultations and negotiations referred above have taken place is no longer the measure on which the WTO Members were given an opportunity to scrutinise, comment and consult. If any modification were allowed without resubmitting the proposed measure to the transparency procedures under Article 12, the door would be open to any possible abuse and arbitrariness. In fact, Article 12 would consequently become a nullity or inutility in substance and its content would be reduced to an empty shell of meaningless formalities.

The EC urges the Panel to reject this interpretation which is implied in the US suggested approach to this issue.

ATTACHMENT 1-9

LETTER FROM THE EUROPEAN COMMUNITY CONCERNING THE UNITED STATES RESPONSE TO THE PANEL'S REQUEST FOR INFORMATION
(11 February 2000)

The EC has examined the US response to the Panel of 8 February 2000. It reacts to the Panel's request to submit documents and data that the US withheld from the published version of its investigation report on the excuse that they were business confidential in nature.

We have attached to this communication the EC's interpretation of the existing legal requirements under the Agreement on Safeguards, based *inter alia* on earlier adopted panel or Appellate Body reports on this matter. As the attached document shows, the course of action suggested by the United States in this procedure finds no justification under any covered agreement. Rather, it constitutes a breach of the procedural and substantive obligations of the US under the relevant WTO rules that should in no way be warranted by this Panel.

The EC wishes to draw the attention of the Panel to the fact that, by its 8 February communication, the US suggests in substance that the documents and data requested by the Panel be submitted only to the Panel "*in camera*", thus by excluding the complainant, i.e. the EC, from the access to that information.

The course of action suggested by the United States is fundamentally at odds with the adversarial nature of the dispute settlement procedures. In addition, it would irreparably damage the fairness of this dispute settlement procedure, since the Panellists and the officials of the WTO Secretariat assisting the Panel would have access to *ex parte* communications, in flagrant breach of Article 18.1 of the DSU and of the Rules of Conduct on the appointment of Panellists. Should the Panel accept the US suggested course of action, the EC's fundamental rights in these proceedings would be inevitably prejudiced.

It is worth noting that the US position expressed in its 8 February communication contradicts a US' statement on the same issue before the Appellate Body in the "*Canada-Aircraft*" procedure (139): "(...) the US argues that the application of procedures for protecting business confidential information promotes important objectives because Members' rights and obligations under the covered agreements can only be preserved if due process is accorded to both the complaining party and the responding party".

The EC submits that the United States cannot rely on any WTO-consistent basis for its refusal to disclose documents and data requested by the Panel to the EC. Its statement that the EC may disclose such documents and data "in the private sector" is entirely gratuitous. It is based on a biased assumption according to which the EC will act in bad faith by violating binding obligations such as Article

18 of the DSU and the specific rules on private confidential information that this Panel has adopted.

While assumptions of this nature do not deserve any comment beyond the legal examination of the relevant WTO provisions that are referred to in the attachment to this communication, they nevertheless raise the issue as to whether the US is "engage[d] in these procedures in good faith in an effort to resolve the dispute", as Article 3.10 of the DSU explicitly requires.

In this respect, the EC would like to underline that the second substantive meeting with the Panel has already taken place 10 days ago and that the US should not be allowed to use delaying tactics in order to postpone the withdrawal of its WTO-inconsistent safeguard measure on wheat gluten. It is barely necessary to recall here that the EC industry is suffering severely from the unjustified, protectionist and discriminatory US safeguard measure, which is still in place.

For the reasons that are set out in detail in the attachment, the EC requests that the Panel rules that the US has refused to provide access to the documents and data requested by the Panel on 1 February 2000 in accordance with the procedures governing private confidential information adopted by the Panel on the same date. The EC requests that the Panel infer from such refusal that the non-disclosed data and documents provide confirmation that the US safeguard measure on wheat gluten violates, *inter alia*, Articles XIX of the GATT 1994 and Articles 2.1 and 4 of the SA.

I am providing a copy of this letter and of its attachment to the mission of the United States.

ATTACHMENT 1-10

COMMENTS OF THE EUROPEAN COMMUNITY ON THE UNITED STATES RESPONSE TO THE PANEL'S REQUEST FOR INFORMATION

(11 February 2000)

Article 3.2 of the Agreement on Safeguard offers no excuse to the US to refuse to the European Communities access to allegedly confidential documents in the context of this dispute settlement procedure

Article 3 of the SA is entitled "Investigation". It deals with the rules that must be applied by the investigating authorities during the investigation procedures.

Article 3.2 SA deals in particular with rules concerning the treatment of confidential information during such investigations. As such, they are binding and applicable by the investigating authorities in that context. This is also true for Article 3.2, second sentence, SA.

However, nothing in Article 3.2 SA, including its second sentence, precludes the US from disclosing allegedly confidential information in an entirely separate procedural framework, i.e. in a dispute settlement procedure governed by the rules of the DSU.

As the Panel is aware, the DSU[1] provides explicitly for rules on good faith and confidentiality. It is these rules that apply to the present dispute settlement proceedings, not Article 3.2 SA. This Panel has, moreover, appropriately adapted the rules on confidentiality under the DSU to the specificities of the confidential treatment of private information in this case by adopting its 1 February 2000 rules. The EC stresses that both the provisions of the DSU itself and the PCI procedure adopted by the Panel provide all necessary guarantees for confidential treatment of the information which is now refused by the US. The Appellate Body stressed this in various paragraphs of its reports on "*Brazil-Aircraft*"[2] and "*Canada-Aircraft*".

In addition, it is stating the obvious to recall that any breach of a Members' obligations under or pursuant to the DSU on the confidential treatment of information disclosed during a dispute settlement procedure can itself be subject to WTO dispute settlement and all that entails.

As far as the complainant in this case is concerned, the EC, Article 287 of the Treaty establishing the European Community imposes strict obligations of confidentiality upon officials and agents, that also extend to the time after they

---

[1] Articles 13, 14, 17 para. 6, 18 and Appendix 3 para. 3 of the DSU.

[2] Para. 119-125.

give up their functions within the EC Institutions. This fundamental provision is compounded by the rules on confidentiality contained in the EC Staff Regulations and the related disciplinary powers, which are applicable in case of violation of such rules. As the Panel will no doubt recall, the EC has indicated as "approved persons" exclusively those EC *officials* who are responsible for the present dispute settlement procedure and their superiors, also EC *officials*.

Moreover, nothing in Article 3.2 SA permits the US to hide behind the US industry's refusal to disclose *exclusively* to the EC the allegedly confidential documents or data requested by the Panel. Article 3.2, second sentence, SA provides that the party submitting the allegedly confidential data or documents can refuse their disclosure in the framework of the investigation procedure. Such refusal is however unqualified: either the documents are disclosed to all participants to the investigation procedure or they are not. No good faith interpretation of Article 3.2 can allow a Member, *in casu* the US, to disclose data and documents to the Panel but not to the other WTO Member, that is the other party to the dispute settlement procedure, even if *both* the Panel and the Members are *all* subject to the *same* rules on treatment of private confidential information within the *same* dispute settlement procedure.

Finally, contrary to the assertions of the US, the way a WTO Member's domestic legislation is drafted or its internal proceedings are organised cannot diminish that Member's obligations under the DSU to provide the necessary PCI when requested by the Panel. Article XVI.4 of the Marrakech Agreement is explicit in this respect.

Pursuant to Article 13.1 of the DSU, the US is under the obligation to "respond promptly and fully to any request by a panel for such information as the panel considers necessary and appropriate".

A refusal to abide by this unequivocal obligation must lead the Panel to make the adverse inferences that logically must follow from such refusal.

In any case, the violation by the US safeguard measure on wheat gluten of Article 4 SA cannot be retrospectively "healed" by providing PCI during the present dispute settlement procedure

The EC would like to recall once more that the US safeguard measure on wheat gluten violates Article 4.2 SA because the published version of the ITC report did not contain many of the essential facts, on which the findings of the US authorities were allegedly based, not even in aggregate, summary or otherwise non-confidential form (e.g. indexed data). The WTO Members, including the EC, had thus no possibility to understand and consider the determinations made and the actions taken by the US. Timely transparency was unlawfully denied.

Furthermore, the findings were not adequately reasoned. In particular, either no reasons or manifestly inadequate reasons were given as to why certain factors did not detract from the findings that "serious injury" occurred and that it was caused by increased imports (taken alone).

The EC could not agree more with the US when it states in its 8 February document at paragraph 28 that "If the USITC's public report does not satisfy the requirements of Article 4,", which the EC submits is clearly the case, "the Panel should hold the United States to have violated the Agreement".

For these reasons, the EC considers that the Panel should already find a violation of the aforementioned Articles due to the deficiencies shortly referred to above, which were extensively dealt with in the EC submissions.

In particular, the EC has – in its letter of 26 January commenting on the proposed PCI procedures – repeated that a violation of (in particular) Article 4 of the SA by failing to provide the relevant information in the public report *at the time of its publication* cannot be healed by providing that information during Panel proceedings.

ATTACHMENT 1-11

FINAL COMMENTS OF THE EUROPEAN COMMUNITY ON THE UNITED STATES LETTER TO THE PANEL OF 22 FEBRUARY 2000

(23 February 2000)

The EC has examined the US letter to the Panel sent on 22 February 2000, i.e. eleven days after the receipt of the EC's reaction to the US 8 February letter. The EC submits that the US additional argument contained in this letter fails to address the compelling legal issues raised by the EC in its 11 February letter and attachment, in particular with regard to the fundamental right of any WTO Member to a dispute settlement procedure adversarial in nature, where fairness, due process and equality of arms are the cornerstones of the Panels' action.

As was indicated in a different context in the EC's second written submission on 17 January 2000, paragraph 71,

> "It would also like to stress that under WTO rules, the US government is *one* entity. It would be absurd if the US were allowed to defend itself by saying that the *US* ITC did not possess the relevant data, although the *US* Department of Agriculture did."

The 22 February 2000 letter is a further attempt to create artificial distinction between the *US* Government and *US* authorities, which has no basis under WTO law. The US is the other party to this dispute. The Panel's request to submit documents is addressed to the US, no matter which internal *US* body or authority materially holds them.

Almost four weeks have already passed after the end of the second substantive meeting with the Panel. The EC respectfully insists that this debate be put swiftly to an end and that the Panel infer from the US persistent refusal to submit the requested data and documents that it provides confirmation that the US safeguard measure on wheat gluten violates, *inter alia*, Articles XIX of the GATT 1994 and Articles 2.1 and 4 of the SA.

I am providing a copy of this letter to the mission of the United States.

ATTACHMENT 1-12

COMMUNICATION OF THE EUROPEAN COMMUNITY CONCERNING NEWLY PROPOSED PROCEDURES GOVERNING PRIVATE CONFIDENTIAL INFORMATION

(28 February 2000)

We acknowledge receipt of your communication of 24 February 2000.

On 1 February 2000, the parties to this dispute received a communication from the Panel setting out the "Procedures Governing Private Confidential Information" which it had adopted. As the communication states, the Procedures "supplement the working procedures already adopted by the Panel" and were adopted after "having given the parties the opportunity to comment on its "Proposed Procedures Governing Business Confidential Information and having considered the communications received from the European Communities and the United States in this regard (...)". In that communication, the Panel has also indicated to both Parties that "the Panel believes that the procedures in effect in this case are adequate to protect the confidentiality of information submitted to it".

The EC continues to be ready to apply fully these procedures that have become binding upon the Parties and the Panel by virtue of the Panel's own decision of 1 February 2000.

Given this context, the EC fails to see any valid reasons which could justify consideration of the proposed procedure on the same subject matter communicated by the Panel on 24 February 2000. The refusal of the United States to accept the ruling of the Panel (after it had already been handed down to the parties to the dispute) and the refusal to submit the requested information can certainly not be a sufficient reason to re-open the issue at this stage. As the Appellate Body has stated in its report of 24 February 2000 in *"United States – Tax Treatment for 'Foreign Sales Corporations'"*, doc. WT/DS108/AB/R, paragraph 166, "the [...] principle of good faith requires that responding Members seasonably and promptly bring claimed procedural deficiencies to the attention of [...] the Panel, so that corrections, if needed, can be made to resolve disputes".

Since the Panel has already ruled on the matter, the persistence of "no convergence of views" on that ruling is no longer relevant. The EC stresses that it is the US which refuses to provide the information requested by the Panel in spite of the fact that appropriate procedures to protect their confidentiality were duly adopted by the Panel.

The EC considers, moreover, that the speculations by the US, contained in its letter of 8 February 2000 and the attachment therewith, according to which "the Panel procedures provide that the Panel will make this confidential business information available to (...) others in the EC or in the private sector who may be designated in the future by the EC as its 'representatives'" or according to which "the Panel, pertinent WTO employees, twenty-two EC officials and unspecified other persons possibly to be designated by the EC in the future *might* keep the information confidential (...)" are unfounded and cannot constitute a valid reason for putting into question the procedure established by the Panel.

In any case, a procedure like the one now proposed which has the effect of seriously unbalancing the position of the Parties involved in a dispute settlement procedure are in conflict with the fundamental requirements of procedural fairness and the equality of arms of the parties to the dispute. A procedure, such as the proposed procedure contained in the 24 February communication by the Panel, whose effects would be to put one of the parties to the dispute settlement procedure in the impossibility of having adequate time and fully using its expertise in order to analyse documents submitted by the other Party, which had of course prior unlimited access to them, is by definition in breach of such fundamental principles.

Furthermore, the EC submits that a PCI procedure, which is meant to manage parts of a dispute settlement procedure, cannot go as far as imposing an obligation upon a WTO Member to take actions which would conflict with its domestic constitutional or institutional rules. *In casu*, EC officials are under a statutory obligation to inform their superiors and cannot therefore undertake to refrain from that. The EC would note in passing that the Appellate Body stressed that the existing provisions in the DSU concerning the confidential treatment of documents or data guarantee already a correct and fair dispute settlement procedure.

ATTACHMENT 1-13

COMMUNICATION OF THE EUROPEAN COMMUNITY ON THE UNITED STATES COMMUNICATION CONCERNING NEWLY PROPOSED PROCEDURES GOVERNING PRIVATE CONFIDENTIAL INFORMATION

(29 February 2000)

The content of the US comments on a new PCI procedure proposed by the Panel on 24 February 2000 has just been brought to our attention.

The US advances in its letter the following new argument:

> "In particular, the United States wishes to know whether the European Communities is in a position to comply with the Panel's condition that "These individuals would be under an obligation not to disclose the information, or to allow it to be disclosed, to any person." In similar circumstances the EC has not been able to warrant that those EC representatives to whom confidential business information was disclosed would not disseminate such information to other EC officials (see WT/DS27/ARB, para. 2.5)."

The EC respectfully submits that the US comments are factually and legally incorrect.

Firstly, the present circumstances are not similar but unprecedented. Indeed, the EC has no knowledge of a WTO Member having opposed a working procedure of a Panel only *after* it was adopted and on grounds that had never been raised *before* those procedures had been adopted. However, the US is doing just that in this case.

Secondly, the reference to the WTO doc. WT/DS27/ARB, paragraph 2.5, does not support the latest affirmations by the US. As a matter of fact, the BCI procedure referred to in that document was based on *personal* commitments from agents and panellists rather than on undertakings from the *WTO Members*, the parties to the arbitration procedure. While that approach was not acceptable as a matter of principle, the EC has already accepted in this case the PCI procedures adopted by this Panel, which were communicated to the Parties on 1 February 2000, because they are based on a legally correct approach. Moreover, the Arbitration decision referred to in the US letter confirms the longstanding position of the EC before this Panel:

> "the European Communities raised further objections concerning practicality, the impossibility of limiting reporting obligations to superiors within the European Communities and concerns that the inviolability of the EC Mission in Geneva had been put into question."

The EC takes this opportunity to re-iterate that the EC institutional system is based on strict confidential treatment of data and information according to Article 287 of the Treaty Establishing the European Communities. Moreover, Article 21 of the Staff Regulations of Officials of the European Communities provides that "[a]n official, whatever his rank, shall assist and tender advice to his superiors". Finally, Article 17 of the Staff Regulations of Officials of the European Communities provides that "[a]n official shall exercise the greatest discretion with regard to all facts and information coming to his knowledge in the course of or in connection with the performance of his duties; he shall not in any manner whatsoever disclose to any unauthorized person any document or information not already made public. He shall continue to be bound by this obligation after leaving the service."

ATTACHMENT 1-14

ORAL STATEMENT OF THE EUROPEAN COMMUNITY AT THE ADDITIONAL MEETING OF THE PANEL WITH THE PARTIES

(18 May 2000)

1. INTRODUCTION

Dear Chairman, Members of the Panel,

1. The European Communities would like, as a first point, to welcome you, Mr. Chairman, in these proceedings and wish you good work. We are aware that it is not easy to join an on-going process, in particular when issues which involve the scrutiny of complex technical aspects are also under examination.

The EC repeats here that it is fully prepared to assist you and the other Members of the Panel, in any way it can, in the follow up of these proceedings. We have brought from Brussels a full-fledged delegation (that we have already introduced to you) in order to respond, immediately if possible, to any additional question you may have. Everybody's time is precious these days, and we thus want to make sure that the Panel has the most ample opportunity to hear from us, directly, any clarification it may still need at this stage.

2. This being said, the EC should also state as from the beginning of this meeting what is the EC's understanding of the stage in which this procedure presently is.

The communication by the Chairman of the DSB, Mr. Harbinson, that the former Chairman of the Panel had resigned was sent to the Parties to the dispute on the 11 April 2000 and was received by the EC the day after, 12 April 2000. According to the timetable circulated by the Panel at the beginning of the procedure, the interim report should have been circulated to the parties on 13 April 2000.

Earlier, the US and the EC had received on 1 March 2000 from the Panel a draft descriptive part on which the Parties were asked to make comments. Comments from Parties were made available to the Panel on 15 March 2000, i.e. according to the original schedule. The US took even the liberty of submitting an unsolicited response to the EC's comments on the descriptive part of the report, which was filed with the Panel on 17 March 2000.

The resignation of the former Chairman has interrupted the procedure. The appointment of a new Chairman of the Panel, as a consequence of the resignation of the former Chairman, cannot and does not entail, in law and in fact, that the procedures that were accomplished before the event could be considered in any way as null or irregular. We all must therefore resume the Panel procedure from where it was suspended, which means just *before* the release of the interim report and the interim review stage but *after* the point in time in which factual issues have been definitively established.

3. Let me say immediately, Mr. Chairman, that the EC is not interested in re-opening before you issues which are closed by now, in particular to come back on the doubtful attitudes that the US has put in place during the days that preceded Mr. Karsz's resignation. However, the EC is determined to have this procedure finalised within the new time table that the Panel has adopted on 2 May 2000: we thus explicitly ask you, Mr Chairman and Members of the Panel, not to allow the US to engage in delaying tactics.

4. Turning now to the substance of the case, the EC has taken note of the Panel's wish that we present a summary of the EC's case. We understand this request as suggesting to introduce, once more, the main claims contained in the EC's complaint that are part of the written record of this Panel. We are of course pleased to go along with your request. It is nevertheless evident that the EC will not repeat all the arguments it made during the proceedings up until now. It will just briefly summarise the main points it has made. For the rest, the EC confirms all the arguments it has made earlier on during these proceedings, including the ones that – for the sake of brevity – it will not explicitly refer back to again today.

2. STANDARD OF REVIEW

5. The EC reiterates that the US domestic procedural rules, or their interpretation, cannot limit the tasks of this Panel whose function is to assist the DSB by performing "an objective assessment of the matter before it". The mission of the Panel cannot consist of a mere "rubber-stamping" of an investigation report, as the US would have it.

Like any WTO Member in a similar situation, the EC has indicated to the Panel the information that the ITC should have properly considered but did not, and the importance of that information to the findings and conclusions made by the US authorities.

6. As was noted, this is entirely consistent with what the Appellate Body considered the correct way of proceeding in its "*Argentina - Footwear*" report, at paragraph 121, third sentence:

> *"Rather, the panel examined whether, as required by Article 4 of the Agreement on Safeguards, the Argentine authorities had considered all relevant facts and had adequately explained how the facts supported the determinations that were made".(emphasis added)*

Finally, as a matter of fact, the objective evidence, which the US authorities have omitted or misinterpreted or downplayed in their investigation and that the EC has submitted to your attention, was prepared by the US authorities themselves before or during the investigation procedure and was in the public domain.

7. The EC refers the Panel back to, in particular, paragraph 3 of its first written submission, paragraphs 5-20 of its oral statement, its answer to question 3 of

the Panel (17 January 2000); paragraphs 3-7 of the EC's second written submission and paragraphs 8-19 of its second oral statement.

3. THE US HAS BREACHED ARTICLE XIX OF THE GATT 1994 ("UNFORESEEN DEVELOPMENTS")

8. According to the Appellate Body report on Korea - Dairy at paragraph 77,

" (...) any safeguard measure imposed after the entry into force of the WTO Agreement must comply with the provisions of both the Agreement on Safeguards and Article XIX of the GATT 1994."

The Appellate Body has also stated that

(...) [I]t seems to us that the ordinary meaning of the phrase "as a result of unforeseen developments" requires that the developments which led to a product being imported in such increased quantities and under such conditions as to cause or threaten to cause serious injury to domestic producers must have been "unexpected" (paragraph 84). (...) "

"Although we do not view the first clause in Article XIX:1(a) as establishing independent conditions for the application of a safeguard measure, additional to the conditions set forth in the second clause of that paragraph, we do believe that the first clause describes certain circumstances which must be demonstrated as a matter of fact in order for a safeguard measure to be applied consistently with the provisions of Article XIX of the GATT 1994" (paragraph 85).

9. The arguments that were exchanged during the earlier part of the panel procedure have shown beyond any possible doubt that nowhere in the ITC report has the US analysed and demonstrated as a matter of fact which facts constituted "unforeseen developments" which led to wheat gluten being imported in such increased quantities ... as to cause serious injury to US domestic wheat gluten producers.

In fact, even the belated attempt in the US second written submission to find an *ex post facto* reconstruction of the ITC report in order to include the "unforeseen developments" element has completely failed. The EC has brought evidence that not only no unforeseen development led to the increase in imports. Rather, all the events had been foreseen by the US authorities and by the US domestic industry itself.

10. We refer in any case the Panel to, in particular, the EC's second oral statement, paragraphs 16 to 32, that was read on 1 February 2000, and to the joint replies 2 and 3 to additional questions from the Panel of 4 February 2000.

4. CONFIDENTIALITY

11. The plain wording of Art. 4.2 (c) of the SA, which refers to Art. 3 of the SA, requires the prompt publication of a report analysing the case, demonstrating the relevance of the factors examined, and containing reasoned conclusions on " *all pertinent issues* " of fact and law.

12. The EC has explained in detail in its various submissions that the ITC report with all its " *** " and with the refusal to provide even data in summary form, i.e. aggregate data or other methods, does not pass that test. The EC has also explained that there are well-known ways by which the ITC could have disclosed the relevant factual elements of confidential information whilst preserving confidentiality. For instance, this could have been done by providing aggregate data or by giving percentages describing developments in a company's performance.

13. The EC would like to stress, as it has done before, that the report required under Art. 4 of the SA has to be published " promptly ". The fact that the US violated that Article by not publishing, before it took the wheat gluten safeguard measure, a report which meets the standards of the SA, can therefore not be "cured " years after the fact. The US finally came forward with certain, very limited, information as an Annex to one of its submissions in this case, information which up until that time it had always kept secret, making it impossible for any WTO Member to review it. This only proves that a violation of Art. 4 of the SA has occurred, since by providing the information the US shows that it could – and therefore should - have made that information public from the very beginning.

14. Regarding this point, the EC refers the Panel back, in particular, to its first written submission, paragraph 49, its first oral statement paragraphs 27-33, its answer to questions 2, 4, 14, 15 and 16 of the Panel (17 January 2000), and to paragraphs 33-36 of its 2nd oral statement.

5. THE ITC DID NOT SHOW THAT "SERIOUS INJURY" OCCURRED

15. The EC has explained at length during the Panel proceedings that the ITC report does not show that the US wheat starch/wheat gluten industry was suffering serious injury at the end of the PoI. In fact many factors indicated that its situation was actually improving during that period. For instance, capacity utilisation,[1] production,[2] and sales out of inventories[3] were going up at the end of the PoI. Also, the market share of imports in 1997 was hardly increasing in comparison with 1996 so that there was no major import surge at the end of the PoI justi-

1 Para. 63 of the EC's first written submission.
2 Para. 62 of the EC's first written submission.
3 Para. 71 of the EC's first written submission.

fying a safeguard measure.[4] (Always note that an "ITC-year" runs from 1 July to 30 June, e.g. "1997" runs from 1 July 1996 to 30 June 1997). With regard to profitability of the US industry, the EC has explained that the complete failure of the ITC to explain the way that industry allocated costs between its various co-products makes this factor wholly unverifiable.

16. On this point of serious injury, the EC refers back, in particular, to its first written submission, pages 19-29, its first oral statement paragraphs. 43-56, its 2nd written submission paragraphs 15-21 and to paragraphs 37-42 of its 2nd oral statement.

6. THE ITC'S FAILURE TO CORRECTLY ADDRESS THE CAUSATION ISSUE

17. The ITC did not fulfil its duty under art. 4.2 of the SA to correctly investigate, in good faith, all pertinent matters. As required under Art. 4.2 of the SA this must be done of the ITC's own initiative. There is even less excuse for the fact that the ITC failed to investigate them since many points have been specifically raised before the ITC, as the EC has shown.[5]

18. The EC has explained at length in its earlier submissions why the US authorities have not addressed the causation issue correctly in various respects. The EC would only like to remind the Panel of some essential points.

19. US wheat prices rose very strongly at the end of the PoI, thus impacting negatively on the US industry's situation. The ITC just assumed, based on oral statements of the two companies requesting the safeguard measure, that this input cost increase could have been passed on by the US industry without limits to its buyers, had it not been for the influence of imports. Even though it acknowledged in its report that the protein content of wheat crops – which varies from harvest to harvest and year to year – determines the demand for wheat gluten and thus its price, the ITC did not investigate at all whether it was not in fact high protein content of wheat crops which was keeping wheat gluten prices low. In this respect, the EC has shown that the price of wheat gluten in the US moved independently from movements in the level of imports. The EC has provided clear evidence that the US wheat gluten price simply followed the developments in the protein content of wheat rather than being determined by the level of imports.[6] The EC has also shown that the protein content of wheat was good in the last years of the PoI, keeping wheat gluten prices low.

20. Moreover, the EC has shown that the US industry has put itself into trouble by creating tremendous overcapacity. Capacity utilisation in 1997 would have been at 74.8 per cent in 1997 if the US industry had not irrationally added enor-

[4] Para. 70 of the EC's first written submission, see also para. 38 of the EC's 2nd oral statement.

[5] See in particular Exhibits EC-16 to 18 to its second written submission.

[6] See Exhibit EC-10 to the EC's first written submission, Figure 4.

mous overcapacity during the PoI.[7] The US authorities however included these self-created difficulties of the US industry in determining whether that industry was suffering serious injury. This means that that they attributed injury caused by other factors to increased imports. They thus violated Art. 4.2(b) of the SA.

21. Finally, the EC has shown that the situation in other co-products of wheat gluten such as wheat starch (which forms a basis for alcohol and ethanol), deteriorated during the PoI.

22. Regarding wheat starch, it is important to note that since wheat starch is a necessary co-product of the wheat gluten production process, the irrational increase by US producers of their capacity also led to increased wheat *starch* capacity. This worsened, for the US wheat starch/wheat gluten producers, the competitive conditions for US wheat starch. The situation deteriorated even more because the cost of production of wheat starch increased during the PoI: for wheat *starch* input cost – the price of wheat (flour) - increased. Moreover, the fact that the US industry has heavily invested to increase its production capacity has had a negative impact on production costs and profits. Like what happened for wheat gluten, these increased costs could not be passed on into wheat starch prices because of the very disadvantageous competitive position in comparison with corn starch. (The price of the raw material – corn – is significantly lower in the US, and the technical yield is much higher).[8]

23. Regarding the wheat starch which can be made into ethanol and food-grade alcohol, the EC has provided evidence that at the end of the PoI there was a weakness in that market.[9]

24. Although Art. 4 of the SA imposes on each WTO Member not to attribute to increased imports difficulties caused by such *other* factors (we recap them once more: strongly increased input prices, self-created overcapacity and difficulties in the co-product markets), the US has failed to do so.

25. Finally, regarding causation, in the *"Argentina-Footwear "* report, the AB agreed with the Panel that in an analysis of causation "it is *the relationship* between the *movements* in imports (volume and market share) and the *movements* in injury factors that must be central to a causation analysis and determination. " The ITC determination is contrary to these principles. For instance, wheat gluten prices developed independently from imports, and in particular went up in 1996 from the last quarter 1995 level even though imports were also increasing. Another example is that inventories were going down – i.e. were being sold in both 1996 and 1997, the years in which imports increased.

26. On the point of absence of a causal link, the EC refers back, in particular, to its first written submission, pages 29-40, its first oral statement paragraphs 57-

---

[7] See graph on p. 24 of EC's first written submission.

[8] See paras. 86-92 of the EC's first written submission.

[9] See paras. 93-95 of the EC's first written submission, Exhibit EC-14, and paras. 78-79 of the EC's second written submission.

86, its answer to questions 6, 7, 8 and 9 of the Panel (17 January 2000), its 2nd written submission paragraphs. 22-83, its 2nd oral statement paragraphs 43-79,and to its reply to question 10 of the Panel after the 2nd substantive meeting.

7. THE US SAFEGUARD MEASURE ON WHEAT GLUTEN IS A PROTECTIONIST MEASURE IN DISGUISE

27. The EC has explained that the US safeguard measure on wheat gluten is in fact *a protectionist measure* in disguise, that is a measure that goes far beyond the exceptional remedies which a WTO member is allowed to adopt in case of proved serious injury caused by increased imports.

28. The US has gone back from the concessions bound in its GATT Schedule beyond what it could possibly be allowed to under the SA and without any justification for doing so. The EC has brought to the Panel's attention in the earlier stages of this dispute settlement procedure numerous elements supporting its claim. They can be summarised as follows:

1. The US has breached the proportionality principle under Articles 4.2 of the SA.

The facts and evidence provided by the EC have shown that the US authorities did not comply with the proportionality principle. The effect of this WTO-inconsistent action is that the US authorities have attributed with no justification to increased imports the cause of an alleged serious injury of US domestic wheat gluten/wheat starch industry.

In fact, the US authorities, when examining the alleged "significant overall impairment in the position of the domestic industry", have completely disregarded the effects that the other co-causes were producing. An objective examination of "all factors having an objective and quantifiable bearing on the situation of" the wheat gluten/wheat starch industry would inevitably have led to the conclusion that none of the causes was sufficient, *taken in isolation*, to create such serious injury.

The "preponderance test" applied by the US pursuant to its internal legislation is inconsistent with the principle of proportionality set out in Article 4.2 of the SA.

Its application to the wheat gluten safeguard procedure has produced the effect of prompting the implementation of a safeguard measure in a situation where the US was not in a position to demonstrate objectively that the alleged "significant overall impairment in the position of the domestic" wheat gluten/wheat starch industry could have been caused by "increased imports" taken in isolation, i.e. after having deducted the effects of the other co-causes.

The EC refers the Panel back to, in particular, chapter 4.6.3 of its first written submission, paragraphs 105 and following of its first oral statement, chapter 5 of its second written submission, answers to questions 8 and 9 from the

Panel (17 January 2000), answer to question 10 from the Panel (4 February 2000).

2. *The US has breached the proportionality principle under Article 5.1, first and third sentence, of the SA*

Article 5.1 of the SA is the second textual application of the principle of proportionality and provides that a Member shall apply safeguard measures "only to the extent necessary to prevent or remedy serious injury and to facilitate adjustment".

Even if one were to assume *arguendo* that a Member has correctly attributed the cause of the serious injury to increased imports (and this hypothesis is certainly *not* correct in the case of the US's safeguard measure on wheat gluten), the corresponding safeguard measure must be commensurate or proportionate to that injury, to the exclusion of any injury caused by other factors.

The EC repeats once more that using the pretext of a safeguard measure in order to remedy the intrinsic uncompetitiveness of the US domestic industry (*in casu* the wheat gluten/wheat starch industry) relative to other domestic competing industry, like the corn milling industry, constitutes a violation of the SA.

Neither can a WTO Member abuse a safeguard measure, in order to remedy situations unrelated to increased imports such as increase in input costs, or fluctuations in price due to variations of protein premiums, or failed business strategies such as over-expansion of production capacity.

However, this is exactly what the US did.

The EC refers the Panel back to, in particular, chapter 5 of its first written submission, paragraphs 99 and following of its first oral statement, chapter 6 of its second written submission, chapter 6.2 of its second oral statement and joint answer to questions 8 and 9 of the Panel (17 January 2000).

3. *Article 5.1 did not allow the US to choose a quantitative restriction without having demonstrated that that was the least trade restrictive measure possible*

The principle of proportionality under Article 5.1 did not allow the US to choose a quantitative restriction without having demonstrated that the applied measure was the least trade restrictive measure possible.

The EC would like to recall once more that the explanation provided by the ITC (I-26) for choosing a quantitative restriction refers *only* to the wheat starch market and to the alleged need to avoid "inequitable" distribution of burden between suppliers from third countries.

There is no explanation on the only relevant issue, i.e. the "suitable" remedy for the alleged serious injury to the US wheat gluten industry caused by increased imports only and the need to facilitate adjustment of that industry to increased imports only.

The ITC's unrelated statements or "*petitiones principii*" do not reach the minimum standard of "reasoned conclusions" required under the SA.

The EC refers the Panel back to, in particular, chapter 5 of its first written submission, paragraphs 99 and following of its first oral statement, chapter 6 of its second written submission and chapter 6.3 of its second oral statement.

4. The US has applied the safeguard measure on wheat gluten inconsistently with the findings of the US authorities about injury and causation

The US authorities have *excluded* from their reasoning concerning causality the effects of the inherently weak position of the US wheat gluten/wheat starch industry on the US *domestic* starch market, thus incorrectly determining that a serious injury was caused solely by the imported wheat gluten

However, the US authorities have *included* as one of their key considerations the wheat starch market conditions in the US when considering the form, the scope and the extent of the safeguard measure against *foreign* wheat gluten.

This inconsistent way of proceeding of the US authorities has *doubly* prejudiced the market access conditions for EC produced wheat gluten by first indicating imports as the sole cause of serious injury and then increasing the restrictions flowing from the safeguard measure in order to remedy *other* causes.

The EC refers the Panel back to chapter 4.6.3.6 of its first written submission, paragraphs 110 and following of its first oral statement and chapter 6.4 of its second oral statement.

5. The US has manipulated the "representative period"

If a Member chooses to implement a quantitative restriction, it has to determine the quantity of imports *in an objective way*, i.e. with reference to the most recent ("last") statistics available.

Such statistics are representative of the legitimate trade in the product concerned *unless* an exceptional event or a violation of WTO rules has distorted the trade. The Member departing from the available statistics for the *last* three years must prove the existence of such exceptional event or violation.

When the objective level of imports is set, it may be adjusted *in a MFN fashion* provided that "a clear justification is given that a different level is necessary to prevent or remedy injury".

A "*clear*" justification corresponds to a *reinforced* burden of proof upon the Member using that possibility. It is a much higher, more demanding standard. Generic explanations or statements do not fulfil that standard.

The US has not followed this correct line of action. Rather, it has argued even in its second written submission that it was entitled to invent a new rule and read in Article 5.1, second sentence, the possibility of choosing another representative period of its choice.

The practical consequence of such action is that the quantities of imports allowed into the US are unjustifiably lower than the level at which they should have been set. In other words, the US domestic industry on wheat gluten is over-protected by the US measure, which is a protectionist measure in disguise.

The EC refers the Panel back to, in particular, chapter 5.2 of its first written submission, paragraphs 114 and following of its first oral statement, chapter 7 of its second written submission, chapter 6.5 of its second oral statement and answer to question 10 from the Panel (17 January 2000).

8. THE US SAFEGUARD MEASURE ON WHEAT GLUTEN IS A DISCRIMINATORY MEASURE

29. The EC has also indicated that the US safeguard measure on wheat gluten is in fact *a discriminatory measure*, i.e. a measure that was designed with the aim of treating in a differentiated fashion imports from different origins. This discrimination is inconsistent with Articles I of the GATT 1994 and 2.1, 4.2 and 5.2 of the SA.

1. The US and Canada have confirmed in their latest submissions that the US authorities have performed the injury and causation investigation in two steps.

They have first (unjustifiably) attributed alleged "serious injury" to increased imports regardless of their origin.

However, the US authorities have then performed a *second causation* investigation and have excluded Canada because its imports allegedly did not contribute "substantially" to the injury.

Finally, they have implemented the allocation of the quantitative restriction in order to reallocate shares among foreign suppliers (ITC I-21 and I-26, *in fine*) without following the appropriate procedures under Article 5.2 (b), as the US itself has explicitly recognised.

The EC states (and requests the panel to rule) that the unequivocal text of Article 4.2 of the SA and of Article I of the GATT clearly prohibit that the US perform a two step injury and causation analysis, and include Canadian imports when determining whether "serious injury" has occurred but exclude Canada from the scope of the safeguard measure. In this case, the facts amply confirm this conclusion in law since since imports from the EC, Australia as well as Canada increased in 1996, and the level of imports from all these sources into the US in 1997 were in any case higher than in 1995.

The US has no justification under the SA or under any other WTO agreement for having breached the principle of parallelism and the fundamental principle of the MFN treatment.

Free trade areas such as the NAFTA are not even mentioned in that text.

The generic reservation contained in footnote 1 to Article 2.1, concerning the interpretation of the relationship between Article XXIV of the GATT 1994 and Article XIX of the same agreement, has evidently no bearing on the interpretation of *Article 4.2 of the Safeguards Agreement*. This is all the more so in light of the General Interpretative note to Annex 1A to the WTO Agreement.

The EC refers the Panel back to, in particular, paragraphs 55 and 60 of its first written submission, paragraphs 87 and following of its first oral statement, chapter 8 of its second written submission, chapter 7 of its second oral statement, answer to question 8 from the panel (4 February 2000) and the comments of the European Communities on US Exhibit 13 (13 February 2000) including the attached table.

2. *The uneven allocation of shares of the quantitative restriction in favour of Australia and to the detriment of the EC is another plain example of discriminatory treatment without justification.*

Since, by its own spontaneous admission, it did not follow the procedures under Article 5.2(b), the US has no explanation left as to how it can justify that despite having a 47 per cent share of the market in the previous representative period, the EC was allocated only a 43 per cent share of the quota. Australia, on the other hand, was allocated a share of 49 per cent, compared to its share in the previous representative period of 38 per cent. More importantly, this allocation has preserved entirely the 1997 record levels of imports from Australia despite the fact that Australia's exports increased continuously in the last three years of the investigative period, by almost 21 per cent.

The EC refers the Panel back to, in particular, chapters 5 and 7 of its first written submission, paragraphs 92 and following of its first oral statement, its answer to question no. 10 of the Panel (17 January 2000), paragraph 100-117 of its second written submission, chapter 7 of its second oral statement and the comments of the European Communities on US Exhibit 13 (13 February 2000) including the attached table.

3. *Finally, the manipulation of the "representative period" by the US authorities, that was examined above, has provided* de facto *a better treatment of wheat gluten of Australian origin when compared to wheat gluten of EC origin. That manipulation is therefore not only a breach of Article 5.1 of the SA but also of Article I of the GATT 1994.*

The EC refers the Panel back to, in particular, chapter 7 of its first written submission, paragraphs 100-117 of its 2nd written submission, and part 7 of its second oral statement.

9. THE US HAS BREACHED A NUMBER OF PROCEDURAL RULES UNDER ARTICLES 8 AND 12 OF THE SA.

30. Without need be to repeat once more the arguments and the evidence which are already on the record of this proceedings and that demonstrate that the US has repeatedly breached these important provisions, the EC would like to draw the attention of the Panel to the fact that the US attitude not only substantially nullifies or impairs benefits expected by the EC upon signing up to the SA. Were the US practice allow to stand, the substantial and procedural interests of *all* Members of the WTO, which are related to transparency and to the predictability and stability of the multilateral trading system, would be severely jeopardised.

The EC refers the Panel back to, in particular, chapter 6 of its first written submission, paragraphs 125-133 of its first oral statement, its answers to questions 11 and 24, 2, and 19-22 of the Panel (17 January 2000), and its answers to questions 13 and 14 of the Panel (4 February 2000).

31. This concludes the EC's brief summary of the most important claims and arguments it has presented during this panel procedure. We are ready as from now to provide any further clarification you may need.

Mr. Chairman, Members of the Panel, thank you for your attention.

ATTACHMENT 1-15

ANSWER OF THE EUROPEAN COMMUNITY
TO THE ADDITIONAL QUESTION FROM THE PANEL

(22 May 2000)

Question No. 1 to the EC

"1. Before the USITC, did the EU producers raise "protein premiums" as a factor that the USITC should take into account? If so, did the EU producers raise it as a factor relevant to the entire period of investigation, or only to certain specific years, i.e. 1993-1994? Please substantiate your answer on the basis of evidence already on the Panel record."

Reply

1. The "protein premium " factor was on many occasions during the ITC procedure mentioned by EC producers as a factor that the USITC should take into account.

(The EC stresses that the issue might even have been mentioned more often than appears from Exhibits EC-16-18. The EC nor its industry can verify this since under USITC procedures the EC producers are not allowed to receive a complete text of the briefs filed on their behalf by their representatives before the ITC ; everything which is alleged to refer to business confidential information must be removed from the version provided to the industry by its counsel).

2. For the sake of brevity, the EC will not discuss *all* occasions at which the protein premium was mentioned by the EC industry. It refers to what was stated in paragraphs 54-55 of the EC's 2nd written submission, and adds the following three observations.

3. First of all, the protein premium factor was mentioned by EC industry from the very beginning of the procedure, and throughout the procedure before the ITC.

In the documents already in the possession of the panel, protein premium is mentioned for the first time by the EC industry in its pre-injury-hearing brief p. 2 and 3, including footnote 54, where the protein content of wheat is mentioned as a factor influencing wheat gluten prices. Also, there the concept of protein premium is explained as follows: " A good indicator of protein content is the premium paid for 13 per cent hard red winter wheat over ordinary hard red winter wheat. "

4. Other examples where protein premium was mentioned by the EC industry also later on during the ITC proceedings, including during the injury hearing be-

fore the ITC and in the post-injury-hearing brief, are cited in the footnote to this sentence.[1]

5. Secondly, the " protein premium " factor was clearly mentioned as one *relevant to the entire period of investigation*. For instance, in the EC industry's pre-injury-hearing brief p. 13 it was explicitly stated that " The simplistic assertion [of the US Wheat Gluten Industry Council requesting the safeguard measure] that only imports can explain *recent industry trends* ignores contemporaneous supply-side and demand-side changes in the US market during this same time-period (e.g. (...) *changes in the protein content of wheat) (...) "* (Emphasis supplied).

6. Also during the hearing before the ITC, the so-called "regression analysis " contained in Petitioners' brief – which served to justify the request for the safeguard measure and thus attributed relatively low wheat gluten prices during the latter part of the PoI to increased imports - was criticised as follows : "First, the regression analysis contained in Petitioner's brief is seriously flawed in that it includes only flour costs as an explanatory variable for changes in vital wheat gluten price. The analysis totally ignores other supply and demand factors that are recognised as affecting price in this industry, *including protein content of wheat* (....) ".[2] (emphasis supplied).

7. This criticism was repeated for the third time in the post-injury-hearing brief.[3]

8. Moreover, a representative of a US customer who shared the EC producers' criticism of the ITC's analysis, Mr Neighbor[4], made the point as a general one, covering the entire PoI. For instance, he stated : "If gluten prices get too high or the premiums between high gluten and patent flour get too low, people

---

1 The EC refers in particular to:

- the injury hearing report (Exhibit EC-17) p. 149-150 (citing a letter by Manildra stating that protein premium is an important factor in determining wheat gluten prices: literally the Manildra representative writes: "the market in the US appears to be headed for further decreases for July forward due to softening demand resulting from weakening high protein premiums (...).)
- page 154 lines 12-16 of that same report of the 16 December 1997 ITC hearing where Mr Klett, who spoke on behalf of the EC producers, made the following statement before the ITC: "I think that one important issue going back to the 1993-1994 period, if you see exhibit 1 (...) it came out that the price spike during that period was due to low protein content of wheat, as well as a shortage situation" (emphasis added)
- the EC industry's post-injury-hearing brief (Exhibit EC-18) page 21, including footnote 57; "Using the first half of 1994 as the base period to measure price suppression is disingenuous, as this was the period when prices were high due to the low-protein content of wheat.".

2 Exhibit EC-17, p. 138, lines 1-10.

3 P. 24 point a, "Petitioners' regression model ignores other significant supply and demand factors that also affect vital wheat gluten price, including the protein content of wheat".

4 Exhibit EC-17, p. 170 line 11 – p. 172 line 5.

will substitute types of flour and use less gluten if gluten prices are too high. " And : " If the premiums between high gluten flour and patent flour are low enough, then you use less gluten again. It's a combination of price of gluten and the premium spread between the two types of flour ".

9. Also Mr Veerman, speaking on behalf of EC producers before the ITC, stated in very general terms : (hearing report Exhibit EC-17 page 174 line 20 – page 175 line 6) : "Once again, wheat gluten as a whole is a global market. It is dictated by supply and demand. It varies from year to year. *If the crop is high quality, the wheat itself, there is less demand, but there is more production. (...)*" (emphasis supplied)

10. Thirdly, contrary to what the US alleges[5], the EC producers *did submit all necessary data.* The exact relevant information on protein premium, covering the entire PoI, was provided to the USITC, both in the form of a graph and in statistical form. For ease of reference, the EC annexes the relevant three pages, which were annexed to the post-injury-hearing brief. (Exhibit EC-20)[6] These pages provide all relevant information for the whole period. In particular, they give not only the proof that protein premium was at an all time-high in 1994 (using the " ITC-year "), but also that it was (relatively) low thereafter, which explained the level of US wheat gluten prices during the latter part of the PoI.

11. In spite of this detailed evidence covering the entire PoI, the USITC did not give any explanation whatsoever of how it arrived at its (implicit) assumption that it was not low protein premium which kept US wheat gluten prices relatively low during the latter part of the PoI. It thus violated the SA, and in particular Art. 4 thereof.

12. By way of a final general observation, the EC would like to note the following. Throughout this procedure[7], the EC has underlined that under the Safeguards Agreement ("SA")[8], the competent authorities of a WTO Member have an obligation to evaluate, of their own initiative, *each* factor of an *objective* and *quantifiable* nature *having a bearing* on the situation of the industry concerned.

They are under this obligation, regardless of whether or not a particular factor has been raised by any party during the proceedings referred to in Article

---

[5] US statement at 3d meeting of Panel with the Parties, para. 20.

[6] In Exhibit EC-18 they are respectively the 5th page, and the 5th-4th before last page of the pages containing evidence.

[7] See in particular the EC's answer to questions no. 6 and 7 of the Panel, 17 January 2000. See also paras. 43-45 of the EC's 2nd oral statement.

[8] See in particular Article 4.2 (a) SA, which provides that "the competent authorities shall evaluate all relevant factors of an objective and quantifiable nature having a bearing on the situation of that industry, in particular (...)" (emphasis supplied). See also AB report on Argentina-Footwear, at para. 136, "Art. 4.2(a) of the Agreement on Safeguards requires a demonstration that the competent authorities evaluated, at a minimum, each of the factors listed in Article 4.2(a) as well as all other factors that are relevant to the situation of the industry concerned." (Emphasis supplied).

3.1 of the SA. Especially since, as the EC has shown[9], the ITC was aware of the fact that the "protein premium " - i.e. the price differential between low- and high protein wheat - influences wheat gluten prices, the USITC should have obtained all relevant information which is necessary to evaluate how that factor developed throughout the entire Period of Investigation (" PoI "). Also, the USITC should have included reasoned conclusions analysing that information in its report. The fact that it failed to do so[10] constitutes a violation of the SA. However, as the EC has also underlined during these proceedings and in this answer, this violation is all the more evident since the "protein premium " factor was at many occasions during the ITC procedure mentioned by EC producers.

[9] See e.g. para. 32 of the EC's second written submission.

[10] In particular the latter, since, as the EC has shown, all the relevant evidence was provided to the ITC by the EC producers.

ATTACHMENT 2-1

FIRST WRITTEN SUBMISSION OF THE UNITED STATES
(6 December 1999)

TABLE OF CONTENTS

I. INTRODUCTION

1. In 1998 the United States established a safeguard measure on imports of wheat gluten after concluding that increased imports were causing serious injury to the domestic wheat gluten industry. The decision to take action came after the US International Trade Commission ("USITC") conducted an exhaustive and transparent investigation of the impact increased imports of wheat gluten were having on the domestic industry.

2. The USITC conducted its investigation in conformity with the procedural requirements of Article 3 of the *Agreement on Safeguards* ("Safeguards Agreement"). Thus, the USITC held public hearings in which producers from the European Union (EU) were permitted active participation. The EC and EU producers were afforded ample opportunity to present evidence and submit their views during the USITC's investigation. Indeed, the EC itself participated in those proceedings. Moreover, the USITC addressed the specific claims raised by the EC and its producers in its published report, which set forth the USITC's findings and reasoned conclusions on the issues of fact and law relevant to this case. In keeping with the mandate of Article 3, the public version of the USITC published report properly did not disclose confidential information.

3. In addition to satisfying the procedural requirements of Article 3, the USITC investigation also conformed to the substantive obligations of Article 4 of

the Safeguards Agreement. After examining the injury factors specifically enumerated in Article 4.2, as well as other relevant factors, the USITC properly concluded that the domestic wheat gluten industry was being seriously injured as a result of increased imports.

4. Following publication of the USITC's findings and recommendation, and after consulting with potentially affected exporting Members, the United States established a safeguard measure on imports of wheat gluten. The US measure consists of a quantitative restriction on wheat gluten imports for 3 years and 1 day, with the quantity of imports increasing progressively over the period. The quantitative restriction is carefully calibrated to ensure that the US safeguard measure is applied only to the extent necessary to remedy the serious injury suffered by the domestic wheat gluten industry and facilitate its adjustment to import competition. The United States notified its investigation, findings, and safeguard measure to the Committee on Safeguards.

5. At the heart of this proceeding, is the EC's effort to convince this Panel to overturn the carefully reasoned and amply articulated evidentiary findings and economic conclusions of the USITC. The EC stakes its case on many of the very same arguments that it, or EU producers, presented and lost before the Commission. The Panel should decline the EC's call for the Panel to substitute its judgment for that of the US competent authorities. The temporary US restriction on wheat gluten imports is based on the USITC's painstaking review and findings regarding all of the evidence and arguments presented to it, including those of the EC. It is fully consistent with all applicable provisions of the Safeguards Agreement, Article XIX of the *General Agreement on Tariffs and Trade 1994,* and all other relevant WTO obligations. The Panel should reject the EC's arguments to the contrary.

II. PROCEDURAL BACKGROUND

6. The EC requested consultations with the United States on 17 March 1999, pursuant to Article 4 of the *Understanding on Rules and Procedures Governing the Settlement of Disputes* ("DSU"), Article XXII:1 of the *General Agreement on Tariffs and Trade 1994* ("GATT"), Article 14 of the Safeguards Agreement and Article 19 of the *Agreement on Agriculture.* The EC's consultation request alleged that the US safeguard – embodied in Proclamation 7103, with an accompanying memorandum from the President of the United States – was inconsistent with Articles 2, 4, 5, 8 and 12 of the Safeguard Agreement, Article 4.2 of the Agreement on Agriculture, and Articles I and XIX of the GATT.

7. Consultations were held in Geneva on 3 May 1999, but failed to settle the dispute.

8. The EC requested establishment of a panel on 3 June 1999, one year after the measure had taken effect, pursuant to Article XXIII of GATT 1994, Articles 4 and 6 of DSU, Article 19 of the Agreement on Agriculture, and Article 14 of the Safeguards Agreement. In its panel request, the EC re-stated the WTO viola-

tions alleged in its earlier request for consultations, except that the EC specified its allegation under Article 2 pertains to Article 2.1 of the Safeguards Agreement.

9. The Dispute Settlement Body established a panel to review the EC's allegations on 26 July1999. Both Australia and Canada reserved third party rights.

III. ACTUAL BACKGROUND

10. After receiving a petition on 19 September 1997 from the domestic wheat gluten industry, the USITC instituted an investigation to determine whether increased wheat gluten imports were a substantial cause of serious injury, or threat of serious injury, to the domestic wheat gluten industry. The USITC conducted its investigation in conformity with both the procedural and substantive requirements of the Safeguards Agreement. After reviewing the economic data, and taking into account the views of all interested parties (including the EC), the USITC properly concluded that the domestic industry was seriously injured.

11. Following the USITC's findings, the United States considered whether to apply a safeguard measure. As part of its deliberative process, the United States consulted with Members that would be affected by a proposed safeguard, including the EC. The United States ultimately determined to impose a safeguard measure on imports of wheat gluten. The measure consists of a quantitative restriction, with specific country allocations, over a period of three years and one day, with the quantity gradually increasing over that period.

12. Both the USITC investigation and the measure adopted by the United States satisfy US obligations under the Safeguards Agreement.

A. *The Investigation*

13. The USITC investigation meets the procedural requirements set out in the Safeguards Agreement. Following is a brief description of the procedures the Commission observed in its wheat gluten investigation.

14. After receiving the domestic industry's petition, the USITC sent out detailed questionnaires to domestic producers and importers/purchasers of wheat gluten. The USITC obtained data on industry financial performance through these questionnaires.[1] The USITC requested that producers provide detailed financial information in four different forms–on the overall operations of the establishments in which they produce wheat gluten, on their combined operations on wheat gluten and wheat starch, on their wheat gluten operations, and on their wheat starch operations. Each of the firms was asked to provide data on net sales, cost of goods sold, selling, general, and administrative expenses, and other income and expenses for each type of operation. The USITC also requested that

---

[1] A copy of the USITC's "producers' questionnaire" is attached as US Exhibit 1.

each firm provide information on capital expenditure, research and development expenditures, property, plant, and equipment, and book value for overall establishment operations, wheat gluten operations, and wheat starch operation. The USITC requested firms that do not maintain separate records for wheat gluten to explain their allocation methodology and provide worksheets with their calculations.

15. After providing prior notice seeking the views of interested parties, the USITC then held extensive public hearings at which interested parties presented relevant views and evidence. Both the EU wheat gluten producers and the EC itself participated in these proceedings, and their views were given full consideration.

16. Once the hearings were completed, the USITC carefully considered all of the evidence, as well as the views of interested parties, and arrived at a determination. The USITC published a report setting out detailed findings and conclusions on all of the pertinent issues relating its determination. This report was notified to the Committee on Safeguards, and it was made available to the public.

17. In addition to satisfying all of the procedural obligations set out in the Safeguards Agreement, the USITC investigation also satisfied the Agreement's substantive obligations. In particular, the USITC examined all of the factors enumerated in Article 4.2, and it published a detailed analysis demonstrating the relevance of the factors it examined.

18. The USITC report documents the state of the domestic industry. The USITC found that the domestic wheat gluten industry was profitable during the first three years of the Commission's period of investigation (POI). While there were some annual fluctuations, domestic production and sales increased, and imports remained basically constant - 128 million pounds in 1993; 124 million pounds in 1994; 128 million pounds in 1995. In anticipation of an increase in domestic demand, the industry made significant capital investments to increase its production capacity and modernize its facilities, and these projects were largely completed in 1995.

19. The USITC also found that the domestic producers had anticipated correctly that domestic demand would increase during the next two years. Domestic consumption increased, and was 15 per cent higher in 1997 than it had been in 1995. However, despite this significant increase in demand, the industry was unable to profit from this increase. Rather, economic indicators turned sharply negative in 1996 and 1997. In particular, the industry operated at a loss in 1996 and 1997, production and sales declined, and virtually all other factors pertaining to industry performance were negative. Although there was a modest upturn in some indicators in 1997, those indicators were still far below previous levels.

20. Correlating with this decline in industry performance, the USITC report found that imports of wheat gluten increased dramatically from their steady 1993-1995 level of 128 million pounds to 156 million pounds in 1996, and still further to 177 million pounds in 1997. Thus, imports increased 38 per cent from 1995 to 1997. Instead of increasing, domestic shipments were sharply lower in

1996 and 1997 than in 1993-1995 because of a surge in low-priced imports and the idling of both old and new capacity.

21. The USITC report concluded that imports had increased significantly, both in absolute terms and relative to domestic production. After reviewing evidence relating to the factors enumerated in Section 4.2 of the Safeguards Agreement, as well as other relevant evidence, the USITC concluded that the industry was seriously injured, given that virtually all such factors were negative. The Commission then considered whether the serious injury was attributable to increased imports. The USITC concluded there was a direct correlation between the dramatic increase in wheat gluten imports and the significant decline in domestic wheat gluten industry performance in 1996 and 1997. In the face of rising domestic demand and consumption, domestic production, shipments, capacity utilization, unit prices, industry financial performance, and worker productivity all declined during the period of greatest import penetration. The USITC further determined that increased imports were a cause greater than any other cause, and that none of the other suggested possible causes - changes in market conditions for co-product wheat starch, ongoing imports of wheat gluten by domestic producers, competition among domestic wheat gluten producers, and rising raw material costs - were as great a cause of serious injury to the domestic industry as increased imports.

1. Serious Injury Caused by Increased Imports

22. *Increased Imports*: The USITC found that wheat gluten imports increased in absolute terms during the POI. From 1993 to 1997 wheat gluten imports rose from 128 million pounds to 177 million pounds. Virtually all of this increase occurred during the last two years of the period examined, when imports surged from 128 million pounds in 1995 to 156 million pounds in 1996, and 177 million pounds in 1997. Between 1995 to 1997 imports increased by nearly 40 per cent Imports also increased when compared with domestic production: the ratio of imports to domestic production rose from 100.6 per cent in 1993 to 145.4 per cent in 19972.[2]

23. *Import Share*: The USITC found that the ratio of imports from all sources to US production rose steadily during the POI, but imports from the EC surged to record levels. In fact, the ratio of EC imports more than doubled relative to US production while the ratio of imports from other sources fluctuated within a narrower range. Thus, during the POI the ratio of imports to domestic production initially fell from 100.6 per cent in 1993 to 88.2 per cent in 1994, then rose steadily to 145.4 per cent in 1997. For the EC, however, the ratio declined initially from 34.4 per cent in 1993 to 29.6 per cent in 1994, and then climbed precipi-

[2] USITC Report at I-10; II-9. US Exhibit 4.

tously from 37.8 per cent in 1995 to 62.6 per cent in 1996 and 74.8 per cent in 1997.[3]

24. *Sales*: With respect to changes in the level of sales – i.e. domestic shipments – the USITC found that domestic shipments followed a similar trend as production, initially rising and then falling — they were at their lowest levels in 1995 and 1997.[4]

25. *Production*: The USITC found that industry production of wheat gluten overall decreased by 4.5 per cent during the POI. Production initially rose from 128 million pounds in 1993 to 143 million pounds in 1995 then fell sharply to 112 million pounds in 1996 and increased to 122 million pounds in 1997.[5]

26. *Capacity Utilization*: The USITC found that capacity utilization in the industry fell significantly during the POI, from 78.3 per cent in 1993 to as low as 42.0 per cent in 1996 before rising slightly to 44.5 per cent in 1997. While some of the decrease can be explained by the fact that the industry had increased capacity during the POI in anticipation of significant increases in domestic consumption, this fact alone cannot account for the decline. Most of the increase in capacity was in place by June 1995, *before* the surge in imports that occurred in crop years 1996 and 1997, and capacity utilization fell sharply to its lowest levels in these two years, from 56.2 per cent in 1995 to 42.0 per cent in 1996 and 44.5 per cent in 1997. Had there been no increase in imports from 1993 levels, the industry likely could have operated at 61per cent of capacity in 1997, a level at which the industry could have operated profitably.[6]

27. *Profit and Loss*: The USITC found that during the POI the domestic industry was unable to operate at a reasonable level of profit in 1996-1997, during the import surge. While domestic operations were profitable during the first three years of the investigative period, the industry operated at a loss in 1996 and 1997. Profitability reflected the trend in average unit value prices, which initially rose and then fell. Average unit values peaked in 1994 and then declined and were at their lowest level in 1997; the decline in average unit values coincided with a rise in average unit costs.[7]

28. *Employment*: The USITC found that statistics on employment and underemployment in the industry provided further evidence of economic decline. While the average number of production and related workers increased during the POI, this does not represent the complete picture. In reality, while the number of hours worked increased from 1993 to 1997, productivity decreased sharply.[8]

---

[3] US Exhibit 4 at II-14-15.

[4] US Exhibit 4 at I-13.

[5] US Exhibit 4 at I-12-13.

[6] US Exhibit 4 at I-12.

[7] US Exhibit 4 at I-13.

[8] US Exhibit 4 at I-13-14.

29. *Other Factors*: In addition to the factors enumerated in Article 4.2(a) of the Safeguards Agreement, the USITC also evaluated other relevant factors, including wages, inventories, new entries/expansion, and price. These factors are discussed in detail in paragraphs 110-124 of the US submission.

2. *Alternative Causes of Injury*

30. In its investigation the USITC specifically examined possible alternative causes of serious injury suggested by certain interested parties, including: (1) changes in co-product markets, (2) domestic producers' importation of wheat gluten, (3) competition among domestic producers, (4) increased capacity, and (5) rising raw materials costs (wheat gluten and wheat flour). After thorough examination of these factors, the USITC concluded, based on the evidence, that increased imports were both an important cause of serious injury and a cause that was greater than any of the alternative causes suggested. A summary of the USITC's findings on these suggested alternative causes follows.

31. *Co-products*.[9] While finding that wheat gluten production decisions are affected by market conditions in the wheat starch market, the USITC concluded that changes in the co-product markets were not a more important cause of serious injury than imports. The USITC arrived at this conclusion after examining US selling prices of wheat starch, which is the major co-product of wheat gluten production. The USITC noted that, in contrast to the domestic selling price of wheat gluten, the domestic selling price of wheat starch showed a gradual increase over the POI. Weighted-average wheat starch prices were at their highest level of the investigative period in 1997. Thus, there was no decline in wheat starch prices that either paralleled the sharp decline since 1994 of domestic wheat gluten prices or explained the sharp decline in the financial performance of domestic wheat gluten producers.

32. Addressing importer arguments about the impact of competition in the US market between corn starch and wheat starch and its impact on wheat gluten production, the USITC found the relative stability, and gradual increase, in domestic wheat starch prices suggested that competition between corn starch and wheat starch was not likely to have had much if any effect on wheat gluten production. The USITC also considered evidence cited by importers that one domestic producer had reduced its wheat gluten production in 1995 for reasons related in part to conditions in the alcohol market, and importers' claim that this explained that firm's poor financial performance. The USITC found that such action by the one producer in 1995 explains only part of the problem faced by one producer and could not be extrapolated to account for the problems facing all domestic producers, nor could not it explain the significant deterioration in 1996 and 1997 of the other three domestic producers, who accounted for the majority of domestic

---

[9] US Exhibit 4 at 16-17.

production. Indeed, the evidence did not even fully explain the declining financial performance of that one producer in its wheat gluten operations.

33. *Imported wheat gluten.*[10] The USITC also found that domestic producers' importation of wheat gluten was not a more important cause of the serious injury. The USITC found that imports by domestic purchasers remained relatively steady during the POI. Thus, US producers were not responsible for the surge in imports that occurred in 1996 and 1997. In addition, the USITC noted that the US market depended on a certain level of imports to meet domestic demand. In all but one year of the POI – 1996 – US apparent consumption of wheat gluten exceeded US producers' capacity to produce wheat gluten.

34. *Competition and increased capacity.*[11] The USITC also considered whether domestic competition and the increase in domestic capacity were more important causes of serious injury than increased imports, and found that they were not. With respect to competition, the USITC found that the domestic wheat gluten market is very competitive, and producers have ample excess capacity to meet higher demand. Moreover, wheat gluten is a commodity product that sells primarily on the basis of price, and wheat gluten from different sources is highly interchangeable. The USITC found that the domestic industry added substantial new capacity. However, the USITC found that the bulk of the increased capacity was added early in the POI in anticipation of continued strong growth in domestic demand and consumption and before the surge in imports. The USITC found that industry projections of continued growth in demand and consumption were largely correct, as apparent consumption increased nearly 18 per cent between 1993 and 1997. The USITC found that, but for the surge in imports, the industry would have operated at 61 per cent of capacity in 1997, which is much closer to previous capacity levels at which the industry was able to operate profitably. Thus, the USITC was able to conclude that neither domestic competition nor increased domestic capacity was a more important cause of serious injury than increased imports.

35. *Raw materials costs.*[12] The USITC examined and rejected the claim that rising prices of wheat and wheat flour, the major inputs into wheat gluten/wheat starch production, was a more important cause of serious injury than increased imports. Raw material costs did increase during the POI, particularly in 1996 and 1997. However, the USITC found the evidence indicates that wheat gluten producers typically are able to pass on the cost increases to their customers, because demand for wheat gluten is relatively insensitive to price changes. In 1996 and 1997, however, unit selling values declined despite increased demand and higher raw material costs. The USITC concluded that this unusual development was

[10] US Exhibit 4 at I-17.
[11] US Exhibit 4 at I-17.
[12] US Exhibit 4 at I-17.

explained by the dramatic increase in relatively low-priced imports during the POI, which had the effect of driving down wheat gluten prices.

36. After making an affirmative injury determination, the USITC conducted a separate analysis of imports from Canada and Mexico to determine whether they accounted for a substantial share of total imports and contributed importantly to the serious injury. The USITC made a negative finding with respect to imports from Mexico, noting that there were no reported imports during the POI. With respect to Canadian imports, the USITC concluded that such imports accounted for a "substantial share" of total imports in that Canada was the third largest supplier of wheat gluten imports to the United States. However, Canadian imports declined significantly during the POI while overall imports increased. By 1997, Canada accounted for only 8.9 per cent of total imports. Moreover, the USITC report found that Canadian imports generally oversold the US market during the POI. Thus, the USITC concluded that Canadian imports were not contributing importantly to the serious injury suffered by the domestic industry. Accordingly, the USITC recommended that Canadian imports be excluded from the proposed safeguard measure.[13]

B. The Remedy

37. Under US law, if the USITC determines that increased imports are a substantial cause of serious injury or the threat thereof to the domestic industry, it is required to recommend to the President the action that will address the serious injury, or threat thereof, to the domestic industry and be most effective in facilitating the efforts of the domestic industry to make a positive adjustment to import competition.[14] The President, after taking into account the USITC's recommendation and certain other factors, including the national economic interest, makes the final decision.

38. In response to the USITC's affirmative injury determination and remedy recommendation, the President carefully considered what action, if any, to take in response.

39. Ultimately, the President adopted a safeguard measure on imports of wheat gluten. The President's Proclamation[15] and accompanying Memorandum[16] and the USITC's recommendation and accompanying explanation[17] together define the US measure in terms of product coverage, form, duration, and level, and provide a reasoned explanation as to how US authorities determined that the

---

[13] US Exhibit 4 at I-19, I-29.

[14] Section 202(e)(1) of the Trade Act of 1974.

[15] Proclamation 7103 of 30 May 1998, To Facilitate Positive Adjustment to Competition From Imports of Wheat Gluten. US Exhibit 2.

[16] Memorandum of 30 May 1998, Action Under Section 203 of the Trade Act of 1974 Concerning Wheat Gluten, published in the Federal Register of June 3, 1998 (63 Fed. Reg. 30359). US Exhibit 3.

[17] US Exhibit 4 at I-3-4, I-21-31.

measure was taken only to the extent necessary to remedy serious injury and facilitate the industry's adjustment.

40. The specific measure the President imposed consists of a quantitative restriction to remain in place for three years and one day. The quota was set at 57,521,000 kg. (126.812 million pounds) for the first year, with annual increases of 6 per cent , and it was allocated on a country basis. Australia, and the European Community received separate allocations, and the third category was for "other countries".[18] In the Proclamation, the President explained that the first year quota level was set at a level equal to the average quantity of wheat gluten that entered the United States during the last three representative years of imports - 1992-95 (July 1-June 30 crop years). The Proclamation further detailed that the country allocations were based on country shares in those same three years[19] and that Canada and Mexico were excluded from the measure. There were no reported imports from Mexico, and Canada was a relatively small and declining supplier.[20]

41. The President adopted a measure that was substantially the same as that recommended by the USITC, except that the measure imposed was less shorter in duration than that recommended: The USITC had proposed a 4-year measure; the safeguard that the President put in place last for just over 3 years. The USITC report details the United States' reasoning and explanations for its adoption of the wheat gluten safeguard measure.

42. The USITC report first described the competitive conditions affecting wheat gluten, including domestic and world market conditions for wheat gluten, demand conditions, and supply conditions.[21] The USITC also closely examined the adjustment plan provided by the domestic wheat gluten industry and company commitments contained therein.[22] The USITC examined the different forms of remedy available, including tariffs, tariff-rate quotas, and quotas, and explained why in this instance it was recommending a quota instead of a tariff or tariff-rate quota.[23]

43. The USITC also explained why it was recommending a quota at an initial level of 126 million pounds, a 6 per cent annual escalator, a duration of four years, country allocations, and the respective choices for recent representative periods.[24] For example, the USITC found, based on its economic analysis, that a quota that restores imports to approximately the market share prevailing in 1993-95 would allow the domestic industry to return to reasonable operating

[18] US Exhibit 2 at 1; and Annex to US Exhibit 2 at 1.
[19] US Exhibit 3 at 1.
[20] US Exhibit 2 at 1; and Annex to US Exhibit 2 at 1.
[21] US Exhibit 4 at I-22-25.
[22] US Exhibit 4 at I-25-26.
[23] US Exhibit 4 at I-26-27.
[24] US Exhibit 4 at I-27-29.

profits.[25] It found that a quota of four years duration would allow the industry sufficient time to make substantial progress in developing the new products described in the adjustment plan and in adjusting to import competition.[26] In recommending a 6 per cent growth rate in the quota in the second and third years, the USITC noted that this would be higher than the 4.2 per cent growth rate in imports over the period of investigation. The USITC found that this would allow for a reasonable rate of growth in imports and further encourage the industry to adjust to import competition.[27]

44. The USITC found that the quota it was recommending would not exceed the amount necessary to remedy the serious injury it found to exist, and that imports would continue to supply a large share of the US market and be an important competitive force in the US market.[28]

C. *Notifications and Consultation*

1. *Notifications*

45. In addition to the substantive requirements, the United States also satisfied the procedural requirements under Article 12 of the Safeguards Agreement. Pursuant to Article 12.1(a) of the Agreement, the United States notified the Safeguards Committee of the investigation initiated by the USITC to examine the domestic industry's serious injury claim on 17 October 1997.[29] The notification informed interested parties of their right to submit written briefs, the dates of USITC hearings and other pertinent information. The United States filed its notification with the Committee promptly after the USITC instituted its investigation. The domestic industry filed its petition on 19 September 1997, and the USITC completed its evaluation and announced institution of the investigation on 1 October 1997.[30]

46. On 15 January 1998, the USITC voted unanimously that wheat gluten was being imported into the United States in such increased quantities as to be a substantial cause of serious injury to the domestic industry. The United States provided a 12.1(b) notification to the Committee on 11 February 1998 notifying Members of the unanimous vote.[31] The USITC published its report and remedy recommendation on 18 March 1998, and the report was provided to the Committee, as part of the United States supplemental Article 12.1(b) notification, on 24 March 1998.[32]

---

25 US Exhibit 4 at I-28.
26 US Exhibit 4 at I-28.
27 US Exhibit 4 at I-29.
28 US Exhibit 4 at I-28.
29 G/SG/N/6/USA/4 (circulated 21 October 1997). US Exhibit 5.
30 See US Exhibit 4 at Appendix A.
31 G/SG/N/8/USA/2 (circulated 12 February 1998). US Exhibit 6.
32 G/SG/N/8/USA/2/Rev.1 (circulated 27 March 1998). US Exhibit 6.

47. The United States imposed a safeguard measure with respect to wheat gluten on 1 June 1998, and provided notification to the Committee on 4 June 1998 pursuant to Article 12.1(c) and Article 9 of the Safeguards Agreement.[33]

2. *Consultation*

48. The United States also satisfied its consultation obligations under the Safeguards Agreement. On 24 April 1998, the United States consulted with the EC and other interested parties having a substantial interest as exporters of wheat gluten.

IV. LEGAL ARGUMENT

49. The EC raises legal claims under both the Safeguards Agreement and GATT 1994. The United States respectfully submits that the EC's claims are unfounded, and as such they should be rejected by the Panel.

50. The United States' submission begins with a discussion of some of the general legal problems arising from the EC's submission: First, the United States reviews the applicable standard of review and identifies critical areas where the EC fails to apply the proper standard. Second, the United States articulates the burden of proof standard and argues that in many instances the EC fails to meet its burden to present a *prima facie* case. Third, based on the findings of prior panels, the United States discounts the EC's claim that a finding of "unforeseen developments" is a necessary prerequisite to taking a safeguard action.

51. Next, the United States addresses the EC's legal claims under the Safeguards Agreement: First, the United States demonstrates that the EC's claims of violation under Articles 2 and 4 are without merit because the USITC investigation and report satisfy the requirements of the Safeguards Agreement. The United States sets out for the Panel the findings and conclusions reached by the USITC in its report regarding the relevant economic factors examined by the USITC – factors enumerated in the Safeguards Agreement and those relevant factors that were not enumerated. Second, the United States addresses the EC's erroneous claim that the safeguard measure violates Article 5's remedy requirements. Third, the United States describes the actions it has taken in fulfilment of Article 12's consultation requirements. Moreover, the United States rebuts the EC's assertion that under Article 8 a Member taking a safeguard must provide compensation to affected exporting Members.

52. Finally, the United States argues that the EC's discrimination claim under GATT Article I is without legal merit.

[33] G/SG/N/10/USA/2, G/SG/N/11/USA/2 (circulated 8 June 1998). US Exhibit 7.

A. *The Standard of Review in Disputes under the Agreement on Safeguards*

1. The Applicable Standard is Now Well-Established

53. In examining disputes under the Safeguards Agreement, it is now well-established that panels are not authorized to review *de novo* the determination made by the domestic investigating authority. Instead, pursuant to Article 11 of the *Understanding on Rules and Procedures Governing the Settlement of Disputes ("DSU"),* a panel must conduct an objective assessment of the matter before it, taking into account: whether the importing Member examined the relevant facts, as specified in Article 4.2(a) of the Safeguards Agreement; whether the importing Member adequately explained its findings and conclusions, and whether the facts support the determination; and consequently, whether the determination made is consistent with importing Member's obligations under the Safeguards Agreement.

54. The United States recalls that in the two previous disputes concerning safeguards, *Korea – Definitive Safeguard Measure on Imports of Certain Dairy Products ("Korea - Dairy")* and *Argentina - Safeguard Measures on Imports of Footwear ("Argentina - Footwear"),* the Panels specifically rejected the notion of engaging in a *de novo* review.[34] Rather, as articulated by the Panel in *Argentina – Footwear,*

> our review will be limited to an objective assessment, pursuant to Article 11 of the DSU, of whether the domestic authority has considered all relevant facts, including an examination of each factor listed in Article 4.2(a), of whether the published report on the investigation contains adequate explanation of how the facts support the determination made, and consequently of whether the determination made is consistent with Argentina's obligations under the Safeguards Agreement.[35]

55. The United States respectfully submits that the above-quoted standard is the appropriate standard of review to be applied in this dispute.

---

[34] Panel Report, *Korea – Definitive Safeguard Measure on Imports of Certain Dairy Products ("Korea – Dairy ")*, WT/DS98/R and Corr. 1, adopted 12 January 2000, DSR 2000:I, 49, para. 7.30; Panel Report, *Argentina - Safeguard Measures on Imports of Footwear ("Argentina - Footwear")*, WT/DS121/R, adopted 12 January 2000, DSR 2000:II, 575, para. 8.117.

[35] *Argentina - Footwear, supra,* footnote 34, para. 8.124; Similarly, the *Korea – Dairy, supra,* footnote 34, para. 7.30 concluded that:

> the Panel's function is to assess objectively the review conducted by the national investigating authority, ... an objective assessment entails an examination of whether the [Korean national authority] had examined all facts in its possession or which it should have obtained in accordance with Article 4 of the Agreement on Safeguards (including facts which might detract from an affirmative determination in accordance with the last sentence of Article 4.2 of the Agreement on Safeguards), whether adequate explanation had been provided of how the facts as a whole supported the determination made, and, consequently, whether the determination made was consistent with the international obligations of Korea.

2. *The EC Misapplies the Standard of Review*

56. While the EC purports to embrace the standard of review espoused in *Argentina - Footwear* and *Korea - Dairy*, the EC's arguments are inconsistent with that standard. In its first submission, the EC advances arguments that it claims undermine the conclusions reached by the USITC. The EC fails to demonstrate, however, why the USITC's explanation of its decision was inadequate. Instead, the EC attempts to persuade this Panel to engage in a *de novo* investigation of the underlying facts and to substitute the *EC's* judgment for that of the national investigating authority. By urging this approach, the EC effectively repudiates the standard of review it claims to endorse.

57. Moreover, to bolster its position, the EC devotes itself at length to complaints that the USITC failed to address factors that are not enumerated in the Safeguards Agreement. As such, the EC illegitimately attempts to expand obligations beyond those provided for in the Safeguards Agreement. DSU Article 3.2 recognizes that the "[r]ecommendations and rulings of the DSB cannot add to or diminish the rights and obligations provided in the covered agreements." Accordingly, the Panel should reject the EC's manufacture of additional obligations not found in the Safeguards Agreement.

58. In addition, the United States notes that Article 4.2(c) of the Safeguards Agreement requires competent authorities to publish an analysis of the case that demonstrates the *relevance* of the factors examined. Consequently, the Safeguards Agreement does not impose an obligation on the competent authority to explain why it found some factors irrelevant and thus did not rely on them.

59. Further, the EC misrepresents the *Argentina - Footwear* panel report as finding that, in addition to the standard of review set forth above, the "panel should *also* verify the adequacy of the [competent authority's] reasoning by reviewing whether the findings made by the USITC are consistent with the evidence.[36] This argument effectively calls on the panel to undertake a *de novo* review of the evidence before the USITC. In fact, the *Footwear* Panel did not impose any test beyond the standard of review identified above. While a competent authority obviously could not adequately explain its findings by citing evidence that plainly contradicts them, the *Footwear* Panel specifically rejected the proposition that it was to undertake a verification of the competent authorities' findings based on a review of the entire evidence.[37] Accordingly, the Safeguards Agreement does not burden the Panel with the obligation to verify through an independent review of the evidence each finding made by the competent authority.

---

36 EC First Submission at ¶ 3 (emphasis added).

37 The Panel concluded that "[i]f we were to conduct our own assessment of the underlying evidence as contained in the entire record of Argentina's investigation, we believe that we would effectively be engaging in a de novo review, which we and both parties agree would be inappropriate." *Argentina - Footwear, supra*, footnote 34, para. 8.126.

60. Rather, as the *Korea - Dairy* notes, the function of a panel is to assess whether the importing Member examined all relevant facts in accordance with Article 4.2 and whether it provided an adequate explanation as to how those facts as a whole supported the determination made.[38] The *Dairy* Panel emphasized that "the Panel should examine the analysis performed by the national authorities at the time of the investigation on the basis of the various national authorities' determinations and the evidence it has collected." Accordingly, the Panel's review is limited to the record that the ITC gathered in its investigation. By seeking to introduce to this Panel evidence that was not before the USITC, the EC repudiates its stated rejection of *de novo* review.

61. The question for this Panel is the adequacy of the USITC's determination as it was made at the time, not whether the Panel itself would have reached a contrary conclusion based on the facts advanced by a complaining Member. Faced with the similar circumstances, the *Diary* Panel endorsed the approach taken in *United States - Imposition of Anti-Dumping Duties on Imports of Fresh and Chilled Atlantic Salmon from Norway* that a panel examine whether the competent authority made a "reasonable explanation of how the facts as a whole supported the determination made.[39] The *Dairy* Panel's articulation of the standard of review comports with Article 3.1's requirement that a Member provide "*reasoned* conclusions reached on all issues of law and fact." (Emphasis added). As will be seen below, by regularly ignoring the USITC's explanation of its conclusions, the EC fails to meet its burden of showing that those conclusions were unreasonable.

B. The EC Fails to Meet its Burden of Proof

62. The EC fails to meet its burden of proof with respect to many of its asserted claims. Instead, in large measure the EC relies on unfounded assertions advanced without supporting evidence or legal grounding. Moreover, the EC neglects to address the specific findings made by the USITC, favoring instead the EC's own view of how the USITC should have conducted its investigation.

63. In *United States - Measures Affecting Imports of Woven Wool Shirts and Blouses from India ("US - Woven Wool Shirts")* the Appellate Body noted that "a party claiming a violation of a provision of the *WTO Agreement* by another Member must assert and prove its claim."[40] The *Korea - Dairy* panel also had occasion to address questions on the burden of proof, and it found that "[a]s a matter of law the burden of proof rests with the European Communities, as complainant, and does not shift during the panel process.[41] Moreover, the *Dairy* Panel

---

[38] *Korea – Dairy, supra*, footnote 34, para. 7.55.

[39] *Korea – Dairy, supra*, footnote 34, para 7.57, quoting US - Salmon at ¶ 492.

[40] Appellate Body Report, *United States – Measures Affecting Imports of Woven Wool Shirts and Blouses from India* ("*US – Woven Wool Shirts*") WT/DS33/AB/R and Corr. 1, adopted 23 may 1997, DSR 1997:I, 323, at 333-338

[41] *Korea – Dairy, supra*, footnote 34, para. 7.24.

noted that in the first instance it is for the EC to submit a *prima facie* case of violation of the Safeguards Agreement.[42] The *Dairy* Panel interpreted this to mean that it was for Korea – as the defending party – to rebut the European Communities' evidence and arguments, once the EC had made its prima facie case, by submitting its own evidence and arguments in support of its assertion that it had respected the requirements of the Safeguards Agreement at the time of its determination.[43] The *Dairy* Panel then concluded that "[a]t the end of this process, it is for the Panel to weigh and assess the evidence and arguments submitted by both parties in order to reach conclusions on whether the EC claims are well-founded.[44]

64. As will be discussed below, in many instances the EC fails to offer legally sufficient evidence and arguments to establish its *prima facie* case. To the extent that the EC offers any claims that are both legally germane and accompanied by sufficient argumentation, the United States has satisfied its own burden to rebut those claims. Accordingly, the United States respectfully requests the Panel to conclude, upon weighing the arguments and evidence presented by both parties, that the EC has failed to meet its burden to show that its claims of violations of the Safeguards Agreement are well-founded.

C. The EC Erroneously Asserts that "unforeseen developments" are a Precondition to the Application of a Safeguard Measure

65. The EC once again asserts that Article XIX:1(a) of GATT 1994 requires a Member, before applying a safeguard measure, to show that the increase in imports results from "unforeseen developments." In each of the two previous dispute settlement proceedings it has initiated to-date challenging safeguards measures - *Korea - Dairy* and *Argentina - Footwear* – the EC advanced similar arguments. In each case those arguments were rejected.

66. A brief review of the findings of both Panels on this question is instructive. After reflecting on this issue, the *Korea - Dairy* Panel concluded:

> 7.41 We recall that the purpose of Article XIX was (and still is) to allow an importing Member to deviate temporarily from its obligations under Articles II and XI of GATT (i.e. to suspend its concessions or other obligations) in situations of increased imports causing serious injury to the relevant domestic industry. We consider that the first paragraph of Article XIX provides only for that:

---

42 *Korea – Dairy, supra*, footnote 34, para. 7.24. As the Appellate Body has noted, a prima facie case is "one which, in the absence of effective refutation by the defending party, requires a panel, as a matter of law, to rule in favour of the complaining party presenting the prima facie case." *EC Measures Concerning Meat and Meat Products (Hormones)* ("*EC – Hormones*"), WT/DS26/AB/R, WT/DS48/AB/R, adopted 13 February 1998, DSR 1998:I, 135, para 104.

43 *Korea – Dairy, supra*, footnote 34, para. 7.24.

44 *Korea – Dairy, supra*, footnote 34, para. 7.24.

> an importing Member is "free", in situations where "any product is being imported into the territory of that Member in such increased quantities and under such conditions as to cause or threaten serious injury to domestic producers in that territory of like or directly competitive products" to deviate temporarily from Articles II and XI of GATT.
>
> 7.42 We consider that the prior section of the sentence, "If, as a result of unforeseen developments and of the effect of the obligations incurred by a contracting party under this Agreement, including tariff concessions..." does not add conditions for any measure to be applied pursuant to Article XIX but rather serves as an explanation of why an Article XIX measure may be needed, taking into account the fact that at the time (1947) the CONTRACTING PARTIES had just agreed (for the first time) on multilateral tariff bindings and on a general prohibition against quotas.
>
> 7.43 For us, the ordinary meaning of the terms "as a result of unforeseen developments and of the effect of the obligations incurred by a contracting party under this Agreement" leads us to conclude that this proposition only describes generally the situations where the binding nature of the obligations contained in Articles II and XI of GATT may need to be set aside (for a certain period). ...

67. The *Argentina – Footwear* Panel was equally unpersuaded by the EC's argument, finding:

> 8.58 Given the reasoning developed by the panel and the Appellate Body in the *Brazil - Desiccated Coconut* case, it is our view that Article XIX of GATT and the Safeguards Agreement must *a fortiori* be read as representing an *inseparable package* of rights and disciplines which have to be considered in conjunction. Therefore, we conclude that Article XIX of GATT cannot be understood to represent the total rights and obligations of WTO Members, but that rather the Safeguards Agreement as applying the disciplines of Article XIX of GATT, reflects the latest statement of WTO Members concerning their rights and obligations concerning safeguards. Thus the Safeguards Agreement should be understood as *defining, clarifying, and in some cases modifying* the whole package of rights and obligations of Members with respect to safeguard measures as they currently exist. By the same token, and in the light of the principle of effective treaty interpretation, the *express omission* of the criterion of unforeseen developments in the new agreement (which otherwise transposes, reflects and refines in great detail the essential conditions for the imposition of safeguard measures provided for in Article XIX of GATT) must, in our view, have meaning.

68. The United States respectfully requests this Panel similarly to conclude that "unforeseen developments" is not a condition that a Member must satisfy before imposing a safeguard measure.

D. The EC's Claims under the Agreement on Safeguards

69. The EC asserts the USITC investigation and published report violate Articles 2 and 4 of the Safeguards Agreement. As demonstrated below, the EC's claims are without merit. The USITC conducted its investigation in conformity with the requirements of Article 4. Thus, the USITC evaluated the relevant factors having a bearing on the situation of the domestic industry, including those factors enumerated in the Safeguards Agreement and certain factors not expressly enumerated therein.

1. Contrary to the EC's Claims, the USITC Report Satisfies the Requirements of Articles 2.1 and 4

70. The arguments advanced by the EC in support of its claims under Articles 2.1 and 4 of the Safeguards Agreement demonstrate a fundamental misapplication of the standard of review in this case and misrepresents the USITC report in critical areas. Further, the EC's factor-by-factor review of the evidence largely obscures, even when it purports to address, the USITC's actual reasoning on injury and causation. The USITC's determination was based on the whole record, including an examination of all relevant factors. The EC fails to address the overall basis for the USITC's determination; instead, the EC isolates individual factors and examines them without reference to the other factors. The EC's arguments concerning individual factors do not address the basis for the USITC's determination and hence do not provide grounds for challenging that determination under the Safeguards Agreement. In particular, the EC's approach of picking and choosing pieces of evidence which it argues support a contrary conclusion does not satisfy its burden to show that the USITC was unreasonable in reaching the conclusion that it did.

71. The EC's factor-by-factor approach suggests implicitly that each factor must equally support a finding of serious injury and causation. As the *Korea - Dairy* Panel noted, however, "[t]he relative importance of particular factors including those listed ... is for each Member to assess in the light of the circumstances of each case.'[45] Thus, the Panel recognized that "the importing Member may decide ... that some of these factors carry more or less weight."[46]

---

[45] *Korea – Dairy, supra*, footnote 34, para. 7.59, quoting *US - Woollen Shirts and Blouses*, para. 7.52.

[46] *Korea – Dairy, supra*, footnote 34, para. 7.56, quoting US - Woollen Shirts and Blouses, para. 7.26.

72. Moreover, many of the EC's arguments assume that there is only one appropriate method for addressing the factors relevant to injury and causation. As prior panels have recognized, this assumption is contrary both to the appropriate standard of review and to the text of Article 4. In fact, the *Korea - Dairy* Panel explicitly found that an importing member "remains free to choose an appropriate method of assessing whether the state of its domestic industry was caused by imports ... or by other factors, but it must be in a position to demonstrate that it did address the relevant issues."[47] The United States is in a position to demonstrate that it did indeed address the relevant factors. In keeping with the requirements of Article 4.2(a), the USITC evaluated all of the factors specifically enumerated therein. The USITC also evaluated the additional factors brought to its attention by the parties before it, encompassing factors now cited by the EC.[48]

73. The EC does not argue that the USITC's findings, as such, would not support a conclusion that, as a result of the increased imports, the domestic industry suffered "serious injury" as defined in Article 4.1(a) of the Agreement - i.e., "a significant overall impairment in the position of a domestic industry." Instead, the EC argues that the competent authority should have found the facts differently. The EC's arguments fail to establish a *prima facie* case of violation of the Safeguards Agreement, and they ignore the applicable standard of review. Accordingly, the United States respectfully submits the Panel should reject the EC's claims under Articles 2 and 4 of the Safeguards Agreement.

74. In keeping with the applicable standard of review, the United States sets out below the USITC's findings and conclusions – as detailed in the USITC report – with respect to the factors set out in Article 4.2(a), and other relevant factors not enumerated therein.

(i) Factors Enumerated in the Safeguards Agreement

75. Article 4.2(a) requires competent authorities in the conduct of safeguards investigations to evaluate "all relevant factors of an objective and quantifiable nature having a bearing on the situation of that industry." In particular, Article 4.2(a) enumerates the following factors: (1) the rate and amount of the increase in imports of the product concerned in absolute and relative terms, (2) the share of the domestic market taken by increased imports, (3) changes in the level of sales, (4) production, (5) productivity, (6) capacity utilization, (7) profits and losses, and (8) employment.

---

[47] *Korea – Dairy, supra*, footnote 34, para. 7.31. See also id. at para. 7.59, quoting US - Woollen Shirts and Blouses at ¶ 7.52. The Argentina - Footwear panel made the same observation particularly with respect to the factor of increased imports, noting, "In our view, each situation is different, and the Agreement certainly does not identify a unique pattern of importation that satisfies the 'increased imports' requirement." *Argentina – Footwear, supra*, footnote 34, para. 8.165.

[48] See US Exhibit 4 at I-10 to I-18.

76. The USITC evaluated all of these factors and more, and the EC does not allege otherwise. Rather, the EC takes exception to the weight the USITC gave to each factor and the conclusions the USITC drew from the available evidence. As previously noted, however, the relative weight accorded each factor is within the discretion of the competent authorities so long as it reaches a reasoned conclusion. Moreover, to argue that a particular factor does not by itself support a serious injury finding does not refute the overall finding. In fact, in its report the USITC noted that "virtually all", but not *all*, factors were negative.[49] Thus, the EC has failed to meet its burden to show that the USITC determination is unreasonable under the circumstances.

Increased Imports

77. The USITC concluded that the criterion of increased imports was satisfied based on the absolute increase in imports from 128 million pounds in 1993 to 177 million pounds in 1997, as well as the relative increase compared to domestic production - the ratio of imports to production increased from 100.6 per cent in 1993 to 145.4 per cent in 1997.[50] In addition to these comparisons, the USITC also analyzed the trends in imports, noting that virtually all of the increase in imports occurred in the last two years of the period, during which imports increased from 128 million pounds in 1995 to 156 million pounds in 1996 to 177 million pounds in 1997.[51] During the investigation the EU producers conceded that imports had increased.[52] Thus, the USITC's conclusion was not only well-founded, it was undisputed.

78. Nor is that conclusion disputed here; indeed, the EC acknowledges that imports increased by 38 per cent during the 1993-1997 period. The EC's point of contention lies in its claim that US demand also increased by 18 per cent and that import market shares "only" went up by 9 percentage points during the period. The EC argues that the USITC was wrong in allegedly downplaying these two other trends.[53] Nowhere does the EC explain, however, why the USITC was required to give precedence to these trends. Nor does the EC address why, even if the USITC did, these trends do not themselves demonstrate that imports increased over the period in question.

79. In particular, the EC advances no reason why a rise in imports relative to consumption should be given greater weight than the absolute rise in imports and their rise relative to production. Article 2.1 requires a finding that the product under consideration is being imported in "increased quantities, absolute or relative to production." Article 4.2(a) lists both "the rate and amount of the increase in imports of the product concerned in absolute and relative terms" and "the share

---

49 US Exhibit 4 at I-12.

50 US Exhibit 4 at I-10.

51 US Exhibit 4 at I-10.

52 US Exhibit 4 at I-10; see also Transcript of hearing before the USITC on 16 December 1997. US Exhibit 8.

53 EC First Submission at ¶ 60.

of the domestic market taken by increased imports" as relevant factors. It does not specify that either factor is to be given greater weight. The EC advances no basis in the Agreement for concluding that the dramatic 38 per cent increase in imports on the US industry must be regarded as negated by the much smaller 18 per cent increase in US demand.

80. Moreover, contrary to the EC's contentions, the USITC did not downplay the trends in demand and in relative market shares, but rather considered them at length in its determination.[54] As the USITC concluded, the increase in the share of US consumption taken by imports from 50.1 per cent in 1995 to 60.2 per cent in 1997 was a sharp increase.[55] Again, the EC advances no reason why this finding would not support the determination that the USITC reached.

81. Instead, the EC presents a different analysis of the evidence that simply fails to address the USITC's findings concerning the critical change in the market in 1996 and 1997 and that employs a methodology that the EC itself rejects. The EC's submission contends that since import market shares were approximately nine percentage points higher at the end of the five year period than at the beginning, it is appropriate to divide that figure by five, from which the EC derives the conclusion that imports increased by less than 2 per cent per year.[56] This calculation is misleading, since, as the USITC found, the increase in import market shares took place in the last two years of the period. Moreover, this analysis is based on a comparison of indicators at the beginning of the five year period (1993) with those at the end of the period (1997) despite the fact that in its submission the EC criticizes reliance on end-point comparisons.[57] The *Argentina - Footwear* Panel raised similar questions concerning such a methodology.[58] In short, the EC' s proposed alternative analysis is contrary to its own arguments and certainly is not required by the Agreement.

82. In connection with its claim that imports did not increase (or at least not as much as the USITC found), the EC also asserts that the United States breached its obligations under Article XIX of GATT and Article 2 of the Safeguards Agreement in that the United States allegedly violated "the principle of parallelism" recognized by the *Argentina - Footwear* Panel.[59] In support of its claim, the EC cites to what it deems to be relevant language in the *Footwear* Panel's discussion of a customs union's application of a safeguard measure. The EC provides no arguments as to why the cited language would be relevant in this case, stating

---

[54] US Exhibit 4 at I-16, I-22 to I-23.

[55] US Exhibit 4 at I-16.

[56] EC First Submission at ¶ 60. Even taken at face value, the EC's calculations are wrong. Given five years of data, there can only be four increases from a previous year, and so such an annualized average would be divided by four rather than five.

[57] EC First Submission at ¶ 55.

[58] The Panel noted that "an end-point- to-end-point comparison, without consideration of intervening trends, is very unlikely to provide a full evaluation of all relevant factors as required." *Argentina – Footwear*, *supra*, footnote 34, para. 8.217.

[59] EC First Submission at ¶ 55.

only that "[e]ven if NAFTA is not a customs union, the EC does not see any reason why this specific principle should not apply equally to free-trade areas..[60]

83. The United States submits the fact that the EC "does not see any reason" cannot constitute the "evidence and arguments" the *Korea - Dairy* Panel recognized as essential for a complaining party to offer in order to meet its burden of proof. The EC's statement is nothing more than a mere assertion, and as the Appellate Body stated in US - *Woven Wool Shirts*, "we find it difficult, indeed, to see how any system of judicial settlement could work if it incorporated the proposition that the mere assertion of a claim might amount to proof."[61] Indeed, the inadequacy of the EC's statement is highlighted by the fact that the *Footwear* Panel, in response to arguments raised by Argentina on NAFTA and the US wheat gluten safeguard in particular, recognized "that MERCOSUR is a customs union, whereas NAFTA is a free-trade agreement, ... "[62] Moreover, the Panel went on to state its view that the provisions of Article 2.1 on which it relied concerned exclusively *customs unions*.

84. Despite the fact that the language cited by the EC is ambiguous as to whether it applies in this case, the United States' nonetheless submits that its actions are consistent with the Safeguards Agreement. While the United States conducted a global investigation and examined imports from all sources, its determination did not attribute injury from NAFTA imports to third countries. The circumstances examined by the *Footwear* Panel were wholly different. In that case, Argentina examined imports from all sources, including from Brazil. Argentina concluded that all of those imports were causing serious injury, but it then fashioned a remedy that excluded Brazilian imports.

85. The United States' investigation simply cannot be compared to Argentina's. In the words of the EC, "the US wheat gluten case is radically different to [Argentina's]."[63] The USITC"s finding make clear that, unlike in *Argentina - Footwear*, the injury determination was not based on effects ascribable to Canadian imports. The USITC found that imports from Canada did not contribute importantly to the serious injury caused by imports because Canadian imports declined significantly during the period of investigation, while overall imports increased.[64] The USITC further found that the 1996-1997 import surge was largely caused by the massive increase in EU wheat gluten capacity.[65] Moreover, the USITC also found that Canadian imports generally oversold the US market

[60] EC First Submission at ¶ 55.
[61] *US - Woven Wool Shirts*, *supra*, footnote 40, at 333-338.
[62] *Argentina – Footwear*, *supra*, footnote 34, para. 8.100.
[63] *Argentina – Footwear*, *supra*, footnote 34, para. 5.123.
[64] US Exhibit 4 at I-19.
[65] US Exhibit 4 at I-22, I-29

during this period.[66] By contrast, in *Argentina - Footwear*, there were no such finding or determination as to the imports from Mercosur.[67]

86. The USITC's methodology in examining NAFTA imports is consistent with the Safeguards Agreement. Indeed, the EC itself provides the rationale for the methodology employed; In its submission to the *Argentina - Footwear* Panel, the EC expressed its view that an importing Member could – and indeed *should* – investigate all imports into its territory in order to "put together a complete file."[68] The EC then specifically noted that "the United States made *separate* determinations concerning imports from NAFTA members and concluded that imports from that source and, in particular, Canada did not cause injury. If Argentina had applied the same procedure as the United States in the wheat gluten case, then Argentina would not have been able to come to the conclusion it did..[69] The United States agrees with the EC on both counts.

87. Accordingly, the United States respectfully submits that the EC's claim with respect to increased imports is unfounded.

Sales

88. The USITC report shows that the USITC examined the evidence regarding changes in the level of US sales in determining that the domestic industry was seriously injured. The USITC report found that domestic industry shipments initially rose and then fell, and were at their lowest levels in 1996 and 1997.[70] The cited record data show that domestic producer shipments were 121.4 million pounds in 1993, 132.4 million pounds in 1994, 127.5 million pounds in 1995, but then declined to 108.7 million pounds in 1996, while increasing to 117.2 million pounds in 1997.[71]

89. Despite the data showing the lows in shipments in the last two years of the period, the EC nevertheless points to the fact that domestic shipments increased in 1997 from their 1996 levels, and argues that this shows the industry is not suffering serious injury.[72] However, as the USITC correctly observed, 1997 shipments, despite the slight improvement from 1996, were still lower than figures for any year, 1993-95, that preceded the import surge. This represented a fall of 8 per cent from the levels only two years earlier. The USITC recognized that industry performance in some factors improved in 1997 over the disastrous performance of 1996 but concluded that such improvements were isolated and did not change the conclusion that the industry was seriously injured.[73] The EC has advanced no reason why these findings may not under the Safeguards Agreement

[66] US Exhibit 4 at I-29.
[67] *Argentina – Footwear, supra*, footnote 34, para. 8.102.
[68] *Argentina – Footwear, supra*, footnote 34, para. 5.130.
[69] *Argentina – Footwear, supra*, footnote 34, para. 5.131.
[70] US Exhibit 4 at I-13.
[71] US Exhibit 4 at II-16, Table 6.
[72] EC First Submission at ¶ 61.
[73] US Exhibit 4 at I-14.

support an injury determination. As the USITC stated, it evaluates such recent data in a broader context, and an upturn in one factor in the most recent year does not by itself mean that serious injury does not exist.[74] The recent *Argentina - Footwear* panel decision reached an identical conclusion.[75]

90. In addition, the EC quotes a statement in the USITC Report showing that the domestic shipments quantity in the last quarter of the last year of the period (1997) was higher than the quantity in the first quarter of the first year of the period (1993) and argues that this refutes the serious injury finding.[76] This contention is contrary to the *Argentina - Footwear* panel decision in not one but two respects. First, the EC again relies on an end-point comparison while ignoring the intervening trends. Second, it again takes a recent upturn (involving only a single quarter, not even a year) out of context to argue that the upturn by itself disproves serious injury. Thus, the EC's contentions simply do not bear on the applicable standard of review.

Production

91. In its determination, the USITC found that domestic production had declined, and that this decline supported the finding of serious injury. The USITC found that production increased early in the period from 128 million pounds in 1993 to 143 million pounds in 1995, but then fell sharply to 112 million pounds in 1996, while increasing somewhat to 122 million pounds in 1997.[77]

92. Nevertheless, the EC now seeks to minimize these facts. It emphasizes that production fell in only one year (1996) and characterizes the decline as "a normal fluctuation," contending that the reason for this 1996 decline was that demand had been especially high in 1994 because of a weather-induced deficiency in protein content in wheat crops in 1993.[78] These contentions are not supported by the facts and ignore the USITC's determination. Certainly the USITC was reasonable in not regarding the production decline as a normal fluctuation; the EC provides no reason for concluding otherwise. As the USITC concluded, the decline in 1996 was a sharp decline of 21.4 per cent from 1995. Even after the modest increase in 1997, production was still 15 per cent below the peak in 1995, just before the import surge, and, as the USITC noted, 4.5 per cent below the previous lowest level in the five-year period.[79]

93. The EC's suggested explanation for the sharp 1996 decline also does not withstand scrutiny, ignoring as it does the USITC's findings on trends in demand. The EC claims that demand had been abnormally high in 1994 because of a wheat protein deficiency, so under this theory demand presumably would decline

74 US Exhibit 4 at I-12.
75 *Argentina – Footwear, supra*, footnote 34, para. 8.214.
76 EC First Submission at ¶ 61, quoting US Exhibit 4 at II-32.
77 US Exhibit 4 at I-12 to I-13.
78 EC First Submission at ¶ 62.
79 US Exhibit 4 at I-12 to I-13.

significantly after the deficiency problem went away, especially in 1996, thereby causing the sharp decline in production. However, US demand (as measured by total US apparent consumption) declined only slightly in 1995 (0.4 per cent), and then actually increased in 1996 and 1997 above the "especially high" 1994 levels.[80] Thus, the EC's explanation fails to explain anything.

94. The EC's purported explanation simply disregards that a major aspect of the USITC's analysis concerned why domestic production and other key indicators were declining (to their lowest levels) in 1996-1997 just as domestic demand was increasing (to its highest levels).[81] The industry was unable to increase production and take advantage of the increased demand in 1996-1997 during the period of greatest import penetration. The EC's arguments not only fail to account for the facts but also fail to put forward any basis for concluding that the USITC acted improperly in finding that the decline in production supported a determination of serious injury.

Productivity

95. The USITC examined data regarding worker productivity, found that it was at its highest level in 1994, and its lowest level in 1997, and concluded that this decline was attributable to the decline in capacity utilization, and was a negative factor supporting the serious injury finding.[82] While admitting that the USITC did evaluate worker productivity, the EC claims that the USITC erred in failing to take into account capital investment, and in failing to separately analyze the productivity of capital.[83] The EC does not suggest why an analysis of worker productivity does not satisfy the requirement of Article 4.2(a) to consider productivity.

96. In any event, the USITC did not fail to take into account capital investment. The USITC assembled and analyzed data regarding the capital investments in the industry, especially the capital projects adding production capacity.[84] The USITC analyzed the effect of these new capital projects on capacity utilization rates.[85] As noted, during the import surge, production declined sharply by 21.4 per cent in 1996, and while it increased somewhat in 1997, it was still 15 per cent below 1995 levels.

97. It is simple mathematics that if production declines (as it did in 1996-1997 from 1995 levels), while the amount of capital in the industry increases (as it did from the capital projects adding capacity), the productivity of capital will correspondingly decline. Thus, since the USITC did analyze worker productivity, and did also analyze the capital projects adding capacity and the effects of those capi-

80 US Exhibit 4 at II-25, Table 17.
81 US Exhibit 4 at I-16
82 US Exhibit 4 at I-14.
83 EC First Submission at ¶ 73.
84 US Exhibit 4 at II-21 and Table 12.
85 US Exhibit 4 at I-12.

tal projects on industry performance, the EC's complaint that the USITC did not do an explicit calculation of "capital productivity" and therefore did not adequately examine productivity, is without merit. In any event, since the productivity of capital demonstrably declined in 1996-1997, the EC's complaint is only that the USITC did not separately enumerate declining capital productivity as another negative factor supporting the serious injury finding, rather than that further analysis might have argued against the serious injury finding.

Capacity Utilization

98. The USITC found that capacity utilization fell significantly, from 78.3 per cent in 1993 to 42.0 per cent in 1996, then rose slightly to 44.5 per cent in 1997. The USITC further noted that some of the decline was attributable to an increase in capacity to produce wheat gluten in anticipation of an expected increase in demand. Most of this capacity increase was in place by June 1995, before imports increased.[86]

99. The EC argues that, given the increased production capacity, the decline in capacity utilization was almost entirely attributable to the capacity increase and was not connected with the import surge.[87] While this was obviously true for the period up to June 1995, as the USITC stated, it was, as the USITC also found, demonstrably not true for the crop years 1996 and 1997. The bulk of the decline in capacity utilization after 1995 was attributable to the decline in production associated with the import surge, not to the increase in capacity.

100. Capacity utilization dropped sharply in 1996, the first year of the import surge, from 56.2 per cent in 1995 to 42.0 per cent. While it improved slightly in 1997 to 44.5 per cent, utilization was still well below the 1995 level. As noted above, production also fell sharply in 1996, and while it increased somewhat in 1997, it was still 15 per cent below the pre-import 1995 levels. However, with the increase in production capacity largely but not entirely completed in 1995, the remaining increase in capacity was much smaller, only about 8 per cent from 1995 to 1997.[88] Thus, the decline in capacity utilization after 1995 is far more attributable to the 15 per cent decline in production (associated with the surge in imports) than it is to the modest 8 per cent increase in capacity. As the USITC concluded, the capacity utilization rate would have been much higher in 1996-1997 if there had been no surge in imports. The USITC found (notwithstanding the improvement from 1996) that capacity utilization in 1997 would likely have been at 61 per cent of capacity rather than at the 44.5 per cent that it turned out to be.[89] .The EC nowhere provides a basis for concluding that this

[86] US Exhibit 4 at I-12.

[87] EC First Submission at ¶¶ 63-64.

[88] US Exhibit 4 at C-4, Table C-1. Furthermore, the trend after 1995 in utilization rate corresponded precisely to the trend in production (sharp decline in 1996, modest increase in 1997, but still well below 1995 levels), but by contrast did not correspond at all to the trend in capacity (small increase in 1996, even smaller increase in 1997).

[89] US Exhibit 4 at I-12.

finding is not reasonable. Once again, the EC's arguments on this factor ignore the significant difference that the USITC found to exist between the 1996-97 time frame and earlier periods covered by the investigation.

101. The EC contends that "the US authorities fail to explain why an industry allegedly suffering 'serious injury' would be increasing its production capacities when it is already operating at substantially less than full capacity."[90] These criticisms do not detract from or even address the USITC's specific findings. First, as the USITC found, industry demand projections turned out to be largely correct, as the US demand did increase significantly in 1996-1997, but that demand was satisfied by imports, which domestic producers did not anticipate.[91] Second, as the USITC stated and the EC admits, the vast bulk of the increased capacity was added by June 1995, before the import surge, and thus before the industry was suffering from serious injury.[92] The EC fails to show why reliance on the fall in capacity utilization in 1996 and 1997 was unreasonable.

Profits and Losses

102. The USITC found that the industry operated at a profit during 1993-1995, and then operated at a loss in 1996 and 1997 during the period in which the surge in imports occurred. The EC does not contend that these findings may not support an injury determination. Rather, it faults the USITC's collection of information on this issue, once again, however, without alleging any basis for finding that the USITC's investigation or determination are in violation of the Agreement.

103. The USITC received usable financial data from three of the four domestic producers of wheat gluten. As the USITC explained in a footnote on page I-13 of its report, the fourth firm, ADM, provided only combined data on its US and Canadian wheat gluten and wheat starch operations. The USITC noted that the three firms that provided data accounted for a substantial majority of domestic production of wheat gluten. The USITC found that each of the firms produced wheat gluten and wheat starch in a joint production process, as well as other by-products or related products. The USITC stated that it carefully considered respondents' arguments about how the domestic industry allocated financial data, and based on a careful review of the allocation methodologies found the allocations to be appropriate.

104. The USITC also found that profitability reflected the trend in average unit value prices, which likewise initially rose and then fell. Average unit values, like profitability, peaked in 1994 and then declined and were at their lowest level in 1997.[93] Since all producers, including ADM, provided unit value data, the parallelism between unit value and profitability data tends to confirm that the profit-

---

90 EC First Submission at ¶ 64.

91 US Exhibit 4 at I-17.

92 US Exhibit 4 at I-12; EC First Submission at ¶ 63

93 US Exhibit 4 at I-13.

ability information that the USITC received was representative of the experience of all producers.

105. In paragraphs 65-67, the EC complains that the USITC had full period data from only two domestic producers, since one entered the market in 1996 and ADM was unable to provide separate data. The EC does not explain, however, how such information limitations might render the USITC's determination in violation of the Safeguards Agreement. Certainly the fact that the USITC did not obtain information from one producer for a period before it became a producer points to no inadequacy in the USITC's investigation. Likewise, the EC cannot claim that the USITC erred in not including in its profitability figures for the United States industry information from one producer that also included profitability information on its Canadian operations. The Agreement does not assume that an investigation will obtain perfect data coverage, since Article 4.1(c) provides specifically that a "domestic industry" may be understood to consist of "those whose collective output of the like or directly competitive products constitutes *a major proportion* of the total domestic production of those products." (Emphasis added). The Safeguards Agreement does *not* require 100 per cent data coverage. Even if the USITC had been able to obtain information on all factors from only two out of the three producers for part of the period and three out of the four producers for the latter two years, its data coverage would have satisfied the requirements of the Agreement. Here, however, it received usable data from all producers except with respect to a particular factor; i.e., profitability. Particularly where other information confirms the representativeness of that information for the industry as a whole, no basis exists for finding the USITC determination in violation of the Agreement.

106. The EC's complaint that the USITC report is inadequately explained, because the USITC did not reveal the particular means that producers used to allocate financial data between wheat gluten and related production, is based on its apparent misunderstanding of this Panel's role. As discussed above, past panels have recognized that it is not a panel's function to verify each piece of information used by a competent authority. Likewise, an authority's determination cannot be found to be in violation of the Agreement because it does not disclose information that is by its nature confidential. Here the EC does not dispute that the cost allocation methodology used by each producer constituted sensitive business confidential information. The USITC's report shows that it took careful precautions to assure the accuracy and probative worth of the information provided.

107. As the USITC made clear in its report, it did not leave the allocation of financial data solely in the hands of domestic wheat gluten producers. The USITC requested domestic producers that do not maintain separate records for wheat gluten to explain their allocation methodology and provide worksheets with their calculations. Respondents in the investigation had access to the questionnaire responses of domestic wheat gluten producers, including their allocation methodologies, under protective order, and had an opportunity to bring to the USITC's attention any concerns about their allocation methodologies. The USITC specifically addressed the allocation issue in its report. It noted the argu-

ments made by respondents about allocations made by domestic producers in providing financial data on their wheat gluten operations, stated that it had carefully reviewed the allocation methodologies, and made a judgment that the allocations were appropriate.[94] The EC provides no argument that the Agreement requires more.

Employment

108. As required by Article 4.2(a), the USITC reviewed the data related to employment in the industry, noting that there had been some recent layoffs and there was underemployment in the industry (average number of hours worked per worker declined), but the overall number of employees and hours worked increased. The USITC also noted that the industry was capital-intensive and employed very few production workers. Ultimately, when summarizing the principal factors supporting the finding of serious injury, the USITC did not not place affirmative reliance on the employment data.[95]

109. The EC's argument that the evidence on employment does not support a serious injury finding completely ignores the fact that the USITC did not cite employment in the list of factors in support of that finding. The EC does not contend that without relying on this factor the USITC could not have properly reached an injury finding. Indeed, the EC itself appears to agree that labour should be regarded as a relatively minor factor in this capital-intensive industry.[96] In any event, the mixed picture provided by the data regarding employment (which included layoffs and underemployment) certainly could not be characterized as favorable, and does not refute the serious injury finding.

(ii) Factors not Enumerated in the Safeguards Agreement

110. In addition to the factors specifically enumerated in Article 4.2(a), the EC also raised objections concerning factors not enumerated in Article 4.2(a), specifically concerning wages, inventories, new entries/expansion, and price. The EC's arguments concerning both the authority's findings as to these factors, and the weight that should be accorded those factors, do not detract from the USITC's determination.

Wages

111. The USITC reviewed data regarding wages, and without characterizing wages as a positive or negative factor, stated in finding serious injury that "hourly wages had been relatively flat."[97]9

---

94 US Exhibit 4 at I-13.

95 US Exhibit 4 at I-13 to I-14.

96 EC First Submission at ¶ 73.

97 US Exhibit 4 at I-14.

112. The EC contends that the evidence regarding wages shows that there was no connection between imports and wages, and that there was no serious injury at all. Once again, the EC has misread the USITC's report. The USITC determination did not cite any connection between wages and imports. Furthermore, the EC incorrectly states that hourly wages increased three times during the period, when the USITC report shows only two increases (from 1993 to 1994, and from 1996 to 1997), as well as declines from 1994 to 1996.[98] In making its finding, the USITC properly considered the evidence regarding wages, and characterized them as relatively flat. The EC's arguments are not contrary and in any event cannot transform this evidence into a refutation of serious injury.

Inventories

113. In finding serious injury, the USITC examined the level of inventories, stating that they more than doubled during the period, and that the ratio of inventories to domestic shipments likewise doubled.[99] The EC contends that inventories do not support a serious injury finding, because, it claims, the entire increase took place in 1995 before the import surge, and inventories declined in 1996-1997 from the 1995 level.[100]

114. However, a review of the inventory data shows that, while inventories were at their highest level in 1995, inventories and the ratio of inventories to shipments were considerably higher during the import surge in 1996-1997 than they were at the beginning of the period. Inventories were 4.5 million pounds in 1993, 7.1 million pounds in 1994, 13.9 million pounds in 1995, 11.5 million pounds in 1996 and 9.1 million pounds in 1997.[101] Thus, despite the reduction in inventories in 1997, they were still twice as much as they had been in 1993 at the beginning of the period. Similarly, the ratio of inventories to shipments was 3.7 per cent in 1993; 5.4 per cent in 1994; 10.9 per cent in 1995; 10.6 per cent in 1996; and 7.8 per cent in 1997. Once again the ratio was over twice as great as it had been in 1993. Thus, the USITC was correct in noting that end of period inventories had more than doubled. While the initial rise in inventories occurred in 1995, and inventories declined in 1996 and 1997, inventories in those last two years were still at much higher levels than at the beginning of the period. Any review of the state of the industry as of 1996-1997 would have to characterize the abnormally high level of inventories (particularly in relation to shipments) as a negative factor, and the USITC properly did so in finding serious injury. In any event, inventory levels are dependent on the relationship between production and shipments, both of which declined during the period. The USITC properly gave more weight to these factors than to inventories.[102]

---

[98] EC First Submission at ¶ 70; US Exhibit 4 at II-17.

[99] USITC Report I-13.

[100] EC Submission at ¶ 71.

[101] US Exhibit 4 at II-16, Table 7

[102] The USITC did not specifically cite inventories as a factor supporting its causation determination. US Exhibit 4 at I-16.

New Entries/Expansion

115. The EC claims that the facts that there was a new entrant into the market and that there were plant expansions during the period show that there was no serious injury.[103] As a legal matter, the EC does not suggest why this fact should be persuasive, much less dispositive. On the evidence, the EC leaves out key facts. Although it emphasizes that Heartland entered the market in 1996, urging that it would be "incomprehensible" to enter the market at a time the industry was being seriously injured, the EC omits that construction of the plant began in 1993, long before the import surge and serious injury.[104] Similarly, the EC stresses upgrades of Midwest's Atchison plant in 1996 and 1997, but omits to mention that this was part of a staged series of upgrades that began in 1992, and continued in 1994 and 1995, before the import surge.[105] Thus, the EC's position relies on selective use of evidence while ignoring evidence to the contrary. Furthermore, the USITC did fully investigate and analyze the facts regarding industry entry, expansion and modernization. As it found, many of these projects were designed to enable the domestic producers to increase efficiency and lower their costs so they could compete with imports.[106] The EC does not dispute these findings.[107]

Price

116. Notwithstanding the USITC's lengthy and detailed causation analysis, the EC, in paragraph 82 of its submission, asserts that the USITC did not fulfill its obligation to publish a detailed analysis of the case or a demonstration of the relevance of the factors examined. It then goes on to suggest, in paragraph 82, that pricing is the only relevant condition to evaluate and to assert that the USITC's finding on EU pricing was inconsistent with the evidence in the USITC's record.

117. The EC is wrong on both counts. As discussed above, the obligation to provide a detailed analysis of the case entails that a competent authority provide a reasonable explanation of the conclusions reached. It does not entail, as the EC appears to contend, that the authority provide in advance a pointed response to every argument that a member might make in a WTO panel proceeding following a determination.

118. Nor does the Agreement fairly lend itself to giving pricing analysis the dispositive position that the EC would give it. The Agreement in fact nowhere mentions price. Although Article 4.2(a) lists numerous "relevant factors of an

---

[103] EC First Submission at ¶¶ 74-75.

[104] US Exhibit 4 at II-8.

[105] US Exhibit 4 at II-6. The EC also fails to mention that an ADM plant opened and then closed during the period. US Exhibit 4 at II-8.

[106] US Exhibit 4 at I-24 to I-25.

[107] The other factors that the EC discusses concerning the injury finding and alleges were inadequately investigated - co-products and imports by domestic producers - will be addressed in the following section concerning causation factors.

objective and quantifiable nature having a bearing on the situation of [the domestic industry]," price does not appear in that enumeration. The EC does not explain why the phrase "under such conditions" in Article 2.1 should be regarded as referring to price at all, much less why it would give to price a relevance greater than the enumerated factors in Article 4.2(a). As has been shown above, the USITC reasonably found the factors listed in Article 4.2(a) to support its conclusion here.

119. As the panel in *Korea–Dairy* made clear, pricing is not the only factor to be considered in this analysis–

> Although the prices of the imported products will most often be a relevant factor indicating how the imports do, in fact, cause serious injury to the domestic industry, we note that there is no explicit requirement in Article 2 that the importing Member perform a price analysis of the imported products and the prices of the like or directly competitive products in the market of the importing country. [Footnote omitted.][108]

120. To the extent that the EC is inferring that the phrase "under such conditions" in Article 2 of the Agreement indicates an additional criterion or analytical requirement, the *Korea-Dairy* panel reached the opposite conclusion:

> We consider that the phrase "and under such conditions" does not provide for an additional criterion or analytical requirement to be performed before an importing Member may impose a safeguard measure.[109]

121. At any rate, the USITC fully considered the evidence on price in this case and found that it supported an affirmative finding. The EC's arguments to the contrary simply misconstrue the authority's report. In noting the relationship between increasing imports and declining EU wheat gluten prices, the USITC stated as follows–

> The ratio of imports to consumption then increased sharply to 58.9 per cent in 1996 and 60.2 per cent in 1997. The record reflects that most of this increase consisted of imports from the EU. The record also shows that imports from the EU *consistently* undersold domestic wheat gluten. This surge in relatively low-priced imports in 1996 and 1997 coincided with the decline in industry performance. [Emphasis added, footnotes omitted.][110]

122. As is made clear by the sentences that precede the sentence containing the phrase "consistently undersold," the phrase refers to underselling during 1996 and 1997 when the surge in imports occurred and industry performance was declining. In fact, in that period, EC imports undersold US wheat gluten in every

108 *Korea – Dairy*, *supra*, footnote 34, para. 7.51.
109 *Korea – Dairy*, *supra*, footnote 34, para. 7.52.
110 US Exhibit 4 at I-16.

quarter during that period by margins of 3.4 per cent to 16.7 per cent, except for one quarter when there was no margin of difference.[111]

123. The evidence in the USITC record that the EC cites as contradicting the USITC finding in fact supports the USITC's conclusion. All six of the quarters in which the EU wheat gluten *oversold* the US product occurred during 1993, 1994, and 1995, *before* the surge in EU imports.[112] Thus, the shift to a consistent pattern of underselling coincided with the surge in EU and total imports.

124. As the USITC also found, profitability reflected the trend in average unit value prices, which initially rose and then fell, reaching their lowest levels in 1997.[113] The EC argument in paragraph 83 that increased imports cannot be the cause of the decline in domestic unit sales values because the value of shipments fell in 1995, before the surge in imports, ignores other forces that the USITC recognized were at work in the market place before 1996. Consumption fell in 1995. However, when consumption rose in 1996 and then again in 1997, the patterns existing in 1993 through 1995 would suggest that unit prices would have risen. Instead, they fell in the face of increases in imports of 22 per cent in 1996 and 13.5 per cent in 1997. The evidence is entirely consistent with the USITC's findings concerning the effects of increased imports.

(iii) Other Asserted Causal Factors

125. Article 4.2(b) requires that a Member not attribute to increased imports injury caused by other factors. This is not a case in which it can reasonably be said that the competent authority did not address the issue of other causes of injury. The USITC examined factors other than imports that may be a cause of serious injury or the threat thereof to the domestic industry and included such findings in its report. The USITC examined explicitly each other possible cause of injury advanced by the parties before it. In each case, the USITC found that the asserted cause did not have the effect on the industry suggested (*e.g.*, co-production, corn starch competition with wheat starch, importation by domestic producers, rising prices for inputs) or had only a demonstrably minor role in the serious injury suffered by the industry (increased capacity).[114] Again, the EC seeks simply to have this Panel re-find the facts as to each of these factors. To the extent that the EC asserts that "the evaluation of other factors in the USITC report did not meet the standard required[115], the EC fails to make any argument

[111] Revised USITC Report at II-33. US Exhibit 10 at II-33. The quarterly pricing data also support the USITC finding in another important respect. For the 5-year period examined, the data show that on an annual basis, EU prices were at their lowest levels in 1996 and 1997, when the surge in EU imports and total imports occurred. *Ibid.*

[112] US Exhibit 10 at II-33.

[113] US Exhibit 4 at I-13.

[114] US Exhibit 4 at I-16-18.

[115] EC First Submission at ¶ 84.

grounded in the text of the Agreement or prior panel or Appellate Body decisions that a particular standard is required.[116]

126. As the very title of this section of the EC's submission shows, its discussion of these factors asks the Panel improperly to re-weigh the evidence. The EC asserts that the USITC gave "insufficient weight" to certain factors that the EC deems important. As other Panels have found, however, it is for the competent authority to decide what weight to give particular factors.[117] The USITC specifically examined each of the other causal factors that the EC now asserts should have led the authority to a different conclusion. The USITC's findings make clear why it did not reach the conclusion that the EC urges.

127. Before addressing further the EC's allegations concerning these specific factors, it is important to consider the EC's arguments that the USITC failed to articulate and apply the correct causation standard. The USITC found that no other factor that might be adversely affecting the wheat gluten industry was more important than the rapid increase in imports. As its findings showed, no factor other than the surge of imports could explain the decline in the performance of the industry as a whole in 1996 and 1997.[118] To the extent that one other factor - namely, additions to US capacity - contributed to the decline in capacity utilization in that period, the USITC demonstrated why it was a less important factor than imports. Indeed, the USITC specifically identified the relative contributions to injury of capacity utilization and import.[119]

128. The EC nevertheless faults the USITC for not articulating a causation standard and for not "deducting" the degree of harm caused by non-import factors to determine the precise amount of injury attributable to increased imports alone. Both objections are without merit. The causation standard relevant to WTO review of an injury determination is set forth in Article 4.2 (b), which re-

---

[116] Cf., e.g., Panel Report *United States – Measure Affecting Imports of Woven Wool Shirts and Blouses from India* (*"US – Woven Wool Shirts"*) WT/DS33/R, adopted 23 may 1997, DSR 1997:I, 343, para. 7.50 (where agreement does not specify method for considering other causal factors, member remains free to choose method of assessment).

[117] *Korea – Dairy, supra*, footnote 34, para. 7.30.

[118] US Exhibit 4 at I-16-18.

[119] As reflected in the USITC Report, the USITC conducted this analysis under provisions of US law that provide that USITC must find not merely the causal link to the serious injury, but also that imports must be a "substantial cause." 19 USC. § 2252(b)(1)(A). It defines "substantial cause" as "a cause which is important and not less than any other cause." 19 U.S.C. § 2252(b)(1)(B). The EC makes some statements regarding US law, but the EC did not challenge US law thus such claims are not within the Panel's terms of reference. See EC First Submission at ¶ 128. The only matter with respect to Articles 2 and 4 that has been referred to this Panel is whether the USITC's findings and conclusions comport with the cited articles. See Appellate Body Report, *Guatemala - Anti-Dumping Investigation Regarding Portland Cement from Mexico*(*"Guatemala – Cement I"*), WT/DS60/AB/R, adopted 25 November 1998, DSR 1998:IX, 3767, para. 73 ("the 'measure' and the 'claims' concerning that measure constitute the 'matter referred to the DSB' which forms the basis for a panel's terms of reference."). The United States' statutory provisions requiring the finding that imports are a "substantial cause" completely satisfy the standard in Article 4.2(c) that the "causal link" to serious injury.

quires that the "investigation demonstrate[], on the basis of objective evidence, the existence of the causal link between increased imports of the product concerned and serious injury or threat thereof." Under Article 3.2, the authority's report must set forth "reasoned conclusions reached on all pertinent issues of fact and law." The USITC determination clearly articulates its reasons for finding "the causal link" between the increased imports and serious injury. Nothing in those provisions requires that an authority articulate a further "causation standard." Indeed, nothing in the Safeguards Agreement requires the competent authority to articulate the causation standard at all; Article 4.2(b) requires merely that it be applied.

129. The EC's further objection - that the USITC should have "deducted the injury caused by other factors"[120] in order to determine the precise extent of injury caused by imports - likewise has no support in the Safeguards Agreement. Article 4.2(b) sets forth the relevant obligation with respect to other causes of injury: "When other factors than increased imports are causing injury to the domestic industry at the same time, such injury shall not be attributed to increased imports." As has been discussed, the USITC's determination more than satisfied this requirement. Not only did it not attribute to increased imports the effects of other factors, it specifically addressed each asserted alternative cause, finding that some were not injuring the domestic industry "at the same time" and specifying why others could not be regarded as more than relatively minor causes of injury.[121]

130. The history and context of Article 4.2(b) demonstrate why the EC's proposal that the USITC must somehow quantify and deduct from total injury the specific effects caused by other factors is not required. The terms used in Article 4.2(b) originate in Article 3:4 of the Agreement on Implementation of Article VI of the General Agreement on Tariffs and Trade (also known as the Tokyo Round Anti-Dumping Code.) Article 3:4 of the Tokyo Round Code stated, "There may be other factors which at the same time are injuring the domestic industry, and the injuries caused by other factors must not be attributed to the dumped imports." Before the adoption of Article 4.2(b), the quoted language from Article 3:4 had been interpreted in *US - Salmon*. In that case, the Panel flatly rejected the very argument that the EC makes here, stating that the requirement "not to attribute injuries caused by other factors to the imports ... did not mean that, in addition to examining the effects of imports under Article 3:1, 3:2 and 3:3, the USITC should somehow have identified the extent of injury caused by these other factors in order to isolate the injury caused by these factors from the injury caused by the imports from Norway."[122] Had the negotiators of the Safeguards

---

[120] EC First Submission at ¶ 104.

[121] See US Exhibit 4 at I-16-17.

[122] United States - Imposition of Anti-Dumping Duties on Imports of Fresh and Chilled Atlantic Salmon from Norway, ADP/87, BISD 41s/229 ¶ 555, adopted by the Committee on Anti-dumping Practices on 27 April 1994.

Agreement intended to impose the requirement that the EC now suggests, they would not have chosen to copy language that had been interpreted as not imposing that requirement.

131. Indeed, the *United States - Salmon* panel considered that the sentence of the Antidumping Code on which the relevant provision of the Safeguards Agreement is modeled "did not contain an express general requirement to consider all possible factors other than the imports under investigation which might be causing injury to the domestic industry."[123] That panel contrasted the provisions of the Antidumping Code that, like Article 4.2(a) of the Safeguards Agreement, specified mandatory factors to examine in determining the effects of imports, to the provision on other factors, which did not do so.[124] It concluded that the provision on other factors specified no particular analysis.[125] The Safeguards Agreement cannot be read to mandate any different conclusion. The USITC analysis in this case, which expressly and with particularity examined such other factors, more than satisfies the requirements in the Agreement. The EC's attempt to require a particular means of analysis of other factors is misguided.

132. Finally, the EC's objection simply ignores the USITC' s actual findings. The USITC specifically found that if the domestic industry, which had the capacity to do so, filled the growth in demand in 1996 and 1997, instead of the increased imports doing so, the industry would have operated at 61 per cent of capacity instead of 44.5 per cent as it actually did.[126] Under these conditions, domestic production, instead of being below all pre-1996 levels, would have stood at 166.3 million pounds in 1997, well above the prior high of 142.6 million pounds. Rather than having fallen below all levels prior to the surge in imports, capacity utilization in 1997 would have exceeded 1995 levels.[127] In short, the fall in virtually all indicators of industry performance in 1996 and 1997 compared with prior periods, which the USITC found to constitute serious injury, would not have occurred. While the United States does not regard such findings to be required by the Agreement, they clearly satisfy the requirements of the Agreement, and the EC does not contest them. The EC has advanced no reason why these findings - regardless of the USITC's specific findings on other asserted causes - do not satisfy the requirement of Articles 2.1 and 4.2.

Wheat Protein Levels

133. In paragraph 83 the EC claims that the USITC elsewhere "acknowledges that the price of wheat gluten is directly related to the protein level in wheat ", implying that the only factor that counts in determining the price of wheat gluten is the protein level in wheat. The USITC made no such statement. In support of

---

123 *Ibid.* at ¶ 552.
124 *Ibid.* at ¶ 550.
125 *Ibid.* at ¶ 551.
126 US Exhibit 4 at I-12, I-17.
127 US Exhibit 4 at II-15, Table 5.

this claim, the EC refers to a page (page I-23), but not specific text, in the remedy section of the USITC views. What the USITC there said was that the protein level of wheat is one of five factors that affect the *demand* for wheat gluten. It noted that a weather-related deficiency in protein content in the wheat crop during 1993 resulted "at least in part" in an increase in the demand for and price of wheat gluten in 1994.[128] The USITC also identified four other factors that affect demand – the level of purchases by pet food producers, increased demand related to the use of high-speed mixing machines at bakeries, increasing popularity of high-fiber breads and other bakery products that use wheat gluten, and anticipation in early 1997 of the filing of a section 301 complaint.

134. The thrust of the EC's argument here is that consumption of wheat gluten and the price of wheat gluten should rise hand in hand. However, as the USITC's findings show, this did not happen in 1996 and 1997. As the USITC made clear in its causation analysis, the price of US wheat gluten prices fell in 1996 and 1997 in the face of rising consumption – a fact the EC does not challenge – and in the face of surging imports. Thus, even if the protein level of wheat is a critical factor in the price of wheat gluten, it does not explain why the price of wheat gluten fell in 1996 and 1997 when consumption was rising.

135. The EC purports to provide evidence in its Exhibit EC-10 that shows that the wheat protein content of wheat, and only that factor, determines the price of wheat gluten in the United States. Figure 3 in Exhibit EC-10, which graphs the EC's construction of wheat gluten prices and wheat protein premiums, appears to represent the heart of the EC's argument. However, figure 3 does not support the EC's premise. Comparing the spread between the price of wheat gluten and the wheat protein premium in 1993 and 1995, the two normal years preceding the surge in imports, and the spread in 1996 and 1997, the years in which the surge in imports occurred, it is clear that the spread was much narrower in 1996 and 1997. To have maintained the same spread in 1996 and 1997, wheat gluten prices would have had to have been substantially higher. They were not because of the surge in imports. Thus, the EC's own analysis does not support its premise. It is noteworthy that none of the parties in the USITC's investigation, including the EU respondents, asserted that a wheat protein related factor was a more important cause of the serious injury. Accordingly, there does not appear to have been a factor to evaluate and there was no need for the USITC to have addressed the issue any further in its report.

Co-product markets

136. The USITC found, in keeping with Article 4.1(c) of the Safeguards Agreement[129], that the "domestic industry" producing the like or directly com-

---

[128] US Exhibit 4 at I-22-23.

[129] "[I]n determining injury or threat thereof, a 'domestic industry' shall be understood to mean the producers as a whole of the like or directly competitive products operating with the territory of a Member, or those whose collective output of the like or directly competitive products constitutes a

petitive product for purposes of its injury analysis consisted of domestic producers of all forms of wheat gluten.[130] The EC does not object to this definition of the like or directly competitive product or the industry. Its arguments, however, at several points posit that the relevant analysis should properly concern a putative "wheat starch/gluten industry."[131] Although firms that produce wheat gluten also produce wheat starch, it is only their condition as producers of wheat gluten that is relevant. Contrary to the EC's current arguments, the USITC properly considered "evidence that wheat gluten production decisions are affected by market conditions in the wheat starch market[132], but did not consider wheat starch and wheat gluten operations as constituting a single industry. As will be shown below, the EC"s contentions concerning the effect of developments in the co-product market, insofar as they may have impacted the wheat gluten industry, are misplaced.

(1) Wheat starch

137. The USITC considered arguments made by EU respondents about co-product markets. The USITC found that wheat gluten production decisions are affected by market conditions in the wheat starch market. The USITC examined wheat starch prices and found that such prices, in contrast to wheat gluten prices, showed a gradual increase over the period of investigation. In particular, it found that weighted-average wheat starch prices were at their highest level of the investigative period in 1997. The USITC also considered the possible impact on wheat gluten production of competition between wheat starch and corn starch. The USITC found the relative stability in domestic wheat starch prices and the gradual increase in such prices to suggest that competition between corn starch and wheat starch is not likely to have had much if any effect on wheat gluten production.[133] Thus, both sets of findings find the logic behind the asserted effects of these factors to be faulty.

138. The EC's analysis of this issue is contradictory both legally and factually. First, by introducing its own exhibits and evidence, the EC is effectively urging the panel to make its own de novo determination based on a new record that includes information newly supplied by the EC, rather than review whether the USITC reached reasoned conclusions based on the record before it. For example, the information in or relied on in EC exhibits 10, 12, 13 and 14 was not part of the record of the USITC investigation. Accordingly, these exhibits and analysis in the EC's first submission based thereon should be disregarded by the Panel. As has been previously discussed, the issue before the Panel is the adequacy of the analysis performed by the national authority at the time of the investigation, and

---

major proportion of the total domestic production of those products." Safeguards Agreement Art. 4.1(c).

130 US Exhibit 4 at I-10 to I-11.

131 See EC First Submission ¶¶ 76, 92.

132 US Exhibit 4 at I-16.

133 US Exhibit 4 at I-16-17.

this question is to be judged on the basis of the evidence collected and considered by that national authority.[134]

139. Second, the EC, having postulated that surging imports could not have had any effect on prices[135], cannot seem to decide what drove down US wheat gluten prices in 1996 and 1997 at the same time that US wheat gluten consumption was increasing. Thus, the EC argues in paragraph 85 that "wheat protein premiums determine the wheat gluten price on the US market" and apparently are critical to the overall situation of the domestic industry, and yet in paragraph 84 argues that the conditions in the wheat starch and alcohol markets "are critical to the overall situation of the domestic industry."

140. Third, the EC does not demonstrate the relevance to the USITC determination of the evidence that the EC insists should have been addressed. For example, the EC asserts at paragraph 88 of its statement that US wheat starch prices fell after 1992-93 until 1994-95 and still remained below 1992-93 levels in 1995-96. On its face, this statement has no relevance to why wheat gluten production, shipments, and capacity utilization in 1996-97 were lower than in any year in the period 1993-95. It is likewise not apparent why it is relevant that wheat starch consumption fell in 1996 and 1997 below 1995 levels. Since wheat starch prices rose in this period in which wheat starch consumption fell, the observation only compounds the dilemma of why during the same period wheat gluten prices fell while wheat gluten consumption rose.

141. Similarly, the discussion in paragraphs 89, 90, 91, and 92 of the EC's statement about competitive conditions between wheat starch and corn starch has no relevance to the findings in dispute. The EC does not allege that competitive conditions between wheat and corn starch changed during the period of investigation. The EC's argument fails to explain how those conditions have any bearing on the question addressed by the USITC - namely, what caused the wheat gluten industry's deterioration in 1996-97.

(2) Ethanol/alcohol

142. The USITC also considered whether conditions in the alcohol market (some wheat starch is further processed into fuel-grade alcohol (ethanol) and food-grade alcohol) impacted wheat gluten production. The USITC noted that while there was evidence that one domestic producer, Midwest, had reduced its wheat gluten production in 1995 for reasons related at least in part to conditions in the alcohol market (the firm further processed wheat starch into alcohol), Midwest was but one of four domestic producers of wheat gluten, and that Midwest's action in 1995 explains, at most, only part of the problem faced by one producer. The USITC concluded that any problems in the alcohol market in 1995 did not explain the significant deterioration in 1996 and 1997 of the other three domestic producers, who accounted for the majority of domestic production, nor

---

[134] *Korea – Dairy, supra*, footnote 34, para. 7.30

[135] EC First Submission at ¶ 84.

did it fully explain Midwest's declining financial performance on its wheat gluten operations.[136]

143. The EC in paragraphs 93-95 claims that the USITC failed to investigate an alleged weakness in the ethanol market. The EC refers to the 1995 information considered by the USITC about Midwest, and also asserts that US ethanol production declined severely in 1995. The EC states in paragraph 93 that it "clearly appears" (but provides no supporting evidence) that many of the US producers have their own facilities to produce food-grade and fuel-grade alcohol and ethanol, and implies in paragraph 94 (but provides no supporting evidence) that Midwest's level of involvement in the alcohol market is typical of firms that produce wheat gluten.

144. As is clear, however, from the USITC's discussion on page I-17 of its report, Midwest was the only domestic wheat gluten producer that internally processes a significant amount of wheat starch slurry into alcohol-related products. Thus, the EC was wrong to suggest that Midwest's involvement in alcohol-related products is typical of other domestic firms that produce wheat gluten, and wrong to imply that any impact that conditions in the alcohol market had on Midwest had a similar impact on other firms that produce wheat gluten.

145. The EC's focus on data relating to conditions in the alcohol market in 1995 misses the mark. What happened in 1995 occurred before the surge in wheat gluten imports and period in which the USITC found the US wheat gluten industry to be seriously injured. Thus, it does not explain the surge in wheat gluten imports in 1996 and 1997 or the decline in the performance of the wheat gluten industry in those years.

146. Finally, whatever change in conditions in the alcohol market may have occurred, it did not lead to a decline in wheat starch prices or to a decline in Midwest's sales of alcohol products. As stated above, wheat starch prices rose in 1996 and 1997 and were at their highest level at the end of the period of investigation. Also, the data on page II-19 of the USITC's report show that Midwest's net sales of alcohol products rose in each year of the period of investigation, particularly in 1996 and 1997. While Midwest's net sales of fuel grade alcohol did fall in 1994, they rebounded sharply in 1995, fell modestly in 1996, and then jumped in 1997 to the highest level of the period.

147. Thus, the USITC conducted an appropriate inquiry into matters relating to the impact of conditions in the alcohol market on domestic production of wheat gluten, and reached reasonable conclusions based thereon.

Input prices

148. The USITC considered whether rising prices of wheat and wheat flour, the major inputs into wheat gluten/wheat starch production, were a more important cause of serious injury. The USITC found that raw material costs rose during the

---

[136] US Exhibit 4 at I-16-17.

period of the investigation, particularly in 1996 and 1997. The USITC also found that domestic wheat gluten consumption increased significantly during this period. The USITC said that it would have expected the domestic industry to have been able to pass on these cost increases in view of the fact that demand for wheat gluten is relatively insensitive to price. The USITC cited testimony of officials of domestic producers at the USITC hearing to the effect that historically they had been able to pass on higher raw material costs to their customers. The USITC found that unit selling values of domestic wheat gluten, instead of rising to reflect increased raw material costs and increased demand, fell in 1996 and 1997. The USITC concluded that this unusual development was explained by the dramatic increase in relatively low-priced imports during the period, which had the effect of driving down wheat gluten prices.[137]

149. The USITC's statement that demand for wheat gluten is relatively insensitive to changes in the price of wheat gluten is supported by the USITC' s findings with respect to the unique nature of wheat gluten. As the USITC found elsewhere in its findings, demand is not sensitive to price changes in wheat gluten because wheat gluten represents only a small cost of producing downstream products and generally lacks substitutes.[138] In addition, the USITC found that about 80 per cent of the wheat gluten consumed in the United States serves as an input by the baking industry to supplement the gluten in the flours, and that wheat gluten must be used in the production of high-fiber and multi-grain breads.[139] In concluding that there are no other domestic products that are "like" domestic wheat gluten, the USITC cited the absence of substitute products with the functional "vitality" of wheat gluten.[140] In addition, information in the USITC's record and cited at page I-22 of the USITC's report shows that all 19 importers/purchasers responding to a question in the USITC's questionnaire stated that there were no substitute products for wheat gluten. The EC's objection to this conclusion is based on the USITC's citation of statements by two US producers that they have been able to pass raw material costs through to their customers.[141] The fact that direct testimony supports conclusions that the authority would reach from the objective evidence cannot reasonably be said to detract from that conclusion.

150. The EC's argument in paragraphs 97-100 is both inadmissible under the standard of review applicable in this proceeding and fails to show the relevance of wheat and wheat flour prices in the United States as an asserted cause of the alleged injury. The EC alleges that wheat prices rose dramatically during the period of investigation. As proof, the EC selectively cites monthly wheat price data that it presents in Exhibit 12 to its statement. The data on which this exhibit is based was not in the record of the USITC investigation. Although wheat price

---

137 US Exhibit 4 at I-17-18.

138 US Exhibit 4 at I-22.

139 US Exhibit 4 at I-6.

140 US Exhibit 4 at I-10.

141 EC First Submission at ¶ 98, citing US Exhibit 4 at I-17.

data were submitted to the USITC, they were not presented on a monthly basis. Indeed, Exhibit 12 contains information from after the period of the USITC's decision. Having accepted that this Panel may not conduct a *de novo* review, the EC should not now be heard to rely on new evidence never presented to the USITC. As indicated above, such evidence cannot be regarded as undermining the adequacy of the reasoned conclusions that the USITC at the time of its determination.

151. Moreover, even if the Panel were to conclude that the EC's submission of new evidence was proper, the data on which the EC seeks to rely does not support its argument. The EC cites the price of wheat in June 1994 and a second price in May 1996, and claims that the price of wheat jumped 95 per cent in the interim and that this huge price increase coincided with the sharp decline in profitability reported in 1995. The EC's focus on industry profitability in 1995 misses the mark as to the USITC determination. The USITC's determination is based on a finding of a surge in imports and serious injury in 1996 and 1997. Indeed, as indicated above, the USITC found that the domestic industry operated at a profit in 1995, but operated at a loss in 1996 and 1997.

Imports of Wheat gluten by Domestic Wheat Gluten Producers

152. The USITC considered whether the ongoing importation of wheat gluten by domestic producers was a more important cause of serious injury than increased imports, and concluded it was not. The USITC found that US producers' imports remained relatively steady during the period of investigation, and thus domestic producers were not responsible for the surge in imports in 1996 and 1997.[142] In view of this finding, the EC has not established the relevance of its contention that the USITC should have excluded from its causation analysis the data for imports from Australia by US producers. Since the USITC found that such imports could not account for the surge in imports, their inclusion would not have affected the USITC's findings concerning the effects of increased imports.

153. The exclusion of such data as proposed by the EC is not required by the Safeguards Agreement. Unlike the WTO Antidumping Agreement, which expressly authorizes (but does not require) a member to exclude imports by related parties under certain conditions[143], the Safeguards Agreement does not authorize a member to exclude related-party imports or even address the issue. Thus, the EC cannot establish that the failure to exclude such companies violated the Agreement.

---

[142] US Exhibit 4 at I-17.

[143] See Agreement on Implementation of Article VI of the General Agreement on Tariffs and Trade 1994, Article 4.1(i).

(iv) The EC's Objections Concerning Non-Disclosure of Confidential Information are not Well-Founded

154. The EC's suggestion that a determination may be found inadequately explained under the Safeguards Agreement due to failure to disclose confidential information flies in the face of the Agreement's plain terms. As the EC acknowledges, Article 3.2 prohibits domestic authorities from disclosing confidential information. Article 3.2 provides, "Any information which is by nature confidential or which is provided on a confidential basis shall, upon cause being shown, be treated as such by the competent authorities. Such information *shall not be disclosed* without permission of the party submitting it." (Emphasis added.). That prohibition contains no exception for disclosure to WTO panels. Accordingly, it would be highly anomalous if the Safeguard Agreement placed on competent authorities a standard for explaining their decisions that required them to disclose confidential information. That anomaly would be all the greater in that the sentences quoted above forbidding the disclosure of confidential information follow immediately the sentence in Article 3.1 that provides for publication of a report setting forth the authority's findings and reasoned conclusions.

155. Article 4.2(c) makes quite clear that the requirement to publish "detailed analysis of the case under investigation" and "demonstration of the relevance of the factors examined" cannot entail the publication of information treated as confidential under Article 3.2. Article 4.2(c) states that such publication shall be "in accordance with the provisions of Article 3." A published analysis that revealed confidential information would violate the provisions of Article 3. Consequently, the degree of detail required in the published report cannot be so great as to require the disclosure of confidential information. To the extent that the EC suggests that the Panel must "verify" all information cited by domestic authorities, its suggestion reflects a misunderstanding of the standard of review, as has been discussed.

156. The USITC accepts confidential information in safeguard investigations subject to release to limited categories of representatives only under protective order during the investigations. USITC regulations and policy give further content to those limitations.[144] In particular, long-established USITC policy[145] provides rules to assure that the publication of aggregate information does not disclose to competitors the confidential information of any firm. Under that policy, when confidential business data come from one or two firms, the published report does not disclose the data. Moreover, to assure that aggregations do not disclose a particular firm's information, aggregate summaries are not provided when the

[144] See, e.g., 19 C.F.R. 201.6 (g) ("Any business information submitted in confidence and determined to be entitled to confidential treatment shall be maintained in confidence by the USITC and not disclosed except as required by law.").

[145] The internal document disclosing the USITC's approval of that policy in 1981 is attached as US Exhibit 9.

information comes from three or more firms, but one firm accounts for 75 per cent of the total or two firms account for 90 per cent.

157. The USITC published report consequently deletes all information from individual companies and aggregated data where disclosure of aggregates would, under the policy, reflect risk of disclosure of particular company information. As the EC's submission reflects, through much of the period, there were only three US producers of wheat gluten and one was not able to provide United States-specific information on aspects of its operations. In other instances, less than all of the US producers engaged in the activity concerning which the USITC sought information. To take an example of which the EC specifically complains, not all US producers imported wheat gluten during the period; consequently, published reporting of aggregate data would have risked disclosure to reporting firms of their competitor's confidential information. Such factors explain virtually all of the deletions in the USITC's publication.

158. Careful review of the published report, however, has established that in some instances the USITC policy was inadvertently misapplied. In particular, although the profile of companies reporting certain pricing information at some periods came close to approximating the policy's criteria, the policy guidelines were not met as to some of the pricing data that were withheld from disclosure. Consequently, the USITC has now prepared a corrigendum to the public report that provides the portion of the pricing data and certain other information that can be disclosed (attached as Exhibit 10 to this submission).[146]

159. Accordingly, the EC's concern that the non-disclosure of this information hampered "verification" of the USITC's conclusions concerning pricing is based on a misreading of the USITC's analysis. Nevertheless, the United States is confident that this greater degree of disclosure will allay the EC's concerns.

2. *The Temporary Import Quota is Neither Being Applied to an Extent Greater than Necessary nor Improperly Allocated*

160. The EC alleges the US safeguard measure is inconsistent with Article 5.1 and 5.2 of the Safeguards Agreement in that the United States allegedly failed to apply the measure "only to the extent necessary" and improperly allocated shares of the quota. As discussed below, the EC's claims are without merit.

(i) The Wheat Gluten Safeguard is not Excessive

161. The EC asserts that the temporary quota established by the United States on wheat gluten imports is inconsistent with the general obligation imposed on Members under the first sentence of Article 5.1. That sentence requires Members

146 A public version of the revised report will shortly be available to the public from the USITC.

to " ... apply safeguard measures only to the extent necessary to prevent or remedy serious injury and to facilitate adjustment." An examination of the USITC's carefully reasoned explanation for the safeguard measure it recommended, demonstrates that the measure falls well within that requirement.

Standard of Review: The Korea – Dairy Test

162. The EC suggests that this Panel should review the temporary wheat gluten import quota using the test adopted by the *Korea – Dairy* Panel, which found that:

> Members are required, in their recommendations or determinations on the application of a safeguard measure, to explain how they considered the facts before them and why they concluded, at the time of the decision, that the measure to be applied was necessary to remedy the serious injury and facilitate the adjustment of the industry.[147]

The *Dairy* Panel went on to say that its role was

> ... *not* to determine for ourselves whether the measure applied by Korea is at a level that is no more restrictive than necessary to remedy the serious injury and facilitate adjustment. Rather, we must evaluate whether in deciding on the type and level of the measure to be applied, the [competent] authorities considered relevant information and explained their decision that the measure chosen was no more restrictive than necessary to prevent or remedy serious injury to the [domestic] industry and to facilitate the industry's adjustment.[148]

163. The EC purports to embrace the standard of review established in the *Korea-Dairy* report. In fact, however, the EC's critique of the safeguard measure at issue in this proceeding invites the Panel to undertake a far more searching inquiry than that contemplated by the *Dairy* report, and effectively asks the Panel to substitute the EC's preferred remedy for that established by the US competent authorities. There is no basis either in the text of Article 5, or under the approach adopted by the *Korea - Dairy* panel, for a *de novo* review of this nature.

164. Nor is there any basis for the EC's evident, but unsupported, conclusion that the US competent authorities were obliged to justify the safeguard measure they selected by publishing detailed findings and conclusions equivalent to those a Member must provide to document its injury and causation determinations. Unlike Articles 3 and 4 of the Safeguards Agreement, Article 5 contains no ex-

[147] *Korea – Dairy*, *supra*, footnote 34, para. 7.102.

[148] *Korea – Dairy*, *supra*, footnote 34, para 7.102 (emphasis added).

press requirement that a member publish findings and reasoned conclusions relating to remedy.[149]

Article 5.1 Does Not Establish a Proportionality Rule

165. Implicitly recognizing that the USITC report easily meets the standard of review set out in the *Korea - Dairy* report, the EC beckons this Panel to embark on an examination of whether the US temporary import quota meets a "proportionality rule"of the EC's invention.[150] This novel standard finds no support either in the text of Article 5, let alone in the *Korea - Dairy* Panel report.

166. As an initial matter, the United States notes that the EC's new "proportionality rule" appears to be based on the erroneous assertion that a Member wishing to apply the safeguard is obliged to justify that the proposed measure is "necessary."[151] The first sentence of Article 5.1 makes plain that the relevant inquiry is not the extent to which the measure is necessary, but the extent to which it is being *applied*.[152]

167. More fundamentally, the text of Article 5.1 provides no support for the notion that the remedy selected must be "proportional" to the serious injury, or threat of serious injury, that the competent authorities have found. Indeed, the first sentence of that article, does not exclusively focus on the relationship between the safeguard measure and injury. It also contemplates that Members will select measures based on their ability to facilitate industry adjustment. The EC's concocted "proportionality test" conveniently ignores this second legal prong of Article 5.1, first sentence.

168. More specifically, Article 5.1 is concerned with ensuring that safeguard measures are not applied beyond the degree necessary to accomplish *two* purposes: (1) preventing or remedying serious injury, and (2) facilitating industry adjustment. Since the two objectives are not identical, a measure that remedies serious injury may be insufficient to facilitate adjustment, and vice versa. By limiting its discussion to the first prong, the EC improperly reads the second prong out of the provision.

---

[149] Article 3.1 requires that the competent authorities "publish a report setting forth their findings and reasoned conclusions reached on all pertinent issues of fact and law." Article 4 of the Agreement expressly requires that a Member publish a detailed analysis of its determination of serious injury or threat of serious injury. Article 4(c) requires as follows–

The competent authorities shall publish promptly, in accordance with the provisions of Article 3, a detailed analysis of the case under investigation as well as a demonstration of the relevance of the factors examined.

[150] EC First Submission at ¶ 109 (emphasis added).

[151] EC First Submission at ¶ 111.

[152] Indeed, the Dairy Panel summarily rejected a similar argument proffered by the EC, concluding that "[Article 5.1] is not concerned with the decision or even the right of a Member to adopt a safeguard measure. The general authorization for a Member to apply a safeguard measure is found in Article 2.1 of the Agreement on Safeguards, ... we cannot conclude that Article 5.1 requires a Member to further justify the necessity of applying a safeguard measure." *Korea – Dairy, supra*, footnote 34, para. 7.99.

169. The *Dairy* Panel, by contrast, recognized the dual objectives of Article 5.1.[153] In examining the USITC's explanation for the safeguard measure it recommended, this Panel should recall that it was entirely permissible, under Article 5.1, for the USITC to the propose, and the President to adopt, a safeguard measure that would place the domestic industry in a situation in which it could make a positive adjustment to import competition.

The "To the Extent Necessary" Language in Article 5.1 Applies to a Safeguard Measure in its Totality

170. The EC misrepresents the *Dairy* Panel when it cites that Panel in support of its assertion that "the requirement to justify [that] the measure chosen is applied only to the extent necessary applies to all elements of the measure: product coverage, form, duration, and level."[154] In fact, the *Dairy* Panel found just the opposite. While the Panel recognized that a safeguard measure is defined by the elements of product coverage, etc., it specifically found that "in order to comply with Article 5.1 a Member must apply a measure which *in its totality* is no more restrictive than is necessary to prevent or remedy the serious injury and facilitate adjustment."[155] Thus, the EC's assertion that each individual element must satisfy a "necessity" requirement is erroneous.

The Wheat Gluten Import Quota Should be Judged under the *Korea - Dairy* Standard

171. The USITC's report fully meets the test set out in the *Korea-Dairy* report. It clearly explains "how [the US competent authorities] considered the facts before them and why they concluded ... that the measure to be applied was necessary to remedy the serious injury and facilitate the adjustment of the industry."[156] A review of the USITC report makes plain that the USITC (1) considered relevant information, and (2) adequately explained the remedy it recommended. Based on the explanation provided by the USITC, the import quota, considered in its totality, plainly conforms with the requirements of Article 5.1, first sentence.

---

[153] *Korea – Dairy*, *supra*, footnote 34, para. 7.99, 7.102.

[154] EC First Submission at ¶ 115.

[155] *Korea – Dairy*, *supra*, footnote 34, para. 7.101 (emphasis added).

[156] *Korea – Dairy*, *supra*, footnote 34, para. 7.102.

The USITC Considered Pertinent Information and Clearly Explained Its Remedy Recommendation

Form of Safeguard: The United States Was Not Obliged to Apply a Tariff Safeguard

172. The EC complains at length that the United States should have imposed a tariff remedy instead of a quota.[157] In the EC's view, the explanations offered by the USITC for the measure it recommended cannot satisfy the requirements of Article 5.1 because " ... a tariff should be used unless ... [it] would not be suitable to remedy the serious injury and facilitate adjustment.[158] The EC provides no textual support for its assertion that the Safeguards Agreement indicates a preference for, or requires an explanation of, a choice of one form of measure over another. In fact, Article 5.1 does not indicate a preference of any kind and nowhere mandates an explanation of the form of remedy selected.

173. The last sentence of Article 5.1 says that "Members should choose measures most suitable for the achievement of these objectives." The term in this context is hortatory rather than obligatory in nature. The United States submits, based on the reasons set out below, that its wheat gluten safeguard measure meets this objective.

174. More importantly for this purpose, however, the silence of Article 5.1 with regard to the form that definitive safeguard measures should take contrasts sharply with the language of Article 6 of the Agreement, which states that provisional measures should take the form of tariff increases. Thus, while Article 6 expresses a preference for tariffs, Article 5.1 expresses no preference for one type of measure or another. Plainly, then, the United States was under no obligation to apply a tariff safeguard in this case.

The USITC Adequately Explained Why It Rejected a Tariff and Recommended an Import Quota

175. In its report, the USITC took pains to describe why it recommended a quantitative restriction rather than a tariff to remedy the serious injury it had found and to facilitate adjustment by the domestic wheat gluten industry. Specifically, the USITC provided three reasons why a tariff remedy would be inappropriate in the case of wheat gluten imports.

176. First, the USITC found that it would be difficult to estimate the effect that a tariff in any given amount might have on imports.[159] The USITC observed that there is a co-product relationship between wheat gluten and wheat starch. It noted that when demand for wheat starch rises, production of wheat starch–and conse-

[157] EC First Submission at ¶ 118-125.
[158] EC First Submission at ¶ 118.
[159] US Exhibit 4 at I-26.

quently wheat gluten–also tends to rise. The USITC found that any assumptions about the effect that a tariff on wheat gluten might have on imports of wheat gluten must take into account both foreign demand for wheat gluten and foreign demand for wheat starch as well as the effect that this demand will have on the supply and price of wheat gluten. The USITC concluded that "[g]iven the large number of variables, we found it impossible to predict the effect of any tariff increase within an acceptable margin of certainty."[160]

177. This explanation plainly articulates one important reason why the USITC considered it appropriate to impose a measure other than a tariff. In the USITC's view, the uncertainties created by these exogenous factors would make it impossible to predict whether a tariff would prevent or remedy serious injury and facilitate adjustment.

178. Second, the USITC concluded that it was possible that EU exporters would choose to absorb any tariff increase while continuing to export the same or greater quantities of wheat gluten to the United States. The USITC noted that pricing data indicated that imports from the EU consistently undersold the US market in 1996 and 1997, and that US market prices in those two years were below US producers' cost of production. The USITC also noted the higher prevailing market prices of wheat starch in the EU, which give EU producers more pricing flexibility than US or other foreign producers.

179. The USITC also cited evidence indicating that EU capacity to produce wheat gluten increased by 44 per cent from 1993 to 1997 and was projected to increase by an additional 30 per cent from 1997 to 1999. The USITC observed that this increase exceeded the projected increase in demand in the US market for wheat gluten. The USITC concluded that, assuming the EU industry continued to operate at a high level of capacity, much of any additional production might be directed towards the US market at whatever price was necessary to produce a sale.[161] Thus, the USITC's second point also supported the choice of a measure other than a tariff.

180. Third, the USITC considered whether a tariff would be equitable with respect to different foreign suppliers. It noted that a tariff would be applied against imports from all suppliers, including those who had maintained a stable market share. The USITC stated that, because it believed EU suppliers have greater pricing flexibility than other foreign suppliers, imposition of a high tariff would be inequitable in that it would be likely further drive these suppliers from the US market.[162]

181. In summary, the USITC considered relevant information, and provided three, well-articulated grounds, for concluding that a tariff remedy would not be effective.

---

160 US Exhibit 4 at I-26.
161 US Exhibit 4 at I-26.
162 US Exhibit 4 at I-26.

182. Moreover, the USITC also considered whether a tariff-rate quota might provide an appropriate remedy, but concluded for much the same reasons as in the case of a tariff that it would not be. The USITC cited in particular the 50 per cent point limitation in US law on the increase in the tariff under a tariff-rate quota.[163]

The EC's Fails in Its Effort to Second-Guess the USITC's Remedy Recommendation on the Form of Relief

183. Implicitly recognizing that the USITC's explanation of the factors it considered, and the reasons it presented, in rejecting a tariff remedy satisfy the standard of review set out in the *Korea - Dairy* report, the EC invites the Panel to embark on a full-scale critique of the USITC's recommendation on this point. As noted previously, there is no basis in the Safeguards Agreement for undertaking what amounts to a *de novo* review of the USITC's remedy findings. Accordingly, the Panel should disregard the EC's invitation to second-guess the USITC on whether it selected an appropriate remedy and focus instead on whether the USITC considered relevant information and provided an adequate explanation of its recommendation. However, even if the Panel were to undertake a more exacting inquiry, the EC's contentions regarding the appropriate form of remedy in this case should be rejected.

184. The EC takes exception to the USITC's first reason for rejecting a tariff - that it would be difficult to estimate the effect of a tariff because of the co-product relationship between wheat starch and wheat gluten. The EC's arguments with respect to the co-product relationship largely rest on the same false assumption that underlay its similar arguments with respect to the USITC's injury determination.[164] Those arguments overlook the fact the USITC's investigation was limited to an examination of alleged serious injury to the US wheat gluten industry - not the combined wheat gluten/wheat starch industry, as the EC would have it. Stated otherwise, the USITC properly considered the question before it, namely whether increased wheat gluten imports were causing serious injury to the US industry producing the *like or directly competitive product.* The USITC found that the domestic industry consisted of firms insofar as they produced wheat gluten.[165]

185. The USITC did consider the co-product relationship to the extent it was relevant in determining the appropriate form of remedy for the domestic wheat gluten industry. In particular, it examined the relationship between production of wheat starch and wheat gluten in Europe in analyzing whether a tariff regime placed on wheat gluten would provide a sufficiently certain remedy. The USITC found that questions about starch demand raised uncertainties about the effec-

[163] US Exhibit 4 at I-27.
[164] EC First Submission at ¶ 120-124.
[165] US Exhibit 4 at I-9.

tiveness of a tariff measure.[166] Nothing in the Agreement on Safeguard compelled the USITC to project the demand for wheat starch with a mathematical degree of certainty before deciding what form of safeguard measure to recommend.

186. The EC also asks the Panel to reject the USITC's second explanation for rejecting a tariff - *i.e.*, price underselling of EC wheat gluten in the US market. Its arguments both ignore the USITC's full record on the issue and mischaracterize its findings. Substantial record evidence exists concerning the factors in the EC wheat starch industry that affect the production of the co-product wheat gluten.[167] In particular, the US Department of Agriculture reported to the USITC that the EU starch production refund was significant and that wheat starch prices in the EU are protected by high levels of import protection and high sweetener prices in Europe that create a demand for wheat starch in Europe.[168] Contrary to the EC's contention, the USITC did not conclude that these factors led to the subsidization of wheat gluten production. Rather, the USITC concluded that, because wheat gluten capacity grew in the EC largely as a byproduct of the desire to increase wheat starch supply in a protected market for wheat starch, the prices at which the EU would sell wheat gluten appeared to the USITC to be relatively unresponsive to changes in wheat gluten prices.[169] The fact that the EU undersold the US industry throughout 1996 and 1997 is consistent with that observation. The EC does not deny, but rather endorses, the relationship between its wheat starch and wheat gluten operations.[170] The USITC made no finding about whether or not the EU sales of wheat gluten were below the cost of wheat gluten production in the EU, or at what prices they would do so, and consequently made no finding concerning "subsidization".[171]

187. Finally, the EC also objects to the USITC's third explanation for rejecting a tariff – *i.e.*, ensuring that the safeguard measure would have an equitable effect on all foreign suppliers. The EU has pointed to no provision of the Safeguards Agreement that would require the United States to choose a measure that would reduce the market share of those countries whose imports have not contributed to the increased imports that caused serious injury – particularly where, as here, such a measure would be liable to be ineffective vis-a-vis imports from the source that did increase rapidly. Moreover, to the extent that the EC's greater capacity to export wheat gluten, and willingness to do so despite falling prices in the US, was driven by increases in wheat starch production that were influenced by market-distorting policies in the EC, there is no reason why the United States should impose a measure that would harm other suppliers. Wheat starch suppliers from other sources are impeded from participating in expansion in the EC wheat starch

---

166 US Exhibit 4 at I-26.
167 US Exhibit 4 at II-20, II-23, and II-38-39
168 US Exhibit 4 at II-24, n. 95.
169 See US Exhibit 4 at I-24.
170 EC First Submission at ¶ 44.
171

market by relatively high EU tariffs. Commensurate with that impediment, wheat gluten production capacity for other sources remained steady for much of the period, declining somewhat in 1997.[172] In contrast to consistent underselling by EU producers in the United States in 1996-97, and their rapidly growing market share in this market, the shares held by the other two major suppliers were stable or declined over the period of investigation and their imports generally oversold the US industry. The USITC reasonably concluded that it would be inequitable to impose safeguard measures that would reward policies that tend to be trade distortive at the cost of foreign supplying countries whose policies had not caused changes in the US market.

188. In sum, each of the USITC's stated reasons for recommending a quota rather than tariff measure was based on the conditions observed. Although Article 5 of the Agreement imposes no obligation to explain the reasons for choosing a quota as opposed to a tariff measure, each basis cited by the USITC supplies a reasonable justification for that recommendation..

The USITC Adequately Explained the Quota Level and Duration of Relief It Recommended

189. With respect to the specific level of the quota, the USITC proposed and the President adopted a quota that would restore imports (other than those from Canada) and domestic product to the market share levels that obtained during the period 1993-95. To determine the initial level of imports needed to attain this objective, the USITC calculated the share that imports excluding those from Canada achieved in 1993-95 (43 per cent) and, to take into account the fact that consumption had risen since 1995, multiplied the 1997 level of consumption (294,238 million pounds) by that percentage.[173] On this basis, the USITC proposed a quota of 126 million pounds, with a 6 per cent annual escalator.[174] As the USITC found, the 6 per cent escalator exceeded the growth in imports that had been the trend over the period of investigation.[175] The President adopted a quota that reflected a more exact figure drawn from this calculation. As opposed to the four-year measure that the USITC recommended as necessary to support the adjustment measures advanced by the industry and prevent industry closures, the President adopted a measure lasting three years and a day.

190. The objective that led the USITC to recommend a measure of this extent is apparent from the face of its determination. As has been discussed, the USITC found that, due to the rapid increase in imports in 1996-97 from prior levels, the industry by 1997 was operating at a capacity utilization level below that at which

[172] See US Exhibit 4 at I-24.
[173] US Exhibit 4 at I-28; see also US Exhibit 4 at II-10, Table 1.
[174] US Exhibit 4 at I-28-31.
[175] US Exhibit 4 at I-29.

it could achieve a reasonable profit level.[176] The USITC found that, because of substantial operating losses in 1996-97, a significant portion of the US industry would have to scale down in the near term and possibly shut down in the long term, if relief were not forthcoming.[177] The need for a reasonable profit level, which in itself the EC does not dispute, is further demonstrated by the USITC's findings that the industry would invest in developing and marketing new products and enhancing its efficiency and productivity.[178] Thus, only by restoring market shares that existed prior to the 1996-97 level could the United States industry be restored to a reasonable profit level. The EC challenges neither the need for the US industry to achieve such a profit level in order to remedy serious injury and facilitate adjustment nor that the restoration of 1993-95 shares is reasonably calculated to achieve that objective. Accordingly, the EC has advanced no basis for claiming that the measure imposed did not meet the requirements of the first sentence of Article 5.1.

The USITC Properly Based the Proposed Import Quota on 1993-95 Levels

191. The EC asserts the USITC should not have recommended a measure that reduced imports below their 1995-97 levels. This allegation ignores the language and purpose of Article 5.1, as well as the USITC's explicit findings.

192. Article 5.1, second sentence, provides that "[i]f a quantitative restriction is used, such a measure shall not reduce the quantity of imports below the level of a recent period which shall be the average of imports in the last three *representative* years for which statistics are available, *unless clear justification is given that a different level is necessary to prevent or remedy or remedy serious injury.*" (emphasis supplied.) Contrary to the EC's claim, that provision does not limit safeguard import quotas to the average level of imports for the most recent three years for which statistics are available.

193. First, the EC's reading of this provision would render the word "representative" mere surplusage. The term would be unnecessary if an authority could only refer to the most recent three years for which statistics were available. The term has meaning, however, in terms of the purpose stated for measures in Article 5.1. A "representative" period, interpreted in view of the purpose of Article 5.1 would normally be a period in which imports did not cause serious injury. To interpret the provision otherwise would mean that a competent authority would be required to choose an import level that would normally not remedy serious injury and facilitate adjustment. Such an interpretation would be contrary to the remedial purpose of safeguard measures permitted under Article 5.1.

194. Second, even if the term "representative" is not given meaning, the USITC's findings satisfy the requirement to provide a clear justification of the reason for choosing a different period. As the USITC found, in 1996 and 1997,

176 US Exhibit 4 at I-12.

177 US Exhibit 4 at I-31.

178 US Exhibit 4 at I-25-26, 30.

US market prices were below US producers' cost of production.[179] The USITC found that choosing a reference period composed in principal part of those two years of crisis would not remedy the serious injury.[180] Selecting the period that the EC has urged would have defeated USITC's objective of proposing a remedy that would allow the domestic industry to achieve a reasonable level of profitability. Accordingly, the USITC proposed, and the President adopted, as an appropriate reference period for establishing the import quota the three years immediately preceding the 1996-97 surge in imports, a time when the domestic industry was profitable.[181] The USITC provided a clear justification for selecting a period other than 1995-1997. The EC has simply ignored the USITC's findings on this point.

(ii) The EC has Failed to Demonstrate that the US Safeguard Measure Improperly Allocates Import Quota Shares Among Supplying Countries

195. The EC asserts that the United States should have allotted quota shares of wheat gluten imports on the basis of supplying country average import market shares during the period 1995-97.[182] Instead, the US safeguard measure allots shares based on averages during the 1993-95 crop year period, a distribution that the EC says runs afoul of the quota allocation rule set out in Article 5.2(a).

The second sentence Article 5.2(a) requires Members that impose quota safeguard measures to allocate the quota between Members having a substantial supplying interest:

> based upon the proportions, supplied by such Members *a previous representative period*, of the total quantity or value of imports of the product, due account being taken of any special factors which may have affected or may be affecting the trade in the product." (emphasis supplied.)

196. Unlike Article 5.1, Article 5.2(a) does not contain a preference for, or indeed any mention, of *the last three representative* years for which statistics are available. Nevertheless, the EC simply assumes that the expression "a previous representative period" in Article 5.2(a) must invariably refer to the most recent three-year period. The EC provides no grounds for that bald assertion, either in the text of Article 5.2(a) or elsewhere. Plainly, however, the burden is on the EC

---

179 US Exhibit 4 at I-26.

180 US Exhibit 4 at I-28.

181 US Exhibit 4 at I-28.

182 The EC also alleges the United States failed to seek agreement with the EC on the allocation of the quota and provided no explanation as to why that method was not "reasonably practicable." EC First Submission at ¶ 142-143. The EC misinterprets the obligations of Article 5.2(a). That Article states that a Member "may" seek agreement, but there is no obligation to do so. Moreover, Article 5.2(a) contains no requirement that a Member provide an explanation as to why it was not reasonably practicable to seek agreement.

to support it legal conclusion on this point (as in others) with reasoned factual and legal arguments.

It has provided none.

197. In particular, the EC has not shown why the period 1993-95 was not "representative" of the historical pattern of import market shares among substantial suppliers. Indeed, the EC has not even suggested, let alone demonstrated, that the period 1995-97 was in some way more "representative" than the period used by the United States in its safeguard measure. With respect to its allegation under Article 5.2 then, the EC has simply failed to meet its burden of legal and factual proof that the United States has improperly allocated its wheat gluten import quota.

3. *The United States Satisfied its Obligations Under Articles 8 and 12*

(i) The United States made timely Notifications to the Committee on Safeguards and provided Adequate Opportunity for Consultations as required under Article 12

Art. 12:

1. A Member shall immediately notify the Committee on Safeguards upon:
   (a) initiating an investigatory process relating to serious injury or threat thereof and the reasons for it;
   (b) making a finding of serious injury or threat thereof caused by increased imports; and
   (c) taking a decision to apply or extend a safeguard measure.
2. In making the notifications referred to in paragraphs 1(b) and 1(c), the Member proposing to apply or extend a safeguard measure shall provide the Committee on Safeguards with all pertinent information, which shall include evidence of serious injury or threat thereof caused by increased imports, precise description of the product involved and the proposed measure, proposed date of introduction, expected duration and timetable for progressive liberalization. ...
3. A Member proposing to apply or extend a safeguard measure shall provide adequate opportunity for prior consultations with those Members having a substantial interest as exporters of the product concerned, with a view to, *inter alia*, reviewing the information provided under paragraph 2, exchanging views on the measure and reaching an understanding on ways to achieve the objective set out in paragraph 1 of Article 8.

198. The EC contends the United States breached its obligations under Article 12 of the Safeguards Agreement both in its alleged failure to timely notify its findings and decision, and in its alleged failure to provide adequate opportunity for prior consultation. The EC's assertions are simply incorrect. Consistent with the requirements of Article 12, the United States made timely notifications to the Committee on Safeguards ("Committee"), and it provided adequate opportunity for prior consultations with Members having a substantial interest in wheat gluten exports.

199. The EC acknowledges that the United States satisfied each of the requirements of Article 12.1, but the EC takes issue with the notifications based on its claim that "these procedural steps, findings and decision had to have been made at a date that would have allowed the Committee on Safeguards, and possibly, the Council for Trade in Goods to request additional information and hold a meaningful discussion in a multilateral forum."[183] The EC attempts to read-in its own interpretation of Article 12, and it provides nothing more in support of its position than a vague reference to "the plain text and meaning of Article 12 of the SA". The actual text of Article 12.2 requires a Member to "immediately notify" the Committee. The *Korea - Dairy* Panel did note that the term "immediately" introduces a certain urgency to the timing of the notification, but it also recognized that no specific number of days is mentioned in Article.[184] The United States timely issued its notification to the Committee on 17 October 1997, only days after the USITC published notice of its investigation in the *Federal Register.* Until the USITC announced it had accepted the petition and set out the scope of the investigation, the United States had nothing to announce. Accordingly, the EC's claim with respect to this point is without merit.

200. Next, the EC claims the United States did not timely file its notification of the findings of serious injury because they "were effected *after* the findings had been made and the measure was enacted."[185] Yet the text of Article 12.1(b) specifically provides that a Member immediately notify upon "*making* a finding of serious injury ..." Article 12.1(b) is clear that a Member's obligation to notify arises only after it has made a serious injury determination. Moreover, the EC's interpretation suggests that a Member is obliged first to issue "preliminary" findings of serious injury that the Committee would then examine and ratify. Again, the EC finds no support in the text of the Safeguards Agreement for its position. In fact, the EC's interpretation directly contradicts Articles 3 and 4 of the Safeguards Agreement, which reserves to competent authorities the ultimate authority to conduct safeguards investigation.

201. Within the same line of argument, the EC takes issue with the United States' notification, based on the alleged failure of the United States to notify the

---

183 EC Submission at ¶ 167.

184 *Korea – Dairy, supra*, footnote 34, para. 7.128

185 EC First Submission at ¶ 168 (emphasis added).

Committee before taking the measure. In the EC's view importing Members are obligated to notify their "proposed measure." The EC's position finds no support in the text of Article 12. First, the text of Article 12.1(c) requires a Member to immediately notify the Committee upon "*taking* a decision to apply or extend a safeguard." In contrast, when the drafters intended a Member to notify the Committee before taking action, they were explicit in that requirement. Thus, Article 12.4 states that "A Member shall make a notification to the Committee on Safeguards *before* taking a provisional safeguard measure ... " (Emphasis added). There is no such statement in Articles 12.1, 12.2 or 12.3, which refer to applying or extending definitive safeguard measures.

202. Even assuming that Article 12 requires Members to notify proposed measures, the United States satisfied that requirement in its Article 12.1(b) notification. While it is true that the United States' proposed measure is somewhat different from the one actually adopted, the change *benefits* the EC and other wheat gluten exporters. The fact that the United States altered its proposed measure is not precluded by any provision of the Safeguards Agreement. In fact, the idea that a Member would alter its provision is specifically contemplated in Article 12. On this point, the United States would add that the object and purpose of Article 12's consultation requirement is to ensure that affected exporting Members have the opportunity to present their views and to impact the measure the importing Member ultimately decides upon. Accordingly, it should be expected that after consulting with potentially affected Members an importing Member may well take into consideration the concerns raised during consultations. There is no basis on which to argue, however, that the importing Member is forced to notify the revised provision anew before it can take action. Indeed, such a requirement provides an incentive for importing Members to ignore concerns raised in consultations. Because safeguards actions are "emergency measures" – that is, measures "requiring immediate action"[186] – time is of the essence and an importing Member does not have the luxury of providing multiple notifications, and then waiting for a period, before it can take action to address the serious injury or threat suffered by its domestic industry.

203. Finally, the EC argues that Article 12.3 imposes on a Member an obligation to "provide adequate opportunity" for prior consultations. The EC then cites *Korea – Dairy* for the proposition that prior consultations means "consultations prior to the application of the measure." The United States would agree that an importing Member must provide the opportunity for consultations before it can take a safeguard action. The EC fails to note, however, that the United States *did* hold consultations with the EC (and other affected Members) prior to imposing the wheat gluten safeguard action. The United States consulted with the EC on 24 April 1998 in compliance with the requirements of Article 12.3.

---

[186] The Concise Oxford Dictionary.

(ii) The United States Satisfied its Obligations under Article 8

Art. 8:

> 1. A Member proposing to apply a safeguard measure or seeking an extension of a safeguard measure shall endeavour to maintain a substantially equivalent level of concessions and other obligations to that existing under GATT1994 between it and the exporting Members which would be affected by such a measure, in accordance with the provisions of paragraph 3 of Article 12. To achieve this objective, the Members concerned may agree on any adequate means of trade compensation for the adverse effects of the measure on their trade.
>
> ...
>
> 3. The right of suspension referred to in paragraph 2 shall not be exercised for the first three years that a safeguard measure is in effect, provided that the safeguard measure has been taken as a result of an absolute increase in imports and that such a measure conforms to the provisions of this Agreement.

204. The EC alleges the United States violated Articles 8 and 12.3 of the Safeguards Agreement by "failing to offer a meaningful opportunity, indeed any opportunity at all, for consultations and negotiations."[187] If the EC's Article 8 claim is limited to the allegation that the United States failed to provide the opportunity for prior consultation, then in the United States' view the claim is redundant and has already been addressed above. Specifically, the EC once again neglects to inform the Panel that the United States indeed did hold consultations with the EC prior to imposing the measure.

205. In addition to its allegation regarding consultations, however, the EC appears to make the additional claim that the United States allegedly failed to maintain a substantially equivalent level of concessions and other obligation pursuant to Article 8. Yet the EC itself acknowledges the ambiguity of Article 8.1 when it informs the Panel that:

> The question may arise as to how a substantially equivalent level of concessions and other obligations can be maintained given conditions on the right to immediately withdraw concessions in the [Safeguards Agreement].[188]

While it identifies the fundamental ambiguity in its interpretation of Article 8, the EC's only response to this dilemma is that "[t]his is not a question the panel needs to answer."[189]

---

[187] EC First Submission at ¶ 178.

[188] EC First Submission at ¶ 175.

[189] EC First Submission at ¶ 175.

206. The United States respectfully submits if the EC's allegation is that the United States violated Article 8, then it is precisely the Panel's duty to determine what obligations, if any, Article 8 imposed and how the United States might have been able to meet that obligation. In the United States' view Article 8.1, when read in conjunction with Article 12.3, imposes on a Member the obligation to hold prior consultations. It does not, however, require a Member to provide concessions before it can take a safeguard action. This interpretation is borne out by the text of Articles 8 and 12, as well as by the object and purpose of the Safeguards Agreement.

207. The text of Article 8.1 provides that a Member proposing to apply a safeguard measure "shall endeavour to maintain a substantially equivalent level of concessions and other obligations ... *in accordance with* the provisions of paragraph 3 of Article 12." Article 12.3, on the other hand, merely provides that a Member shall provide opportunity for prior consultations with a view to, among other things, "reaching an understanding on ways to achieve the objective set out in paragraph 1 of Article 8." Thus the only obligation on a Member proposing to apply a safeguard is to provide an opportunity for prior consultations. As previously stated, the United States satisfied that obligation.

208. The United States finds further support for its interpretation of Article 8 in the object and purpose of the Safeguards Agreement. The preamble to the Agreement recognizes the need "to re-establish multilateral control over safeguards and eliminate measures that escape such control." Specifically, drafters of the Safeguards Agreement intended to eradicate so-called grey-area measures. To ensure this objective, they permitted Members to impose safeguards for a limited period without fear of "having to pay" for such action. For the EC to now argue that a Member must provide substantially equivalent concessions before taking a safeguard action jeopardizes the objective to re-establish multilateral control because it ensures that Members will find methods outside of the Safeguards Agreement to protect their injured domestic industries. Such an outcome would defeat the very purpose of the Agreement.

209. Accordingly, the United States respectfully submits it satisfied its obligations under Articles 12 and 8 of the Safeguards Agreement.

E. The EC's GATT Article I Claim is Without Merit

> *Art. I*: With respect to customs duties and charges of any kind imposed on or in connection with importation or exportation or imposed on the international transfer of payments for imports for exports, and with respect to the method of levying such duties and charges, and with respect to all rules and formalities in connection with importation and exportation, and with respect to all matters referred to in paragraphs 2 and 4 of Article II, [citation omitted] any advantage, favour, privilege or immunity granted by any contracting party to any product originating in or destined for any other country shall be accorded immediately and unconditionally to the

like product originating in or destined for the territories of all other contracting parties.

210. The EC alleges that the US measure violates the most-favoured-nation provision of GATT Article I. In the EC's view, the mere fact that Australia's quota allocation is greater than the EC's is sufficient to support a claim of discrimination.

211. The United States respectfully submits the EC's claim is without merit either factually or legally. First, the EC 's accusation that the United States deliberately chose a representative period most favorable to Australia because one US producer is a subsidiary of an Australian producer is baseless and without foundation.[190] The USITC Report provided a reasoned analysis as to the appropriateness of using the representative period the United States chose.[191]

212. Second, and more importantly, other Panels that have examined the issue consistently have found that claims of discrimination in the administration of quotas are more appropriately raised as a violation of Article XIII rather than Article I. In *EEC – Restrictions on Imports of Dessert Apples*, the Panel examined a claim raised by Chile that the EEC's import quota on apples violated Article I. The Panel found that "it [was] more appropriate to examine the consistency of the ECC measures with the most-favoured-nation principles of the General Agreement in the context of Article XIII ... this provision deals with the non-discriminatory administration of quantitative restrictions and is thus the *lex specialis* in this particular case.[192] The Appellate Body has agreed as well that the allocation of quantitative restrictions is outside the scope of Article I, in finding that the EC's tariff rate quota on bananas under the Lomé Convention was not within the scope of the "Lomé waiver" of Article I.1.[193]

213. Accordingly, the United States respectfully submits that the EC's discrimination claim under GATT Article I must fail.

V. CONCLUSION

214. For the foregoing reasons, the United States respectfully submits its safeguard measure on imports of wheat gluten satisfy US obligations under the Safeguards Agreement and the GATT. Accordingly, the EC's claims to the contrary are without merit and should be rejected by the Panel.

[190] EC First Submission at ¶ 41 and ¶ 182.

[191] See paras. 182-183 supra.

[192] L/6491, adopted on 22 June 1989, 36S/93, 133, para. 12.28; See also, EEC –Restrictions on Imports of Apples from Chile, L/5047, adopted on 10 November 1980, 27S/98, 112, para. 4.1.

[193] Appellate Body Report, *EC – Regime for the Importation, Sale and Distribution of Bananas* ("*EC – Bananas III*"), DS27/AB/R, adopted 25 September 1997, DSR 1997:II, 591, paras. 180-188.

UNITED STATES LIST OF EXHIBITS

United States - Definitive Safeguard Measure on
Imports of Wheat Gluten from the European Communities

Exhibit Number	Description of Exhibit
1	USITC Producers Questionnaire.
2	Presidential Proclamation 7103, 30 May 1998.
3	Memorandum from the President, 30 May 1998, Accompanying Proclamation 7103.
4	USITC Report on Investigation No. TA-201-67, *Wheat Gluten,* USITC Pub. No. 3088, March 1998.
5	US Notification to the Committee on Safeguards under Article 12.1(a).
6	Original and revised US Notifications to the Committee on Safeguards under Article 12.1(b).
7	US Notification to the Committee on Safeguards under Article 12.1(c).
8	Transcript of USITC hearing, injury phase, 16 December 1997.
9	USITC Memorandum Describing USITC Policy on Confidentiality.
10	Revised USITC Report on Investigation No. TA-201-67, *Wheat Gluten*

ATTACHMENT 2-2

UNITED STATES ORAL STATEMENT

(20-21 December 1999)

Ms. Florestal

Mr. Chairman, Members of the Panel,

On behalf of the United States delegation, I would like to thank the Panel for agreeing to take on this task. At the conclusion of our statement, we would be pleased to receive any questions you may have.

This case concerns a safeguard measure that the United States took when its authority, the US International Trade Commission, determined that a surge of imports of wheat gluten in 1996 and 1997 caused serious injury to the United States wheat gluten industry. As my colleague, Mr. Toupin, will discuss today, the Commission's determination of injury and causation was entirely in accord with Articles 2.1 and 4 of the Safeguards Agreement. I will demonstrate why the measure taken by the United States, which specifically addresses the injury found, is consistent with Article 5, and fully comports with Articles 8 and 12.

I would like to make two preliminary remarks before we turn to those issues. First, the Appellate Body's recent decisions in *Argentina - Footwear* and *Korea - Dairy* make clear that no issue of failure to comply with Article XIX of the GATT 1994 exists in this case. Article XIX refers to "unforeseen developments". The two Appellate Body Reports expressly contrast "unforeseen" (that is, "unexpected") with "unforeseeable" (that is, "incapable of being foreseen, foretold or anticipated"). Both conclude that Article XIX's provisions must be interpreted with the ordinary meaning of the word "unforeseen" and not with that of "unforeseeable."

Here the European Communities' first written submission admits that the surge of imports at issue in this case was unforeseen. It agrees with the USITC that the US wheat gluten producers did not foresee the import surge when they added production capacity during 1993 to 1995 in anticipation of a large increase in domestic demand. As the USITC found, the US industry was correct that demand would grow. But imports increased at a rate greater than the growth in demand. Though the EC claims that the import surge was foreseeable, the Appellate Body Reports in *Argentina - Footwear* and *Korea - Dairy* demonstrate conclusively that such a showing, even if made, would not satisfy the requirement to make a *prima facie* case under Article XIX.

Second, although the parties agree that the standard of review in this matter is not *de novo*, the EC's first written submission disregards that standard. In examining a serious injury determination, a Panel must address three questions:

- First, whether the authority considered all relevant factors, including those listed in Article 4.2(a);

- Second, whether its published report contains an adequate explanation of how the facts support the determination made, and
- Third, whether the determination made is consistent with the Safeguards Agreement.

Many of the EC's arguments are irrelevant under this standard. In one respect, however, the EC acts here in plain defiance of the standard. The EC has presented to this Panel evidence that was not before the national authority. In doing so, the EC seeks to have the Panel review the authority's decision on a basis clearly outside this Panel's authority. The Panel should disregard the new evidence that the EC seeks to present and the arguments that it has made on that basis.

Mr. Toupin will now discuss the International Trade Commission's injury and causation determination.

Mr. Toupin

Mr. Chairman, Members of the Panel,

As the USITC's findings are discussed at considerable length in the United States' first written submission, I will highlight a few salient points, paying particular attention to the Appellate Body decision in *Argentina - Footwear*. The USITC's report conclusively demonstrates that it considered all relevant factors during its investigation. In reaching its affirmative determination, the USITC found that the "surge in relatively low-priced imports in 1996 and 1997 coincided with the decline in industry performance" in almost all performance indicators. This decline coincided with rising domestic demand and consumption.

It is undisputed that imports increased. In the last two years investigated, 1996 and 1997, imports increased 38 per cent from 1995 levels. Moreover, even though consumption in the US market was rising, imports gained a 20 per cent increase in market share during that two-year period. Coming as it did after a period in which import market share fell slightly, such a rise was, in the terms that the Appellate Body recently used in *Argentina - Footwear,* "recent enough, sudden enough, sharp enough, and significant enough, both quantitatively and qualitatively, to cause serious injury."

Though the industry was profitable in the first three years of the period, it suffered growing operating losses in 1996 and 1997, when imports, particularly from the EC, surged and consistently undersold the US product. As the USITC found, the industry's gross profit, operating income, and market share all declined in both 1996 and 1997. Likewise, both the domestic industry's production and shipments fell sharply when imports surged, and were at their lowest levels in 1996-1997. The EC would have the Panel place controlling weight on the fact that, after the sharp declines in 1996, there were slight upturns in production and sales in 1997. As the USITC found, however, both indicators remained in 1997 far below their pre-import surge levels. Moreover, since other injury indicators continued to decline, the USITC found that minor improvements in some factors in 1997 were "isolated".

The USITC's analysis is in perfect accord with the recent statements of the Appellate Body in *Argentina - Footwear.* As the Appellate Body stated, while an authority must examine all relevant factors, not all of those factors must be declining to support a conclusion that an industry is seriously injured. Rather, an authority considers whether the overall picture demonstrates "significant overall impairment" of the industry. The USITC performed just such an analysis here. The EC has not advanced any reason why the minor improvement in some factors in the last year - particularly when those indicators remained at seriously depressed levels - should have required the USITC to find no serious injury.

The USITC's determination also fully satisfies the requirement of Article 4.2(b) not to attribute to increased imports the injury caused by other factors. It did so in two ways. First, each of the causal factors it addressed is specific to the increased imports. In particular, the USITC found that capacity utilization fell to its lowest levels in the 1996-97 period, when imports surged. It estimated what the capacity utilization of the US wheat gluten industry would have been in 1997 but for the increase in imports. The USITC found that, at that level of capacity utilization, the industry would have approached levels at which it had been profitable in the past. This analysis took into account that the growth in the US industry's capacity in 1993-95 would have had some effect on capacity utilization. However, by estimating how much the severe decline that actually occurred in 1996-97 resulted from the growth in imports, the USITC assured that it did not attribute to increased imports the effects of other causes.

Second, the USITC specifically addressed each of the other factors that importers and foreign producers suggested were causing injury. The EC's argument that the USITC's analysis was inadequate is based on the false premise that the USITC should have quantified the amount of injury caused by each factor. This argument is directly contrary to the GATT panel report in *United States - Salmon*, which interpreted virtually identical language in the Antidumping Code before that language was incorporated into the Safeguards Agreement.

The USITC's findings on each proposed alternative cause of injury are discussed at length in the United States' first written submission. To summarize briefly, the USITC found that each proposed alternative cause could not to any significant extent explain the severe deterioration in the industry's position in 1996 and 1997. The EC's arguments in its written submission fail uniformly to show how other factors affecting the industry could have led to its losses in the last two years investigated.

In short, an objective assessment of the USITC's Report shows that it examined all the relevant factors, adequately explained why the facts supported its conclusion, and reached its conclusions in accordance with the Safeguards Agreement. At most, the EC has advanced suggestions on how an authority might have reached a different conclusion. It has not, and cannot, show that a different conclusion was required.

Ms. Florestal will now discuss the issues relating to Articles 5, 8 and 12 of the Agreement.

Ms. Florestal

Mr. Chairman, Members of the Panel,

My colleague has discussed with you the USITC's thorough determination, which found that the US wheat gluten industry was being seriously injured as a result of increased imports. I will now discuss with you the actions the United States took to respond to those findings.

The United States' safeguard remedy comports with all applicable provisions of the Safeguards Agreement. The EC has demonstrated no violation of the covered agreement. Instead, the EC has relied on extraordinary allegations of collusion and conspiracy to attempt to meet its burden. Those allegations have no basis in fact. They merely demonstrate that the EC is unhappy with the temporary US safeguard measure. The EC has not shown that, in taking such action, the United States violated the Safeguards Agreement.

Our discussion of the US safeguard action today examines two aspects of the remedy the United States put in place: First, the level at which the quota was set, and second, the distribution of shares of the quota between supplying Members.

First, regarding the overall quota amount: The President established a quota based on the historical market share level that wheat gluten imports had obtained during the representative period 1993 to 1995. But, in order to take into account the increase in consumption that had occurred, the President applied the 1993 to 1995 import market share to the higher level of consumption reached in 1997. The President thus set the quota at a level higher than the average level of imports during 1993 to 1995.

The EC's position reads Article 5.1 as if the term "representative" were not present, effectively requiring a Member to choose the most recent three years regardless of conditions in those three years. The question that Article 5.1 poses, however, is "representative" of what? By choosing as its benchmark the most recent three years preceding the increased imports and operating losses, the United States chose a period "representative" of conditions in which its industry can survive. Such an interpretation is in accord with the object and purpose of Article 5.1 to remedy serious injury and facilitate adjustment. The USITC, moreover, clearly justified this choice of a period in its finding that setting a quota level at the average of 1995 to 1997 would not remedy the serious injury. For these reasons, the quota amount chosen was perfectly appropriate both to remedy the serious injury and to facilitate the industry's adjustment to import competition.

I will next turn to the question of how the quota was allocated. The United States chose as "a previous representative period" in accordance with Article 5.2, the same years - 1993 to 1995. The United States chose those years because they were the most recent period that was representative of the historical pattern in the market place. Before 1996 and 1997, import market shares were relatively stable. Only the market share from one source - the EC - grew dramatically during the surge years of 1996 and 1997. Likewise, only imports from that source – the EC – consistently undersold the US product during that surge. The surge years were unrepresentative because the surge itself distorted the relative distribution of market shares among foreign suppliers. Thus, the quota allocation chosen by the United States comports with Article 5.2(a). The EC cites Article 5.2(b), but that Article is irrelevant because the United States did not take action under Article 5.2(b).

As we have shown, the US measure comports with the requirements of Article 5. The EC also raises questions about the fact that Canada is not subject to the measure, and tries to draw similarities between the US safeguard and the safeguard taken by Argentina on footwear imports. The Appellate Body's report in *Argentina – Footwear* demonstrates why the EC' s claims in this area are without merit. The Appellate Body explicitly stated that what was at issue in *Argentina – Footwear* was whether Argentina could take a safeguard remedy solely against third country imports when its investigation found injury from all sources. That is simply not the case here. The USITC conducted a separate examination of wheat gluten imports from Canada. As the USITC found, Canadian imports were not contributing importantly to the injury. They did not participate in the surge. Canada was a relatively small and declining supplier to the US market, whose product oversold the US product during the surge period. On the basis of the specific finding that Canadian imports were not contributing importantly to the injury, the United States excluded Canada from the measure. Therefore, there is no basis on which the EC can argue that third country imports were being punished for the injury caused by imports from an excluded country, as occurred in *Argentina - Footwear.*

In closing, I would like to discuss briefly the EC's complaints that the United States did not satisfy its consultation obligations under Articles 8 and 12 of the Agreement. That claim is simply incorrect. As US Exhibit 6 shows, the United States invited all affected Members to participate in consultations. Its invitation stated that consultations would be held with a view to "reviewing the information provided, ... exchanging views on the measure and reaching an understanding on ways to achieve the objective set out in Article 8.1 of the Agreement on Safeguards." The EC accepted the United States' invitation to consult under those terms. Consultations were held on 24 April 1998. The United States satisfied its consultation obligations.

Mr. Chairman, Members of the Panel, that concludes the United States' oral statement. We thank you for this opportunity to further elaborate our position.

ATTACHMENT 2-3

UNITED STATES CLOSING ORAL STATEMENT
(21 December 1999)

Ms. Florestal

Mr. Chairman, Members of the Panel,

On behalf of the United States delegation, I would like to thank the Panel for the opportunity to comment on some of the allegations raised by the EC in its oral statement yesterday. We will reserve much of our response for our second submission, but we feel compelled to respond to certain claims raised by the EC that attempt to distort the record in this case.

Mr. Toupin will briefly address certain issues raised by the EC's arguments concerning the injury determination, while I will address some of the EC's claims regarding the remedy the United States chose.

Mr. Toupin

Mr. Chairman, Members of the Panel,

First, I would like make some comments concerning the EC's bald claim yesterday that this Panel should engage in new fact finding on injury based on new evidence never presented to the competent authority. In doing so, I do not mean to suggest that the evidence that the EC seeks to introduce here in any way detracts from the USITC's determination. For reasons given in the United States' first written submission, it does not. Nevertheless, the EC should not be permitted to disregard the respective roles of this Panel and the competent authorities.

At the outset, I should highlight an area of agreement between the United States and the EC on the vexed subject of the standard of review. The United States agrees completely with the EC, as it states at paragraph 12 of its statement, that a Panel may not be "engaged itself in redoing the Member's procedure, thus getting to 'its' determination on the appropriateness to adopt 'that' or 'another' safeguard measure". Yet this is precisely what the EC asks the Panel to do by presenting new evidence for the first time to this body. Under Article 3 of the Safeguards Agreement, it is a member's competent authority that investigates the facts. The USITC did so by sending questionnaires to foreign producers, importers, domestic producers, and purchasers; by gathering other publicly available information; and by entertaining any information that interested parties desired to submit, both through written submissions and at its hearings. I note that the EC itself appeared at the hearings as a witness, as shown on page B-8 of the USITC report.

The EC would have this Panel become another authority before which evidence could be submitted on the underlying facts. The EC would have this Panel find that, if only the USITC had gathered just one more piece of evidence, the authority should have reached a different determination. The evidence that the EC mentioned yesterday illustrates the harm that such an approach would do to the ability of national authorities to conduct investigations under Article 3 of the Agreement. This is not a case, as the EC seems to suggest, in which the issue of input prices cannot be discussed except by reference to new information. As the United States' first written submission discusses, the USITC obtained information on input prices. The USITC had before it, for instance, data obtained directly from the US wheat gluten producers on the costs of their inputs. It had before it quarterly data on wheat costs provided by the EC producers. The USITC made findings concerning the rise in input costs, particularly the prices of wheat and wheat flour.

The mischief that the EC does by suggesting that this Panel should make new findings because monthly official wheat cost data was also available is apparent. Quite apart from the fact that the EC's arguments from that evidence are irrelevant to the USITC's determination, the EC's approach would undermine the ability of member's competent authorities to conduct investigations under the Safeguards Agreement. It is hard to imagine a case in which some piece of information could not be obtained somewhere that was not before a competent authority. Interested parties could submit one set of information to the competent authorities, and, on review of determinations before the WTO, the WTO members could seek to relitigate the case based on a new set of information. Moreover, Article 3 of the Safeguards Agreement provides for fact-finding to occur through proceedings that accord an opportunity for all commercially interested parties to present evidence and their views. The government-to-government dispute settlement process in the WTO has a different purpose. It is not designed to provide the procedures that the negotiators of the Safeguards Agreement considered essential to fair and open administration of national safeguard regimes. As the Appellate Body reports have indicated, a Panel's role is limited to conducting an objective assessment of the matter to ascertain whether the United States acted in accordance with the Agreement. The EC would take this Panel outside of that role.

Second, we would like to correct a misstatement that the EC made yesterday in characterizing the United States' position concerning the adequacy of the USITC' s public report. The EC told you yesterday, and I quote, "The US has explicitly recognized in its first written submission that it has 'misapplied' the provisions of Article 3 and 4". This is simply not so. What the United States said, at paragraph 158 of its first written submission, was that in certain instances the USITC had inadvertently misapplied its own policies concerning reporting of aggregate data. The USITC is correcting its misapplication of its own policies. In the interest of transparency, the United States has supplied that correction to the Panel. The United States maintains its position that the USITC's findings are adequately explained in the published report as originally issued. As further explained in the first written submission, the EC's contention that certain findings were inadequately explained was based on a simple misreading by the EC of those findings.

Third, the EC's oral presentation here yesterday continued to fail to address the basis for the USITC's determination. The EC continued instead to present a beginning point to end point analysis of the period of investigation that is contrary to its own statements about the proper analysis. Nevertheless, taking the EC's presentation on its own terms, it is startling how the EC 's oral presentation makes out a case for finding injury caused by increased imports. The EC told us yesterday that, over the course of the period investigated, demand rose. It told us that the US industry's costs also rose. Hearing those facts alone, one would expect also to hear that prices rose. But that is not what the EC told us, because it did not happen. What the EC told us, at paragraph 38, was that prices of EC imports at the end of the period of investigation were essentially the same as they were at the beginning. That prices did not rise when demand and costs rose suggests that something must have been happening on the supply side. It cannot have been an increase, however, in domestic supply. The EC characterized the overall trend of US production as remaining relatively steady. Only the supply of imports grew. The EC's presentation seems to leave no option but to conclude that increased imports held prices down at a level lower than the domestic industry's cost of production.

Ms. Florestal

The EC's oral statements on Article 5 distorts the United States' position, misstates the findings of the Appellate Body, and wholly ignores those findings in certain areas.

The EC's claim of violation under Article 5.2(a) of the Safeguards Agreement is without merit. Recently, the Appellate Body in *Korea - Dairy* expressly cautioned against reading obligations into Article 5 that are not found in the text of that Article. Yet, the EC asks the Panel to do exactly that. The EC's claims under Article 5.2(a) must be rejected for two reasons: First, the United States has specifically and repeatedly contested the EC's allegation that the US failed to consult on the measure. That simply is not true. Moreover, Article 5.2(a) does not establish a duty to consult. The consultation obligation is found in Article 12. The United States satisfied that obligation.

Second, regardless of whether one argues that Article 5.2 or GATT Article XIII is the *lex specialis* in this case, the reality is that GATT Article I is not implicated because the US measure is a quota and not a tariff. The EC's discrimination claim is particularly incomprehensible given that the measure at issue is applied in the same manner to all Members subject to the measure. There is no discrimination in the US safeguard measure.

The EC also suggests to this Panel that Article 5.1 requires a Member to provide clear justification for its choice to impose a quantitative restriction rather than a tariff measure. The EC's position is directly contrary to the Appellate Body's findings in *Korea – Dairy*. The Appellate Body specifically found, and I quote "a Member is *not* obliged to justify in its recommendation or determination a measure in the form of a quantitative restriction which is consistent with the average of imports in the last three representative years for which statistics are available. . (AB Report at para. 99). The United States imposed a safeguard measure in the form of a QR set *above* the level of imports in the last three representative years. Thus, the Appellate Body has held that the United States was *not* required to justify the measure.

The EC's arguments that the United States has the burden of proof to justify the level of the measure it imposed is incorrect. The United States imposed a measure in accordance with Article 5.1. The EC argues that the measure is inconsistent with that Article. Therefore, the burden is on the EC as the complainant to assert and prove its claim.

The EC's allegation of a supposed "proportionality rule" in Article 5.1 not expressed in the text is also contrary to the admonition of the Appellate Body in *Korea - Dairy* to avoid reading obligations into Article 5 that are not expressed in the text. The EC fails to focus on the express terms of Article 5.1 in its rush to create a new "rule". Article 5.1 imposes an obligation on Members to apply a measure "only to the extent necessary to prevent or remedy serious injury and to facilitate adjustment". The United States' measure satisfies that obligation.

The EC next attempts a contorted argument that succeeds only in reading the term "representative" out of Article 5.1. The United States' response to the EC 's allegation on this point is simple: If the negotiators had intended that the term "last three representative years" should always refer to the most recent three years, they would have said so.

Finally, on the EC's claim that the United States failed to consult on the provisions of Article 8, the United States notes that the EC' s statement itself undermines that assertion. The EC acknowledges that the United States invited affected Members to participate in consultations. While the EC chooses to ignore the fact that consultations were held on 24 April 1998, it does not deny it.

Mr. Chairman, Members of the Panel, that concludes the United States comments on the EC's oral presentation. Once again, we thank the Panel for this opportunity.

ATTACHMENT 2-4

UNITED STATES REPLIES TO QUESTIONS

A. *Questions to both parties*

Q.1 We note that the ITC Report (p. I-9) states: "[w]e find that domestically produced wheat gluten is "like" imported wheat gluten and that the domestic industry consists of the domestic producers of all forms of vital wheat gluten, including modified wheat gluten that is used in the baking and pet food industries." Do the parties agree that, for the purposes of this proceeding, the domestic industry consists of the domestic producers of all forms of vital wheat gluten?

Reply

1. The United States agrees that the domestic industry consists of the domestic producers of all forms of vital wheat gluten, including modified wheat gluten used in the baking and pet food industries, which is how the USITC defined the industry. While the EC has made references to a wheat gluten/wheat starch industry, the EC has not challenged the USITC's like product finding or its finding that the domestic industry consists of the domestic producers of wheat gluten. Furthermore, during the USITC investigation neither the EC nor the EU producers contested the fact that the domestic industry should be defined as something other than the domestic producers of all form of vital wheat gluten.[1]

Q.2 In para. 9 of its third party submission, New Zealand asserts: "New Zealand does not contest that the protection of such confidential information, including from the respondents in the safeguards investigation, may be appropriate at the time of the investigation. However, New Zealand considers that a Member cannot justify a measure as being consistent with its obligations under the WTO without disclosing to the panel and the parties the information on which it relies." How do the parties react to this statement?

Reply

2. New Zealand makes this assertion without citing any provision of the Safeguards Agreement (or any other authority) in support of its contention that a party must release all such confidential information to the panel and the parties. In fact, there is no such requirement in the Safeguards Agreement or elsewhere. To the contrary, Article 3.2 states: "Any information which is by nature confidential or which is provided on a confidential basis shall, upon cause being shown, be treated as such by the competent authorities. *Such information shall not be disclosed without permission of the party submitting it*". (Emphasis added). Furthermore, the requirement in Article 4.2 (c) that the competent au-

[1] US Exhibit 4 at I-9.

thority publish a detailed analysis of the case is expressly provided to be "in accordance with the provisions of Article 3". Thus, not only does the Safeguards Agreement not require disclosure of such confidential information by a Member, the Agreement forbids such disclosure without the consent of the party that submitted the confidential information. Finally, it should be noted that Article 3 protects the confidentiality of information furnished by domestic producers as well as importers. Disclosure carries with it the inherent danger of compromising the commercial interests of the companies that supplied the information. It would also likely impede the ability of competent authorities to gather such information, thereby limiting the quality of the information before them at the time they make their decisions.

3. Article 3.2 sets no time limit on the obligation to keep this information confidential. Contrary to New Zealand's suggestion, there is no provision that magically transforms information that is confidential in the USITC investigation into non-confidential information that may be disclosed once the matter goes to a WTO panel.

4. Apart from its inconsistency with the Safeguards Agreement, adoption of New Zealand's proposal would harm not only domestic producers in importing countries, but also importers and producers from exporting countries. For example, the USITC Report redacted not only confidential information submitted by domestic producers, but also confidential information submitted by exporting producers from Canada, Australia and the European Union, as well as by US importers of wheat gluten.[2]

5. Furthermore, notwithstanding the redaction of confidential information, the USITC report adequately discloses the information on which the USITC based its findings. The panel's role is to determine: (1) whether, in making its findings and determination, the competent authority considered all relevant factors, including those listed in Article 4.2(b); (2) whether the published report contains an adequate explanation of how the facts support the determination made; and (3) whether the determination made is consistent with the Safeguards Agreement. Nothing in this proceeding suggests that in order to accomplish this task, the Panel needs to examine and verify all the data examined by the USITC during its investigation.

6. New Zealand purports to base its argument on the decision of the Appellate Body in *Canada – Aircraft.*[3] But *Canada –Aircraft* is irrelevant in this proceeding because it provides no guidance with regard to Article 3.2 of the Safeguard Agreement. The Appellate Body did not address how and under what circumstances a member should or could disclose confidential information to a Panel consistent with the specific requirements of Article 3.2.

---

[2] US Exhibit 4 at II-22-24.

[3] Appellate Body Report, *Canada - Measures Affecting the Export of Civilian Aircraft* ("*Canada – Aircraft*"), WT/DS70/AB/R, adopted 20 August 1999, DSR 1999:III, 1377.

Q.3 In the view of the parties, is the Panel able to perform an "objective assessment of the matter before it" within the meaning of Article 11 of the DSU on the basis of the ITC Report issued in March 1998 (with the "corrigendum" submitted by the United States in these proceedings)?

Reply

7. Yes. The Panel's role consists of evaluating on an objective basis issues on which it finds that the EC has made the required *prima facie* case. The USITC report in its public version (with or without the recently produced "corrigendum") provides sufficient information for the Panel to conduct the analysis required by Article 11 of the DSU regarding the relevant facts and circumstances considered by the USITC that underlay its determination that increased imports were causing serious injury to the domestic wheat gluten industry.

8. The redaction of confidential information in the published USITC report does not materially affect the Panel's ability to conduct this review. In its first submission, the EC raised two issues regarding the redaction of confidential information in the USITC report: (1) questions about the pricing data for the US wheat gluten market (EC First Submission at Paragraphs 49, 82); and (2) questions about the allocations methodologies used by the US producers in determining profitability. (EC First Submission at Paragraph 67).

9. As to the first issue, pricing data, the EC's initial objection was based on a misunderstanding of the USITC report. In discussing the import surge, the report stated that EU imports had consistently undersold domestic wheat gluten.[4] The context made it clear that this statement referred to consistent underselling during the import surge of 1996-1997. The EC's criticism was based on another statement in the USITC report showing six quarters of overselling during the overall 1993-1997 period, which the EC argued was inconsistent with the USITC's findings.[5] However, the six quarters in which EU imports oversold the market all took place during 1993-1995, before the import surge.[6] Thus, as the USITC found, the consistent underselling in 1996-1997 coincided with the surge in EU and total imports. Accordingly, the submission by the United States of the corrigendum only confirms that the EC's argument was based on a misunderstanding of the USITC Report.

10. As to the second issue, the EC complains about the redaction of certain information regarding the allocation methodology used by individual firms. This kind of data, however, is manifestly business sensitive in nature, and the USITC is prohibited from disclosing it - both as a matter of domestic law and as required by Article 3.2 - without the consent of the submitting firms. While the EC has complained about the redaction of aggregate data, it has acknowledged the

4 US Exhibit 4 at I-16.

5 EC First Submission at Para. 82; US Exhibit 4 at II-36.

6 US Exhibit 10 at II-33.

need to protect business confidential data relevant to individual firms. EC First Submission at Paragraph 49. The allocation methodology information redacted from the USITC report is precisely of this nature.

Q.4 Could the parties clarify whether the EU had access to the "confidential information" in question in the domestic proceedings before the ITC? If the EC did have access, under what conditions?

Reply

11. Under the USITC's rules, the EC could have applied to be a party to the USITC administrative protective order governing the confidential information at issue, pursuant to which its counsel would have had access to the information. But the EC never made such an application, and thus did not have such access. The counsel for the European producers (Association des Amidonneries de Cereales de l'U.E.) did agree to the administrative protective order and thus did have access to the confidential information.

12. Under USITC rule 206.17(a)(3)(D)(iii)(B), concerning governments as interested parties, the EC qualified as an interested party and could have applied to be a party to the administrative protective order. While the EC filed an entry of appearance early in the USITC investigation, and participated in the remedy hearing, it chose not to actively participate during the injury phase and did not exercise its right to obtain the confidential information available under the administrative protective order.

Q.5 We note the recent statement of the Appellate Body that the phrase "as a result of unforeseen developments and of the effect of the obligations incurred by a Member under this Agreement, including tariff concessions" in Article XIX:1(a) of the GATT 1994 does not establish independent conditions for the application of a safeguard measure additional to the conditions set out in the second clause of Article XIX:1(a), but it "describes certain circumstances which must be demonstrated as a matter of fact in order for a safeguard measure to be applied consistently with the provisions of Article XIX of the GATT 1994.[7]

What could constitute such "unforeseen developments"? By whom must such developments be "unforeseen"? In this case, what precisely were the circumstances constituting "unforeseen developments" and where are these addressed in the ITC Report?

[7] Appellate Body Report, *Argentina –Safeguard Measures on Imports of Footwear* ("*Argentina – Footwear*"), WT/DS121/AB/R, adopted 12 January 2000, DSR 2000:I, 515, paras. 92 ff.; Appellate Body Report, *Korea – Definitive Safeguard Measure on Imports of Certain Dairy Products* ("*Korea – Dairy*"), WT/DS98/AB/R, adopted 12 January 2000, DSR 2000:I, 3, paras. 85 ff.

Reply

13. The introductory language in Article XIX was intended to ensure that any increase in imports that may result in serious injury or threat of serious injury to a domestic industry is not simply the result of (1) negotiated tariff reductions; or (2) factors of which the negotiating WTO Member was aware at the time of the tariff concession. Thus, unforeseen developments would include significant, unexpected changes in the marketplace as compared to the situation that pertained at the time of the tariff concession. The developments summarized below, which resulted in a surge of low-priced EC imports into the US in 1996-1997, were not foreseen - and indeed could not have been expected - by the United States at the time the wheat gluten tariff concession was negotiated in 1994 as part of the Uruguay Round.

14. Moreover, the 1996-97 import surge, and accompanying underselling of EC wheat gluten, was not the result of the modest decrease in the US wheat gluten tariff negotiated in the Uruguay Round. The decline in the average price of EU wheat gluten from approximately $0.78 per pound in 1994 before the tariff reduction to approximately $0.57 per pound in 1997 - a decline of approximately 27per cent - cannot be accounted for by the much smaller declines of 1.1 per cent and 0.6 per cent in the US general rates of duty on wheat gluten between 1994 and 1997.[8]

15. Indeed, in considering whether to recommend that the wheat gluten safeguard take the form of a tariff increase, the USITC found that wheat gluten appears to be largely insensitive to changes in wheat gluten price and tariff levels.[9] Thus, the modest drop in the US wheat gluten tariff does not explain the massive increase in imports during the 1996-97 period.

16. In fact, the USITC's findings show that the 1996-97 import surge reflected a change in market conditions that could not have been anticipated from prior market conditions. The USITC found that during 1993-95, imports both oversold and undersold the US wheat gluten market, and import market share fell slightly.[10] These trends gave no reason to believe that the mixed pricing pattern would suddenly be replaced by a pattern of consistent underselling by EC imports, causing such a massive increase in imports that domestic production and shipments actually declined during a period of growth in demand.

---

[8] US Exhibit 4 at II-33, Table 18. The general US rate of duty on wheat gluten (other than wheat gluten to be used as animal feed) was 8 per cent ad valorem in 1993-1994, and under concessions negotiated in the Uruguay Round the United States agreed to reduce this rate in six stages to 6.8 per cent ad valorem in 2000. In 1997, the rate was 7.4 per cent ad valorem. The United States agreed to reduce the general US rate of duty on wheat gluten to be used as animal feed from 4 per cent ad valorem (in 1993-1994) to 1.8 per cent ad valorem in 2000; the rate was 2.9 per cent ad valorem in 1997. EC First Submission at Para. 42; EC Exhibit EC-9; US Exhibit 4 at II-6.

[9] US Exhibit 4 at I-26; see also US Exhibit 4 at I-17, I-24.

[10] US Exhibit 4 at I-16, II-36.

17. As the USITC findings show, this dramatic change in market conditions did not result from developments in the wheat gluten market itself. Rather, the USITC found that it resulted primarily from a huge increase in EC production capacity aimed at increasing production of wheat starch (a co-product of wheat gluten).[11] The EC wheat starch market is protected by high tariffs from import competition, and its high domestic wheat starch prices encourage EC domestic production.[12] In addition, the EC operates a number of programmes, including starch production refunds, to enhance the production of wheat starch.[13]

18. The USITC specifically found that EC wheat gluten production was not responsive to changes in wheat gluten prices, but rather was driven by EC production of wheat starch.[14] The USITC also found that the high prices for wheat starch in its protected home market allowed the EC the flexibility to sell wheat gluten at low prices, including its exports to the United States.[15] Thus, developments in the EC wheat starch market led to an increase in EC production of wheat gluten, and to increased EC exports of wheat gluten to the US at relatively low prices, for reasons unrelated to conditions in the US or European market for wheat gluten.

19. Even the participants in the US wheat gluten market did not foresee these developments. As proof, one need only consider the fact that the US industry considerably expanded its capacity (largely completed by June 1995), and a new US market entrant, Heartland Wheat Growers, began building a new plant in 1993 and started production in 1996.[16] As the EC itself has observed, such investments were inconsistent with the expectation that imports would grow substantially in excess of the increase in demand, as they did. In short, circumstances in the marketplace would not and did not lead the United States to foresee the developments that led to increased imports in 1996-97.

20. As the Panel's question recalls, the unforeseen developments are circumstances to be demonstrated, not conditions that must be found by the competent authority in order to make an affirmative injury finding under the Safeguards Agreement. In any event, the USITC Report makes clear that the United States did not foresee the developments that led to increased wheat gluten imports from the EC.

Q.6 In paras. 73-77 of its first written submission, the EC argues that the ITC failed to take several "relevant" factors into account in its "serious injury" analysis (i.e. capital investment; new entries/expansion; developments as to co-products, "imports as positive business strategy"). We note that, in the summary

---

11 US Exhibit 4 at I-24.

12 US Exhibit 4 at I-24, II-38-39, and n. 95.

13 US Exhibit 4 at I-24, n. 119.

14 US Exhibit 4 at I-24.

15 US Exhibit 4 at I-24-25, II-38.

16 US Exhibit 4 at I-12, II-8.

of parties' arguments in the relevant section of the ITC Report (pp. I-11, I-12), while it appears that the EC raised arguments concerning "profitability" with respect to wheat starch/wheat gluten, it is not clear that the EC raised the other factors just mentioned as "relevant" in this context in the ITC proceedings. Can the parties clarify whether or not the EC did raise these issues in this context before the ITC? If the EC did not raise them before the ITC in this context, what considerations should guide the Panel in any examination of these factors or of their "relevance" in this context?

Reply

21. The EC itself did not raise any of these issues in the USITC proceedings, although it could have do so had it wished. According to the USITC's public docket list, the EC filed a notice of appearance with the USITC early in the investigation, did not participate during the injury/causation phase of the investigation, but then did appear and argue at the USITC remedy hearing. The EC's arguments at the remedy hearing did not address the issues pertaining to the USITC's "serious injury" analysis.

22. The European producers raised some but not all of these issues during the USITC proceedings, although not necessarily in the same way that the EC has raised them before this Panel. It appears that the European producers did raise arguments, in at least some form, about developments in co-product markets, about new entries and expansion in the US market, and about imports as an alleged business strategy.

23. A review of the record shows that no party in the USITC investigation raised the EC's argument regarding the productivity of "capital investment." Thus, at least one of the arguments now raised by the EC in paragraphs 73-77 of its first submission is being raised in this Panel proceeding for the first time. The Panel should treat the failure by the parties to raise that issue during the USITC investigation as supporting the conclusion that the issue is not relevant for the reasons stated in the United States' response to Panel Question #7.[17]

Q.7 Does the language of Article 4.2(a) of the Safeguards Agreement ("¼the competent authorities shall evaluate all relevant factors of an objective and quantifiable nature having a bearing on the situation of that industry") impose an obligation on the competent authorities to themselves undertake an inquiry into "all relevant factors" even if these are not raised in the proceedings before it? If so, what is the nature and scope of this obligation?

[17] Moreover, as the United States demonstrated in its first submission, the EC's belated claims regarding capital productivity are without merit, in that in its injury analysis the USITC fully considered and evaluated the facts concerning capital investments in the industry, as well as the effects of increased imports on productivity. United States First Submission at Paras. 95-97.

Reply

24. Article 4.2(a) goes on to enumerate certain factors that the competent authorities "shall evaluate." Thus, there is no doubt that a competent authority should undertake an inquiry as to these specifically enumerated factors regardless of whether they are raised by the parties.

25. However, with respect to injury causation factors not specifically enumerated in Article 4.2(a), the competent authority should in general be able to rely on the interested parties (e.g., importers and foreign producers, as well as domestic producers) to bring them to the authority's attention and raise arguments regarding the weight that the authority should attribute to them. In view of their intimate familiarity with the marketplace and their own commercial interests, the market participants are in the best position to know of, and have every incentive to point out additional factors - such as other sources of injury to the domestic industry - meriting examination by the competent authority. Indeed, the USITC has long relied on the comments and arguments of the market participants to help it identify and analyze relevant causation factors. If the parties fail to mention particular factors during the course of the investigation, it strongly suggests that those in the best position to know did not view those factors as significant.

26. The proposition that a competent authority may properly rely on the interested parties to identify factors other than imports that may have caused or contributed to injury finds strong support in a related context. As the United States pointed out in paragraphs 130-131 of its first submission here, in United States – Salmon-[18] the Panel addressed arguments about the interpretation of Article 3.4 of the Agreement on Implementation of Article VI of the General Agreement on Tariffs and Trade (also known as the Tokyo Round Anti-Dumping Code). The terms of Article 4.2(b) of the Safeguards Agreement were drawn from that earlier provision.

27. The panel noted first that there was another provision, Article 3.3 of the Tokyo Round Anti-Dumping Code (comparable to Article 4.2(a) of the Safeguards Agreement) that provided that the investigating authorities must conduct "an evaluation of all the relevant economic factors and indices having a bearing on the state of the industry," and specifically enumerated certain factors that must be considered. United States - Salmon at Paragraphs 493, 557. In interpreting the language in Article 3.4, which, like Article 4.2(b) of the Safeguards Agreement, provides that the competent authority may not attribute injury caused by other factors to increased imports, the Panel stated "there is no express requirement that investigating authorities examine in each case on their own initiative the effects of all other possible factors other than imports under investigation." Id. at

[18] United States - Imposition of Anti-Dumping Duties on Fresh and Chilled Atlantic Salmon From Norway, ADP/87, BISD 41s/229, adopted by the Committee on Anti-dumping Practices on 27 April 1994.

Paragraph 550. Thus, in construing comparable provisions of the Anti-Dumping Code, the United States - Salmon panel concluded that, in contrast to the requirement that enumerated factors must be considered, there was no requirement that the competent authority investigate the effects of non-enumerated factors that had not been raised by the parties.

28. Accordingly, the USITC could properly rely on the parties to identify and raise arguments about causation factors other than those enumerated under Article 4.2(a).

Q.8 Article 4.2(b) of the Safeguards Agreement states : "When factors other than increased imports are causing injury to the domestic industry at the same time, such injury shall not be attributed to increased imports." We note that the term used in this sentence is "injury" rather than "serious injury". What is the meaning and relevance, if any, of this distinction?

Reply

29. The language that the Panel has identified in Article 4.2(b) recognizes that in any given case, factors other then increased imports may play a greater or lesser role in any injury sustained by the domestic industry. The choice of the term "injury" as opposed to "serious injury" in this context is appropriate, since the role that non-import factors may play in any particular case may be small and thus may not amount to "serious injury" within the meaning of Article 4.1(a). By using the term "injury," Article 4.2(b) avoids specifying a threshold or limit for the degree of injury that may be caused by such other factors. In its larger context, the language suggests that in establishing "the causal link" between increased imports and serious injury, the competent authority must avoid attributing to increased imports any degree of injury caused by other factors.

Q.9 What is the legal basis in the Safeguards Agreement for a causation analysis that examines whether or not certain factors are "a more important cause of serious injury than increased imports"? What guidance, if any, can be found on this issue in past GATT/WTO practice?

Reply

30. Article 4.2(b) of the Agreement on Safeguards provides that a safeguards determination under Article 4 requires that the investigation demonstrate "the existence of the causal link between increased imports of the product concerned and serious injury thereof."

31. As the United States discussed in its first submission[19] the USITC Report reflects that the USITC conducted its examination under provisions of US law that provide that it must find not merely the "causal link" to the serious injury,

---

[19] United States First Submission at Paras. 127-128.

but also that imports must be a "substantial cause." 19 U.S.C. § 2252(b)(1)(A).[20] US law defines substantial cause as "a cause which is important and not less than any other cause." 19 U.S.C. § 2252(b)(1)(B).

32. This aspect of US law requires the USITC to make a finding related to causation that, while not required by Article 4.2, helps to ensure that its objectives are realized. The requirement to examine the relative weight of other factors ensures that the USITC both thoroughly examines the causal link between increased imports and serious injury, as required by Article 4.2(b), and avoids attributing to imports the effects of other causes of injury that are more important. While they result in findings that provide more detail than required under Article 4.2(b), the relevant US procedures are entirely consistent with its letter and spirit.

33. The United States wishes to stress that the EC has not challenged the compatibility of US law on this point with the Safeguard Agreement, and thus this issue is not within the Panel's terms of reference. The only matter with respect to Articles 2 and 4 of the Safeguard Agreement that has been referred to this Panel is whether the USITC's findings and conclusion comport with those articles. See Guatemala - Anti-Dumping Investigation Regarding Portland Cement From Mexico, AB-1998-6 at Paragraph 73 (2 November 1998) ("the 'measure' and the 'claims' made concerning that measure constitute the 'matter referred to the DSB' which forms the basis for a panel's terms of reference."). See also United States - Measure Affecting Imports of Woven Wool Shirts and Blouses from India, WT/DS33/AB/R, at Paragraph 6 ("Given the explicit aim of dispute settlement that permeates the DSU, we do not consider that Article 3.2 of the DSU is meant to encourage either panels or the Appellate Body to 'make law' by interpreting existing provisions of the WTO Agreement outside the context of resolving a particular dispute. A panel need only address those claims which must be addressed in order to resolve the matter in issue in the dispute").

Q.10 What is the legal relationship between Article 5.2 of the Safeguards Agreement and Article I of the GATT 1994? What legal principles and/or past GATT/WTO practice give guidance in this context?

Reply

34. Article 5.2(a) sets forth the MFN principle for safeguard quotas, which is the lex specialis in this case. Any challenge to a safeguard quota should be judged under the terms of Article 5 and not under the general MFN principle of GATT Article I. Although no previous Panel has examined this question under the Safeguards Agreement, GATT disputes relating to the relationship between Article XIII and Article I are instructive because the language in Article 5.2(a)[21]

[20] US Exhibit 4 at I-14.

[21] The United States assumes that the Panel's question is limited to Article 5.2(a).

is identical to Article XIII:2(d) of the GATT with respect to the requirement that:

> In cases in which a quota is allocated among supplying countries, the Member applying the restrictions may seek agreement with respect to the allocation of shares in the quota with all other Members having a substantial interest in supplying the product concerned. In cases in which this method is not reasonably practicable, the Member concerned shall allot to members having a substantial interest in supplying the product shares based upon the proportions supplied by such members during a previous representative period, of the total quantity or value of imports of the product, due account being taken of any special factors which may have affected or may be affecting the trade in the product.

35. GATT panel determinations that have addressed the question consistently have found that claims of discrimination in the allocation of a quota properly should be raised under GATT Article XIII, rather than Article I. In EEC Restrictions on Imports of Apples from Chile I, Chile argued that the EEC's import restriction against Chilean apples violated GATT Article I. Contrary to its present arguments, in that dispute the EC "maintained that its action, being a quantitative restriction, should be examined in connection with the most-favoured-nation type commitment contained in Article XIII".[22] The panel concluded that the restriction constituted a quota, and it concurred with the EC that it was "more appropriate to examine the matter in the context of Article XIII which deals with the non-discriminatory administration of quantitative restrictions, rather than Article I:1.

36. Similarly, in a second adopted report in EEC - Restrictions on Imports of Dessert Apples, Chile again argued that the EC's import quotas were discriminatory and thus a breach of Article I. The EC maintained that, as this was a question on the administration of quantitative restrictions, it should be examined "solely under Article XIII, which was the lex specialis." The panel again concurred with the EC, noting that the issue concerned the non-discriminatory administration of quantitative restrictions, thus Article XIII is the lex specialis in that case. Finally, as noted in the US first submission, the Appellate Body in EC - Regime for the Importation, Sale and Distribution of Banana[23] endorsed the notion that allocation of quantitative restrictions is outside the scope of Article I in finding that the EC's tariff rate quota on bananas under the Lome Convention was not within the scope of the "Lome Waiver" of Article I.

[22] EEC Restrictions on Imports of Apples from Chile I, L/5047 - 27S/98, adopted 10 November 1980.

[23] Appellate Body Report, *European Communities – Regime for the Importation, Sale and Distribution of Bananas* ("*EC – Bananas III*"), WT/DS27/AB/R, adopted 25 September 1997, DSR 1997:II, 591.

37. The reasoning in those panels applies equally in this instance. No matter what the EC's legal theory, the underlying claim is that the allegedly discriminatory application of a quota measure – either as a violation of Article 5.2(a) or 5.2 (b) - leads to a violation of Article I. The EC's position that Article I addresses quotas is incorrect as a matter of law. A claim of discrimination relating to quotas properly is raised either as a violation of Article 5, in the case of safeguards, or GATT Article XIII. But the US safeguard measure cannot be inconsistent with GATT Article I because it is a quota, not a tariff measure.

Q.11 Can the parties indicate whether consultations took place on 24 April 1998 as the United States is suggesting, and, if so, whether the parties discussed the measure proposed in the United States notification of 24 March 1998?

38. The United States has provided exhibits to the Panel conclusively demonstrating that the parties held several consultations, including the consultations that took place on 24 April 1998.

39. In a letter dated 8 May 1998, the EC representative noted that consultations concerning the wheat gluten investigation took place on 24 April 1998 and that "it was mentioned that the US was considering a possible remedy in the form of a quota which would involve a departure from the method of proportionate allocation provided for in Article 5.2(a).[24] The letter further sates that "if such a departure from Article 5.2(a) is envisaged," the EC expected that further consultations would take place under Article 12.3

40. In a letter dated 14 May 1998, the EC representative referenced "formal" consultations on the wheat gluten issue that occurred as far back as 11 July 1997. The letter goes on to request "informal" consultations without prejudice to the further "formal" WTO consultations that were scheduled for 22 May 1998. The EC representative provided a list of six questions to the United States on 21 May 1998, in preparation for consultations scheduled for the following day. These questions raised the EC's concerns regarding the US "recommended measure". The United States' records indicate that consultations did in fact take place, and the EC does not appear to deny that contention. Thus, the EC's own documents demonstrate that, far from refusing to consult, the United States engaged in multiple consultations with the EC on the measure.[25]

Q.12 On page 34 of its oral statement, the EC refers to an "informal meeting" held on 19-20 May 1999. Do the parties consider that this meeting constituted "consultations" within the meaning of Article 12.3 of the Safeguards Agreement?

---

[24] Letter of 8 May 1988 from J-J. Bouflet, Minister Counsellor of the European Commission to B. Kasper, Second Secretary Permanent Mission of the United States.

[25] See US Exhibit 11 and 12.

Reply

41. Article 12.3 of the Safeguards Agreement makes no mention of "formal" or "informal" meetings, it refers merely to "prior consultations." The object and purpose of Article 12.3, as clearly stated, is to provide Members with a substantial interest the opportunity to consult with the Member proposing to apply the measure. That objective is satisfied when the parties concerned meet and discuss the matter, regardless of whether that meeting is designated as "formal" or "informal." Therefore, as the EC itself admits, the parties met on 19-20 May 1999 and discussed the matter. Accordingly that meeting forms a part of the "consultations" between the parties. As noted above, however, the meeting on 19-20 May does not constitute the only consultations between the parties. In view of the multiple consultations held with the EC – both "formal" and "informal" – the United States has amply satisfied that requirement.[26]

Q.13 With respect to production, capacity and capacity utilization, what is the meaning and relevance of the following statement at p. II-14 of the ITC Report: "ADM, Manildra and Midwest reported that dryer capacity defines the limit on production capacity for wheat gluten."

Reply

42. According to what these producers reported to the USITC, their dryers are the piece of equipment that constrains and sets the upper limit on their production capacity for wheat gluten. In other words, other pieces of equipment may allow them to produce more in a given period of time, but their dryers serve as a bottleneck. The relevance is that the piece of equipment that serves as a bottleneck determines their practical capacity for that product.

43. Separate dryers are used for wheat gluten and wheat starch. After the starch and gluten are separated from each other, they are submitted to special processes, including drying.[27]

B. Questions to the EC

Q.14 In its first written submission, the United States indicates that the ITC has now prepared a corrigendum to the public report that provides the portion of the pricing data and certain other information that can be disclosed, and attached it as Exhibit 10. The United States also expresses that it is "confident that this greater degree of disclosure will allay the EC's concerns." How does the EC react to this statement? What, in your view, is the status of this corrigendum in these proceedings?

---

[26] Presumably, the EC would define "informal" to mean those consultations that are not specifically designated in writing as consultations held under Article 12.3 of the Safeguards Agreement.

[27] US Exhibit 4 at II-7, Figure 1.

Reply

44. The Safeguards Agreement sets out two requirements concerning the publication of reports: (1) Article 3.1 requires that the competent authorities "publish a report setting forth their findings and reasoned conclusions reached on all pertinent issues of fact and law", and (2) Article 4.2(c) requires that the competent authorities "publish promptly, in accordance with the provisions of Article 3, a detailed analysis of the case under investigation ... ." Neither provision specifies the level of detail required, and neither provision specifically requires that all information be published.

45. The United States submits that the report as initially published by the USITC satisfied the publication requirements of Articles 3.1 and 4.2(c). The United States brought forward these previously unpublished facts in response to a claim made by the EC in 56 and 82 of its First Submission. The EC claimed that the USITC did not have evidence to support its finding that imports of wheat gluten from the EC consistently undersold US wheat gluten in 1996 and 1997. This previously unpublished information (it was included in the confidential version of the USITC's report but not in the public version) supports the USITC's finding.

46. There is no transparency issue here despite the EC's claim to the contrary in 29 of its Oral Statement. The USITC's finding was clear on its face and was supported by evidence in the record of the investigation. Furthermore, in the course of the USITC 's investigation, the European producers had access to all the confidential business information in the record of the USITC investigation , including the pricing data at issue here, under an administrative protective order. Accordingly, they had full opportunity to review the information and make any arguments they deemed appropriate. Moreover, as pointed out in the response to panel question 4, the EC could have had access to the confidential information itself, but chose not to apply to become a party to the administrative protective order. Thus, the EC complaint about a lack of transparency vis-a-vis the exporting Member are without merit.

47. The United States further notes that the EC has not challenged the USITC's redaction procedures. Although the EC has not disputed that publishing aggregate data in certain circumstances can have the effect of disclosing a company's confidential information to competitors, the EC has simply stated that any redaction of aggregate information is improper. Thus, the EC has not raised a legal claim with respect to these pricing data that this Panel must decide.

Q.15 What is the motivation underlying the assertion in paragraph 49 of the EC first written submission that "[t]his requirement presupposes that the detailed analysis and the demonstration of the relevance of factors are published and not held secret, unless confidentiality is really an issue"? Is the EC asserting that confidentiality is not really an issue here?

Reply

48. The EC has acknowledged the obligation to protect business confidential data submitted by individual firms, but questions the USITC 's redaction of aggregate data. EC First Submission at Paragraph 49. However, the US had ample reason to redact the aggregate. Throughout much of the investigative period there were only three US producers, one of which was not able to provide US-specific information on its operations, and not all producers engaged in each activity for which the USITC sought information (e.g., not all US producers imported wheat gluten).

49. Thus, in many instances the USITC had data for only two firms, and publication of aggregate data would have risked disclosure of each firm's confidential competitive information to its competitors. Pursuant to its long-standing policies, the USITC redacted all aggregate data that risked such disclosure. The EC's arguments do not provide any basis for disputing the confidentiality claims of the competing firms involved, and likewise do not suggest any way for the United States to disclose the confidential information consistent with its obligations to preserve the confidentiality of the information submitted to it.

Q.16 Is the EC arguing that it was/is prejudiced in any way in these WTO dispute settlement proceedings from the ITC's treatment of confidential information in the public version of its report? If so, in what way?

Reply

50. The EC was not prejudiced by the USITC's treatment of confidential material. As pointed out in the response to Panel question 4, the EC could have had access to confidential information in the USITC proceeding, as the European producers did, but chose not to apply to be a party to the administrative protective order governing that material.

51. The redaction of confidential information in the published USITC report does not materially affect the Panel's ability to conduct this review. The Panel's role does not entail verifying all the data examined by the USITC during its investigation.

52. Furthermore, as explained in response to Panel question 3, the EC's only specific objections concerning the redactions of confidential information in the USITC report were based on a misreading of that report, and fail to show any prejudice to it in these WTO dispute settlement proceedings.

Q.17 We note that the EC did not refer to Article 3 of the Safeguards Agreement in its panel request. In what way and on what legal basis is the EC referring to Article 3 of the Safeguards Agreement in these proceedings?

53. In 28 and 29 of its First Oral Statement the EC sets out a new claim against the United States under Article 3.2 of the Safeguards Agreement. Because the EC did not reference Article 3 in its panel request, this claim falls outside the terms of reference of this Panel. Accordingly, the Panel should disregard the claim and any arguments made by the EC under it.

54. In 28 of its statement, the EC asserts in pertinent part that–

> Article 3.2 of the SA certainly allows that information which *truly* must be kept confidential, is not included in the public version of the report of a safeguard investigation without permission by the company concerned. However, the ITC report oversteps this provision by not even providing *aggregate* data. [Emphasis in the original.]

The EC then asserts in 29 of the statement that "The EC submits that the US refusal to disclose pertinent information even in an aggregate form constitutes a very serious violation of the US WTO obligations ..." and then cites several reasons.

55. The United States agrees that Article 4 requires that the competent authorities publish, in accordance with the provisions of Article 3, "a detailed analysis" of the case under investigation and a demonstration of the relevance of the factors examined. Article 4 does not require the competent authorities to publish all non-confidential information, but only to publish a detailed analysis and demonstration of the relevance of the factors examined. Any further claim based on Article 3.2 of the Agreement is beyond this Panel's terms of reference, and the Panel's terms of reference with respect to Article 3 are limited to the extent that a claim arises under Article 4. As was made clear by the Appellate Body in European Communities – Hormones, "Panels are inhibited from addressing legal claims falling outside their terms of reference".[28]

56. The United States has explained its reasons for not publishing confidential business information in its responses to panel questions 2, 3 and 15 above.

Q.18 At p. I-13 of its Report, the ITC states that it "received usable financial data on wheat gluten operations from three of the four domestic producers of wheat gluten. The three firms accounted for the substantial majority of domestic production of wheat gluten." Why precisely does the EC object to this degree of data coverage and on what legal basis?

Reply

57. The USITC findings fully complied with all the requirements of Article 4 of the Safeguards Agreement, including with regard to consideration of profit and loss data relating to the condition of the domestic industry. As noted in the excerpts from the USITC report quoted in the question, the USITC received usable data from three firms accounting for the great majority of domestic production.

[28] Appellate Body Report, *EC Measures Concerning Meat and Meat Products (Hormones)* ("*EC – Hormones*"), WT/DS26/AB/R, WT/DS/48/R, adopted 13 February 1998, DSR 1998:I, 135, para. 156. This finding in European Communities – Hormones was cited by the Appellate Body in *Korea – Dairy, supra*, footnote 7, para. 139.

58. As explained in Paragraph 105 of the First Submission of the United States, the data furnished by one of the four domestic wheat gluten producers included financial information on that firm's Canadian and United States operations combined, and thus did not provide usable data on the profitability of the US operations alone. The Safeguards Agreement does not require 100 per cent data coverage, and the data coverage that the USITC received on profitability of US operations, representing a major proportion of the total domestic production of wheat gluten, is fully consistent with Article 4.1(c) of the Safeguards Agreement.

Q.19 In paragraph 165 of its first written submission, the EC argues that paragraph 3 of Article 12 "provides further clarification that the measure should be notified immediately when it is proposed, not after it has been put into place". Does the EC consider that both the proposed measure and the final measure have to be notified?

Reply

59. The United States notes that it notified both its proposed measure (Article 12.1(b) supplemental notification), and its final measure (Article 12.1(c)). The EC appears to take exception to the United States' Article 12.1(c) notification, which identified the final measure, because it was notified one day after the measure became effective. Under the EC's reading, the United States was obligated to notify the measure it actually imposed - i.e., the final measure - before it could be imposed.

60. The EC's reading simply ignores the fact that Article 12 refers to "proposed measures" and not final measures. The purpose of Article 12's notification requirements, as the Appellate Body has found, is to provide transparency so that potentially affected Members may have information concerning the facts of the case in order that they might decide to request consultations, which in turn may lead to modification of the proposed measure.[29] The EC had just such an opportunity. The United States fully and repeatedly consulted with the EC (and other affected Members) on the proposed measure. After consultations were concluded, the United States reflected on the views of affected Members and it imposed a measure consistent with the obligations of the Safeguards Agreement.

Q.20 If a proposed measure is altered before it is imposed, must the modification be notified prior to imposition of the measure?

Reply

61. The Safeguards Agreement does not require a Member to notify the modification of a proposed measure before the final measure can be applied. Article 12.2 states that in making their 12.1(b) and 12.1(c) notifications, Members shall

[29] *Korea – Dairy*, *supra*, footnote 7, para. 111.

provide to the Safeguards Committee "all pertinent information" which includes a "precise description of the product involved and the proposed measure" (emphasis added). The purpose of that provision, as clarified in Article 12.3, is to permit Members during consultations to exchange views on the measure proposed. Once consultations have been completed, there is no provision in the Safeguards Agreement that prevents a Member from modifying its measure – consistent with substantive requirements of the Agreement - in order to take into account the results of consultations.

62. Indeed, the EC's reading of Article 12 would render consultations a meaningless exercise of form over substance. Under the EC's reading a Member proposing to apply a safeguard would simply ignore any suggestions offered up by potentially affected Members because incorporating those suggestions would trigger another round of notifications which would delay the Member from applying the measure.

63. The objective of consultations is to provide potentially affected Members with ample opportunity to comment on the competent authority's investigation and to actively express their views at a time when the Member proposing to apply a measure is deliberating on a course of action. The EC had exactly such an opportunity. The United States consulted with the EC extensively prior to applying the measure, thus the objectives of Article 12 were properly met.

Q.21 In paragraph 166 of its first written submission, the EC submits that the United States failed to notify each and every step in Article 12.1 Safeguards Agreement in a timely manner. In paragraph 200 of its first written submission, the United States is arguing that the EC's interpretation of Article 12 Safeguards Agreement suggests that a Member is obliged first to issue "preliminary" findings of serious injury that the Committee would then examine and ratify. Does the EC agree with this interpretation of its argument?

Reply

64. Paragraph 200 of the first US submission addressed the argument in paragraph 168 of the EC's submission that "[i]n particular, the US notifications of the findings of serious injury and of the decision were effected after the findings had been made and the measure was enacted". The EC considered this to be a violation of Article 12 because the "findings and decision had to have been made at a date that would have allowed the Committee on Safeguards and, possibly, the Council for Trade in Goods to request additional information and hold a meaningful discussion in a multilateral forum." The United States' comment merely suggested that if its notifications on the findings of serious injury were effected before the findings had been made they would constitute "preliminary" findings.

Q.22 The United States argues that it notified the proposed measure and that consultations were held. The United States refers to its notification pursuant to Article 12.1 (b) of the Safeguards Agreement of 24 March 1998 (United States Exhibit 6). Could the EC explain why it does not consider this notification to be a notification of the proposed measure?

Reply

65. The EC's contention appears based on an erroneous reading of Article 12 that would require notifications before a Member takes a decision to apply a safeguard measure. In fact, Article 12 requires notification "upon taking a decision to apply ... a safeguard measure." In other words notification is to take place *after* the decision is made.

Q.23 The United States is suggesting in paragraphs 205 and 208 of its first written submission that the EC is claiming that Article 8 of the Safeguards Agreement requires that substantially equivalent concessions be provided before a Member, in casu the United States, can take a safeguard action. Is this a correct reflection of the EC's argument under Article 8 of the Safeguards Agreement?

Reply

66. In paragraphs 205 - 208 of its submission, the United States sought clarification as to paragraph 177 of the EC's submission, which argued that:

> By imposing certain specific conditions on the right of an affected Member to withdraw substantially equivalent concessions, paragraph 3 of Article 8 is addressing only the last step of the process. It does not relieve Members from the obligation to make every effort to maintain a substantially equivalent level of concessions when imposing a measure under the Safeguards Agreement. An affected Member would be fully within its rights to request temporary concessions on other products to offset the concessions impaired by the safeguard measure.

67. In response to the EC's claim, in paragraph 205 of its first submission, the United States noted that "if the EC's allegation is that the United States violated Article 8, then it is precisely the Panel's duty to determine what obligations, if any, Article 8 imposed and how the United Sates might have been able to meet that obligation". The United States went on to articulate its interpretation of the obligations contained in Article 8.

Q.24 Does the EC agree with the United States that consultations within the meaning of Article 12.3 of the Safeguards Agreement were held on 24 April 1998 regarding the proposed wheat gluten safeguard measure?

Reply

68. See US Response to Panel Question 11.

Q.25 Could the EC expand on the relationship between Article XXVIII of the GATT 1994 and Article 8 of the Safeguards Agreement?

Reply

69. The United States looks forward to reviewing the EC's response to this important question, and the United States reserves its right to provide its views on the matter during its second oral presentation.

C. *Questions to the United States*

Q.26 At p. I-13 of its Report, the ITC states: "Based on a careful review of the allocation methodologies used by domestic wheat gluten producers in responding to the Commission's questionnaire, we find those allocations to be appropriate." Could the United States clarify the nature of the "careful review" and clarify and elaborate upon the "allocation methodologies" referred to?

Reply

70. In the financial section of the producers' questionnaire sent to domestic wheat gluten producers, the USITC provided specific instructions with respect to the submission of the financial data.[30] The USITC directed that questionnaire recipients provide financial data on overall establishment operations, combined wheat gluten/wheat starch operations, wheat gluten operations, and starch operations. Firms that did not maintain separate internal profit-and-loss and cost of production data for wheat gluten operations were directed to allocate costs between wheat gluten and wheat starch to explain their allocation methodology and provide worksheets with their calculations. They were also instructed to indicate the accounting basis that they used (US generally accepted accounting principles (GAAP), tax, cash, or other).[31]

71. All reporting firms stated that their financial data were prepared in accordance with GAAP. The majority of the responding firms maintained separate internal profit-and-loss and cost of production data for wheat gluten on a regular basis and furnished such data to the USITC. The responding firm that did not maintain separate data made allocations, and provided the USITC with an explanation of the basis for those allocations.

72. The accounting methodologies used by all the producers were reviewed by the USITC accounting staff and checked for reasonable allocation methods to the extent the revenues and costs were not directly attributable to a particular product. The USITC accounting staff found all of the allocation methods to be in accordance with US generally accepted accounting principles. It found that differences among the methodologies used by the responding companies were principally a function of differences in operations and reflected commercial realities. Copies of the confidential questionnaires submitted by domestic wheat gluten

[30] A copy of the this questionnaire was attached as Exhibit 1 to the United States' First Submission.

[31] US Exhibit 1, US First Submission, USITC producers' questionnaire at 8.

producers were made available to authorized representatives of the parties to the administrative protective order, including representatives of the EU producer respondents. The USITC considered the arguments made by EU producer respondents with respect to the allocations in finding the allocations to be appropriate.[32]

73. In addition, the USITC selected the largest producer, Midwest Grain Products, Inc., for a two day on-site verification in Atchison, Kansas on 3 and 4 December 1997. This verification was conducted by a USITC auditor, an independent certified public accountant (CPA). The auditor prepared a 50-page verification report, including exhibits, which was made a part of the USITC's record in the investigation. Virtually all of the information in the report is confidential business information. However, the United States can provide the following information about the report without disclosing confidential business information. Midwest Grain, the company selected for verification, is a public corporation whose stock is traded on the NASDAQ stock exchange. The USITC auditor confirmed that Midwest's overall financial statements were prepared in accordance with GAAP and were audited by an independent certified public accounting firm in accordance with US generally accepted auditing standards. Midwest made these audits available to the USITC auditor.

74. To derive the wheat gluten financial data from the overall corporate financial data, the USITC auditor at the verification conducted a reconciliation which entailed a detailed evaluation of the firm's operations and the accounting system. The USITC auditor reconciled Midwest Grain's questionnaire data on wheat gluten for each period with the product income and loss statements which were derived from the audited financial statements. This was possible as Midwest Grain prepares separate income and loss statements on a monthly basis for each of its divisions, one of which is the wheat gluten division. The USITC auditor reviewed the financial statements for each division and any allocations that might have been used, and tested their reasonableness with alternative allocation methods.

75. In addition, the USITC auditor confirmed that the allocation methods used by Midwest to measure the financial performance of each division, to the extent allocations were necessary, had been in use for a number of years and were not changed for purposes of the USITC wheat gluten investigation. The auditor concluded that the verification objectives were fully satisfied. number of years and were not changed for purposes of the USITC wheat gluten investigation. The auditor concluded that the verification objectives were fully satisfied.

Q.27 At p. I-14 of the ITC Report, the ITC states: "While there has been minor improvement in several factors during the most recent year, these improvements are isolated and do not change our conclusion that the domestic industry is presently seriously injured." Could the United States explain how these "im-

[32] US Exhibit 4 at I-13.

provements" in each of the "several factors" referred to are "isolated" and why did they not affect the determination of serious injury?

76. As the United States pointed out in 75-76 of its First Submission in this proceeding, Article 4.2(a) of the Safeguards Agreement requires competent authorities to evaluate "all relevant factors of an objective and quantifiable nature having a bearing on the situation of that industry," in particular the several factors enumerated therein. But Article 4.2(a) leaves to the competent authorities the discretion to decide the relative weight to be accorded to each factor, so long as they reach a reasoned conclusion. Thus, neither Article 4.2(a) nor any other provision in the Agreement requires that any particular factor or number of factors be declining in any given year of the investigative period, but only that the evidence with respect to the relevant factors provide a basis for the competent authority to make a reasoned conclusion that the domestic industry is seriously injured.

77. The USITC noted that several indicators rose slightly in 1997 from very depressed levels in 1996. For example, it found that domestic wheat gluten industry capacity utilization declined from 78.3 per cent in 1993 to as low as 42.0 per cent in 1996 before rising slightly to 44.5 per cent in 1997.[33] It also found that domestic production of wheat gluten rose from 128 million pounds in 1993 to 143 million pounds in 1995, fell sharply to 112 million pounds in 1996, and then increased to 122 million pounds in 1997. However, the USITC noted that domestic wheat gluten production in 1997 remained at a depressed level and that it was 4.5 per cent lower than the 1993 level.[34]

78. At the same time, the USITC found that other indicators of serious injury declined in 1997 and reached their lowest level of the investigative period in that year. For example, USITC found that the share of the domestic market held by domestic wheat gluten producers fell to its lowest level of the investigation period in 1997.[35] It found that the profitability of the domestic wheat gluten industry fell in 1996 and again in 1997, and that the industry operated at a loss in both years.[36] The USITC also found that average unit values for wheat gluten were at their lowest level of the investigative period in 1997, and that this decline in average unit values occurred at the same time that average unit costs were rising[37] The USITC also found that worker productivity was at its lowest level in 1997, and that as a result unit labour costs almost doubled during the period of the investigation.[38]

33 US Exhibit 4 at I-12.
34 US Exhibit 4 at I-13.
35 US Exhibit 4 at I-16.
36 US Exhibit 4 at I-13.
37 US Exhibit 4 at I-13.
38 US Exhibit 4 at I-14.

79. The USITC reasonably concluded that those trends did not contradict the overall picture that the domestic industry was in a state of serious injury. The USITC appropriately characterized the indicia that showed improvement in 1997 as "isolated" because: (1) major financial indicators continued to fall, and (2) the indicators that did improve, improved only slightly and remained at substantially depressed levels.

Q.28 In its causation analysis, in what manner did the ITC take into account injury attributable to causes other than increased imports (inter alia, those that the United States refers to at para. 125 of its first written submission as having "only a demonstrably minor role in the serious injury suffered by the industry")?

Reply

80. In its causation analysis the USITC first established the existence of a clear causal link between increased imports of wheat gluten and the serious injury being suffered by the domestic wheat gluten industry. The USITC found that virtually all of the increase in wheat gluten imports occurred in 1996 and 1997, and that most of this increase consisted of imports from the EU. The USITC found that imports from the EU consistently undersold domestic wheat gluten in 1996 and 1997. It also found that the share of the US market held by wheat gluten imports increased sharply in 1996 and 1997 to its highest level of the period of investigation.

81. The USITC found a direct correlation between the increase in wheat gluten imports and the significant decline in domestic wheat gluten industry performance in 1996 and 1997. Specifically, the USITC found that domestic production, shipments, capacity utilization, unit prices, industry financial performance, and worker productivity all declined during the period of greatest import penetration and in the face of rising domestic demand and consumption.[39]

82. The USITC then examined factors other than imports which might be a cause of serious injury to the domestic industry. The USITC separately examined each of the possible causes identified by the participants in the investigation, including changes in co-product markets, imports of wheat gluten by domestic producers, competition among domestic producers, increased domestic wheat gluten capacity, and rising raw material costs (for wheat and wheat flour), to determine whether any of these possible causes was a more important cause of the serious injury than increased imports. The USITC analysis clearly demonstrates that none of these other factors played more than a minor role in contributing to the injury experienced by the domestic industry in 1996 and 1997 when the surge in imports took place and the USITC found the US industry seriously injured.

[39] US Exhibit 4 at I-10, 16.

83. The first of the other possible causes addressed by the USITC was the alleged change in co-product markets.[40] The USITC examined US selling prices of wheat starch, which is the major co-product of wheat gluten production. The USITC found that, in contrast to the domestic selling price of wheat gluten, the domestic selling price of wheat starch showed a gradual increase over the period of investigation ("POI"). The USITC found that weighted-average wheat starch prices were at their highest level of the investigative period in 1997.

84. Thus, there was no decline in wheat starch prices that either paralleled the sharp decline since 1994 of domestic wheat gluten prices or explained the sharp decline in the financial performance of domestic wheat gluten producers. In effect, the USITC found no causal link between developments in the US wheat starch market and the 1996-97 decline in the condition of wheat gluten producers. Similarly, the USITC found the relative stability, and gradual increase, in domestic wheat starch prices suggested that competition between corn starch and wheat starch was not likely to have had much if any effect on wheat gluten production.

85. The USITC also considered evidence cited by importers that one domestic producer had reduced its wheat gluten production in 1995 for reasons related in part to conditions in the alcohol market, and considered importers' claim that this explained that firm's poor financial performance. The USITC found that this action explains only part of the problem faced by one producer and could not be extrapolated to account for the problems facing all domestic producers, nor could it explain the significant deterioration in 1996 and 1997 of the other three domestic producers, who accounted for the majority of domestic production. Indeed, the evidence did not even fully explain the declining financial performance of that one producer in its wheat gluten operations. Accordingly, since the USITC found the industry as a whole to be seriously injured in 1996-97, this factor, which had a partial effect only on the condition of one producer, was demonstrably minor in relation to the overall cause of injury.

86. As for the alleged impact of imports of wheat gluten by domestic wheat gluten producers,[41] the USITC found that imports by domestic purchasers remained relatively steady during the POI. Thus, US producers were not responsible for the surge in imports that occurred in 1996 and 1997. Again, this factor could not be linked to the deterioration in 1996 and 1997 that the USITC found constituted serious injury.

87. The USITC found that the domestic industry added substantial new capacity.[42] However, the USITC found that the bulk of the increased capacity was added early in the POI in anticipation of continued strong growth in domestic demand and consumption and before the surge in imports. The USITC found that

[40] US Exhibit 4 at I-16-17.
[41] US Exhibit 4 at I-17.
[42] US Exhibit 4 at I-17.

industry projections of continued growth in demand and consumption were largely correct, as apparent consumption increased nearly 18 per cent between 1993 and 1997. The USITC found that, had the domestic industry satisfied the growth in demand rather than lost sales to the surge in imports, the industry would have operated at 61 per cent of capacity in 1997.

88. The USITC found this to be a level much closer to previous capacity levels at which the industry was able to operate profitably. Accordingly, the severe profitability and operating income losses in 1996-97 could not be ascribed to increased capacity. Nor would increased capacity explain why US shipments and production in 1996-97 fell below prior levels. Accordingly, although increased imports could account for the conditions the USITC identified as serious injury, the increase in capacity could not.

89. The USITC examined and rejected the claim that rising raw material prices as reflected in the prices paid for wheat and wheat flour, the major inputs into wheat gluten/wheat starch production, were a more important cause of serious injury than increased imports.[43] Raw material costs did increase during the POI, particularly in 1996 and 1997.[44] However, the USITC found the evidence indicates that wheat gluten producers historically were able to pass on the cost increases to their customers, finding that demand for wheat gluten is relatively insensitive to price changes.[45]

90. This finding is supported by evidence in the confidential version of the USITC report which shows that when raw materials costs rose in 1994, the average unit selling value of wheat gluten also rose, and when the raw materials costs fell in 1995, the average unit selling value of wheat gluten also fell.[46] In 1996 and 1997, however, average unit selling values declined despite increased demand and higher raw material costs. The USITC concluded that this unusual development was explained by the dramatic increase in relatively low-priced imports during the POI, which had the effect of driving down wheat gluten prices.

91. In summary, the causation analysis employed by the USITC was fully consistent with Article 4.2(b) of the Safeguards Agreement. The USITC investigation demonstrated, on the basis of objective evidence, the existence of the required causal link between increased imports and serious injury. Through its examination of other alleged causes of injury, the USITC ensured that it did not ascribe to increased imports the effect of other causes of injury.

Q.29 In the United States first written submission (para. 84), the United States asserts: "While the United States conducted a global investigation and examined imports from all sources, its determination did not attribute injury from

---

43 US Exhibit 4 at I-17.
44 US Exhibit 4 at I-17.
45 US Exhibit 4 at I-17.
46 Confidential version of USITC Report at II-29; US Exhibit 4 at C-4.

NAFTA imports to third countries" We also note that in the ITC report (p I-18), it states: "Section 311 of the NAFTA Implementation Act provides that if the Commission makes an "affirmative injury determination in an investigation under section 202 of the Trade Act ¼", the Commission must also "find" whether – (1) imports of the Article from a NAFTA country, considered individually, account for a substantial share of total imports; and (2) imports of the Article from a NAFTA country ¼ contribute importantly to the serious injury, or threat thereof, caused by imports".

Is the Panel therefore correct in understanding that imports from Canada were taken into account in order to reach a finding of serious injury, but that a separate causation analysis was then performed on imports from Canada? If so, what is the legal basis in the Safeguards Agreement for such a separate causation analysis?

Reply

92. In its analysis, the Commission found that the serious injury sustained by the domestic wheat gluten industry was attributable to a surge in imports from the EU in 1996 and 1997, accompanied by sustained underselling by EU producers.[47]

93. In a second step, the USITC examined Canadian imports alone and determined that they were not a significant cause of the serious injury. In particular, the USITC pointed to the fact that Canadian imports declined significantly during the period, while overall imports increased, and that Canadian imports generally oversold the market.[48] Thus, the Panel is correct in its understanding that the USITC conducted a separate causation analysis of Canadian imports to determine whether they contributed importantly to the serious injury. The results of that analysis make clear that the USITC's overall causation finding did not depend on the inclusion of Canadian imports.

94. Nothing in the Safeguards Agreement proscribes an independent causation analysis for imports originating in the territory of another free-trade area (FTA) participant or, indeed, suggests that only a single causation analysis is appropriate. Article 4.2(b), which addresses causation procedures generally, says nothing about the number or sequence of causation analyses that the competent authority may undertake. Rather, it establishes general rules for the authority to follow when it examines causation issues. Moreover, the EC has pointed to no relevant Article 4.2(b) defect in either of USITC's causation analysis. Thus, there is no basis for the EC to challenge either causation finding.

Q.30 In connection with the exclusion of Canada from the application of the United States wheat gluten safeguard measure, is the United States relying on Article XXIV of the GATT 1994? If so, in what way?

---

47 US First Written Submission at ¶ 85.

48 US Exhibit 4 at I-19, I-29.

Reply

95. As noted above, the USITC conducted a separate causation analysis of NAFTA imports, pursuant to US law and as required under Article 802 of the NAFTA. The President adopted the USITC's recommendation to exclude Canadian imports on the ground that they did not contribute importantly to the serious injury that the USITC had found.

96. Article 2.2 of Safeguards Agreement establishes a general rule that "[a] safeguard measure shall be applied to a product being imported irrespective of its source." In addition, Article 5.2 establishes specific rules for allocating safeguard quotas. Neither article makes specific reference to application of safeguard measures by the participants of customs unions and FTAs to imports from other countries participating in the union or FTA.

97. Specific provisions addressing these issues are found in footnote 1 of the Safeguards Agreement, appended to Article 2.1. The last sentence of footnote 1 states that "Nothing in this Agreement prejudges the interpretation of the relationship between Article XIX and paragraph 8 of Article XXIV of GATT 1994."

98. Footnote 1 establishes two important principles. First, it demonstrates that the framers of the Safeguards Agreement recognized a connection ("the relationship") between safeguards measures (Article XIX) and customs unions and FTAs, as defined in Article XXIV:8. Second, the footnote makes clear that the negotiators of the Safeguards Agreement sought to avoid any implication that the provisions of the Safeguards Agreement could be invoked to change that nexus ("Nothing in this Agreement prejudges the interpretation").

99. Thus, to determine Members' rights and obligations regarding the application of a safeguard measure in the context of an FTA, one must look to the applicable provisions of the GATT 1994, namely Articles XIX and XXIV:8 in the first instance. In particular, the footnote makes clear that the non-discrimination requirement of Article 2.2 of the Safeguards Agreement, and the quota allocation rules of Article 5.2, are not pertinent in assessing the safeguards treatment accorded by a customs union or FTA member to goods originating in other participant countries.

100. To sum up, the question of how an FTA member may (or must) treat imports from its FTA partners when it applies a safeguard measure cannot be answered by reference to the Safeguards Agreement. Rather, the answer is to be found in the rights and obligations associated with FTAs as those rights and obligations may apply in the context of safeguards measures contemplated by Article XIX.

101. GATT Article XXIV:8(b) provides as follows:

> A free-trade area shall be understood to mean a group of two or more customs territories in which the duties and other restrictive regulations of commerce (except, where necessary, those permitted under Articles XI, XII, XIII, XIV, XV and XX) are eliminated on

substantially all the trade between the constituent territories in products originating in such territories.

102. We do not understand the EC to question as a factual matter that the US is a participant in the NAFTA, that the NAFTA constitutes an FTA for purposes of Article XXIV:8, or that the NAFTA requires the United States to exempt Canadian and Mexican wheat gluten imports from a global safeguard measure, unless those imports "contribute importantly" to injury and "account for a substantial share" of imports.

103. That the NAFTA constitutes a free trade area for purposes of Art. XXIV:8 is well documented in the relevant working party reports. The safeguard exemptions set out Article 802 of that agreement, were introduced upon the formation of the NAFTA. The EC has not questioned the fact that Article 802 constitutes a critical component of the free-trade. The importance the NAFTA parties attached to this provision is illustrated by the fact that NAFTA Article 802 was also included, in slightly different form, in Article 1102 of the 1988 United States - Canada Free-Trade Agreement. Article 1102 required Canada and the United States to exempt each other's products from any global safeguard measures they imposed while the agreement was in effect, subject to the same sort of exceptions included in NAFTA Article 802.[49]

104. Finally, we do not understand the EC to contest the proposition that under GATT Article XXIV, the governments of a free-trade area may agree to exclude each other's goods from Article XIX safeguard measures as part of an agreement to eliminate "duties and other restrictive regulations of commerce" on "substantially all the trade between the[ir] constituent territories in products originating in such territories." In a similar vein, the EC has stated that "the European Communities does not question the right of a member of a customs union to exclude other members of that customs union from the scope of a safeguards measure".[50]

105. In fact, the EC's complaint in respect of US treatment of Canadian imports is procedural in nature. It argues that the United States was prohibited from excluding Canadian imports from its wheat gluten safeguard measure because they were included for purposes of assessing global injury causation. But the EC fails to point to any provision of GATT Article XIX (or of the Safeguards Agreement) that imposes such a rule. See response to Question 29.

---

[49] Article 1102 of the US – Canada FTA provides in relevant part:

> 1. With respect to an emergency action taken by a Party on a global basis, the Parties shall retain their respective rights and obligations under Article XXI of the General Agreement on Tariffs and Trade subject to the requirement that a Party taking such action shall exclude the other Party from such global action unless imports from that Party are substantial and are contributing importantly to the serious injury or threat thereof caused by imports. For purposes of this para., imports in the range of five per cent to ten per cent or less of total imports would normally not be considered substantial.

[50] Panel Report, *Argentina – Safeguard Measures on Imports of Footwear* ("*Argentina – Footwear Safeguard*"), WT/DS121/R, adopted 12 January 2000, DSR 2000:II, 575, para. 5.71.

106. Nor does GATT Article XXIV address the sequencing, or number, of causation analyses that may be undertaken as part of an Article XIX safeguards investigation. Article XXIV:8(b) addresses "duties and other restrictive regulations of commerce." To the extent that this language applies to safeguards measures, it addresses the measures themselves, not procedures for conducting serious injury investigations.

107. Therefore, there is no basis for the EC's claim that the United States could not exclude Canadian imports from its safeguard measure having included them for purposes of its causation analysis.

108. Lastly, the EC argues that the Appellate Body endorsed the notion of "parallelism" crafted by the panel in Argentina – Footwear and that the procedures employed by the United States in respect to Canadian imports were inconsistent with that concept. The United States does not understand the Appellate Body to have established a broad requirement of "parallelism" given the fact-specific nature of the Footwear dispute.[51] Nevertheless, the procedures contemplated by NAFTA Article 802, and employed by the United States in the case of its wheat gluten safeguard, satisfies the purpose of the "parallelism" notion the Footwear panel articulated, which is to ensure that when a Member attributes serious injury to imports originating in the territory of a country that is a party to a customs union (or FTA, in this case), those imports should be included in the safeguard measure the Member determines to apply.

109. NAFTA Article 802, and US law implementing that provision, provide for the inclusion of FTA imports in a US safeguard measure in such cases. Conversely, Article 802 and US implementing provisions, provide for the exclusion of Mexican and Canadian imports from an eventual safeguard measure where they did not play a significant role in causing serious injury or threat of injury. Thus, in both cases, the NAFTA and US law comport with the notion of "parallelism."

Q.31 Does the United States believe there is a difference between "taking the decision to apply a measure" (wording used in Article 12.1(c) of the Safeguards Agreement) and "taking a measure" (term used in Article 12.4 of the Safeguards Agreement regarding provisional safeguard measures)? If so, how does this dif-

[51] The Appellate Body noted:

> 112. Argentina applied the safeguard measures at issue after conducting an investigation of products being imported into Argentine territory and the effects of those imports on Argentina's domestic industry. In applying safeguard measures on the basis of this investigation in this case, Argentina was also required under Article 2.2 to apply those measures to imports from all sources, including from other MERCOSUR member States.
>
> 113. On the basis of this reasoning, and on the facts of this case, we find that Argentina's investigation, which evaluated whether serious injury or the threat thereof was caused by imports from all sources, could only lead to the imposition of safeguard measures on imports from all sources.
>
> (Emphasis in original).

ference, according to the United States, affect the notification requirements under Article 12 of the Safeguards Agreement?

Reply

110. Article 12.4 of the Safeguards Agreement requires Members that apply a provisional measure to make a notification "before taking a provisional safeguard measure ....." Article 12.1(c) requires immediate notification once a Member has taken a decision to apply or extend a safeguard measure ("A Member shall immediately notify ... upon taking a decision to apply ... a measure"). The United States is of the view that Article 12.4 requires notification prior to applying the safeguard, whereas Article 12.1(c) requires notification once the decision to apply the measure is taken. In the case of wheat gluten, the President took the decision to apply the safeguard measure on 30 May 1998, and the United States notified the Safeguards Committee of that action on 4 June 1998.

Q.32 In paragraph 203 of its first written submission, the United States argues that it agrees that an importing Member must provide the opportunity for consultations before it can take a safeguard action. However, in paragraph 201 of the same submission, the United States argues that there is no obligation to notify a proposed measure. Can the United States explain on what basis consultations will be held, if there is no obligation to notify proposed measures?

Reply

111. The argument the United States sought to address in paragraph 201 of its first written submission is the EC's claim that the United States did not notify the "proposed measure," which the EC appears to define as the final measure. Paragraph 201 makes the point that there is no such requirement. With respect to the basis consultations on which consultations will be held, Article 12.3 contemplates that a number of issues will be reviewed at that time, including "exchanging views on the measure." The Korea – Dairy panel noted that "the basis for the serious injury finding, and the details of the measure that the notifying member proposes to apply" are among the information to be discussed in consultations.[52] The United States provided all of the requisite information in its original and supplemental notifications under Article 12.1(b) prior to holding consultations with the EC.

Q.33 We note that the United States made two notifications pursuant to Article 12.1(b) of the Safeguards Agreement regarding a finding of serious injury (on 11 February 1998 and 24 March 1998, respectively). What factors determined this course of action?

---

[52] Panel Report, *Korea – Definitive Safeguard Measure on Imports of Certain Dairy Products* ("*Korea – Dairy*"), WT/DS98/R and Corr. 1, adopted 12 January 2000, DSR 2000:I,49, para. 7.120.

Reply

112. The United States made its first notification under Article 12.1(b) of the Safeguards Agreement after the USITC found that increased wheat gluten imports were causing serious injury to the domestic industry. At that time, the USITC had not published a report on its findings nor had it decided on an appropriate remedy to recommend to the President. On 18 March 1998 the USITC forwarded its injury report and remedy recommendation to the President. Subsequently, the United States provided a revised 12.1(b) notification to the Committee on Safeguards that included pertinent information on the evidence of serious injury, the amount of the increase in imports, and a description of the proposed measure. The United States also provided a copy of the USITC's non-confidential report to the Committee.

Written Questions by the Panel to the Third Parties

To Canada

Q.1 In the United States first written submission (para. 84), the United States asserts: "While the United States conducted a global investigation and examined imports from all sources, its determination did not attribute injury from NAFTA imports to third countries" We also note that in the ITC report (p I-18), it states: "Section 311 of the NAFTA Implementation Act provides that if the Commission makes an "affirmative injury determination in an investigation under section 202 of the Trade Act ", the Commission must also "find" whether – (1) imports of the Article from a NAFTA country, considered individually, account for a substantial share of total imports; and (2) imports of the Article from a NAFTA country contribute importantly to the serious injury, or threat thereof, caused by imports".

Is the Panel therefore correct in understanding that imports from Canada were taken into account in order to reach a finding of serious injury, but that a separate causation analysis was then performed on imports from Canada? If so, what is the legal basis in the Safeguards Agreement for such a separate causation analysis?

Reply

113. See US Response to Panel Question 29.

Q.2 Is the exclusion of Canada from the application of the United States wheat gluten safeguard measure based on, or related to, Article XXIV of the GATT 1994? If so, in what way?

Reply

114. See US Response to Panel Question 30.

Written Questions From the European Communities to the United States

Q.1 Please indicate in which of its findings the ITC determined that increased imports were due to unforeseen developments; i.e. to unexpected developments which led to a product being imported in such increased quantities and under such conditions as to cause serious injury?

Reply

115. The USITC findings demonstrating the circumstances constituting "unforeseen developments" are summarized in the response to Panel question 5.

116. The assumption in the EC's question - that the USITC should have made findings in which it explicitly "determined" that increased imports were due to unforeseen developments - is not supported by the recent Appellate Body reports addressing safeguards measures. The Appellate Body has stated that Article XIX does not establish "independent conditions" for the application of a safeguard measure, but rather describes "certain circumstances which must be demonstrated as a matter of fact in order for a safeguard measure to be applied consistently with the provisions of Article XIX of the GATT 1994." Argentine - Footwear at Paragraph 92.

117. Thus, what is required is not a USITC "determination" of such conditions, but rather a demonstration as a matter of fact of the circumstances constituting "unforeseen developments". The portions of the USITC Report summarized in the response to Panel question 5 amply demonstrate as a matter of fact the circumstances constituting "unforeseen developments."

Q.2 Nowhere in the ITC report an explanation is given of the methodology used to assess profitability of the US industry. However, the ITC claims on the one hand that at 78.3 per cent of capacity utilization, the US wheat gluten industry operated "reasonably profitably." On the other hand, the ITC equally claims that if there had been no increase in imports since 1993, industry would have operated at 61 per cent capacity utilisation in 1997.

Where in its report does the ITC show that at this 61 per cent level of capacity utilisation the industry could have operated profitably in 1996 and 1997?

How is this second claim consistent with the fact recognized by the ITC that in particular in 1996 and 1997 wheat prices, i.e. 75 per cent of input cost, were at their highest level?

Reply

118. The EC's contentions here (and in its first oral statement) misstate the findings of the USITC report. Contrary to the suggestion in the EC's first question here, the USITC did not make any statements or predictions as to whether the industry would or could have been profitable at 61 per cent of capacity in 1996 or 1997. What the USITC report said is that this 61 per cent of capacity is "much closer [than the 44.5 per cent of capacity actually reported in 1997] to the level at which the industry operated early in the investigative period when it op-

erated reasonably profitably.[53] The statement the USITC actually made is fully consistent with the record. The industry was profitable in 1993 and even more so in 1994, when capacity utilization was 78.3 per cent and 67.4 per cent, respectively. While profitability dropped in 1995, when capacity utilization was 56.2 per cent, the industry was not yet suffering losses. The record further shows that the industry was unprofitable in 1996 and 1997, when capacity utilization was 42.0 per cent and 44.5 per cent, respectively.[54] Thus, as the USITC Report shows, the industry had its most profitable year (both in terms of gross profit and net operating income) during the period in 1994, when capacity utilization was at 67.4 per cent. Accordingly, even the EC must concede that, as the USITC stated, 61 per cent is much closer than 44.5 per cent to the level at which the industry had operated profitably early in the period.

119. Somewhat higher wheat prices in 1996-1997 would not affect this analysis. Historically, demand for wheat gluten had been relatively inelastic, and the industry had been able to pass on increases in input costs to wheat gluten purchasers in the form of higher prices, which should not have been difficult given the substantial increase in demand in 1996-1997. Instead, as the USITC found, prices declined, despite the increase in input costs and the increase in demand, as a result of the surge of relatively low-priced imports.[55]

Q.3 How and where does the ITC explain in its report why the US producers had reason to assume, when massively increasing their production capacity, that increased domestic consumption (domestic market demand) would turn to them only for supply?

Can the US indicate where in the ITC report an explanation is provided on how the assumption referred to in the previous question could hold in light of the fact that one of the major US domestic producers, Manildra, controlled a dominant part of the imports.

120. The USITC made no findings that the US producers assumed that increased domestic consumption would turn to them only for supply. As the USITC Report stated, the US producers expanded production capacity in expectation of a significant increase in domestic demand. This increase in demand in fact occurred in 1996-1997. Furthermore, as part of its analysis pursuant to Article 4.2(b) of the Safeguards Agreement, the USITC analyzed the effects of increased imports on capacity utilization, in which it held other factors constant, and thus isolated the effects of increased imports on capacity utilization. For purposes of this analysis, the USITC did a calculation of what capacity utilization would have been in 1997, using the assumptions that there had been no increase in imports since 1993, and that domestic producers would have supplied all of the increase in domestic demand, and came up with a figure of 61 per cent capacity utiliza-

53 US Exhibit 4 at I-17.
54 US Exhibit 4 at I-13, II-15, Table 5.
55 US Exhibit 4 at I-17-18.

tion. The USITC analysis did not make a prediction of what would have actually happened in 1997 if the increased imports had not occurred. Nor did the USITC making any factual findings or statements as to what portion of the expected increase in demand the domestic producers expected to capture.[56] Nor is such an expectation by the US producers required by any provision of the Safeguard Agreement.

121. Thus, the EC's question about whether the US producers had good reason for expecting that the increased domestic consumption would go to them is not relevant.[57] Given the irrelevance of this issue, the USITC made no explicit findings about it as such. Nevertheless, the USITC Report shows that the US producers had every reason to expect that they would capture at least a large portion of the increased demand. The share of domestic consumption taken by imports fell somewhat between 1993 and 1995.[58] In addition, a new US producer, Heartland Wheat Growers, which had begun construction of a plant in 1993, opened the plant and began production in 1996.[59] Its entry would normally have been expected to take market share from both importers and domestic producers, particularly given pricing patterns while the plant was being built, when imports from all sources both oversold and undersold the domestic product from 1993.[60] Thus, there was every reason to assume that a new entrant to the domestic industry would take market share from the imports, leading to a significant increase in the domestic producers' overall share of the market, and no reason for the domestic producers to expect that imports would grow to take the increased demand.

---

[56] It is the EC that has contended that the US producers foresaw that they would capture the entire increase in US demand, and did not foresee that the increase would instead be captured by imports. EC First Submission at Para. 53, 63. While conceding that the dramatic import surge was unforeseen by the US industry, the EC has instead argued that the US was "irrational" to have expanded production capacity and not to have foreseen that imports would increase dramatically and would capture the increased demand.

[57] It is likewise irrelevant whether the US producers were unreasonable in not foreseeing the unexpected developments that led to the surge in imports in 1996-1997. This question is irrelevant, under the plain language of Article XIX of GATT and the holdings in the recent Appellate Body Reports in Argentina - Footwear and Korea – Dairy, *supra*, footnote 7. The pertinent clause in Article XIX refers to "unforeseen developments" and makes no reference to "unforeseeable developments." Article XIX likewise imposes no requirement that the failure by the US industry or government to foresee such developments be reasonable or well-founded. Similarly, the two Appellate Body Reports both contrast the meaning of "unforeseen" (synonymous with "unexpected") with that of unforeseeable" (meaning "incapable of being foreseen, foretold or anticipated"), and both conclude that Article XIX's provisions must be interpreted with the ordinary meaning of the word "unforeseen." Argentina - Footwear at Para. 91; Korea - Dairy at Para. 84. Thus, whether the US producers had good reasons for not foreseeing the import surge is not relevant. Nevertheless the USITC response provides ample information demonstrating why they had no reason to foresee it. See Response to Panel Question #5.

[58] US Exhibit 4 at C-3, Table C-1.

[59] US Exhibit 4 at II-8.

[60] US Exhibit 10 at II-36.

122. Since the reasonableness of the US producers' expectations regarding capturing the expected increase in US demand is not relevant, the EC's further question about the reasonableness of such expectations given the relationship between Manildra and any imports it may have controlled is likewise irrelevant. Furthermore, Manildra hardly controlled a "dominant" part of US imports. According to the USITC Report, Manildra is the subsidiary of a parent company that has as additional subsidiaries two Australian producers of wheat gluten that exported wheat gluten to the United States, while there was one other Australian firm not controlled by Manildra that also produced wheat gluten.[61] As a share of total imports, Australian imports declined during the period, suffering declines in 1995, 1996 and 1997, with its share of imports falling further behind the EU's rapidly growing share each year.[62]

Thus, it was not imports from Australia, and hence not any imports controlled by Manildra, that constituted the surge in increased imports that captured the increase in domestic demand in 1996 and 1997 that the US producers had hoped to capture. The USITC specifically found that imports of wheat gluten by US producers remained relatively steady during the period, and that the US producers were not responsible for the surge in imports in 1996.[63] Moreover, since imports from Australia, as well as Australia's share of total imports, were falling in 1995, when the US producers were adding capacity, the US producers would not have had any basis for expecting that Australian imports would increase to capture the increase in US consumption.[64]

---

61 US Exhibit 4 at II-8, II-22.

62 US Exhibit 4 at II-12, Table 2.

63 US Exhibit 4 at I-17.

64 US Exhibit 4 at II-12, Table 2.

ATTACHMENT 2-5

SECOND WRITTEN SUBMISSION OF THE UNITED STATES (17 January 2000)

TABLE OF CONTENTS

I. INTRODUCTION

1. The European Communities has failed to assert and prove its claim that the United States' safeguard measure is inconsistent with US obligations under the *Agreement on Safeguards*. In its first written submission, filed on 6 December 1999, the United States addressed the claims raised by the EC alleging violations of Articles 2, 4, 5, 8 and 12 of the Safeguards Agreement as well as GATT Article I. The United States demonstrated that the findings and economic conclusions of the USITC in this matter were carefully reasoned and amply articulated, and that the safeguard measure applied by the United States is fully in accordance with US obligations under the Safeguards Agreement and GATT 1994. The United States also demonstrated that it fully satisfied the notification and consultation provisions of the Safeguards Agreement.

2. In its second written submission, the United States addresses the written questions of the Panel and the EC as well as certain elaborations of the EC's arguments raised in its first oral statement on 20 December 1999. The United States' submissions and responses together demonstrate that the EC's claims are without merit and properly should be rejected by the Panel.

II. THE EC HAS FAILED TO ESTABLISH THAT THE USITC'S INVESTIGATION WAS INCONSISTENT WITH THE SAFEGUARDS AGREEMENT

A. *Standard of Review*

3. As the Appellate Body recently confirmed, in examining a serious injury determination, a Panel must address three questions: (1) whether the competent authority considered all relevant facts, including each factor listed in Article 4.2(a); (2) whether its published report contains an adequate explanation of how the facts support the determination made; and (3) whether the determination made is consistent with the Safeguards Agreement.[1] A panel should not conduct

[1] Appellate Body Report, *Argentina –Safeguard Measures on Imports of Footwear* ("*Argentina – Footwear*"), WT/DS121/AB/R, adopted 12 January 2000, DSR 2000:I, 515, para. 116 (quoting and

a *de novo* review, and it is accordingly inappropriate for a panel to attempt to conduct its own assessment of the raw data reviewed by the competent authority during its investigation.[2]

4. The Appellate Body further stated that Article 11 of the *Understanding on Rules and Procedures Governing the Settlement of Disputes* ("DSU") requires that "... a panel should make an objective assessment of the matter before it, including an objective assessment of the facts of the case and the applicability of and conformity with the relevant covered agreements ...".[3]

5. While the EC admits that the Panel is not to undertake a *de novo* review, it nevertheless asks the Panel to do just that by conducting a review of new evidence that was not before the USITC during its investigation.[4] The EC's argument that the Panel should consider its new evidence is based on a play on words. The EC argues that the Panel should review the EC's new evidence because under Article 11 of the DSU the Panel is to conduct an "objective assessment of the facts of the case. " Under Article 3.1 of the Safeguards Agreement, a competent

endorsing the standard stated in the Panel Report, *Argentina –Safeguard Measures on Imports of Footwear* ("*Argentina – Footwear*"), WT/DS121/R, adopted 12 January 2000, DSR 2000:II, 575, para. 8-124.

[2] In *Argentina - Footwear, supra*, footnote 1, the panel concluded that it would be inappropriate for it to review the raw data in the record before Argentina's competent authority: "[i]f we were to conduct our own assessment of the underlying evidence as contained in the entire record of Argentina's investigation, we believe that we would effectively be engaging in a de novo review, which we and both parties agree would be inappropriate." Argentina - Footwear Panel Report, *supra*, footnote 1, para. 8.126. The Appellate Body subsequently held that the panel had correctly stated the standard of review, although the Appellate Body questioned the Panel's reliance on several previous panel reports reviewing investigations under the Tokyo Round Agreements. Appellate Body Report, *Argentina – Footwear, supra*, footnote 1, para. 117.

[3] Appellate Body Report, *Argentina – Footwear, supra*, footnote 1, para. 120.

[4] Despite the EC's request to the Panel to engage in what would amount to a de novo review of the USITC's findings, the United States notes that European courts have themselves declined to implement such a standard. The European Court of Justice, for example, pointedly avoids substituting its own assessment of the facts for that of the competent authority in matters involving the evaluation of complex economic situations. See, e.g., Joined Cases C-248/95 and C-249/95 SAM Schiffahrt v. Germany [1997] ECR I-4475, ¶¶ 23-25, citing Case 138/79 Rouquette Freres v. Council, [1980] ECR 3333, ¶ 25; and Case 166/78, Italy v. Council, [1979] ECR 2575, ¶ 15. Therefore, it employs a deferential standard of review which focuses on whether the action being reviewed "contains a manifest error or constitutes a misuse of power or whether the authority in question did not clearly exceed the bounds of its discretion." Case 138/79 Rouquette Freres v. Council, [1980] ECR 3333, ¶ 25. And as observed in Case C-122/94 Commission v. Council, [1996] ECR 881, ¶ 18, "the discretion which [the Council] has does not apply exclusively to the nature and scope of the measures to be taken but also to some extent to the finding of the basic facts inasmuch as, in particular, it is open to the Council to rely if necessary on general findings." See also, Case C-169/95 Spain v. Commission, [1997] ECR 135, ¶ 34 wherein it was recognized that in applying the terms of the Treaty, the competent authority "enjoys a significant freedom of assessment." Therefore, "the Courts, when examining the lawfulness of the exercise of such freedom, cannot substitute their own assessment of the matter for that of the competent authority but must restrict themselves to examining whether the assessment of the competent authority contains a manifest error or constitutes a misuse of power (see, in particular, Case 57/72 Westzucker v. Einfuhr- und Vorratsstelle Für Zucker {1973} ECR 321, para. 14)."

authority conducts an investigation, after which it publishes a report setting forth its findings "on all pertinent issues of fact and law." Hence, the EC implies, a Dispute Settlement Body (DSB) panel may make the same kind of inquiry into " facts" that a competent authority makes.[5]

6. However, the "facts" that are the subject of the two different kinds of proceeding are very different. A competent authority determines whether a domestic industry has been seriously injured by increased imports. A panel resolves a dispute between member governments about whether, in doing so, the competent authority violated the Safeguards Agreement. The "facts" examined by the competent authority concern the economic condition of the domestic industry. The "facts" to be examined by a panel concern whether the member's actions complied with the Safeguards Agreement. Since under the Safeguards Agreement, injury determinations are made by competent authorities, the facts before the Panel concern what the competent authority did and the findings it made.

7. As pointed out in the United States' Oral Statement[6], the EC's contention that the Panel should gather additional evidence on the economic conditions of the industry would be contrary to the balance of concessions and benefits in the Safeguards Agreement.[7] Article 3 makes it clear that it is the competent authorities established by WTO Members that are authorized to conduct investigations of whether increased imports have caused serious injury. There is nothing in the DSU that suggests that it was intended to operate in derogation of the fact-finding responsibilities reserved by the underlying WTO Agreements to the Members and their competent authorities. Article 3 likewise establishes conditions for these investigations, including notice and public hearings, that guarantee interested parties, including both domestic and foreign commercial interests, the opportunity to present evidence and comment on the other presentations and evidence received by the competent authority. The government-to-government procedures established in the DSU do not create any equivalent process in panels.

8. The new evidence that the EC now seeks to have this Panel consider concerning monthly spot market prices for wheat illustrates the pitfalls of a panel entertaining new evidence. When such new evidence is presented, a panel will not have had the benefit of comment on it by the interested parties or the evaluation of it by the competent authority.

9. Two points are relevant here. First, the USITC investigated input prices and obtained information directly from US wheat gluten producers and foreign producers. The raw data were made available to representatives of the interested parties, including the European producer respondents, under administrative pro-

---

5 See EC Oral Statement at ¶¶ 11, 14.

6 See United States Oral Statement, December 21, 1999, at 2-5.

7 As pointed out in he United States' first submission, EC exhibits 10,12, 13 and 14 were not part of the record of the USITC investigation and those exhibits (and the EC's arguments based on those exhibits) should be disregarded by the Panel. US First Submission at Para. 138.

tective order, and they had the opportunity to comment on it. The USITC made findings concerning the rise in input costs, including wheat prices.[8]

10. Second, the monthly public data that the EC now wishes the Panel to consider were equally available to the EC and to the EU producers at the time of the investigation, but they chose not to submit such data to the USITC. (The EC appeared as a party during the investigation, and the EU producers participated very actively in the investigation). The EU producers in fact submitted other official data (from the US Department of Agriculture) on this subject, and may have viewed those data as more probative than the data that the EC now submits to the Panel. However, neither the EU producers nor any of the other parties are here before the Panel to clarify or otherwise address these evidentiary matters.

11. Moreover, the new data presented by the EC are not probative of raw material costs, as some US wheat gluten producers purchase wheat flour rather than wheat as their raw material (wheat gluten is made from wheat flour), and those with their own flour milling operations obtain a substantial portion of their wheat through long-term contracts and not through the spot market. Again, the interested parties are not present in this proceeding to clarify this question.

12. Regardless of the EC's characterization of its new evidence as "official US government statistics," permitting a party to submit data to a WTO panel that it could have submitted to the competent authority during the investigation, but did not, invites strategic manipulation by parties of the process before the competent authority. In almost every investigation, there is likely to be some additional source of information, perhaps including government information, that may have some relevance to the industry under review, and may be contrary to some other piece of information. If parties know that they can withhold such information from the scrutiny and evaluation of the interested parties and the competent authority during the investigation and then introduce it for the first time before the WTO panel to cast doubt on the competent authority's findings, then it will be in a party's interest to engage in such strategic gamesmanship. The WTO will undermine proceedings before competent national authorities if it encourages such practices.

13. For all these reasons, a WTO panel is not a proper tribunal to review new evidence on the factors investigated by the designated competent authorities, and the Panel should decline the EC's invitation to conduct such a review.

B. *Burden of Proof*

14. The EC further contended in its Oral Statement that there is a special burden of proof in safeguards cases resting with the Member that adopted the safeguards measure.[9] This contention is not supported by the Safeguards Agreement

---

[8] See US Exhibit 4 at I-17 to I-18.

[9] EC Oral Statement at ¶ 9.

or by any other authority, and the EC is unable to cite any authority for it. To the contrary, the *Korea - Dairy* panel stated that the complainant must first submit a *prima facie* case of violation of the Safeguards Agreement, and that "[a]s a matter of law the burden of proof rests with the ... complainant, and does not shift during the panel process."[10] The Appellate Body concluded that the panel did not err in its application of the burden of proof. *Korea - Dairy* Appellate Body report at ¶ 150. Thus, here the EC, the complainant, first has the burden of submitting a *prima facie* case, and the burden rests with the EC throughout the entire process and never shifts to the United States.

15. As demonstrated in this submission, as well as in our First Written Submission, the EC has failed to make out a *prima facie* case of violation of the Safeguards Agreement and its claims should accordingly be dismissed. Contrary to the EC's assertions, the EC has not shown that the USITC failed to consider all the relevant evidence; it has utterly failed to show that there was any evidence that the USITC should have considered but did not. Nor has the EC shown that the USITC's conclusions were deficient, and it has not shown any biased, deficient or subjective presentation of the facts.[11]

C. *Unforeseen Developments*

16. The United States has addressed the issue of "unforeseen developments" at length in its response to the Panel's Question #5. In sum, the USITC Report makes clear that the United States did not foresee the developments that led to increased wheat gluten imports from the EC in 1996-1997. As the USITC findings show, this dramatic change in market conditions did not result from developments in the wheat gluten market itself. Rather, the USITC found that it resulted primarily from a huge increase in EC production capacity in an effort to increase production of wheat starch (a co-product of wheat gluten) to meet demand for wheat starch in the EC market. Thus, developments in the EC wheat starch market led to an increase in EC production of wheat gluten, and to increased EC exports of wheat gluten to the US at relatively low prices, for reasons unrelated to demand for wheat gluten. While there was mixed overselling and underselling by imports from 1993-1995, during the import surge in 1996-1997 imports consistently undersold the US market.

17. These developments were not attributable to the modest reduction in the US wheat gluten tariff negotiated in the Uruguay Round. Moreover, the participants in the US wheat gluten market clearly did not foresee such developments. The US industry's substantial addition of production capacity during 1993-95, and the entry of a new producer into the market, are inconsistent with the fact that even US industry failed to foresee the dramatic jump in imports during 1996-97.

---

[10] Panel Report, *Korea – Definitive Safeguard Measure on Imports of Certain Dairy Products* ("*Korea – Dairy*"), WT/DS98/R and Corr. 1, adopted 12 January 2000, DSR 2000:I,49, para. 7.24.

[11] EC Oral Statement at ¶ 10.

18. The USITC Report amply demonstrates that the import surge resulted from significant changes in the marketplace that occurred after the tariff concession was negotiated. Accordingly, the USITC Report demonstrates as a matter of fact circumstances constituting unforeseen developments, and the "unforeseen developments" provision of Article XIX:1(a) of GATT 1994 is fully satisfied.

D. *Confidential Data*

19. The concerns that the EC raised in its Oral Statement about the redaction of confidential data in the USITC report are insubstantial, as shown in the United States' response to Panel Question #3 . In summary, the EC contends that *any* redaction of aggregate data is improper.[12] However, the EC's sweeping assertion fails to take account of the fact that in some circumstances, such as those present in the USITC's wheat gluten investigation, the disclosure of aggregate data may reveal sensitive, proprietary information, as the United States explained in its first submission.[13]

20. Contrary to the EC's contentions in ¶¶ 30-33 of its oral statement, the USITC's treatment of aggregate data did not violate any provisions of Articles 3 and Article of the Safeguards Agreement. That the USITC staff made some mistakes in applying its policy on aggregate data with respect to pricing data (mistakes corrected in the corrigendum) in no way involves a violation of Articles 3 and 4, and the correction does not constitute an acknowledgement of such a violation.

21. Article 3 of the Safeguards Agreement imposes a requirement to protect confidential data; contrary to the EC's contention it imposes no requirement on a competent authority to publish every piece of non-confidential data it receives. Moreover, the requirement in Article 4.2(c) to publish a detailed analysis of the case and a demonstration of the relevance of the factors examined does not impose an obligation to publish all evidence. Nor does Article 3 contain such a requirement. What is required is that the competent authority must set out its findings and reasoned conclusions on the issues. The USITC Report does so, and, as set forth in the United States' response to Panel Question 3, the specific questions raised by the EC about confidential information do not raise any issues that the Panel must address.

22. Moreover, if the EC's point is that aggregate information must be made available to the Panel, its objection that the USITC's release of additional aggregate data in the corrigendum comes too late (EC Oral Statement at ¶¶ 31-32) is without merit. If there the competent authority were required to provide the Panel with the means to verify particular findings, that duty would arise during the panel proceeding, not before. The United States has provided the Panel with all

---

[12] EC Oral Statement at ¶ 28.

[13] See US First Submission at ¶¶ 156-157, and Exhibit 9.

aggregate information whose publication would not disclose confidential information. Moreover, the aggregate information provided to the panel confirms the accuracy of the only specific USITC finding (regarding underselling and overselling) attacked by the complaining Member with respect to confidentiality. Thus, the EC has not suggested, much less established, why any additional information would be needed.

23. The United States notes that the EC has not in its initial submissions urged the extreme position espoused by New Zealand's third party submission. New Zealand contends that the duty not to disclose confidential information applies only during the competent authority's investigation, and does not apply during a WTO proceeding.[14] This argument has no basis in the Safeguards Agreement. Article 3.2 requires authorities not to disclose confidential information without the permission of the party submitting it. Article 3.2 does not, on its face, place any time limit on that duty. Contrary to New Zealand's suggestion, there is no provision in the Safeguards Agreement or the DSU that magically transforms information that is confidential in the USITC investigation into non-confidential information that may be disclosed once the matter goes to a WTO panel. Apart from its inconsistency with the Safeguards Agreement, adoption of New Zealand's proposal would harm not only domestic producers that submit confidential information, but importers and producers from exporting countries as well. For example, the USITC Report redacted not only confidential information submitted by domestic producers, but also confidential information submitted by producers from Canada, Australia and the European Union.[15]

24. New Zealand purports to base its argument on the decision of the Appellate Body in *Canada – Aircraft.*[16] But *Canada –Aircraft* is irrelevant in this proceeding because it provides no guidance with regard to Article 3.2 of the Safeguard Agreement. The Appellate Body did not address how and under what circumstances a member should or could disclose confidential information to a Panel consistent with Article 3.2.

25. [Deleted]

E. EC arguments on "conditions" and price

26. The EC's argument on price in ¶¶ 34 et seq. of its Oral Statement are difficult to fathom. In its First Written Submission, the EC attacked the USITC's finding on price underselling, failing to understand that the USITC's finding of consistent underselling applied to 1996-97, not the entire investigatory period. The EC in its Oral Statement does not advert again to that argument. Instead, it

---

14 New Zealand Third Party Submission at ¶¶ 9-10.

15 US Exhibit 4 at II-22 to II-23.

16 Appellate Body Report, *Canada - Measures Affecting the Export of Civilian Aircraft* ("*Canada – Aircraft*"), WT/DS70/AB/R, adopted 20 August 1999, DSR 1999:III, 1377.

makes a vague allegation about a failure to find "conditions" without specifying what conditions need be found.

27. It would appear that the EC seeks some finding about the substitutability of imports and domestic product - that is, whether the products were so related that differences in price would matter. In one sense, the issue is academic. The record shows that when Australian and EC imports both were mixed in their overselling and underselling of the US product, their relative market shares remained relatively steady. US production rose. When in 1996-97, the EC alone consistently undersold the US industry, its market share rose 20 per cent, while the Australian market share remained stable. US production and market share fell. The trends speak for themselves.

28. Nevertheless, the USITC made findings that showed why the conditions were such that these price and volume trends would arise. In making its findings on the like or directly competitive product, the USITC made specific findings on the substitutability of imported and domestic wheat gluten. It found that, overwhelmingly, purchasers found them to be of roughly the same quality, to be used for the same purpose, and to be sold to the same end users. This finding suggests that purchasers would tend to change suppliers if price relations changed, as indeed occurred in 1996-97.

29. The United States does not deny that factors other than imports, such as the protein content of the domestic wheat crop, can affect domestic demand for and the domestic price of wheat gluten. As the USITC report noted and as the EC again pointed out in its oral statement on 20 December 1999[17], domestic wheat gluten demand and prices rose in early 1994 in response to the low protein level in the 1993 domestic wheat crop, and then fell in 1995 when the protein content of the domestic wheat crop returned to a more normal level. However, this only reinforces the finding of the USITC that domestic prices should have increased in 1996 and 1997 when domestic demand and consumption were rising. However, domestic prices fell substantially in 1996 and 1997 in the face of rising demand and consumption. The only explanation for this substantial price decline was the surge in imports in 1996 and 1997 – virtually all of which was attributable to EU imports.

F. Consideration of injury factors

30. As evidenced by its arguments in ¶¶ 43-56 of its Oral Statement, the EC continues to ignore the USITC's explanation of its conclusions regarding the factors that relate to serious injury and causation, and continues to misunderstand the role of the Panel. Instead, the EC implicitly urges the Panel to draw its own conclusions based on the selective evidence the EC would have the Panel consider. As the United States pointed out in ¶ 61 of its First Written Submission, the

---

[17] Oral Statement of the EC, 20 Dec. 1999, ¶¶ 38, 63-68.

question for this Panel is the adequacy of the USITC's determination as it was made at the time, not whether the Panel itself would have reached a contrary conclusion based on the facts advanced by a complaining Member. The United States believes that standard of review comports with Article 3.1's requirement that a Member provide "*reasoned* conclusions reached on all issues of law and fact." (Emphasis added). By picking and choosing pieces of evidence which it argues support a contrary conclusion, the EC does not satisfy its burden to show that the USITC was unreasonable in reaching the conclusion that it did.

31. Specifically, the EC ignores the fact that the USITC's findings relating to increased wheat gluten imports and the increased share of the US wheat gluten market taken by imports were supported by findings of fact based on the record in the USITC investigation. In particular, the EC ignores the fact that the USITC found that wheat gluten imports increased by nearly 40 per cent between 1995 and 1997, more than twice the 18 per cent rate of increase in wheat gluten consumption during the same period; ignores the fact that the share of the US wheat gluten market held by imports increased from 50.1 per cent in 1995 to 60.2 per cent in 1997, or by 20 per cent; and ignores the fact that virtually all the factors relating to wheat gluten industry health declined in 1996 and 1997 in the face of the surge in imports.[18] Instead, the EC selectively notes that US consumption increased in 1996 and 1997, wrongly implies that imports increased at no more than this rate, and concludes without explanation that "the increase in imports in terms of domestic market share cannot support a finding of injury, let alone serious injury."[19]

32. The USITC found that domestic wheat gluten production and shipments (sales) rose during the first 3 years of the investigation period, fell sharply in 1996 and then increased in 1997, but to a level that was still below the level in the first 3 years of the investigation period, notwithstanding the increase in domestic demand and consumption.[20] The EC again ignores the data. It notes the uptick in production and shipments in 1997, and concludes that the trend in production and shipments "has remained relatively steady.[21] The EC ignores the fact that domestic wheat gluten production and shipments in 1996 and 1997 remained well below the levels in the pre-1996 period, before the surge in imports, and it ignores the fact that this decline in domestic wheat gluten production and shipments occurred at the same time that domestic wheat gluten demand and consumption were rising.

33. Although the USITC did not place much weight on inventory data, other than to note that end of period inventories and the ratio of domestic producer inventories to shipments both more than doubled during the period of investigation, the EC summarily ignores these findings and asserts that inventories "were

---

[18] US Exhibit 4 at I-10, 16.

[19] EC oral statement of 20 December 1999 at ¶ 44.

[20] US Exhibit 4 at I-13.

[21] EC oral statement of 20 December 1999 at ¶ 46-47.

strongly going down in 1996 and 1997."[22] While inventories did in fact decline in 1996 and 1997, the EC ignores the fact that domestic wheat gluten production and shipments were also down in 1996 and 1997 from pre-1996 levels. Consequently, the trend in inventories would simply reflect decisions about whether to let production fall faster than shipments, rather than the other way around. A fall in inventories would simply reflect a deeper cut in production. In such a depression period, inventory trends are of little probative value with respect to causation, and the USITC did not cite them in finding that the causal link was satisfied.

G. *Profits and losses*

34. In ¶¶ 50-54 of its Oral Statement, the EC called into question the allocation methodologies employed by US wheat gluten producers in submitting profit and loss data to the USITC. The USITC stated that it carefully reviewed the allocation methodologies used by domestic wheat gluten producers in responding to the Commission's questionnaire, and found those allocations to be appropriate.[23] As the Panel will recall, on the basis of those data, the USITC found that the domestic industry was profitable during 1993-95, before the surge in imports, and operated at a loss in 1996 and 1997, when the surge in imports occurred.[24]

35. As the United States explained in its response to the Panel's question #26, the USITC provided clear instructions to domestic firms on how they were to submit financial data in response to the USITC's domestic producers' questionnaire.[25] Firms that maintained separate internal profit-and-loss and cost of production data for wheat gluten operations were directed to provide those data, and firms that did not were directed to allocate costs between wheat gluten and wheat starch to explain their allocation methodology and provide worksheets with their calculations.[26] The majority of the responding firms maintained separate internal profit-and-loss and cost of production data for wheat gluten on a regular basis and furnished such data to the USITC. The responding firm that did not maintain separate data made allocations, and provided the USITC with an explanation of the basis for those allocations.

36. USITC accounting staff reviewed the accounting methodologies used by all the producers and checked for reasonable allocation methods to the extent the revenues and costs were not directly attributable to a particular product. The USITC accounting staff found all of the allocation methods to be in accordance with US generally accepted accounting principles. It found that differences among the methodologies used by the responding companies were principally a function of differences in operations and reflected commercial realities. Copies

22 EC oral statement of 20 December 1999 at ¶ 48.
23 US Exhibit 4 at I-13.
24 US Exhibit 4 at I-13.
25 A copy of the this questionnaire was attached as Exhibit 1 to the United States First Submission.
26 US Exhibit 1, US First Submission, USITC producers' questionnaire at 8.

of the confidential questionnaire responses submitted by domestic wheat gluten producers were made available to authorized representatives of the parties in the investigation that were parties to the administrative protective order, including representatives of the European producer respondents.[27] The European producer respondents set out their concerns in their posthearing brief submitted during the injury phase of the USITC investigation, arguing *inter alia* that the USITC should give little or no weight to reported profitability data.[28] The USITC considered the arguments made by respondents with respect to the allocations in finding those allocations to be appropriate.[29]

37. In addition, the USITC selected the largest producer, Midwest Grain Products, Inc., for a two day on-site verification in Atchison, Kansas on December 3 and 4, 1997. This verification was conducted by a USITC auditor, an independent certified public accountant (CPA). The auditor prepared a 50-page verification report, including exhibits, which was made a part of the USITC's record in the investigation. The USITC auditor reconciled Midwest Grain's questionnaire data on wheat gluten for each period with the product income and loss statements which were derived from the company's audited financial statements. This was possible because Midwest Grain prepares separate income and loss statements on a monthly basis for each of its divisions, one of which is the wheat gluten division. The USITC auditor reviewed the financial statements for each division and any allocations that might have been used, and tested their reasonableness with alternative allocation methods. In addition, the USITC auditor confirmed that the allocation methods used by Midwest to measure the financial performance of each division, to the extent allocations were necessary, had been in use for a number of years and were not changed for purposes of the USITC wheat gluten investigation. The auditor concluded that the verification objectives were fully satisfied.

H. Imports by US producers

38. In its Oral Statement, the EC again raised the issue of wheat gluten imports by domestic producers, particularly by Manildra, which is owned by an Australian firm that also has Australian production operations. The EC argues in its Oral Statement (at ¶ 55) that a policy of importation by Manildra that corresponds to its business strategy of optimizing profits cannot be considered an injury.

---

27 As pointed out in the United States' response to Panel question 4, the EC could have had access to those questionnaire responses, but chose not to apply to be a party to the administrative protective order.

28 Posthearing Brief on Injury of Association des Amidonneries de Cereales de L'U.E, at 35 (Dec. 23 1997).

29 US Exhibit 4 at I-13.

39. The USITC addressed this issue in its causation analysis and made two findings. First, it found that US producers' wheat gluten imports remained relatively steady during the period examined, and thus US producers were not responsible for the surge in imports that occurred in 1996 and 1997. Second, it noted that the US market has historically depended in part on imports to meet domestic demand, and noted that in all but one year of the investigative period domestic apparent consumption of wheat gluten exceeded US producers' capacity to produce wheat gluten.[30]

40. The point the EC is trying to make here is unclear. Even the Antidumping Agreement, which contains a specific provision for domestic producers who import, does not permit the authority to disregard such imports. Moreover, as the USITC made clear, the 1996-1997 surge in imports that caused serious injury was due to EC imports not wheat gluten imports by US wheat gluten producers, including from Australia.

41. The USITC found that wheat gluten imports by domestic producers remained steady during the investigation, and thus US wheat gluten producers were not responsible for the surge in imports that occurred in 1996 and 1997. The USITC found that the bulk of the increase in imports was from the EU.[31] US wheat gluten imports from the EU increased by 69 per cent between 1995 and 1997.[32] While US wheat gluten imports from Australia also increased in 1996 and 1997, the rate of increase was comparable to the rate of increase in domestic wheat gluten consumption. As a share of total US wheat gluten imports, US wheat gluten imports from Australia declined from 40.5 per cent in 1995 to 35.3 per cent in 1997.[33] Thus, there was no evidence of a change in the pattern and level of imports by domestic wheat gluten producers in 1996 and 1997 that would explain the surge in imports and decline in industry performance in those 2 years.

I. Competition with corn processors

42. As explained above in our response to the Panel's Question #28, the USITC considered arguments about the impact of competition in the US market between corn starch and wheat starch and its impact on wheat gluten production. The USITC found that the relative stability, and gradual increase, in domestic wheat starch prices suggested that competition between corn starch and wheat starch was not likely to have had much if any effect on wheat gluten production. The USITC also considered evidence cited by importers that one domestic producer had reduced its wheat gluten production in 1995 for reasons related in part to conditions in the alcohol market, and considered importers' claim that this ex-

---

30 US Exhibit 4 at II-17.

31 US Exhibit 4 at I-16.

32 US Exhibit 4 at II-12.

33 US Exhibit 4 at II-13.

plained that firm's poor financial performance. The USITC found that such action by the one producer in 1995 explained only part of the problem faced by one producer and could not be extrapolated to account for the problems facing all domestic producers, nor could not it explain the significant deterioration in 1996 and 1997 of the other three domestic producers, who accounted for the majority of domestic production. In fact, the evidence did not even fully explain the declining financial performance of that one producer in its wheat gluten operations.

43. The EC asserts in ¶¶ 61-62 of its Oral Statement that domestic wheat starch producers operate at a relative competitive disadvantage to domestic corn starch producers, and that the USITC should have investigated more thoroughly the conditions of competition between wheat starch and corn starch. However, the EC does not assert how the USITC's alleged failure to further investigate this issue might have contravened the Safeguards Agreement, nor does the EC demonstrate the relevance of this assertion to the USITC findings in dispute.

44. As the United States explained in ¶ 141 of its First Submission to this Panel, the EC's statement about competitive conditions between wheat starch and corn starch has no relevance to the findings in dispute. The EC does not argue that competitive conditions between corn and wheat starch changed during the period of investigation, nor does it contest the USITC's finding that wheat starch prices rose during the period of the investigation. The fact that the price of wheat is higher than the price of corn, as the EC alleges in ¶ 61 of its oral statement, is not only irrelevant, but simply confirms the statement in the USITC report that premium wheat starch prices usually enjoy a price premium over corn starches and low grade wheat starches.[34] In short, the EC fails to explain how conditions of competition between wheat starch and corn starch had any causal effect on the deterioration in the wheat gluten industry that took place in 1996 and 1997. Accordingly, in the absence of a showing of relevance, there is no reason to believe that there is a causal link, and no basis for attributing the decline in the performance of the domestic wheat gluten industry in 1996 and 1997 to conditions of competition between wheat starch and corn starch.

J. Input costs

45. The USITC examined and rejected the claim that rising raw material prices as reflected in the prices paid for wheat and wheat flour, the major inputs into wheat gluten/wheat starch production, were a more important cause of serious injury than increased imports.[35] Raw material costs did increase during the POI, particularly in 1996 and 1997. However, the USITC found the evidence indicates that wheat gluten producers typically are able to pass on the cost increases to their customers, because demand for wheat gluten is relatively insensitive to price changes. In 1996 and 1997, however, unit selling values declined

---

[34] US Exhibit 4 at II-21.

[35] US Exhibit 4 at I-17.

despite increased demand and higher raw material costs. The USITC concluded that this unusual development was explained by the dramatic increase in relatively low-priced imports during the POI, which had the effect of driving down wheat gluten prices.

46. In ¶¶ 84-86 of its Oral Statement, the EC makes much of the fact that the USITC cited testimony presented by the presidents of two of the domestic producers, Midwest and Manildra, to support its finding that domestic wheat gluten producers typically are able to pass on cost increases to their customers. The EC argues that oral assertions by persons interested in the outcome of an investigation do not fulfill US obligations under Article 4.2(b) of the Safeguards Agreement. The EC claims that these assertions are factually incorrect because customers can substitute high protein wheat or wheat flour.[36]

47. The USITC's finding with respect to the ability of domestic producers to pass on cost increases is supported by quantifiable data in the record of the USITC's investigation. Data in the confidential version of the USITC report show that when raw materials costs rose in 1994 from the 1993 level, the unit selling value of wheat gluten also rose, and when the raw materials costs fell in 1995, the unit selling value of wheat gluten also fell.[37] In 1996 and 1997, however, unit selling values declined despite increased demand and higher raw material costs. The USITC concluded that this unusual development was explained by the dramatic increase in relatively low-priced imports during the POI, which had the effect of driving down wheat gluten prices.

48. Furthermore, the EC's claim about substitute products is not consistent with what wheat gluten purchasers told the USITC. US purchasers generally reported in their questionnaire responses that wheat gluten has no substitutes when used in bakery products that require the vitality/binding properties of wheat gluten.[38] The evidence in the USITC report indicates that the amount of wheat gluten used in the production of bakery products varies by type of product and with the nature of the production process. For example, the USITC found that the wheat gluten must be used in the production of high-fibre and multi-grain breads and in the production of bagels. The USITC also found that the shift to high-speed mixing equipment has led to increased use of wheat gluten because the higher mixing speed tends to break down the vitality of the flour.[39] Thus, while most flours contain gluten in varying amounts and the hard wheat flour used in bread making typically has a high gluten content[40], this does not mean that bakers do not need to supplement the protein content of their flour by adding wheat gluten. The EC implies that high gluten wheat flour has a sufficiently high gluten content so as not to require the addition of wheat gluten to enhance the gluten level. This is

36 EC oral statement of 20 December 1999, ¶¶ 84-86.
37 Confidential version of US Exhibit 4 at II-29 and C-4].
38 US Exhibit 4 at II-27.
39 US Exhibit 4 at I-23.
40 US Exhibit 4 at II-4.

contrary to the evidence in the record of the USITC investigation[41], and the EC offers no support in the USITC record for its claim.

49. As stated above, the testimony of the two domestic company presidents was thus supported by the record as a whole. The United States does not agree that the testimony of a company official on conditions affecting the industry should automatically be regarded as unobjective just because the official may have an interest in the outcome of the investigation. Most participants in an investigation, whether representing a domestic producer, purchaser, distributor, or an importer, have at least some interest in the outcome of the investigation.

50. As a practical matter, company officials who are involved in the day-to-day pr oduction, sale, purchase, or importation of the product are likely to be the most knowledgeable persons about the factors affecting the economic performance of the industry and the conditions of competition between the domestic and imported products and are the source of much of the information obtained in the course of the investigation. For example, most of the information of a quantifiable nature is obtained through questionnaires filled out by officials of companies involved in the production, importation, or purchase of the product under investigation. Accordingly, there was no reason why the USITC should have disregarded the testimony of the two company presidents when the testimony was given under oath and described the experiences of their respective companies, particularly when the testimony was not rebutted, and was consistent with other evidence before the Commission.

K. Capacity Utilization

51. In its injury determination, the USITC performed a calculation analyzing the effects of increased imports on capacity utilization, pursuant to the requirement of Article 4.2(a) of the Safeguards Agreement to examine the specific enumerated factors.[42] The USITC calculated what the capacity utilization level would have been in 1997 (61 per cent) if the domestic industry had increased production to match the increase in domestic consumption, rather than seeing it captured by increased imports. This calculation explicitly held constant the other possible effects of increased imports (*e.g.*, their effect in driving down prices) to isolate the effects of imports on capacity utilization in accordance with Article 4.2(a). The EC makes no argument that this methodology is not in accordance with the plain language of Article 4.2(a).

---

[41] See, e.g., testimony at the 16 December 1997 USITC injury hearing by Charles A. Sullivan, Chairman and Chief Executive Officer of Interstate Bakeries Corp., at 80: "If we had a crop of wheat that had significantly high protein, we would use a less amount of the gluten, but I have not seen a crop in all the years that I have been in the business that we haven't had to use some."

[42] US Exhibit 4 at I-12, I-17. The EC's criticism (EC Oral Statement at ¶ 73) of the description of this USITC analysis in the United States ' First Submission as an "ex post facto justification" is obviously wrong, since this analysis comes directly from the USITC Report.

52. Given that the USITC conducted this analysis of the effects of increased imports on capacity utilization in accordance with the requirements of Article 4.2(a), the EC's complaint in ¶ 76 of its Oral Statement that this analysis shows "protectionist aims" is without merit. By conducting such an Article 4.2 analysis, the USITC was hardly "assuming," as the EC claims it was, that the entire increase in domestic demand (much less "the entire domestic consumption") "should have" turned to US domestic suppliers.[43] Article 4.2(a) requires an examination of what effects on the domestic industry have been caused by increased imports, including the effects on specific enumerated factors such as capacity utilization. In its capacity utilization finding in its injury analysis, the USITC isolated the effects of increased imports on capacity consistent with Article 4.2(a); it was not making assumptions about which suppliers "should have" satisfied domestic demand.

53. In its Question #3 to the United States, the EC implicitly criticizes the USITC's determination because it did not make an explicit analysis of how much of the expected increase in demand the US industry expected to capture. This criticism has no basis in the Safeguards Agreement, which imposes no duty to make any such finding. The EC would in effect require an analysis that would subdivide increased imports. It would limit USITC analysis to only that portion of increased imports that the USITC affirmatively found that the industry could not have expected, and treat as illegitimate any consideration of the effects of the other portion of increased imports. Whether or not such an analysis might be permissible under the Safeguards Agreement, there is no suggestion in the Agreement that such an analysis is required. Article 4.2(a) directs the competent authorities to investigate the effects caused by "increased imports," not some of the increased imports.

54. Whether or not the US producers had good reason for expecting that the increased domestic production would go to them is not relevant. Given the irrelevance of this issue, the USITC made no explicit finding about it as such. Nevertheless, the USITC Report shows that the US producers had every reason to expect that they would capture a large portion of the increased demand. They did not foresee, and had no reason to foresee, that the increased demand would instead be captured by low-priced EC imports, which increased due to developments in the EC wheat starch market exogenous to the wheat gluten market. Between 1993 and 1995 import market shares fell somewhat.[44] In addition, a new US producer, Heartland Wheat Growers, which had begun constructing its plant in 1993, began production in 1996.[45] Its entry would normally have been expected to take market share from both importers and domestic producers. Certainly that would have been expected as the plant was being built, given pricing patterns before 1996, when imports from all sources both oversold and undersold

[43] EC Oral Statement at ¶ 75.

[44] US Exhibit 4 at C-3, Table C-1.

[45] US Exhibit 4 at II-8.

the domestic product.[46] Thus, there was every reason to assume that a new entrant to the domestic industry would take market share from the imports, leading to a significant increase in the domestic producers' overall share of the market.

55. The EC also asks in its Question 2 where in its findings the USITC showed that at 61 per cent capacity utilization, the industry would have been profitable in 1996 and 1997. Contrary to the EC's suggestion, the USITC made no statements or predictions as to whether the industry could or would have been profitable at 61 per cent of capacity in 1996 and 1997; the Safeguards Agreement requires no such statement. What the USITC Report stated was that the 61 per cent capacity utilization level was "much closer [than the 44.5 per cent of capacity actually reported in 1997] to the level at which the industry operated early in the investigative period when it operated reasonably profitably." This observation was directly relevant to analyzing whether the effects of increased imports were causing serious injury.

56. Moreover, this statement is entirely consistent with the record. As the USITC Report stated, the industry was profitable in 1993 and even more so in 1994, when capacity utilization was 78.3 per cent and 67.4 per cent, respectively.[47] Accordingly, even the EC must concede that, as the USITC stated, 61 per cent is much closer than 44.5 per cent to the level at which the industry had operated profitably early in the period. Furthermore, since the industry had its most profitable year in 1994 when capacity utilization was 67.4 per cent, the EC' s suggestion that the 78 per cent capacity utilization level of 1993 was the only level at which the industry could operate profitably is just plain wrong.[48]

III. THE REMEDY THE UNITED STATES IMPOSED COMPORTS WITH US OBLIGATIONS UNDER ARTICLE 5.1 OF THE SAFEGUARDS AGREEMENT

A. *The United States applied its safeguards quota "only to the extent necessary"*

1. *The quota was not applied beyond the extent necessary*

57. The EC has characterized the first sentence of Article 5.1 as establishing a "proportionality test." The United States has made clear why that characterization is incorrect.[49] However, there can be no disagreement regarding the fact that Arti-

---

46 [US Exhibit 4 at II-36 and Corrigendum].

47 US Exhibit 4 at I-13, II-15 at Table 5.

48 EC Oral Statement at ¶ 71. In addition, the industry was still profitable (although less so) in 1995, before the import surge, when capacity utilization was 56.2 per cent. US Exhibit 4 at I-13, II-15 at Table 5. The EC's repeated efforts to argue that it was the domestic industry's expansion of capacity in 1993-1995, and not the import surge of 1996-1997, that caused the serious injury to the industry are simply inconsistent with the record.

49 US First Submission at ¶ 165-169.

cle 5.1, first sentence, establishes a specific obligation. That obligation is to apply a measure "only to the extent necessary to prevent or remedy serious injury and to facilitate adjustment." The EC has argued that the United States violated that requirement in two ways.[50]

58. First, the EC alleges that the US wheat gluten safeguard is being applied beyond the extent necessary because it purportedly seeks to address *all* of the injury suffered by the industry, including injury caused by sources other than imports. Second, the EC contends that the US resort to a quantitative restriction amounted to the application of a safeguard measure beyond the extent necessary because, in the EC's view, quotas are disfavoured under the Safeguards Agreement and the GATT. The EC's arguments are without merit on both claims.

59. The United States took care to ensure that its safeguard measure was applied "only to the extent necessary" to remedy the serious injury caused by imports. While the EC alleges that the United States attributed injury from other sources to imports and then applied a remedy that addressed *all* of the injury, it cites no findings by the USITC identifying factors other than imports that were a significant cause of serious injury to the domestic industry.

60. In ¶ 105 its oral statement, the EC crafts a hypothetical situation, based on its reading of the US safeguards statute[51], in which the United States allegedly *could* apply a remedy that "punishes" imports for the injury caused by other sources. The EC's hypothetical plainly does not apply to the facts of this case, where the USITC identified no significant sources of injury other than imports. The hypothetical thus has no relevance for purposes of assessing whether the US wheat gluten safeguard measure has been applied beyond the extent necessary to remedy the serious injury attributable to increased imports.

61. Moreover, the EC's argument seems to assume that the United States was required to quantify the specific amount of injury that was due to imports as opposed to other causes. As pointed out in the first US written submission, the specific language that the negotiators of the Safeguards Agreement adopted in Article 4.2(b) concerning injury due to other factors had previously been interpreted not to require such quantification.[52] Article 5.1 does not impose any particular

[50] The EC also asserts the United States violated Article 5.1 through its alleged "inherent inconsistency" in considering the co-product nature of wheat gluten for purposes of the remedy but not in its injury investigation. The United States previously addressed this erroneous argument in para. 184 - 185 of its first submission, and the EC's oral statement adds nothing new to that argument.

[51] The EC cites the provisions of 19 USC. 2252(b)(1) as "evidence" of its assertion that the United States has disproportionately restricted wheat gluten imports. The United States does not understand the EC, in citing this provision of US law, to have challenged its compatibility with the Safeguards Agreement as such. Indeed, the EC could not purport to do so at this stage, having not included the US safeguard statute in its request for a panel. Moreover, the EC stated in its First Written Submission that the compatibility of the US safeguard law "is not under the scrutiny of this Panel. " First Written Submission of the EC, ¶ 128. See US response to Panel Question # 9.

[52] US First Written Submission at ¶ 130.

methodology by which Members must ensure that their safeguard measures are not applied beyond "the extent necessary".

62. The EC's contention that the US safeguard measure did not take account of the injury caused by other factors, but instead sought to remedy all of the industry's injury, simply disregards the actual remedy imposed and the findings underlying that remedy. The USITC conducted an analysis in addition to its injury findings and causation findings to ascertain what would be necessary to remedy the injury caused by imports and facilitate adjustment. Both that analysis, and the action taken by the President, ensure that the remedy taken was as modest as possible to address the injury caused by imports and facilitate adjustment by the industry.

63. In particular, the remedy does not seek to offset each element of injury that the USITC found was caused by increased imports. For example, as noted at, in evaluating the injury factor concerning capacity utilization, the USITC held all other factors constant and ascertained what the difference in US capacity utilization would be if the US producers had captured the increase in demand acquired by increased imports in 1996-1997. By contrast, in its remedy findings, the USITC conducted a different analysis that was directed toward determining the effect its recommended safeguard measure would have on the US industry's operations in the future.[53] This analysis did not assume that the domestic industry would capture all of the increase in domestic demand in 1997 from earlier levels. Although the safeguard remedy was based on the 1993-1995 market shares held by imports, the USITC applied those market shares to 1997 domestic consumption/demand levels in setting quota levels. Thus, the remedy the USITC proposed, and that the President adopted, does not seek to recoup for the domestic industry the full increase in domestic demand.

64. In addition, the remedy analysis did not attempt to isolate the effects of increased imports on capacity utilization from its effects on price. The remedy analysis assumed that domestic producers, relieved from pressure from low-priced imports, would prefer to raise their prices above their operating costs, even though this meant that they would be foregoing some increase in sales, and consequently in production and capacity utilization. This different kind of analysis is consistent with the Safeguards Agreement, which prescribes certain factors for competent authorities to consider in making their injury determination, but by contrast does not specify any particular method of estimating the effects of proposed safeguard remedies.

65. For both of these reasons, the USITC's projection of the capacity utilization level that the domestic industry would reach if the proposed safeguard remedy were implemented (50.7 per cent-53.3 per cent) is lower than the USITC's calculation of the capacity utilization level (61 per cent) in its injury analysis. Because this estimate assumes that the US industry will sell at a price that covers

---

53 USITC Report at I-30 to I-31.

its operating costs, it seeks to ensure that the US industry will operate at a level at which it will achieve a reasonable profit.

66. Nevertheless, although the projected capacity utilization is considerably closer to the utilization levels at which the US industry operated profitably, it remains below the 56.2 per cent level achieved in the last year of profitability (1995) and well below the 78.3 per cent level achieved in 1993.[54] The USITC found that this remedy would allow US producers "to more fully utilize their recently increased capacity ... , thereby raising productivity and lowering unit operating costs."[55] The remedy was not designed, however, to ensure that domestic producers could come close to completely utilizing their increased capacity. Thus, the US remedy plainly does not seek to remedy all ills facing the US industry, but rather seeks specifically to facilitate the US industry's adjustment to those specific problems posed by increased imports.

67. Moreover, although the USITC found that a 4-year remedy would be necessary to facilitate adjustment, the President did not impose a remedy of that duration. Instead, he chose a remedy of only 3 years. Thus, both the USITC's recommendations and the President's action were calculated to ensure that the United States would *not* apply a safeguard measure beyond the extent necessary to remedy the serious injury attributable to imports and facilitate adjustment. Under these circumstances, the EC has no basis on which to argue that the United States imposed an overly expansive remedy that addressed not only injury caused by imports, but also injury from other sources.

2. *The United States was not required to use a tariff safeguard measure*

68. The EC further alleges that the form of the remedy the United States applied - a quantitative restriction - automatically means that the United States applied a remedy beyond the extent necessary to remedy the serious injury. The EC arrives at that conclusion based on its supposition that Article 5.1 disfavours quota measures over tariffs. In support of its claim, the EC points to the third sentence of Article 5.1, which states that "Members should choose measures most suitable for the achievement of these objectives," and argues that sentence, read in conjunction with the "only to extent necessary" language of Article 5.1, first sentence, disfavours quotas. The EC also points to "basic principles of the GATT 1994" as evidenced in the preamble to the Safeguards Agreement, and the panel report in *Turkey - Restrictions on Imports of Textiles and Clothing Products.*[56]

[54] USITC Report at II-15, Table 5.
[55] USITC Report at I-30.
[56] WT/DS34/R 31 May 1999.

69. There is no basis for the claim that the Safeguards Agreement disfavours quotas for purposes of applying definitive safeguard measures. Indeed, Article 5, which treats definitive safeguard remedies, *specifically* provides for quotas and fails to mention duties at all. Moreover, whereas Article 6, which provides for provisional safeguard measures, establishes a preference (although not a requirement) for provisional tariff remedies, Article 5 contains no such admonition. Had the framers of Article 5 preferred tariff remedies over quantitative restrictions for purposes of definitive safeguards measures, they would have included in Article 5 language akin to that in Article 6.

70. Plainly, Article 5.1 contemplates that Members may establish safeguard measures in the form of quantitative restrictions. Rather than subordinating them to tariff measures, Article 5.1, second sentence, simply places restrictions on the extent to which they may be applied. That sentence provides:

> If a quantitative restriction is used, such a measure shall not reduce the quantity of imports below the level of a recent period which shall be the average of imports in the last three representative years for which statistics are available, unless clear justification is given that a different level is necessary to prevent or remedy serious injury.

71. Where a Member satisfies that obligation, and assuming that the quota is not otherwise applied beyond the extent necessary to prevent or remedy serious injury, it is free to apply a quantitative restriction. The EC's citation to the fourth preamble of the Safeguards Agreement, that the Safeguards Agreement is "based on the basic principles of GATT 1994," and its reference to *Turkey – Textiles* are irrelevant. The preambular language the EC cites may establish context for the interpretation of Article 5, if the plain meaning of its terms are in doubt. But they are not in doubt, since they plainly provide for definitive safeguard measures in the form of quantitative restrictions and do not create any preference for tariff remedies.

72. The EC next tries to fashion an argument out of the third sentence of Article 5.1, which provides that "Members should choose measures most suitable for the achievement of these objectives." The EC argues in its first submission (but did not further elaborate in its oral statement) that "a tariff should be used unless, as provided by the third sentence of paragraph 1, a tariff would not be suitable to remedy the serious injury and facilitate adjustment."[57] This is a contorted reading of Article 5.1, to say the least.

73. The second sentence of that article specifically provides for quantitative restrictions without the slightest hint that they may be used only where a tariff remedy is unsuitable. In fact, as noted above, Article 5.1 nowhere mentions tariff remedies, which hardly suggests that they are to be preferred. The last sentence

[57] EC First Submission at ¶ 118.

of Article 5.1, which admonishes Members to choose the most suitable remedy, does not exalt tariff remedies over quantitative restrictions as a matter of principle. Rather, it admonishes the importing government to choose a measure - whether tariff- or quantitative-based - that, in the particular case, is most suitable for remedying or preventing injury and facilitating adjustment. In fact, the USITC provided extensive explanations as to why, in the case of wheat gluten, a tariff measure would not meet the objectives of remedying the industry's serious injury and facilitating its adjustment.[58] Thus, a tariff measure was not the "most suitable" remedy in the case of wheat gluten imports.

74. Both the EC's first written and oral statements acknowledge the USITC's explanations, but in the EC's view these "short arguments" are inadequate.[59] If by that the EC means to imply that there is a specific page limit requirement – that position is both erroneous and absurd. The USITC's reasoned explanations as to why a tariff measure was an unsuitable remedy amply satisfy US obligations under Article 5.1.

B. *The Wheat Gluten Quota is Set at a Level in Excess of Import Levels in the Last Three Representative Years*

75. In its oral statement the EC continues to argue that the burden of proof shifts to the United States to demonstrate that the wheat gluten quota conforms to the second sentence of Article 5.1 – *i.e.*, a quantitative restriction cannot reduce the level of imports below the last three representative years of imports. In the EC's view, Article 5 establishes a special rule that is "not the usual burden of proof.."[60] This argument simply ignores GATT jurisprudence on this issue, most recently articulated in *Korea – Dairy* where the Panel found that "the burden of proof rests with the ... complainant, and does not shift during the panel process."[61] Accordingly, the burden, at all times remains with the EC to prove its claim. It has failed to do so in this instance.

76. The substance of the EC's claim is that the United States failed to use the "representative" period 1995 to 1997. The EC argues that the most recent three years of wheat gluten imports are representative because they "represent exactly the pattern of trade on-going before the entry into force of the measure ... "[62] But this argument is entirely circular. A three-year pattern of trade is not "representative " merely because it occurred in the last three years. Rather, a three-year pattern of trade is "representative" if it is characteristic of pre-existing patterns. The EC resorts to doublespeak because the pattern of trade that pertained during the 1995 to 1997 period was unlike – that is, *unrepresentative* – of the historical

[58] The United States previously discussed these issues in detail in ¶ 194 of this submission.
[59] EC First Oral Statement at ¶ 109.
[60] EC Oral Statement at ¶ 122.
[61] *Korea – Dairy*, *supra*, footnote 10, para. 7.24.
[62] EC Oral Statement at ¶ 199.

pattern of US wheat gluten import trade. That is so because 1996-97 were surge years, with imports far in excess of historical averages and rising faster than the increase in demand. Moreover, the EC's complaints about the size of the quota are particularly unpersuasive in light of the fact that the United States set the quota at a level *higher* than that accounted by imports during the 1993-95 period.

77. The EC discounts the United States' position that the term "representative," as used in Article 5.1, normally would be a period in which imports did not cause serious injury. The EC's contrary reading would undermine the remedial purpose of the Safeguards Agreement since a quota set at the average level of imports during the period in which the industry sustained serious injury would be unlikely to remedy that injury or facilitate adjustment. The EC responds that "if an increase in imports were a 'clear' justification for using a representative period other than the 'last three representative years for which statistics are available,' this situation would always apply, rendering the provision meaningless."[63] Yet, by arguing that Article 5.1 normally would require a Member to set its quota level at the level that pertained during the most recent three years, it is the *EC* that is rendering "representative" meaningless.

78. Moreover, assuming *arguendo* that the EC's interpretation of " representative" is correct, Article 5.1 provides for deviation from that level when "clear justification is given that the different level is necessary to prevent or remedy serious injury." As noted in the United States' first submission, the USITC's findings satisfy the "clear justification" requirement.[64] The USITC found that choosing a period comprising the two years of crisis - 1996 and 1997 - would not remedy the serious injury; thus selecting that period would have defeated the objectives of remedying serious injury and facilitating adjustment set out in Article 5.1.[65]

IV. THE UNITED STATES COMPLIED WITH ARTICLE 5.2(A) QUOTA ALLOCATION RULES

79. In its oral statement, the EC added nothing to bolster its claim that the United States allocated the wheat gluten quota in violation of Article 5.2(a). Rather, the EC continues to assert that the United States failed to consult with Members with a view to achieving an agreed allocation and did not explain why that method was not "reasonably practicable." Conspicuously absent from the EC's allegations are any arguments that would support its conclusion that the hortatory or permissive language of Article 5.2(a) should be read as mandatory in nature.

---

63 EC Oral Statement at ¶ 119.

64 See US First Submission at ¶ 194.

65 See US First Submission at ¶ 194.

80. Article 5.2(a) provides that "in cases in which a quota is allocated among supplying countries, the Member applying the restrictions *may* seek agreement." The EC reads the term "may" as "shall," but provides no textual basis for this extraordinary interpretation nor does it cite to any WTO jurisprudence that would sanction such a leap. It is apparent from the plain terms of Article 5.2(a) that the EC's claim is incorrect as a legal matter.

81. Moreover, to the extent that this purported "obligation" in Article 5.2(a) imposes an obligation to hold consultations, the United States satisfied that requirement. That fact is confirmed in letters drafted by the EC on this issue. Specifically, in a 8 May 1998 letter to the United States from Jean-Jacques Bouflet, Minister-Counsellor to the EC Commission Delegation in Geneva, Mr. Bouflet notes that the parties indeed did consult on 24 April 1998, and further confirms that the parties discussed the quota allocation issue. Therefore, the EC's allegation that the United States breached Article 5.2(a) by failing to consult on the quota allocation is factually incorrect, as evidenced by the EC's own document.[66]

V. THE UNITED STATES OBSERVED THE NOTIFICATION AND CONSULTATIONS REQUIREMENTS OF ARTICLES 8 AND 12

A. *The United States Satisfied its Consultation Obligations Under Article 12*

82. The EC alleges that because of the "unilateral" nature of safeguards measures, the Safeguards Agreement imposes heightened consultation and negotiations obligations on the Member imposing the measure.[67] To that end, the EC discerns an obligation to consult under practically every article of the Safeguards Agreement, even where the plain terms of the article in question do not call for such consultation "obligations." Thus, the EC alternately alleges violations of consultation obligations under Articles 5, 8 and 12 of the Safeguards Agreement.[68] The United States submits that it amply satisfied its consultation obligation, to the extent such obligations exist. Therefore, the EC's allegations on this point cannot be sustained.

83. The EC has not denied that it actually consulted with the United States under Article 12.3 on 24 April 1998. In its response to Panel Question 11 the United States provided documentation supporting its claim and demonstrating that the parties discussed the proposed measure (US Exhibits 11 and 12). Those facts alone are sufficient to establish that the United States satisfied its consultation obligations under Article 12.3. Rather than respond to the facts brought for-

---

[66] Letter dated 8 May 1998 from Mr. Bouflet to Mr. Bob Kasper of the United States. US Exhibit 11.

[67] EC Oral Statement at ¶ 174.

[68] The United States previously discussed in Section III herein the fact that Article 5.2 does not establish a consultation "obligation."

ward by the United States, the EC has made conclusory assertions. The EC's oral statement alleges that at certain "informal meetings" held after the Article 12.3 consultations, the United States failed to accede to EC demands. In short, the EC has not met its burden of proof with respect to its claim of a violation of Article 12.3.

B. The United States Timely Filed its Notification on the Investigation and on the Proposed Measure

84. The EC maintains that the United States failed to notify the "proposed measure," because the US safeguard measure was notified three days after it had taken effect. The EC further alleges that the United States "made findings of serious injury on 15 January 1998, but notified the WTO only on 11 February 1998." In the EC's view "[a]ll these notifications were thus effected *ex post facto*, i.e. after the action or the measure had been adopted and not at the stage of proposed action or measure, in clear breach of the letter and the spirit of Article 12 SA."

85. The EC's claim regarding the US notification of serious injury is incomprehensible in light of the plain terms of Article 12.1(b), which requires immediate notification "upon ... making a finding of serious injury ... " The United States simply could not have provided notification of the USITC's serious injury findings until *after* the USITC made those findings. Thus, the EC's complaint that the notification was inconsistent with Article 12.1(b) because it was "effected *ex post facto*" cannot be taken seriously.

86. The EC's allegations regarding the US remedy notification are equally unfounded. Article 12.1(c) requires immediate notification "upon ... taking a decision" to apply a safeguard measure. The United States effected a notification of this type once it had taken the decision to impose the wheat gluten safeguard, in conformity with the plain terms of Article 12.1(c).

87. Detailed below is a brief chronology of the relevant consultation and notification events in this matter, which may help the Panel to address the various notification and consultation issues raised in this proceeding.

Date	Action
19 September 1997	Domestic industry files petition with USITC
1 October 1997	USITC completes evaluation and announces institution of investigation
17 October 1997	United States files Article 12.1(a) notification
15 January 1998	USITC votes unanimously that increased imports are causing serious injury to the domestic industry
11 February 1998	US files Article 12.1(b) notification
18 March 1998	USITC issues confidential report and recommendation
24 March 1998	US files supplementation 12.1(b) notification along with a copy of the public version of the USITC's report
24 April 1998	US holds first consultations with the EC
19-20 May 1998	The US holds "informal" consultations with the EC (alleged by EC)
22 May 1998	US holds second consultations with the EC
1 June 1998	US measure on wheat gluten becomes effective
4 June 1998	US files Article 12.1(c) and Article 9 notification

88. In light of these facts, the EC's complaint regarding the timing and notifications on the investigation and the proposed measure cannot be sustained.

VI. CONCLUSION

89. The EC has failed to assert and prove its claim that the US safeguard measure is inconsistent with US obligations under the Safeguards Agreement or the GATT 1994. For the reasons presented in the US first and second submissions and first oral statement, the United States respectfully requests that the Panel reject the EC's claims in this dispute and affirm that the United States has acted consistently with its obligations.

UNITED STATES LIST OF EXHIBITS

United States – Definitive Safeguard Measure on Imports of Wheat Gluten from the European Communities

Exhibit Number	*Description of Exhibits*
11	Letter dated 8 May 1998 from Mr. Jean-Jacques Bouflet, Minister-Counsellor of the EC Commission Delegation to Mr. Bob Kasper of the United States regarding consultations on 24 April 1998.
12	Letter dated 21 May 1998 from Mr. Juan Monfort of the EC Commission Delegation to Mr. Bob Kasper regarding consultations on 22 May 1998 (with attachment).

US Exhibit 11

US Exhibit 12

ATTACHMENT 2-6

COMMUNICATION OF THE UNITED STATES CONCERNING PROPOSED PROCEDURES GOVERNING PRIVATE CONFIDENTIAL INFORMATION
(27 January 2000)

My authorities have instructed me to respond to the Panel's fax of 25 January 2000, wherein the Panel proposes procedures for providing and safeguarding Business Confidential Information. The United States has carefully reviewed the Panel's fax. As the United States has noted in its submissions to the Panel, under Article 3.2 of the *Agreement on Safeguards*, as well as US law, US competent authorities are precluded from disclosing confidential information provided to them in the course of a US safeguards investigation, absent the express consent of parties that supplied the information. In this case, that would include not only the consent of US producers but also producers of the European Communities, Australia, and Canada, as well as US purchasers and importers.

While the United States has reservations about the basis on which the Panel is seeking the information in question, the United States nevertheless wishes seeks to facilitate the Panel's work and to that end is prepared to make every effort to secure authorization to provide relevant Business Confidential Information that the Panel is seeking for its deliberations. It would greatly facilitate our efforts in this regard, however, if we were in a position to specify for the companies concerned the precise nature and scope of the information that the Panel is seeking, as well as the use to which the information will be put. This information would help the companies concerned to assess the extent of commercial risk they may face in the event of an inadvertent or unauthorized disclosure of any sensitive information they have provided. To this end, it would be highly desirable if the Panel could indicate to the Parties the type and extent of the information it is seeking; whether the business information to be supplied is solely that contained in the confidential report of the US International Trade Commission or would also include raw data that US and/or other suppliers, importers, and purchased furnished directly to the Commission; and whether the Panel would expect to use the information solely for its own purposes in verifying arguments advanced by the Parties to date or for some other purpose.

In the absence of an enforceable mechanism for ensuring the nondisclosure of confidential information, our efforts to secure consent from the companies concerned may be enhanced to the extent that there are strict and verifiable restrictions on the degree of access provided to the information, both in terms of the place in which it is made available and the affiliation and number of persons accorded access to it. Once we have been apprised of the nature and extent of business confidential information that the Panel is seeking we will consult with the firms in question and provide a detailed response to the Panel's proposed procedures. In our view, the appropriate procedures may varying depending on the particular information being sought.

We should hasten to point out, that even if the United States is successful in obtaining permission from US producers, importers, and purchasers to disclose some or all of the information the Panel is seeking, we may not be well situated to secure such permission from companies located outside the United States or with non-US ownership. In those instances we very likely would need to seek the cooperation of the Members concerned, in particular the EC, Canada, and Australia.

ATTACHMENT 2-7

UNITED STATES ORAL STATEMENT
SECOND MEETING
(1 February 2000)

Final Version

Mr. Chairman, Members of the Panel,

On behalf of the United States delegation, I would like to thank the Panel for its hard work to date in examining the questions raised in this dispute. In this oral statement, the United States will not repeat the arguments made in its previous submissions, but rather will briefly respond to the issues raised in the EC's Second Written Submission and its response to the Panel 's questions.

The United States will begin its presentation with a statement by Mr Henderson addressing the EC's recent arguments regarding standard of review, unforeseen developments and confidential information. Mr. Gearhart will address new arguments the EC has raised regarding the so-called wheat protein premium. Ms. Florestal will close the United States' presentation with a discussion of the EC's claims under Articles 5 and 12 of the Safeguards Agreement.

At the conclusion of our statement, we would be pleased to receive any questions you may have.

Mr. Henderson,

Standard of Review and Burden of Proof

1. The EC begins its second written submission with a list of questions purporting to set forth the issues to be examined by the Panel. Yet upon closer examination, each of the EC's questions concerning the USITC's injury and causation findings directs this Panel away from its task under the WTO Agreements. The EC's questions reverse the burden of proof, create false definitions of terms, and manufacture obligations that are not contained in the Safeguards Agreement.

2. Contrary to the wording of the EC's questions, it is the EC as complainant that bears the burden of proof, a burden that does not change throughout this panel process. Thus, after the EC has submitted its arguments and the United States has responded to the EC's claims, the Panel must weigh the evidence and arguments submitted by both parties to determine whether the EC has met its burden.

3. In addition to reversing the burden of proof, the EC also supplies its own definitions of terms in the Safeguards Agreement, and then tries to argue that the US has failed to satisfy those newly-created definitions. The EC does this, for example, in discussing the requirement in Article 4.2(b) that the investigation must demonstrate the causal link between increased imports and serious injury on

the basis of "objective evidence." The EC argues that this means that the United States must show that the evidence the USITC cited in its causation findings was not "biased by subjective, political or unrelated aims." The EC's twisted definition of "objective evidence" is not based on anything in the Safeguards Agreement or any decision construing the Agreement. Moreover, it reverses the burden of proof, and seeks to distract the Panel's attention to irrelevant matters. The Panel is fully capable of determining whether the pertinent evidence in the USITC investigation constitutes "objective evidence" under Article 4.2(b) without undertaking a separate inquiry into the existence of such alleged other motives.

4. In addition, the EC suggests that Article 4.2(b) required the USITC to establish with "positive and irrefutable evidence" the existence of the causal link between increased imports and serious injury. There is no such language in Article 4.2(b). Neither the Safeguards Agreement nor the Dispute Settlement Understanding nor Panel or Appellate Body reports require "positive and irrefutable evidence." As the EC itself acknowledged in its first oral statement, the Panel's job is to examine the USITC report and determine whether the USITC's decision was reasonable.

5. Again and again in its submission the EC offers evidence that it says the USITC report did not consider, and claims that such omissions constitute, in themselves, a violation of Article 4.2. The EC in effect argues that it can demonstrate a violation of Article 4.2 simply by demonstrating that some piece of evidence that it considers relevant was not included in the USITC report.

6. The EC makes a fundamental mistake, misreading Article 4.2 by confusing the term "factors" with particular "facts" or "evidence." Article 4.2(a) requires a competent authority to evaluate "all relevant *factors*" bearing on the situation of the domestic industry. Article 4.2(c) requires the competent authority to publish a report containing a detailed analysis of the case, as well as a demonstration of the relevance of the "*factors*" examined. Similarly, Article 3.1 requires a competent authority to publish a report setting forth findings and conclusions of law reached on "all pertinent *issues* of fact or law."

7. Thus, while the competent authority's report should address all relevant "factors" and resolve all relevant "issues of fact," the Safeguards Agreement contains no requirement that it explicitly mention each "fact," much less each piece of evidence. To show that a particular fact or piece of evidence is not mentioned does not establish a violation of the Safeguards Agreement. Moreover, as the United States has demonstrated in its previous submissions, the specific examples cited by the EC do not show that the USITC report failed to address any relevant factor or issue of fact, or that the United States in any way violated the Safeguards Agreement.

8. Similarly, the Safeguards Agreement does not require the competent authority's report to contain every specific fact that may support the authority's

findings. Consequently, the EC's complaint that the USITC report redacted some non-confidential information states no claim under the Safeguards Agreement.

9. The United States has previously set forth in its response to Panel Question 7 why the USITC did not have an obligation on its own initiative to hypothesize other possible causes of injury to the domestic industry besides increased imports beyond those raised by the parties, including the EC or the European producers, during the USITC investigation. However, in its treatment of this issue, the EC misrepresents the role of the USITC in gathering information during the investigation. The EC claims that the USITC did not actively search for information during its wheat gluten investigation, but rather relied solely on the information that the parties placed before it. As the EC knows very well, this is absolutely incorrect.

10. As was demonstrated in the United States' prior submissions, the USITC conducted a very thorough investigation. The USITC sent questionnaires to domestic producers, importers, and purchasers, and gathered publicly available information. The USITC held public hearings in both the injury and remedy phases of the investigation, at which all parties expressing an interest - including the EC - were permitted to appear and make their views known. At these hearings, the USITC Commissioners and staff directly questioned the witnesses and requested additional information and clarification of arguments. The record was supplemented by additional information and arguments supplied by the parties. Through the investigative process, the USITC developed a substantial body of information and arguments relating to the questions of injury and remedy, and the USITC made its determination and recommendation on the basis of that detailed record.

Unforeseen Developments

11. As set forth in the United States' response to Panel Question 5, the USITC'S detailed report amply demonstrates as a matter of fact the unexpected developments that caused the increased imports. These developments concerned the European producers' expansion of capacity as part of an effort to increase their production of wheat starch for the protected European market, for reasons unrelated to developments in the wheat gluten market, and were in fact unforeseen by the United States and the domestic wheat gluten industry. These USITC findings fully satisfy the ruling of the Appellate Body in *Argentina - Footwear* that this provision of Article XIX of the GATT 1994 does not establish "independent conditions" for the application of a safeguard measure, but rather "describes certain circumstances which must be demonstrated as a matter of fact in order for a safeguard measure to be applied."

12. In its second submission, the EC attempts to add an obligation not found in the Safeguards Agreement or in Article XIX and that does not flow from the recent Appellate Body decisions addressing unforeseen developments. According to the EC, the Appellate Body stated that such unforeseen developments must be "demonstrated in [the competent authority's] investigation report." That is simply incorrect. The Appellate Body made no such statement. The Appellate Body in

Argentina - Footwear considered "whether the Argentine authorities have, *in their investigation*, demonstrated that the increased imports in this case occurred as a result of unforeseen developments and of the effect of the obligations incurred by a Member under this Agreement, including tariff concessions." Thus, the relevant question is whether the USITC demonstrated in its investigation that unforeseen developments occurred, not whether the USITC made a specific determination regarding unforeseen developments. It is plain that the USITC report shows that those developments took place.

Ms. Florestal,

13. Mr. Chairman, at this point I would like to briefly depart from the text of our prepared statement to discuss the fax the Panel sent over this morning regarding certain Business Confidential Information it would like the United States to provide, and the procedures for that information.

14. The United States seeks to be responsive to the Panel's request. We note that the Panel's working procedures do not include a reference to the language in Article 3.2, which provides that "[confidential information] shall not be disclosed without permission of the party submitting it." The United States believes that it is important for the working procedures to reflect the obligation contained in Article 3.2.

15. In addition, the Panel's fax makes reference to the recent Appellate Body report in *Canada – Aircraft*. The United States believes that *Canada - Aircraft* is not applicable to the situation here. The United States recalls that the information at issue in *Canada – Aircraft* was information in the government's possession. It is not at all similar to this case, where the information the Panel is requesting is business confidential information relating to private parties. Moreover, the *Canada - Aircraft* case did not involve an express prohibition on providing that information without the express consent of the parties, as is the case under Article 3.2 of the Safeguards Agreement.

Confidential Information

16. While acknowledging that the USITC could properly redact from its report confidential data of individual companies, the EC continues to argue that the redaction of aggregate data is improper in every case. However, the EC carefully avoids acknowledging why the USITIC redacted aggregate data in this case. The USITC did so for an entirely justifiable reason, namely because of the small number of firms that submitted data. Disclosing aggregate data in such circumstances would have made it easy for competing companies to discern the individual confidential information supplied by other firms. Article 3.2 states that such confidential information submitted to the competent authority "shall not be disclosed without the permission of the party submitting it." Moreover, Article 4.2(c) expressly requires that publication of the competent authority's report shall be in accordance with these provisions of Article 3.

17. In its Second Submission, the EC adds another new claim. It says that because the USITC redacted confidential information from its report, the United States violated an obligation to provide non-confidential summaries of confidential information. The EC is once again misreading the Safeguards Agreement, which contains no such obligation. Article 3.2, which addresses non-confidential summaries of confidential information, states only that "parties providing confidential information may be requested to furnish non-confidential summaries thereof, or if such parties indicate that such information cannot be summarized, the reasons why such a summary cannot be provided." Thus, this provision deals only with the submission of non-confidential summaries by interested parties that make submissions during the course of a safeguards investigation. Article 3.2 does not impose any requirement on a competent authority such as the USITC to provide a non-confidential summary, nor does any other provision of the Safeguards Agreement. Moreover, Article 3.2 does not impose an obligation on a competent authority to require that interested parties provide such non-confidential summaries during the investigation. Article 3.2 states only that non-confidential summaries "may be requested" of submitting parties.

18. Finally, the EC's claims of prejudice from the USITC's redaction of confidential information cannot be taken at face value. Under USITC rules the EC could have applied to be a party to the administrative protective order governing the confidential information, and could have had access to that information during the USITC proceeding. The European producers did exactly that, and their counsel had such access. While the EC appeared at the beginning of the investigation, it chose not to apply to be a party to the protective order. Its lack of access to the confidential information was due to its own choice.

New Claims

19. Indeed, this panel should not consider the EC's misplaced arguments that a competent authority must provide non-confidential summaries of confidential information and that the USITC must have made a specific determination of unforeseen circumstances. These are among several contentions that the EC raises for the first time in its most recent submission. Also new is the EC's claim that US law requiring the USITC to determine that other possible causes of injury are not a more important cause of serious injury to the domestic industry than increased imports is inconsistent with Article 4 of the Safeguards Agreement. Those claims were not included in the EC's panel request, and it would prejudice the United States if such claims were now to be considered, when briefing is almost completed. If these new claims are allowed to be heard now, the United States will have been deprived of its ability to address these claims in both its first and second written submissions, at the December 21-22 oral argument, and in its responses to the Panel's questions.

20. In addition, the EC now claims in response to Panel Question 18 that the United States somehow violated Article 4.2(a) of the Safeguards Agreement because one producer, ADM, did not maintain separate financial records for its US

and Canadian operations, and thus submitted combined data for its US and Canadian operations to the USITC. Although the EC never explains why this producer's data problems constitute a violation of the Safeguards Agreement, it is clear that the EC raised no such claim in its panel request and that its attempt to introduce such a claim at this late date is prejudicial to the United States and outside the panel's terms of reference.

21. Mr. Chairman, I would now like to turn to my colleague, Mr. Gearhart, who will address the EC's new arguments relating to the so-called wheat protein premium.

Mr. Gearhart,

Protein premium

22. Mr. Chairman and members of the Panel, we would now like to address the new arguments that the EC makes about a so-called wheat protein premium factor, which the EC now asserts explain why US wheat gluten prices declined in 1996 and 1997 at the same time that US consumption increased. These arguments are contrary to USITC findings that the EC has never challenged. In its Second Written Submission the EC claims that supplies of high-protein wheat in 1996 and 1997 were good and that the protein premium for wheat was low. This, the EC claims, enabled bakers to force down wheat gluten prices and also allowed bakers and pet food producers to buy more wheat gluten. The EC claims that because input costs (wheat prices, fuel, and depreciation) were rising, US wheat gluten producers were caught in a cost-price squeeze caused by domestic factors. The trouble with the EC's new argument is that it is contrary to the USITC's uncontested findings that demand increased for reasons not based on the price of wheat gluten. The EC is asking this Panel to substitute its judgment for that of the US competent authority in analyzing the factors that affect demand.

23. The USITC addressed the reasons for the increase in demand for wheat gluten in 1997 and indirectly for 1996 on page I-23 of its report. The USITC listed four reasons. First, the increase in demand for canned cat food formulations that feature product in gravy instead of the regular loaf-style canned cat food. Second, the shift by bakeries to high-speed mixing equipment, which requires a higher protein content in the dough. Third, the increasing popularity of high-fibre bread and other products, like bagels, that are particularly high in wheat gluten. Fourth, anticipation by purchasers and importers of the section 301 petition submitted by the domestic wheat gluten industry in January 1997. The EC has never challenged these findings.

24. Nor is there any support in the record for the EC's new hypothesis. As we have previously stated, the USITC also recognized that the protein content of the wheat crop can affect demand for wheat gluten. This was the case in 1993 and 1994. As the USITC observed, both demand for wheat gluten and the price of wheat gluten rose in 1994 in response to the decline in the protein content of the

1993 wheat crop. However, when the protein content returned to a more normal level in the following year, prices came back down.

25. There was no evidence before the USITC of a drop in the protein content of the wheat crop in 1996 and 1997, or of any other change relating to the protein content of the wheat crop that would explain the increase in wheat gluten consumption in those two years. Nor did any of the parties in the USITC investigation make the argument the EC has advanced in this proceeding. While EU producers during the USITC proceeding cited the 1993/94 supply shortage, fluctuating prices of wheat, and the price premium of wheat over *corn* as factors affecting the domestic wheat gluten market, they did not allege a "wheat protein premium factor" or protein shortfall in the 1996 and 1997 wheat crops. If the protein content of wheat during 1996 and 1997 was a serious factor affecting price and demand for wheat gluten, it is surprising that it was only discovered by the EC long after the conclusion of the USITC investigation.

26. In arguing that high protein wheat is a substitute for wheat gluten, the EC continues to misstate the role that wheat gluten plays in the bakery industry, particularly in the production of certain bakery products such as high-fibre and multi-grain breads and bagels. Without sufficient protein content, the dough will lack the necessary elasticity and will not rise properly. Some wheat gluten must be added to the production process to bring the protein content up to the required level. The protein content of wheat flour - even high-protein wheat flour - is simply not high enough to do the job.

27. Thus, the demand for wheat gluten by producers of the bakery and pet food products that require wheat gluten does not rise or fall with the price of wheat gluten. Demand for wheat gluten is instead driven by the amount of protein required to make the various bakery and pet food products. In the absence of some abnormality in the wheat crop, this demand is dependent on the mix and quantity of bakery and pet food products made and the production processes used. Moreover, as the USITC found, wheat gluten represents only a small share of the cost of the downstream products.

28. As we have stated previously, what changed in 1996 and 1997 was imports. Between 1995 and 1997, imports surged by 40 per cent, which was more than double the increase in domestic consumption. As a result, domestic producers' shipments fell in 1996 and 1997, and were below the levels of 1993, 1994, and 1995. Domestic prices should have increased to offset the increased costs of inputs, as they had done in previous years. Instead, as the USITC report shows, domestic prices fell in response to the surge in low-priced imports.

29. In short, the EC and the United States agree that the US wheat gluten industry experienced a cost-price squeeze in 1996 and 1997. However, as the USITC found, the reason for the *squeeze* was the surge in low-priced EC imports that consistently undersold the US product. The US authority reasonably concluded that those increased imports displaced US wheat gluten and held down prices. Without the increased imports, the US industry would have been able to

sell a greater amount of its product at a higher price as demand increased. The USITC report amply demonstrates the causal link between increased imports and serious injury.

Ms. Florestal,

30. Mr. Chairman, Members of the Panel, I would like to make a few brief remarks on the EC's claims under Articles 5 and 12 of the Safeguards Agreement.

Article 5.1: Setting the Quota Level

31. The EC has made two principal arguments under Article 5.1. First, the EC has argued that the United States should have used a tariff remedy rather than a quota. Second, the EC claims that the US should have set the quota at a higher level than we did. Specifically, the EC complains that the United States should have set the quota at the level of imports during 1995 to 1997.

32. The EC's second written submission in large part merely restates the EC's position without responding to many of the legal claims asserted by the United States. The United States will not repeat all of its arguments here. Rather, we would direct the Panel to the relevant portions of the US submissions on this issue. In this statement, the United States will highlight the key legal problems with the EC's arguments under Article 5.1.

33. First, contrary to the EC's position, Article 5.1 does not favor tariff measures over quotas. When the Safeguards Agreement *does* establish such a preference, it does so explicitly. For example, Article 6 refers to provisional measures. Article 6 specifically states that provisional measures should be in the form of tariff increases. There is no such language in Article 5. Therefore, the conclusion to be drawn is that the Framers of the Safeguards Agreement did not intend to state a preference for one remedy over another under Article 5.1.

34. The EC recognizes that the terms of Article 5.1 itself do not favor tariffs over quotas. Therefore, the EC attempts to shift the Panel's focus from the plain terms of Article 5.1. The EC does this by creating "rules" and "tests" that are not found in the Safeguards Agreement. The United States asks the Panel to examine the actual language of Article 5.1, rather than to focus on the EC's tests.

35. Article 5.1 sets out a specific rule for the application of quotas as a safeguard measure. It states that if a Member chooses to impose a quota, it may not set the quota level below a specified floor unless there is a clear justification as to why a lower level is necessary. Thus, under Article 5.1 a Member may not impose a quota level below the level of imports in the last three representative years unless it provides clear justification.

36. The most recent representative three-year period in this instance was 1993 to 1995. Thus, under Article 5.1 the United States could have set the quota level based on imports during the 1993 to 1995 period. Instead, the United States established a quota well above 1993 to 1995 import levels. The United States chose

to establish a higher quota level in order to allow imports an equitable share of the increase in US consumption that occurred during 1996 to 1997.

37. The EC argues that the US should have established an even larger quota level. In the EC's view, the United States should have set the quota at the level of imports during 1995 to 1997. The EC's position is incorrect for a number of reasons:

38. First, the EC simply mis-reads the plain terms of Article 5.1. Article 5.1 provides that the quota level cannot fall below the average of imports in the last three *representative* years. The 1995 to 1997 period the EC points to is not representative because imports surged during that period. The EC tries to read the word representative out of Article 5.1 by arguing that the importing country must always choose the most recent three year period. It is not surprising that the EC wants this Panel to ignore the word "representative" because there was nothing representative about the level of imports during the surge period 1996 to 1997.

39. The Panel should reject the EC's effort to render meaningless a term specifically included in the Safeguards Agreement. The word representative must be given meaning. The task for this Panel is to determine what the term representative means. The Oxford dictionary defines representative as that which is typical of a class or category. Article 5.1 must be defined in its context. Article 5.1 is a provision regarding setting import levels. In the context of Article 5.1 the term representative logically means a period that is typical of import levels. The level of imports that occurred in 1993 to 1995 was the most recent that is typical of the historical level of imports. Thus, 1993 to 1995 was representative.

40. The EC fails to satisfactorily answer the question of why the surge years of 1996 to 1997 are typical of the historic level of wheat gluten imports into the United States. The EC argues that the most recent three years of imports is representative merely because it is the most recent period. Yet that claim cannot logically hold true. A period is not representative merely because it is the most recent period. It is representative only if it is typical of the historical pattern of trade in the product. A surge period generally is an anomaly - that is, a departure from typical import levels. Thus, a surge period would normally not be representative of import levels. The EC ignores the fact that the surge in imports occurred during the last two years of the 1995 to 1997 period, thus rendering the period unrepresentative.

41. Second, even if the EC were correct that the term representative is mere verbiage without meaning, the United States has nonetheless satisfied the requirements of Article 5.1. As demonstrated in its first submission, the United States provided clear justification in the USITC's report as to why a quota level different from the surge levels of 1995 to 1997 was necessary to remedy serious injury. At that level of imports, the USITC found that the domestic industry was seriously injured. Thus, to establish relief based on 1995 to 1997 import levels would simply not achieve the objectives of remedying serious injury and facilitating adjustment.

Article 5.2: Quota Allocation

42. The EC also objects to how the United States allocated the quota between supplying countries. The EC makes two principal arguments under Article 5.2 of the Safeguards Agreement. First, the EC alleges that the United States failed to seek agreement with supplying countries before allocating the quota and failed to explain why reaching agreement was not reasonably practicable. Second, the EC asserts that the United States should have allocated shares of the quota based on the market shares that existed during 1995 to 1997.

43. The EC's first complaint that the United States violated Article 5.2(a) by failing to seek agreement on allocating the quota is incorrect. In the first instance, the EC wholly fails to address the question of why the permissive language in Article 5.2(a) that Members may seek agreement on allocating the quota constitutes an obligation to seek agreement.

44. Moreover, the United States held consultations with the EC on at least two separate occasions before allocating the quota. The EC admits that these consultations did take place. Having made that admission, the EC now argues that Article 5.2(a) contains not just an obligation to consult but a higher obligation to "seek to reach agreement." (EC Response to Panel Question 10). There is no basis for the EC's claim. During consultations, the parties discussed the quota allocation issue but were not able to come to an agreement on the point. There is no requirement in Article 5.2(a) that parties actually achieve agreement, thus there is no violation of Article 5.2(a).

45. Following consultations, the United States allocated shares of the quota based on the shares held by individual supplying Members during the most recent representative period, namely 1993 to 1995. This allocation is consistent with the terms of Article 5.2(a), which requires allotting shares of the quota based upon the proportions supplied by Members during "a previous representative period".

46. The EC has failed to make any arguments to support its claim that in using the 1993 to 1995 period for allocating the quota, the United States violated the provisions of Article 5.2. The EC merely asserts without explanation or justification that 1995 to 1997 constitute the only possible previous representative period. The EC simply does not address the fact that in the last two years of that period imports from the EC surged to injurious levels, while imports from other Members remained relatively stable. In the EC's view, setting quotas on any basis other than the most recent three year period is discriminatory and violates US MFN obligations.

47. The EC puts forward conclusory statements without any serious legal argumentation. These statements are inadequate to meet the EC's burden of proof on this claim. Based on that fact alone, the United States asks the Panel to reject the EC's claim under Article 5.2.

48. Moreover, an analysis of Article 5.2 demonstrates that the EC's claim is incorrect as a matter of law. The question presented for this Panel is the meaning

of the term "a previous representative period." In the context of Article 5.2, which addresses the allocation of import shares among supplying countries, the term "a previous representative period" should be given a meaning that addresses the question of import distribution. Based on this logic, "a previous representative period" means a period that is typical of the historical distribution of import market shares between supplying countries.

49. To that end, the United States would direct the Panel's attention to US Exhibit 13, which is a chart of market shares of Members supplying wheat gluten to the US market from 1990 to 1999. The EC's market share during the period 1995 to 1997 rose dramatically from 42.2 per cent in 1995 to 45.0 per cent in 1996 and 51.5 per cent in 1997. This is in contrast to the EC's historical market share, which ranged from 29.5 per cent in 1990 to 42.2 per cent in 1994. Thus, the EC's market share from 1995 to 1997 level was not representative. During 1993 to 1995 the EC's share went from 34.1 per cent to 33.6 per cent to 42.2 per cent Those figures are more representative of the EC's historical market share levels.

50. Thus, the evidence demonstrates that the EC's preferred quota allocation period - 1995 to 1997 - was truly unrepresentative of the historical pattern of market shares in the United States over the past 10 years. This is because imports from the EC surged during the last two years of that period. By contrast, consistent with Article 5.2(a), the United States recognized that 1993 to 1995 was a recent representative period and allocated shares based on that period.

51. Even assuming, for purposes of argument, that the 1995 to 1997 period could be viewed as representative, the EC has not demonstrated that the quota allocation period the United States used was inconsistent with Article 5.2. The EC fails to show why the period the United States chose - 1993 to 1995 - is not also "a recent representative period". The plain text of Article 5.2(a) refers to *a* representative period, not *the* representative period. The text itself suggests that there may be more than one representative period for quota allocation purposes. That makes sense because the distribution of import shares may have been relatively stable over many years so that any number of previous periods may be representative.

52. The EC claims that the way in which the United States allocated shares of the wheat gluten quota was inconsistent with MFN treatment under GATT Article I. But that Article plainly does not apply to quota allocations. The EC wants to direct the Panel's attention away from the express terms of Article 5.2(a), which plainly call for safeguard quotas to be allocated on the basis of a representative period, not the last three years, which may not be representative. The EC has not pointed to anything in the GATT which overrules the specific language of Article 5.2(a), which the United States has followed in this case.

53. Moreover, in choosing the most recent period that is representative of historic market share levels, the United States ensured equitable treatment among its trading partners. The EC's claim that the United States discriminated in favor

of Australia is without merit. The United States chose the representative period and then applied the same period to all Members that were granted a quota allocation. Australia received no favorable treatment, merely the same treatment that was accorded to the EC and all other affected Members.

Article 12: Consultations

54. The last issue the United States would like to address is the EC's allegations under Article 12 of the Safeguards Agreement. The United States has repeatedly stated that it fulfilled its obligations to consult with the EC under Article 12 of the Safeguards Agreement. We are pleased that in their second submission the EC now acknowledges that these consultations did indeed take place. Having made that acknowledgement, the EC is reduced to one last argument. The EC complains that it was deprived of the opportunity to consult on the United States' proposed measure. The EC argues that the United States notified the USITC's proposed safeguard measure. The EC characterizes the USITC's proposal as an internal recommendation that does not qualify as a "proposed measure". The EC also argues that the USITC's proposed remedy cannot be considered to be the US "proposed measure" because it was notified under Article 12.1(b) rather than 12.1(c) of the Safeguards Agreement.

55. The problem with the EC's argument is that the United States plainly did notify the Safeguards Committee of its proposed measure. The proposed measure was clearly set out in the United States12.1(b) notification, which contained the USITC's report and proposed remedy recommendation to the President. The United States provided this information to the Committee on 24 March 1998, well over two months before the President put the quota into effect. The President deliberated on the USITC's proposed measure. The safeguard measure that the President put into effect was based very closely on the USITC's proposal, with alterations that simply made the final measure more trade-liberal. The EC had every opportunity to provide its views to the United States during that two-month period, and in fact did so.

56. The EC says that the United States should have notified the USITC 's proposed measure under Article 12.1(c) instead of Article 12.1(b). In effect, the EC is complaining because it received more advance notice of the proposed US measure, rather than less. More importantly, there is no provision in Article 12 that requires or suggests that a Member is obliged to notify its proposed measure under Article 12.1(c). Once again, the EC merely asserts that such an obligation exists without finding support for its position in the text.

57. In addition, the Appellate Body has found that the principal purposes of Article 12 are to promote transparency and information sharing. (*Korea - Dairy* AB report at ¶ 111). Surprisingly, in an effort to find a violation where none exists, the EC calls into question these very important purposes. The EC argues that before the United States notified its proposed measure, it should have first fully completed its internal deliberative process. Under the EC's reading of Article 12, only after already deciding what it intended to do should the United States

have notified its proposed safeguard measure and elicited views from affected exporting Members. In effect, the EC argues that the United States should have decided on the safeguard measure to be applied without any input from supplying countries.

58. The EC's position is puzzling because it is antithetical to the notion of transparency and information sharing. In effect, the notification procedure that the EC is suggesting calls for the United States to make its decision in secrecy and without input from affected Members.

59. In addition to the fact that the EC's position is inconsistent with the object and purpose of Article 12, the EC's reading also renders the consultations that would follow after this late-stage notification practically useless. If, as the EC suggests, a Member may satisfy the consultation requirements of Article 12 only after it has taken a decision to apply a safeguard and decided on the measure it intends to apply, then it greatly reduces the likelihood that a Member will subsequently modify its decision based on information provided by affected Members during consultations. At the late stage in which the EC is suggesting that consolations should take place, a Member would have already considered and addressed fundamental questions about the nature and extent of the measure. It would have decided what it intended to do without having heard the views of affected Members. That outcome would be inconsistent with the object and purpose of Article 12.

60. The EC's reading of Article 12 calls for consultations not on the proposed measure but rather on what is very likely to be the final measure because the importing Member will have already made its decision. Moreover, the EC's view makes it very unlikely that a government would ever modify its measure because under the EC's reading a Member would have to re-notify the new proposal and start the consultation process again. That is because if the Member decided to change its proposed measure, the new measure would then be its proposed measure. This could lead to an endless round of consultations and notifications. To avoid that result, and the attendant delay in providing relief for their industries, governments would very likely decide not to modify their proposed measures. That would mean that they would not seriously consider the views of importing Members. In addition, any announcement by the importing government that it intends to impose import relief is likely to prompt a surge in imports as suppliers seek to ship their products before the measure is put into effect. Again, to avoid that result importing governments would be very unlikely to make a change in their proposed measures, which under the EC's interpretation, would require a further round of notification and consultations.

61. Finally, the United States would draw the Panel's attention to the essential fact that the measure the USITC proposed was not markedly different from the measure the president actually applied. Indeed, the only significant difference between the two is that the measure the USITC proposed was for a term of 4 years, while the measure the president applied was for only 3 years. Thus, the United States notified and consulted on almost exactly the same measure as the

one applied. It is difficult to understand under those circumstances how the EC has been harmed or how the United States failed to meet its obligations under Article 12.

62. Mr. Chairman, Members of the Panel, that concludes the United States' oral statement.

ATTACHMENT 2-8

UNITED STATES RESPONSES TO QUESTIONS FROM THE PANEL AT THE SECOND MEETING OF THE PANEL

(4 February 2000)

Q1. Please comment on the EC statement (pages 8, paras. 33-35) during the second substantive Panel meeting that there are ways in which information of a "confidential" nature can be given – e.g. in an indexed or ranged form – while maintaining its confidentiality.

Response

1. Unfortunately, the use of percentages and indexes, as proposed by the EC, would not be adequate to alleviate the disclosure problem posed in this case. When the universe of reporting companies is small, the USITC faces the same problem in reporting data in percentage and index forms that it faces in reporting the actual aggregate data – the percentages and indexes may also reveal confidential data. The confidential information is most likely to be revealed to competitor companies that have furnished data reflected in the percentages and trends. Each competitor can index its own data or restate its own information in percentage terms. Taking that information, as well as aggregate information the USITC report already discloses on other factors, such as sales and production, competitors can use aggregate indices and percentages to derive confidential information about their competitors.

2. Thus, the USITC report necessarily used other methods to give the maximum public disclosure of information without compromising confidentiality. There are numerous examples in the USITC report where the USITC has characterized confidential data without revealing the underlying confidential information. For example, on page I-13 of its report the USITC characterized data relating to wheat gluten industry financial performance in terms of trends and whether the overall industry was profitable or operated at a loss, without revealing actual overall industry profit and loss data, which would have revealed confidential business information.

3. Finally, we note that, even if the EC approach could be adopted, it would not solve the confidentiality problems posed on this record. Its approach would only apply to aggregate statistical information. It would not be effective with respect to individual firm statistical information or confidential descriptive information.

Q3. In connection with question 2 above, could the parties please indicate to the Panel, what, if any, they consider the difference between "demonstrating" such unforeseen developments in an "investigation" – the terms used by the Appellate Body at para. 98 of the *Argentina – Footwear* report –

and "making a specific determination" regarding such unforeseen developments.

Response

4. The requirement that unforeseen developments be demonstrated "in the investigation" (to use the language of the Appellate Body in *Argentina – Footwear*) is satisfied if the competent authority's report contains evidence or information demonstrating the existence of unforeseen developments as a matter of fact. A specific determination of unforeseen developments is not required by Article XIX or by the recent Appellate Body reports. Accordingly, specific findings of fact and conclusions of law on the issue are likewise not required. The evidence and information in the USITC report amply demonstrate the existence of unforeseen developments as a matter of fact, and therefore fully satisfy the requirements of Article XIX, and are in accordance with the ruling of the Appellate Body in *Argentina – Footwear.*

Q4. How does the United States respond to the statements of the European Community at para. 25 of its oral statement to the second substantive Panel meeting concerning "unforeseen developments"?

Response

5. Although the United States reserves the right, granted by the Panel, to respond more fully once the EC has provided the document on which it relies, a preliminary response can be made. The prediction that, according to the EC, a wheat gluten association representative made to USTR in 1992 is not relevant to what the United States government foresaw in 1994, when trade concessions were negotiated. Indeed, that prediction, if it had ever been believed, would have appeared to have been disproved in 1994. As Table 15 of the USITC report shows, not only had EU production not increased substantially, it fell slightly from 1993 to 1994; EC capacity had risen only slightly and remained at only about 55 per cent of the level that been predicted for 1995. More importantly, EC exports to the United States had fallen by 24 per cent. In short, whatever the domestic wheat gluten industry representative had predicted in 1992 would have had no bearing on what the United States government would have foreseen as occurring in 1994 when trade concessions were negotiated. Trends after 1992 were contrary to that prediction. Moreover, the substantial US industry investment in additional capacity in 1993 and 1994 demonstrated through the industry's actions that, whatever one of its spokesmen may have said in 1992, after 1992, the industry did not believe that there would be substantial increases in EU exports to the United States.

6. As Table 15 of the USITC report also shows, another development occurred after 1992 that would tend to render moot the relevance to imports to the US of any prediction made in 1992 concerning increased wheat gluten production in the EU. From 1993 to 1994, EU exports to the United States as a share of total EU production fell 23 per cent, from 10.4 per cent to 8.0 per cent. Continuation of this trend would have suggested that exports to the United States would

not have increased as much as production even if the EU expanded its production. However, this trend reversed after 1994. EU exports to the United States expanded as a share of EU production to 13.3 per cent by 1996 and 14.3 per cent in 1997, an increase of 79 per cent over the 1994 level. In contrast, EU shipments to other foreign markets as a percentage of total EU production were lower in 1996 and 1997 than in 1993 and 1994. EU home market shipments as a percentage of total EU production were at their highest level, for the period investigated, in 1994 and at their lowest level in 1997. In short, not only did the EU expand production and exports after 1994, it also substantially increased its concentration on exportation to the United States market. There was no ground to foresee such a development in 1994, or, for that matter, in 1992.

7. Moreover, the EC's statements in Paragraph 25 fail to address other information in the USITC report that demonstrated the existence of unforeseen developments. The increase in EC wheat gluten capacity, on which the EC's statements focus, was only one part of the information detailed in the United States' response to the Panel's earlier Question 5, particularly the change in the pricing of EC imports in the US market. The USITC found that EC wheat gluten production was driven not by changes in wheat gluten prices, but by EC wheat starch production. The EC producers were aiming to increase their production of wheat starch for the protected EC market. The high prices for wheat starch in the protected home market allowed the EC to export wheat gluten to the US market at relatively low prices. Thus, for reasons unrelated to conditions in the wheat gluten market, there was a dramatic change in market conditions, resulting not only in an increase in wheat gluten imports, but also in a change from mixed overselling and underselling to a pattern of consistent underselling by EC imports. As previously discussed, the US producers who built new capacity and the domestic company that entered the market would not have done so if they had foreseen these developments.

Q6. In connection with question 5 above, please comment on the relevance of the fact that Article 2.1 SA refers to the increase in imports relative to domestic *production* only. (We note that the Anti-Dumping Agreement (article 3.2) and the SCM Agreement (article 15.2) refer to the amount of imports relative both to production and consumption).

Response

8. Under the Safeguards Agreement, the term imports "relative to production" refers to a legal requirement. Article 2.1 requires that a competent authority find that the product is being imported "in such increased quantities, absolute or relative to domestic production," as to cause or threaten to cause serious injury. The requirement is satisfied if the increase is either in absolute terms or relative to domestic production. That comparison is not to be made relative to consumption.

9. In contrast to the threshold legal determination required in Article 2.1, Article 4.2(a) cites trends in imports as compared either to consumption or production as relevant factors in evaluating the situation of the industry. As exam-

ples of such factors it includes both "the rate and amount of the increase in imports of the product concerned in absolute and relative terms" and "the share of the domestic market taken by increased imports". Since the share of the market taken by imports is their share relative to consumption, Article 4.2(a)'s reference to their increase in relative terms refers to the basis of comparison set forth in Article 2.1, namely, "relative to domestic production". In short, both criteria are relevant factors in evaluating whether increased imports cause serious injury. Article 4.2(a) does not make any of the factors that it lists dispositive or entitled to greater weight than other factors.

10. The Anti-Dumping Agreement and Part V of the Subsidies Agreement likewise make both increases in imports relative to production and consumption relevant to a determination of whether dumped or subsidized imports cause material injury. Unlike the Safeguards Agreement, however, neither of these other agreements makes any particular measure of increase legally necessary to an affirmative determination.

Q7. Does the United States rely on Article XXIV *alone* for the manner in which it treated imports from Canada in its injury and causation analysis and the application of its safeguard measure? Or does the United States believe that imports from another WTO Member who is not a participant in an FTA could also be treated in a similar manner in a safeguard investigation and the application of a safeguard measure?

Response

11. Footnote 1 to the Safeguards Agreement and Article XXIV of the GATT 1994 are both relevant for purposes of determining how a Member may treat its customs union and FTA partners in conducting a safeguards investigation and applying a remedy.

12. The United States does not believe that imports from WTO Members that are not participants in FTAs or Customs Unions could be treated in a similar manner. The United States notes, however, that Article 9 of the Safeguards Agreement calls for special treatment for imports from developing Member countries that meet certain requirements.

Q8. Could Article XXIV of the GATT 1994 provide an "exception" or "derogation" to provisions of the Safeguards Agreement? Please give the legal basis for your response.

Response

13. Article XXIV provides neither an exception nor a derogation to the provisions of the Safeguards Agreement. Rather, Article XXIV provides an exception to Article XIX of the GATT 1994 and the other provisions of GATT 1994.

14. The relevant provision for purposes of the Safeguards Agreement is footnote 1. Footnote 1 provides that the Safeguards Agreement should not be interpreted in such a manner as to prejudge the existing relationship between Article XIX and Article XXIV of the GATT. In order to determine how a Member may

treat its FTA partners for purposes of safeguards, the Panel must look not to the Safeguards Agreement but to Article XXIV – as directed by footnote 1. In this regard, the United States would note that contrary to the EC's allegation, footnote 1 is not limited to customs unions. The last sentence of footnote 1applies to all of Article XXIV, including the provisions relating to free trade area agreements.

15. An examination of Article XXIV demonstrates that the United States' treatment of Canada both with respect to the injury investigation and the remedy applied are consistent with Article XXIV, as noted in the United States' earlier submissions.

Q9. How do you react to the argument made by the European Communities concerning "discrimination" at paras. 115-137 of its oral statement at the second substantive Panel meeting, particularly with respect to GATT Article I?

Response

16. At this late stage in the proceedings, the EC has raised the novel claim that the US measure is discriminatory because it treats imports from Canada more favorably than EC imports. The EC suggests that it has only just become aware of the fact that the United States examined Canadian imports and determined that such imports were not contributing seriously to the injury.

17. First, to the extent that the United States treated Canadian imports differently, this action is permissible under Article XXIV, which permits more favorable treatment for FTA partners.

18. Second, it is surprising that the EC now takes issue with the fact that the United States separately examined Canadian imports to ensure that it was not ascribing injury from that source to imports from third countries. In *Argentina – Footwear*, the EC took exception to the fact that Argentina did *not* perform such an analysis. The EC specifically cited with approval the United States' actions in its wheat gluten investigation. According to the EC, "the United States made separate determinations concerning imports from NAFTA members and concluded that imports from that source, and in particular, Canada did not cause injury. If Argentina had applied the same procedure as the United States in the wheat gluten case, then it would not have been able to come to the conclusion it did." (*Argentina - Footwear* at ¶ 5.131). For the EC now to argue either that it was unaware of the United States' actions, or that the US action is inconsistent with the Safeguards Agreement, is simply not credible.

19. Moreover, the EC's argument that the two-step causation analysis performed by the USITC was discriminatory because it departed from principles of parallelism is simply wrong. As we have noted, we do not understand the Appellate Body to have established a broad requirement of "parallelism" in the *Footwear* dispute. Nevertheless, US procedures satisfy the purpose of the "parallelism" notion the *Footwear* panel articulated. That purpose is to ensure that where a Member attributes serious injury to imports originating the territory of a country that is a party to a customs union (or FTA, in this case), those imports should be included in the safeguard measure the Member determines to apply.

20. The very procedures that the EC complains of ensure that is the case. Conversely, those procedures provide for the exclusion of Mexican and Canadian imports from an eventual safeguard measure where they did not play a significant role in causing serious injury or threat of injury. Thus, in both cases, the two-step US causation analysis comports with the notion of "parallelism."

21. The EC would like this Panel to focus on the number and sequence of the USITC's causation analyses, issues the Safeguards Agreement does not address. The real question is whether the United States attributed injury occasioned by Canadian imports to those from the EC. The answer plainly is "no."

22. The EC also argues that the allocation of shares of the wheat gluten quota discriminates in favor of Australia over the EC in violation of GATT Article I. As fully explained in our previous submissions, GATT Article I is simply not implicated when the claim at issue relates to quota allocation. The relevant GATT provision governing this subject generally is Article XIII. For purposes of the allocation of a *safeguards quota*, however, the more relevant provision is Article 5.2 of the Safeguards Agreement. For the reasons we have made plain in our submissions, the EC does not have a sustainable claim under that provision.

23. Moreover, the United States simply did not discriminate in allocating the wheat gluten quota. The United States determined "a" representative period consistent with the requirements of Article 5.2. Supplying Members were then allocated shares of the quota on the basis of the shares of the market they held during the representative period.

24. In its oral statement of 2 February 2000, the EC purports to respond to US Exhibit 13 by providing a chart and written statement to the Panel regarding market share levels in 1998 and 1999. The Panel will recall that US Exhibit 13 demonstrated in precise numerical terms what the United States has noted all along: That is, the 1995 to 1997 period was not representative of the historical market share levels of supplying Members – either the EC's or Australia's. The United States therefore allocated the quota based on a period that *was* representative – namely the 1993 to 1995 period.

25. The EC's statement and chart are irrelevant for purposes of evaluating the information in US Exhibit 13. The EC provides the Panel with an alleged analysis of market share levels in July of 1998 to May of 1999. The EC's views with respect to the distribution of import market shares *after* the US safeguard measure went into effect are simply not germane to the question of whether the United States based its quota allocation on an appropriate representative period.

Q10. Is the causation analysis under Article 4.2 SA to be conducted in terms of imports as a "necessary" or "sufficient" condition (or both) for serious injury?

Response

26. Under Article 4.2, there are two different inquiries. One is whether there is serious injury or threat thereof. The other is whether the serious injury or threat thereof is caused by increased imports.

Q11. Does the phrase "prevent or remedy serious injury" in Article 5.1 SA mean that a Member should or may aim to restore the market situation that existed prior to the period of serious injury determined to have been caused by imports?

Response

27. Article 5.1 permits Members to apply safeguards measures only to the extent necessary to both prevent or remedy serious injury and to facilitate adjustment. In some cases, it will be necessary to restore the market situation that existed prior to the period of the injury in order to remedy the injury and place the industry in a position to adjust. In other cases, a Member will be able to achieve its dual objectives without restoring prior market conditions. It will depend on the facts of each case.

Q12. On what basis was the decision taken to increase the level of the US wheat gluten quantitative restriction by 6 per cent per year?

Response

28. The United States would first like to clarify that it did not *increase* the level of the restriction by 6 per cent. Rather, the United States *decreased* the level of the restriction by increasing the overall amount of the quota. This is in keeping with Article 7.4, which requires that Members progressively liberalize safeguards measures that are applied for longer than one year.

29. The United States provided for a 6 per cent growth rate for imports in order to avoid restricting imports over the life of the safeguard beyond the extent necessary. Import growth during the period of investigation had averaged 4.2 per cent. (USITC Report at I-29). By setting a growth rate at 6 per cent, the United States sought to allow imports a reasonable rate of growth and further encourage the industry to adjust to import competition.

Q15. We note that section 311(a) of the NAFTA Implementation Act provides for certain actions to be taken after the Commission makes an affirmative determination in an investigation under Section 202 of the Trade Act. Is it a determination that the domestic industry is "seriously injured"? Or is it a determination that the domestic industry is "seriously injured" and that this "serious injury" is caused by imports? Please cite the relevant portions of your legislation.

Response

30. The reference is to an affirmative determination under section 202(b)(1)(A) of the Trade Act of 1974, that is, to a determination that a product is being imported into the United States in such increased quantities as to cause or threaten to cause serious injury to a US industry producing a like or directly competitive product.

ATTACHMENT 2-9

LETTER OF THE UNITED STATES RESPONDING TO THE PANEL'S REQUEST FOR INFORMATION

(8 February 2000)

My authorities have instructed me to respond to the Panel's fax of 1 February 2000, in which the Panel requests certain confidential business information furnished by the domestic industry, or derived from information furnished by the domestic industry, in the United States International Trade Commission (USITC) safeguard investigation on wheat gluten. The Panel procedures provide that the Panel will make this confidential business information available to its members, the Secretariat officers serving the Panel, and 22 European Commission (EC) officials and unknown others in the EC or in the private sector who may be designated in the future by the EC as its "representatives."

The confidential business information that the Panel has requested represents some of the most sensitive information that companies provide to competent authorities that conduct safeguards investigations. The requested information involves everything from the cost structures of individual companies to their profit margins and pricing practices. Access to that information would reveal to competitors, customers, and suppliers the submitting companies' financial and operational strengths and weaknesses. This knowledge would aid competitors in setting their own prices and provide an unfair advantage to suppliers and customers in their negotiations with the companies whose information is revealed. The result would be further damage to an industry that the USITC has already found to be seriously injured. Even more important, the unauthorized dissemination of such sensitive information could damage the reputation of WTO dispute settlement in the business community worldwide, whose support and confidence is essential to the future of the WTO. The impact of such an unauthorized disclosure cannot be overstated.

This information was submitted to the USITC by US wheat gluten producers under strict assurances of non-disclosure. The USITC is prohibited from disclosing the information absent consent from the submitting companies, under provisions of US law that implement Article 3.2 of the *Agreement on Safeguards*. That article prohibits a competent authority from disclosing CBI it receives in the course of a safeguard investigation without permission from the submitting parties.

Promptly after receiving the Panel's request, the United States contacted the companies concerned in an effort to obtain their permission for the release of the information the Panel has requested. We have attached to this communication a copy of a letter from the Wheat Gluten Industry Council responding to our request (US Exhibit 15). The WGIC represents all of the parties whose consent is required.

We are pleased to inform the Panel that the United States expects to receive permission from the various domestic producers for release of all of the information the Panel has requested. As the attached letter makes clear, the producers will grant that permission subject to two adjustments in the Panel's procedures intended to provide greater assurances against unauthorized disclosures. In particular, the procedures should be amended to make clear that: 1) the Panel will review the CBI exclusively *in camera*; and 2) any Panel member, or WTO employee, who views or hears such information shall be under an obligation not to disclose the information, or allow it to be disclosed, to any person. For the reasons set out in the WGIC letter, the companies concerned are not prepared to grant permission for the CBI to be divulged to EC representatives.

By swiftly seeking permission from US wheat gluten producers to provide the information in question to the Panel, and by reporting to the Panel on the steps that will allow the United States to obtain that permission, the United States has responded "promptly and fully" to the Panel's request, as contemplated by Article 13.1 of the *Understanding on Rules and Procedures Governing the Settlement of Disputes*.

We have attached to this communication further US comments on the Panel's request for confidential business information. As the Panel is aware, the United States had reserved its comments on the procedures pending identification by the Panel of the information it was seeking and an explanation of the purpose for which the information is being sought. The Panel identified the information in its 1 February 2000 communication, but has not as yet informed the Parties of the reason that the information is required. That explanation would have permitted the United States to make specific suggestions regarding the Panel's procedures tailored to uses to which the Panel intends the CBI to be put.

Finally, the United States would reiterate its view that, consistent with the appropriate standard of review in proceedings under the *Agreement on Safeguards*, the Panel may not undertake a *de novo* review of the evidence before the USITC, whether based on CBI or non-confidential data. To the extent that the Panel requires access to CBI from the USITC report, it should be for the purpose of confirming the compliance with the *Agreement on Safeguards* of the USITC's injury and causation determinations, not for developing or documenting alternative injury or causation theories.

ATTACHMENT 2-10

COMMENTS OF THE UNITED STATES ON THE PANEL'S PROCEDURES GOVERNING PRIVATE-CONFIDENTIAL INFORMATION

(8 February 2000)

1. As the Panel is aware, in the United States' letter dated 27 January 2000 the United States reserved its comments on the Panel's proposed "Procedures for treatment of business confidential information" pending identification of which information the Panel sought and the reason why the information is required. The Panel has now provided "Procedures for treatment of private confidential information" dated 1 February 2000, and has identified the information it is seeking. The United States has responded promptly and fully to the Panel's request.

2. The United States hopes that the terms proposed by the domestic industry submitters of the information sought by the Panel will become the basis for the Panel's obtaining the information that it seeks. The United States wishes to address at this time both the procedures that the Panel has adopted and statements that the Panel has issued in adopting them. Those statements and procedures may be interpreted as asserting authority contrary to the Safeguards Agreement and the Dispute Settlement Understanding and to the sound operation of proceedings under both agreements.

3. The Panel's communication of 2 February 2000, citing the *Canada-Aircraft* Appellate Body report, suggests that the United States may be required to provide the Panel and the EC certain confidential business information (CBI) subject to the imposition of possible adverse inferences if the United States does not do so. However, in *Canada-Aircraft* the Appellate Body was not addressing a Panel's request for information first obtained subject to a provision, such as Article 3.2 of the Agreement on Safeguards, that imposes a specific requirement on the Member not to disclosure confidential information without consent from the supplying parties. Thus, the Appellate Body was not addressing a case, such as this one, in which a Panel's request for CBI creates a tension between a Member's responsibilities under the Dispute Settlement Understanding (DSU) and its specific obligations under another covered agreement. Applying the approach taken by the Appellate Body in *Canada-Aircraft* in this very different context risks undermining the carefully negotiated balance of benefits reflected in the Safeguards Agreement without advancing the objectives of the DSU.

4. For the reasons given below, the terms of those agreements, properly construed, indicate how the objectives of the two agreements are to be properly reconciled when a panel desires access to confidential information. In reviewing the determination of a competent authority under the Safeguards Agreement, a panel should, if it seeks confidential information:

(1) recognize that a Member that has conducted a safeguard investigation is bound under the Safeguards Agreement not to disclose confidential business information in its possession in the absence of consent for its release;

(2) find that such a Member satisfies its obligation under the DSU if it makes a good faith effort to obtain consent for disclosure to the Panel of such information; and

(3) determine, if the Member is unable to obtain consent, whether the competent authority's published report on the investigation nevertheless contains an adequate explanation of its injury and causation determinations to satisfy the requirements of the Safeguards Agreement.

The United States Satisfies the Requirements of DSU Article 13.1 by Requesting, in Keeping with Article 3.2 of the Safeguards Agreement, that the Private Parties Consent to Disclosure of Information to the Panel

5. The United States recognizes, as the Appellate Body indicated in *Canada - Aircraft*, that under DSU Article 13.1 a panel may seek information from any body that it deems appropriate. That article also states that a Member "should respond promptly and fully to any request by a panel for such information as the panel deems necessary and appropriate." Although the Appellate Body indicated that "should" in that context may be read as imposing a mandatory requirement, it did not address cases such as that presented by the present dispute, in which the Member is subject to an affirmative obligation under another covered agreement to protect the information from disclosure.

6. Article 13.1 does not state that a Member shall in all cases provide a panel the information the panel seeks. Instead, it speaks in more general terms, stating that a Member "should respond promptly and fully". The use of the term "should" in DSU Article 13.1 assumes that in some cases a Member may not be able to respond fully to a panel's request. "Should" cannot be read as "shall" in this context, because such a reading would compel a violation of Article 3.2 of the Safeguards Agreement, and the WTO Agreement is to be read so as to avoid such conflicts between agreements. The phrasing of Article 13.1 contemplates that in some cases a Member may satisfy its obligation to respond although it is not able to provide the requested information.

7. The United States submits that this is such a case. Article 3.2 of the DSU states the fundamental principles that the DSU "serves to preserve the rights and obligations of Members under the covered agreements" and that "recommendations and rulings of the DSB cannot add to or diminish the rights and obligations provided in the covered agreements." Accordingly, the panel 's authority under Article 13.1 of the DSU to seek information reaches its limit when providing the information requested would cause a Member to violate its obligations under another covered agreement.

8. Article 3.2 of the Safeguards Agreement governs treatment by the United States International Trade Commission (USITC) of the information that the Panel

is seeking. The USITC collected that information from domestic producers in the course of its wheat gluten investigation. Article 3.2 provides that any such information that is by nature confidential or is provided on a confidential basis shall be treated as such by the competent authority conducting the safeguard investigation. The second sentence of that article states, "Such information *shall not be disclosed* without permission of the party submitting it" (emphasis added). This provision makes no exception for disclosure of confidential information to panels or to complaining parties in WTO dispute settlement proceedings. Thus, for the United States to provide to the Panel or the EC information that was submitted to the USITC on a confidential basis without the consent of the submitting companies would violate the Safeguards Agreement.

9. The fact that Article 13.1 of the DSU, and paragraph 3 of Appendix 3 to the DSU, both provide that when documents are submitted to a panel they shall be kept confidential does not affect this conclusion. Article 3.2 of the Safeguards Agreement does not make provision for the competent authority to release the information on a limited basis so long as the information is not divulged to the public at large. Rather, it categorically forbids a competent authority from *disclosing* the information without consent. That the Panel, pertinent WTO employees, twenty-two EC officials and unspecified other persons possibly to be designated by the EC in the future might keep the information confidential does not detract from the fact that the United States would be *disclosing* the information to them. Under Article 3.2, disclosure requires consent.

10. Unlike the provisions of the Subsidies Agreement at issue in *Canada - Aircraft*, the Safeguard Agreement ensures that a panel has the means to undertake a review of the matter before it without recourse to confidential information. Specifically, Articles 3.1 and 4.2(c), respectively, provide for the competent authority to issue a public report and to publish a detailed analysis of the case under investigation. Where, as here, a complaining Member has raised a challenge under Article 4, the question before the Panel is whether the public report that the USITC issued pursuant to Article 3.1 contains an adequate explanation of how the facts support the USITC's injury and causation determinations. Accordingly, the Safeguards Agreement provides a means through which a panel can review the competent authority's determinations, and take account of the fact that Article 3.2 may preclude a Member from providing a panel with confidential information.

11. The United States meets its obligation to respond to a panel's request for confidential information under Article 13.1 of the DSU when it takes the one step contemplated by Article 3.2 of the Safeguards Agreement. That step is to seek from those who submitted the information consent to disclose the information to the panel. As the accompanying letter from the Wheat Gluten Industry Council makes clear, the United States has done so. This is not a case in which the United States, to use the phrasing of the Appellate Body, has "refus[ed] to collaborate" with the Panel. *Canada - Aircraft* at ¶ 204. The United States' submission informing the Panel of its efforts to obtain consent for disclosure of the information constitutes a full and prompt response under DSU Article 13.1. Moreover, as the

Industry Council's letter states, the United States may be able to obtain such consent if the confidentiality of the information is protected to the satisfaction of the original providers of the information.

Requiring the Disclosure of CBI Under Threat of Adverse Inferences Would Interfere with the Conduct of Safeguards Investigations

12. Strict conformity with Article 3.2 of the Safeguards Agreement provides the necessary framework for the effective conduct of the safeguards investigations as required by Article 3.1 of the Agreement. Article 3.2 provides more than a right for Members to complain in the WTO if their companies' confidential information is improperly released. The operation of national laws that conform to Article 3.2 provides the basis for competent authorities to obtain the cooperation they need to conduct safeguard investigations. The Agreement recognizes that the injury and causation information that authorities must gather in order to make the findings required by Article 4.2 will commonly be confidential, because this information will include firm-specific data on prices, profits and losses, production, productivity, costs of production, capacity utilization, and imports. This information is highly commercially sensitive. If the producers, importers, and consuming industries whose information a competent authority seeks cannot be assured that they will enjoy the benefits of Article 3.2, they will be deterred from submitting necessary information.

13. This assurance is necessary to obtain the cooperation of both foreign and domestic interests - both of those who may oppose safeguard relief and of those who support it. Although in the current case, the Panel has requested information provided to the USITC by domestic producers only, the authority it has claimed to obtain access to confidential information would apply to all submitters of information in safeguard proceedings. Authorities in these investigations obtain critical confidential information from importers, consuming industries, and foreign producers. All of these firms rely on the protections afforded by members' laws pursuant to Article 3.2. Without strict observance of those protections, competent authorities can expect that these firms will become substantially more reluctant to provide necessary information. Both the willingness of domestic industries to petition their governments for relief, a right the Safeguards Agreement guarantees, and the ability of others to provide evidence defending their interests, would be compromised.

14. In short, the ability of Members to perform the investigation required by Article 3.1 would be substantially impaired if firms believed that the WTO dispute resolution process constituted an unstated exception to the plain language of Article 3.2. As the United States has previously stressed in the current proceedings, the Safeguards Agreement leaves the crucial task of gathering information and weighing the evidence to the competent authorities. Insofar as the procedures that the Panel has adopted suggest that a Member must provide information regardless of the consent of those who submitted confidential information, those procedures threaten to undermine the functioning of the Safeguards Agreement. Article 3.2 constitutes a negotiated benefit both to Members whose exports may

become the subject of an investigation and to Members whose competent authorities are conducting those investigations. The DSU should be interpreted so as not to disrupt that balance of benefits.

15. Thus, Article 3.2 protects both domestic and foreign interests concerned with safeguards investigations. In keeping with Article 3.2, US law prohibits the USITC from releasing CBI of all firms, even if, to the extent it originates with a domestic producer, the United States might not be subject to a WTO proceeding if the information were released. It may be noted, however, that, in the current case, the United States would not be free from complaint from other WTO Members if it were, in violation of Article 3.2, to disclose information without the consent of submitting US companies. As the EC has frequently noted in these proceedings, one of the US producers is related to an Australian company. Australia might well have a basis for complaint under Article 3.2 if the United States were, without consent, to disclose information of a company related to one of its enterprises. And as one of the US firms producing wheat gluten is related to an EC producer, the EC might have the same basis for complaint. Indeed, the EC has just requested consultations with Argentina concerning two antidumping measures, in document WT/DS189/1, with the complaint that "the Argentinean investigating authority appears to have rejected without any valid justification the requests for confidential treatment submitted by the EC exporters with respect to highly sensitive business information, including information on prices and production costs."

The Procedures Adopted by the Panel Would Undermine the Guarantees Provided for the Treatment of Confidential Information Under the Safeguards Agreement

16. The circumstances of this case demonstrate the reasons why the negotiators of the Safeguards Agreement did not authorize competent authorities to release confidential business information to anyone, including panels, without the consent of the providers of that information.

17. Although Articles 13.1 and 18.2 of the DSU provide that confidential information must be held confidential, those provisions impose no enforceable legal obligation on panelists, on officials of the Secretariat who may assist them, or on Members.[1]. In contrast, US law provides criminal penalties for disclosure of trade secret information, as well as other legal remedies. *See* 18 U.S.C. §§ 1831, 1832, 1905. Thus, it is quite a different matter for firms to provide information to the US government than for the United States to forward that information to the WTO. Indeed, this difference between the strong assurances against disclosure that national authorities can and, by virtue of Article 3.2, must provide, and the lack of any significant protections offered under DSU rules, goes a long way to-

[1] The United States would have further detailed comments on the Panel's procedures if the private submitters of the confidential business information were willing to consent to the release to parties that the procedures anticipated.

ward explaining why the Safeguards Agreement does not include an exception for the disclosure of confidential business information to WTO panels.

18. The facts of this case point up the lack of protection that is available for CBI if it leaves the custody of the investigating authority. The EC was a party to the USITC proceeding, but did not seek access to the CBI at issue in this panel proceeding and did not challenge its authenticity, its evidentiary value, or even its confidential nature. Every item of the CBI now at issue was available to the EC, under the USITC's administrative protective order procedure, which releases information to specific individuals under penalty of disbarment and criminal sanction. The EC declined to submit itself to this procedure to obtain the information. Nonetheless, it now stands to receive that same information subject to no individual undertakings, no enforceable legal obligation to refrain from disclosing it and no sanctions in the event of unauthorized disclosure. Private enterprises may be understandably hesitant when the EC declines to obtain access to information when to do so would subject its representatives to sanctions, and designates 22 persons to receive that information when no sanctions are provided.

19. Moreover, to the extent that DSU Article 13.1 contemplates the disclosure of CBI, it addresses the disclosure of such information to a Panel, not other parties. The procedures that the Panel has adopted, however, operate contrary to DSU Article 13.1, in that they provide that without the USITC's consent the CBI shall be made available not only to the Panel but to the EC as well. Article 13.1 provides that "[c]onfidential information which is provided shall not be revealed without formal authorization from the individual, body, or authorities of the member providing the information." The United States' authority has not provided such authorization in this case.

20. The EC's response to the Panel's announced procedures provides an unfortunate demonstration of the need for the authorization mechanism provided in Article 13.1. The EC has named no fewer than 22 officials as possible recipients of the CBI. The rather astonishing number of officials that the EC has designated would tend to make it impracticable to trace the source of any further release if it should occur. By allowing the EC unlimited discretion in deciding which, and how many, of its officials may have access to the CBI in this case, contrary to Article 13.1 and without any showing of need, the procedures further undermine the ability to protect that information from disclosure. As the Wheat Gluten Industry Council's letter makes plain, the EC's undisciplined designation of 22 representatives has undercut whatever ability the United States might have had to persuade its industry to consent to release of confidential information to the EC.

21. The procedures also operate contrary to the Safeguards Agreement and the DSU in suggesting that the Panel may overrule the designation by the United States of the information it submits as "confidential." If the Panel disagrees with the US designation, the United States would be put in the position of either withdrawing the information (under threat of adverse inferences) or withdrawing the confidentiality designation. There is no basis for this procedure. To the contrary, Article 3.2 of the Safeguards Agreement requires the competent authority to treat

as confidential any information that is by its nature confidential or that is provided on a confidential basis. Thus, the USITC in accepting information as confidential has, in keeping with Article 3.2, affirmatively obligated itself to the submitters to keep that information confidential. The United States would thus be prohibited by the Safeguards Agreement from obeying a Panel demand to release certain information as non-confidential if the USITC has accepted it as confidential. Under the general principles governing the dispute settlement process as set forth in Article 3.2 of the DSU, panel procedures may not properly subject a Member to such a dilemma.

22. The possibility that, under the announced process, the Panel might declare information non-confidential that the USITC has accepted as confidential is all the more inappropriate when the EC had an opportunity to participate fully in the USITC proceeding. Although the EC was a party in that investigation, neither it nor any EC producers raised any objection that the USITC improperly treated as confidential individual company information that it received in the course of its investigation. The EC received the public staff report of the USITC during that investigation and, despite having the opportunity at that time, never objected that the public report excised aggregate data, which is the only objection it has raised here. Those who submitted information to the USITC relied on the understanding that any objections to confidential treatment would be raised before the USITC. Had objection been raised at that stage, submitters could, if the USITC granted the objection, have exercised the right guaranteed by US law pursuant to Article 3.2 to withdraw the information from the USITC record.

23. For a panel to undertake to reconsider confidentiality designations after the investigation is concluded would undermine the expectations - guaranteed by Article 3.2 - of those from whom the competent authority obtained information. Since that provision plainly entrusts designations of confidentiality to competent authorities during investigations, there is no basis for a panel to reject a party's determination that information is to be accorded confidential status. Procedures that would allow for such a result understandably erode any confidence producers, importers, and consuming industries may have that their commercially sensitive information will be protected, and undermine the United States' ability to obtain their consent to disclosure of that information to the Panel.

Consideration of Adverse Inferences is Inappropriate in this Case

24. The statement that accompanied the procedures adopted by the Panel suggests the possibility of drawing adverse inferences if the United States fails to provide the requested confidential information. Although the Appellate Body in *Canada - Aircraft* advised that panels might issue such reminders, the application of adverse inferences is inappropriate in this case. First, the statements in *Canada - Aircraft* affirming the possibility o f drawing adverse inferences were predicated on the legal finding that Canada had violated Article 13.1 of the DSU. Where, however, as shown above, a Member has complied with Article 13.1 by responding in a manner contemplated by the Safeguards Agreement, adverse inferences would be inappropriate.

25. Moreover, as the Appellate Body made clear, panels may not use adverse inferences to punish Members for failing to provide certain information. Rather, they may draw adverse inferences only where, in the circumstances, those inferences "could be logically or reasonably derived from a panel from the facts before it." *Canada - Aircraft* at ¶ 200. Consideration of whether to draw an adverse inference is, as the Appellate Body indicated, an aspect of the "objective assessment of the facts" that a panel undertakes under Article 11 of the DSU. *See Canada - Aircraft* at ¶ 198.

26. An objective assessment of the facts cannot lead to the conclusion that the United States is withholding information because of its "inculpatory character". *Canada - Aircraft* at ¶ 204. Nor has the EC suggested this is the case. The United States is doing so because of what it regards, in good faith, as its obligations under the Safeguards Agreement and US law to protect the information in question. There is no basis for the Panel to infer that disclosure of the information might disadvantage the United States' case before the Panel. The only appropriate inference under the circumstances is that the United States is attempting in good faith to fulfill its WTO obligations, not that it is attempting improperly to shield information from disclosure. Even on issues to which the parties have disagreed in this proceeding, there is no fundamental difference concerning the nature of the evidence. For example, although the parties in this case have argued at length about input costs, one of the types of CBI that the Panel requests, there is agreement on what the data show - namely, that input costs rose in 1996-97.

27. In sum, panel review of determinations made under the Safeguards Agreement must take into account the specific requirements of that Agreement, including Article 3.2. That Article imposes a requirement on competent authorities not to disclose confidential information and makes no provision for disclosure to panels absent consent of the private parties. It can thus be inferred that the negotiators of the Safeguards Agreement considered that competent authorities would normally obtain confidential information during investigations, but that panel review of determinations pursuant to Article 14 of the Safeguards Agreement would not require panels to review that information. Nothing in the DSU supersedes that judgment of the negotiators of the Safeguards Agreement.

28. This case should be decided in the manner contemplated by the Agreement under which the EC has claimed a violation. If the USITC's public report does not satisfy the requirements of Article 4, the Panel should hold the United States to have violated the Agreement. If the report does satisfy them, the Panel should hold that the United States satisfied the Agreement.

ATTACHMENT 2-11

RESPONSE OF THE UNITED STATES TO THE EUROPEAN COMMUNITY LETTER OF 11 FEBRUARY 2000

(22 February 2000)

The United States appreciates the opportunity that the Panel has afforded to the United States to respond to the letter submitted by the European Communities on 11 February 2000.

The United States has addressed previously much of what the EC discusses in that letter and in the attachment to it, and will not burden the Panel with further argument on these points. Likewise, this letter will not dignify with a response the EC's allegations concerning the United States' good faith in these proceedings. The United States' previous submissions set forth legitimate and serious concerns with respect to the operation of the Safeguards Agreement and panel proceedings under the Dispute Settlement Understanding. The United States is confident that the Panel will not be distracted by unwarranted and unseemly accusations from giving these issues its well considered attention.

One point raised by the letter of 11 February, however, does deserve a response. That is the EC's conclusory accusation that the *in camera* submission of the information that the Panel has requested would violate Article 18.1 of the Dispute Settlement Understanding. With respect, the United States submits that the EC has failed adequately to read the Dispute Settlement Understanding.

The Panel has requested information from the report of the US International Trade Commission under the Panel's authority granted in Article 13 "to seek information ... from any individual or body which it deems appropriate" and to "seek information from any relevant source." The US International Trade Commission is certainly a "body" and a "relevant source" within the meaning of Article 13. Article 13.1 further provides, "Confidential information which is provided shall not be revealed without formal authorization from the individual, body, or authorities of the Member providing the information." Thus, Article 13.1 on its face contemplates that when a Panel requests confidential information from the authorities of a Member (not excluding an authority whose decision is before the Panel), the Panel may not further reveal that information without formal authorization from the authority. As discussed in the United States' earlier submission, the Safeguards Agreement prohibits a competent authority from providing such authorization without the consent of those who provided the confidential information to the authority in the first place. In effect, the EC is arguing that Article 18.1 forbids the Panel from gathering information in a way that Article 13.1 specifically authorizes.

The EC has misread what is contemplated by Article 18.1 by an "*ex parte* communication". The United States agrees that, if it were to submit any form of argument or make any communication to the Panel calculated in any way to persuade the Panel with respect to matters that are *sub judice*, Article 18.1 would forbid such a communication. The United States would not in providing the requested information make any *ex parte* communication to the Panel concerning the information. As this case exemplifies, such a communication is quite different from the provision of information pursuant to a Panel request under Article 13.1. The information that the Panel has requested is pre-existing material not prepared in the course of this panel proceeding. The requested information constitutes summaries of confidential data prepared before the Commissioners of the USITC reached any decision in the matter; most of the data in tabular form. Article 18.1 is not violated and the EC is in no way prejudiced by the United States' provision of information to the Panel under the procedures contemplated by Article 13.1.

Finally, we note that, while the EC has alleged that receipt of such information *in camera* would violate the Rules of Conduct on the appointment of Panelists, the EC has decided not to indicate what provision of the Rules it would regard as being violated. It is thus impossible for the United States to reply to such a claim. In any event, a procedure that is contemplated by the DSU cannot be contrary to the Rules of Conduct.

ATTACHMENT 2-12

COMMUNICATION OF THE UNITED STATES CONCERNING NEWLY PROPOSED PROCEDURES GOVERNING PRIVATE CONFIDENTIAL INFORMATION

(28 February 2000)

I am writing to convey the reactions of my authorities to the Panel's fax message of 25 February 2000 proposing a procedure for the viewing of the requested information, as follows:

> No more than two representatives of the United States would bring the requested information to a designated location at the premises of the WTO in Geneva on Thursday 2 March 2000. The Panel, two professional staff of the Secretariat, and no more than two representatives of the European Communities would review the information exclusively in camera. No photocopies of the information would be permitted. The Panel, the two professional staff of the Secretariat, and the [two] representatives of the European Communities may take written summary notes of the information for the sole purpose of the Panel process. These individuals would be under an obligation not to disclose the information, or to allow it to be disclosed, to any person. Any such notes would be destroyed at the conclusion of the Panel. While the Panel would be under an obligation not to disclose the information in its report, it could make statements of conclusion drawn from such information.

In the view of the United States, the procedure that the panel has proposed is helpful and constructive. The United States continues to maintain that there is no need for, or legal basis on which to require, disclosure of the information in question to representatives of the European Communities. Nonetheless, the United States is actively seeking to secure permission from the US firms in question for the release of the information under the terms the Panel has suggested.

In this regard, we request clarification on one very important aspect of the proposed procedure. In particular, the United States wishes to know whether the European Communities is in a position to comply with the Panel's condition that "These individuals would be under an obligation not to disclose the information, or to allow it to be disclosed, to any person." In similar circumstances the EC has not been able to warrant that those EC representatives to whom confidential business information was disclosed would not disseminate such information to other EC officials (see WT/DS27/ARB, para. 2.5).

Upon receiving a clear answer to this question, the United States will provide a definitive answer (within 24 hours if at all possible) from the US firms in question regarding whether they will consent to release of the information the Panel has requested.

Again, we appreciate the Panel's effort to resolve this problem.

ATTACHMENT 2-13

FINAL COMMENTS OF THE UNITED STATES CONCERNING NEWLY PROPOSED PROCEDURES GOVERNING PRIVATE CONFIDENTIAL INFORMATION

(3 March 2000)

Thank you for your communication of 1 March 2000 concerning the issue of special procedures to protect confidential business information ("CBI"). The United States considers it perfectly appropriate for the Panel to proceed with its review, as it decided on 1 March, on the basis of the existing record. As the United States has previously stated, all of the European Communities' ("EC") claims may be objectively evaluated based on that record. Moreover, we believe that the EC has no ground to complain that the public record is inadequate given that:

(1) it was a party to the United States International Trade Commission ("USITC") proceeding but failed to avail itself of the opportunity to review the CBI then; and (2) by its letters of 28 and 29 February the EC has rejected a constructive proposal, offered by the Panel on 24 February, under which the EC could have reviewed the CBI in this proceeding.

However, in the event that the Panel continues to believe that there would be some benefit in the Panel having access to the CBI, my authorities have instructed me to inform the Panel that the United States remains prepared to assist the Panel in this regard. Accordingly, the United States would like to inform the Panel, as foreseen in the letter of the United States to the Panel of 28 February 2000, of the action that the United States took in response to the Panel's 24 February communication and the EC's letters of 28 and 29 February.

In its 24 February communication the Panel proposed, *inter alia*, that the Panel, two WTO professional staff members, and two representatives of the EC be permitted to examine the CBI *in camera* and to make summary written notes, subject to an obligation not to disclose the information, or allow it to be disclosed to any person. Under the procedure, the notes would be destroyed at the conclusion of the Panel proceedings.

The United States considers that the Panel's proposed procedure represented a reasonable basis on which to reconcile both the obligation of the United States to protect sensitive proprietary information submitted to the USITC under a guarantee of confidentiality and the EC's desire to have access to any information that the Panel seeks to review. In its 28 and 29 February communications, however, the EC made clear that it is not in a position to honour the Panel's proposed requirement that the two designated EC representatives refrain from disseminating the CBI to other EC officials. In its letters of 28 and 29 February, the EC insisted on the right to distribute the CBI up through the entire EC chain of command, presumably to include at least those 22 individuals designated by the EC in its communication of 1 February.

The EC's position that it must be free to disseminate the CBI to such EC officials as it sees fit is plainly at variance with the compelling need, recognized both in Article 3.2.of the *Agreement on Safeguards* and in the Panel's proposed procedure, to provide meaningful protection against inadvertent or unauthorized CBI disclosures. As a result of its self-imposed procedures, the EC cannot rule out the possibility that any data its representatives record during the course of an *in camera* review would be widely distributed in the Commission. Understandably, the US producers are unwilling to grant permission for disclosure to the EC of their commercially-sensitive data under circumstances in which widespread dissemination of the data in the EC Commission must be presumed - particularly in the absence of any enforceable remedies available to the United States or US producers in the event of dissemination outside the EC.

After reviewing the EC's letters of 28 and 29 February, and before receiving the Panel's communication of 1 March, the United States discussed with the US producers ways in which to modify the Panel's constructive proposal to accommodate the EC's internal rules while providing adequate safeguards against dissemination of the CBI. To this end, the United States obtained from US wheat gluten producers consent to make the CBI available to the Panel and the EC for *in camera* review under the Panel's proposed procedure - - subject to two changes. The changes would be designed to address the EC's inability to prevent the dissemination of the CBI beyond those EC representatives participating in the review.

Specifically, the domestic producers have stated that they would be willing to permit the CBI to be disclosed to EC representatives *in camera* provided those representatives refrain from making written notes of the data. With that change, the producers would not insist that the EC representatives not make further disclosures to other EC officials for purposes directly related to this proceeding - with the strict understanding that the information could not be revealed to persons outside the EC. These modifications would minimize the possibility of significant data leakage while permitting the EC representatives both to review the data and comply with the EC's internal reporting requirements.

The United States is providing this information in order to make the Panel aware of the consent it had received with the US producers regarding the *in camera* disclosure of the CBI. In the US view, if implemented this arrangement could have served to facilitate the Panel's work and accommodate the EC.

The US producers' consent to a modified *in camera* review procedure, as described above, remains in place. (See enclosed letter.) Thus, if the Panel continues to have an interest in reviewing the requested information, the United States offers this procedure as a possible way forward.

ATTACHMENT 2-14

ORAL STATEMENT OF THE UNITED STATES AT THE ADDITIONAL MEETING OF THE PANEL WITH THE PARTIES

(18 May 2000)

Mr. Chairman, Members of the Panel,

1. On behalf of the United States delegation, I would first like to thank the Panel for providing us this opportunity to summarize our case to the reconstituted Panel. In particular we appreciate the willingness of the Chairman to step in and serve in the unusual circumstances in which we found ourselves, and we appreciate the indulgence of the other panelists in meeting with the parties. We are pleased to see you once again today. The United States will not attempt today to address each of the points raised in the 314 pages of text in the draft descriptive part and the further pages of additional correspondence, but rather will focus on the key issues.

1. The investigation by the USITC

2. Before turning to the issues in dispute, I will begin with a summary of the situation found by the USITC. At the beginning of the investigation period, in 1993, the US wheat gluten industry was performing well. Its members were profitable. They projected growth in consumption, and expected based on past performance that this situation would lead to a growth in their own sales. The outlook was sufficiently good that a new producer sought to enter the industry.

3. Imports were a factor in the wheat gluten market, but at a steady level. From 1993 to 1995, the volume of imports remained at approximately 130 million pounds. Then, the volume surged, increasing to 156 million pounds in 1996 and 177 million pounds in 1997 – an increase of 38 per cent all together. (Report, p. II-12.) For US wheat gluten producers, the 1993 to 1995 period saw roughly flat sales, varying between 121 and 132 million pounds. But in 1996, sales fell to 109 million pounds, before rising somewhat to 117 million pounds in 1997, which was still lower than at any time before 1996. (Report, p. II-10) As a result, positions in the market were reversed. Where US wheat gluten producers had had a slight majority of total sales from 1993 to 1995, by 1997, imports had a 58 per cent market share, and US producers only 42 per cent.

4. Import pricing also changed in 1996. The USITC examined the quarterly average prices for imports and for domestic merchandise. For the 1993 to 1995 period there were 12 such comparisons, and EC wheat gluten sold for less than US wheat gluten in them exactly half of the time. But in 1996 and 1997, EC wheat gluten sold for less than US wheat gluten in every single quarter. Starting in the second quarter of 1996, the price for US wheat gluten decreased consistently, and by the end of the investigation period had dropped 12 per cent lower than its previous low point. At the same time, input prices were increasing. As a

result, the profits that the industry had experienced in 1993 to 1995 became losses in 1996, and deeper losses in 1997. The USITC determined that these conditions constituted an overall impairment in the condition of the industry caused by increased imports.

5. The USITC arrived at this conclusion after a thorough investigation. It first reviewed the petition filed by the US wheat gluten industry in September 1997, and issued a notice in the Federal Register announcing the commencement of the investigation in October 1997. That notice invited any persons who wished to participate in the process to file an entry of appearance. In addition to the US producers, five parties appeared before the USITC: the industry association representing producers of wheat gluten in the European Union, the European Commission, the sole Australian producer of wheat gluten, the government of Australia, and the government of Canada. The Federal Register notice indicated that, if they satisfied the requirements of the USITC regulations, the representatives of each of these parties could obtain access to confidential business information gathered during the investigation. Representatives of the US producers, the European producers, the Australian producer, and the Government of Canada all requested and received access to confidential information. However, the EC did not do so.

6. The USITC gathered information on the wheat gluten industry through questionnaires issued to US producers, to foreign producers, and to US importers. All of the US producers responded, along with 26 importers, and 14 foreign producers. In addition, persons who appeared before the USITC were entitled to submit argument and information in two rounds of briefing, the first related to whether imported wheat gluten was a substantial cause of serious injury to the domestic industry and the second to the nature of the safeguard that should be imposed. The US producers, the EC producers, the Australian producer, the Australian government, and the Canadian government all submitted briefs, which contained argument and supporting information that the USITC had not previously received. The EC itself did not submit any briefs during the course of the proceedings and did not appear at the injury hearing.

7. In their brief on serious injury, the EC producers argued that improvements in certain financial indicators in 1997 proved that the US wheat gluten industry was not seriously injured, and that the domestic producers' profitability data were distorted by improper allocation of costs between the production of wheat gluten and wheat starch. The EC producers also argued that any injury sustained by the domestic industry was not attributable to increased imports, but instead to five unrelated factors.

8. The USITC found that the imports of wheat gluten were a substantial cause of serious injury in a vote in January 1998, and held a hearing on potential remedy measures in February 1998. All of the parties presented testimony at that hearing.

9. The USITC voted to recommend that the safeguard take the form of a quantitative restriction in March 1998, and issued its public report on the investi-

gation two weeks later. The report addressed the arguments raised by all of the parties and, in particular, those of the EC producers. The USITC recognized that certain indicators of the US wheat gluten industry's performance improved in 1997, but found that those improvements were isolated because other indicators continued to decline. The USITC also evaluated each of the other possible causes of injury identified by the EC producers, and found that none of them could explain to a significant degree the serious injury experienced by the US wheat gluten industry in 1996 and 1997.

10. Thus, as you can see the USITC sought information from a wide variety of sources and carefully considered the views of each party that displayed an interest in the outcome of its investigation. This evaluation established that the United States had the right to impose a safeguard, as contemplated under Article XIX of the GATT 1994 and by the Safeguards Agreement.

2. *Standard of review*

11. Before I move to our rebuttal of the arguments raised by the EC, I would like to discuss briefly the standard of review, both because it is the basis for the Panel 's consideration of each of the issues in dispute, and because the EC has thoroughly distorted that standard in its arguments.

12. Article 11 of the Understanding on Dispute Settlement states that "a panel should make an objective assessment of the matter before it, including an objective assessment of the facts of the case and the applicability of and conformity with the relevant covered agreements." The Appellate Body recently emphasized that in applying these guidelines to the Agreement on Safeguards, "the applicable standard is neither *de novo* review as such, nor 'total deference', but rather the 'objective assessment of the facts.' "

13. However, in paragraph 5 of its second written submission, the EC states that the Panel must examine whether "the US authorities established, as they should, the 'existence (i.e. a positive and irrefutable evidence of its reality) of the causal link between increased imports of the product concerned and serious injury.' " That is decidedly not the approach embodied in the Safeguards Agreement. Article 3.1 requires that the competent authorities make "findings and reasoned conclusions" on "all pertinent issues of law and fact," and Article 4.2(c) requires a demonstration of the "relevance of the factors examined." Neither of these provisions suggests that irrefutable evidence is necessary.

14. In fact, by affording all interested parties the opportunity to present argument and evidence before the competent authorities, the Safeguards Agreement ensures that on almost all matters in dispute, there will be evidence to support both sides. Then, should a WTO Member dispute the competent authority's decision before the WTO, the Appellate Body has stated in *Korea - Dairy* that the "significance and weight properly pertaining to the evidence presented by one party is a function of a panel's appreciation of the probative value of all the evidence submitted by both parties considered together." (Para. 137) Therefore, the proper question is not whether the evidence supporting the findings of a compe-

tent authority is "irrefutable." In most cases, it will have been vigorously contested before both the competent authority and the Panel. Rather, the Panel must determine whether an objective assessment of the facts indicates that the USITC demonstrated the relevance of the factors it examined and made reasoned conclusions as to all pertinent issues of law and fact.

3. *Serious injury*

15. The USTIC finding of serious injury amply meets these criteria. As I described earlier, the domestic industry first began to suffer poor financial performance in 1996, when the surge in imports began. Its performance worsened in 1997. The EC argues that certain small positive developments in 1997, especially an increase in the volume of sales by the domestic industry, defeat a finding of serious injury. However, the USITC considered this information, along with other indicators of the performance of the domestic industry, such as a precipitous reduction in operating margins and market share that resulted in financial losses, and concluded that the information demonstrated a significant *overall* impairment. The USITC subjected the data it used to a variety of checking procedures, including verification of one domestic producer' s information by a certified public accountant, and found the data to be reliable. The EC has provided absolutely no reason to doubt the validity of this analysis. Therefore, the United States has satisfied the Safeguards Agreement requirement of establishing that the domestic industry was being seriously injured.

4. *Causation*

16. An objective assessment also supports the USITC finding that increased imports caused the serious injury suffered by the US wheat gluten industry. As I described earlier, the USITC found that the volume of imports rose, while imports from the EC began to sell consistently for less than wheat gluten produced in the United States. The USITC found that these conditions prevented the domestic industry from increasing its prices to match rising input costs, which resulted in decreasing profits. Thus, there was a direct link between the increased imports and an overall impairment in the condition of the domestic industry.

17. The EC couches its arguments against this finding in terms of violations of Articles 3 and 4 of the Safeguards Agreement, but the foundation of these claims is a factual argument – that the USITC incorrectly attributed the condition of the industry to increased imports when other factors were responsible for any injury that the industry suffered. This legal argument fails because the USITC carefully examined each of the four alternative causes posited by the EC, and explained why they did not cause serious injury to the US wheat gluten industry.

18. First, I will address the EC claim that fluctuation in the so-called "protein premium" is the primary impetus for changes in wheat gluten demand. I will do this in some detail because this issue only became central to the EC argument in the second written submission. It is not one of the five alternative explanations of

injury identified by the EC producers in their arguments before the USITC. The protein premium is the price differential between low- and high-protein wheat, and the EC claims that a decrease in the differential is responsible for declining wheat gluten prices after 1995. There can be no question that the USITC addressed this issue. It specifically found that "the increase in demand for wheat gluten in 1994 ... resulted at least in part from a weather related deficiency in protein content in the wheat crops." (Pub. 3088, p. I-22.) It also found that "demand for wheat gluten is expected to continue to grow, with possible sharp fluctuations in demand due to weather related effects on the wheat crop." (Pub 3088, p. I-23.) However, the USITC found that most of the increase in demand during 1993-97, and particularly in 1997, was due to long-run factors – the growing popularity of high-gluten bread products and pet foods, the need for heightened gluten content in bakery products made with high-speed mixers, and larger orders from purchasers who were concerned that a potential WTO action by the United States would affect the market.

19. Thus, it is clear that the USITC did consider the effect of the protein content of wheat on demand for wheat gluten. It found protein content to be just one among many factors that varied in importance from year to year, and one that was not particularly important after 1994. The report cited to evidence to support these findings. The USITC also analyzed how changes in demand would affect prices and consumption of wheat gluten. (Pub. 3088, pp. I-16 - I-18.)

20. In fact, the protein premium is just one aspect of the relationship between the protein content of wheat and demand for wheat gluten, which the USITC examined in terms of whether the protein content itself had an effect on the marketplace. If the EC or the EC producers of wheat gluten truly felt that the protein premium was central to the determination of wheat gluten prices, they had every opportunity to emphasize that point in their briefs and submit the necessary data. When they did not, the USITC was entitled to conclude that the protein premium was not a significant factor. In the context of this Panel's inquiry, the failure by the EC and EC wheat gluten producers to press this issue is one of the facts that the Panel should consider in its objective assessment of the USITC findings.

21. I will cover the EC's remaining factual claims in a more summary fashion. The second of the alternative causes now posited by the EC is that wheat gluten prices were depressed after 1995 because domestic producers had unwisely committed to major capacity expansions, which forced them to compete more vigorously with each other to fill the capacity. The USITC found that, in light of the expected growth in demand for wheat gluten, domestic producers acted reasonably in deciding to increase capacity in the early 1990s. The extra capacity only became a problem when increasing imports deprived the domestic producers of the growth in sales that they reasonably expected to enjoy. (Pub. 3088, p. I-17)

22. The third of the alternative causes claimed by the EC is that sales of low-priced corn starch were depressing demand for wheat starch, an additional output of the production of wheat gluten, and that these developments influenced the performance of the wheat gluten industry. The USITC considered this possi-

bility, but found that wheat starch prices *increased* throughout the investigation period and peaked in 1997, when the wheat gluten industry performance was worst. Therefore, the USITC concluded that competition between corn starch and wheat starch did not have a significant effect on the wheat gluten market. (Pub. 3088, p. I-16)

23. The fourth alternative cause identified by the EC is that these other factors were already causing prices to decline when the industry's input costs increased, placing the domestic wheat gluten producers in a cost-price squeeze that caused their profits to fall. The USITC considered this possibility and found that in light of the domestic industry's historic experience and the prevalent conditions of competition, the industry's inability to raise prices to cover higher raw material costs was "unusual." As I have just described, the USITC found that other factors were not significantly affecting the wheat gluten industry. It concluded that the new development of increased imports at relatively low prices was responsible for the serious injury that the industry had experienced. (Pub. 3088, pp. I-17 - I-18.)

24. In addressing each of these factors, the USITC referenced the arguments of the parties and cited evidence in support of its findings. That the EC can identify contrary evidence is not strange, since most of the issues were subject to intensive argument during the investigation. An objective assessment of the facts will reveal that the USITC considered all of the relevant facts and adequately explained its determination.

4. Confidential information

25. I would now like to turn briefly to the role of confidential information in the Panel's deliberative process. In its second oral statement, the EC recognized that the report of a competent authority need not include confidential information that supports the various findings. Thus, the only issue remaining for the Panel's resolution is whether the summary of confidential information in the report is adequate. Nothing in the Safeguards Agreement even requires a competent authority to prepare a non-confidential summary of confidential information. The only mention of such a summary appears in Article 3.2, third sentence, which states that parties providing confidential information to the competent authority "*may* be requested to furnish non-confidential summaries." (emphasis added.) Therefore, the USITC was under no obligation to include summarized data in its confidential report, let alone to use the particular methodologies that the EC suggested for summarizing those data.

26. There is an additional question as to whether the Panel needs to consider confidential information to assess the USITC's decision. As before, we submit that the public report is fully sufficient to evaluate the findings of the USITC. However, if the reconstituted Panel feels that a review of confidential information would be useful, the domestic producers have already specified that they do not object to disclosure of that information to the Panel, or to the EC's participation

in that process in a manner consistent with the requirements of the Safeguards Agreement.

27. Finally, we note that should the Panel decline to review confidential information, it would be inappropriate to draw an adverse inference against the United States. The Appellate Body in *Canada - Aircraft* authorized the use of adverse inferences by a panel only when a party refuses to provide information, and the inference "could be logically or reasonably derived from the facts before it." (¶¶ 200 & 205.) The United States has never refused to supply information to the Panel. Rather, it has consistently worked with the Panel to ensure that the information is submitted and evaluated in compliance with the requirements of Article 3.2 of the Safeguards Agreement, which states that the information "not be disclosed without permission of the party submitting it." Therefore, there is no reason to make any inference based on actions taken by the United States to protect confidential information.

5. *Unforeseen developments*

28. The United States safeguard also satisfies the requirement of Article XIX:1 of GATT 1994 that the increase in imports be the result of "unforeseen developments." The EC argues that the USITC never examined this issue. However, a separate determination as to unforeseen circumstances has never been required. The Appellate Body stated in paragraph 92 of its report in *Argentina - Footwear* that:

> Although we do not view the first clause in Article XIX:1(a) as establishing independent *conditions* for the application of a safeguard measure, additional to the *conditions* set forth in the second clause of that paragraph, we do believe that the first clause describes certain *circumstances* which must be demonstrated as a matter of fact ... (emphasis original)

This passage establishes that "unforeseen developments" is not one of the determinations the competent authority must make pursuant to Article 2 of the Safeguards Agreement, or one of the factors that must be examined pursuant to Article 4. The question, then, is not whether the competent authorities made a finding or conducted an investigation of unforeseen developments, but as the Appellate Body stated in *Argentina - Footwear*, whether they "in their investigation, demonstrated that the increased imports in this case occurred 'as a result of unforeseen developments.' " (¶ 98)

29. The USITC report and evidence on the administrative record show that the investigation did just that. The EC concedes that US producers did not foresee an increase in imports when they concluded in the early 1990s that wheat gluten demand would grow strongly, and commenced capacity expansions on that basis. (Pub. 3088 at I-17.) Since they did not foresee the growth in imports, US producers plainly did not foresee the conditions that spurred that growth in imports. There is no basis to conclude that the US government had reached a con-

clusion different from that of the domestic producers when it agreed to the tariff reduction on wheat gluten implemented in the Uruguay Round.

30. In describing the reasons for the increase in imports, the USITC report lists several developments that occurred at the end of the investigation period, which were not foreseen at the time that the United States agreed to the reduction in the wheat gluten tariff. First, the EC producers unexpectedly expanded their wheat gluten production capacity. (Pub. 3088, p. I-24.) Second, the surge in imports was accompanied by consistent price undercutting on the part of EC producers, who had previously sold at average prices both above and below domestic producers' prices. (Pub. 3088, pp. I-16, II-36.) Third, in 1995-97, EC producers devoted an ever-increasing portion of their total production to exports to the United States. These findings by the USITC, which are cited to evidence on the record, show that the investigation did demonstrate that increased imports occurred as a result of unforeseen developments.

6. *Exclusion of imports from NAFTA parties*

31. Our last point on causation is that the decision to place imports from the NAFTA parties outside of the safeguards measure on wheat gluten is fully consistent with GATT 1994 and the Safeguards Agreement. In *Argentina - Footwear*, the Appellate Body stated that "Argentina's investigation, which evaluated whether serious injury or the threat thereof was caused by imports from *all* sources, could only lead to the imposition of safeguard measures on imports from *all* sources." (Emphasis original.)

32. The Appellate Body emphasized that its decision turned on the facts of the case, in which Argentina evaluated all imports, including those from Brazil, determined that that group of imports caused serious injury, but excluded Brazil from the remedy. Thus, it had attributed injury caused by an outside factor – imports from Brazil – to imports covered by the safeguard measure. The USITC did not do this. It performed two evaluations – one of all imports and one of imports from the NAFTA parties. This two-step process ensured that the injury finding underlying the safeguard did not depend upon the effects of imports from countries that were excluded from the measure. As such, the result is equivalent to an evaluation restricted to non-NAFTA countries, and conforms with the requirement that the competent authorities not attribute injury caused by other factors to the imports that are subject to a safeguard.

33. In *Argentina - Footwear*, the Appellate Body refers several times to the fact that the investigation covered imports from all sources. That, by itself, cannot be an infirmity. Even if a competent authority decides from the outset to exclude imports from within a free trade area, it must still include such imports in its investigation to ensure that there is no inconsistency with the Article 4.2 requirement not to attribute injury caused by other factors to the increased imports.

34. In addition, imports from NAFTA parties fell over the course of the investigation and, thus, did not participate in the increase in imports. Therefore, the

exclusion of wheat gluten from NAFTA parties would not affect the determinations of serious injury or causation.

35. GATT 1994 and the Safeguards Agreement, read together, authorize this result. The analysis begins with GATT Article XXIV, paragraph 8, which defines a free trade area. The last sentence of footnote 1 of the Safeguards Agreement cross references this definition, stating that "[n]othing in this Agreement prejudges the interpretation of the relationship between Article XIX and paragraph 8 of Article XXIV of GATT 1994." Thus, it is GATT 1994, and not the Safeguards Agreement, that governs the applicability of Article XIX to safeguards measures among members of a free-trade area.

36. The definition of a free trade area in GATT Article XXIV establishes that among members of a free trade agreement, "duties and other restrictive regulations of commerce (except, where necessary, those permitted under Articles XI, XII, XIII, XIV, XV and XX) are eliminated on substantially all trade between the constituent territories." To untangle this somewhat complex provision, free trade areas eliminate trade restrictions on substantially all trade, but may maintain measures permitted under several other GATT articles. Measures under Article XIX, namely safeguards, are not listed as among those that a free trade area may specifically maintain. This silence indicates that members of a free trade area may choose to "eliminate" safeguard measures on substantially all trade among themselves. Since the United States has done that with regard to Canada and Mexico, its action fully comports with the Safeguards Agreement.

7. *Validity of the safeguard measure*

37. Finally, we turn to the permissibility of the safeguard measure chosen by the United States. As required under Article 4.2, the USITC examined whether factors other than increased imports could have been responsible for the serious injury experienced by the domestic industry and found that they were not responsible for that injury. Accordingly there is no basis for the EC claim that the US impermissibly applied its safeguard measure to remedy injuries unrelated to the increased exports.

38. Article 5.1, second sentence, states a general rule that a safeguard in the form of a quantitative restriction may not restrain imports to a level less than "the level of a recent period which shall be the average of imports in the last three representative years" without clear justification. And Article 5.2 states that when the Member imposing a quantitative restriction cannot reach agreements with other Members as to the level of the restriction, it may allot to each a share "based upon the proportions, supplied by such Members during a previous representative period, of the total quantity or value of imports of the product, due account being taken of any special factors which may have affected or may be affecting the trade in the product." The use of 1993-95 as the period for determining both the volume of the quantitative restriction imposed by the United States and the shares allocated to the major suppliers also comports fully with the Safeguards Agreement.

39. Neither Article 5.1 nor Article 5.2 elaborates on the factors that make a period "representative." Therefore, to determine the meaning of the clause the Panel must "examine these words in their ordinary meaning, in their context and in light of the object and purpose of Article XIX." The ordinary meaning of representative is "typifying" or "serving as a characteristic example." (Webster's New 3d Int'l Dictionary 1926 (1981). Thus, in the context of Article 5.1, which calls for a consideration of the overall volume of imports, a period is representative if it reflects the typical level of imports. Similarly, in the context of Article 5.2, which calls for a consideration of the distribution of imports among various sources, a period is representative if it reflects a typical distribution.

40. It is also significant that the Appellate Body recently found that Article XIX and the Safeguards Agreement addresses "emergency action" which "is not the language of ordinary events in routine commerce." In the context of setting the overall quota level pursuant to Article 5.1 of the Safeguards Agreement, the requirement that a particular period be "representative" would appear to preclude any year in which unforeseen developments resulted in unprecedented import volumes.

41. In any event, basing the quota levels on years in which there was an import surge would frustrate the remedial purpose of the Safeguards Agreement by guaranteeing imports access to the imposing country's market at levels already determined to cause serious injury. This is the position advanced by the EC, and it simply makes no sense.

8. *Conclusion*

42. In the interests of brevity, the United States has focused on the complicated central issues. This should not be interpreted as a de-emphasis of the many additional points that we have made in our submissions and oral presentations. We note the following discussions in particular:

- paragraphs 82-88 of the US second written submission, showing that the US complied with the notification requirements of Articles 8 and 12 of the Safeguards Agreement; and
- paragraphs 70-124 of the US first written submission, which show that the USITC report met all of the requirements of Articles 2.1 and 4.

43. Mr. Chairman, Members of the Panel, that concludes the United States' oral statement.

ATTACHMENT 2-15

RESPONSES OF THE UNITED STATES
TO THE ADDITIONAL QUESTIONS FROM THE PANEL
(22 May 2000)

Question 1 (to the EC)

Before the USITC, did the EU producers raise "protein premiums" as a factor that the USITC should take into account? If so, did the EU producers raise it as a factor relevant to the entire period of investigation, or only to certain specific years, i.e., 1993-1994? Please substantiate your answer on the basis of evidence already on the Panel record.

1. The United States would like to take this opportunity to provide information relevant to the Panel's question to the European Communities ("EC"). The USITC's review of its files, particularly the briefs submitted during the serious injury phase of the safeguard inquiry and at the injury hearing, shows very little discussion of the so-called "protein premium." The prehearing brief submitted on behalf of the producers of wheat gluten in the EU contains only one mention of the protein content of wheat, in a footnote on page 15 of a 43-page document. The 211-page transcript of the USITC hearing contains only four pages in which the EU producers discussed the protein content of wheat – pages 151 and 170-172. The EC producers' 48-page posthearing brief mentions protein content only twice, on pages 26 and 31, along with a supporting attachment. EC Exhibit 18 at 31, n. 81. The paucity of references to protein content shows that that issue was not a major element in the EU producers' presentation to the USITC.

2. The nature of the discussion in the EU producers' posthearing brief is revealing. They stated that the low protein level in the wheat harvested in 1993 resulted in a protein shortage in 1993-94 that caused prices to increase. The protein premium is mentioned only once, in a footnote that describes it as "one indicator of the protein level in wheat." The EU producers then continue to observe that the protein premium spiked in 1993-94. They made no observation with regard to previous or later years, and did not claim that protein content had any effect on the price of wheat gluten at any time other than 1993-94.

3. These materials establish that the EU producers cited the protein premium exclusively as an indicator that wheat harvested in 1993 had a lower protein content than in other years, and not as an independent factor affecting wheat gluten prices. Thus, in analyzing the effect on the marketplace of the low protein content of wheat harvested in 1993, the USITC fully addressed the protein argument as raised by the EC producers.

Question 2 (to the United States)

Beyond the information given in your response dated 17 January 2000 to question 26 of the Panel on the nature of the "careful review" performed by the

USITC pertaining to the financial data submitted by the United States producers, was there any additional basis for the statement in the USITC Report that the allocation methodologies were "appropriate" (USITC Report, p. I-13). If so, where is this indicated in the USITC Report?

4. The statements on page I-13 of the USITC Report regarding the USITC's "careful review" of the domestic producers' allocation methodologies, and its determination that those methodologies were "appropriate," contain a footnote (footnote 57) referring to pages II-20, II-19-21 of the USITC Report, which further address the allocation issues. This footnote states that the "supporting information on these pages of the report is confidential business information." Thus, the place in the USITC Report where this information is discussed is on pages II-19 to II-21, in particular in two paragraphs on page II-20. However, as the footnote states, most of this information is business confidential, because it discusses the particular allocations used by individual companies, and is thus redacted from the public USITC report.

5. The USITC's staff report reflects its resolution of issues that arose in its careful review of producers' cost allocations, a review that included extensive input from respondents and included scrutiny not discussed in the Report. After the petition was filed on 19 September 1997, the USITC prepared draft questionnaires, and submitted them to the parties, including the EU producers, for comments. On 3 October, counsel for the EC producers submitted a letter to the USITC with eight pages of comments on the draft producer questionnaire, including several directed at allocation issues. In response to comments by EC producers, the final USITC producer questionnaires specifically asked domestic producers to explain their allocation methodology and to supply worksheets (US Exhibit 1 at 8). After the questionnaires was sent out, USITC staff travelled to Kansas and Missouri later in October to visit the facilities of the domestic producers, and to interview their personnel about a wide range of matters, including allocation issues. *(See* USITC Report at II-4, II-6, II-8).

6. After the USITC received the questionnaire responses on or about 31 October, USITC staff examined the questionnaire responses in detail. A USITC accountant examined the financial information in the questionnaire responses and called all of the producers for clarification of the data, and for more information, including on allocation issues. USITC staff followed up with letters seeking additional information, and received more information from the domestic producers. These procedures and the evidence of the appropriateness of domestic producers' accounting procedures are documented in USITC staff memoranda of the meetings with the parties, staff notes of the phone calls to the parties, and letters to the parties, as well as the parties ' questionnaire responses and additional submissions of information in response to these USITC requests. Much of the information involved is business proprietary information and, therefore, confidential. However, it was all placed in the record of the USITC investigation, and was available to representatives of parties subject to the USITC's administrative protective order, including representatives of the EU producers.

7. After reviewing these materials, on 25 November counsel for the EU producers sent a letter to the USITC, contending that there were deficiencies in the domestic producers' questionnaire responses, including on allocation issues, and urging the USITC to collect additional information from the domestic producers. The next day a USITC accountant followed up with a call to a domestic producer seeking certain information that the EC producers had requested, and USITC staff followed up with a written request. On 1 December Manildra responded to USITC staff requests by producing allocation worksheets that had been requested.

8. That same week, on 3 and 4 December, a USITC auditor, a certified public accountant, travelled to Kansas and verified the financial information submitted by Midwest, the largest US wheat gluten producer, including the allocation methods used. The auditor interviewed Midwest personnel, reviewed numerous documents, and verified the financial data in Midwest's questionnaire response against its internal records. The USITC auditor prepared a detailed verification report, dated 12 December which was placed in the record of the USITC investigation, and available to parties to the USITC protective order, including representatives of the EU producers.

9. On 11 December, the parties submitted pre-hearing briefs to the USITC. The EU producers again raised questions about the allocation methodologies used by the domestic producers. (EC Exhibit 16 at 7-13). At the public USITC hearing on 16 December 1997, the attorney on the USITC investigative team asked the domestic producers several questions about their allocation methodologies: " for each of the firms that you represent, does each of the firms regard wheat gluten as a separate profit center, and do they have a formulation for coming up with figuring out what their financial data is for gluten versus starch? If they do have such a formulation, did they use the same formulation in supplying data in their questionnaire responses, or did they develop a different formulation for purposes of this investigation?" The domestic producers' counsel answered the questions at the hearing, and submitted a fuller response in the posthearing brief in order to discuss confidential information without revealing it publicly. (EC Exhibit 17 at 111-114).

10. In addition, after the hearing, USITC Commissioner Crawford posed additional questions to the domestic producers about their allocation methodologies. She asked the domestic producers (1) to explain why their allocation methodologies would not result in the mis-attribution of costs to wheat gluten; and perhaps the under- or over-estimation of profitability; (2) to report the value of wheat starch and any products that might be considered waste; and (3) to explain differences between financial statistics for the two main wheat gluten producers.

11. In their posthearing briefs, the petitioners answered the questions of USITC Commissioner Crawford and the USITC attorney, and explained the allocation methodologies in a detailed 12-page response. The domestic producers argued, *inter alia*, that the USITC auditor's verification report put to rest the EU producers' questions concerning the accuracy of the challenged profit and loss

information. In their posthearing brief, the EU producers addressed the allocation methodologies of two of the domestic producers, but did not question the USITC's verification report, which had been made available to them under the administrative protective order. (EC Exhibit 18 at 35-39).

12. Although the business confidential content of the confidential staff report's discussion of the staff's examination of the producers' allocations methodologies cannot be disclosed absent permission from the submitters, the nature of that discussion can be generally characterized in pertinent part. As the public version of the report discloses, each firm used its own methodology and each method was found to have been consistently applied from year to year. The confidential discussion in the report addressed the results of review of each producer's information, in particular addressing the staff's analysis of the cost allocation methodologies of the two producers whose allocations EC producers had challenged. As to one, the staff report reflected the result of staff's verification of its methodology, particularly recounting how an alternative allocation using a different methodology had been conducted and did not yield significantly different results. As to the other, the report explained why the complaints that the EC producers raised in their posthearing brief, which concerned allocation of certain overhead charges, were based on a mistaken interpretation of the data provided. The discussion also describes how the cost allocation methodologies of the two firms differ from each other.

ATTACHMENT 3-1-1

SUBMISSION OF AUSTRALIA
(16 December 1999)

TABLE OF CONTENTS

1. Introduction

1. Australia thanks the Panel for the opportunity to make a third party submission. Australia will supplement this through its oral statement on 21 December 1999 at the Panel's session with third parties. Australia's submission focuses on: the size of the quota; the allocation of market shares to individual suppliers; and the issue of alleged discrimination in favour of Australia. In that context, Australia will also rebut comments made by the EC in its First Submission about the Australian-owned company, Manildra.

2. Size of quota

2. At pages I-21 to I-31 of its report, in particular on pages I-27 and I-28, the USITC provided a detailed justification of the necessity of the measure to prevent or remedy serious injury and to facilitate adjustment. The US was permitted under SG Article 5.1 to impose a quantitative restriction at the levels recommended by the USITC provided that they were justified. This was done by the USITC.

3. In section 5.2, in particular paragraph 134 of the EC's First Submission, the EC relies on a quotation from EC - Bananas - Recourse to Article 21.5 by Ecuador.[1] Australia submits that this quotation is being made out of context. This report was discussing whether certain years were representative because of distortions. For example, paragraph 6.45 of that report says: "Accordingly, in our

[1] Panel Report, *European Communities – Regime for the Importation, Sale and Distribution of Bananas – Recourse to Article 21.5 of the DSU by Ecuador* ("*EC – Bananas III (Article 21.5 – Ecuador)*"), WT/DS27/RW/ECU, 12 April 1999, DSR 1999:II, 803.

view, the 1994-96 period could not serve as a previous representative period because of the presence in the market of the foregoing distortions." This justifies the omission of years where there are distortions, rather than being seen to limit the discretion of a Member to exclude a non-representative year. Moreover, the EC - Bananas case was about the allocation of country share, not about the size of the quota. SG Article 5.1 does not use the phrase "a previous representative period" but rather "last three representative years". The EC provides no argument why past findings in respect of GATT Articles XIII should apply to SG Article 5.1. The relevant fact in the context of the level of the quota is that the USITC did justify the necessity of looking at the level of imports during the period before the surge, in order to reach a recommendation on what level of import restriction was necessary to prevent or remedy injury, and to facilitate adjustment. In doing this, it justified basing its recommendation on the level of imports during the period (crop years) 1993-1995.

4. The period used by the United States in the case (1993-1995) is particularly appropriate because it covers the period prior to the surge in wheat gluten imports found by the USITC to be the cause of serious material injury to the domestic wheat gluten industry. This was the surge that distorted the domestic market and caused serious injury. An effective remedy could not be fashioned at that level of imports of wheat gluten.

5. Despite the trade-distorting European conditions that caused the surge in imports, the Safeguards Agreement requires only that a surge occurred, and that the surge caused serious injury. The EC does not dispute that the surge occurred. Under the Safeguards Agreement, the USITC was entitled to recommend, and the President of the US was entitled to choose and implement, an effective and efficient safeguard remedy based on the period before the surge caused injury.

3. Allocation of quota to supplying countries

6. The US is entitled to allocate quota to supplying countries, since this is explicitly provided for under SG Article 5.2. The basis for such a share is set out in SG Article 5.2(a) as being based on the proportions during "a previous representative period ... due account being taken of any special factors which may have affected or may be affecting the trade in the product".

7. The USITC analysed what was appropriate for determining the "previous representative period" in this case. Moreover, the allocation of country shares on the basis of 1993-95 reflected the choice of the period for determining the quota. Accordingly, this period was also appropriate for the choice of country shares, since "these years preceded the significant increase in imports that occurred in 1996 and 1997.[2]

8. A Member is allowed discretion here in determining "a previous representative period". There is no necessary link between the "last three representative

[2] USITC Report, page I-28, lines 15 and 16.

years" referred to in SG Article 5.1 and "a previous representative period" in SG Article 5.2(a). If the intent had been for such a link, then the term "previous representative period" would have been defined in SG Article 5.1.

9. Paragraph 144 of the EC's First Submission claims that:

> "Paragraph 2(a) of Article 5 requires a quantitative restriction to be allocated among substantial suppliers on the basis of proportional shares in a previous representative period for which reliable statistics are available. In this case, the previous representative period was 1995-97."

10. This is no more than an implied assertion by the EC that "a previous representative period" must be the latest period for which reliable statistics are available. There is no basis in the text of the Safeguards Agreement for this. If that is what the term "a previous representative period" is supposed to mean, then surely the text would have said so. On the contrary, "a previous representative period" should be one that is representative of the normal flow of imports, which the USITC judged was 1993-95, the same period on which it based its recommendation for the quota. This did not require recourse to SG Article 5.2(b).

11. The EC never provides any argument or evidence that 1993 - 1995 period used for allocation among country suppliers is not, as a matter of fact, "a previous representative period" for the purpose of SG Article 5.2(a). The resulting allocation amounts implemented by the US are simply a function of the representative period selected, and in no way targets any country. Moreover, in the context of the USITC's recommendation, which was accepted by the US Government to base the quota on this period, it was clearly not an arbitrary period.

12. Moreover, SG Article 5.2(a) cannot be read to imply some obligation that the "most suitable" or "most representative" period must be found, whatever that would mean. It only requires that "a previous representative period" be chosen. The necessity test in SG Article 5.1 only applies to the level of the quota applied. The issue of the allocation amongst supplying countries is a different issue. Without evidence that the 1993-1995 period is not "a previous representative period" within the meaning of SG Article 5.2(a), there is no justification for the EC's claim.

13. As the same EC - Bananas report[3] cited before said at paragraph 6.50: "Members have a degree of discretion in choosing a previous representative period". The period used by the US in this case is particularly representative because it covers a time prior to the surge in wheat gluten imports found by the USITC to be the cause of serious material injury to the domestic wheat gluten industry, and is coincident with the period for the overall quota.

---

[3] Panel Report, *EC – Bananas III (Article 21.5 – Ecuador)*, *supra*, footnote 1.

4. Manildra

14. Australia is obliged to comment on the EC's references to an Australian owned company, Manildra, that is part of the US wheat gluten industry. The EC seeks to make something out of the fact that Manildra has an investment in the US and that its Australian operations also export to the US. In some cases the comments are not even accurate. For example, the EC complains at paragraphs 41, 71 and 158 of its First Submission that the Manildra Group "owns two Australian producers of wheat gluten" that "account for the dominant share of exports of wheat gluten from Australia to the US" (citing the USITC report at page II-8). However, the USITC report, confirms at page II-22 that Manildra's Tasman Starches production facility was closed in 1997, thereby reducing considerably Australia's capacity at the very time the EC was radically expanding wheat gluten production.

15. The EC at paragraph 41 of its First Submission finds it "necessary to draw attention to the fact" that an Australian company has interests in wheat gluten production in both Australia and the US. The EC goes as far as to claim that such a legitimate business relationship "may explain the discriminatory structure given to the safeguard measure by the US." Australia disagrees with the EC characterization of the US's safeguard measure as discriminatory. Australia also objects to the insinuation here, and indeed throughout the EC First Submission, especially again in paragraph 180, that the US somehow colluded with Australia in fashioning the safeguard remedy. The US's determination of the safeguard remedy and its implementation of that remedy were legal and fair. The EC provides no evidence for its insinuations, nor is there any.

16. There is no obligation on the US under the Safeguards Agreement to take account of the nationality of the ownership of a company in its domestic industry. Indeed, it could be inconsistent with the Safeguards Agreement for it to do so.

17. In paragraph 77 of its First Submission, the EC says that the USITC report fails to address the issue of Manildra's imports. Then again in paragraph 102 of its First Submission, the EC argues that "imports from Australia to the US by US producers should have been excluded entirely from the causation analysis and findings." The EC gives no textual reason why this was required by SG Articles 2 and 4.2, but merely affirms that it was. This issue was addressed at page I-17 of the USITC report. However, there was no obligation for it to be addressed. The Safeguards Agreement is about the impact of imports from all sources on the "domestic industry" as defined in SG Article 4.1(c). The issue of who the importer is irrelevant. Just because one of the companies in the US industry is an importer does not make those imports a "factor other than increased imports".

18. While it is not clear what the EC is actually proposing in terms of the Safeguards Agreement, presumably the EC is in effect arguing that importing firms should be excluded from the definition of domestic industry for injury purposes. The EC may be thinking by analogy of a provision such as Article 4.1(i) of

the Anti-Dumping Agreement[4], or Article 16.1 of the Subsidies Agreement.[5] Even in those agreements the provision is discretionary. This ability to exclude companies from the domestic industry in anti-dumping (and countervailing duty) cases is exercised to obtain affirmative findings of injury, and so to make it easier to impose anti-dumping duties. However, SG Article 4.1(c) does not contain any such provision. The presence of such flexibility in the Anti-Dumping and Subsidies Agreements and its omission from the Safeguards Agreement mean that a Member does not have the discretion, let alone the obligation, to exclude such companies from the definition of "domestic industry" under the Safeguards Agreement.

5. Article I of GATT 1994

19. A recurrent theme of the EC First Submission, aside from its attempts to get the Panel to conduct what would essentially be a *de novo* review of the USITC finding of injury (which the US has addressed in detail), is its unfounded insistence that the quota remedy is discriminatory and favours Australia. The EC fails to identify any inconsistency with the Safeguards Agreement where the US made quota allocations. The EC alleges in paragraph 144 of its First Submission that the US "unfairly reallocates market share from one WTO Member to another" and concludes in paragraph 147 that the US "clearly and repeatedly breached Article 5.2(a)" of the Safeguards Agreement. This claim that the US breached Article 5.2(a) of the Safeguards Agreement is trivially incorrect, since there was no "re-allocation" of market shares.

20. The EC claims that the US's safeguard measure breaches Article I of GATT 1994 through the allocation of country shares on the basis of the representative period, 1993-1995. This is despite no attempt by the EC to show that this period was not representative. Indeed given that the quota is based on the same period it is difficult to see what other period would have been representative, even without taking into account the distortions inherent in the period subsequent to 1995. The EC claim is without merit and amounts to no more than an assertion that the EC has been treated unfairly.

21. Australia does not accept that the EC has been treated in a "flagrantly discriminatory manner".[6] This is just empty rhetoric. The US has complied with its obligations under SG Article 5.2(a). The US was allowed to provide individual shares to principal suppliers under SG Article 5.2(a). If the US's obligations under the Safeguards Agreement are satisfied, then any conflict with GATT 1994

---

[4] "when producers are related [footnote 11 omitted] to the exporters or importers or are themselves importers of the allegedly dumped product, the term "domestic industry" may be interpreted as referring to the rest of the producers."

[5] "except that when producers are related [footnote 48 omitted] to the exporters or importers or are themselves importers of the allegedly subsidized product or a like product from other countries, the term "domestic industry" may be interpreted as referring to the rest of the producers".

[6] At para. 180 of the EC's First Submission.

Article I would be subject to the General Interpretative Note to Annex 1A of the WTO Agreement. Accordingly, the choice of 1993-1995 as a previous representative period does not constitute a violation of Article I of GATT 1994.

6. Conclusion

22. In conclusion, Australia considers that the US complied with the Safeguards Agreement and in its choice of the level of quota and in its choice of 1993-1995 as a previous representative period for the apportionment of country shares. In addition, Australia rejects the EC's rhetoric about discrimination in respect of Australia and that the business activities of Manildra in the US should have been treated differently by the US Government because it is has Australian ownership.

ATTACHMENT 3-1-2

ORAL STATEMENT OF AUSTRALIA
(21 December 1999)

1. Australia welcomes this opportunity to elaborate its views on this case. Our submission set out our main thinking regarding the legal standing of the remedy imposed by the US.

2. While Australia does not normally support the imposition of import restraint measures, in this case, Australia considered that the USITC had in this particular case demonstrated that serious injury was being caused by imports of wheat gluten from the EC. Accordingly, Australia recognized the right of the US to impose a safeguard measure. Further, Australia recognized that the measure had to be imposed on imports from all sources and not just from the EC.

3. Australia considers that the US was justified in deciding to impose a quota as the remedy. Australia also agrees that the US justified the necessity of its choice of the quota level.

4. In order to prevent or remedy the serious injury caused by the surge of imports after the 1995 crop year, it was necessary to look to the situation preceding that surge to see what level of quota was necessary. The level during the crop years 1993-1995 is clearly justified as the basis for such a calculation. Indeed, the US imposed a level of quota that even included imports from countries such as Canada that were not covered by the quota. The amount of the quota was correctly determined by the USITC to be an amount that the US industry could absorb and that would ensure a continued steady and sure supply of wheat gluten to the US market.

5. While Australia considers that a quota was needed as the remedy in this particular case, Australia disagrees with the EC that the US had a WTO obligation to justify its choice of a quota over a tariff or tariff rate quota. Section 5.1.2 of the EC's First Submission about the form of the remedy is based on the broad interpretation of the Korea - Dairy report[1], which was reversed by the Appellate Body.[2] In particular the point made by the EC in paragraph 125 of its First Submission in regard to the third factor cited by the USITC in support of a quota over a tariff, viz.

> "a high tariff would be inequitable in that it is likely to further drive [other foreign] suppliers from the US market"[3]

---

[1] See Panel Report, *Korea - Definitive Safeguard Measure on Imports of Certain Dairy Products* ("*Korea –Dairy Safeguard*"), WT/DS98/R and Corr. 1, adopted 12 January 2000, DSR 2000:I, 49.

[2] Appellate Body Report, *Korea - Definitive Safeguard Measure on Imports of Certain Dairy Products* ("*Korea –Dairy Safeguard*"), WT/DS98/AB/R, DSR 2000:I, 3.

[3] At page I-26 of the USITC Report.

is irrelevant to the matters before this Panel. In any case, the EC mischaracterizes the USITC's consideration as the protection of the market share of other importers as against the EC, when the USITC was in fact responding to the concern of domestic consumers that the wheat gluten supply be diverse and competitive. The USITC was fully within its rights to consider the equitable impact of a tariff on all foreign suppliers and to recognize that setting a tariff sufficiently high as to restrict the quantity of imports would necessarily prevent countries, which do not provide subsidies, from continuing to export to the US.

6. The EC has also made play of the fact that one of the companies in the US industry was Australian owned and is also an importer of wheat gluten from Australia. As we pointed out in our submission, these facts are irrelevant to the matters before the Panel. The EC's points amount to no more than an *ad hominem* argument.

7. While it is not entirely clear what the EC considers that the US should have done about producers of wheat gluten who are also importers, the implication at least is that they or their imports should have been excluded in one way or another from the injury consideration. As we noted it would have been inconsistent with the Safeguards Agreement to exclude elements of the domestic industry on such grounds. Similarly it would not be consistent to exclude consideration of some imports. While these considerations may be seen by the EC to bolster its *ad hominem* argument in this particular case, it would significantly weaken the disciplines under the Safeguards Agreement to allow a Member to make such exclusions. In the case of anti-dumping investigations, the flexibility arrogated to themselves by some Members to exclude some parts of a domestic industry can serve to make affirmative findings on injury all that much easier to achieve.

8. Article 5.2(a) of the Safeguards Agreement only requires that the country shares be on the basis of "a previous representative period". This does not have to meet the necessity test of Article 5.1. The EC has not addressed this issue directly apart from claiming that it was disadvantaged as compared to Australia. The EC's arguments are made in the context of the size of the quota. Even there the citation of EC - Bananas (with regard to GATT Article XIII) misrepresents the finding of the panel. In that case, it is clear that the point at issue was about the obligation to exclude distorted years and the discretion that is afforded the importing Member to choose a previous representative period. Indeed to assume that "a previous representative period" means no more than "the last three years" would be to render the drafting meaningless. Moreover, to assume that the choice is unique, i.e. to say that it should be "the previous representative period" rather than "a previous representative period" would again be to change the drafting in order to remove the deference afforded the importing Member in the choice of period for the allocation of quota.

9. The choice of the crop years 1993-1995 for the allocation of quota was not arbitrary. On the one hand it was the same period as used for the basis for the calculation of the overall quota. On the other hand it was the period before the surge of imports that caused the injury, which the safeguard action seeks to rem-

edy. Thus it was genuinely "representative". It is difficult to see how the period distorted by the surge of imports causing the injury at issue could be regarded as being "representative" for the purpose of a measure to remedy that injury.

10. There was no favourable action taken by the US in respect of Australian exports to the US. There was no breach of equitable treatment. What the EC appears to be saying amounts to no more than that: its exporters used their excess capacity to injure the US industry; its exporters should be allowed to continue to injure the US industry; and so its exporters should be allowed to maintain their level of exports achieved before the safeguard measure was imposed. This interpretation of the EC has no basis under the Safeguards Agreement and is inconsistent with the purpose of the safeguard action, which is to prevent or remedy serious injury.

11. In conclusion, Australia would like to reiterate that it considers that in this particular case the USITC did justify its injury finding and the level of quota recommended. In addition, the country allocation between Australia and the EC recommended by the USITC and adopted by the US is consistent with the United State's obligations under the Safeguards Agreement and GATT 1994.

ATTACHMENT 3-2-1

SUBMISSION OF CANADA
(16 December 1999)

TABLE OF CONTENTS

1. Introduction

1. Canada is a third party in these proceedings and is appreciative of the opportunity to provide its views to the Panel on certain matters arising in the dispute.

2. The dispute concerns a safeguard measure imposed by the US in the form of a quantitative limitation on imports of wheat gluten effective as of 1 June1998.[1]

3. The dispute was initiated by a request for consultations on 17 March 1999, by the European Communities (EC) in respect of a safeguard measure imposed by the US on imports of wheat gluten.[2] Such consultations with the US were held in Geneva on 3 May 1999, but no mutually satisfactory solution was reached.

4. On 3 June 1999, the EC requested the establishment of a panel pursuant to Article 6.1 of the DSU.[3] The Dispute Settlement Body (DSB) established this Panel on 26 July 1999, with the standard terms of reference.[4]

---

[1] Proclamation 7103 of 30 May 1998 - To facilitate Positive Adjustment to Competition From Imports of Wheat Gluten, submitted as US Exhibit 2; Memorandum of 30 May 1998 - Action Under Section 203 of the Trade Act of 1974 Concerning Wheat Gluten by the President of the US, published in the Federal Register Vol. 63, No. 106, pp. 30359 and 30363 on 3 June 1998, submitted as US Exhibit 3.

[2] WT/DS166/1.

[3] WT/DS166/3.

[4] WT/DS166/4.

5. Canada, Australia and New Zealand reserved their rights to participate as third parties pursuant to Article 10.3 of the DSU.

6. Canada has a substantial interest in the matter, particularly with respect to the EC claim regarding the exclusion of Canada from the application of the safeguard measure imposed by the US.

7. Canada has had an opportunity to review those portions of the First Submission of the US as it pertain to this particular issue, and is fully supportive of the points made by the US.

8. Canada maintains that the US International Trade Commission (USITC) findings and recommendations regarding imports of wheat gluten from Canada, as well as the subsequent US decision to exempt Canada from the safeguard measure on wheat gluten, are consistent with US obligations under the WTO agreements, in particular Article XIX of the GATT 1994 and Articles 2 and 4 of the Agreement on Safeguards. Canada further maintains that the EC claim to the contrary is unfounded and as such should be rejected by the Panel.

2. Exemption of Canada from the US safeguard measure on wheat gluten

9. Pursuant to the obligations of the US under the North American Free Trade Agreement (NAFTA), Canada was exempted from the safeguard measure imposed by the US after the USITC found that imports of wheat gluten from Canada and Mexico did not contribute importantly to the serious injury.[5] Article 802 of the NAFTA provides that "any [NAFTA] Party taking an emergency action under Article XIX or any such agreement shall exclude imports of a good from each other Party from the action unless:

(a) imports from a [NAFTA] Party, considered individually, account for a substantial share of total imports; and

(b) imports from a [NAFTA] Party, considered individually, or in exceptional circumstances imports from Parties considered collectively, contribute importantly to the serious injury, or threat thereof, caused by imports."[6]

Thus, unless affirmative findings on both conditions are made, NAFTA Parties must be exempted from a safeguard measure taken by another NAFTA Party.

10. Article 802 of the NAFTA was incorporated into US law through Sections 311 and 312 of the NAFTA Implementation Act.[7] Accordingly, after the USITC

---

5 Proclamation 7103 of 30 May 1998, submitted as US Exhibit 2; USITC Report, Investigation No. TA-201-67, Publication 3088, March 1998, submitted as US Exhibit 4, pp. I-5 and I-18/19.

6 NAFTA, Art. 802. The full text is reproduced in Annex 1.

7 19 U.S.C. 3371, 3372 (Supp. 1993).

instituted a safeguard investigation on wheat gluten imports and made an affirmative injury determination[8], it conducted a separate analysis of imports from Canada and Mexico to determine whether they accounted for a substantial share of total imports and contributed importantly to the serious injury.[9] The USITC found that "imports from Canada declined significantly during the period examined, while imports overall increased.[10] It concluded that imports from Canada were not contributing importantly to the serious injury caused by imports, and recommended that the President exclude Canada (and Mexico[11]) from any relief action. The definitive safeguard measure imposed by the US in the form of a quantitative limitation on imports of wheat gluten, effective as of 1 June 1998, excluded imports of wheat gluten from Canada, as well as imports from certain other countries.[12]

3. Argument

11. The EC raises legal claims under both the GATT 1994 and the Agreement on Safeguards regarding the US decision to exclude imports from Canada from the application of the safeguard measure on wheat gluten. The EC asserts that, by doing so, the US breached its obligations under Article XIX of GATT and Articles 2 and 4 of the Agreement on Safeguards.

12. The EC argument rests solely on certain parts of the Panel Report in *Argentina - Safeguard Measures on Imports of Footwear*[13] (*Argentina - Footwear*). This Panel Report was appealed, and the decision of the Appellate Body was released on 14 December 1999. Given the very short time between the release of this decision and the due date of the submission of Canada (16 December 1999), Canada has not had an adequate opportunity to review this decision. Therefore, Canada will limit its comments at this point to Panel Report in *Argentina - Footwear*. Canada will present its views on the Report of the Appellate Body, as they are relevant to this dispute, orally to this Panel.

---

[8] US First Submission, para. 10-48, for a factual description of the USITC investigation and the measure adopted by the US.

[9] US First Submission, para. 36 and 40.

[10] USITC Report, submitted as US Exhibit 4, p. I-19.

[11] USITC Report, submitted as US Exhibit 4, p. I-19; the USITC investigation concluded that there were no reported imports of wheat gluten from Mexico during the period examined (1993-1997); the USITC therefore found that Mexico did not account for a substantial share of total imports and recommended that the President exclude Mexico from any relief action.

[12] Proclamation 7103 of 30 May 1998, submitted as US Exhibit 2; Memorandum of 30 May 1998, submitted as US Exhibit 3.

[13] Panel Report, *Argentina –Safeguard Measures on Imports of Footwear* ("*Argentina – Footwear*"), WT/DS121/R, adopted 12 January 2000, DSR 2000:II, 575. This Panel Report has been appealed.

13. The EC claims that the US violated " the principle of parallelism" elaborated by the *Argentina - Footwear* Panel.[14] In support of its claim, the EC cites comments in the Panel Report describing the principle of parallelism, with regard to a safeguard measure imposed by a member of a customs union.[15] In particular, the EC cites the comment of the Panel that the provisions of Article 2 of the Agreement on Safeguards "imply a *parallelism* between the scope of a safeguard *investigation* and the scope of the *application* of safeguards measures.[16]

14. In its submission, the US indicates that the EC provides no arguments as to why the language from *Argentina-Footwear* would be relevant in this case.[17] Canada agrees with this conclusion. The Panel itself, in response to arguments raised by Argentina on NAFTA and the US wheat gluten safeguard in particular, recognised "that MERCOSUR is a customs union, whereas NAFTA is a free-trade agreement".[18] Moreover, as the Panel also pointed out, the provisions of footnote 1 to Article 2.1 on which it relied to elaborate the principle of parallelism concern only regional integration in the form of a customs union. Canada therefore further agrees with the US that the EC has not, with this particular claim, met its burden of proof.

15. In any event, the US submits that its actions, i.e. its decision to exclude Canada from the safeguard measure on wheat gluten, are consistent with the Agreement on Safeguard.[19] The US further submits that the circumstances examined by the *Argentina – Footwear* Panel were wholly different. Canada agrees with the US on both counts.

16. The USITC report clearly shows that the methodology used by the USITC in examining NAFTA imports is consistent with both the GATT 1994 and the Agreement on Safeguards. While the US conducted a global investigation and examined imports from all sources, its determination did not attribute injury from NAFTA imports to third countries. After the USITC made an affirmative injury determination, it conducted a separate analysis of imports from Canada and Mexico. Its investigation and analysis demonstrated clearly that Canadian imports declined significantly during the period of investigation, while overall imports increased.[20] The USITC rightly concluded that imports from Canada did not contribute importantly to the serious injury. Based on this conclusion, the US exempted imports from Canada from the safeguard measure.

17. The EC claims that by doing so, i.e., excluding Canada from the safeguard measure on wheat gluten, the US breached the principle of parallelism recognised

---

[14] EC First Submission, para. 55, 60 and 103.

[15] EC First Submission, para. 55.

[16] *Argentina - Footwear, supra*, footnote 13, para. 8.87.

[17] US First Submission, para. 83.

[18] *Argentina - Footwear, supra*, footnote 13, para. 8.100.

[19] US First Submission, para. 84.

[20] USITC Report, submitted as US Exhibit 4, p. I-19.

by the *Argentina – Footwear* Panel Report.[21] It was the EC itself that provided the rationale for "the principle of parallelism" in its submission in the *Argentina – Footwear* dispute. The EC thesis was aimed directly at demonstrating the inconsistency of the Argentine actions under the GATT 1994 and the Agreement on Safeguards. Accordingly, the EC expressed the view that Argentina, after having investigated imports from all sources, and determined *that serious injury* had been caused by *all* imports, "failed to construct a safeguard measure that addressed the imports that were causing the injury".[22] In this particular case, both the EC and the US agreed that what is troubling "is Argentina's use of MERCOSUR imports for its increased-imports analysis when there was no possibility that those imports could be included in any safeguard action, *even where those imports are demonstrably the cause of the injury suffered by the domestic industry*"[23] (emphasis added).

18. In *Argentina - Footwear*, the facts of the case are important and, we believe, critical to the conclusions of the Panel.[24] Given that MERCOSUR members were the source of more that half of the imports used to determine the injury, excluding MERCOSUR imports from the application of the safeguard measure while using these imports for the injury determination could not be justified, especially considering the object and purpose of the Agreement on Safeguards.[25]

19. Canada therefore agrees also with the EC, to use its own words in the *Argentina – Footwear* case, that the "US wheat gluten case is radically different to [*Argentina – Footwear*]".[26] It is self evident that the methodology used by Argentina in the *Argentina – Footwear* case is easily distinguishable from that used by the US in this matter. As the EC specifically noted in the context of the *Argentina - Footwear* dispute, "the US made *separate* determinations concerning imports from NAFTA members and concluded that imports from that source and, in particular, Canada did not cause injury. If Argentina had applied the same procedure as the US in the wheat gluten case, then Argentina would not have been able to come to the conclusion it did."[27]

---

[21] EC First Submission, para. 55, 60 and 103.

[22] *Argentina - Footwear, supra*, footnote 13, para. 5.124.

[23] *Argentina - Footwear, supra*, footnote 13, para. 5.124.

[24] MERCOSUR imports of footwear in Argentina accounted in 1991 for only 1.90 million pairs of 8.86 million total imports (i.e. 21.4 per cent) and in 1995, for roughly 1/4 of the total imports, i.e. 5.83 of 19.84 million pairs; in 1996, MERCOSUR supplied the largest percentage (55.7 per cent) of total imports of 13.47 million pairs, i.e. 7.5. million pairs (as oppose to 5.97 million pairs from third countries); *Argentina - Footwear, supra*, footnote 13, footnote 474.

[25] The objectives of the Agreement on Safeguards are to "re-establish multilateral control over safeguards and eliminate measures that escape such control"; Preamble, Agreement on Safeguards.

[26] *Argentina - Footwear, supra*, footnote 13, para. 5.123.

[27] *Argentina - Footwear, supra*, footnote 13, para. 5.131.

20. Canada agrees with the US in this case[28], and the EC as it expressed itself in the *Argentina – Footwear* case, that an importing Member is free to – and indeed *should* – investigate all imports into its territory in order to "put together a complete file".[29] The US methodology includes all sources of imports (including NAFTA sources) in the injury determination, and excludes a NAFTA member from a safeguard measure *only* after having made a separate determination concerning the imports from that Member and having concluded that imports from that source *did not contribute importantly to the injury*. The US applied this methodology in the wheat gluten investigation, and found that imports from Canada did not contribute importantly to the serious injury. Based on this conclusion, the US exempted imports from Canada from the safeguard measure. If Canadian imports had contributed importantly to the serious injury, they would not have been excluded from the safeguard measure. This last distinction is very important and distinguishes clearly the USITC methodology from the circumstances of the *Argentina – Footwear* case, in which "the principle of parallelism" was elaborated.

21. Canada further submits to the Panel that pursuant to Article 802 of the NAFTA, a NAFTA member contributing importantly to the injury will not be excluded from the safeguard measure imposed by another NAFTA member. Conversely, only a NAFTA member found not contributing importantly to the injury will be excluded from the safeguard measure. Thus, the *parallelism* between the scope of the *application* of safeguards measures and the actual source of the serious injury is respected, because a separate determination has been made that the imports from that source are not an important cause of injury.[30]

4. Conclusion

22. Accordingly, Canada respectfully submits that the USITC findings and recommendations regarding imports of wheat gluten from Canada, as well as the subsequent US decision to exempt Canada from the safeguard measure on wheat gluten, are fully consistent with the WTO obligations of the US.

---

[28] US First Submission, para. 86.

[29] *Argentina - Footwear, supra*, footnote 13, para. 5.130.

[30] Given the nature of the NAFTA Article 802 exclusion (contingent on imports from the NAFTA party not accounting for a substantial share of total imports of the product and not contributing importantly to the serious injury or threat thereof caused by imports of the subject goods), inclusion of a NAFTA partner - not contributing importantly to the serious injury - in the injury inquiry would, by necessary implication, only make a de minimis contribution to the total level of injury found to have been caused by imports.

ANNEX 1 - FULL TEXT OF ARTICLE 802 OF THE NAFTA

Article 802: Global Actions

1. Each Party retains its rights and obligations under Article XIX of the GATT or any safeguard agreement pursuant thereto except those regarding compensation or retaliation and exclusion from an action to the extent that such rights or obligations are inconsistent with this Article. Any Party taking an emergency action under Article XIX or any such agreement shall exclude imports of a good from each other Party from the action unless:

(a) imports from a Party, considered individually, account for a substantial share of total imports; and

(b) imports from a Party, considered individually, or in exceptional circumstances imports from Parties considered collectively, contribute importantly to the serious injury, or threat thereof, caused by imports.

2. In determining whether:

(a) imports from a Party, considered individually, account for a substantial share of total imports, those imports normally shall not be considered to account for a substantial share of total imports if that Party is not among the top five suppliers of the good subject to the proceeding, measured in terms of import share during the most recent three-year period; and

(b) imports from a Party or Parties contribute importantly to the serious injury, or threat thereof, the competent investigating authority shall consider such factors as the change in the import share of each Party, and the level and change in the level of imports of each Party. In this regard, imports from a Party normally shall not be deemed to contribute importantly to serious injury, or the threat thereof, if the growth rate of imports from a Party during the period in which the injurious surge in imports occurred is appreciably lower than the growth rate of total imports from all sources over the same period.

3. A Party taking such action, from which a good from another Party or Parties is initially excluded pursuant to paragraph 1, shall have the right subsequently to include that good from the other Party or Parties in the action in the event that the competent investigating authority determines that a surge in imports of such good from the other Party or Parties undermines the effectiveness of the action.

4. A Party shall, without delay, deliver written notice to the other Parties of the institution of a proceeding that may result in emergency action under paragraph 1 or 3.

5. No Party may impose restrictions on a good in an action under paragraph 1 or 3:

(a) without delivery of prior written notice to the Commission, and without adequate opportunity for consultation with the Party or Parties against whose good the action is proposed to be taken, as far in advance of taking the action as practicable; and

(b) that would have the effect of reducing imports of such good from a Party below the trend of imports of the good from that Party over a recent representative base period with allowance for reasonable growth.

6. The Party taking an action pursuant to this Article shall provide to the Party or Parties against whose good the action is taken mutually agreed trade liberalizing compensation in the form of concessions having substantially equivalent trade effects or equivalent to the value of the additional duties expected to result from the action. If the Parties concerned are unable to agree on compensation, the Party against whose good the action is taken may take action having trade effects substantially equivalent to the action taken under paragraph 1 or 3.

ATTACHMENT 3-2-2

Oral Statement of Canada
(21 December 1999)

TABLE OF CONTENTS

1. Introduction

1. The Government of Canada is appreciative of this opportunity to provide its views to the Panel on certain matters arising in this dispute. Canada reserved its right to participate as third party in these proceedings because of its substantial interest in the matter, particularly with respect to the EC claim regarding the exclusion of Canada from the application of the safeguard measure on wheat gluten imposed by the United States.

2. We are fully supportive of the position of the United States on this particular issue. We maintain that the United States International Trade Commission (USITC) findings and recommendations regarding imports of wheat gluten from Canada, as well as the subsequent US decision to exempt Canada from the safeguard measure on wheat gluten, are consistent with US obligations under the WTO agreements, in particular Article XIX of the GATT 1994 and Articles 2 and 4 of the Agreement on Safeguards. We further maintain that the EC claim to the contrary is unfounded and as such should be rejected by the Panel.

2. Argument

3. The EC raises legal claims under both GATT 1994 and the Agreement on Safeguards regarding the US decision to exclude imports from Canada from the application of the safeguard measure on wheat gluten. The EC asserts that, by doing so, the United States breached its obligations under Article XIX of GATT and Articles 2 and 4 of the Agreement on Safeguards.

4. Canada was exempted from the safeguard measure imposed by the United States, after the USITC found that imports of wheat gluten from Canada and Mexico did not contribute importantly to the serious injury. This was done in accordance with US obligations under the North American Free Trade Agreement (NAFTA), more particularly Article 802.

5. The EC argument appears to rely solely on the "principle of parallelism", as found in the Panel Report in *Argentina - Safeguard Measures on Imports of*

Footwear (Argentina – Footwear).[1] This Panel Report was appealed, and the decision of the Appellate Body[2] was released last week. We take this opportunity to present our views on the decision of the Appellate Body, as it is relevant to this matter.

6. In its Report, the Appellate Body stated, after a short discussion of Articles 2 and 4 of the Agreement on Safeguards, that "On the basis of this reasoning, and on the facts of this case, we find that Argentina's investigation, which evaluated whether serious injury or the threat thereof was caused by imports from *all* sources, could only lead to the imposition of safeguard measures on imports from *all* sources. Therefore, we conclude that Argentina's investigation, in this case, cannot serve as a basis for excluding imports from other MERCOSUR member States from the application of the safeguard measures."[3]

7. For these reasons, the Appellate Body ruled that "Argentina, on the facts of this case, cannot justify the imposition of its safeguard measures only on non-MERCOSUR third country sources of supply on the basis of an investigation that found serious injury or threat thereof *caused* by imports from *all sources*, including imports from other MERCOSUR member State." [4] [emphasis added]

8. It is clear from this decision that the Appellate Body's legal conclusions regarding the imposition of safeguard measures by a member of a customs union are directly linked to the particular facts of the *Argentina - Footwear* case.

9. The US wheat gluten case is radically different from the *Argentina – Footwear* case. This is clearly demonstrated in Canada's Third Party Written Submission. Now that we have the benefit of the recent decision of the Appellate Body in *Argentina – Footwear*, we will reiterate these differences in the context of the Appellate Body's Report.

10. The USITC report clearly shows that while the United States conducted a global investigation and examined imports from all sources, its determination did not attribute injury from NAFTA imports to third countries. After the USITC made an affirmative injury determination, it conducted a separate analysis of imports from Canada and Mexico. Its separate examination demonstrated clearly that Canadian imports declined significantly during the period of investigation, while overall imports increased.[5] The USITC rightly concluded that imports from Canada did not contribute importantly to the serious injury. Based on this conclusion, the United States exempted imports from Canada from the safeguard measure.

---

1 Panel Report, *Argentina –Safeguard Measures on Imports of Footwear* ("*Argentina – Footwear*"), WT/DS121/R, adopted 12 January 2000, DSR 2000:II, 575

2 Appellate Body Report, *Argentina –Safeguard Measures on Imports of Footwear* ("*Argentina – Footwear*"), WT/DS121/AB/R, adopted 12 January 2000, DSR 2000:I, 515.

3 *Argentina - Footwear, supra*, footnote 2, para. 113.

4 *Argentina - Footwear, supra*, footnote 2, para. 114 and 151 (d).

5 USITC Report, submitted as US Exhibit 4, p. I-19.

11. The separate USITC examination served as the basis for excluding imports from Canada from the application of the safeguard measure. The USITC, unlike the process followed in Argentina, investigated not only whether serious injury or the threat thereof was caused by imports from *all* sources, it also conducted a separate examination of imports from Canada and Mexico. In this separate examination, the USITC concluded that imports from Canada did not contribute importantly to the serious injury. On the basis of this process, the United States was therefore justified in excluding Canada from its safeguard measure.

12. The methodology used by the United States thus excludes a NAFTA member from a safeguard measure *only* after having made a separate determination concerning the imports from that member and having concluded that imports from that source *did not contribute importantly to the injury*. The United States applied this methodology in the wheat gluten investigation. If Canadian imports had contributed importantly to the serious injury, then presumably they would not have been excluded from the safeguard measure. This last distinction is very important and distinguishes clearly the USITC methodology from the facts of the *Argentina – Footwear* case, as well as from the conclusions of the Appellate Body in the same case.

3. Conclusion

13. Accordingly, we respectfully submit to the Panel that the USITC findings and recommendations regarding imports of wheat gluten from Canada, as well as the subsequent US decision to exempt Canada from the safeguard measure on wheat gluten, are fully consistent with the WTO obligations of the United States.

ATTACHMENT 3-2-3

REPLIES OF CANADA TO QUESTIONS FROM THE PANEL AND THE EUROPEAN COMMUNITY
(17 January 2000)

TABLE OF CONTENTS

1. The Questions

The Panel has asked Canada the following questions:

Q.1. In the United States first written submission (para. 84), the United States asserts: "While the United States conducted a global investigation and examined imports from all sources, its determination did not attribute injury from NAFTA imports to third countries" We also note that in the ITC report (p I-18), it states: "Section 311 of the NAFTA Implementation Act provides that if the Commission makes an "affirmative injury determination in an investigation under section 202 of the Trade Act ...", the Commission must also "find" whether - (1) imports of the Article from a NAFTA country, considered individually, account for a substantial share of total imports; and (2) imports of the Article from a NAFTA country ... contribute importantly to the serious injury, or threat thereof, caused by imports".

Is the Panel therefore correct in understanding that imports from Canada were taken into account in order to reach a finding of serious injury, but that a separate causation analysis was then performed on imports from Canada? If so, what is the legal basis in the Safeguards Agreement for such a separate causation analysis?

Q.2. Is the exclusion of Canada from the application of the United States wheat gluten safeguard measure based on, or related to, Article XXIV of GATT 1994? If so, in what way?

In addition, the European Commission (EC) has asked:

Q.1. The EC should welcome further elaboration from Canada on its view that the AB report in *Argentina – Footwear* was, in its opinion, confined to the circumstances of that case, and on how this in Canada's opinion is consistent with Article 2(1) of the SA, and in particular its footnote No. 1, and the text of Article 2.2 that reads as follows:

> "Safeguard measures shall be *applied* to a product being imported irrespective of its source". (emphasis added)

2. Response by Canada

1. The United States excluded Canada from the US wheat gluten safeguard measure, on the basis of Canada's membership in the North American Free Trade Agreement (NAFTA) and after having performed a separate examination of imports from Canada and Mexico.

2. With respect to the legal basis in the Safeguards Agreement for such a "separate causation analysis", Canada notes that there is nothing in the Safeguards Agreement preventing such an analysis. Articles 3 and 4 of the Agreement identify some general parameters for the conduct of the injury investigation. These Articles do not, in any way, imply that a separate analysis is prohibited.

3. A further point to recognize in this respect is that the interpretation of any particular article of a WTO agreement cannot be conducted in isolation. It is a well-established principle that the WTO agreements form a single undertaking. Therefore, all WTO obligations are cumulative and Members must comply with all of them simultaneously.[1]

4. Moreover, the text of the Safeguards Agreement itself indicates that its provisions, and Article 2.2 of the Safeguard Agreement in particular, are not to be considered in isolation from Articles XIX and XXIV of GATT 1994. Footnote 1 to Article 2.1 of the Safeguards Agreement states, *inter alia*, that "Nothing in this Agreement prejudges the interpretation of the relationship between Article XIX and paragraph 8 of Article XXIV of GATT 1994." [2] The negotiators of the Safeguards Agreement clearly recognized that there was a special relationship between Articles XIX and XXIV:8 of GATT 1994 and that the Safeguards Agreement was to be interpreted consistently with that relationship as it stood. Thus the Safeguards Agreement, read in conjunction with the other relevant WTO provisions, leaves open the possibility that, as the United States has done

[1] Appellate Body Report, *Korea – Definitive Safeguard Measure on Imports of Certain Dairy Products* ("*Korea – Dairy Safeguard*"), WT/DS98/AB/R, 12 January 2000, DSR 2000:I, 3, para. 74; Appellate Body Report, *Argentina – Safeguard Measures on Imports of Footwear* ("*Argentina – Footwear Safeguard*"), WT/DS121/AB/R, 12 January 2000:I, 515, paras. 76-98. This finding of the Appellate Body is of course consistent with the fundamental rule of treaty interpretation as set out in Article 31(1) of the Vienna Convention on the Law of Treaties, done at Vienna, 23 May 1969, 1155 U.N.T.S. 331.

[2] We note that the Appellate Body in *Argentina - Footwear, supra*, footnote 1, para. 106-108, commented that the footnote only applies where customs unions take action, not the Member State. A plain reading of the text indicates that these comments would not apply to the last sentence of the Footnote, the language of which clearly suggests a general application to all provisions of the Safeguards Agreement, with no exception. In any event, the Appellate Body's reasoning in paras. 84-95 in Argentina – Footwear would confirm that the Safeguards Agreement does not change or overrule the established meaning of Article XIX of GATT 1994, including its relationship with to Article XXIV:8.

in this case pursuant to Article 802 of the NAFTA, members of an FTA may exclude other members from the application of a safeguard measure.[3]

5. We wish to underscore that none of the Parties in this case have challenged this principle.[4]

6. Regarding the question posed by the EC, Canada's view is that the facts of this case are fundamentally different from those under consideration in the *Argentina – Footwear* case.

7. The Appellate Body decision in the *Argentina – Footwear* case concluded that:

> "In applying safeguard measures on the basis of *this investigation in this case*, Argentina was also required under Article 2.2 to apply those measures to imports from all sources, including those from other MERCOSUR states. On the basis of this reasoning, and on the facts of this case, we find that Argentina's investigation, which evaluated whether serious injury or the threat thereof was caused by imports from *all* sources, could only lead to the imposition of safeguard measures on imports from *all* sources. Therefore, we conclude that Argentina's investigation, in this case, cannot serve as a basis for excluding imports from other MERCOSUR member States from the application of the safeguard measures.[5] (*emphasis added*)

8. "This investigation in this case" refers to the fact that Argentina had investigated and found injury from all sources, including and in particular, MERCOSUR sources. Argentina did not conduct any separate analysis with respect to its MERCOSUR partners. Therefore, under Article 2.2 of the Safeguards Agreement, Argentina had to apply its safeguard measure to injury from those sources. In contrast, in the present case, the United States found, on the basis of its investigations, that Canadian imports were not contributing importantly to the serious injury. Accordingly, it is fully consistent with Article 2.2 of the Safeguards Agreement, interpreted in accordance with Footnote 1 and the decision in *Argentina - Footwear*, for the United States to exclude Canadian imports from the application of its safeguard measure.

---

[3] This analysis is not inconsistent with the analysis of the Panel in *Argentina – Safeguard Measures on Imports of Footwear* ("*Argentina – Footwear*"), WT/DS121/R, 12 January 2000:II, 575, para. 8.97.

[4] Appellate Body Report, *Argentina – Footwear, supra*, footnote 1, para. 114. The Appellate Body itself stated in Argentina – Footwear that, "as the issue is not raised in this appeal, we make no ruling on whether, as a general principle, a member of a customs union can exclude other members of that customs union from the application of a safeguard measure"

[5] Appellate Body Report, *Argentina – Footwear, supra*, footnote 1, para. 113.

ATTACHMENT 3-3-1

SUBMISSION OF NEW ZEALAND
(16 December 1999)

TABLE OF CONTENTS

1. Factual Background

1. Following a safeguards investigation initiated on 1 October 1997 the United States imposed a safeguard measure on imports of wheat gluten on 1 June 1998 which consisted of a quantitative restriction on those imports. The United States decision to impose this safeguard measure was notified to Members through the Committee on Safeguards on 4 June 1998.

2. On 3 June 1999, following consultations with the United States on the wheat gluten safeguard measure, the European Communities requested the establishment of a panel to rule on the consistency of the measure with the WTO Agreement on Safeguards (the Safeguards Agreement). A panel was established on 26 July 1999. New Zealand, as well as Australia and Canada, reserved its third party rights in this panel.

2. New Zealand's Interest

3. New Zealand has a systemic interest in the issues before the panel. The Safeguards Agreement was one of the key reform commitments achieved during the Uruguay Round. The Agreement, which was developed in response to concerns over the use of "grey-area measures", was intended to clarify and reinforce the disciplines of GATT 1994 and specifically those of Article XIX. As stated in the preamble, the Agreement also aimed "to re-establish multilateral control over safeguards and eliminate measures that escape such control", and to encourage

"structural adjustment and the need to enhance rather than limit competition in international markets".

4. In broad terms, safeguard measures under the Agreement take the form of the suspension of concessions or obligations, which can consist of quantitative import restrictions or increases of duties beyond bound rates. Accordingly, the Safeguards Agreement falls into the narrow category of WTO provisions allowing for suspension or modification of applicable WTO obligations, subject to meeting specific legal requirements. As an exporting nation, the proper implementation of the legal requirements of the Safeguards Agreement is of fundamental importance to New Zealand.

5. Against this background, New Zealand wishes to make the following comments on certain issues raised in the first submissions of the European Communities and the United States.

3. Standard of Review

6. In the consideration of safeguard measures, panels are not authorised to review *de novo* the determination made by a domestic investigating authority.[6] Rather, the appropriate standard of review by a panel is to objectively assess whether the Member imposing the safeguard measure has examined the relevant facts, whether it has adequately explained its findings and conclusions, whether the facts support the determination, and consequently whether the determination made is consistent with the obligations of that Member under the Safeguards Agreement.

7. In its submission, the United States stated that:

> Article 4.2(c) of the Safeguards Agreement requires competent authorities to publish an analysis of the case that demonstrates the *relevance* of the factors examined. Consequently, the Safeguards Agreement does not impose an obligation on the competent authority to explain why it found some factors irrelevant and thus did not rely on them.[7]

However, relevance and irrelevance are opposite sides of the same coin. Something that is relevant cannot be irrelevant, and vice versa. Accordingly, an assessment of whether all relevant factors have been adequately examined in a

---

[6] See Panel Report, *United States - Restrictions on Imports of Cotton and Man-Made Fibre Underwear* ("*US -Underwear*") WT/DS24/R, adopted 25 February 1997, DSR 1997:I, 31, paras 7.12 and 7.13; Panel Report, *United States - Measure Affecting Imports of Woven Wool Shirts and Blouses from India* ("*US - Woven Wool Shirts*"), WT/DS33/R, adopted 23 May 1997, DSR 1997:I, 343, para 7.17; Panel Report, *Korea - Definitive Safeguard Measure on Imports of Certain Dairy Products* ("*Korea – Dairy Safeguard*"), WT/DS98/R and Corr. 1, adopted 20 August 2000, DSR 2000:I, 49, para. 7.30; Panel Report, *Argentina - Safeguard Measures on Imports of Footwear* ("*Argentina – Footwear Safeguard*"), WT/DS121/R, DSR 2000:II, 575, paras 8.117 to 8.121.

[7] First submission of the United States, para 58.

safeguards investigation necessarily requires an assessment of whether those factors considered irrelevant were in fact not relevant. In order for the panel to carry out such an assessment, explanations must be given for the conclusions of the competent authority that certain factors were not relevant. A Member cannot justify its refusal to consider factors on the basis simply of a claim that they are irrelevant.

4. Confidential Information

8. In making safeguards investigations, a Member may consider information from the petitioners of a confidential nature.[8] New Zealand does not contest that the protection of such confidential information, including from the respondents in the safeguards investigation, may be appropriate at the time of the investigation. However, New Zealand considers that a Member cannot justify a measure as being consistent with its obligations under the WTO without disclosing to the panel and the parties the information on which it relies. A panel cannot determine whether a measure is in conformity with the Safeguards Agreement without access to all relevant information.[9]

9. The Appellate Body in *Canada – Aircraft*[10] has recently made clear that the provisions of the Understanding on the Rules and Procedures of Disputes Settlement (DSU) for the protection of confidential information are adequate to protect that information in dispute settlement proceedings. New Zealand therefore considers that parties must release to a panel and to the parties involved all information, including confidential information, on which it relies to justify its safeguard measure.

5. Causation

10. The Safeguards Agreement provides in Article 2.1 that:

> A Member may apply a safeguard measure to a product only if that Member has determined, pursuant to the provisions set out below, that such product is being imported into its territory in such increased quantities, absolute or relative to domestic production, and under such conditions as to cause or threaten to cause serious injury to the domestic industry that produces like or directly competitive products.

This provision does not say that increased imports need only be "a" cause, a partial cause, or just a substantial cause of serious injury to the domestic industry. It

[8] Safeguards Agreement, Article 3.2.

[9] See also para 49 of the first submission of the European Communities.

[10] Appellate Body Report, *Canada - Measures Affecting the Export of Civilian Aircraft* ("*Canada – Aircraft*"),WT/DS70/AB/R, adopted 20 August 1999, DSR 1999:III, 1377.

requires that serious injury to the domestic industry must *be caused* by increased imports.

11. Article 4.2(b) of the Agreement provides that:

> When factors other than increased imports are causing injury to the domestic industry at the same time, such injury shall not be attributed to increased imports.[11]

The United States claimed that this provision does not require Members imposing a safeguard measure to quantify and deduct from total injury the specific effects caused by other factors.[12] It cited in support *United States - Salmon*[13], a case that examined Article 3:4 of the Tokyo Round Anti-Dumping Code which contains similar language to that in Article 4.2(b) of the Safeguards Agreement. The panel in *United States - Salmon* said that, in making its determination on causation, a Member need not seek out on its own initiative other possible factors of injury beyond those raised by the parties. The panel did not, however, state or imply that the language of Article 3:4 of the Anti-Dumping Code meant that a Member need not quantify or deduct from total injury the specific effects of other factors shown to have caused injury.[14]

6. Application of Remedy

12. Once the legal conditions for taking a safeguard measure have been established, the Safeguards Agreement imposes obligations on Members with regard to the application of the particular safeguard measure selected. These include restrictions on the extent of application of the measure (Article 5), and procedural requirements to notify the measure and consult with affected Members (Article 12). These obligations apply to measures actually taken by Members and not to measures previously considered as possible measures to be taken, or measures recommended by the competent authorities.[15]

7. Necessity

13. Thus, the obligation in Article 5.1 of the Safeguards Agreement to apply safeguard measures only to the extent necessary to prevent or remedy serious

---

11 This language first appeared in negotiating drafts of the Safeguards Agreement in the "Brussels text" of 6 December 1990.

12 First submission of the United States, paras 130 and 131.

13 United States - Imposition of Anti-Dumping Duties on Imports of Fresh and Chilled Atlantic Salmon from Norway (ADP/87), BISD 41s/229, adopted by the Committee on Anti-Dumping Practices on 27 April 1994.

14 United States - Imposition of Anti-Dumping Duties on Imports of Fresh and Chilled Atlantic Salmon from Norway (ADP/87), BISD 41s/229, adopted by the Committee on Anti-Dumping Practices on 27 April 1994, paras 550 to 555.

15 See the first submission of the European Communities, paras 106, 107, 115, and 116.

injury and to facilitate adjustment is not fulfilled if it is applied to a measure previously considered as a possible measure to take, or recommended by the competent authorities, which is not then imposed without modification. The obligation is only fulfilled if it is applied to the actual safeguard measure imposed by a Member.[16]

8. Notification

14. Articles 12.1 and 12.2 of the Safeguards Agreement require a Member "proposing to apply" a safeguard measure to notify that measure to the Committee on Safeguards, and to provide the Committee with all pertinent information on the measure. This obligation to notify applies to the actual measure imposed, and is not fulfilled by notification of a different measure from the one imposed.[17]

Furthermore, Article 12 of the Agreement imposes the obligation to notify on "the Member proposing to apply a measure". These words indicate that the actual measure imposed must be notified to the Committee on Safeguards prior to that measure being imposed. After the measure has been imposed, the Member will no longer be "proposing to apply" the measure, but rather will be "applying" the measure.[18]

9. Consultation

15. Article 12.3 of the Safeguards Agreement requires a Member imposing a safeguard measure to provide adequate opportunity for prior consultations with Members having a substantial interest in the measure as exporters of the product concerned. Those consultations must have as an objective, *inter alia*, reaching an understanding on ways to maintain a substantially equivalent level of concessions and other obligations to that existing under GATT 1994 between it and the exporting Members which would be affected by the measure.[19]

16. In these circumstances too, the obligation contained in Article 12.3 relates to the actual safeguard measure imposed. Adequate opportunity for meaningful consultations on that measure must be provided prior to the measure coming into effect. The consultations must also address the issue of maintaining a substantially equivalent level of concessions.[20]

---

[16] See the first submission of the European Communities, paras 106, 107, 115, and 116.

[17] See the first submission of the European Communities, paras 163 to 170.

[18] See the first submission of the European Communities, paras 165 and 168.

[19] The objective of maintaining a substantially equivalent level of concessions is set out in Article 8.1 of the Safeguards Agreement.

[20] See the first submission of the European Communities, paras 171 to 178.

10. Conclusion

17. The Safeguards Agreement seeks to ensure that emergency action by Members is taken only in a form consistent with their WTO obligations. As such, the Agreement allows Members to suspend obligations and modify and withdraw concessions, provided that in doing so they fulfil the requirements of the Agreement. These include requirements that safeguard measures may be used only to address serious injury caused by increased imports, and that safeguard measures must be applied only to the extent necessary to prevent or remedy serious injury and to facilitate adjustment.

ATTACH MENT 3-3-2

ORAL STATEMENT OF NEW ZEALAND
(21 December 1999)

TABLE OF CONTENTS

1. Introduction

1. New Zealand's Oral Statement today is a brief synopsis of our written third party submission which was forwarded to the Panel and other parties on 16 December 1999. It attempts to highlight some of the key issues that were discussed more fully in that submission.

2. The Safeguards Agreement

2. The Safeguards Agreement establishes rules for the application of safeguard measures as provided for in GATT Article XIX. It was a key achievement of the Uruguay Round, aimed at meeting concerns over the use of "grey-area measures" by clarifying and reinforcing the disciplines of that Article, re-establishing multilateral control over safeguards and eliminating measures that escape such control, encouraging structural adjustment, and enhancing rather than limiting competition in international markets.

3. The Safeguards Agreement allows safeguard measures in the form of the suspension of GATT concessions or obligations, by quantitative restrictions or by tariff increases beyond bound rates. Accordingly, it falls into the narrow category of WTO provisions allowing for suspension or modification of applicable WTO obligations, provided specific legal requirements are met.

4. As an exporting nation, the proper implementation of the legal requirements of the Safeguards Agreement is therefore of fundamental importance to New Zealand.

3. Legal Arguments

5. Against this background, New Zealand wishes to make a few comments on certain issues raised in the first submissions of the European Communities and the United States.

3.1 Standard of Review

6. It is now well-established that in the consideration of safeguard measures, panels are not authorized to review *de novo* the determination made by a domestic investigating authority. Rather, the appropriate standard of review by a panel is to objectively assess whether the Member imposing the safeguard measure has examined the relevant facts, whether it has adequately explained its findings and conclusions, whether the facts support the determination, and consequently whether the determination made is consistent with the obligations of that Member under the Safeguards Agreement.

7. For the purposes of such an assessment, relevance and irrelevance are opposite sides of the same coin. Something that is relevant cannot be irrelevant, and vice versa. An assessment of whether all relevant factors have been adequately examined in a safeguards investigation necessarily requires an assessment of whether those factors considered irrelevant *were* in fact not relevant. In order for the panel to carry out such an assessment, explanations must be given for the conclusions of the competent authority that certain factors were not relevant. A Member cannot justify its refusal to consider factors on the basis simply of a claim that they are irrelevant.

3.2 Confidential Information

8. In making safeguards investigations, a Member may consider information from the petitioners of a confidential nature. Article 3.2 of the Safeguards Agreement provides for the protection of that confidential information, including from the respondents in the safeguards investigation, at the time of the investigation. However, a Member cannot justify a measure before a panel as being consistent with its obligations under the WTO without disclosing to the panel and the parties the information on which it relies. A panel cannot determine whether a measure is in conformity with the Safeguards Agreement without access to all the relevant information.

9. The Appellate Body has recently made clear that the provisions of the DSU for the protection of confidential information are adequate to protect that information in dispute settlement proceedings. New Zealand therefore considers that parties must release to a panel and to the parties involved all information, including confidential information, on which it relies to justify its safeguard measure.

3.3 Causation

10. Article 2.1 of the Safeguards Agreement provides that a safeguard measure may be applied to a product only where that product is being imported into its territory in such increased quantities and under such conditions as to cause or threaten to cause serious injury to the domestic industry that produces like or directly competitive products. It does not say that increased imports need only be "a" cause, a partial cause, or just a substantial cause of serious injury, or threat thereof, to the domestic industry. It says that serious injury, or threat thereof, to the domestic industry must *be caused* by increased imports.

11. Article 4.2(b) of the Agreement then says that when factors other than increased imports are causing injury to the domestic industry at the same time, such injury shall not be attributed to increased imports. The panel ruling in the case of *United States - Salmon* considered similar language in the context of Article 3:4 of the Tokyo Round Anti-Dumping Code. That panel said that a Member making its determination on causation need not seek out on its own initiative other possible factors of injury beyond those raised by the parties. Contrary to the assertion contained in the submission of the United States, however, the panel did not state or imply that this language means a Member need not quantify or deduct from total injury the specific effects of other factors shown to have caused injury.

3.4 Application of Remedy

12. Once the legal conditions for taking a safeguard measure have been established, the Safeguards Agreement imposes obligations on Members with regard to the application of the particular safeguard measure selected. These include restrictions on the extent of application of the measure in Article 5, and procedural requirements to notify the measure and consult with affected Members in Article 12. These obligations apply to safeguard measures actually taken by Members and not to measures previously considered as possible measures to be taken, or measures recommended by the competent authorities but not imposed in the form recommended.

13. For example, the obligation in Article 5.1 of the Safeguards Agreement to apply safeguard measures only to the extent necessary to prevent or remedy serious injury and to facilitate adjustment is only fulfilled if it is applied to the actual safeguard measure imposed by a Member. Similarly, the obligation in Articles 12.1 and 12.2 of the Safeguards Agreement on a Member proposing to apply a safeguard measure to notify that measure applies to the actual measure imposed, and is not fulfilled by notification of a different measure from the one imposed. In addition, the obligation contained in Article 12.3 to provide adequate opportunity for prior consultations with Members having a substantial interest in the measure relates to the actual safeguard measure imposed. Adequate opportunity for meaningful consultations on *that* measure must be provided prior to the measure coming into effect.

4. Conclusion

14. The Safeguards Agreement seeks to ensure that emergency action by Members is taken only in a form consistent with their WTO obligations. As such, the Agreement allows Members to suspend obligations and modify and withdraw concessions, provided that in doing so they fulfil the requirements of the Agreement. These include requirements that safeguard measures may be used only to address serious injury caused by increased imports, and that safeguard measures must be applied only to the extent necessary to prevent or remedy serious injury and to facilitate adjustment.

ATTACHMENT 4

PROCEDURES GOVERNING PRIVATE
CONFIDENTIAL INFORMATION

(1 February 2000)

I. BASIC PRINCIPLE

1. The treatment of information as "private confidential" under these procedures imposes a substantial burden on the Panel and the parties. The indiscriminate designation of information as "private confidential" could limit the ability of a party to include fully in its litigation team individuals who have particular knowledge and expertise relevant to presenting the party's case, impede the work of the Panel and complicate the Panel's task in formulating credible public findings and conclusions. Accordingly, while the Panel recognizes that parties have a legitimate interest in protecting sensitive "private confidential" information, *the Panel expects that parties will exercise the utmost restraint in designating information as "private confidential"*.

II. DEFINITIONS

"approved person" means:

(i) a Panel member;

(ii) a representative; or

(iii) a Secretariat employee.

"capital city office" means the buildings and grounds of the United States Trade Representative in Washington, DC, United States of America, and buildings and grounds of the European Commission in Brussels, Belgium.

"conclusion of the Panel" means when, pursuant to DSU Article 16.4, the Panel report is

(i) adopted;

(ii) not adopted;

(iii) the Panel report is appealed and the report of the Appellate Body is adopted; or

when the authority for establishment of the Panel lapses pursuant to DSU Article 12.12.

"private confidential information" means any information that is designated as such by the party submitting the information, that is not otherwise available in the public domain, and that was identified by the United States International Trade Commission (the "ITC") as confidential business information for the purposes of ITC Investigation No. TA-201-67 concerning Wheat Gluten and, for this reason, was deleted from the public version of the ITC Report of March 1998 (Publication 3088).[1]

"designated as private confidential" means:

(i) for printed information, clearly marked with the notation 'PRIVATE CONFIDENTIAL INFORMATION' and with the name of the party that first submitted the information;

(ii) for binary-encoded information, clearly marked with the notation 'PRIVATE CONFIDENTIAL INFORMATION' on a label on the storage medium, and clearly annotated in the binary-encoded files with the notation 'PRIVATE CONFIDENTIAL INFORMATION' and with the name of the party that first submitted the information; and

(iii) for uttered information, declared by the speaker to be "Private Confidential information" prior to the disclosure, and identified with the name of the party that first submitted the information.

"dispute" means the complaint brought by the European Communities concerning the imposition by the United States of the definitive safeguard measure in the form of a quantitative limitation on imports of wheat gluten effective as of 1 June 1998, WT/DS166, entitled "United States – Definitive Safeguard Measures on Imports of Wheat Gluten from the European Communities".

"DSU" means the WTO Understanding on Rules and Procedures Governing the Settlement of Disputes.

"Geneva mission" means the buildings and grounds of the United States and the European Communities at 1-3 Avenue de la Paix, 1211 Geneva and 37-39 Rue de Vermont, 1202 Geneva, respectively.

"information" means:

(i) printed information;

(ii) binary-encoded information stored in computer diskettes, computer disc drives, CD roms, or other electronic media; or

(iii) uttered information.

"Panel" means the WTO panel established pursuant to DSU Article 6 by the 26 July 1999 decision of the WTO Dispute Settlement Body to examine the dispute.

"Panel meeting" means a substantive meeting of the Panel with the parties or any interim review meeting of the Panel with the parties, as described in the working procedures of DSU Appendix 3.

"Panel member" means a person serving on the Panel.

---

[1] For greater clarity, such information shall not include the additional information submitted by the United States in US-Exhibit 10 in this dispute.

"Panel process" means the process of the Panel as described in relevant provisions of the DSU.

"party" means the European Communities or the United States.

"premises of the WTO" means buildings and grounds of the WTO at Centre William Rappard, Rue de Lausanne 154, Geneva, Switzerland.

"representative" means any person that a Member selects to act as its representative, counsel or consultant during the dispute and whose selection as such has been notified to the Chairman of the Panel and to the other party, but in no circumstances shall this definition include an employee, officer or agent of a private company engaged in wheat gluten production.

"Secretariat" means the Secretariat of the World Trade Organization.

"Secretariat employee" means a person employed or appointed by the Secretariat who has been authorized by the Secretariat to work on this dispute and whose authorization has been notified to the Chairman of the Panel, including without limiting the generality of the foregoing, interpreters and transcribers present at the Panel hearings.

"secure location" means a locked storage receptacle on the premises of the WTO chosen by the Secretariat to provide secure storage for private confidential information.

"submit" means:

(i) the filing by a party of printed or binary-encoded information at the Secretariat during the dispute;

(ii) the filing by a party of printed or binary-encoded information with the Panel during a Panel hearing; or

(iii) the uttering of information during a Panel hearing.

III. SCOPE

1. These procedures apply to all private confidential information submitted during the Panel process, but do not apply to a party with respect to private confidential information first submitted by that party, including in derivative form.

IV. OBLIGATION ON PARTIES

1. Each party shall ensure that its representatives comply with these procedures.

V. SUBMISSION BY A PARTY

1. When submitting information, a party may designate all or any part or parts of that information as private confidential information. Private confidential

information shall be submitted in three copies: one copy of the private confidential information shall be provided to the Secretariat, and two copies shall be provided to the other party. Of the two copies for the other party, one copy is for that party's Geneva mission, and one copy is for that party's capital city office.

2. Where a submission by a party incorporates private confidential information first submitted by the other party, that submission shall clearly identify all such information, as set forth in Article II of these procedures concerning "designated as private confidential".

3. If, taking into the account the Basic Principle stated in Article I, the Panel considers that a party has designated as private confidential information which is not reasonably entitled to such treatment, the Panel may decline to consider such information. In such a case, the party submitting the information may, at its discretion:

(i) withdraw the information, in which case the Panel and the other party shall promptly return the information to the party submitting it; or

(ii) withdraw the designation of the information as private confidential.

4. When submitting printed or binary-encoded private confidential information, the party shall also provide:

(i) a non-private confidential edited version, redacted in such a manner as to convey a reasonable understanding of the substance of the information;

(ii) a non-private confidential summary in sufficient detail to convey a reasonable understanding of the substance of the information; or

(iii) in exceptional circumstances, a written statement:

(a) that such a non-private confidential edited version or non-private confidential summary cannot be made, or

(b) that such a non-private confidential edited version or non-private confidential summary would disclose facts that the party has a proper reason for wishing to keep private confidential.

5. If the Panel considers that a non-private confidential edited version or summary does not fulfill the requirements of paragraph 4(i) or (ii), or that such exceptional circumstances as justify a statement pursuant to paragraph 4(iii) do not exist, the Panel may decline to consider the private confidential information in question. In such a case, the party submitting the information may, at its discretion,

(i) withdraw the information, in which case the Secretariat and the other party shall promptly return the information to the party submitting it; or

(ii) comply with the provisions of paragraph 4 to the satisfaction of the Panel.

6. When uttering private confidential information at a Panel meeting, the speaker shall also provide a brief non-private confidential oral statement in sufficient detail to convey a reasonable understanding of the substance of the information that will be uttered.

VI. STORAGE

1. The Secretariat shall store all private confidential information submitted in the secure location when not in use by an approved person.

2. Each party shall store all private confidential information submitted to it by the other party in a locked storage receptacle, to which only approved persons have access, at the premises of its Geneva mission or its capital city office, when not in use by an approved person.

3. An approved person shall take all necessary precautions to safeguard private confidential information when in use and when being stored.

VII. VIEWING AND SUMMARIZING

1. Private confidential information submitted by a party and stored at the Geneva mission or capital city office of the other party may only be viewed by an approved person acting as representative of that other party.

2. An approved person viewing or hearing private confidential information may take written summary notes of that information for the sole purpose of the Panel process.

VIII. COPYING, DISTRIBUTION AND REMOVAL

1. Private confidential information shall not be copied, distributed, or removed from the premises of the WTO, or from the premises of a party's Geneva mission, or from the premises of a party's capital city office, except as specifically provided in these Procedures.

2. Notwithstanding paragraph 1. above, a party may bring with it to a Panel meeting, for the sole purpose of that meeting, one of the two copies of private confidential information that it has received from the other party under these procedures, and shall immediately thereafter return any and all such information to the locked storage receptacle at its premises.

3. Notwithstanding paragraph 1. above, a Panel member may make and remove from the premises of the WTO a copy of private confidential information. Any copies of private confidential information removed from the premises of the WTO by a Panel member shall be used exclusively by that Panel member for the purpose of working on the dispute, and shall be returned to the Secretariat upon conclusion of the Panel. Copies of private confidential information removed from

the premises of the WTO by a Panel member shall be stored in a locked receptacle.

IX. DISCLOSURE AT A PANEL MEETING

1. A party that wishes to submit private confidential information during a Panel meeting shall so inform the Panel prior to doing so. The Panel shall exclude persons who are not approved persons from the meeting for the duration of the submission of such information.

X. PANEL REPORT

1. The Panel shall not disclose private confidential information in its report, but may make statements of conclusion drawn from such information.

XI. TAPES AND TRANSCRIPTS

1. Any tapes and transcripts of Panel meetings at which private confidential information is uttered shall be treated as private confidential information under these procedures.

XII. RETURN OR DESTRUCTION

1. After the conclusion of the Panel, the Secretariat and the parties shall:

(i) return any printed or binary-encoded private confidential information (including any notes taken pursuant to paragraph VIII:2 above) in their possession to the party that first submitted such private confidential information, or certify in writing that any such private confidential information has been destroyed, unless that party agrees otherwise;

(ii) destroy all tapes and transcripts of the Panel hearings that contain private confidential information and certify in writing that this has been done, unless the parties mutually agree otherwise.

2. If the Panel Report is appealed, the Secretariat shall transmit any printed or binary encoded private confidential information, plus all tapes and transcripts of the Panel hearings that contain private confidential information, to the Appellate Body as part of the record of the Panel proceedings. The Secretariat shall transmit such information to the Appellate Body separately from the rest of the record and shall inform the Appellate Body of the special procedures that the Panel has applied with respect to such private confidential information. The parties shall comply with any directive of the Appellate Body regarding disclosure of private confidential information to parties or third parties as the Appellate Body may deem appropriate.

9 780521 829809